Math Survival Guide

to accompany

Data Structures, Algorithms, and Software Principles in C

Sum of the Integers from 1 to n

$$S = 1 + 2 + 3 + \ldots + n$$

$$S = n\left(\frac{n+1}{2}\right)$$

Sum of an Arithmetic Progression

n = number of terms
a = first term
d = common difference
l = last term, $l = a + (n-1)d$

$$S = a + (a+d) + (a+2d) + \ldots + [a + (n-1)d]$$

$$S = n\left(\frac{a+l}{2}\right) = \frac{n}{2}\{2a + (n-1)d\}$$

Sum of a Geometric Progression

n = number of terms
a = first term
r = common ratio, $r \neq 1$
l = last term, $l = ar^{(n-1)}$

$$S = a + ar + ar^2 + \ldots + ar^{(n-1)}$$

$$S = a\left(\frac{r^n - 1}{r - 1}\right) = a\left(\frac{1 - r^n}{1 - r}\right)$$

Special Case—Sum of the Powers of $1/2^i$

$$S = \sum_{k=i}^{j} \frac{1}{2^k} = \frac{1}{2^i} + \frac{1}{2^{i+1}} + \ldots + \frac{1}{2^j}$$

$$S = \frac{2}{2^i} - \frac{1}{2^j} = (\text{twice the first minus the last})$$

Sum of the Squares

$$\sum_{i=1}^{n} i^2 = \frac{n(n+1)(2n+1)}{6}$$

Sum of the Cubes

$$\sum_{i=1}^{n} i^3 = \frac{n^2(n+1)^2}{4}$$

Sum of the Odd Numbers

$$S = 1 + 3 + 5 + \ldots + (2n - 1) = n^2$$

Sum of $i*d^i$

$$\sum_{i=1}^{n} i d^i = \left(\frac{d}{(d-1)^2}\right)[(nd - n - 1)d^n + 1]$$

Sum of Floors of Base Two Logarithms

$$L_n = \sum_{i=1}^{n} \lfloor \lg i \rfloor = (n+1)q - 2^{(q+1)} + 2,$$

$$\text{where } q = \lfloor \lg(n+1) \rfloor$$

Number of Integers in the Integer Range:

bottom : top = { i | bottom $\leq i \leq$ top }

$$\text{top} - \text{bottom} + 1$$

The nth Harmonic Number, H_n

$$H_n = \sum_{i=1}^{n} \frac{1}{i} = \ln n + \gamma + O(1/n),$$

$$\text{where } \gamma = 0.57721566$$

Floor and Ceiling Laws

Let a be an integer, and
Let x and y be real numbers. Then

$$\lfloor a \rfloor = \lceil a \rceil = a$$

$$\lfloor x \pm a \rfloor = \lfloor x \rfloor \pm a, \text{ and } \lceil x \pm a \rceil = \lceil x \rceil \pm a$$

$$\lceil x \pm y \rceil \geq \lceil x \rceil \pm \lceil y \rceil, \text{ and } \lfloor x \pm y \rfloor \leq \lfloor x \rfloor \pm \lceil y \rceil$$

$$-\lfloor x \rfloor = \lceil -x \rceil, \text{ and } -\lceil x \rceil = \lfloor -x \rfloor$$

$$\text{if } x \leq y, \text{ then } \lfloor x \rfloor \leq \lfloor y \rfloor \text{ and } \lceil x \rceil \leq \lceil y \rceil$$

Laws for Powers and Exponents

$$x^a x^b = x^{a+b}$$

$$x^a / x^b = x^{a-b}$$

$$x^0 = 1, \text{ provided } x \neq 0$$

$$x^{-b} = 1/x^b$$

$$x^{1/n} = \sqrt[n]{x}$$

$$1^a = 1, \text{ and } x^1 = x, \text{ for any } a \text{ and } x$$

$$(xy)^a = x^a y^a$$

$$(x^a)^b = x^{ab}$$

$$(x/y)^a = x^a / y^a$$

Definition of the *mod* Operator

Let a and b be any two real numbers.
We define $a \bmod 0 = a$, and if $b \neq 0$,
we define $a \bmod b = a - b \lfloor a/b \rfloor$.

Logarithm Laws

$$\log_b(xy) = \log_b x + \log_b y$$

$$\log_b(x/y) = \log_b x - \log_b y$$

$$\log_b(1/x) = -\log_b x$$

$$\log_b(x^n) = n \log_b x$$

$$\log_b(1) = 0$$

$$\log_b b = 1$$

$$x \,\Re\, y \Leftrightarrow \log_b x \,\Re\, \log_b y, \text{ for } \Re \in \{=, \leq, <, >, \geq\}$$

$$\log_b x = \frac{\log_c x}{\log_c b}$$

$$\log_b c = \frac{1}{\log_c b}$$

Congruence Laws

(A) If $a \equiv b \ (modulo\ m)$ and $r \equiv s \ (modulo\ m)$,
then $(a \pm r) \equiv (b \pm s) \ (modulo\ m)$
and $(ar) \equiv (bs) \ (modulo\ m)$

(B) Provided c and m are relatively prime,
if $ac \equiv bc \ (modulo\ m)$
then $a \equiv b \ (modulo\ m)$

Solution to Recurrence Relations

$$T(1) = a \text{ and } T(n) = b + c\,T(n-1)$$

Condition $\Rightarrow$ Solution

$$c = 1 \Rightarrow T(n) = b\,n + (a - b)$$

$$c \neq 1 \Rightarrow T(n) = \left(\frac{a-b}{c} + \frac{b}{c-1}\right)c^n - \left(\frac{b}{c-1}\right)$$

Solution to Recurrence Relations

$$T(1) = a \text{ and } T(n) = b\,n + c + d\,T(n-1)$$

Condition $\Rightarrow$ Solution

$$d = 1 \Rightarrow$$

$$T(n) = \left(\frac{b}{2}\right)n^2 + \left(\frac{b}{2} + c\right)n + (a - b - c)$$

$$d \neq 1 \Rightarrow$$

$$T(n) = \left(\frac{a-b-c}{d} + \frac{b+c}{d-1} + \frac{b}{(d-1)^2}\right)d^n$$
$$- \left(\frac{b}{d-1}\right)n + \left(\frac{c - (b+c)d}{(d-1)^2}\right)$$

Solution to Recurrence Relations

$$T(1) = a$$
$$T(n) = b\,n + c + d\,T(n/p), \text{ where } p > 1, d > 0$$

Condition $\Rightarrow$ Solution

$$d = p \Rightarrow$$

$$T(n) = b\,n \log_p n + \left(a + \frac{c}{d-1}\right)n - \left(\frac{c}{d-1}\right)$$

$$d = 1 \Rightarrow$$

$$T(n) = \left(\frac{bp}{p-1}\right)n + c\log_p n + \left(a - \frac{bp}{p-1}\right)$$

$$d = 1 \text{ and } b = 0 \Rightarrow T(n) = c\log_p n + a$$
$$d \neq 1 \text{ and } d \neq p \Rightarrow$$

$$T(n) = \left(a + \frac{bp}{d-p} + \frac{c}{d-1}\right)n^{\log_p d}$$
$$- \left(\frac{bp}{d-p}\right)n - \left(\frac{c}{d-1}\right)$$

Data Structures, Algorithms, and Software Principles in C

Data Structures, Algorithms, and Software Principles in C

Thomas A. Standish

Computer Science Department
University of California, Irvine

▲ **ADDISON-WESLEY PUBLISHING COMPANY**
Reading, Massachusetts
Menlo Park, California • New York
Don Mills, Ontario • Wokingham, England
Amsterdam • Bonn • Sydney • Singapore
Tokyo • Madrid • San Juan • Milan • Paris

Preface

This book covers material recommended for a second course in computer science—Computer Science 2 (or CS 2, for short). Not only does it cover the CS 2 material recommended by ACM's *Curriculum '78* (as revised in 1984[1]), it also covers the material recommended in the new *Computing Curricula 1991*, as set forth in the *Report of the Joint Curriculum Task Force*[2, 3, 4] of the ACM and the IEEE Computer Society. The Curricula 1991 material is presented in a format called *Knowledge Units* (KUs) in the Curricula 1991 Report. Accordingly, this book supports the KUs recom-

---

[1] E. B. Koffman, D. Stemple, and C. E. Wardle, "Recommended Curriculum for CS2, 1984," *Communications of the ACM* 28:8 (August 1985), pp. 815–18.

[2] A. B. Tucker, B. H. Barnes, et al, *Computing Curricula 1991: Report of the ACM/IEEE-CS Joint Curriculum Task Force.* Association for Computing Machinery, New York, ACM Order Number 201910 (Dec. 17, 1990).

[3] A. Joe Turner, "Introduction to the Joint Task Force Report," *Communications of the ACM* 34:6 (June 1991), pp. 68–70.

[4] A. B. Tucker, "Computing Curricula 1991," *Communications of the ACM* 34:6 (June 1991), pp. 70–84.

mended for a second course in computing covering data structures, algorithms, and software principles.

In addition, Curricula '91 specifies a number of *recurring concepts* that it advocates covering. Recurring concepts are central ideas—such as *recursion, levels of abstraction, efficiency,* and *tradeoffs*—that occur throughout computer science. Such recurring concepts are used as *integrators* in this book in order to tie the material together conceptually and to help reveal its underlying unity and interrelationships.

The book is therefore appropriate to use either to support a traditional revised Curriculum '78 CS 2 course or to use during the transition period from Curriculum '78 to the new Curricula '91, as we evolve our computer science courses to meet the new challenges of the 1990s.

Prerequisites for the C Programming Language

It is assumed that students using this book for a CS 2 course will have already taken a first course covering introductory programming using C. Such students should be familiar with C's statements (such as assignments, for-statements, if-statements, while loops, do-while loops, and switch statements) and with C's block structure and control flow. Input and output using **scanf** and **printf** should have been covered.

In addition, students should have been introduced to C's basic data types—ints, floats, doubles, chars, and enum types—as well as to C's composite types—arrays, structs, unions, and strings (not including pointers, which are covered from the start in this book).

Finally, the declaration and use of functions should have been covered, not including recursion, which is covered in this book.

The Approach to Mathematical Foundations

A very careful approach is taken toward the mathematical foundations of computer science. The detailed mathematical demonstrations in the book are specially marked with two trailing asterisks (**) so that they may be either skipped entirely or covered to varying degrees of depth. Consequently, the mathematical developments in the book can be engaged at different levels, and a range of philosophies toward the inclusion of mathematics by instructors can be accommodated.

Our approach is to structure the material so that different levels of contact with the mathematics are possible, without destroying the continuity of the material, and to provide a gentle introduction to the mathematical background needed in an appendix called the *Math Reference and Tutorial*. In addition, a tear-out card called the *Math Survival Guide* accompanies the book and provides a handy reference giving useful mathematical formulas and tables of solutions to recurrence relations.

The *Math Reference and Tutorial* appendix reviews useful mathematical facts at the level of precollege algebra that are used frequently in the derivations in the book.

For example, some of the topics covered are the sums of arithmetic and geometric progressions, exponentials and logarithms, various facts concerning the divisibility of integers, and so forth. Calculus is neither used in nor required for this book.

The *Instructor's Manual*, provides several options for structuring CS 2 courses based on the material in this book, including courses having differing levels of coverage of the mathematical foundations and the mathematical skills that are useful for practical programmers.

Software Engineering Principles

The book also aspires to cover a range of important topics in contemporary software engineering. In addition to covering traditional software engineering concepts and principles, the book introduces new material in software engineering, such as risk-based software lifecycle models, rapid prototyping, and reusable software components. It also highlights recently popular programming trends, such as object-oriented programming (OOP) based on C++, and tries to identify their value and utility.

Why Is This Book Special?

Several key features distinguish the approach of this book:

- Coverage both of *Curriculum '78* and the KUs for *Curricula '91*
- Focus on key *recurring concepts* of *Curricula '91* as integrators
- Mathematical foundations that can be engaged at a variety of depths
- Coverage of important software engineering concepts and principles
- Introduction to object-oriented programming

The author's hope is that instructors will find this book to be a great resource to use for offering CS 2 courses that meet the challenges of the 1990s.

Supplements

Supplemental materials include source code for sample programs, a solutions manual, and an instructor's manual. These items are on-line.

The **source code** and **Instructor's manual** is available via anonymous FTP. The address is ftp aw.com. Once in the FTP site, you will be asked for a name; respond with **anonymous**. You will then be asked for a password; respond with your e-mail address. From here, change directory to aw.computer.science/Stan.C (to do this type cd aw.computer.science/Stan.C at the UNIX prompt). Consult the README file in the directory Stan.C for more detailed information. (to get this file type get README at the UNIX prompt). Individuals without direct internet access can send mail to StanC@aw.com. Include the line **send information** in the body of the message.

The sample programs have been complied and run under C on Macintoshes and under Unix ANSI C, except for the program in Chapter 15 which run under C++ on the Macintosh. Most programs have been written in a subset of ANSI C and should run on most ANSI C systems with the exception of the object-oriented programs in Chapter 15, which are written in C++ to run under Symantec C++ on Macintoshes.

The **solutions manual** is available on-line to professors adopting the text. To receive this file, contact our local Addison-Wesley representative.

Acknowledgments

The author is grateful to computer science editors at Addison-Wesley who persuaded him to write this book and who helped shape the book into its present form. Lynne Doran Cote shaped the project and encouraged the author in numerous important ways. Bob Woodbury, executive editor of computer science, supported the project enthusiastically. Maite Suarez-Rivas, assistant to Lynne Doran Cote, helped greatly with obtaining reviews and with the preparation of the *Instructor's Manual*.

The author is also grateful to many fine people at Addison-Wesley who participated with great excellence and professionalism in the design and production of this book. Mona Zeftel did a superb job as production supervisor. Tom Ziolkowski helped immensely with the marketing strategy. Joya Faretra helped with the marketing materials. Katherine Harutunian did a fine job setting up the network server providing on-line access to the programs and instructional materials. Peter M. Blaiwas designed the cover. In addition, Lisa Delgado did an outstanding job of book design. Susan London-Payne helped with the artwork, which was drawn by Scot Graphics and revised by DPI. Jackie Davies did an outstanding job as compositor and helped the author immensely as he struggled to learn the subtleties of the composition system we used. Stephanie Magean was superb at copyediting. Roberta Brent proofread the book.

The author also wishes to express his thanks to faculty colleagues and students at UC Irvine who test-taught CS 2 courses based on earlier drafts of the book and who provided suggestions for improvement. In particular, Michael B. Dillencourt, Norman M. Jacobson, and Ray Watkins gave excellent feedback from the faculty's perspective. The following students and teaching assistants were of tremendous help in finding errors and suggesting improvements: Manny Powers, Theresa Millette, Deborah Dubrow, Denise McElroy, and Keith Marino. The author is particularly grateful to Dinesh Ramanathan who helped translate the programs from Pascal into C, test-ran the C programs and examples, and helped with the C-version of the *Instructor's Manual*.

Wendy Lasher, Assistant to the Chair of Computer Science at UC Irvine, helped copy and express mail numerous drafts and artwork. Juancho Banaag provided unfailingly cheerful and efficient service with copying, binding, and mailing of many drafts and versions of the book and instructional materials.

Finally, the author and Addison-Wesley are indebted to the following reviewers who contributed their experience and knowledge to improving this text throughout its development: Richard Weinand, Wayne State University; Beth Weiss, University of Arizona; Khosrow Kaikhah, Southwest Texas State; Steve Vinoski, Hewlett-Packard; Harry W. Tyrer, University of Missouri-Columbia; and Rayno Niemi; Rochester Institute of Technology.

The author is most of all indebted to his wife, Elke, for providing the devotion and encouragement without which this book could not have been written.

T.A.S.
Laguna Beach, California

Contents

≡ **Chapter 1**　Preparing for the Journey 1

1.1　Where Are We Going? 1
　　　Plan for the Chapter 2
1.2　Blending Mathematics, Science, and
　　　Engineering 3
1.3　The Search for Enduring Principles in Computer
　　　Science 6
1.4　Principles of Software System Structure 8
1.5　Efficiency and Tradeoffs 11
1.6　Software Engineering Principles 11
1.7　Our Approach to Mathematics 13
1.8　Some Notes on Programming Notation 15
1.9　Preview of Coming Attractions 18
　　　Chapter Summary 20
　　　Problems and Exercises 21

≡ **Chapter 2**　Linked Data
Representations 22

2.1　Introduction and Motivation 22
　　　Plan for the Chapter 24
2.2　What Are Pointers? The Basic Intuition 24
　　　Two Examples of Linked Representations 25
2.3　Pointers in C — The Rudiments 27
　　　Question and Answer Time 29
　　　Some Fine Points — Aliases, Recycling, and
　　　　Dangling Pointers 30
　　　The Lifetime of Dynamic Storage 32
　　　Dereferencing 32
　　　2.3 Review Questions 32
　　　2.3 Exercises 33
2.4　Pointer Diagramming Notation 35

2.4 Review Questions 37
2.4 Exercises 37
2.5   Linear Linked Lists 38
       Inserting a New Second Node on a List 39
       Declaring Data Types for Linked Lists 42
       Searching for an Item on a List 43
       Deleting the Last Node of a List 46
       Inserting a New Last Node on a List 48
       How to Print a List 48
       Getting Our Act Together 51
       Where to From Here? 52
       2.5 Review Questions 52
       2.5 Exercises 53
2.6   Other Linked Data Structures 54
       2.6 Review Questions 57
       2.6 Exercise 57
       Pitfalls 57
       Tips and Techniques 58
       References for Further Study 60
       Chapter Summary 60

Chapter 3   Introduction to Recursion 62

3.1   Introduction and Motivation 62
       Plan for the Chapter 63
       Preview of Later Discussions of Recursion 63
3.2   Thinking Recursively 64
       How to Make Things Add Up Recursively 64
       Call Trees and Traces 69
       Multiplying Things Recursively 71
       Reversing Lists and Strings 75
       Reversing Strings 78
       The General Idea 80
       3.2 Review Questions 80
       3.2 Exercise 81
3.3   Common Pitfall—Infinite Regresses 83
       3.3 Review Questions 85
       3.3 Exercises 85
3.4   Quantitative Aspects of Recursive
       Algorithms** 86

Towers of Hanoi 86
3.4 Review Questions 90
3.4 Exercise 90
Pitfalls 90
Tips and Techniques 91
References for Further Study 91
Chapter Summary 91

Chapter 4   Modularity and Data Abstraction 93

4.1   Introduction and Motivation 93
       Plan for the Chapter 94
4.2   The Structure of C Modules 95
       4.2 Review Questions 96
4.3   Priority Queues—An Abstract Data Type 97
       A Priority Queue Interface File 97
       Two Implementations for Priority Queues 99
       Implementing Priority Queues Using Sorted
          Linked Lists 101
       Implementing Priority Queues Using
          Unsorted Arrays 104
       4.3 Review Questions 107
       4.3 Exercises 107
4.4   A Pocket Calculator Interface 107
       4.4 Review Questions 110
       4.4 Exercises 110
4.5   How to Hide Data Representations 111
       4.5 Review Questions 128
       4.5 Exercises 128
4.6   Modularity and Information Hiding in Program
       Design 131
       4.6 Review Questions 134
       Pitfalls 134
       Tips and Techniques 134
       References for Further Study 135
       Chapter Summary 135

Chapter 5   Introduction to Software Engineering Concepts 137

5.1   Introduction and Motivation 137
       Plan for the Chapter 138

5.2   Top-Down Programming by Stepwise
       Refinement 139
          Do You Have a Winning Ticket? 139
          Choosing a Data Representation for the
             Table 144
          A Note on Program Modularity 147
          A Second Refinement 148
          5.2 Review Questions 153
          5.2 Exercises 153
5.3   Proving Programs Correct 155
          A Subtle Bug 160
          A Bit of Formal Logic 161
          5.3 Review Questions 165
          5.3 Exercises 165
5.4   Transforming and Optimizing Programs 166
          5.4 Review Questions 172
          5.4 Exercise 172
5.5   Testing Programs 172
          Bottom-Up Testing 173
          Unit Testing, Formatted Debugging Aids, and
             Test Drivers 174
          Integration Testing 175
          Acceptance Testing and Regression
             Testing 175
          Top-Down Testing and Stubs 176
          Test Plans 178
          Comparing the Roles of Testing and
             Verification 178
          5.5 Review Questions 179
          5.5 Exercises 179
5.6   The Philosophy of Measurement and
       Tuning 179
          Comparing Some Methods for Binary
             Searching 180
          5.6 Review Questions 185
          5.6 Exercises 185
5.7   Software Reuse and Bottom-up
       Programming 186
          5.7 Review Questions 189
          5.7 Exercises 189
5.8   Program Structuring and Documentation 190
          Programming Style Disciplines 196
             Documentation 197
          5.8 Review Questions 198
          5.8 Exercises 199
       Pitfalls 200
       Tips and Techniques 201
       References for Further Study 202
       Chapter Summary 202

Chapter 6   Introduction to Analysis
             of Algorithms   205

6.1   Introduction and Motivation 205
          Plan for the Chapter 206
6.2   What Do We Use for a Yardstick? 207
          6.2 Review Questions 212
          6.2 Exercise 212
6.3   The Intuition Behind O-Notation 213
          A Word of Caution 217
          What We'll Discover Later 217
          6.3 Review Questions 219
          6.3 Exercises 220
6.4   O-Notation—Definition and Manipulation 220
          An Example of a Formal Proof of
             O-Notation 221
          Practical Shortcuts for Manipulating
             O-Notation 222
          6.4 Review Questions 224
          6.4 Exercises 225
6.5   Analyzing Simple Algorithms** 225
          Analysis of Sequential Searching 225
          Analysis of SelectionSort 227
          Analysis of Recursive SelectionSort 230
          Analysis of Towers of Hanoi 232
          Analysis of MergeSort 236
          Analysis of Binary Searching 241
          6.5 Review Questions 246
          6.5 Exercises 247
6.6   What O-Notation Doesn't Tell You 247
          6.6 Review Questions 249
          6.6 Exercise 249
       Pitfalls 249
       Tips and Techniques 250

References for Further Study 250
Chapter Summary 251

Chapter 7   Linear Data Structures—
               Stacks and Queues 253

7.1   Introduction and Motivation 253
      Plan for the Chapter 255
7.2   Some Background on Stacks 256
      7.2 Review Questions 258
      7.2 Exercises 258
7.3   ADTs for Stacks and Queues 259
      Interfaces for Stack and Queue
          Operations 261
      7.3 Review Questions 263
      7.3 Exercises 263
7.4   Using the Stack ADT to Check for Balanced
      Parentheses 263
      7.4 Review Questions 266
      7.4 Exercises 266
7.5   Using the Stack ADT to Evaluate Postfix
      Expressions 267
      7.5 Review Questions 270
      7.5 Exercises 270
7.6   Implementing the Stack ADT 271
      The Sequential Stack Representation 271
      The Linked Stack Representation 273
      7.6 Review Questions 274
      7.6 Exercises 275
7.7   How C Implements Recursive Function Calls
      Using Stacks 275
      7.7 Review Questions 280
      7.7 Exercise 280
7.8   Implementations of the Queue ADT 280
      Sequential Queue Representations 281
      Linked Queue Representations 284
      Comparing Linked and Sequential Queue
          Representations 286
      7.8 Review Questions 288
      7.8 Exercises 288
7.9   More Queue Applications 289
      Queues in Operating Systems 289
      Queues in Simulation Experiments 291
      7.9 Review Questions 293

7.9 Exercise 293
Pitfalls 294
Tips and Techniques 294
References for Further Study 295
Chapter Summary 295

Chapter 8   Lists, Strings, and Dynamic
               Memory Allocation 296

8.1   Introduction and Motivation 296
      Plan for the Chapter 297
8.2   Lists 298
      A List ADT 298
      Sequential List Representations 298
      The One-Way Linked Representation 299
      Comparing Sequential and Linked List
          Representations 301
      Other Linked List Representations 302
      Circular Linked Lists 303
      Two-Way Linked Lists 303
      Linked Lists with Header Nodes 304
      8.2 Review Questions 304
      8.2 Exercises 304
8.3   Generalized Lists 305
      8.3 Review Questions 308
      8.3 Exercises 308
8.4   Applications of Generalized Lists 308
      8.4 Review Questions 312
      8.4 Exercises 312
8.5   Strings 312
      A String ADT 313
      Some String Representations 314
      String Representations in Text Files and
          Word Processors 316
      8.5 Review Questions 318
      8.5 Exercises 319
8.6   Dynamic Memory Allocation 319
      Available Space Lists and Garbage
          Collection 321
      Heaps and Dynamic Memory Allocation 323
      First-Fit 325
      Best-Fit 326
      Fragmentation and Coalescing 326
      Compacting to Deal with Allocation

Failures 328
Comparing Uses of Heaps in
Applications 330
Reference Counts 330
8.6 Review Questions 331
8.6 Exercises 332
Pitfalls 332
Tips and Techniques 333
References for Further Study 334
Chapter Summary 334

=== **Chapter 9**   Trees 337

9.1   Introduction and Motivation 337
Plan for the Chapter 338
9.2   Basic Concepts and Terminology 339
9.2 Review Questions 341
9.2 Exercises 341
9.3   Binary Trees 342
9.3 Review Questions 343
9.3 Exercises 343
9.4   A Sequential Binary Tree Representation 344
9.4 Review Questions 345
9.4 Exercises 346
9.5   An Application—Heaps and Priority
Queues 346
Converting to the Sequential
Representation 352
A Few Mathematical Facts About
Heaps** 355
9.5 Review Questions 358
9.5 Exercises 358
9.6   Traversing Binary Trees 359
Traversals Using the Linked Representation of
Binary Trees 361
9.6 Review Questions 364
9.6 Exercises 364
9.7   Binary Search Trees 365
Analyzing Performance Characteristics** 366
9.7 Review Questions 374
9.7 Exercises 375
9.8   AVL Trees and Their Performance 376
Building an AVL Tree Using Insertions and
Rotations 380

Balance Factors and Comments on Rotation
Algorithms 383
Analysis of Performance** 384
9.8 Review Questions 387
9.8 Exercises 388
9.9   Two–Three Trees** 388
B–Trees—A Generalization of 2–3 Trees** 391
9.9 Review Questions 392
9.9 Exercises 392
9.10   Tries 392
9.10 Review Questions 394
9.10 Exercise 394
9.11   An Application—Huffman Codes** 394
9.11 Review Questions 399
9.11 Exercises 399
Pitfalls 399
Tips and Techniques 400
References for Further Study 401
Chapter Summary 401

=== **Chapter 10**   Graphs 405

10.1   Introduction and Motivation 405
Plan for the Chapter 406
10.2   Basic Concepts and Terminology 408
Some Formal Definitions 409
Paths, Cycles, and Adjacency 410
Connectivity and Components 410
Adjacency Sets and Degrees 410
10.2 Review Questions 411
10.2 Exercises 411
10.3   Graph Representations 412
10.3 Review Questions 414
10.3 Exercises 414
10.4   Graph Searching 415
10.4 Review Questions 419
10.4 Exercises 419
10.5   Topological Ordering 419
10.5 Review Questions 422
10.5 Exercises 422
10.6   Shortest Paths 423
10.6 Review Questions 428
10.6 Exercises 428
10.7   Task Networks 428
Critical Path Algorithms 431

10.7 Review Questions 438
10.7 Exercises 438
10.8   Useful Background on Graphs 439
        Minimal Spanning Trees 439
        Flow Networks 441
        The Four-Color Problem 442
        NP-Complete Graph Problems 443
        Concluding Remarks 445
        10.8 Review Questions 445
        10.8 Exercises 446
        Pitfalls 446
        Tips and Techniques 446
        References for Further Study 447
        Chapter Summary 447

Chapter 11 Hashing and the Table ADT 450

11.1   Introduction and Motivation 450
        Plan for the Chapter 453
11.2   The Table ADT 453
        11.2 Review Questions 455
        11.2 Exercises 455
11.3   Introduction to Hashing by Simple
        Examples 455
        11.3 Review Questions 461
        11.3 Exercises 461
11.4   Collisions, Load Factors, and Clusters 461
        Collisions 462
        The von Mises Probability Argument ** 463
        Load Factors and Clustering 465
        11.4 Review Questions 468
        11.4 Exercises 468
11.5   Algorithms for Hashing by Open
        Addressing 469
        Two Examples of Primary Clustering and Its
            Absence 470
        Ensuring That Probe Sequences Cover the
            Table ** 476
        Performance Formulas 478
        Derivations for Half of the Performance
            Formulas ** 480
        Comparing Theoretical and Empirical
            Results 482
        11.5 Review Questions 483

        11.5 Exercises 484
11.6   Choosing a Hash Function 486
        The Division Method 487
        Other Hash Function Methods 488
        11.6 Review Questions 488
        11.6 Exercises 488
11.7   Comparison of Searching Methods Using the
        Table ADT 489
        11.7 Review Questions 491
        11.7 Exercises 491
        Pitfalls 492
        Tips and Techniques 493
        References for Further Study 493
        Chapter Summary 494

Chapter 12 External Collections of Data 497

12.1   Introduction and Motivation 497
        Plan for the Chapter 498
12.2   Characteristics of External Storage Devices 499
        Tapes 499
        Disks 501
        12.2 Review Questions 504
        12.2 Exercises 504
12.3   Techniques That Don't Work Well 505
        12.3 Review Questions 507
        12.3 Exercises 507
12.4   Techniques That Work Well 507
        Sorting Large External Files 507
        The Indexed Sequential Access Method 509
        Using B-Trees 513
        Hashing with Buckets 514
        12.4 Review Questions 516
        12.4 Exercises 516
12.5   Information Retrieval and Databases 517
        File Inversion Techniques 517
        Queries and Information Retrieval 518
        Databases 519
        12.5 Review Questions 520
        12.5 Exercises 520
        Pitfalls 521
        Tips and Techniques 521
        References for Further Study 521
        Chapter Summary 522

Chapter 13 Sorting 524

13.1   Introduction and Motivation 524
          Plan for the Chapter 525
13.2   Laying Some Groundwork** 527
          13.2 Review Questions 531
          13.2 Exercises 532
13.3   Priority Queue Sorting Methods 532
          Some Preliminary
             Assumptions 532
          Priority Queue Sorting 533
          SelectionSort 535
          HeapSort 537
          13.3 Review Questions 539
          13.3 Exercises 539
13.4   Divide-and-Conquer Methods 540
          MergeSort 540
          QuickSort 541
          13.4 Review Questions 547
          13.4 Exercises 547
13.5   Methods That Insert Keys and Keep Them
        Sorted 547
          InsertionSort 548
          TreeSort 550
          13.5 Review Questions 550
          13.5 Exercises 551
13.6   O(n) Methods—Address Calculation
        Sorting 551
          ProxmapSort 552
          RadixSort 563
          13.6 Review Questions 565
          13.6 Exercises 565
13.7   Other Methods 566
          ShellSort 566
          BubbleSort 569
          13.7 Review Questions 571
          13.7 Exercises 571
13.8   Comparison and Perspective 572
          Some Simple Wisdom 575
          13.8 Review Questions 575
          13.8 Exercises 575
        Pitfalls 576
        Tips and Techniques 576
        References for Further Study 577
        Chapter Summary 577

Chapter 14 Advanced Recursion 581

14.1   Introduction and Motivation 581
          Plan for the Chapter 582
14.2   Recursion as a Descriptive Method 583
          14.2 Review Questions 585
          14.2 Exercises 585
14.3   Using Recursion to Build a Parser 586
          14.3 Review Questions 595
          14.3 Exercises 595
14.4   Translating from Infix to Postfix 596
          14.4 Review Questions 600
          14.4 Exercises 600
14.5   Recursion and Program Verification 601
          Proving that Recursive Tree Reversal Works
             Correctly 601
          14.5 Review Questions 605
          14.5 Exercises 605
14.6   Pitfalls 606
14.7   Tips and Techniques 607
14.8   References for Further Study 607
14.9   Chapter Summary 607

Chapter 15 Object-Oriented
                     Programming 610

15.1   Introduction and Motivation 610
          Plan for the Chapter 612
15.2   Exploring OOP Through Progressive Examples 613
          Defining Derived Classes 618
          Using the Shapes Module in the Main
             Program 619
          Drawing Filled Shapes — The Second Stage
             OOP Example 624
          Building and Moving Lists of Shapes — The
             Third Stage OOP Example 627
          Conclusions 638
          15.2 Review Questions 638
          15.2 Exercises 639
15.3   Building Systems Using Object-Oriented
        Programming 639
          Imagining a Drawing Application 639
          Implementing File and Printing Subsystems
             Using Object-Oriented Programming 643

Developing User Interfaces Using Object-
Oriented Programming 646
15.3 Review Questions 650
15.3 Exercises 650
15.4 Advantages and Disadvantages of Object-
Oriented Programming 651
The Importance of Using Good Class
Browsers 652
15.4 Review Questions 654
15.4 Exercises 654
Pitfalls 655
Tips and Techniques 655
References for Further Study 656
Chapter Summary 656

Chapter 16 Advanced Software
Engineering Concepts 659

16.1 Introduction and Motivation 659
Plan for the Chapter 660
16.2 The Software Lifecycle 660
Requirements Analysis 661
Specification 662
Design 663
Coding and Debugging 664
Testing and Integration 665
Operations, Maintenance, and Upgrade 666
16.2 Review Questions 667
16.2 Exercises 667
16.3 Software Productivity 667
The Software Learning Curve 668
High Variance in Individual Productivity 669
Productivity Differences as a Measure of
Comparative Difficulty Among
Projects 670
Boehm's COCOMO Model 670
16.3 Review Questions 674
16.3 Exercises 675
16.4 Software Process Models 675
The Waterfall Model 676
The Spiral Model 681
16.4 Review Questions 684
16.4 Exercises 684
Pitfalls 685
Tips and Techniques 685
References for Further Study 686
Chapter Summary 686

Appendix Math Reference and
Tutorial 689

A.1 Arithmetic Progressions 689
Applying the Formulas for Arithmetic
Progressions 692
A.1 Review Questions 694
A.1 Exercises 694
A.2 Geometric Progressions 695
Applications of Geometric Progressions 698
A.2 Review Questions 700
A.2 Exercises 700
A.3 Floors and Ceilings 701
Manipulating Floors and Ceilings 702
A.3 Review Questions 704
A.3 Exercises 704
A.4 Logarithms and Exponentials 704
Exponentials 704
Logarithms 705
Application to Inequalities 709
A.4 Review Questions 710
A.4 Exercises 710
A.5 Modular Arithmetic 710
A.5 Review Questions 713
A.5 Exercises 713
A.6 Sums 713
Changing Index Variables 715
Application 715
Finding Closed Formulas for Sums 716
Sums of Sums 718
Useful Formulas for Some Special Sums 720
A.6 Review Questions 723
A.6 Exercises 723
A.7 Recurrence Relations 724
A.7 Review Questions 727
A.7 Exercises 727
A.8 Manipulating Logical Expressions 727
Problem 1 728
Problem 2 729
Applications 731
A.8 Review Questions 731
A.8 Exercises 731

Index 733

1

Preparing for the Journey

1.1   Where Are We Going?

Before beginning a journey, it's always a good idea to ask, "Where are we going?" and "Why are we going there?"

Computer science itself has been on a fast-paced journey of formulation and discovery since it got rolling in the early 1940s. It has introduced astonishing innovations, never before seen in human history, which have transformed our thought and our civilization in ways undreamed of a half-century ago. Learning about computer science is a journey filled with excitement and adventure.

This book covers material for a second course in computer science. Such a course is only the second leg of a longer journey—that of learning about computer science as a whole. The book makes the assumption that you have already covered the first leg of the journey by taking a first course in computer science.

Principally, this book covers *algorithms*, *data structures*, and *software principles*— these being fundamentals needed as essential groundwork for making the rest of the journey of learning computer science. It also emphasizes fundamental questions of computer science, and explains significant accomplishments that all well-educated computer scientists should know about.

An important goal is to help you develop competence in the field. By weaving together skills from mathematics, science, and engineering, you will be helped to develop competence in computer science that harmoniously integrates theory, experimentation, and design. Some of these skills are analytic and some are creative.

mathematics, science, and engineering

In order to help tie the material in the book together, attention is paid throughout to important *recurring concepts*. Some of these concepts relate to how computing systems or large software systems are structured, and they involve organizational principles, such as *layers*, *hierarchies*, *information-hiding*, *abstraction*, and *interfaces*. Others relate to important properties of algorithms and data structures, such as *efficiency*, *tradeoffs*, and *resource consumption* characteristics. Yet others relate to software engineering, and they involve aspects of the organization of human effort required to build large software systems so that they exhibit certain key properties such as *reliability*, *affordability*, *efficiency*, *correctness*, and *safety*.

Plan for the Chapter

As a starting point, it's important to grasp why computer science, unlike other sciences, blends mathematics, science, and engineering. Section 1.2 discusses how you should try to develop competence in each of these three aspects of computer science.

searching for enduring principles

Section 1.3 focuses on the process of searching for enduring principles in computer science. Even though hardware technology has been changing rapidly, other features of hardware and software systems have been much more stable over time. Section 1.4 discusses some of the enduring principles that have been discovered about the structure of software systems. Such systems involve the recurring concepts of *representation*, *abstraction*, *information-hiding*, and *interfaces*.

Section 1.5 discusses the recurring concepts of *efficiency* and *tradeoffs*. It is vital for computer science to discover the best ways of performing commonly occurring algorithmic tasks, used often as building blocks in the creation of larger systems. Insights into efficiency and tradeoffs can be gained sometimes by performing mathematical analyses of algorithms and sometimes by conducting experiments that measure the performance of algorithms and systems.

Software engineering principles, discussed in Section 1.6, are related to organizing and managing the human effort and resources needed to build software systems.

Section 1.7 comments on the approach to mathematics used in this book and Section 1.8 covers a few brief points about the programming notation used. Mostly, we use ANSI C. However, in Chapter 15, we introduce various object-oriented programming features from C++, an object-oriented extension of the C language. Because the other chapters are written using only ANSI C, there is little drawback if the version of C you are using does not have the C++ object-oriented programming features. We also give an example of the style for indentation and line numbering of C programs used in the book.

Finally, Section 1.9 provides a brief description of what is covered in the remaining chapters.

1.2 Blending Mathematics, Science, and Engineering

Computer science is a bit different from other contemporary sciences, because it blends mathematics, science, and engineering activities more intimately than other sciences do. It's worth spending a few minutes discussing this topic in order to understand why computer science has this distinction.

First, let's get clear in our minds how mathematics, science, and engineering are different. Science tries to discover fundamental laws and principles of nature. Engineering is the design and construction of artifacts to suit human purposes. It applies the sciences to build artifacts and systems. Mathematics attempts to discover significant facts and relationships that can be expressed precisely using symbolic or quantitative language.

how science, engineering, and mathematics differ

For example, let's look at superconductivity, a phenomenon in which an electric current flows through an electrical conductor without resistance. A physicist might try to understand how and why superconductivity occurs while an engineer might try to build a magnetic levitating train or an efficient electrical power transmission system based on superconductivity. A mathematician might develop useful mathematical models that might help the physicists express their theories of superconductivity, or that might help engineers solve problems relating to how strong superconducting magnets need to be to support levitating trains.

Mathematics deals in the realm of pure thought, rather than in the realm of material artifacts. And yet, mathematics has a great deal to say about what is true and what is possible in this world of pure ideas. Furthermore, experience has shown that mathematics is vitally important for expressing the precise understanding that the sciences have achieved. Mathematics has been a key source of models and descriptions used by scientists in their fundamental quest to develop descriptive and predictive theories of nature.

In the contemporary academic world, physics, engineering, and mathematics are separate disciplines that are pursued in separate departments by separate groups of investigators. In computer science, however, there appears to be a blending of the mathematical, scientific, and engineering aspects of the investigation of computing into a single enterprise, typically housed in a single academic department. It is not entirely clear why computer science differs from the classical sciences, and from mathematics and engineering, in this regard—nor is it clear whether this difference will endure in the future.

It is nevertheless informative and interesting to try to make an educated guess as to why computer science has integrated mathematics, science, and engineering (see Fig. 1.1 on the next page), while the other traditional fields have kept them separate. One such speculation goes like this: Computer science is a science that concerns artificial things—things made by human beings—instead of things that occur in nature that were not made by human beings. That is, rather than being a *natural science*, computer science is a *science of the artificial*.

While an astronomer can study the phenomena of the stars and heavenly bodies, and can develop astronomical theories that are both descriptive and predictive (as in predicting when Halley's Comet will next appear), an astronomer cannot change the nature of the things astronomy studies. Likewise, the physicist Isaac Newton studying

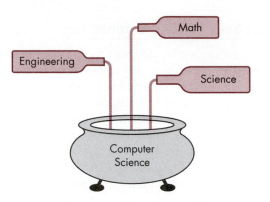

Figure 1.1 Blending Mathematics, Science, and Engineering

the nature of light, developed astonishing theories describing its properties and behavior, but Newton did not have the option of changing the nature of light to make his theories easier to discover or formulate.

By contrast, a computer scientist studies phenomena—such as the behavior of operating systems or algorithms—that are exhibited by artifacts created by the human imagination. Moreover, the objects of study can be changed by further creative acts of the human imagination. Thus computer science is a science in which it is possible to change the things you are studying and trying to understand.

Consequently, computer scientists can alter the objects they study to make them reveal better theories or yield better understanding. Because this opportunity is *open* in computer science, rather than being *shut* as it is in the traditional sciences, it is not surprising that computer scientists take advantage of it by interweaving activities of design and analysis: An episode of design produces something worthy of study because it exhibits interesting behavior. An episode of analysis follows, which reveals that if the design were changed, the behavior might be even more interesting and valuable to study. This is followed by more design activities, which in turn are followed by more analysis activities. The process ends when some important discoveries are made, providing key insights into how things work, or what is possible or impossible. Moreover, the process tends to lead to discoveries that reveal how to build things having useful applications—knowledge that answers the questions "How to?" as well as "What is?"

weaving design and
analysis together

Suppose we accept as a matter of historical observation that design and analysis have tended to be interleaved during the past evolution of computer science. Let's now focus more concretely on the nature of these design and analysis activities. First, let's look at design. Design activities in computer science are sometimes very close in style to traditional engineering activities. You build a computer system or write a program to satisfy some requirements. (These requirements may have resulted from a requirements analysis process that is a traditional engineering practice.)

development of theory

Sometimes, however, the design activities are very close in style to the process of formulation, definition, and conjecture that mathematicians perform when they are developing new mathematical theories. Formulating a new mathematical theory (consisting of definitions, theorems, and proofs) involves inventive acts of the human imagination. Unlike engineering activities that design new material artifacts and systems, the creative design of the mathematician is directed at discovering (or inventing) new systems of mathematical ideas that are found to exhibit interesting and profound properties.

For example, one of the important problems faced in the early days of computer science was how to get a computer to translate and execute programs written in high-level programming languages. There was a critical need to develop some theories of parsing, translation, and compiling. In order to develop the theory of parsing (in which *parsing a program* is the process of grammatically analyzing how it is composed of its parts), computer scientists behaved like mathematicians. From linguistics, they borrowed definitions of grammars, called *context-free grammars*, useful for precisely describing the structure of programming languages. (We will learn a little bit about these context-free grammars in Chapter 14 when we study advanced recursion.) They formulated algorithms for parsing programs written in such programming languages, and they conjectured and then proved some powerful theorems characterizing exactly when such parsing algorithms would work and how efficiently they could be made to operate. The result was a body of discoveries that yielded deep understanding of what was possible in the realm of parsing, and which had important practical applications to the development of compilers.

Sometimes the analysis activities conducted by computer scientists resemble those in traditional experimental science. Experiments are conducted, observations are made, data are collected, and theories and laws are devised to account for the data. A successful theory is one that is both descriptive and predictive. Its laws describe the data and these laws can be used to predict the future behavior of computational systems. Scientific understanding has been achieved by this traditional scientific method when (1) the experiments can be repeated by independent observers under precisely understood experimental conditions, and (2) the results of these experiments agree with the predictions generated by the theory.

experiments and the scientific method

But the analysis activities undertaken by computer scientists sometimes also resemble those undertaken by pure mathematicians. An algorithm is an object expressed in a precise symbolic language with precise rules of operation. As such, it is a mathematical object. Mathematical reasoning can be applied to discover its properties and implications.

Sometimes the consequences of such mathematical reasoning can be very startling. For example, using a mathematical style of investigation, it has been discovered that (1) it is impossible to write a computer program P_1 that will look at another computer program P_2 and tell whether P_2 will halt or get into an endless loop when it is executed; (2) it is impossible to write a computer program that will take a look at a context-free grammar, G, and tell whether the language it describes is ambiguous or not (where an ambiguous sentence is one having two or more different grammatical structures, as in the sentences, "They are flying planes." or "He saw the man in the park with the telescope."); and (3) it is impossible to write a program that will simplify algebraic expressions in a general way (as in simplifying $x^2 - 2xy + y^2$ to become $(x - y)^2$). Historically, investigations conducted in the style of mathematical analysis have contributed important and deep results about what is possible and impossible in computer science.

One conclusion that we can draw from this discussion is that instead of investigating a part of nature that is already there and can't be changed, computer science is investigating a subject that is undergoing vigorous and rapid evolution. Fascinating new computing artifacts appear on the scene at a fantastic rate and tantalize the computer scientist to study and understand them. Consequently, computer science is a journey of *formulation* and *discovery*—formulation of interesting new artifacts and new systems of mathematical ideas and discovery of important fundamental principles of computation.

formulation and discovery

The creative acts of building computer systems or designing algorithms are essentially engineering activities (i.e., building things to suit purposes). Experimentation to collect data and study the behavior exhibited by the things created in this way is essentially a scientific activity. Moreover, the discovery and development of formal theories that express essential ideas underlying a class of computations are essentially mathematical activities. Historically, these three strands of activity—mathematics, science, and engineering—have been carried out by computer scientists in an interwoven fashion. And aspects of each activity have been essential to making progress in computer science.

implications for you

The main implication of these observations for you as a student is that you should adopt the goal of gaining competence in each of the three kinds of computer science activities—mathematics, science, and engineering—by (1) becoming skilled at conducting mathematical analyses and performing mathematical reasoning; (2) gaining understanding of the experimental scientific method and learning to conduct experiments, collect data, and discover meanings; and (3) learning how things work and developing creative capacities to design algorithms, choose appropriate data structures, and build software or computational systems to solve problems.

This book is written with an eye toward supporting the learning of these three kinds of skills. There are opportunities to learn how to conduct mathematical analyses and to learn how to reason about programs by doing it. Experiments are described in the text in which data are collected and then analyzed. Opportunities for you to conduct your own experiments are given in the exercises. And, of course, there are many opportunities to design algorithms and data structures to solve both small and large programming problems, leading to opportunities to develop skills in software engineering.

1.3 The Search for Enduring Principles in Computer Science

searching for ideas that have lasting value

Computer science is intimately involved with the search for enduring fundamental principles that help us understand the nature of computation and help us create useful new computing applications. In our computer science courses we certainly hope to present topics that have lasting value, rather than short-lived topics that will turn out to be useless a short while later. But it is often difficult to have the foresight to know ahead of time which discoveries will have lasting value and which will have only temporary value. On the other hand, by looking backward and observing which things lasted and which things were short-lived, we can determine important clues that can help us to choose topics that are likely to have enduring value.

An example of something that didn't last and has been in flux is the nature of computer hardware, which has changed four times since the 1940s. Computers were first built from electromechanical parts, such as relay circuits and mercury delay line memories. They were then built from vacuum tube circuits and magnetic drum memories. Following this, processors were built from transistors and the memories began to use magnetic cores. (You will still occasionally hear old-timers refer to primary memory as "core" even though memory isn't built from magnetic cores any more—which proves that some language habits can be more long-lasting than computer hardware.) Most recently, both processors and memories have been built from chips. VLSI chips (meaning very large scale integrated chips) contain tens of thousands of transistors in a space smaller than your thumbnail, and operate with astonishing speed and reliability.

At the moment, we don't know what the future holds with regard to hardware. Perhaps the next few decades will see the introduction of hardware based on optical devices—computing based on light valves or holograms. Or perhaps biologically engineered macromolecules will be used to store massive amounts of data in tiny spaces. While it is likely that new kinds of hardware will be faster, cheaper, and more reliable than today's hardware (otherwise why bother changing things), we really can't foresee which new ideas will be successful.

Nevertheless, it doesn't matter. Although computer hardware has changed four times in the past half-century and is likely to continue changing in the future, the essential nature of basic computer instructions and the basic building blocks of data (such as bits, bytes, and words) didn't change very much at all and probably won't change very much in the future. The basic machine-level instructions still perform arithmetic and logical operations on sequences of bits, they still perform branches in the execution of instruction sequences depending on the outcome of comparisons, and they still transfer information between processors and memory. Moreover, the underlying laws of arithmetic and logic didn't change at all—two plus two still equals four. And it is likely that none of them will change if we replace the current generation of computers with future optical or biological computers.

basic machine organization principles survived hardware changes

Since the fundamental arithmetic, logical, and data movement operations of computers stayed nearly the same, things built on top of them could survive the change from one generation of hardware to the next. In fact, many programming languages, such as COBOL, FORTRAN, LISP, C, and Pascal, survived hardware generation changes, as did many kinds of computer software written in these languages. The compilers for these programming languages turned out to be portable from one generation of hardware to the next, since not much needed to be changed in the way they were written. Their basic organizational principles—consisting of algorithms and data structures—stayed the same, even though the underlying machine instruction sets from which they were programmed changed slightly. They still used context-free grammars and parsers based on them to detect program structure. They still used tables in which to store and retrieve values. And the structure of these entities did not have to change at all, even though the hardware device technology was rapidly changing underneath in a fundamental way.

Let's pause now to introduce a new word—*abstraction*. When you form an abstraction from a set of instances, you ignore inessential differences, and identify common features that are important. For example, when building a radar air traffic control system, the only features of an airplane that are useful to display on a radar screen are the airplane's *position*, *velocity*, *altitude*, and *identification*. All other features, such as the aircraft's manufacturer and color, are inessential (and would hopelessly clutter the radar scope, if one were so foolish as to attempt to display them). In this case, we could say that we had *abstracted* from the set of instances of airplanes under air traffic control just four essential features to display on controllers' radar scopes.

the concept of abstraction

Returning now to our discussion of what did and did not survive the changes in hardware generations, we can observe (with the benefit of hindsight) that the right kind of *abstractions* survived changes in the underpinnings. Because these abstractions turned out to have lasting value and utility, we are entitled to believe that they are fundamental, and that the principles by which they are organized and which describe how they operate are fundamental principles. And that's what computer science is partly about—finding enduring fundamental principles that govern the nature of computation and that can be applied to build new software and systems.

1.4 Principles of Software System Structure

Let's push this line of exploration a bit further. What other fundamental principles can we discover by studying with hindsight the way software systems have come to be organized?

In such a discussion it is helpful to focus on a specific example—for instance, an airline reservation system, where customers can phone in to make reservations to fly to various destinations on various future dates. Figure 1.2 shows some of the data structures that might be used to implement such a system. At the top level, the system must be programmed to deal directly with the entities of direct concern to users—things like schedules, flights, dates, and reservations. These top-level entities are rep-

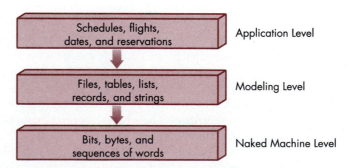

Figure 1.2 Data Structures Used in an Airline Reservation System

resented using intermediate-level data structures—things like files, tables, lists, records, and strings. For example, the overall schedule of available flights might be represented using a big table of some sort. Reservations for a flight on a future date might be stored as lists of records in a file associated with that flight. The records in this file might contain strings and numbers representing names, phone numbers, and some other coded data for each passenger who has made a future reservation. The intermediate level data structures are in turn ultimately represented using the primitive data structures available on the naked machine—things like bytes and linear sequences of machine words.

The process of writing programs to create computer applications involves the *representation* of objects, operations, and behaviors required in the application in terms of the primitives available in the computational medium. In this representational process, the surface behaviors displayed by solutions are synthesized from compositions of primitive behaviors available in the computational medium. From this point of view, we could look on the computer as fundamentally being a *representation machine*.

representation—a main idea in computer science

We can construct a representation by organizing the data and processes of a given representational medium to exhibit the required properties and behaviors of some specified system of objects and operations being represented. Often two distinct conceptual levels are involved in the representational process, with each one using different levels of language and notation. One level describes the structures being modeled, and the other level describes the objects and operations in the underlying representational medium. In most large software systems more than two levels of representation are used, with intermediate layers serving both as representational media for higher layers and as specifications for underlying representations by lower layers.

Thus representations are often composed one or more times, using several layers of abstraction, spanning the gap from the machine domain to the application domain. In Fig. 1.2, the intermediate level of representation is called the "modeling level."

In building application systems, it is interesting to ask, "Why do we use general-purpose, intermediate-level data structures, such as files, lists, trees, arrays, and strings?" Why are they even needed? These entities do not actually exist in the naked machine. They are fictional entities that we create in our imaginations. They provide no essential capacity that cannot be implemented in terms of machine primitives by using assembly language directly.

why use intermediate-level data structures?

The answers to these questions penetrate to the heart of the reason why the material in this book is of fundamental importance in computer science. The basic answers have to do with assisting the human mind in dealing with complexity and with software economics—the problem of how to build reliable, efficient systems as cheaply and rapidly as possible.

First, on purely economic grounds, it is more efficient to build systems out of intermediate-level components than it is to start from scratch. For example, to build a radio, you might want to start with intermediate-level components such as power supplies, voltage regulators, antennas, speakers, and potentiometers (i.e., dials). It would be costly for you to have to start with tin-foil and wax and wrap your own capacitors, or, worse, with iron ore that had to be smelted into iron to make magnets for the speakers. Likewise, to build software systems, it is often cheaper to use libraries of reusable software components than it is to start from scratch by using a programming language to "roll your own." Much of the substance of several later chapters in this book covers the powerful basic ideas and concepts which are the foundation of such reusable software components. Equipped with a stock of such powerful ideas, you will find you have tremendously enhanced skill for crafting software representations and solutions.

Second, the human mind has limits to its capacity to deal with intellectual complexity. Human short-term memory can deal with only seven plus-or-minus two "chunks" of information at a given time. Constructing software representations often requires great mental precision, which cannot be attained if the things being thought about are too complex. Consequently, there is a premium on discovering ways to break the structure of a complex system into simpler parts. Ideally, such parts should consist of interacting subsystems that are simple, concise, and lucid, and that can be dealt with easily by the human mind.

It has been found, after much exploration and by virtue of much trial-and-error experience, that certain organizational principles greatly help the human mind to deal with the design and construction of software. (These organizational principles also help teams of programmers to build big systems cooperatively.) Such principles include (1) the use of intermediate-level modeling structures to help break the overall representational mapping (of application-level entities into machine primitives) into simple steps that the human mind can deal with more easily one step at a time; and (2) packaging representational entities into *modules* and *layers* that hide the inner details of their operation from view and present clean, simple interfaces to their users, thus making them easier to handle. Here, *information-hiding* is the act of concealing the internal details from view, and *abstraction* is used to extract a few simple details to put into the interfaces for users to employ, while deciding which things to conceal from view in order to reduce complexity.

Third, experience has shown that even though the intermediate-level data structures are figments of the human imagination, they have a high utility in solving programming problems. They present programmers with a stock of ideas to use for constructing representations in a remarkably broad range of application areas. In this sense, programming is analogous to mathematics. Mathematics abounds with imaginary objects that are creations of human thought—geometric figures, algebraic quantities, sets, differential equations, permutations, probabilities, and so forth. These mathematical entities are highly useful for constructing theories and models—especially because they are rich with important properties that have been extensively explored.

The situation is similar in computer science, although computer science is at a more primitive stage of development than mathematics. Computer science abounds with general purpose, intermediate-level data structures that are highly useful in con-

abstract data types   structing representations—things like lists, trees, arrays, strings, tables, stacks, queues, sets, and graphs. The notion of *abstract data types* (ADTs) refers to a way of packaging some intermediate-level data structures and their operations into a useful collection whose properties have been carefully studied. These ADTs have been organized to have clean, simple interfaces. They can be represented in many ways by lower-level representations (such as sequential or linked representations)—but the several ways in which they can be represented have been hidden from view (through the use of information-hiding) so that they can be used, simply by knowing only their abstract interface properties. Moreover, they have precisely defined behaviors, permitting clear reasoning about them to take place.

Major parts of this book are devoted to presenting various kinds of ADTs and to developing their properties and uses, in order to enrich your knowledge of ideas and concepts useful for crafting practical representations and systems.

1.5 Efficiency and Tradeoffs

When we develop the properties of ADTs, we often focus on algorithms supporting the useful operations we can perform with them. In this connection, the recurring concept of *efficiency* is a major concern. It is useful to discover algorithms that work as efficiently as possible and to be able to characterize their efficiency with suitable mathematical formulas. Sometimes it is even possible to prove that certain algorithms work at maximum efficiency, and that it is impossible to do any better.

On other occasions, we shall be concerned with the recurring concept of *tradeoffs*. Among ADTs that have more than one representation, some representations take very little space but the algorithms that implement their operations take substantial time. Other representations of the same ADT take more space but have algorithms using less time. In such a case, we say that space and time *trade off* against one another.

1.6 Software Engineering Principles

There are two levels at which this book covers software engineering principles: those concerning small programs and those concerning large software systems. The first is called *programming-in-the-small*. The second is called *programming-in-the-large*.

Programming-in-the-small concerns concepts that help us create small programs—those that vary in length from a few lines to a few pages. Sometimes the creation of small programs involves great subtlety of thought and requires great precision and ingenuity. It is important to be able to reason about small programs with clarity and mental precision.

programming-in-the-small

We are also interested in ideas for program structuring that help make the flow of control during program execution mirror the textual structure of the program—this being called *structured programming*. By using good program structuring, our reasoning about programs is made easier and more effective, and programs are made easier to understand. One technique that is useful for creating structured programs is called *top-down programming by stepwise refinement*. We will explore this technique in Chapter 5.

structured programming

In programming-in-the-large, we are concerned with principles that organize large, long-lived software systems, and we are concerned with processes for organizing

programming-in-the-large

the large-scale human effort needed to build such systems. You might think of *large* software systems as those having over 100,000 lines of code, and you might think of *long-lived* software systems as those having useful service lifetimes of twenty-five years or longer. There are many topics to cover in learning about what has been discovered to be useful by software engineers for programming-in-the-large. We survey only some key ideas in this book, since a CS2 course cannot provide you with the opportunity to build a big system. Nonetheless, it can help you appreciate many of the important concepts and issues involved.

For instance, the *lifecycle* of a software system is the period of time that stretches from the system's initial conception to its eventual retirement from service. The human activities related to the lifecycle involve processes such as requirements analysis, design, coding, testing, verification, documentation, and maintenance.

During the *requirements analysis* process, software engineers develop precise definitions of the properties of the software system that they intend to build. The *design* process produces a detailed plan for building the system. The *coding* process translates the design into actual working computer programs. The *testing* process subjects both individual software components and the entire integrated software system to trial runs to see if they work properly. The *verification* process involves the construction of mathematical proofs (or the development of other kinds of convincing evidence) to help determine whether programs do what they are supposed to do. *Documentation* consists of producing written explanations of what the system does, how its parts work, and how the system is used. The *maintenance* process follows the release of the system into active service, and consists of correcting defects and upgrading the system to meet evolving conditions during its useful service lifetime.

There are many fascinating questions that arise in connection with lifecycle processes and methods. For instance, when is it useful to build a *prototype* of a system (or a part of a system) and to try it out? Automotive and aeronautical engineers frequently build and test prototypes to try out new design concepts. In the case of software engineering, a good answer is that you use prototyping to buy information to reduce risk. We'll explore what this means in the context of risk-based software process models in Chapter 16.

Software engineers also need to be concerned with the skills related to the organization and management of large software projects. Concepts such as schedules, budgets, resource management policies, risk assessment, and risk item resolution come into play. These will be discussed in Chapter 16.

Overall, software engineers try to build software systems on time and within budget, to exhibit the characteristics defined in the system requirements definition. Often such characteristics include general software system properties such as *reliability*, *affordability*, *efficiency*, *correctness*, and *safety*. Everyone wants to buy software that is cheap; that is reliable, safe, and efficient; and that does what it is supposed to do. (A *safe* system is defined as one whose operation causes no harm to persons or property.) Organizing human effort in large software projects is a demanding and subtle business, fraught with risks. Software engineering is the art of organizing people and resources to achieve such aims with the highest quality possible. While the development of a

software lifecycle processes

full complement of software engineering skills must await more advanced courses, the present CS2 course can certainly survey many of the important ideas and can build an appreciation for the issues. Chapters 5 and 16 do this.

1.7   Our Approach to Mathematics

Mathematics is used for two purposes in this book. The first is to help you learn how to apply just a little bit of the right kind of simple mathematics that is useful in the activity of programming—mainly to help you to reason about the efficiency and correctness of the programs you write. The second purpose is to support and clarify the important discoveries and principles of computer science.

For the practical programmer, this book will demonstrate that just by applying a few simple kinds of precollege mathematics, one can go an amazingly long way toward being able to characterize the efficiency of many of the algorithms that programmers write. In Chapter 6, there is a gentle, easy introduction to *O-notation*, which computer scientists use to characterize the efficiency of algorithms. You will

mathematics for the practical programmer

discover how easy it is to find the O-notation for many simple algorithms. More importantly, you will find you will be able to grasp the *intuition* behind O-notation. Being able to do so is important for practical programmers, because it enables them to determine whether their programs are good solutions to the programming tasks they have been given. The language of O-notation is truly simple and absolutely everybody who makes a small but honest effort to learn how to speak it and understand it can master it.

In certain sciences, mathematics plays a central role in the development of the subject matter. For example, in college textbooks on physics or economics, you can expect to find mathematical formulas that describe important laws and relationships. Moreover, you can expect to find mathematical justifications, in which these formulas are derived from basic assumptions and in which their truth is demonstrated under carefully defined conditions. Computer science is one of the sciences in which mathematics plays a central role. Computer scientists have discovered many important laws and principles that are expressed in mathematical form. Oftentimes, to understand why such laws hold true, one needs to follow the steps of the mathematical argument that establishes their validity.

As we noted before, an important goal of computer science is knowing how to perform certain common algorithmic tasks as efficiently as possible. It could be said that the job of developing computer science fully isn't finished until we know absolutely the best ways of solving important algorithmic problems. Ideally, we would

identifying the best possible solutions

like to be able to exhibit the best algorithms and data structures that are possible, and to prove that it is not possible to do any better.

In practical terms, discovering efficient ways to solve algorithmic problems has important impact on the enterprise of building good hardware and software systems. For example, the performance of a software application, such as a spreadsheet or a word processor, may influence how well it sells. If it is blazing fast, when the competition's product is as slow as a snail, it may do much better in the marketplace.

There is a reason why computer scientists use mathematics to characterize the efficiency of algorithms and data structures. Every algorithm ultimately breaks the solution of a big problem into compositions of tiny steps (since that's the nature of computer programs). Consequently, the mathematics needed to describe the efficiency of an algorithm often mirrors an algorithm's decomposition of the overall problem into smaller subproblems. Sometimes, for example, the mathematics needed consists of summing up contributions that measure the work needed to solve the subproblems. As a result, skill in manipulating sums is quite valuable. Even knowing how to take sums of arithmetic and geometric progressions, something usually taught in high school, has tremendous payoffs, as we will see.

Also, certain problems have a natural decomposition into subproblems that has a special mathematical pattern that can be expressed in the form of special types of equations called *recurrence relations*. Learning how to recognize these special mathematical patterns, and knowing how to characterize the overall result is often the key to knowing precisely how efficient an algorithm will be.

This book takes just a few preliminary steps in the direction of explaining important mathematically expressed truths of computer science relating to fundamental data structures and algorithms. We do not go very far along this path, nor do we use any mathematics beyond precollege algebra. For example, we do not use calculus and we do not expect students to apply calculus in solving problems given in the text.

the kinds of mathematics we will need

Instead, we rely on a few specific kinds of precollege algebra that are both useful and appropriate for discussing beginning computer science. This involves topics such as finding the sums of arithmetic and geometric progressions, manipulating logarithms and exponentials, dealing with two special ways of rounding real numbers into integers (called *floors* and *ceilings*), manipulating relations involving the divisibility of integers, manipulating summation notation, and setting up and solving recurrence relations.

The appendix to this book, entitled the *Math Reference and Tutorial*, provides a gentle introduction to these topics. For high school students who are already familiar with topics such as sums of arithmetic and geometric progressions, this appendix can serve as a useful review. (For those who didn't study these subjects, the appendix provides a quick introduction.)

getting a head start

This book is also accompanied by a card called the *Math Survival Guide*, which contains some of the useful formulas and tables developed in the appendix. This card can serve as a handy refresher when doing homework problems or taking exams.

In addition, there are self-contained developments in several places in the text that explain how to set up and solve recurrence relations and introduce basic mathematical logic. With respect to solving recurrence relations, we do nothing fancy. We use only simple techniques, such as expanding terms and summing, that rely on the mathematics for sums already introduced. We neither mention nor apply the heavy artillery, such as generating functions or setting up and solving characteristic equations. Instead, we summarize our findings in three short tables that present solutions to three general forms of recurrence relations that are commonly used in analyzing algorithms. It is amazing how often these three forms can be applied and how most of the recurrence relations in the text and in the exercises can be solved by using these tables.

Finally, those sections containing challenging mathematical arguments are identified with two asterisks (**) so that they can be skipped if desired. In the case of texts in physics or economics, it is possible to learn about overall conclusions, such as the laws of gravity or price elasticity, without going through the mathematical details of how these conclusions are derived, and there is certainly some value in learning about these high-level conclusions and about their importance and impacts elsewhere in the subject. Similarly, it is possible to learn about high-level conclusions in algorithms and data structures without going through the mathematical derivations—although there is definitely value in doing that too.

challenging mathematics is marked with two stars (**)

For example, suppose you are trying to write a program that sorts n numbers into increasing order based on comparing and exchanging pairs of numbers stored in an array of n numbers. It turns out that it is *impossible* for such a program to use less than $n * \log n$ comparisons in the average case. It is not necessary to follow the mathematical argument that demonstrates this fact in order to learn this important conclusion. And you can apply this conclusion in practical circumstances to help you evaluate whether a proposed sorting algorithm is as good as it should be or not.

Some of the mathematical derivations in this book are forced to appeal to formulas that can't be derived on the spot and are beyond the scope of the book. For example, the derivation of the lower bound of $n * \log n$ comparisons for comparison-based sorting uses Stirling's Approximation for $n!$. (Here, $n!$ is the *factorial of n*, where the factorial of n is the product of all the integers from 1 to n). Deriving Stirling's Approximation is beyond the scope of this book.

On the other hand, most of the derivations in this book appeal only to the mathematical facts developed in the appendix, and the facts in this appendix are all within easy reach of high school graduates. Consequently, you will be pleasantly surprised at how many of the derivations in this book can be followed using only a little precollege algebra and the facts developed in the appendix.

Even though there is certainly value in learning only the high-level conclusions, while skipping the mathematical derivations, there is even more value in trying to follow the derivations, since the derivations often provide key insights into how things work in computer science, and also introduce important techniques that can be applied in other circumstances to gain insight and understanding. Thus you are urged to try your hand at following the derivations, even in the optional sections. Each derivation you succeed in understanding will give you a sense of accomplishment and self-confidence, in addition to giving you insight into the fundamentals of computer science.

1.8 Some Notes on Programming Notation

using ANSI C

In this section, we cover a few brief points about the version of C used in this book and about the form in which C programs are presented. In recent years, a standard for C has been defined, called ANSI Standard C (where ANSI is an abbreviation for the American National Standards Institute). Moreover, the use of C has become popular among software professionals to implement industrial applications of substantial size and utility. In this book, we use ANSI Standard C, with only one exception—the use of C++ in Chapter 15 to introduce some of the significant concepts in object-oriented programming.

There is one convenient notational convention that lies outside the domain of the C language which we need to introduce at this moment, because it will be used frequently throughout the remainder of the book. This concerns the notation for an *integer range* consisting of all the integers from m to n, which is denoted by $m{:}n$. In symbols, $m{:}n = \{\, i \mid m \leq i \leq n \,\}$, meaning that "the integer range $m{:}n$ equals the set of all integers i such that i is greater than or equal to m and i is less than or equal to n."

integer ranges

We will often use integer ranges to denote subarrays of an array or to denote the range of integer indexes for an entire array. For example, suppose we have an array A that consists of the 100 locations A[0], A[1], A[2], . . . , A[99]. We could describe these array locations using the expression A[0:99] in which the integer range 0:99 gives the set of integer indexes for the array A. Also, to designate, for example, the subarray of A consisting of locations A[10], A[11], A[12], . . . , A[20], we could write A[10:20].

In the C language, the indexes of a declared array always start at 0 and increase in steps of 1 until reaching a number which is one less than the number of items in the array. For instance, suppose that, in C, we were to write:

```
#define MaxIndex 100                              /* 100 is the array size */

typedef int SearchArray[MaxIndex];      /* a SearchArray is an integer array */
                                        /* with indexes in the range 0:MaxIndex − 1 */

SearchArray A;              /* declares A to be a SearchArray with indexes 0:99*/

int B[MaxIndex];            /* declares B to be an integer array with indexes 0:99*/
```

The first line above declares **MaxIndex** to be equivalent to **100**. The next line establishes a type definition, **SearchArray**, which consists of arrays of integers indexed by the **100** integers in the range **0:99**. The third line declares **A** to be a **SearchArray**. The fourth directly declares **B** to be an integer array indexed by **0:99** also.

our format for C programs

To introduce the format in which we display C programs in this book, let's state and solve a simple search problem. (In the remainder of this section, the word "C" will be used to refer to ANSI Standard C.)

Problem: Search an array of integers A[0:99] to find the first negative integer. If one exists, return its position in the array. If A contains no negative integer, then return the position −1. In order to avoid doing useless work, the solution should exit as soon as the first negative integer is discovered.

In this book, we will pretend that our C programs have been printed by an imaginary *line printer listing program* that prints both line numbers and vertical bars to the left of each program to aid the reader in finding parts of the program referenced in the discussion in the text. Program 1.3 illustrates the output from this imaginary program in which line numbers are explicitly given every five lines in the margin to the left of a series of vertical bars.

```
|   #define MaxIndex 100
|
|   int Find( int A[ ] )                        /* Find operates on integer arrays, A */
|   {
5  |       int j;                               /* j is an index variable used in the search */
|
|           for ( j = 0; j < MaxIndex; ++j ) {   /* search upward starting at position 0 */
|               if (A[j] < 0) {                          /* if A[j] is negative */
|                   return j;                       /* return its index j as the result */
10 |               }
|           }
|
|           return −1;                       /* return −1 if no negative integers were found*/
|   }
15 |
|   int main(void)
|   {
|       int   A[MaxIndex];                        /* declare A to be an integer array*/
|       int   i;                       /* let i be an index variable used for initialization */
20 |
|   /* Initialize array A to squares of integers. Then make A[17] negative. */
|       for ( i = 0; i < MaxIndex; ++i ) A[i] = i*i;
|       A[17] = − A[17];
|
25 |   /* Print test results */
|       printf("First negative integer in A found at index = %2d.\n",Find(A));
|   }
```

Program 1.3 Finding the First Negative Integer in an Integer Array

using line numbers
to refer to parts
of programs

Throughout the book, line number ranges are used to identify parts of programs discussed in the running text. For example, in Program 1.3, the function Find(A) is defined on lines 3:14. The function prototype int Find(int A[ ]) is given on line 3, and declares that Find is a function which returns an integer value (int) and takes as a parameter (a pointer to) an array of integer values, A. (Recall that, in C, when an array is passed as an actual parameter to a function, a pointer to the zeroth array position is passed instead of passing a copy of the values in the entire array.)

Line 5 of Program 1.3 declares j to be an integer variable using the declaration int j;. Various lines of Program 1.3 have comments in color that are in the rightmost position on their lines. For example, the comment on line 5, to the right of the declaration int j; is /*j is an index variable used in the search */. Comments given in color at the rightmost end of a line *explain* how the statement or declaration to the left works, or else describe its *purpose*.

Another kind of comment is a *goal comment*, such as the one given on line 25 which states /* Print test results */. Goal comments are given in black and they describe a goal which is achieved by executing the indented statements following them. Such goal comments are analogous to topic headers in an outline.

1.9   Preview of Coming Attractions

Our discussion so far should have given you the big picture of what this book covers. But how are the individual chapters in the book organized to help you along your journey?

As mentioned previously, several chapters later in the book cover various fundamental abstract data types (ADTs). These aim at developing the properties of important data types such as: stacks, queues, trees, graphs, and tables. Chapters 7 through 11 cover these individual ADTs and develop their properties. Before studying such individual ADTs, however, it is important to lay some fundamental groundwork. This is the purpose of Chapters 2 through 6.

linked data representations

Chapter 2 develops the concepts of *linked data representations*, which are created by linking individual blocks of storage together using pointers. There are some specific programming skills that need to be covered regarding how to use pointers in C, which are not usually covered thoroughly in CS1 courses, due to lack of time.

The notion of *representation* is one of the key recurring concepts that ties together the material in this book. Knowing about both linked representations and sequential representations is essential to the study of data abstraction that comes later. Oftentimes, a given ADT, such as the *list* ADT, will have both sequential and linked representations. Often these will exhibit tradeoffs. It is assumed that your previous CS1 course covered the use of basic sequential representations based on C arrays.

recursion

Chapter 3 is an introduction to *recursion*, another key recurring concept in computer science. It can be used to define algorithms, data structures, programming language grammars, and much more. Becoming skilled in writing recursive algorithms, and in understanding the implications of recursion, provides important preparation for understanding the various representations of ADTs covered later. It is also important to master the rudiments of recursion before studying topics such as recurrence relations, which are used to analyze the efficiency of algorithms mathematically.

Along with linked representations, recursion is not normally covered sufficiently well in many CS1 courses, again because of lack of time. Chapters 2 and 3 therefore provide opportunities to review or deepen the study of topics that may have been begun in many CS1 courses, but which need to be finished properly in order to provide a good foundation for covering topics which depend on knowing them well.

One of the places where recursion really pays off is in the expression of elegant, concise algorithms for manipulating certain linked representations, such as linked lists. Consequently, the study of linked representations in Chapter 2 is prerequisite for studying these important uses of recursion in Chapter 3.

modularity and information hiding

Chapter 4 covers modularity, information hiding, and data abstraction. It uses the vehicle of separately compiled C program segments to focus on essential concepts of modularity, information hiding, and interfaces. After explaining how C program segments work, it presents examples of segments that define abstract data types, and that use information hiding to conceal whether linked or sequential representations have been used underneath. This helps reveal the benefits of data abstraction and information hiding. Understanding the topics in this chapter is essential for understanding software engineering concepts presented in Chapter 5.

Chapter 5 introduces software engineering topics. It focuses mainly on issues relevant to programming-in-the-small. Another later chapter on advanced software engineering concepts, Chapter 16, covers issues relevant to programming-in-the-large, such as the processes and methods used in the software lifecycle. Building on concepts

programming by stepwise refinement

such as modularity and abstraction discussed in Chapter 4, Chapter 5 introduces additional structuring concepts for writing easily modifiable programs, and it covers the method of *top-down programming by stepwise refinement*. In addition, it introduces program verification and proofs of correctness. Also covered are practical topics, such as testing strategies, principles of good program documentation, and the importance of taking advantage of reusable software components.

Chapter 6 introduces the mathematical analysis of algorithms. It starts by posing the question, "What do we use for a yardstick?"—meaning how can we compare algorithms meaningfully when the same algorithm will run at different speeds and will require different amounts of space when run on different computers or when implemented in different programming languages? This leads to an introduction to the important concept of *O-notation*. The chapter gives examples of how to analyze several important algorithms and includes an introduction to the solution of recurrence relations.

At this point, the groundwork has been laid for studying individual ADTs. The next several chapters cover the important ADTs and develop their properties.

studying individual ADTs

Chapter 7 studies linear ADTs such as *stacks* and *queues*. Chapter 8 studies *lists* and *strings*. Chapter 9 studies *trees*. Chapter 10 studies *graphs* and graph processing algorithms. Chapter 11 studies the *table* ADT, and various important associated algorithms, such as hashing. Then in Chapter 12, the special problems of large data collections and externally stored data are investigated.

sorting

Chapter 13 studies important sorting algorithms. It is essential for well-educated computer scientists to know about a few of these algorithms, and to know a few of the main results of the mathematical analysis of their efficiencies. Some of the classical results are studied and compared.

Chapter 14 covers advanced topics in recursion that build on and extend the topics introduced in Chapter 3. It is shown how recursion is useful for defining things and recognizing things. In addition, proofs of correctness based on recursion induction are studied.

object-oriented programming

Chapter 15 covers new concepts in object-oriented programming (OOP). The concepts of *subclassing*, *inheritance*, and *overriding* are introduced. C++, an object-oriented extension of C, is the natural vehicle used to gain access to these concepts, since it builds on the concepts of C.

advanced software engineering

Chapter 16 covers advanced software engineering concepts. It studies various process models for supporting the activities in the software lifecycle. For example, it introduces risk-based software process models, including the concepts of risk analysis and risk item resolution. Issues relevant to programming-in-the-large are covered in this chapter.

Chapter Summary

Computer science blends skills from *science, engineering,* and *mathematics.* To become a competent computer scientist, it is important for you to master skills in these three areas, including skills in experimentation, design, and theory.

enduring concepts and principles

Computer scientists have tried to identify enduring concepts and principles that are useful for understanding the possibilities and limits of computing, and the useful forms of organization of software and hardware systems. Finding the right *abstractions* has been of value in this search. The right abstractions are of lasting value instead of being transitory.

The ideas of *abstraction* and *representation* help us organize and understand the structure of large software systems. Such software systems tend to be structured using several layers of representations. Using *abstraction* and *information-hiding,* such systems can be partitioned into subsystems having simple *interfaces,* making them easier to understand and use.

abstract data types

Computer scientists have discovered many kinds of useful data structures and algorithms that can be used as intermediate level representations in large software systems. These are best presented and studied as *abstract data types* (or ADTs). The ADTs studied in this book, such as lists, trees, queues, stacks, graphs, and tables, provide a useful stock of ideas for crafting new representations to use in new software applications. The properties of such ADTs have been extensively studied, including their useful algorithms and their alternative underlying representations.

Efficiency and *tradeoffs* are two additional recurring concepts that are important to study and master. It is an important goal of computer science to discover the most *efficient* algorithms possible. When studying different representations for a given ADT, we often find that space and time *trade off* against each other.

software engineering

Software engineering methods and processes are also important to learn about. Many helpful things have been learned about how to organize people and resources in the enterprise of building software systems. The activities in the software lifecycle include many processes such as *requirements analysis, design, coding, testing, verification, documentation,* and *maintenance. Risk-based software process models* have recently been introduced incorporating new concepts such as the use of *prototyping* to buy information that reduces risk. Traditional topics such as *top-down structured programming by stepwise refinement* and *program verification* using *correctness proofs* are also important to know about.

the role of mathematics

Mathematics plays an important role in the development of computer science and has been used to discover many central results. Among the benefits of using mathematics to practical programmers are: being able to reason about why programs work, being able to determine the efficiency of algorithms, knowing what is possible and impossible in computing, being able to improve programs, and gaining the advantages of precision and structure that come from using precisely-defined mathematical models whose properties and implications have been carefully studied. The more mathematics you can master in connection with your study of computer science, the more competent you will become as a programmer and a computer scientist. Even a little bit of mathematics helps.

We imagine that C algorithms are printed by a *line-number listing program*, using line numbers and vertical bars in the left margin, to the immediate left of each C program text given. This aids the reader in following the discussion in the text since various parts of C programs can be referenced directly by the line numbers on which such parts occur.

Problems and Exercises

Note: To solve Problems 1 and 2, refer again to the problem solved by Program 1.3.

1. One programmer suggested the following version of the function, Find(A):

```
|    int Find(SearchArray A)
|    {
|        int i = 0;
|
5  |        while ((A[i] >= 0) && (i < MaxIndex)) {
|            ++i;
|        }
|
|        return (i < MaxIndex) ? i : –1;
|    }
```

Can you discover a flaw in the implementation of this program? [*Hint:* suppose that the array A contains no negative integers, and that your version of C has array index bounds checking that has been turned on. What happens when you execute Find(A)?] Can you suggest a way to fix this program by changing just one line?

2. Another programmer claims that the following version of the program for Find(A) correctly solves the problem:

```
|    int Find( int A[ ] )
|    {
|        int i, result;
|
5  |        result = –1;
|        for ( i = MaxIndex–1; i >= 0; – – i ) if (A[i] < 0) result = i;
|        return result;
|    }
```

In what respect, if any, does this proposed solution fail to satisfy the statement of the problem?

3. Looking back over your own experience with computers and over what you have learned in previous computer science courses, describe some things that were temporary (here one year, and gone the next) and then describe some truths you learned that survived all the turmoil and change. What are the characteristics of the truths that endured, and what are the characteristics of the temporary things that did not survive?

2

Linked Data Representations

2.1 Introduction and Motivation

Linked data representations, and the algorithms that use them, are a major topic of study in computer science. Sometimes, linked representations support efficient algorithms. Linked data representations are especially useful for applications in which it is difficult to predict the size and shape of the data structures needed.

For example, linked representations can be used to overcome problems with predicting how much array space to allocate for tables and lists before running a program. The size to which a table or list might grow when a program runs may depend on the inputs to the program. The number or size of those inputs may not be easy to predict in advance. Yet we may be forced to allocate arrays of a given size before program execution begins. If we have guessed wrongly, the space for one kind of table or list might run out while unused space still exists inside another table. We can use linked representations of tables and lists to overcome these problems.

To create linked representations, we use *pointers* to connect separate blocks of storage together. A pointer is just the memory address of a block of storage. If a given block contains

handling unpredictable space requirements

pointers

22

a pointer to a second block, we can follow this pointer to access the second block. By following pointers one after another, we can travel along an access path contained in a linked data representation. In diagrams of linked data structures, we will represent pointers by arrows.

Moreover, starting with a given linked data structure, we can add or delete a particular block of data by adding or deleting pointers that point to it. This means that linked representations can grow or shrink piece-by-piece—in small increments—enabling them to change shape a step at a time, using just a few pointer operations on each piece. This possibility opens up a very interesting class of growth and combining properties for linked representations that computer scientists have explored extensively.

The class of linked data representations that become possible using these techniques can have important advantages when compared to other data representation methods, such as sequential data representations that are allocated inside arrays.

Our journey in this chapter on linked representations, and later in Chapter 4 when we cover *modularity* and *information hiding*, will eventually reveal to us that certain high-level data structures, such as lists, stacks, sets, trees, and queues, can be represented in many ways by lower-level data representations. Two broad classes of such lower-level representations are *sequential representations* and *linked representations*. These observations will, in turn, lead us to introduce the idea of *levels of data abstractions*. This idea is fundamental to computer science and is another of the recurring concepts that unifies the explanations in this book.

Objects and operations at higher levels of data abstraction are represented by organizing objects and operations at lower levels. For example, at the highest level of abstraction, we find *abstract data types* (ADTs)—structures such as *lists*, *stacks*, *sets*, *trees*, and *queues*. Each of these ADTs can be represented in a variety of different ways by lower-level representations, including those in the two broad classes— *sequential representations* and *linked representations*. At still lower levels, the linked representations can be represented in a variety of different ways, such as using arrays of records, C's built-in pointer data types, or parallel arrays.

Later we will extensively develop the themes that surround the levels of data abstraction illustrated in Fig. 2.1. Introducing the key notion of linked representations in this chapter lays groundwork essential to the understanding of how alternative representations can support more abstract data types. Later, chapters 7 through 11 develop various ADTs and their different representations.

growth and combining laws

levels of data abstraction

essential groundwork

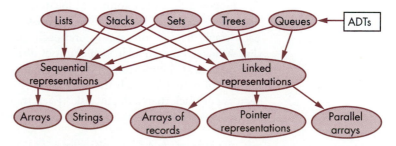

Figure 2.1 Levels of Data Abstraction

Plan for the Chapter

We start with an intuitive discussion of pointers. Then we give two specific examples of linked representations in order to provide an intuitive feeling for how linked representations are used in important, real-world applications. Next, we study the technical details of managing pointers in C by introducing perhaps the simplest

managing pointers in C

example of pointers—namely, pointers to integers. Even though this sounds simple, there are a few tricky issues, such as *dangling pointers*, *aliases*, how to recycle used storage for further use, and the creation of *inaccessible garbage* through failure to recycle used storage. We then introduce the diagramming language that will be used for pointers and linked representations in the remainder of this book.

A topic of key importance—*linear linked lists*—is discussed next. We show how to declare the pointer data types for list nodes in C, how to create and delete list nodes,

linear linked lists

and how to link them together. Following this, we study how to perform various important list operations such as insertion and deletion of nodes in lists. We also investigate how to search for a node on a linked list containing a given search key.

The last section presents brief examples of linked representations that can be constructed from nodes having two links per node, such as two-way linked lists and linked binary trees. These illustrate that a given building block can be used to form a variety of different kinds of linked data representations, having differing shapes and organizational principles.

2.2 What Are Pointers? The Basic Intuition

Learning Objectives

1. To understand what pointers are and how they can be used.
2. To appreciate the importance of pointers in real-world systems.

Linked data representations can be supported by any addressable storage medium. The random-access memory (RAM) of a computer, the read-write memory on a flop-

addressable storage media

py disk, and the read-only memory (ROM) on a CD-ROM, illustrate three different kinds of addressable storage media. In the case of the RAM in a computer's main memory, the units of addressable storage might be words or individual bytes.

Floppy disks can be formatted for storage in many ways. One computer company formats its floppy disks as follows: The disk is formatted into 80 circular tracks, with each track divided into sectors and each sector containing a block of 512 bytes of disk storage. Thus an addressable unit of disk storage is a 512-byte block with a two-part address (t,s) consisting of a track number t and a sector number s. A CD-ROM can be formatted in much the same way, only it would have many more tracks and sectors per track than a floppy disk.[1] Even though the CD-ROM is a *read-only* device, it is still possible to use pointers in the data structures stored on it.

---

[1] Some CD-ROMs contain a single spiral track up to three miles long, which can be formatted into addressable blocks of storage. Here, CD is an abbreviation for *compact disk*.

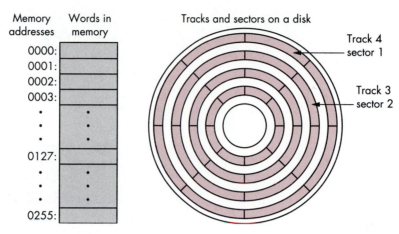

Figure 2.2 Addressable Storage Media

Two Examples of Linked Representations

Using arrows to denote pointers, let's look at two practical uses of pointers to help develop intuition about what linked representations are good for.

Example 1—Storing Files on Disks

First, let's look at how a file can be stored on the floppy disk shown in Fig. 2.2. On many computers, a file is defined as a finite sequence of bytes. We can break this sequence of bytes into successive blocks of 512 bytes each and we can store each 512-byte block in an empty sector of the disk. We link the successive sectors together by storing in each sector the address of another sector that contains the next 512-byte block of the file. Thus each sector contains not only a 512-byte block of data, but also a *pointer* to the next block in sequence in the file.

It is also usual to save some of the empty sectors on the disk to contain a file directory. You can imagine this as a table that contains one record for each file on the disk. Each record in the directory contains the characters spelling the file name, such as **MyProgram.c**, some file attributes, such as the length of the file in bytes, its date of creation, a code designating the type of the file, and finally a pointer to the first 512-byte block in the series of linked blocks containing the contents of the file. If the directory containing these individual file records fills more than one 512-byte sector, additional sectors can be allocated and "linked on" to the end of the directory in order to extend it. Figure 2.3 presents a diagram of this situation.

Example 2—Window Lists

window lists

Consider a window package for the user-interface of a desktop computer. The windows displayed on the screen can be layered on top of one another in an overlapping fashion, as shown in Fig. 2.4. Inside the main memory of the desktop computer, the

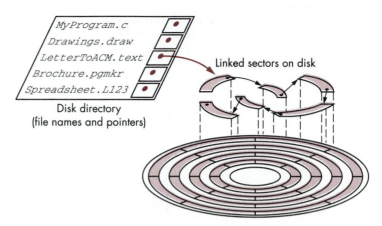

Figure 2.3 Files and Directories on a Disk

operating system has to keep track of these windows. One way of doing this is with a *window list*, which keeps one record per window. Each window record in the window list contains a pointer to the record for the window immediately underneath it on the screen. Each window record also contains information such as the window's size, its position on the screen, and its visible region (which is the part of the window that can be seen because it is not overlapped with parts of other windows lying on top of it).

Suppose a user issues a command to bring one of the partially overlapped background windows, W, to the front of the screen. To carry out this command, the operating system can execute a routine to remove the record for window W from its position somewhere in the middle of the window list and insert it as the new first record on the window list (giving it a new status as the topmost window). It then

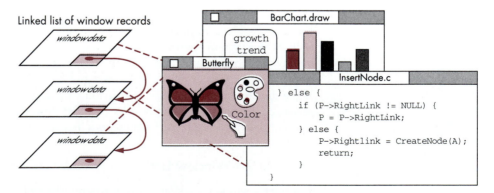

Figure 2.4 A Stack of Windows and a Window List

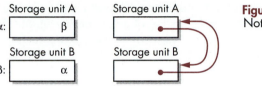

Storage unit A

α: [β]

Storage unit B

β: [α]

Storage unit A

Storage unit B

Figure 2.5 Two Equivalent Notations for Pointers

goes down the window list drawing the contents of each window from top to bottom, making sure to clip the drawing of each window's contents so that it will occur only in its visible region.

Pointers Defined

When we store the address α of a storage unit A inside another storage unit B, we say that B contains a *pointer* to A, and we say that α is a *pointer*. In Fig. 2.5 we can also say that B *links to* A, or that B contains a *reference* to A. Also, we can say that A is B's "*referent*." When we follow a pointer to the unit of storage for which the pointer value is the address, we *dereference* the pointer.

> A **pointer** is a data value that references a unit of storage.

On the right side of Fig. 2.5, the upward pointing arrow (●⟶) gives an alternative way to represent a pointer to the storage unit A. The tail of the arrow (●—) represents a stored copy of a data value equal to the address of the storage unit that the tip of the arrow (⟶) touches. Thus the left and right sides of Fig. 2.5 depict identical situations.

2.3   Pointers in C—The Rudiments

Learning Objectives

1. To understand how pointers work in C.
2. To be able to declare pointer data types.
3. To know how to allocate and deallocate memory dynamically.
4. To be able to perform operations, such as dereferencing, on pointers.
5. To understand the concepts of aliasing, dangling pointers, and the scope of dynamic storage allocation.

Suppose we want to create some pointers to blocks of storage containing integers. To do this in C, we could first make the following declaration:

```
typedef int *IntegerPointer;
```

pointers to integers

The asterisk (*) in this type definition appears before the type name **IntegerPointer** to indicate a type consisting of a "pointer to an **int**." Thus the above declaration says, "define a type consisting of an integer pointer having the name **IntegerPointer**."

We can now declare two variables **A** and **B** to be of a "type" that requires them to contain pointers to integers:

    IntegerPointer A, B;   /* the declaration, int *A, *B; has the same effect */

This means that the C compiler will constrain the values of the variables **A** and **B** to be "pointers to integers." There are two aspects of this constraint: (1) **A** and **B** have to contain *pointers* to other storage units, and (2) these other storage units, to which the pointer values in **A** and **B** refer, are required to contain integers.

dynamic storage allocation

Now, to create some pointers to some empty integer storage units and to make **A** and **B** point to them, we use the special C *dynamic storage allocation procedure*, **malloc** (which is used for dynamic <u>me</u>mory <u>alloc</u>ation).

    /* Create a new block of storage for an integer, and place a pointer to it in A. */
    /* Here (IntegerPointer) type casts the void pointer returned by malloc */
    /* into a pointer to a block of storage containing an integer. */

    A = (IntegerPointer) malloc(sizeof(int));

A diagram of what is created is given immediately above.

    /* Then, create another block of storage for an integer, and put a pointer to it in B.*/
    /* This time, type cast the void pointer to storage for an int directly with (int *).*/

    B = (int *) malloc(sizeof(int));   /* sizeof(int) == no. of bytes to store an int */

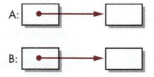

A diagram of the newly created storage that results from executing the latter statement after executing the former statement is shown immediately above.

Now let's store the integer **5** in the block of storage referenced by the pointer in variable **A**. In what follows, we'll continue to give the diagram that portrays the storage structures created immediately after executing each new statement. So to store **5** in the block of integer storage to which the pointer in **A** refers, we need to execute a special assignment statement:

> /* Store the integer 5 in A's referent. */
>
> *A = 5;

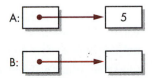

By placing the asterisk (*) before the variable **A** on the left side of the assignment *A = 5; we designate the storage location *A to which the pointer value in **A** refers. Similarly, we can store the integer 17 in the block of integer storage to which **B**'s pointer refers:

> /* Store the integer 17 in B's referent. The result is shown in Fig. 2.6. */
>
> *B = 17;

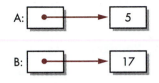

Figure 2.6 Pointers to Integers

Question and Answer Time

type mismatches

Question: Suppose you try to store **17** directly into **B** by performing the assignment statement **B = 17**. What happens? *Answer:* The C compiler won't compile the program, since this is a "type mismatch error." The right side of the assignment is a value, **17**, of type **int**, but the left side of the assignment, **B**, is a variable which is required to contain a pointer to an integer. In C's type system, an **int** and a pointer to an **int** are not the same type. Since the types don't match, and since there is no defined automatic conversion to change the type of the right side into a pointer value, C considers **B = 17** to be an "illegal pointer arithmetic" in an assignment statement.

are pointers invisible?

Question: Suppose you try to print the value of the pointer stored in **B** by executing the statement printf("B == 0x%x",B). What happens? *Answer:* In contrast to compilers for some other hard-typed languages, C permits pointer values to be printed. The **printf** statement just given prints an answer such as **B == 0xf6da**, which is given in hexadecimal (because the conversion specification %**x** prints values in hexadecimal).

Question: Starting with the situation in Fig. 2.6, which of the following diagrams results if we perform the assignment **A = B;**—the left diagram or the right diagram?

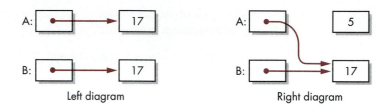

Left diagram   Right diagram

Answer: The right diagram. Why? Because the assignment, **A = B**, takes a copy of the value of **B**, which is a *pointer* to the block of storage containing **17**, and places this pointer in **A**, so that **A** now points to the same block of storage that **B** points to.

copying pointers

Question: What assignment statement would we perform if we wanted to create the situation shown in the left diagram, starting with Figure 2.6? *Answer:* The assignment ***A = *B**; which says to take a copy of the value **17** stored in **B**'s referent, and put it in the location given by **A**'s referent, ***A**.

copying integers

Some Fine Points—Aliases, Recycling, and Dangling Pointers

Now, focus for a moment on the right diagram above, which resulted from performing the assignment A = B on Figure 2.6.

Aliases

Note that **A** and **B** contain identical pointer values, pointing to the same (shared) storage location, which contains the integer **17**. Because **A**'s referent, ***A**, and **B**'s referent, ***B**, "name" the same storage location, they are called *aliases*. In general, *aliases* are two different naming expressions that name the same thing. Starting with the right diagram, the effect of performing either the assignment ***A = 23**; or the assignment, ***B = 23**; is identical. Namely, the value **23** is put in the location that used to contain **17**. Similarly, starting with the right diagram, **19** is the common value of the expressions ***A + 2** and ***B + 2** because ***A** and ***B** are both aliases that designate the same value **17** when used inside expressions.

aliases

Recycling Used Storage

Again starting with the right diagram, note that the block of storage containing the integer **5** has no pointer pointing to it. If such a situation should develop, we say that this storage block has become *inaccessible*—meaning that nobody can access it to read its value or to store a new value into it.

inaccessible storage

It is potentially wasteful to allocate blocks of storage and then abandon them when they become inaccessible, since the pool of storage for allocating new blocks of storage could easily become used up. This could result in a *storage allocation failure*, in which, when we called the function **malloc**, there would be no more storage to allocate.

In order to guard against this possibility, we can execute the special C *storage reclamation function*, **free(X)**. This returns the block of storage, to which the pointer in

storage reclamation

X points, to the pool of unallocated storage so that it can be used again. (In C, this pool of unallocated storage is often called *dynamic memory*.) Reclaiming storage this way is analogous to recycling used bottles and newspapers.

Sometimes, we use the word *garbage* to refer to inaccessible storage. Some programming languages, such as the list-processing language, LISP, have procedures for storage reclamation called garbage collection procedures that are triggered when available unallocated storage is used up. These garbage collection procedures have a way of identifying which blocks of storage are inaccessible and of returning them to the pool of unallocated storage. C does not have such an automatic garbage collection procedure, however, so the recycling of storage must be explicitly managed by the programmer who writes C programs.

garbage collection

If we want to recycle the storage block containing **5** in Fig. 2.6, before destroying the pointer to it in **A** (by overwriting this pointer with a copy of **B**'s pointer), we could first perform the function call, **free(A)**, as in the following sequence of actions:

*disposing of
unused storage*

```
/* First, dispose of A's referent. Then, replace A with B.*/

    free(A);        /* First, recycle the storage block to which A refers.*/
    A = B;          /* Then, put a copy of B's pointer in A.*/
```

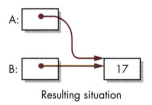

Resulting situation

Dangling Pointers

Once we have *aliases* pointing to the same storage location, a new *programming danger* arises. Starting with the resulting situation immediately above, suppose we called the function **free(B)**. What would happen then, if we tried to evaluate the expression *A + 2? We don't know, but, since *A might no longer contain a valid integer value, the result could be unexpected.

First, the call to **free(B)** would return the storage location containing **17**, which is **B**'s referent, to the pool of available storage. (When it does this, it might erase the value contained in the block, or join the block to another block of storage to make a bigger block—just to name two of several possibilities.) Now, **A** contains a pointer, called a *dangling pointer*, which points to the same location that **B**'s pointer used to point to. This dangling pointer might now point into the middle of a large block, formed when **free(B)** caused **B**'s referent block to join another block in the storage reclamation process. The possibility exists that the referent of the dangling pointer doesn't even have a meaningful existence anymore in C. It is reasonable to consider this to be a programming error, even though neither the C compiler nor the running

dangling pointers

C system may have any means of detecting it. Consequently, the creation of dangling pointers is a pitfall that should be avoided.

The Lifetime of Dynamic Storage

The blocks of storage that pointers refer to are created dynamically during the running of the program and can be thought of as *anonymous variables*.[2] Such variables have no explicit textual names in the program, and their lifetimes exist beyond the lifetimes of local variables in the program. For example, even though an anonymous variable might be created by a function having its own local variables that vanish after the function has terminated execution, the pointer values and the locations they reference nonetheless have an existence outside the (temporary) existence of the function's local storage. One way to think of this is that dynamic storage allocated for anonymous variables by **malloc** exists from the moment it is allocated until the moment when its storage is reclaimed, using **free(X)**, or until the program's execution terminates (if its storage is not reclaimed previously, using **free(X)**).

anonymous variables

Dereferencing

When the asterisk (*) precedes the name of a variable, as in *A, we say that the pointer value of **A** is *dereferenced*. Thus dereferencing is a fancy name for *pointer following*. When the asterisk (*) precedes a new type name identifier **T** in a type definition, it defines a *pointer type*. For example,

> typedef T *TPointer;

means that the type **TPointer** is the set of pointers to storage units containing values of type **T**. Thus, the asterisk precedes pointer variables when they are dereferenced and precedes type name identifiers when they are defined. When a dereferenced variable, *V, occurs on the left side of an assignment, *V = X, it signifies that a copy of the value in **X** is to be stored in the location to which the pointer value in **V** points..

pointer following

2.3 Review Questions

1. What does it mean to *dereference a pointer*? If **A** is a pointer variable in C, what is the notation for dereferencing the pointer value stored in **A**?

---

[2] The word *anonymous* means "having no name." For example, anonymous donors to a charity are donors whose names are not revealed. Thus an *anonymous variable* is a variable that has no name but acts like a variable in all other respects. If an ordinary variable is defined to be a named storage location that can contain values that can be varied (i.e., changed) over time, then an *anonymous variable* is an unnamed storage location that can contain values that can be varied over time.

2. What are some other ways of describing the situation in which a unit of storage B contains a pointer to a unit of storage A?

3. How would you declare a data type in C called **IntegerPointer** to be a type consisting of pointers to integers? Give the C syntax for the type definition needed to accomplish this.

4. Suppose **A** is a variable declared in C to be a pointer variable containing pointers to storage of type **T**. How do you dynamically allocate a new block of storage of type **T** and obtain a pointer to it in C?

5. Suppose **A** has been declared to be an **IntegerPointer** variable. How would you write an assignment statement to assign the integer **19** to be the value of **A**'s referent? How would you write an expression whose value is twice the value of **A**'s referent?

6. Suppose **A** has been declared to be an **IntegerPointer** variable. What is wrong with the assignment **A = 5**; for assigning **5** to be the value of **A**'s referent?

7. What are aliases?

8. How do you recycle dynamically allocated storage when it is no longer needed so that its space can be reused to meet further storage allocation needs?

9. How can dynamically allocated storage become inaccessible in C?

10. What is garbage?

11. What is a dangling pointer?

12. What is the lifetime of dynamically allocated storage?

13. What is an anonymous variable?

2.3 Exercises

For the following problems, assume that the following types and variables have been declared in C, and are available for use:

```
typedef int *IntegerPointer;

IntegerPointer A , B;
```

1. What does the following procedure print when it is executed?

```
      |    void P(void)
      |    {
      |        A = (IntegerPointer)malloc(sizeof(int));
      |        B = (IntegerPointer)malloc(sizeof(int))
    5 |        *A = 19;
      |        *B = 5;
      |        A = B;
      |        *B = 7;
      |        printf("%d\n",*A);
      |    }
```

2. What does the following procedure print when it is executed?

```
|    void P(void)
|    {
|        A = (int *)malloc(sizeof(int));
|        B = (int *)malloc(sizeof(int))
5  |        *A = 19;
|        *B = 5;
|        *A = *B;
|        *B = 7;
|        printf("%d\n",*A);
|    }
```

3. How does storage allocation failure manifest itself in your C system? If your instructor will authorize you to do so, try running the following program. What does it tell you if it terminates and prints its final message properly?

```
|    void AllocationFailureTest(void)
|    {
|        typedef int BigArray[1000];
|        BigArray *A;
5  |
|        while ((A = (BigArray *)malloc(sizeof(BigArray))) != NULL)
|            ;
|
|        printf("storage allocation failure occurred");
|    }
```

Caution: Don't try executing this procedure in your C system unless you know in advance how to interrupt a running program, how to terminate its execution, and how to regain control of events. It is possible that the above program will result in an endless loop, if allocation failure does not result in setting A to **NULL**, when **malloc(sizeof(BigArray))** is called with insufficient storage available to satisfy the request. As a precaution, you can rewrite the program above to count the number of times **malloc(sizeof(BigArray))** is called, and to pause and ask you if you want to continue, say, every 5000 times it is called.

4. What happens in your C system if you try to dereference the null pointer, as in the following C fragment?

```
|    A = NULL;          /* set A to NULL */
|    A = *A;            /* dereference the pointer NULL */
```

Caution: Don't try to execute this on your computer unless your instructor authorizes you to do so, and you know how to recover from crashes.

2.4 Pointer Diagramming Notation

Learning Objectives

1. To understand how to interpret the pointer diagrams used in this book.
2. To learn a notation for picturing linked representations that is helpful when reasoning about them.

nodes

Diagrams illustrating pointers in this book follow a few simple conventions. The boxes represent different units of addressable storage. We will refer to these boxes as *nodes*. By convention in these diagrams, we assume that different nodes represent storage locations with different addresses. The three rows in Fig. 2.7 represent the same linked list. When addresses are represented explicitly, they are signified by Greek letters, such as α, β, and γ, as shown in the topmost linked list of Fig. 2.7. For instance, α is the address of the following node:

Info   Link

α: | x_1 | β |

fields

It is written to the left of the node, followed by a colon. β signifies an address stored as a pointer value in the Link field of this node. If a node is divided into fields (representing a C structure with members), the names of the fields are attached to the border of the box representing the node. Thus the node above has two fields: an Info field, containing the value x_1, and a Link field containing the pointer β.

the null address

There exists a special *null* address, which by convention is not the address of any node. It is depicted by a solid dot (●) that represents an arrow with no tip that points

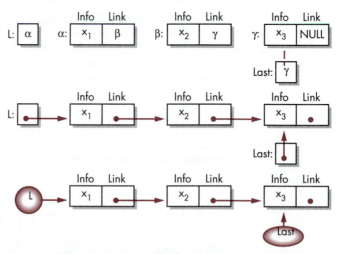

Figure 2.7 Three Equivalent Diagrams in Pointer Diagramming Notation

nowhere. In C, the null pointer is represented by the special pointer value **NULL**. This special null address is used to show where a linked list ends, and it is used to represent an empty structure (such as a linked list having no nodes).

Finally, Fig. 2.7 shows some examples of the diagramming notation for the pointer variables **L** and **Last**. In the diagram below, the two notations for **L** and **Last** are equivalent.

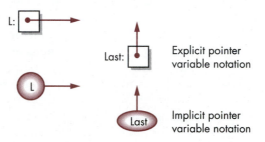

Pointer variables can be written two ways: either (1) *explicitly* as a box containing a pointer value labeled on the left side with the name of the variable followed by a colon, or (2) *implicitly* as an oval (or circle) containing the variable name and pointing to the node the pointer value references.

We can use a pointer to **NULL** to represent the null pointer in diagrams where we want to show explicitly how the null pointer is replaced by a non-null pointer value. For instance, Fig. 2.8 shows how we can insert a new second node into a linked list by changing the link of the first node to point to it, and by replacing its null link with a pointer to the previous second node. The arrows that are "crossed out" represent pointer values that were replaced with new pointer values during the operation shown in the diagram.

We will use the implicit notation for pointer variables (as ovals containing variable names) in diagrams with many nodes in which we use pointer variables to contain pointers to point at places in the overall linked data structure (1) where change is about to occur or (2) to keep track of a location we will need to use in the future. The implicit notation tends to be more compact and less cluttered than the explicit notation in such circumstances, but we should always remember that it is equivalent to the explicit notation in which the variable name, followed by a colon, is to the left of a box containing a pointer.

Finally, when the value of a variable or the value of a field in a node is unknown (as happens sometimes at the outset of an algorithm before initialization), we may symbolize the unknown value by a question mark (?) for nonpointer values, or a

pointer variable notation

using implicit pointer variable notation

unknown values

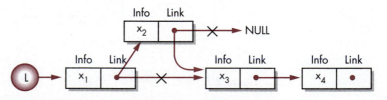

Figure 2.8 Inserting a New Second Node into a Linked List

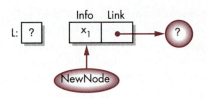

Figure 2.9 Unknown Values and Pointers

pointer to a circle containing a question mark, for an unknown pointer value, as in Fig. 2.9. We will use these explicit denotations of unknown values in situations where we want to emphasize that a newly allocated structure needs to be initialized with known values, and where we need something to "cross out" to indicate the replacement of an old value with a new value.

2.4 Review Questions

1. What is the null address?
2. How is null address depicted in pointer diagramming notation?
3. What value represents the null address in C?
4. How is the end of a linked list indicated in pointer diagramming notation?
5. What is an empty linked list, and what value is used to indicate it?
6. Explain the difference between explicit pointer variable notation and implicit pointer variable notation.
7. How is an unknown value signified in pointer diagramming notation?

2.4 Exercises

[*Note:* The exercises below introduce an important new –> notation.] For these exercises assume that the following diagram specifies the values of the variables N and L:

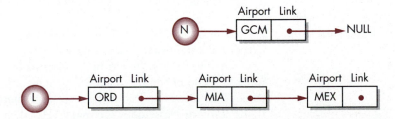

(*Note:* Here, the three-letter codes ORD, MIA, GCM, and MEX are the codes airlines use on baggage tags: ORD = Chicago's O'Hare airport; MIA = Miami, Florida; MEX = Mexico City, Mexico; and GCM = Grand Cayman in the Cayman Islands.)

1. In the diagram above, if you assume L's referent, *L, is a node containing a **struct** with an **Airport** field containing **ORD**, then you could write: (*L).Airport == ORD. Also, given that L–>Airport is a preferred equivalent notation for (*L).Airport, you could conclude that L–>Link–>Airport == MIA. Using this line of reasoning, what

are the values of the following four **struct** field selection expressions: (a) N–>Link, (b) N–>Airport, (c) L–>Link–>Link–>Airport, and (d) L–>Link–>Link–>Link?

2. Write C expressions possibly using: (a) the variables L and N, (b) the **struct** member names **Airport** and **Link**, (c) the dereferencing operator (*), the **struct** member selection operator (.) or the operator (–>), having the following values: (i) a pointer to the node containing MIA, (ii) a pointer to the node containing MEX, (iii) a pointer to the node containing ORD, and (iv) the node containing ORD.

3. Write two C assignment statements that (when executed) will insert N's referent as the new third node of the list L. Before these assignments are executed, the airport codes of the nodes in the list referenced by L are ORD, MIA, MEX. After the assignments are executed, the airport codes should be in the sequence ORD, MIA, GCM, MEX.

4. Draw the picture of the result of executing the two assignment statements that solve problem 3, starting with the diagram for the values of L and N above.

5. In C, executing the string copy function strcpy(L–>Airport,"JFK") starting with the diagram above, replaces the airport code ORD by JFK. Write a function call using strcpy that replaces MIA by JFK. (*Note:* JFK is the airport code for John F. Kennedy International Airport in New York City.)

6. Write statements in C that replace the node containing MIA with the node containing GCM. After execution, L should point to nodes with airport codes given in the sequence ORD, GCM, MEX. Remember to free the storage for the node containing MIA.

2.5 Linear Linked Lists

Learning Objectives

1. To understand how to represent and manipulate linked lists using C's pointer data types.
2. To develop skill in designing and implementing linked list algorithms.
3. To learn a set of useful basic linked list operations.

linear linked lists

A *linear linked list* (or a *linked list*, for short) is a sequence of nodes in which each node, except the last, links to a successor node.

The link field of the last node contains the null pointer value, **NULL**, which signifies the end of the list. Figure 2.10 represents a linear linked list containing the three-letter airport codes for the stops on American Airlines flight number 89. This flight starts in Düsseldorf, Germany (DUS), it stops at Chicago's O'Hare Airport (ORD), and it continues on to its final destination at San Diego (SAN).

Figure 2.10 A Linear Linked List

The pointer variable L contains a pointer to the first node on this list. We will sometimes say "L's value is the list (DUS, ORD, SAN)," imagining that the whole linked list is a single entity, and that this list is the value of the variable, L, even though L contains a pointer referencing only the first node of the list.

Inserting a New Second Node on a List

Suppose we want to add a new stop to the route of flight 89 represented by the list in Fig. 2.10 so that it stops in Brussels, Belgium (BRU) before flying to O'Hare. To represent this change, we need to insert a node for BRU as the new second node on the list.

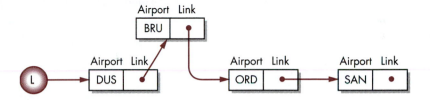

A method for linking the new second node into the given list is shown in Program Strategy 2.11. Program strategies such as these specify high-level goals to accomplish. In this book, we use them as starting points for the development of C programs. They are intended to help you grasp how algorithms work, by expressing concisely the essential plans, methods, and goals that lie at the heart of an algorithm's design. If the actual programming details are given too soon, they can often obscure what is really going on.

program strategies

The goals in a program strategy can be achieved by supplying more specific programming details. The process of filling in such details in a series of specific steps is called *stepwise refinement*. The method of starting with a top-level design and expanding its details progressively until an actual program is developed is called *top-down programming*.

stepwise refinement and top-down programming

We will comment in greater detail on the method of top-down programming using stepwise refinement in Chapter 5, where software engineering concepts are discussed. However, we will actually use this method many times before studying it in Chapter 5. Thus, you will have encountered numerous examples of this method,

```
| void InsertNewSecondNode(void)
| {
|     (Declare a pointer variable N, that points to list nodes)
|
|     (Allocate a new node and let the pointer variable N point to it)
|     (Copy the string "BRU" into the Airport field of N's referent)
|     (Change the Link field of N's referent to point to the second node of list L)
|     (Change the Link field of the first node of list L to point to N's referent)
| }
```

Program Strategy 2.11 Inserting a New Second Node in a Linked List

allowing you to develop intuition for how it works before being asked to understand its significance.

We will now expand the goals in Program Strategy 2.11 into a specific C program in two separate steps. In the first, we use pointer diagramming notation to illustrate what is happening in addition to giving C code. In the second step, we delete the diagrams and shorten the comments. What remains is a concise final C program.

```
void InsertNewSecondNode(void)
{
    /*Declare a pointer variable, N, that points to nodes of type NodeType. */
        NodeType *N;

    /* Allocate a new node and let the pointer variable N point to it.*/
        N = (NodeType *)malloc(sizeof(NodeType));
```

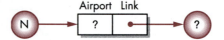

```
    /* Copy the string "BRU" into the Airport field of N's referent. */
        strcpy(N->Airport,"BRU");
```

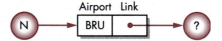

```
    /* Change the Link field of N's referent to point to the second node of list L. */
        N->Link = L->Link;
```

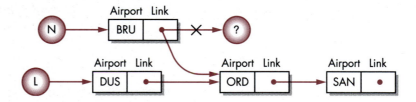

```
    /* Change the Link field of the first node of list L to point to N's referent. */
        L->Link = N;
```

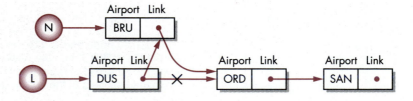

```
}
```

Next, we strip the pictures from this intermediate version of our procedure, and we shorten the original comments. The following C program results:

```
void InsertNewSecondNode(void)
{
    NodeType *N;                                          /* let N be a list node */

    N = (NodeType *)malloc(sizeof(NodeType));        /* allocate a new node, N */
    strcpy(N–>Airport,"BRU");                         /* set N's Airport to "BRU" */
    N–>Link = L–>Link;                        /* let N link to the second node of list L */
    L–>Link = N;                                /* let L's first node link to N */
}
```

In this program, note that in order to make the comments short, we have used language imprecisely. The shortened language makes it sound as if N were a variable containing a node, rather than being a variable containing a pointer to a node. Thus instead of giving the untruthful comment, "allocate a new node, N," we should have given the truthful comment, "allocate a new node and let the pointer variable N contain a pointer to it." Although we will not usually engage in this kind of falsifying brevity in this book, you should be aware that real-world programmers, in an attempt to achieve brevity and conciseness, sometimes use short comments that are slightly out-of-correspondence with the truth expressed by the underlying code. This is not an unreasonable programming practice. Any competent programmer can infer from the underlying code exactly what is going on. Not only do the brief comments give valid descriptions of top-level goals being achieved by the code, they also help make the program concise and easy to read.

the problem of slightly untruthful comments

Another important thing to note about the function, InsertNewSecondNode, is that the variable N is a *local* variable. N exists only during the execution of the function, and it contains a pointer to a newly allocated node only when it is in existence. N's pointer value is placed in the Link field of the first node of list L before the function terminates, causing the first node of list L to link to the newly allocated node. After the function terminates execution, the variable N and its contents vanish. However, the dynamically allocated storage for the new second node of list L created during this function's execution remains in place after the execution of the function has terminated:

dynamically allocated storage remains in existence

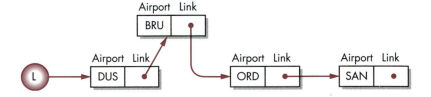

Actually, the process of stepwise refinement is not complete yet, since we haven't yet given any declarations for the C data types needed to make the above program work properly. So, let's proceed to finish the job. This is the subject of the next subsection.

Declaring Data Types for Linked Lists

First, we have to specify some way of representing the three-letter airport codes. A reasonable way to do this is to define a type **AirportCode** to be an array of four characters capable of storing a C-string consisting of the three letters for the airport code followed by a fourth null character (\0) which terminates the string. We can then use string literals, such as "BRU", in string copy statements in a C program to copy airport code strings into fields of structs representing nodes. Thus, in the type definition section of our program, we could write,

declaring types for three-letter airport codes

```
typedef char AirportCode[4];
```

node types

Next, we need to define a system of nodes and pointers to serve as the foundation for manipulating linked lists. To do this, we define a structure type for list nodes, called **NodeType**, in the type definition section of our program as follows:

```
typedef  struct NodeTag {
              AirportCode       Airport;
              struct NodeTag *Link;
         } NodeType;
```

This defines a **NodeType** to be a **struct** having two *members* (or *components*, or *fields*, as we shall sometimes call them) which are: (1) an **Airport** field containing a three-letter **AirportCode**, and (2) a **Link** field containing a pointer to a **NodeType**.

In order to make it possible for the **Link** field of a **NodeType** struct to contain a pointer to another **NodeType** struct, the **typedef** above introduces the tag **NodeTag** after the word **struct** and then specifies the second member of the struct using **struct NodeTag *Link**; while it is illegal in C to attempt to define a struct which contains itself as a member, it is nonetheless legal to define a struct having a member which is a pointer to structs of the same type, as is accomplished above.

pointer types

To define a pointer type in C consisting of pointers to nodes of type **NodeType**, we could write,

```
typedef NodeType *NodePointer;
```

We could then write,

```
NodePointer N, L;
```

to declare **N** and **L** to be two variables holding pointers to nodes of type **NodeType**. Another equivalent way of defining such node pointers is,

```
NodeType *N, *L;
```

Because the second form of declaration is common in professional practice among C programmers, we shall use it in what follows.

Another important idea is that the special null pointer, **NULL**, is automatically considered to be a value that belongs to every pointer type that is defined in C. Thus it is possible to write assignments such as **L–>Link = NULL**; to put the null pointer into the **Link** field of the node that the pointer in **L** references, or to test a pointer value to see if it is null, as in **if (L–>Link == NULL) { /*L points to the last node in the list */ }**. [*Note:* In ANSI C, the null pointer simply has the value 0 and **NULL** is just a form of "visual documentation" for its value.]

NULL belongs to every pointer type

Searching for an Item on a List

Suppose we are given the task of finding the node **N** on a list of airport codes **L** containing the airport code **A**. Assume that all types and variables have been declared using the declarations just given. Suppose that the problem statement asks us to write a function to return a pointer to the node on list **L** containing airport code **A**, if there is such a node. If no such node exists, we are to return the null pointer, **NULL**. To access the linked list, **L**, assume that **L** is a variable declared by **NodeType *L**, containing a pointer to the first node of the linked list (or containing the value **NULL**, in case **L** is the *empty list*, consisting of a list with no nodes).

strategy for list searching

One strategy for solving this search problem is to let **N** be a pointer to a **NodeType** and to let it point to each node of list **L** in succession, checking each node to see if it contains the string for the airport code **A**. As soon as a node containing airport code **A** is found the search terminates. The general idea is sketched in Program Strategy 2.12.

```
     |   NodeType *ListSearch(char *A, NodeType *L)
     |   {
     |         (Declare N to be a variable that points to nodes)
     |
  5  |         (Initially, set N to point to the first node of list L)
     |
     |         while (N points to a non-null node on list L ) {
     |
     |               if (the Airport code of N's referent equals A) {
 10  |
     |                     (return the node pointer in N)
     |
     |               } else {
     |
 15  |                     (advance the pointer N to point to the next node on list L)
     |               }
     |         }
     |
     |         (return N's value, NULL, as the result of the list search)
 20  |
     |   }
```

Program Strategy 2.12 Strategy for List Searching

Using the method of top-down programming by stepwise refinement, we proceed to fill in actual C code that accomplishes the goals given in this program strategy. Program 2.13 is a refinement of the program strategy with specific C code inserted and more generous comments added.

To make sure that you understand how this program works, it is useful to go over a specific worked example that uses diagrams generously to help make the explanation clear. Suppose we are searching for the airport code A == "ORD" on the list L == (DUS, BRU, ORD, SAN). This search would be initiated if we made the function call ListSearch("ORD",L). On line 6, we perform the assignment N = L, which makes N point to the same node that L does. This initializes the search, so that the pointer N is pointing to the first node of the list, as shown in the following diagram:

a worked example with diagrams

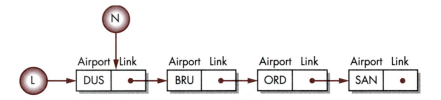

We are now set up to perform the while-loop on lines 11:23. Inside this while-loop we advance N along the list, so that it points to each node in sequence.

Each time N points to a new nonempty node, we check to see if that node's airport code is equal to the string "ORD" using the string comparison function call strcmp(L–>Airport,A), which returns the value 0 if and only if the string in the L–>Airport field is identical to the string A. If N points to a node having an airport code ORD, the search terminates successfully and returns the node pointer value in N. In this specific case, when N advances to point to the third node of list L, we find that N is pointing to a node containing the airport code ORD, so the value returned by the ListSearch function will be N's current value, which is a pointer to the node containing ORD.

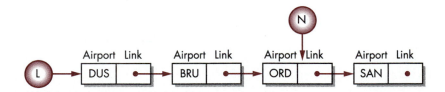

On the other hand, if the node to which N points does not contain the airport code we are searching for, we change the pointer in N to point to the next node in the list. To do this, we replace N's pointer with the pointer in the link field of the node that N

```
   |   NodeType *ListSearch(char *A, NodeType *L)
   |   {
   |       NodeType *N;                    /* N points to successive nodes on the list L */
   |
 5 |       /* Initialization */
   |           N = L;                      /* let N start by pointing to the first node of the list L */
   |
   |       /* While N points to a non-null node on list L */
   |       /* examine the node to which N points */
10 |
   |           while (N != NULL) {
   |
   |               if (strcmp(N–>Airport,A) == 0) {        /* if N's Airport == A */
   |
15 |                   return N;                           /* return the node pointer in N */
   |
   |               } else {                                /* otherwise */
   |
   |                   N = N–>Link;        /* advance N to the next node on the list */
20 |
   |               }
   |
   |           }
   |
25 |       return N;                       /* return NULL if no node's Airport == A */
   |
   |   }
```

Program 2.13 List Searching Program

is currently pointing to. The statement, N = N–>Link, on line 19, advances the pointer in N to the next node in this fashion.

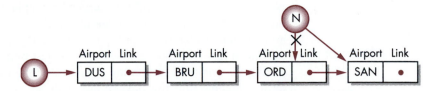

As we travel step-by-step down the list, with N pointing at each node in sequence, either we find a node with airport code ORD, or we come to the end of the list. This brings us to consider what happens in cases of unsuccessful search. If the list is empty to begin with (meaning L == NULL), or the airport code ORD that we are searching for is not on the list, the pointer N eventually takes the value NULL.

In the case of a nonempty list that does not contain an airport code ORD, this happens as follows. As N is advanced to point to each node of the list in sequence, it eventually is made to point to the last node of the list.

unsuccessful search

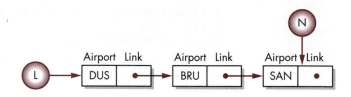

The last node of a list always has **NULL** as the value of its **Link** field. When it is discovered that this last node does not contain airport code **ORD**, we attempt to advance the pointer to the next node by executing **N = N–>Link**, on line 19. But since there is no next node, the value **NULL** in the **Link** field of the node that **N** points to becomes the next value of **N**.

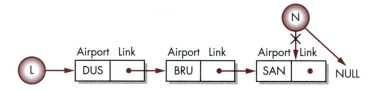

At this point, when we return to the beginning of the while-loop, on line 11, the condition **N != NULL** becomes false. Control exits the while-loop and passes down to the statement on line 25, which returns **NULL** as the value of the function, to signify that the result of the search was unsuccessful. (Recall that the problem statement required us to return a **NULL** pointer value in place of a pointer to an actual nonempty node in order to designate the result of an unsuccessful search.)

Deleting the Last Node of a List

list termination

Now let's turn to a second fully worked example. Suppose we are asked to write a procedure to delete the last node of a linked list. Again assume that the C type and variable declarations for linked lists are the same as those we have been using for linked lists of airport codes. Since the last node of a linked list is designated by setting its **Link** field to contain **NULL**, to delete the last node of a linked list, we must somehow find the next-to-last node so we can set its **Link** field to contain **NULL**.

In the solution that follows, we will use two node pointer variables called **PreviousNode** and **CurrentNode**. As we advance the **CurrentNode** pointer to point to each successive node on the list, we will advance the **PreviousNode** pointer to point to the node immediately before the one that **CurrentNode** points to. The two pointers therefore travel down the list as a *pointer pair*.

When **CurrentNode** gets to the last node of the list, **PreviousNode** will be pointing to the next-to-last node of the list. At this moment, we can set the **Link** of this next-to-last node to be **NULL**, designating it as the new last node of the list. Then we can return the storage for the unused former last node to the pool of unallocated storage, using the **free** function.

In order for our pointer-pair process to work properly, we need to use lists with at least two nodes on them. But since the empty list, L == NULL, and the list having only one node do not fit this requirement, we need to treat them as special cases at the beginning of the function. In the case of an empty list, we don't need to do anything, since there is no last node to delete. In the case of a list with one node, we need to dispose of the node's storage, and then we need to set L to be the empty list. This will require us to pass the address of L as an actual parameter (in the form &L) enabling us to change L's contents inside the DeleteLastNode function. A summary of these considerations is given in Program Strategy 2.14.

handling two special cases first

```
     void DeleteLastNode(&L)          /* &L gives the address of the variable L */
     {

         (Let PreviousNode and CurrentNode contain pointers to list nodes)
5

         if (L is not the empty-list) {

             if (L has exactly one node) {
10
                 (free the node's storage, replace L with the empty list,)
                 (and return from the procedure)

             } else {              /* otherwise, L must have two or more nodes */
15
                 (Initialize a pair of pointers, (PreviousNode,CurrentNode) )
                 (to point to the first and second nodes.)

                 (Advance the pointer pair along L until CurrentNode)
20               (points to the last node}

                     while (CurrentNode does not point to the last node)  {
                         (advance the pair of pointers to the next pair of nodes)
                     }
25
                 (Now PreviousNode points to the next-to-last node on the list)
                 (and CurrentNode points to the last node on the list.)

                 (Finally, change the next-to-last node into the new last node)
30               (and free the space for the discarded last node)

             }

         }
35
     }
```

Program Strategy 2.14 Strategy for Deleting the Last Node of a List

A diagram of what needs to happen on line 23 when we advance the pointer pair to the next pair of nodes is given below:

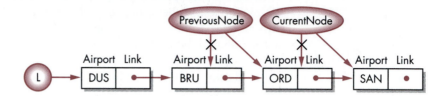

We now make a top-down, stepwise refinement of this program strategy so that it contains the actual working details in C shown in Program 2.15. Note that the last two programs we have developed (Programs 2.13 and 2.15) share a common theme. They both use a while-loop to step down the successive nodes of a linked list until a specific condition is satisfied. The strategy for this theme is **while (condition not satisfied) { (move to next node on list) }**. This strategy can be used to solve the problem of inserting a new last node on a list.

Inserting a New Last Node on a List

Another important building block to learn about is the function for inserting a new node on a list. Suppose we are given an airport code, **A**, and the address **&L** of a variable **L**, which contains a pointer to the first node of list **L**. We want to insert a new node, containing the airport code, **A**, at the end of this list. A function with the calling form, **InsertNewLastNode(A,&L)**, that accomplishes this is given in Program 2.16.

On line 8, a new node is allocated. A pointer to it is placed in the pointer variable **N**, and its **Airport** and **Link** fields are set to contain **A** and **NULL**, respectively.

Lines 12:14 handle the special case that the list, **L**, was empty to begin with. In this case, we need to put **N**'s node pointer into **L**. Since the address of **L** is used in the call **InsertNewLastNode(A,&L)**, we need to use the assignment ***L = N;** to do this.

On the other hand, if the original list, **L**, was not empty, we can be assured that it contains one or more nodes. In this case, we need to search for the last node. We do this on lines 19:20 using a pointer variable, **P**, which is made to step along the nodes of **L** until it comes to rest on **L**'s last node.

Initially, **P** is made to point to the first node of **L**, using the assignment **P = *L;** on line 19. The while-loop on line 20 is now executed to locate the last node of **L**. Note that this while-loop is an instance of the strategy **while (condition not satisfied) { (move to next node on list) }** which shares the same theme as Programs 2.13 and 2.15.

Once **P** has been made to point to the last node of **L**, the new last node, **N**, can be linked to it. This is accomplished on line 23.

How to Print a List

Before we can write a small program that meaningfully builds up an airport code list, changes it, and shows us the changes, we need to define the list printing function illustrated in Program 2.17. The heart of the **PrintList** function is also a while-loop

```
      void DeleteLastNode(NodeType **L)          /*Note: **L is the address of the */
      {                                          /* variable L, whose value points */
                                                 /* to the first node of list L */

5         NodeType * PreviousNode, *CurrentNode;

          if (*L != NULL) {                      /* do nothing if *L was the empty list */

             if ((*L)–>Link == NULL) {           /* if *L has exactly one node, then */
10
                free(*L);                        /* free the node's storage, */
                *L = NULL;                       /* set L to be the empty list, and terminate */

             } else {                            /* otherwise, list L must have two or more nodes */
15
                /* initialize a pair of pointers, (PreviousNode,CurrentNode) */
                /* to point to the first and second nodes. */

                   PreviousNode = *L;
20                 CurrentNode =(*L)–>Link ;


                /* Advance the pointer pair along L until CurrentNode */
                /* points to the last node */
25
                   while (CurrentNode–>Link != NULL) {
                      PreviousNode = CurrentNode ;
                      CurrentNode = CurrentNode–>Link;
                   }
30
                /* Now PreviousNode points to the next-to-last node on the list */
                /* and CurrentNode points to the last node on the list. */

35                 PreviousNode–>Link= NULL;  /* last node gets NULL link */
                   free(CurrentNode);  /* recycle storage for discarded node */

             }

40        }

      }
```

Program 2.15 Deleting the Last Node of a List

```
      |    void InsertNewLastNode(char *A, NodeType **L)        /* Again, expect **L */
      |    {                                                    /* to be the address of */
      |                                                         /* a variable L containing a */
      |                                                         /* pointer to the first node of the list */
  5   |        NodeType *N, *P;
      |
      |        /* Allocate a new node N with Airport == A and Link == NULL */
      |            N = (NodeType *)malloc(sizeof(NodeType));
      |            strcpy(N–>Airport, A);
 10   |            N–>Link = NULL;
      |
      |        if ( *L == NULL ) {                                  /* If list *L is empty,*/
      |
      |            *L = N;                               /* let N become the new value for *L */
 15   |
      |        } else {                                                  /* Otherwise, */
      |
      |            /* Locate the last node of list L, using pointer variable P */
      |                P = *L;
 20   |                while (P–>Link != NULL) P = P–>Link;
      |
      |            /* Finally, link node N onto the end of the list */
      |                P–>Link = N;
      |        }
      |    }
```

Program 2.16 Inserting a New Last Node on a List

```
      |    void PrintList(NodeType *L)
      |    {
      |        NodeType *N;                        /* N points to successive nodes on list L */
      |
  5   |
      |        /* First, print a left parenthesis */
      |            printf( "(" );
      |
      |        /* Let N start by pointing to the first node on the list L */
 10   |            N = L;
      |
      |        /* Provided N doesn't point to an empty node, print N's Airport */
      |        /* and advance N to point to the next node on the list */
      |
 15   |            while (N != NULL) {
      |                printf("%s",N–>Airport);                    /* print airport code */
      |                N = N–>Link;                      /* make N point to next node on list */
      |                if (N != NULL) printf(", ");           /* print comma between items */
      |            }
 20   |
      |        /* Finally, print a closing right parenthesis */
      |            printf(")\n");
      |
      |    }
```

Program 2.17 Printing a List

that steps down the list, visiting each successive node. In this case, the pointer variable N is made to point to each such node.

Inside the while-loop, the airport code for each node, N, is printed (using the statement printf("%s",N–>Airport);, which does *not* advance to the next line). Following this, N is made to point to the next node on the list, by executing the statement N = N–>Link;. In order to print commas *between* the airport codes on the list but not *after* the last airport code, the statement if (N != NULL) printf(", "); is executed. The reason this does not print a comma after the last node of the list is because the variable N is made to point to NULL immediately beforehand.

Getting Our Act Together

At this point, we have developed a small library of building blocks useful for writing linked list programs. Consequently, we are in a position to assemble some of the pieces together to make a complete C main program. Program 2.18 is an example of one such program. When we run this program, it prints three lines:

```
( DUS , ORD , SAN )
( DUS , BRU , ORD , SAN )
( DUS , BRU , ORD )
```

```
         /* Here, insert the typedefs and functions defined above for the types */
         /* AirportCode and NodeType and the functions InsertNewLastNode, */
         /* InsertNewSecondNode, DeleteLastNode, and PrintList. Then declare */
         /* a node pointer variable L as shown below: */
5
         int main (void)
         {
                 NodeType *L;

10               /* First, construct the list L == (DUS,ORD,SAN) and print it */

                 /* To start things off, let L be the empty list */
                 L = NULL;

15               /* Insert a new last node in L with airport code "DUS" */
                 InsertNewLastNode("DUS",&L);

                 /* Insert a new last node in L with airport code "ORD" */
                 InsertNewLastNode("ORD",&L);
20
                 /* Insert a new last node in L with airport code "SAN" */
                 InsertNewLastNode("SAN",&L);
```

Program 2.18 An Example That Puts Some Pieces Together (continued)

Program 2.18 An Example That Puts Some Pieces Together (continued)

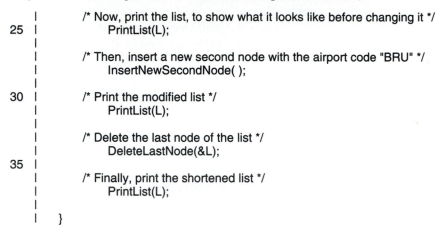

```
25 |          /* Now, print the list, to show what it looks like before changing it */
   |              PrintList(L);
   |
   |          /* Then, insert a new second node with the airport code "BRU" */
   |              InsertNewSecondNode( );
   |
30 |          /* Print the modified list */
   |              PrintList(L);
   |
   |          /* Delete the last node of the list */
   |              DeleteLastNode(&L);
35 |
   |          /* Finally, print the shortened list */
   |              PrintList(L);
   |
   |      }
```

Where to From Here?

We have now studied five examples that illustrate key foundations of linked list programming in C. But if you have never programmed with linked lists before, you might need further development of your skills before you can attain an intermediate level of mastery. An excellent way to improve your skills is to write perhaps seven to twelve new linked list functions implementing basic linked list operations.

building your skills

Exercises 2.5 ask you to write programs to do typical list operations such as: (1) inserting a node as the new first node on a list, (2) deleting the first node on a list, (3) making a copy of a list, (4) reversing the order of the nodes on a list, and (5) joining two lists together to make a single combined list.

2.5 Review Questions

1. What is top-down programming using stepwise refinement?
2. When defining a struct for a **NodeType** in C, how can we arrange for a **Link** field to contain a pointer to the **NodeType** we are defining?
3. What value in C is automatically a value of every C pointer type?

2.5 Exercises

Assume that the following types and variables have been defined in C and are available for use:

```
typedef char AirportCode[4]

typedef  struct NodeTag {
            AirportCode      Airport;
            struct NodeTag   *Link;
         } NodeType;


         NodeType *L, *M, *N;
```

1. Write a function, InsertNewFirstNode(A,&L), which inserts a node having the airport code A as the new first node of list, L, where &L is the address of variable L.
2. Write a function, DeleteFirst(&L), which deletes the first node of a linked list L.
3. Given a non-null pointer N to a node of a list L, and a pointer M to a new node to be inserted, write a C function to insert the node that is M's referent *before* the node that is N's referent on list L. [*Hint:* Adjust pointers to insert M after N and then swap the airport codes in N and M.]
4. Write a function, Copy(L), which makes a copy of a linked list, L, and returns a pointer to the first node of the copy.
5. Write a function, Reverse(&L), which reverses the order of the nodes on list L. For example, if L == (ZRH, GLA, YYZ) beforehand, then executing Reverse(&L) changes L to be the list L == (YYZ, GLA, ZRH). [*Hint:* Write two subroutines to remove the first node N of a list L1, and to insert a node N as the new first node on a list L2. Then, starting with an empty list L2 = NULL, successively remove nodes from L1 and insert them on L2 until L1 is empty.] (*Note:* The airport codes: ZRH, GLA, and YYZ stand for Zürich, Switzerland; Glasgow, Scotland; and Toronto, Ontario, respectively.)
6. What is wrong with the following search program for finding the node on list L containing the airport code A and returning a pointer to it?

```
    |    NodeType *FindNode(char *A, NodeType *L)
    |    {
    |
    |        while ( (strcmp(L–>Airport,A) != 0) && (L != NULL) ) {
  5 |            L = L–>Link;
    |        }
    |
    |        return L;
    |    }
```

How could you fix the bug in the program above by changing only one line?

7. Given two lists **L1** and **L2**, write a function, **Concat(L1,L2)**, to return a pointer to a list in which the nodes of **L2** follow the nodes of **L1**. For example, if, beforehand, **L1 == (ARN, BRU)** and **L2 == (JFK, SAN, HKG)**, then the node pointer returned by **Concat(L1,L2)** should point to the list **(ARN, BRU, JFK, SAN, HKG)**. (*Note:* ARN is Stockholm, Sweden, and HKG is Hong Kong.)

8. What is wrong with the following algorithm for finding the last node of a list **L** and returning a pointer to it?

```
   |     NodeType *LastNode(NodeType *L)
   |     {
   |         if (L != NULL) {
   |             do
 5 |                 L = L–>Link;
   |             while (L–>Link != NULL);
   |         }
   |
   |         return L;
10 |
   |     }
```

9. In Program 2.15, **DeleteLastNode(NodeType **L)**, if you want to delete the last node of a list, **L**, why does the parameter have to be a pointer to a variable containing a node pointer? Give an example of a list that would fail to have its last node deleted if the parameter had been only a node pointer as in the function prototype **void DeleteLastNode(NodeType *L)**.

2.6 Other Linked Data Structures

Learning Objectives

1. To understand some possibilities for linked data representations other than simple, one-way linked lists.
2. To illustrate how nodes with two links can be linked into representations such as two-way linked lists, rings, and trees.

As you might expect, the simple linked lists we studied in the previous sections in this chapter are not the only kinds of linked data representations that are possible. For example, starting with nodes that contain **AirportCodes** and two separate link fields—a **LeftLink** field and a **RightLink** field—we can build linked data structures using a variety of different organizational principles. We proceed to illustrate just three of the many possibilities.

First, we need to declare some data types in C to represent the nodes of these structures. We do this as follows.

```
typedef  struct NodeTag {
            AirportCode        Airport;
            struct NodeTag    *LeftLink;
            struct NodeTag    *RightLink;
         } NodeType;
```

We assume that the **AirportCode** type is the same as that used in the previous examples of linked lists of airport codes. Note that a node of type **NodeType** contains *two* pointer fields, a **LeftLink** field and a **RightLink** field, both of which contain pointers to other nodes.

Figure 2.19 illustrates a typical node used to construct various linked representations. One type of data structure that we can build by linking such nodes is called a *two-way linked list* (or, sometimes, a *symmetrically linked list*). Figure 2.20 gives an example of a two-way list of airport codes. If we were to replace the null links marking the left and right ends of the list in Fig. 2.20 with links to the respective opposite ends of the list, we would get the two-way ring structure illustrated in Fig. 2.21.

Figure 2.19 Typical node with two links

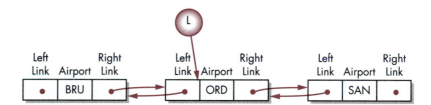

Figure 2.20 A Two-Way Linked List of Airport Codes

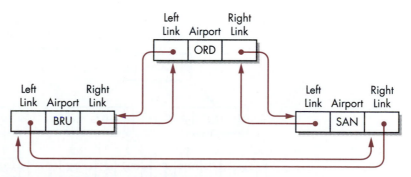

Figure 2.21 Two-Way Ring of Airport Codes

ARN	Stockholm, Sweden
BRU	Brussels, Belgium
DUS	Düsseldorf, Germany
GCM	Grand Cayman, Cayman Islands
GLA	Glasgow, Scotland
HKG	Hong Kong
JFK	Kennedy Airport, New York
MEX	Mexico City, Mexico
MIA	Miami, Florida
NRT	Narita Airport, Tokyo, Japan
ORD	O'Hare Airport, Chicago, Illinois
ORY	Orly Field, Paris, France
SAN	San Diego, California
YYZ	Toronto, Ontario
ZRH	Zürich, Switzerland

Table 2.22 Three-Letter Airport Codes

linked binary trees

Let's now take a look at another type of linked representation—a *linked binary tree*. Table 2.22 gives 15 airport codes in alphabetical order, and Fig. 2.23 shows these codes arranged in a linked binary tree, constructed from nodes of the type illustrated in Fig. 2.19. It is a common convention in computer science to picture such trees *upside-down*, with their branches growing downwards.

We will have more to say about various different kinds of linked list representations in Chapter 8, and about linked binary tree representations in Chapter 9. In Chapter 9 when we discuss the anatomy of trees, we will define terms such as the *root*, *leaves*, and *branches* of a tree. In Chapter 3, on recursion, we will see several instances of binary trees when we discuss call trees for evaluating recursive functions and procedures.

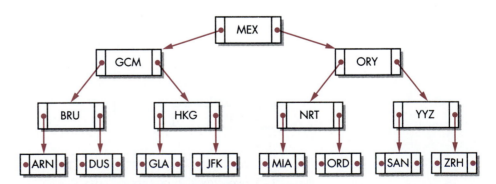

Figure 2.23 A Linked Data Structure for a Binary Tree

2.6 Review Questions

1. Name some linked data structures that can be constructed from nodes having two separate pointer fields.
2. What is a symmetrically linked list?

2.6 Exercise

1. Write a C function to delete the node of a two-way linked list pointed to by the variable **L** in Fig. 2.20. Assume **L** is declared with the declaration **NodeType *L**, and that the nodes of Fig. 2.20 are of type **NodeType**, as defined in the text above.

 Pitfalls

- *Creating dangling pointers*

    Recall that dangling pointers are created when a pointer points to a block of storage that has been returned to the pool of available unallocated dynamic storage. This is likely to happen when there are two or more aliases (or access paths) pointing to the same block of storage. This can occur when **free(X)** is called to dispose of the storage referenced by **X**, while another alias, **Y**, still refers to the same storage that **X** did before **free(X)** was called. Misuse of aliases is not the only way that dangling pointers can be created, however.

- *Failing to deallocate nodes not in use—or forgetting to recycle used memory*

    If you have lots of memory available, and you forget to free a few small blocks of storage that are no longer needed, there may be no problem. In fact, you may not want to make storage deallocation a part of time critical operations if there is a danger that calls on the **free** function could take additional (but unknown) amounts of time.

    On the other hand, if a function **P** is executed many thousands of times in the course of a running program, and if **P** both allocates new blocks of dynamic storage and creates inaccessible blocks of garbage that it fails to recycle, there is a danger of a storage allocation failure when dynamic storage is used up.

    Therefore a good habit to cultivate is that of freeing unused storage immediately after it is known that it will not be needed any further, rather than allowing it to become inaccessible garbage.

- *Dereferencing the null pointer*

    It is easy to run off the end of a path formed by successive links in a data structure, leading to an accidental attempt to dereference the null pointer, **NULL**.

- *Forgetting to mark the end of a list*

  By convention, the **Link** field of the last node on a list should contain **NULL** to designate it as the end node of the list. If you forget to mark the last node in this fashion when constructing or altering a list and then use another algorithm that assumes the last node has a null link, the algorithm could fail to work properly.

- *Detecting storage allocation failure*

  Recall that the function call **malloc(sizeof(NodeType))** produces a **void** pointer to a new block of dynamic storage of size equal to the size of a node of type **NodeType**. This pointer is then type cast (i.e., converted) into a pointer to a node using the operator **(NodeType *)** as in **P = (NodeType *)malloc(sizeof(NodeType))**.

  But what happens if dynamic storage has been used up so that **malloc** cannot find any more blocks of storage of size **sizeof(NodeType)** to allocate? In this case, **malloc** returns the **NULL** pointer to signal storage allocation failure. It is therefore good practice to guard against storage allocation failure with a statement such as:

```
     if (  (P = (NodeType *)malloc(sizeof(NodeType))  ) == NULL ) {

             /* invoke storage allocation failure policy of some sort */
                error("dynamic storage exhausted");
  5
     } else {

             /* use the new block of storage pointed to by P */
     }
```

- *Watching out for the boundary cases*

  When algorithms are being designed to operate on linked data structures, it is dangerous to forget to consider the *boundary cases* that often require special treatment. Boundary cases occur at the *boundaries* of the range of problem situations—such as the *empty list* on the one hand or the largest possible list to which the algorithm applies, on the other hand. For example, in Program 2.15, which deletes the last node of a linked list, both the empty list and the list with exactly one node need to be given special treatment. It is important to check the operation of an algorithm design carefully for proper operation on these boundary cases, since experience indicates that is where bugs are frequently found.

Tips and Techniques

- *Using pointer diagrams during design*

  When designing an algorithm that processes linked representations, it helps to use pointer diagramming notation to draw pictures of typical situations that can arise. Pointer diagramming notation can be used in the pre-C stage of program design when program strategies are being sketched. Later, C types can (usually) be declared to provide specific stepwise refinements of the linked data structures designed earlier using pointer diagramming notation.

- *Preserving access to nodes needed later on*

   There is a basic (usually unwritten) law to observe when programming with linked data structures, which might be called "The Law of Preservation of Access." Loosely stated, it says that access must be preserved to all nodes that will be needed later in the solution of a problem. Bugs can arise from failure to observe this law.

   For example, consider the following diagram of a linked list of three nodes L == (GLA, ORD, NRT) in which we intend to replace the node with airport ORD in list L with the new node YYZ, which is given as the referent of pointer variable N.

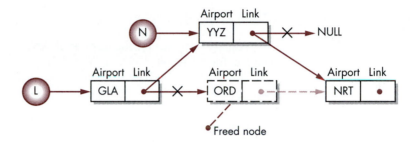

   Suppose someone wrote the following C function to attempt this replacement:

```
    |   void Replace(void)
    |   {
    |           /* link the "YYZ" node to the "NRT" node */
    |               N–>Link = L–>Link–>Link;
5   |           /* link the "GLA" node to the "YYZ" node */
    |               L–>Link = N;
    |           /* free the storage node for "ORD", which is no longer needed */
    |               free(L–>Link);
    |   }
```

   The problem here is that we lost access to the ORD node when we overwrote the only pointer referring to it, which was located in the link field of the GLA node. So when we tried to dispose of the storage for the ORD node, there was no pointer left to give us access to it. Instead, by accident, we disposed of the YYZ node, while the ORD node was inaccessible garbage.

   The cure is either to perform the operations in a correct order or to declare and use a new pointer variable to retain access to a node to which later access is required. For example, the following procedure correctly solves the problem:

```
    |   void Replace2(void)
    |   {
    |           /* link the "YYZ" node to the "NRT" node */
    |               N–>Link = L–>Link–>Link;
5   |           /* free the storage node for "ORD", which is no longer needed */
    |               free(L–>Link);
    |           /* link the "GLA" node to the "YYZ" node */
    |               L–>Link = N;
    |   }
```

The procedure in Program 2.15 for deleting the last node of a list implicitly uses the law of preservation of access. The ultimate purpose of the **PreviousNode** pointer is to retain access to the next-to-last node. The **CurrentNode** pointer is used to locate the last node, by stepping it along the nodes of the list until it points to a node whose **Link** field is **NULL**. At this moment, access to the next-to-last node is needed in order to mark it as the new end of the list by setting its **Link** field to **NULL**.

References for Further Study

A good reference on the features of ANSI C is the second edition of Kernighan and Ritchie (often referred to as "K & R").

Brian W. Kernighan and Dennis M. Ritchie, *The C Programming Language*, *Second Edition*, Prentice-Hall, Englewood Cliffs, N.J., (1988).

One of the great classic references in computer science for algorithms and data structures is the three volume set by Knuth.

Donald E. Knuth, *The Art of Computer Programming*, 3 vols., Addison-Wesley, Reading, Mass. The titles of the three volumes are:

a classic reference

- *Fundamental Algorithms*, vol. 1, 2nd ed., 1973 (Linked lists are covered in depth on pp. 252–72.)
- *Seminumerical Algorithms*, vol. 2, 2nd ed., 1980.
- *Sorting and Searching*, vol. 3, 1973.

Chapter Summary

Linked data representations are a major topic of study in computer science. Sometimes, they support efficient algorithms. They are also useful for applications requiring data structures of unpredictable size and shape. Because they can grow piece-by-piece, they can support elastic data representations that have important growth and combining laws. Consequently, they provide one of the principal ways for representing various important abstract data types.

Linked representations are created by using pointers to link blocks of data storage together. Pointers are data values that represent the memory addresses of these data blocks.

Managing pointers in C is tricky. By studying simple examples of the use of pointers to integers in C, several of the subtle problems can be mastered. Among the tricky issues are dangling pointers, aliases, how to recycle used storage for further use, and the creation of inaccessible garbage through failure to recycle used storage.

This chapter introduces a pointer diagramming language that is used for pointers and linked representations in the remainder of the book. This pointer diagramming language is handy to use in the initial stages of program design. It is also helpful to use it to reason precisely and pictorially about various linked data structures.

Linear linked lists are of key importance. Several skills are important in relation to them: (1) knowing how to declare the pointer data types for list nodes in C; (2) knowing how to create and delete list nodes, and how to link them together; and (3) knowing how to perform various important list operations such as insertion and deletion of nodes in lists, searching for items in lists, printing lists, and joining lists together.

Of course, linked representations come in many different shapes and patterns. For example, using nodes with two separate pointer fields, we can create linked representations for two-way lists and rings and for linked binary trees, to name just three examples.

3

Introduction to Recursion

3.1 Introduction and Motivation

recursion is a key
recurring concept

Recursion is an important recurring concept in computer science. It can some-times be used to formulate unusually simple and elegant solutions to problems that are hard to solve otherwise. It can sometimes be used to define things simply and concisely. Occasionally, recursion can help express algorithms in a form that makes their performance easy to analyze. It can also be used to help recognize things, as in the use of recursive descent parsers (which will be explored in Chapter 14).

This chapter tells only part of the story about recursion. Even though it is only an introduction, it aims at covering the heart of the concept. It also gives you opportuni-ties to build your skills for dealing with recursion. An important goal is for you to be able to implement algorithms that use recursion.

First, what is *recursion*? Let's answer this question by first talking about circular definitions. In elementary school, teachers usually instruct students to avoid circular definitions such as the following:

> **mandiloquy.** (1) The conduct of mandiloquy between nations; (2) Skill in doing this.

Circular definitions are not helpful because they do not do what definitions are supposed to do—namely, tell you about something new by rendering its meaning in terms of what is already known. Instead, they exchange the unknown for more unknowns.

recursive definitions are circular

In this chapter, we will study a useful kind of circular definition called *recursion*. Recursive definitions are just circular definitions. When we define something recursively, we define it in terms of itself.

Initially, this sounds as if it might get us in the same unhelpful mess that ordinary circular definitions do. But what makes a recursive definition of an X work is that it shows how to define a big version of an X in terms of simpler versions of X. This enables us to solve a big problem by breaking it down into simpler subproblems of the same kind, until, at some point, we reach subproblems simple enough that we can give their solutions directly. Then subproblem solutions can be combined to get the solution to the original problem.

Plan for the Chapter

learning to think recursively

Our approach is to discuss a graduated sequence of examples of recursive programs that aim at helping you learn to "think recursively." We begin by studying some simple programs to compute sums and products and to reverse several kinds of data structures. Studying simple examples first can help build intuition for how recursive programs work.

we generalize

we cover a pitfall

We then generalize briefly to try to capture the essence of what a recursive program is. At this point, you are invited to try your hand at solving some programming problems recursively. Next we pause to study a commonly occurring pitfall—a recursive program that keeps on calling itself forever, producing an infinite regress. We'll study some examples of infinite regresses in order to become aware of the danger. We move on to investigate some quantitative aspects of recursive programs. The famous Towers of Hanoi problem is solved recursively, and we analyze the number of steps it takes to achieve a solution (in Section 3.4). When we discover that it takes an exponential number of steps, the notion of exponential complexity classes is introduced. Finally, we give some useful tips and techniques for dealing with recursion.

Preview of Later Discussions of Recursion

While this chapter introduces recursion, it does not finish the job. There are several places later in the book where additional aspects of recursion are revealed.

One such place is in Chapter 5, which discusses software engineering concepts. There we compare iterative and recursive binary searching in an attempt to see which is more efficient—iteration or recursion. The results are somewhat surprising, and lead to a discussion of the philosophy of *measurement and tuning* as a good software engineering practice.

Recursive algorithms are also used in Chapter 6, which explores the analysis of algorithms. There we investigate the use of recurrence relations to analyze algorithms. Chapter 7 illustrates how C can use run-time stacks to implement recursion. Chapter 13 uses recursive algorithms to solve sorting problems in a way that makes them easy to analyze.

Finally, Chapter 14 explores advanced topics in recursion, such as the use of recursion as a descriptive tool to define things and recognize things. Also explored is the relation between recursion and proofs of correctness by structural induction.

3.2 Thinking Recursively

Learning Objectives

1. To learn to think recursively.
2. To learn how strategies for recursion involve both base cases and recursion cases.
3. To learn how to search for different ways of decomposing a problem into subproblems.
4. To understand how to use call trees and traces to reason about how recursive programs work.

a gradual introduction

A good way to get a gradual introduction to the idea of recursion is to examine a sequence of solutions to simple problems. First, we study the simple problem of adding up the squares of some integers. Three different recursive solutions are presented to illustrate different ways of breaking problems into subproblems. We also discuss base cases and show how they are used to terminate the execution of recursive procedures. Then we introduce call trees and traces and show how they can reveal the way recursive programs work.

After showing how the decomposition techniques explored in summing squares of integers can be applied to multiplying integers as well, we study a nonstandard way of computing the factorial function recursively. We also briefly mention the use of factorials in computing permutations and combinations.

We then broaden the range of examples of recursion to show how we can treat nonnumeric data such as linked-lists and strings. We study some recursive solutions for reversing linked-lists and strings in order to illustrate some possibilities. Then it's time to generalize. We look back on our examples and try to extract the essence of what recursion involves.

How to Make Things Add Up Recursively

adding up squares

Our first example is a simple program to add up all the squares of the numbers from m to n. That is, given two positive integers, m and n, where $m \leq n$, we want to find

```
|     int SumSquares(int m, int n)
|     {
|         int i, sum;
|
5 |       sum = 0;
|         for (i = m; i <= n; ++i) sum += i*i;
|         return sum;
|     }
```

/* Recall that the assignment */
/* sum += i*i has the */
/* same effect in C as the */
/* assignment sum = sum + i*i */

Program 3.1 Iterative Sum of Squares

$\text{SumSquares}(m,n) = m^2 + (m + 1)^2 + \ldots + n^2$. For example, $\text{SumSquares}(5,10) = 5^2 + 6^2 + 7^2 + 8^2 + 9^2 + 10^2 = 355$.[1]

the iterative way

An ordinary iterative program to compute **SumSquares**(m,n) is shown in Program 3.1. The strategy for this program is familiar to beginners. The variable **sum** holds partial sums during the iteration, and, initially, **sum** is set to 0. On line 6, a for-statement lets its controlled variable, i, range over the successive values in the range m:n (where the range m:n consists of the integers i, such that m ≤ i ≤ n).

iteration builds up solutions stepwise

For each such integer i, the partial sum in the variable, **sum**, is increased by the square of i (by adding i∗i to it). After the iteration is finished, **sum** holds the total of all the contributions of the squares i∗i, for each i in the range m:n. The value of **sum** is finally returned as the value of the function on line 7.

In an iterative solution such as this, a typical pattern is to build up the final solution in stages, using a repetitive process that enumerates contributions step-by-step and combines the contributions with a partial solution that, stepwise, gets closer and closer to the overall solution.

recursion combines subproblem solutions

To compute **SumSquares(m,n)** recursively, a new way of thinking needs to be used. The idea is to find a way of solving the overall problem by breaking it into smaller subproblems, such that some of the smaller subproblems can be solved using the *same* method as that used to solve the overall problem. The solutions to the subproblems are then *combined* to get the solution to the overall problem.

refining the strategy

Program Strategy 3.2 illustrates one such way of thinking about the solution. To refine this program strategy into an actual recursive solution, all we have to do is to replace the comments with appropriate implementations in C, as illustrated in Program 3.3.

recursive calls

Line 4 of Program 3.3 contains the *recursive call*, **SumSquares(m+1,n)**. A recursive call is one in which a function calls itself *inside* itself. In effect, what line 4 says

---

[1] When implementing practical applications, professional programmers would be unlikely to write iterative or recursive programs to compute **SumSquares**(m,n), since this sum can be computed more directly and efficiently by evaluating a simple algebraic formula involving m and n, such as **SumSquares**$(m,n) = (n^3 - m^3)/3 + (n^2 + m^2)/2 + (n - m)/6$. But for the purpose of this chapter, the value of writing iterative and recursive programs to compute **SumSquares**(m,n) lies not in their efficiency but rather in their value as a device for illustrating the principles of recursion.

```
 |   int SumSquares(int m, int n)
 |   {
 |       (to compute the sum of the squares in the range m:n, where m ≤ n)
 |
5|       if (there is more than one number in the range m:n) {
 |           (the solution is gotten by adding the square of m to)
 |           (the sum of the squares in the range m+1:n)
 |       } else {
 |           (there is only one number in the range m:n, so m == n, and)
10|          (the solution is therefore just the square of m)
 |       }
 |   }
```

Program Strategy 3.2 Recursive Sum of Squares

is that the solution to the overall problem can be gotten by adding (a) the solution to the smaller subproblem of summing the squares in the range m+1:n, and (b) the solution to the subproblem of finding the square of m. Moreover, the smaller subproblem (a) can be solved by the same method as the overall problem by making the recursive call, SumSquares(m+1,n), in which the function SumSquares calls itself *within* itself.

base cases

It is important to be aware that there is always a potential danger that a recursive function could attempt to go on endlessly splitting problems into subproblems and calling itself recursively to solve these subproblems, without ever stopping. Consequently, each properly designed recursive function should have a *base case* (or several base cases).

Line 6 of Program 3.3 contains the base case that occurs when the range m:n contains just one number, in which case m == n. The solution can then be computed directly by returning the square of m. This stops the recursion, since SumSquares is *not* called recursively on line 6.

the general pattern

Now let's generalize. The overall pattern of a recursive function is that it breaks the overall problem into smaller and smaller subproblems, which are solved by calling the function recursively, until the subproblems get small enough that they become

```
 |   int SumSquares(int m, int n)                          /* assume m ≤ n */
 |   {
 |       if (m < n) {
 |           return  m*m + SumSquares(m+1,n);              /* the recursion */
5|       } else {
 |           return m*m;                                    /* the base case */
 |       }
 |   }
```

Program 3.3 Recursive Sum of Squares

base cases and can be solved by giving their solutions directly (without using any more recursive calls). At each stage, solutions to the subproblems are combined to yield a solution to the overall problem. Let's look at two more recursive solutions to SumSquares(m,n) that fit this overall general pattern.

Program 3.4 gives a new solution that is only slightly different than the first solution given in Program 3.3. The process of reading what a program such as this does involves inferring the goals that the individual parts of the program achieve and describing how the program achieves these goals. Therefore one way of summarizing the results of reading what a program does is to replace the program by the program strategy that describes its goals and methods. (This can be thought of as the reverse of the process of refining a program strategy into a specific realization of the strategy—a process of *antirefinement*, so-to-speak, in which we infer the program strategy from the specific program text.) The result of this process is shown in Program Strategy 3.5. Comparing Program 3.4 with Program 3.3 reveals that the decomposition of the overall problem into subproblems is slightly different. Program 3.3 specifies that to get the sum of the squares in the range m:n, we add m^2 to the sum of the squares in the range m+1:n, whereas, Program 3.4 gets the same sum by adding n^2 to the sum of the squares in the range m:n−1. The former could be called a *going-up recursion* since the successive subproblems called in the recursive calls "go upward," starting with the full range m:n, progressing next to subranges (m+1:n), (m+2:n), …, and finally stopping at the uppermost subrange containing the base case (n:n). Program 3.4 could be called a *going-down recursion* since the successive subproblems called in the recursive calls "go downward," starting with the full range m:n, progressing next to subranges (m:n−1), (m:n−2), …, and finally stopping at the bottommost subrange containing the base case (m:m).

The final example for computing SumSquares(m,n) uses yet another decomposition principle to break the overall problem into subproblems—namely, splitting the overall problem into two *halves*.

In Program 3.6, if a range of numbers, m:n, contains just one number (i.e., if m == n), then the base case solution m^2 is given on line 6. Otherwise, the range m:n

(margin notes:)
reading what a program does

going-up recursions

going-down recursions

splitting a range in halves

```
|     int SumSquares(int m, int n)                        /* assume m ≤ n */
|     {
|
|         if  (m < n) {
5 |             return SumSquares(m, n − 1) + n*n;          /* the recursion */
|         } else {
|             return n*n;                                  /* the base case */
|         }
|
|     }
```

Program 3.4 Going-Down Recursion

```
  |    int SumSquares(int m, int n)
  |    {
  |        (to compute the sum of the squares in the range m:n, where m ≤ n)
  |
5 |        if (there is more than one number in the range m:n) {
  |            (the solution is gotten by adding the square of n to)
  |            (the sum of the squares in the range m:n–1)
  |        } else {
  |            (there is only one number in the range m:n, so m == n, and)
10|            (the solution is therefore just the square of n)
  |        }
  |
  |    }
```

Program Strategy 3.5 Strategy for Going-Down Recursion

```
  |    int SumSquares(int m, int n)                        /* assume m ≤ n */
  |    {
  |        int middle;
  |
5 |        if (m == n) {
  |            return m*m;                                 /* the base case */
  |        } else {
  |            middle = (m+n) / 2;
  |            return SumSquares(m, middle) + SumSquares(middle +1, n) ;
10|        }
  |    }
```

Program 3.6 Recursion Combining Two Half-Solutions

contains more than one number and is split into two half-ranges. Assuming that middle is a midpoint for the range m:n, then the left half-range, m:middle, goes from m up to and including the middle. The right half-range, middle+1:n, goes from the number just past the middle up to and including n.

The recursion case on line 9 simply says that the sum of the squares of the entire range of integers m:n can be obtained by adding the sum of the squares of the left half-range, m:middle, to the sum of the squares of the right half-range, middle +1:n.

Let's take a closer look at the method used on line 8 to compute the middle. An example, shown in Fig. 3.7, is splitting the range 5:10 into two half-ranges.

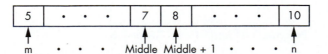

Figure 3.7 Splitting a range m:n into two halves

computing the middle

In this example, the range **5:10** is split into a left half-range, **5:7**, and a right half-range, **8:10**, using a **middle == 7**. To compute the middle of the range **m:n**, we divide **m + n** by 2, using *integer division* by 2, which keeps the quotient and throws away the remainder. The / operator in C performs integer division on two integer operands.

In the case of the range **5:10**, we set **middle = (5 + 10) / 2**, on line 8 of Program 3.6, which gives **middle** the value 7, since (5 + 10) = 15, and 15 divided by 2 gives a quotient of 7 and a remainder of 1/2. This remainder is discarded in the integer division, **15 / 2**. (If the range **m:n** contains an odd number of integers, as in the example **10:20**, which contains 11 integers, then the middle value 15 divides the range into two half-ranges of unequal size. In this case, the left half-range, **10:15**, contains six integers, and the right half-range, **16:20**, contains only five integers.)

In summary, Program 3.6 presents a way of decomposing the overall problem into two subproblems different from that in Programs 3.3 and 3.4, because it uses two subproblems whose size is (roughly) half the size of the overall problem, and, whenever the range includes more than one number, it uses two recursive calls to compute the sum of the squares of the numbers in the two half-ranges.

Call Trees and Traces

It is informative to look at the *call tree* of Program 3.6, when the function call **SumSquares(5,10)** is evaluated. This is illustrated in Fig. 3.8. The evaluation of the calling expression, **SumSquares(5,10)**, causes a function call on Program 3.6 generating two more recursive calls, **SumSquares(5,7)** and **SumSquares(8,10)**. These latter two calls are shown as the descendants of the topmost call, **SumSquares(5,10)**. In Fig. 3.8, we see that the calls of the form **SumSquares(m,m)** have no descendants beneath them in the call tree since they do not generate any further recursive calls. This is because calls of the form **SumSquares(m,m)** result in base cases in Program 3.6, in which m^2 is returned as the direct result.

annotating call trees

Suppose we annotate each calling expression in the call tree of Fig. 3.8 with the results returned by each recursive call. To do this, assume each call resulting in a base

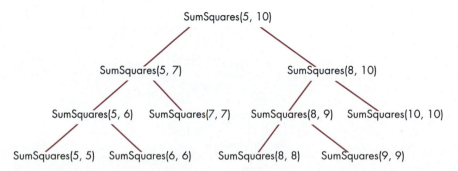

Figure 3.8 Call Tree for SumSquares(5,10) of Program 3.6

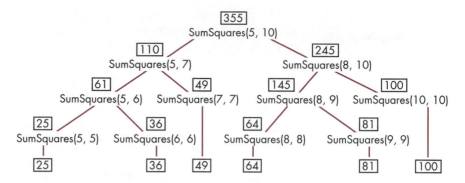

Figure 3.9 Annotated Call Tree for SumSquares(5,10) of Program 3.6

case has the value computed by the base case placed in a box directly beneath the calling expression, and also directly above the calling expression to indicate the value returned by the call. Then to compute the value returned by each calling expression, E, that does not result in a base case, we add the values in the annotation boxes above E's two immediate descendant calling expressions and place the sum in a new annotation box directly above E itself. For example, we can see how the topmost final value, **355**, for the calling expression, **SumSquares(5,10)**, is computed by adding the solutions, **110** and **245**, returned by the recursive calls, **SumSquares(5,7)** and **SumSquares(8,10)**. The entire annotated call tree is shown in Fig. 3.9. The call trees for Programs 3.3 and 3.4 are much simpler, consisting of the chains of calls, shown in Fig. 3.10.

call traces

Another way of conceptualizing what happens when we call **SumSquares(5,10)** recursively is to use a *call trace*. Some C systems can print the trace of their function calls when appropriate debugging commands are given. Some traces of the call **SumSquares(5,10)** are shown on the following page.

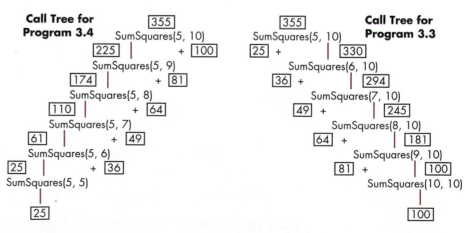

Figure 3.10 Annotated Call Trees for Programs 3.3 and 3.4

Trace of "going-up" recursion from Program 3.3

```
SumSquares(5,10) = (25 + SumSquares(6,10))
                 = (25 + (36 + SumSquares(7,10)))
                 = (25 + (36 + (49 + SumSquares(8,10))))
                 = (25 + (36 + (49 + (64 + SumSquares(9,10)))))
                 = (25 + (36 + (49 + (64 + (81 + SumSquares(10,10))))))
                 = (25 + (36 + (49 + (64 + (81 + 100)))))
                 = (25 + (36 + (49 + (64 + 181))))
                 = (25 + (36 + (49 + 245)))
                 = (25 + (36 + 294))
                 = (25 + 330)
                 = 355
```

Trace of "going-down" recursion from Program 3.4

```
SumSquares(5,10) = (SumSquares(5,9) + 100)
                 = ((SumSquares(5,8) + 81) + 100)
                 = (((SumSquares(5,7) + 64) + 81) + 100)
                 = ((((SumSquares(5,6) + 49) + 64) + 81) + 100)
                 = (((((SumSquares(5,5) + 36) + 49) + 64) + 81) + 100)
                 = (((((25 + 36) + 49) + 64) + 81) + 100)
                 = ((((61 + 49) + 64) + 81) + 100)
                 = (((110 + 64) + 81) + 100)
                 = ((174 + 81) + 100)
                 = (255 + 100)
                 = 355
```

Trace of "division in halves" recursion from Program 3.6

```
SumSquares(5,10) = (SumSquares(5,7) + SumSquares(8,10))
                 = (SumSquares(5,6) + SumSquares(7,7))
                     + (SumSquares(8,9) + SumSquares(10,10))
                 = ((SumSquares(5,5) + SumSquares(6,6))
                         + SumSquares(7,7))
                     + ((SumSquares(8,8) + SumSquares(9,9))
                         + SumSquares(10,10))
                 = ((25 + 36) + 49) + ((64 + 81) + 100)
                 = (61 + 49) + (145 + 100)
                 = (110 + 245)
                 = 355
```

Multiplying Things Recursively

If we multiply together the integers from 1 to n, we get the *factorial of* n, which is denoted by n!. Thus n! = 1 * 2 * 3 * ... * n. It is easy to write an iterative program in C to compute n!, as shown in Program 3.11. The program builds up the final product by repeatedly multiplying an initial partial product, F == 1, by each successive integer in the range 2:n.

```
  |    int Factorial(int n)
  |    {
  |        int i, f;
  |
5 |        f = 1;                                    /* Recall that f *= i has the */
  |        for (i=2; i <= n; ++i)  f *= i;           /* same effect as f = f*i in C */
  |        return f;
  |    }
```

Program 3.11 Iterative Factorial

recursive factorial

The factorial of n can also be computed recursively. As usual, we need a base case and a recursive call that solves the overall problem by solving a smaller subproblem of the same kind. The base case is computed on line 4 of Program 3.12. It specifies that to multiply together the numbers in the range 1:1, we directly return 1 as the answer, without making any recursive calls. But if the range 1:n consists of more than one integer, we can multiply all the integers in 1:n together by multiplying the product of all the numbers in 1:n–1 by the multiplier n. This is the purpose of the recursive call on line 6. A trace of the call Factorial(6) is as follows:

Trace of the call Factorial(6)

```
Factorial(6) = (6 * Factorial(5))
             = (6 * (5 * Factorial(4)))
             = (6 * (5 * (4 * Factorial(3))))
             = (6 * (5 * (4 * (3 * Factorial(2)))))
             = (6 * (5 * (4 * (3 * (2 * Factorial(1))))))
             = (6 * (5 * (4 * (3 * (2 * 1)))))
             = (6 * (5 * (4 * (3 * 2))))
             = (6 * (5 * (4 * 6)))
             = (6 * (5 * 24))
             = (6 * 120)
             = 720
```

several ways of computing
the factorial

Program 3.12 uses a "going-down" recursion in which the parameter n in the recursive calls of Factorial(n) goes down by one on each successive recursive call. We

```
  |    int Factorial(int n)
  |    {
  |        if (n == 1) {
  |            return 1;                             /* base case */
5 |        } else {
  |            return  n * Factorial(n – 1);         /* recursion */
  |        }
  |    }
```

Program 3.12 Recursive Factorial

```
|    int Product(int m, int n)
|    {
|        (to compute the product of the integers from m to n)
|
5 |      if (the range m:n has only one integer in it) {
|            (return m as the solution, since m == n)          /* the base case */
|        } else {
|            (the range m:n must have more than one integer in it, so)
|            (compute the midpoint of m:n as the value of the variable middle)
10 |           (and return the product of the integers in the range m:middle)
|            (times the product of the integers in the range middle+1:n)
|        }
|
|    }
```

Program Strategy 3.13 Multiplying m:n Together Using Half-Ranges

can also multiply together the numbers in the range 1:n, using a "going-up" recursion or by dividing the range into halves, similar to the way we summed the squares in the range m:n earlier. To do this, we can first write an auxiliary function, Product(m,n), which multiplies together the numbers in the range m:n, and then we can compute n! using Factorial(n) = Product(1,n).

Let's write the Product function using recursive division of the range into halves, as shown in Program Strategy 3.13. A refinement of this program strategy is given in Program 3.14. Having defined this auxiliary function, it is now easy to compute Factorial(n) by calling Product(1,n). It is also easy to write Product(m,n) so that it uses a "going-up" recursion (see Exercise 6 at the end of this section). Note, however, that it is hard to write a going-up recursion for Factorial(n), in which the parameter m, for the lower end of the range of numbers to be multiplied, is absent. Sometimes, writing an auxiliary function first, helps you get a handle on the solution of a problem to be solved recursively.

auxiliary functions can be helpful

```
|    int Product(int m, int n)                                /* assume m ≤ n */
|    {
|        int middle;
|
5 |      if (m == n) {
|            return m;                                         /* the base case */
|        } else {
|            middle = (m+n) / 2;
|            return Product(m, middle) * Product(middle+1, n);
10 |       }
|
|    }
```

Program 3.14 Multiplying m:n Together Using Half-Ranges

Some Uses for Factorials**

We will see a number of uses for the factorial of n in later chapters. One use of factorials is to compute the number of possible *permutations* of n different objects (where the permutations are different ordered sequential arrangements). For example, we may need to consider all possible sequential arrangements of keys as being equally likely in order to analyze the average running time of a sorting algorithm. There are $n!$ such equally likely arrangements. We use this fact in Chapter 13 when we analyze sorting algorithms. Also, $n!$ is used in Chapter 13 to compute the $n*\log n$ lower bound for the average number of comparisons needed by all comparison-based sorting methods.

combinations

Another example of factorials occurs in defining the number of combinations of n things taken k at a time:

$$\binom{n}{k} = \frac{n!}{k!(n-k)!} \qquad \qquad 3.1$$

The quantity

$$\binom{n}{k}$$

is sometimes pronounced as "n choose k." Formula 3.1 is needed in Chapter 12 to compute the average seek time for moving read-write heads on a disk from a starting track to a destination track.

As another example of the use of

$$\binom{n}{k},$$

several state lotteries use numbers games in which players choose six numbers out of a possible 49. We might ask, "How many possible different ways can six numbers be chosen from 49?" The answer is

$$\binom{49}{6},$$

** Recall that sections marked with two asterisks indicate more challenging mathematical topics.

which is computed using the above formula by

$$\frac{49!}{6!*43!}.$$

This in turn equals 13,983,816. In other words, you have about a one-in-fourteen-million chance of winning the jackpot in a 6–49 type lottery if you buy a single ticket.

Formula 3.1 also gives coefficients in binomial expansions. For example, if we expand $(x + y)^{49}$, into a polynomial by multiplying it out, the coefficient of the term involving y^6 is

$$\binom{49}{6}.$$

These coefficients may have been introduced to you in precollege algebra when you studied Pascal's triangle.

Reversing Lists and Strings

Continuing with our graduated sequence of introductory examples, let's look at two reversal problems: (1) reversing the order of the items in a linked list, and (2) reversing the order of the characters in a string. An iterative solution to the list reversal problem (although not the one suggested in the hint to problem 5 in Exercises 2.5 in Chapter 2) is as given in Program 3.15 (assuming that **NodeTypes** and pointers to **NodeTypes** are defined as given at the beginning of Exercises 2.5).

recursive list reversal

Let's rethink this solution to see if we can come up with a recursive way to solve the same problem. Consider a typical list, such as L = (SAN, ORD, BRU, DUS). We might imagine breaking this list into two lists called the Head and the Tail, where: Head(L) = (SAN), and Tail(L) = (ORD, BRU, DUS). That is, the **Head** is a list containing the first node of L, and the **Tail** of L is the remainder of the list, after the first node has been removed. In other words, the **Tail** of L is the list consisting of L's sec-

```
   |   void Reverse(NodeType **L)                              /* to Reverse a list L */
   |   {
   |       NodeType *R, *N, *L1;
   |
 5 |       L1 = *L;                        /* L1 points to the first node of the list to reverse */
   |       R = NULL;                       /* initialize R, the reversed list, to the empty list */
   |       while (L1 != NULL) {
   |           N = L1;                                     /* let N point to L1's first node */
   |           L1 = L1->Link;                  /* now, let L1 point to the remainder of L1 */
10 |           N->Link = R;                                    /* link N to the rest of R */
   |           R = N;                              /* and make R point to its new first node */
   |       }
   |       *L = R;                  /* finally, replace L by a pointer to the reversed list R */
   |   }
```

Program 3.15 Iterative List Reversal

ond and succeeding nodes. (Let's also agree that if L = NULL, Head(L) and Tail(L) are not defined. But if L consists of just one node, as in L = (SAN), then Head(L) = (SAN), and Tail(L) = NULL.)

partitioning a list into its Head and Tail

Now, supposing we had a way to partition a nonempty list L into its **Head** and its **Tail**, what strategy could we use to reverse the entire list? (Before peeking at the solution, try conceptualizing it yourself, starting with the hint that since **Tail(L)** is a subproblem of smaller size, you might somehow be able to combine **Reverse(Tail(L))** into a solution to the overall problem.)

To go after the solution systematically, let's take our example list L and write out both L and its reversal, together with L's **Head** and **Tail** and their reversals:

$$L = (\text{SAN, ORD, BRU, DUS})$$
$$\text{Reverse(L)} = (\text{DUS, BRU, ORD, SAN})$$
$$\text{Tail(L)} = (\text{ORD, BRU, DUS})$$
$$\text{Reverse(Tail(L))} = (\text{DUS, BRU, ORD})$$
$$\text{Head(L)} = (\text{SAN})$$
$$\text{Reverse(Head(L))} = (\text{SAN})$$

Now we can ask, "Which of the above pieces combine to yield the needed solution, **Reverse(L)**?" One possible answer is indicated in Fig. 3.16. We see that (except for the base cases, which are not yet considered), a possible solution could result if we could concatenate (i.e., join together) the two lists **Reverse(Tail(L))** and **Head(L)** into a single list. This partial solution is shown in Program Strategy 3.17.

we can concatenate to get a solution

To refine this strategy into a final working C program, we need to solve three subproblems: (1) deciding how to reverse the empty list, (2) finding out how to partition a nonempty list into its **Head** and its **Tail**, and (3) writing a function to concatenate (or join together) two lists into a single list. It seems reasonable that the reverse of an empty list () is another empty list (), so let's let **Reverse(NULL) = NULL**. The next problem is to partition L into a **Head** and a **Tail**. The solution to this is shown in Program 3.18. Note that the function **Partition(L,&Head,&Tail)** is not defined if L is the empty list.

identifying and solving the subproblems

concatenation

The final subproblem to solve is that of joining two lists, L1 and L2, together to make a single list in which the items on list L2 follow the items on list L1. This process is called concatenation. The following program returns a **NodeType** pointer to

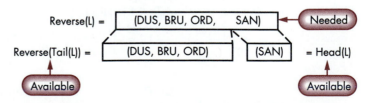

Figure 3.16 A Possible Solution

```
   |    NodeType *Reverse(NodeType *L)
   |    {
   |        /* to Reverse a list L */
   |
 5 |        if (L is the empty list) {
   |            (the result is the reverse of the empty list)        /* base case */
   |        } else {
   |            (In the case that L is non-empty,)
   |            (partition the list L into its Head and Tail.)
10 |            (Then, concatenate the Reverse of the Tail of L)    /* recursion step */
   |            (with the Head of L)
   |        }
   |
   |    }
```

Program Strategy 3.17 For Reversing a List, **L**

```
   |    void Partition(NodeType *L, NodeType **Head, NodeType **Tail)
   |    {
   |        /* to divide list L into its Head & Tail */
   |
 5 |        if ( L != NULL) {
   |            *Tail = L–>Link;         /* Tail contains all nodes of L after the first */
   |            *Head = L;                /* Head contains just the first node of L */
   |            (*Head)–>Link = NULL;     /* mark the end of the Head node */
   |        }
   |    }
```

Program 3.18 Partitioning a List L into its **Head** and **Tail**

the result of concatenating the two lists pointed to by the **NodeType** pointers given in **L1** and **L2** respectively:

```
   |    NodeType *Concat(NodeType *L1, NodeType *L2)
   |    {
   |        NodeType *N;
   |
 5 |        if (L1 == NULL) {
   |            return L2;
   |        } else {
   |            N = L1;                               /* let N point to the first node of L1 */
   |            while (N–>Link != NULL) N = N–>Link;  /* find the last node of L1 */
10 |            N–>Link = L2;                         /* set the link of the last node of L1 to L2 */
   |            return L1;                            /* return the pointer to the concatenated lists */
   |        }
   |    }
```

we used top-down
programming

Now that we have solved our three subproblems, we are ready to refine Program Strategy 3.17 into an actual C program to reverse a list. This is given as Program 3.19.

```
    |   NodeType *Reverse(NodeType *L)
    |   {
    |       NodeType *Head, *Tail;
    |
 5  |       if (L == NULL) {
    |           return NULL;                        /* base case */
    |       } else {
    |           Partition(L, &Head, &Tail);         /* divide L into Head and Tail */
    |           return Concat(Reverse(Tail), Head); /* recursion step */
10  |       }
    |
    |   }
```

Program 3.19 Refinement for Reverse(L)

Note that we used the process of top-down programming by stepwise refinement to create the function for **Reverse(L)**. We started with a strategy providing the topmost goals we would need to achieve in order to accomplish list reversal in Program Strategy 3.17. This presented us with three subproblems to solve. After solving these, we combined the three solutions in the last step—creating a final refinement of Program Strategy 3.17 to yield Program 3.19.

In fact, according to good software engineering practice, we are not yet finished with our task. Having created Program 3.19 as a refinement, we really don't know that it works properly yet. We should test it, together with its components, and/or we should verify that it works by attempting to prove mathematically that it terminates and gives the correct outputs. Moreover, we should analyze it for its efficiency and see if it runs as well as might be expected. It turns out that Program 3.19 is an example of a recursive program with a clear design structure that, nonetheless, is not as efficient as it should be. We will return to this subject later. Furthermore, we will go over the rudiments of good software engineering practice covering design, programming by stepwise refinement, testing, and verification in Chapter 5. For now, we note the fact that the solution in Program 3.19 is not optimal, and that we need to build up the necessary skills in analysis of algorithms and software engineering practice in order to design a good reversal function for lists. Stay tuned! This topic will be pursued in Chapter 5 and thereafter in stages throughout the remainder of the book.

but we're not finished yet

Reversing Strings

enlarging our bag of tricks

Let's now take a moment to expand our repertoire of decomposition methods for splitting an overall problem into subproblems. In the case of linked-list reversal, just considered, we decomposed a list L into its **Head** and its **Tail**. This is a natural decomposition for linked lists, since the **Tail** can be accessed starting with a pointer to L, just by accessing the link of L's first node. Other decompositions of a linked-list into sublists, such as dividing the list into two half lists, are more cumbersome and expensive to implement.

However, if we have a string whose components can be accessed by integer indexes, the kinds of decompositions into subproblems that can be arranged conveniently increases. Let S be a string, and let S[m:n] denote the substring of S consisting of the mth through the nth characters of S. Here are three different types of decompositions we can use:

Decomposition 1. First and Rest
    Split S[m:n] into its **First** character, S[m], and the **Rest** of them, S[m+1:n]
Decomposition 2. Last and All but Last
    Split S[m:n] into its **Last** character, S[n], and **AllButLast** == S[m:n − 1]
Decomposition 3. Split into Halves
    Compute **middle** = (m + n) / 2, and then Split S[m:n] into its **LeftHalf** == S[m:middle] and **RightHalf** == S[middle+1:n]

We have actually seen these three different decompositions in slightly different dress before. For instance, when considering how to compute the sum of the squares of the numbers from m to n, the "going-up" recursion of Program 3.3 split m:n into "First and Rest." The "going-down" recursion of Program 3.4 split m:n into "Last and All but Last." Moreover, Program 3.6 split m:n into two halves. Also, the list reversal Program 3.19 split the list L into "First and Rest," where the "First" of a list L was its **Head**, and the "Rest" was its **Tail**.

three familiar ways to decompose a range

Now, let's expand the set of ideas available for splitting problems into subproblems by considering a fourth decomposition method—splitting a range m:n into its "Edges and Center."

and a new one

Decomposition 4. Edges and Center
    Split S[m:n] into its **Edges**: (S[m], S[n]), and **Center** == S[m +1:n − 1]

This decomposition can form the basis for a recursive string reversal algorithm, such as that given in Program 3.20. For example, when applied to a string, S = "abc...xyz", consisting of the letters of the alphabet, ReverseString(S,0,25) first swaps the first and last letters 'a' and 'z' (on line 6) and then reverses the middle of the alphabet "bc...xy" (using the recursive call on line 7).

```
    |    void ReverseString(char *S, int m, int n)       /* to reverse the characters */
    |    {                                               /* from m through n in string S */
    |        char c;
    |
  5 |        if (m < n) {
    |            c = S[m]; S[m] = S[n]; S[n] = c;         /* first, swap the edges */
    |            ReverseString(S, m + 1, n – 1);       /* and then, reverse the center */
    |        }
    |    }
```

Program 3.20 Reverse Characters m:n of String S

The General Idea

Let's now generalize from our experience with this series of graduated examples to reach some conclusions about how recursive programs work.

what are recursive programs?

Recursive programs are just programs that call themselves in order to obtain a solution to a problem. The reason that they call themselves is to compute the solution to a subproblem that has three general properties: (1) the subproblem is *smaller* than the overall problem to be solved (or is *simpler*, in the sense that it is closer to a final solution), (2) the subproblem can be solved either directly (as a base case) or recursively by making a recursive call, and (3) the subproblem's solution can be combined with solutions to other subproblems to obtain the solution to the overall problem.

divide and conquer

Inherent in this overall strategy is the implication that you can break a big problem into smaller subproblems of the same kind that can be solved by application of the same method, and that you can combine subproblem solutions back into the overall solution. This breakdown of a big problem into similar component problems is an instance of the *divide and conquer strategy*. We'll see more examples of this strategy later in the book.

how to think recursively

To *think recursively*, then, you can try asking yourself a series of questions. You first ask, "How can I break this big problem into smaller problems of the same kind that can be solved by the same method?" Second, you ask, "When the problems get small enough, how can they be solved directly, without breaking them down any further and making more recursive calls, so the process of recursion can stop?" Finally, you ask, "If I assume I've got the solutions to the subproblems, how can I combine these solutions to get the overall solution to the original problem?"

considering a typical example

It sometimes helps to consider a typical example. From the example of the overall problem, you apply the problem decomposition method you have chosen, yielding examples of the subproblems. Then, you assume you have the solutions to the subproblems (either as results of base cases or recursion cases) and you write out the examples of the subproblem solutions. Finally, you have a table of parts, consisting of the subproblems and their solutions, and you can gain insight into what method of combination is needed to compose the subproblem solutions into the overall solution. Sometimes, through trial and error, you may have to back up and try several different decomposition methods before discovering one that works.

Perhaps you are ready to solve some recursive programming problems on your own now. Experience indicates that it is difficult to gain mastery of recursion just by reading about it. You should thus try solving, say, a dozen recursion problems. The wider the range of problems you solve, the better your recursive programming skills will become.

3.2 Review Questions

1. What is the base case in a recursive program?
2. Give four different decomposition methods for splitting an integer interval, m:n, into parts that can be helpful in determining subproblems to solve in a recursive program.

3. What is a call tree?
4. What is the trace of a recursive function call?
5. How can the factorial of n, denoted $n!$, be used to compute the number of possible combinations of n items taken k at a time?
6. What is a natural way to consider decomposing a linked list into substructures helpful for devising a recursive solution to a problem?

3.2 Exercises

1. Write a recursive function that computes x^n, called Power(x,n), where x is a floating point number and n is a nonnegative integer. [*Hint*: Power(x,n) can be defined by the following two equations: Power($x,0$) = 1.0 and for $n \geq 1$, Power(x,n) = x * Power($x, n-1$)].
2. Write an improved recursive version of Power(x,n) that works by breaking n down into halves (where half of $n = n / 2$), squaring Power($x,n / 2$), and multiplying by x again if n was odd. For example, $x^{11} = (x^5)*(x^5)*x$, whereas $x^{10} = (x^5)*(x^5)$. Find a suitable base case to stop the recursion.
3. Write a recursive function, Mult(m,n), to multiply two positive integers, m and n, using only repeated addition.
4. According to Euclid's algorithm for finding the greatest common divisor, gcd(m,n), of two positive integers m and n, one can take successive pairs of remainders, and when one of the remainders is zero, the other number in the pair is the gcd. Letting (m,n) be the first remainder pair, we can write $m = q * n + r$, such that $0 \leq r < n$. Here, q is the quotient of m upon division by n ($q = m / n$), and r is the remainder of m after division by n ($r = m \% n$). Any divisor (including the gcd) that divides m and n must also divide r, since $r = m - q*n$. Consequently, the gcd of m and n must be the same as gcd(n,r). In Euclid's algorithm, one starts with the pair (m,n) and computes the pair (n,r). Then, if $r = 0$, the gcd(m,n) = gcd(n,r) = n. But if $r \neq 0$, the pair (n,r) is replaced by the next successive remainder pair, which is guaranteed to have the same gcd. Write a recursive version of Euclid's algorithm to compute gcd(m,n).
5. Prove that your solution to the previous exercise correctly computes the gcd. Divide your proof into two parts: (a) *termination*: a proof that your algorithm must terminate, and (b) *correctness*: a proof that after termination, the result is the gcd.
6. Write a "going-up" recursive version of **Product(m,n)**, which gives the product of the integers in the range m:n.
7. Write a recursive string reversal program by refining Program Strategy 3.17, in which the word **List** is replaced by the word **String**. In order to do this, you will need to develop auxiliary functions to: (a) get the **Head** of a string, (b) get the **Tail** of a string, (c) concatenate two strings, and (d) determine whether a string is empty. How does the efficiency of this method compare with the efficiency of the recursive string reversal Program 3.20?
8. Write another recursive string reversal program, **ReverseString(S,R)**, which uses two string parameters. It repeatedly removes the first character from **S** and puts it on the front of **R** until **S** is empty. It is originally called with the string, **S**, to be

reversed and an empty string, R. The result is given as the modified value of R after returning from the call.

9. Write a recursive function to find the length of a linked list, where the length of a linked-list, L, is defined to be the number of nodes in list L.

10. Write a recursive function Min(A) to find the smallest integer in an integer array A[n]. [*Hint:* Define an auxiliary function Min2(A,k,j) that finds the smallest integer in A[k:j], and let Min(A) = Min2(A, 0, n − 1).]

11. Ackermann's function, $A(m,n)$, is a two argument function defined as follows:

$$
\begin{aligned}
A(0,n) &= n + 1 & &\text{for } n \geq 0, \\
A(m,0) &= A(m - 1, 1) & &\text{for } m > 0, \\
A(m,n) &= A(m - 1, A(m, n - 1)) & &\text{for } m,n > 0.
\end{aligned}
$$

Write a recursive function that gives the value of Ackermann's function.

12. For what range of integer parameters, (m,n), does the output of your implementation of Ackermann's function, $A(m,n)$, *not* exceed the value of the maximum integer in your C system?

13. Describe in words what the following function P(int n) does:

```
 |    void PDigit(int d)        /* auxiliary procedure used below in P to write the */
 |    {                              /* character corresponding to the digit d */
 |         printf("%c", (char) ( (int)'0' + d ) );
 |    }
5|
 |    void P(int n)                     /* assume n is a non-negative integer */
 |    {
 |         if (n < 10) {
 |              PDigit(n);
10|         } else {
 |              P(n / 10);
 |              PDigit(n % 10);
 |         }
 |    }
```

14. What does the following function do?

```
 |    void R(int n)                          /* where n is a non-negative integer */
 |    {
 |         /* Output the rightmost digit of n in a one character field */
 |              printf("%1d", (n%10) );
5|
 |         if ((n / 10) != 0)  R(n / 10);
 |    }
```

15. Let x be a positive real. To calculate the square root of x by Newton's Method, so that the square of the solution differs from x to within an accuracy of *epsilon*, we start with an initial approximation $a = x/2$. If $|a*a − x| \leq$ *epsilon*,

we stop with the result a. Otherwise we replace a with the next approximation, defined by $(a + x/a)/2$. Then, we test this next approximation to see if it is close enough and we stop if it is. In general, we keep on computing and testing successive approximations until we find one close enough to stop. Write a recursive function, Sqrt(x), that computes the square root of x by Newton's Method.

16. The binomial coefficients,

$$\binom{n}{k}$$

can be specified recursively. Letting

$$C(n,k) = \binom{n}{k},$$

we can use the following relationships:

$$C(n,0) = 1 \text{ and } C(n,n) = 1 \qquad \text{for } n \geq 0.$$
$$C(n,k) = C(n-1, k) + C(n-1, k-1) \quad \text{for } n > k > 0$$

Develop a recursive program to compute $C(n,k)$.

17. If your solution to the previous exercise does not already do so, modify it so that it avoids wasteful recomputation of the results previously computed by other recursive calls, so that it computes the result efficiently. Does your solution do the best job possible of ensuring that intermediate partial results do not violate the maximum limits of the numerical variables it uses? How can you compute $C(n,k)$ in a way that is efficient and that works for the largest range of integer inputs n and k?

3.3 Common Pitfall—Infinite Regresses

Learning Objectives

1. To learn about infinite regresses.
2. To understand the symptoms caused by the occurrence of infinite regresses.

We now pause briefly to explore a common pitfall with recursive programs—*infinite regresses*. An infinite regress in a recursive program is somewhat analogous to an endless loop in an iterative program. It occurs when a recursive program calls itself endlessly and never encounters a base case that forces it to stop its execution.

infinite regresses

There are two reasons that a recursive program can call itself endlessly: (1) there is no base case to stop the recursion, or (2) a base case never gets called. The second possibility tends to happen more frequently, and sometimes it happens because the set of values used in a recursive call is bigger than the set of values that the recursive program was designed to handle. It may therefore not be the fault of the program designer, or even the fault of the user who made the call with a value lying outside the set for which the design works. Rather, the fault could lie in faulty or incomplete documentation about the set of values for which the given recursive program is designed to work.

To take a specific example of this, let's reconsider the program for Factorial(n) given earlier as Program 3.12. Now, let's ask two questions: (1) What happens if we call this function with n == 0, by making the call Factorial(0)?, and (2) What happens if we make the function call Factorial(− 1)?

prepare to crash

Warning: Don't fire up your computer, type in Program 3.12, and try out the calls Factorial(0) and Factorial(− 1) without first knowing how to recover from program crashes. Do you know how to perform the crash recovery procedure?

Why this warning? Let's try our method for writing out a call trace, starting with the call, Factorial(0).

$$
\begin{aligned}
\text{Factorial(0)} &= 0 * \text{Factorial}(-1) \\
&= 0 * (-1) * \text{Factorial}(-2) \\
&= 0 * (-1) * (-2) * \text{Factorial}(-3) \\
&= 0 * (-1) * (-2) * (-3) * \text{Factorial}(-4) \\
&= 0 * (-1) * (-2) * (-3) * (-4) * \text{Factorial}(-5) \\
&= \text{and so on, in an infinite regress.}
\end{aligned}
$$

a base case that never gets called

This happens because, when n == 0 or n is any negative integer, the condition, n == 1, in the if-condition on line 3 of Program 3.12 evaluates to *false*, after which the else-part is evaluated, causing an evaluation of the expression n*Factorial(n − 1). This results in a recursive call of Factorial(n − 1) with a new argument one less than the previous argument, for which the base case will not be encountered. So yet another recursive call on Factorial(n − 2) will occur—and so on, endlessly.

running out of resources

Well, to be truthful, the process can go on almost endlessly, except for the fact that the computer may run out of resources sooner or later. One thing that may happen is that the computer can run out of space in the region of memory where it stores separate structures containing information about each function call that has been initiated but which has not yet been completed. Each time a function is called in C, some space for a *call frame* for the call is allocated in a call-frame region of memory where call frames are stored for all previous calls that have been made but have not yet been completed. Since each such frame uses up a finite amount of space, an unending sequence of recursive calls results in an unending sequence of frame allocations. This may cause the program to request additional space for call frames, without limit.

Eventually, this call-frame region may try to expand into memory devoted to some other purpose (the *wild case*, resulting in who knows what kind of mayhem), or a request for more program call-frame space by the C run-time administration program gets made to the computer's operating system and is denied (usually resulting in *civilized termination* by C), or a *memory protection violation* is incurred when the operating system notices that the C program is attempting to access memory beyond its assigned limits (the *authoritarian intervention case*, in which the operating system overrides C and intervenes to prevent undesirable invasion of unassigned memory).

or integer values can cycle beyond their limits

A second possibility is that the integers used as actual parameters will cycle through all values in their range, allowing the infinite regress to terminate, when the value n == 1 is reached but returning an incorrect result. A third possibility is that the range of the integer value being returned by the factorial function will be exceeded, and the result returned will be taken modulo C's maximum integer value, yielding incorrect results once again. Evidently, the situation is fraught with confusing possibilities.

It is a common occurrence for programmers to encounter infinite regresses accidentally—especially during the phase when they are first learning about recursive programs. Rather than "flying blind" into a situation where you accidentally encounter infinite regresses, it might be best if you could first find out what your C system is likely to do if a recursive function with an infinite regress is executed. By this means, you might become prepared to recognize the symptoms of an accidental encounter with an infinite regress, and you might be prepared with knowledge of the proper recovery procedure.

a useful precaution

A *word of caution*: It is especially irritating to lose the entire C program text you have typed in when you encounter an accidental program crash. This can happen in some C systems. A useful habit to acquire is that of saving in a file the text of any program you have written that contains recursive procedures *before* you start trial executions for debugging or testing purposes. This way, if your program gets into an infinite regress that causes a system crash, the text of your program will already have been safely stored in an external storage medium, preventing it from vanishing in a crash that wipes out the contents of the internal computer memory.

3.3 Review Questions

1. What is an infinite regress?
2. What are two programming errors that cause infinite regresses?
3. Why can executing a recursive function that causes an infinite regress result in a C run-time system's running out of space?
4. Why might Program 3.12 have returned 0 when Factorial(0) was called?

3.3 Exercise

1. The following function, F(n), is intended to be defined for all non-negative integers.

```
   |    int F(int n)
   |    {
   |        if (n == 0) {
   |            return 1;
 5 |        } else if (n == 1) {
   |            return 2;
   |        } else {
   |            return F(n – 1) * F(n – 3);
   |        }
   |    }
```

Is there any non-negative value, n, for which F(n) does not terminate properly?

3.4   Quantitative Aspects of Recursive Algorithms**

Learning Objectives

1. To understand why some recursive algorithms have exponential running times.
2. To see an example of an analysis of the number of steps a recursive program takes before it terminates.

In this section, we investigate some quantitative aspects of recursive programs. The famous Towers of Hanoi problem is solved recursively, and we analyze the number of steps it takes to achieve a solution. We discover that it takes an exponential number of steps. The notion of exponential complexity classes is introduced.

Towers of Hanoi

when will the universe dissolve?

It is rumored that somewhere in Asia a group of spiritually advanced monks is hard at work transferring golden disks. When they are finished moving a tower of 64 of these golden disks from the first peg to the third peg of a sacred three-peg stand, then the next *Maha Pralaya* will begin, in which the universe will dissolve and revert to its unmanifested state. The 64 disks have different sizes, and the monks must obey two rules: (1) only one disk can be moved at a time, and (2) a bigger disk can never be placed on top of a smaller disk. If the monks work nonstop in shifts, 24 hours a day, moving one disk every second and never wasting any moves, how long after they started their task will the next *Maha Pralaya* begin?

This puzzle is popularly known as the Towers of Hanoi. The four-disk version of this puzzle is shown in Figure 3.21.

the solution is forced to work a certain way

Suppose the objective is to move the tower of four disks from peg 1 to peg 3. In order to solve this puzzle, we could reason as follows. In any solution, we must move the bottommost disk from peg 1 to peg 3. Since it is the biggest disk, there can be no smaller disk on peg 3 at the time we try to move it. Consequently, we must move the three disks on top of it from peg 1 to peg 2. Following this, we can move the bottom

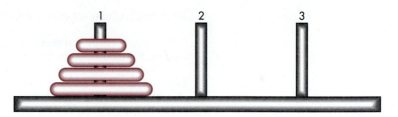

Figure 3.21 Towers of Hanoi with Four Disks

disk from peg 1 to peg 3. Finally, we need to move the three-disk tower from peg 2 to peg 3. To summarize:

To Move 4 disks from Peg 1 to Peg 3:

Move 3 disks from Peg 1 to Peg 2

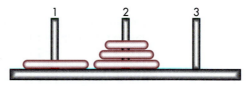

Move 1 disk from Peg 1 to Peg 3

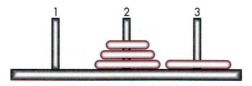

Move 3 disks from Peg 2 to Peg 3

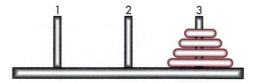

This breaks down the solution of the overall problem (moving four disks) into a composition of three smaller subproblems (two of which involve moving three disks). Thus we have discovered a basis for the recursive solution shown in Program Strategy 3.22. It's easy to see how to refine this strategy into a program that prints disk move instructions. All we need to do is to implement the base case of the recursion with a single **printf** instruction, by letting (Move one disk directly from start-peg to finish-peg) refine to printf("Move a disk from peg %1d to peg %1d\n", start, finish). The finished program is shown in Program 3.23.

```
 |      void MoveTowers(int n, int start, int finish, int spare)
 |      {
 |          /* To move a tower of n disks on the start-peg to the finish-peg */
 |          /* using the spare-peg as an intermediary. */
5|
 |          if (n == 1) {
 |              (move one disk directly from start-peg to finish-peg)
 |          } else {
 |              (move a tower of n − 1 disks from start-peg to spare-peg)
10|             (move one disk directly from start-peg to finish-peg)
 |              (move a tower of n − 1 disks from spare-peg to finish-peg)
 |          }
 |      }
```

Program Strategy 3.22 Recursive MoveTowers Procedure

If we call this program to move a tower of three disks from peg 1 to peg 3, the program prints the following list of instructions:

```
MoveTowers(3 /*disks*/, /*from peg*/ 1, /*to peg*/ 3, /*using spare peg*/ 2) prints:
    Move a disk from peg 1 to peg 3
    Move a disk from peg 1 to peg 2
    Move a disk from peg 3 to peg 2
    Move a disk from peg 1 to peg 3
    Move a disk from peg 2 to peg 1
    Move a disk from peg 2 to peg 3
    Move a disk from peg 1 to peg 3
```

now for the important question

Now the burning question remains, "When will the universe dissolve?" To answer this question, we need to be able to discover a formula that gives the length of the list of move instructions in terms of the number of disks in the tower to be moved. If n is the number of disks in the tower to be moved, we could define $L(n)$ to be the length of the list of move instructions.

setting up some recurrence relations

Clearly, $L(1) = 1$, since it takes just one move instruction to move a tower of one disk from a start-peg to a finish-peg. This covers the base case. But now, what hap-

```
 |      void MoveTowers(int n, int start, int finish, int spare)
 |      {
 |          /* To move a tower of n disks on the start-peg to the finish-peg */
 |          /* using the spare-peg as an intermediary.*/
5|
 |          if (n == 1) {
 |              printf("Move a disk from peg %1d to peg %1d\n", start, finish);
 |          } else {
 |              MoveTowers(n − 1, start, spare, finish);
10|             printf("Move a disk from peg %1d to peg %1d\n", start, finish);
 |              MoveTowers(n − 1, spare, finish, start);
 |          }
 |      }
```

Program 3.23 Recursive Towers of Hanoi Solution

pens in the general recursion case? Looking at Program 3.23, if $n > 1$, we have to move a tower of $n - 1$ disks on line 9 of the program, which takes $L(n - 1)$ instructions, then we have to move a single disk on line 10 of the program, which takes one more instruction, following which we have to move the tower of $n - 1$ disks again on line 11 of the program, which takes an additional $L(n - 1)$ instructions. Adding up these contributions, $L(n) = L(n - 1) + 1 + L(n - 1)$ whenever $n > 1$. To summarize:

$$L(1) = 1$$
$$L(n) = 2 * L(n - 1) + 1 \quad \text{for } n > 1$$

(3.2)

Recurrence Relations

but how do we solve them?

Learning how to solve recurrence relations, such as these, will turn out to be an important skill in our arsenal of techniques for analyzing the running time of algorithms. We will delve into this subject in more detail in Chapter 6. For now, you might take pleasure in trying to guess the solution by looking at Table 3.24. Can you figure out the solution? [*Hint* (1): The number of instructions printed is the same as the number of calls in the call tree for **MoveTowers**, since each call prints exactly one instruction. The call trees for the procedure **MoveTowers** are binary trees shaped just like the ones we saw in Chapter 2 in Fig. 2.23. In such completely balanced binary trees (with full bottom rows), there is one node at the top level, two nodes at the second level, then four at the third level, and so on. The number of nodes in such a tree is a sum of the form $1 + 2 + 4 + \ldots + 2^k$. If you read how to find the sum of a geometric progression in the *Math Reference* appendix, you may be able to discover a tidy formula for sums of this form. *Hint* (2): You can apply the solution method summarized in Table A.12 of the *Math Reference* appendix to solve the Recurrence Relations 3.2, by plugging in values into the general solution and simplifying.]

can you find the solution?

Alternatively, a keen observer might note that the solutions for n, given in Table 3.24, are each one less than a corresponding power of two. So $L(n) = 2^n - 1$. This means that the length of the instruction sequence needed for the monks to move a

we learn when tragedy will strike

Number of Disks, n	Number of Instructions, $L(n)$, Needed to Move the Tower
1	1
2	3
3	7
4	15
5	31
6	63
7	127
8	255

Table 3.24 Lengths of Instruction Sequences for Towers of Hanoi

tower of 64 golden disks is just $L(64) = 2^{64}-1$. If the monks move one disk every second, then it will take $2^{64}-1$ seconds to move all 64 disks. Since there are 31,536,000 $= 3.1536 * 10^7$ seconds in a year, the universe will dissolve in approximately $(2^{64}-1)/(3.1536 * 10^7) \cong 584,942,417,355$ years after the monks started moving disks. We need not worry that the universe will dissolve soon unless the monks started a long, long time ago. In fact, if the sun lasts only another 5 to 10 billion years before it burns out, we might want to worry first about how to escape from the solar system before we worry about how to survive the dissolution of the universe.

The solution to the Towers of Hanoi puzzle is an *exponential running-time algorithm*, since it takes time proportional to 2^n to print the instructions required to move a tower of size n. For this reason it is said to belong to the *exponential complexity class*. We will have much more to say about exponential running-time algorithms in Chapter 6. Generally, we try to avoid such exponential algorithms like the plague in computer science (but it is not always possible to do so).

3.4 Review Questions

1. What is the name of the complexity class that characterizes the running time of the recursive solution to the Towers of Hanoi puzzle given in Program 3.23?
2. What is the principal disadvantage of solutions in the complexity class which is the answer to Question 1?

3.4 Exercise

1. Assume that the Tower of Hanoi puzzle must be solved completely in one year's time. If disks are moved at one disk per second and no wasteful moves are made, what is the largest number of disks, n, that can be used in the puzzle?

Pitfalls

- *Infinite regresses*

   Infinite regresses can happen when you write a recursive program with no base case, or when you call a recursive program with a value for which no base case will ever be invoked in order to stop the recursion.

- *Ranges that are not checked carefully*

   Be careful about the ranges of acceptable values to use as parameters when calling a recursive function—particularly for fast-growing functions with exponential growth properties. The range of acceptable input values can be surprisingly small in order not to exceed the allowable numerical precision, or the maximum size of the output, or the permissible maximum size of the C run-time call-frame memory region.

Tips and Techniques

- *Use auxiliary functions*

  Sometimes the definition of a recursive function can be simplified by introducing an auxiliary function with more parameters. The additional parameters can serve to transmit critical data across recursive calls that can be helpful in determining when the base case has been reached or to avoid solving the same subproblems over and over. For example, consider the problem of writing a "going-up" recursive function to compute the sum, 1 + 2 + 3 + . . . + n. We could write Sum(n) = Sum2(1,n), where Sum2(m,n) is an auxiliary function that adds the numbers from m to n and which has the value:

  $$Sum2(m,n) \ = \ (\ m == n\ ?\ m\ :\ m + Sum2(m + 1, n)\ )$$

- *Use call traces and call trees to help understand and debug recursive programs*

  Sometimes it is difficult to understand how a recursive program works. One technique that sometimes proves helpful is to choose a small problem size and to write out the call trace or the call tree of the recursive program to observe the pattern by which it splits its inputs into subproblems and solves them. Once the patterns for the base cases are understood, it can usually be readily seen how to combine the base case solutions into larger non–base-case solutions.

  Writing out the call trace of a recursive program you are trying to debug can sometimes provide the clues you need to discover your mistakes. Sometimes, C programming systems permit traces to be generated when programs are executed. Using such a feature, if it is available in your C system, can be helpful when testing or debugging your programs.

References for Further Study

programming pearls

Jon Bentley, *Programming Pearls*, Addison-Wesley, Reading, Mass., (1986) and *More Programming Pearls: Confessions of a Coder*, Addison-Wesley, Reading, Mass., (1988).

Jon Bentley, author of the "Programming Pearls" column in the *Communications of the ACM* offers many elegant recursive algorithms along with helpful programming tips.

thinking recursively

Eric S. Roberts, *Thinking Recursively*, Wiley, New York, (1986).
Eric Roberts has written a helpful book on the subject of thinking recursively.

Chapter Summary

Recursion is an important recurring concept in computer science. This chapter offers an introduction to this topic, although it does not finish telling the whole story.

In a recursive solution to a problem, the overall problem is solved by combining solutions to smaller subproblems. These smaller subproblems either can be solved by applying the recursive method itself, or are base cases that can be solved directly without using recursion. Often, there are many ways to decompose the overall problem into smaller subproblems of the same nature. It is worthwhile to search for different kinds of decompositions in order to devise several different alternative recursive solutions whose characteristics can be compared and from which the best solution can be chosen.

Infinite regresses occur when recursive programs call themselves endlessly. A recursive program can get into an infinite regress if (a) it has no base cases, or (b) its base cases never get called.

Sometimes, there are problems that have recursive solutions that are simple, concise, and elegant, for which it is hard to devise iterative solutions having the same simplicity and clarity. For example, the recursive solution to the Towers of Hanoi problem is an example of a recursive solution to a problem for which it has been hard to find iterative versions that are as clear and simple.

Recursion is a thread that ties material in this book together and it will occur again in Chapters 6, 13, and 14.

4

Modularity and Data Abstraction

4.1   Introduction and Motivation

The goal of this chapter is to learn about *modularity*, *information hiding*, and *data abstraction*.

Generally speaking, a *module* is a unit of organization of a software system that packages together a collection of entities (such as data and operations) and that carefully controls what external users of the module can see and use. Ordinarily, modules have ways of hiding things inside their boundaries to prevent external users from accessing them. In this way modules can protect their internal mechanisms from external tampering. This is called *information hiding*, and it can be used as a basis for implementing *abstract data types*.

Abstract data types are collections of objects and operations that present well-defined abstract properties to their users, meanwhile hiding the way they are represented in terms of lower-level data representations. When a module is used to implement an abstract data type, it provides an *interface* that makes the ADT's abstract operations available to outside users, meanwhile hiding the ADT's actual data representation inside part of the module called its *private part*.

To give a rough analogy for a *module*, consider a microwave oven. You can use a microwave by setting its dials or buttons, without knowing how it works internally (which relies on the miracles of magnetron tubes and microwave technology). In order to use a microwave, you, the user, need know only the available operations in the microwave's external user interface. You do not need to know any of its internal details.

separate compilation modules

Many modern programming languages offer *modules* that have several important features: (1) they provide a way of grouping together collections of related data and operations; (2) they present clean, well-defined interfaces to users of their services; (3) they hide internal details of operation to prevent interference; and (4) they can be separately compiled.

modules in C

By means of careful use of header files we can arrange for separately compiled C program files to have the four properties of modules mentioned above. In this chapter, we will call these separately compiled C files "modules" because they are similar to what are called *packages* or *modules* in recent advanced programming languages such as Modula-2 and Ada.

In this book, we use C modules as a vehicle to explore concepts of modularity, information hiding, and data abstraction, since they provide the way that such concepts can be expressed in C. In addition, the use of C modules has other benefits that we will explore.

the importance of modules

For instance, since using C modules permits large programs to be designed by combining separate components that interact cleanly, they aid in "dividing and conquering" a large software task by enabling it to be broken into separate pieces that can be worked on by different teams. Also, they ease software maintenance by supporting the use of abstractions and information hiding that allow changes to be made locally instead of having to spread changes throughout a large program text.

Plan for the Chapter

In this chapter, we first study how C modules work by illustrating their structure and use. Each C module is composed of a pair of files: (1) its *interface*—a header file which is made public, and which is included at the beginning of other programs using the module; (2) its *implementation*—a separately compiled C program file which contains the module's private part.

the parts of a module

Three examples of C modules are studied next. These enable us to illustrate some important concepts in preparation for the introduction to software engineering in Chapter 5. Two of these are (1) using modules to hide data representations and to provide access only to defined features of an *abstract data type* (by making them publicly available in the module's interface header file) and (2) using modules in a software system project to help provide a work breakdown structure for project teams.

We next summarize the benefits of modules and information hiding. Specifically, we state a philosophy of software system structuring, centering on concepts of modularity, which stresses the importance of clarity of program structure and ease of program modification.

4.2 The Structure of C Modules

Learning Objectives

1. To learn about the parts of a C Module.
2. To understand the purpose of the separate interface and implementation files in a C Module.
3. To learn how to use the services provided by a C Module.

You can think of a module as a set of declarations that can be placed into service inside a C program. Modules tend to consist of collections of related entities all of which work together to offer a set of capabilities or to provide a set of components that can be used to solve some class of problems.

the structure of C modules

A C module, M, consists of two files MInterface.h and MImplementation.c, having the structure shown in Program Template 4.1. The file MInterface.h is the *interface file*, which declares all the entities in the module that are visible to (and therefore usable by) the external users of the module. Such visible entities can include constants, typedefs, variables, and functions. Only the prototype of each visible function is given (and only the argument types are given, not the argument names). The full definitions of such functions must be given later in the implementation file of the module.

the implementation file

Below the text for the interface file is the text for the *implementation file* of the module, MImplementation.c. It contains all the private entities in the module that are not visible to outside users, and it contains the full declarations of functions whose prototypes have been given in "extern" declarations the interface file.

```
    |   /*-----------< the text for the file MInterface.h begins here >------------ */
    |
    |      (declarations of entities visible to external users of the module)
    |
 5  |   /*---------------------< end of file MInterface.h >----------------- */
    |
    |
    |   /*-------< the text for the file MImplementation.c begins here >-------- */
    |
10  |   #include <stdio.h>
    |   #include "MInterface.h"
    |
    |      (declarations of entities private to the module plus the)
    |      (complete declarations of functions exported by the module)
15  |
    |   /*------------------< end of file MImplementation.c >-------- */
```

Program Template 4.1 Interface and Implementation Files for Module M

```
    |   #include <stdio.h>
    |   #include "ModuleAInterface.h"              /* external modules used */
    |   #include "ModuleBInterface.h"              /* by your main program */
    |
  5 |   (declarations of entities used by your main program)
    |
    |   int main(void)
    |   {
    |       (statements to execute in the main part of your program)
 10 |
    |   }
```

Program Template 4.2 A Main Program Using Two Modules A and B

using modules

In order to use the entities in a module M, your main program has to include the interface header file, MInterface.h, with a file *include directive*. For example, the include directive, #include "ModuleAInterface.h", on line 2 of Program Template 4.2 tells the C compiler preprocessor to substitute the lines of the interface header file ModuleAInterface.h in place of the include directive on line 2. The effect is as if the declarations in the interface header file had been made at the place the include directive was given in your main program. In the case of a main program having the structure shown in Program Template 4.2, lines 2:3 include the declarations given in the two interface header files ModuleAInterface.h and ModuleBInterface.h. The effect is as if the declarations in the interface files of modules A and B had been given one after another in place of the include directives on lines 2 and 3. The remaining entities you declare in your program (on line 5) and the executable statements (on line 9), can each use entities declared in ModuleAInterface.h and ModuleBInterface.h.

Suppose that int gcd(int x, int y) is an integer valued function of two integer arguments, and suppose that gcd is defined in module A. Suppose you want to use gcd in your main program. Then all you have to do is give an *extern declaration* of the form extern int gcd(int,int); in the text of ModuleAInterface.h and to give the full function definition for gcd(x,y) inside the implementation file ModuleAImplementation.c. The occurrence of the extern declaration for gcd in your main program tells the C linker to find the definition of gcd in the compiled code for a separately compiled external module and to link properly with it.

4.2 Review Questions

1. What is a C module?
2. What is the interface file of a module?
3. What is the implementation file of a module?
4. How do you use the services provided by a module?

4.3   Priority Queues—An Abstract Data Type

Learning Objectives

1. To learn what an abstract data type is.
2. To understand how it is possible to replace the underlying representation for an ADT without changing the operations it presents to its external users through its interface.
3. To learn how to use the information-hiding features of C modules to hide the implementation details of an ADT's operations.

In this section, we study an example of an abstract data type called a *priority queue*. We then present the interface file of a C priority queue module, which provides the services that external users can use. We show how to use these services to perform sorting using priority queues. But while this is going on, we still don't know how priority queues are implemented. That's because the implementation file of the module has not been specified yet.

Next, we provide two implementation files for the priority queue module. Each of the two implementations implements priority queues differently. This allows us to make the point that the data type that users of the module can access externally is *abstract*—since nothing in the way its operations are expressed reveals the particular implementation details that were chosen for its hidden representation.

A Priority Queue Interface File

You can think of a *priority queue* as a container that holds some prioritized items. It is assumed that these items can be compared to one another and that they can be ranked in their order of priority. One scale of priorities useful for ranking might simply be the items' magnitudes, with the item of largest magnitude having the highest priority. Another possible priority scale might be defined in terms of urgency for processing. Each item might be stamped with a specific processing time deadline. The highest priority item might be defined to be the most urgent item to process next. This, in turn, could be defined as the item having the earliest deadline for processing. No matter which way you define priorities, when you remove an item from a priority queue, you always get the item of highest priority.

For example, you might decide to put all the bills you have to pay into a pile, and you might decide to pay them in the order defined by their payment deadlines, with the earliest payment deadline having the highest priority. If you remove and pay bills from your pile, one-at-a-time, in earliest-to-latest order of their payment deadlines, you are using a priority queue. (In fact, priority queues are used in this fashion by deadline-driven scheduling algorithms in operating systems.)

We begin defining an abstract data type by defining the operations that external users can use, without constraining how to represent the underlying data structures or how to program the operations in C.

Priority Queues

A *Priority Queue, (PQ)* is a finite collection of items for which the following operations are defined:

1. Initialize the priority queue, *PQ*, to be the *empty priority queue.*
2. Determine whether or not the priority queue, *PQ*, is *empty.*
3. Determine whether or not the priority queue, *PQ*, is *full.*
4. *Insert* a new item, *X*, into the priority queue, *PQ*.
5. If *PQ* is nonempty, *remove* from *PQ* an item, *X*, of highest priority in *PQ*, (where the highest priority item in *PQ* is defined as an item *X* in *PQ* such that $X \geq Y$ for all items *Y* in *PQ*).

You can see from these definitions that you can insert items into a priority queue *PQ* in any order of priority, but when you remove an item from *PQ*, you always get a highest priority item in *PQ*. (There may be more than one item of highest priority in *PQ* in the event that *PQ* contains several items of equal priority value all having a common priority higher than that of the other items in *PQ*. Thus, while the item you remove will have highest priority, it may not be the unique item of highest priority.)

If we define the interface file, **PQInterface.h**, to contain the operations on priority queues just defined, we can immediately begin using priority queues in our program designs. For example, Program 4.3 gives one possible interface file. To illustrate with a simple example, suppose we have defined an array, **A**, to hold ten items of type **PQItem**, where to begin with we have defined **PQItems** to be simple integer values,

```
     |    /* Use a file include directive to import data type definitions for */
     |    /* priority queue items and the priority queue data type. */
     |
     |        #include "PQTypes.h"        /* defines types PQItem and PriorityQueue */
   5 |
     |    /* Define the function prototypes for functions that can be used by */
     |    /* external users of the priority queue module. */
     |
     |        extern void Initialize(PriorityQueue *);          /* creates an empty PQ */
  10 |
     |        extern int Empty(PriorityQueue *);                 /* true if PQ is empty */
     |
     |        extern int Full(PriorityQueue *);                    /* true if PQ is full */
     |
  15 |        extern void Insert(PQItem, PriorityQueue *);        /* puts the PQItem */
     |                                                        /* into the PriorityQueue */
     |
     |        extern PQItem Remove(PriorityQueue *);              /* removes an item */
     |
```

Program 4.3 The Interface File, **PQInterface.h**, for a Priority Queue Module

```
      |      void PriorityQueueSort(SortingArray A)
      |      {
      |          int i;  PriorityQueue PQ;
      |
   5  |          Initialize(&PQ);                          /* let PQ be initially empty */
      |
      |          for (i = 0; i < 10; ++i) Insert(A[i],&PQ);
      |
      |          for (i = 9; i >= 0; − − i) A[i] = Remove(&PQ);
      |      }
```

Program 4.4 A Priority Queue Sorting Procedure

such that bigger integers have higher priority than smaller ones:

```
typedef  int         PQItem;

typedef  PQItem  SortingArray[10];

SortingArray A;
```

It is now possible to employ the priority queue operations declared in Program 4.3 to define a simple sorting procedure that sorts the elements in array A into increasing order of priority.

how to sort using priority queues

You can see that the sorting procedure in Program 4.4 works by first taking the items in array A one-by-one and inserting them into a priority queue, PQ, and, second, by removing the items from PQ in order of highest-to-lowest priority while putting them back into array A in decreasing order of the index positions in A.

Assembling these pieces into a complete program, together with a test case, gives Program 4.5. The interesting thing about this program is that it successfully uses the abstract data type—priority queues—without knowing any of the details of its implementation. We have cleanly separated the *what* from the *how*.

This is our first illustration of the benefits of abstract data types. Program 4.3 gives the operations we are allowed to use to manipulate the ADT called priority queues. The interface specifications in Program 4.3 give external users the calling forms to be used to invoke operations on priority queues. But this interface does not reveal the implementation details for priority queues. Consequently, we can write programs that use priority queues in a way that makes them independent of the way priority queues are represented using lower-level data representations.

Two Implementations for Priority Queues

different ways to implement priority queues

A moment's thought reveals that there are a variety of ways that we could implement priority queues. For example, we could let *PQ* be represented by a linked list in which the succeeding nodes in the list contain items sorted in decreasing order of priority.

```
     |   #include <stdio.h>                      /* access standard input-output operations */
     |   #include "PQInterface.h"                    /* access operations and types for PQs */
     |
     |   typedef PQItem SortingArray[MAXCOUNT];        /* Note: MAXCOUNT == 10 */
  5  |
     |   void PriorityQueueSort(SortingArray A)
     |   {
     |        int i;                                  /* i is an index variable for array A */
     |        PriorityQueue PQ;                             /* PQ is a priority queue */
 10  |
     |        Initialize(&PQ);                            /* let PQ be initially empty */
     |        for (i = 0; i < MAXCOUNT; ++i) Insert(A[i],&PQ);
     |        for (i = MAXCOUNT − 1; i >= 0; − − i) A[i] = Remove(&PQ);
     |   }
 15  |
     |   int SquareOf(int x) { return x*x; }           /* computes x², the square of x */
     |
     |   int main(void)
     |   {
 20  |        int i; SortingArray A;
     |
     |        /* initialize array A to ten values to sort and print them */
     |            for (i = 0; i < 10; ++i) {
     |                A[i] = SquareOf(3*i − 13);
 25  |                printf("%d, ",A[i]);    /* prints: 169,100,49,16,1,4,25,64,121,196 */
     |            }
     |            printf("\n");
     |
     |        /* sort array A, using priority queue sorting */
 30  |            PriorityQueueSort(A);
     |
     |        /* print the values in A after sorting */
     |            for (i = 0; i < 10; ++i) {
     |                printf("%d,",A[i]);    /* prints: 1,4,16,25,49,64,100,121,169,196 */
 35  |            }
     |            printf("\n");
     |   }
```

Program 4.5 Sorting Using a Priority Queue

Removing an item from *PQ* is easy, since all we have to do is remove the first node of the linked list, which is guaranteed to contain the item of highest priority. To insert a new item, we have to link in a new node containing the item in the proper position in the linked list, immediately beyond the nodes containing items whose priority is higher than that of the item we are inserting.

Another possibility is to keep an unsorted array of items, *PQ*. In this case, inserting an item is easy, since all we have to do is add a new item to the end of the array *PQ*. But in removing an item, we have to search for the item of greatest priority, then delete it, and then move the last item into the hole created by the deletion. In this case, removal is expensive while insertion is cheap. In the previous case, removal was cheap, but insertion was expensive.

We will study another representation for priority queues in Chapter 9 that has greater efficiency than the two representations just mentioned. This particular representation places items into nodes of a binary tree in a clever way. Before undertaking this study, however, we first need to master some techniques for analyzing the efficiency of algorithms in Chapter 6. Consequently, we do not discuss this specially efficient representation for priority queues here.

At this point, we have laid the groundwork for understanding the importance of data abstraction in the rest of this book by successfully using an ADT without knowing its representation. We have shown that we need to know only *what* an ADT does, not *how* it does it, in order to use it successfully as a building block for doing something else. This is an extremely important principle for two reasons: (1) It is easier to use something if you don't need to know how it works in order to use it. This is a great help in making complex systems more intellectually manageable. (2) It is easier to change the internal mechanics that determine how something works (in order to improve it, for instance) if the description of how it works is concentrated in one place and if you don't have to make changes in each place it was used. Since the details of how the priority queue ADT works have not been revealed yet, we did not make use of priority queue operations in Program 4.5 in a way that depended on the details of their implementation.

Before giving the implementation details for the sorted linked list representation of priority queues, we first provide a header file, **PQTypes.h**, that defines the data type for priority queue items, called **PQItem**, and for the linked-list representation of priority queues themselves, which are of the type **PriorityQueue**. These are given in Program 4.6. When this header file is included, using the include directive **#include "PQTypes.h"** (given on line 4 of the **PQInterface.h** file of Program 4.3), you can imagine that the declarations of Program 4.6 are substituted for the include directive at that place. Now it is time to reveal the details of the first of the two priority queue implementations we shall study.

Implementing Priority Queues Using Sorted Linked Lists

The first implementation of priority queues we will examine uses a sorted, linked-list representation. The essence of the idea is that the hidden representation of a priority queue uses a linked list of **PQItems** kept in decreasing sorted order of priority—meaning that the integers used as **PQItems** are stored in descending order in the succeeding nodes of the linked list representing the priority queue.

To insert a new item, **X**, into *PQ* in priority order (on lines 48:74 of the implementation file **PQImplementation.c**, defined in Program 4.7) there are three cases to consider. First, if *PQ*'s **ItemList** is empty, then we need to replace it with a new list having a single node, **N**, having **X** as its **NodeItem** and **NULL** as its **Link** (see lines 52:56). Second, if the new item, **X**, to insert has a priority greater than or equal to

```
     /* Exports the data types PQItem and PriorityQueue */

     #define MAXCOUNT 10          /* PQ's can hold at most MAXCOUNT items */
5

     typedef int PQItem;                 /* to start with, PQItems are just integers */


10   typedef  struct PQNodeTag {
                 PQItem              NodeItem;
                 struct PQNodeTag  *Link;
             } PQListNode;

15
     typedef  struct {
                 int           Count;
                 PQListNode  *ItemList;
             } PriorityQueue;
```

Program 4.6 Header File **PQTypes.h** for Priority Queue Data Types

that of the first item on the ItemList (see lines 52:56), then we need to insert a new first node N on the ItemList having X as its NodeItem. Treatment of these first two cases is combined by the statements on lines 52:56. Finally, if X's priority is less than that of the first node on the ItemList, we need to insert X recursively in the *tail* of the ItemList (where the *tail* is the linked list consisting of the second and succeeding nodes of the ItemList). This is done on lines 58:59.

Removal of the highest priority item is simple—you just delete the item in the first node of the linked list representing *PQ* (see lines 78:88 in Program 4.7).

```
     /*
      *     The file "PQImplementation.c" for the Sorted Linked List
      *     Representation of Priority Queues
      */
5
     /* First, provide access to standard input-output functions. */
     /* Then, include the PQInterface.h file giving exactly one common, shared */
     /* set of definitions of types, constants and extern function prototypes. */

10   #include <stdio.h>                  /* include standard input-output file */
     #include "PQInterface.h"            /* access operations and types for PQs */
```

Program 4.7 Sorted Linked List Priority Queue Implementation (continued)

Program 4.7 Sorted Linked List Priority Queue Implementation (continued)

```
15

    /*
     * Next, give full definitions for all functions including both those
     * that are exported to external module users via the extern function
     * prototypes in the PQInterface.h file, and those which are used
20   * internally and privately by the PQImplementation.c file.
     */


    /*--------------------------------------------------------------------*/
25
        void Initialize(PriorityQueue *PQ)
        {
            PQ->Count = 0;              /* let PQ's item count be zero, and */
            PQ->ItemList = NULL;     /* let the link to its list of items be NULL */
30      }

    /*--------------------------------------------------------------------*/

        int Empty(PriorityQueue *PQ)
35      {
            return (PQ->Count == 0);   /* PQ is empty if its item count is zero */
        }

    /*--------------------------------------------------------------------*/
40
        int Full(PriorityQueue *PQ)
        {                                       /* PQ is full if it contains */
            return (PQ->Count == MAXCOUNT);   /* the maximum number of */
        }                                       /* items allowed in PQs */
45
    /*--------------------------------------------------------------------*/

        PQListNode *SortedInsert(PQItem Item, PQListNode *P)
        {
50          PQListNode *N;               /* N points to priority queue list nodes */

            if ((P == NULL) || (Item >= P->NodeItem)) {    /* if old list is NULL */
                N = (PQlistNode *) malloc(sizeof(PQListNode)); /* or new item */
                N->NodeItem = Item;         /* is of highest priority, insert a node */
55              N->Link = P;              /* with new item on front of PQ's ItemList */
                return (N);
            } else {                               /* otherwise, insert a node for the new Item */
                P->Link = SortedInsert(Item,P->Link);        /* in sorted order */
                return (P);                            /* into the tail of PQ's ItemList */
60          }
        }

    /*--------------------------------------------------------------------*/
```

Program 4.7 Sorted Linked List Priority Queue Implementation (continued)

```
65  |
    |       /*----------------------------------------------------------------*/
    |
    |               void Insert(PQItem Item, PriorityQueue *PQ)
    |               {
70  |                   if ( ! Full(PQ)) {
    |                       PQ–>Count++;                   /* increase PQ's item count and insert */
    |                       PQ–>ItemList = SortedInsert(Item,PQ–>ItemList);   /* the new */
    |                   }                                              /* Item on PQ's ItemList */
    |               }
75  |
    |       /*----------------------------------------------------------------*/
    |
    |               PQItem Remove(PriorityQueue *PQ)
    |               {
80  |                   PQItem temp;
    |
    |                   if ( ! Empty(PQ)) {                    /* result undefined if PQ empty */
    |                       temp = PQ–>ItemList–>NodeItem;    /* otherwise, remove the */
    |                       PQ–>ItemList = PQ–>ItemList–>Link;   /* highest priority item */
85  |                       PQ–>Count – –;                          /* from the front of the list */
    |                       return (temp);                          /* and decrease the item count */
    |                   }
    |               }
    |
90  |       /*----------------------------------------------------------------*/
    |
```

Implementing Priority Queues Using Unsorted Arrays

We now study a second implementation of priority queues that uses an unsorted array representation. This hidden representation uses an array of **PQItems** kept in arbitrary order. The following type definition include file, which replaces the file **PQTypes.h** given by Program 4.6, defines a *PQ's* hidden internal **ItemArray** differently from the **ItemList** of the linked list *PQ* type of Program 4.6.

```
   |   #define MAXCOUNT 10
   |
   |   typedef int PQItem;
   |
5  |   typedef PQItem PQArray[MAXCOUNT];
   |
   |   typedef  struct {
   |                   int              Count;
   |                   PQArray       ItemArray;
   |           } PriorityQueue;
```

After including this file on line 4 of Program 4.3, we are ready to write the implementation of the priority queue operations based on unsorted item arrays.

```
     /*
      *    The file "PQImplementation.c" for the Unsorted Array
      *    Representation of Priority Queues
      */
 5

     #include <stdio.h>                          /* include standard input-output file */
     #include "PQInterface.h"                    /* access operations and types for PQs */


     /*
10    *    Next, give full definitions for all functions including both those
      *    that are exported to external module users via the extern function
      *    prototypes in the PQInterface.h file, and those which are used
      *    internally and privately by the PQImplementation.c file.
      */
15
     /*-------------------------------------------------------------------*/

     void Initialize(PriorityQueue *PQ)
     {
20       PQ->Count = 0;                           /* let PQ's item count be zero */
     }


     /*-------------------------------------------------------------------*/

25   int Empty(PriorityQueue *PQ)
     {
         return (PQ->Count == 0);     /* PQ is empty if its item count is zero */
     }


30   /*-------------------------------------------------------------------*/

     int Full(PriorityQueue *PQ)
     {                                                  /* PQ is full if it contains */
         return (PQ->Count == MAXCOUNT);   /* the maximum number of */
35   }                                                  /* items allowed in PQs */


     /*-------------------------------------------------------------------*/

     void Insert(PQItem Item, PriorityQueue *PQ)
40   {
         if ( ! Full(PQ)) {                               /* insert item at end */
             PQ->ItemArray[PQ->Count] = Item;          /* of array and */
             PQ->Count++;                              /* increase PQ's item count */
         }
45   }
```

Program 4.8 Unsorted Array Priority Queue Implementation (continued)

Program 4.8 Unsorted Array Priority Queue Implementation (continued)

```
      /*-----------------------------------------------------------------------*/

50    PQItem Remove(PriorityQueue *PQ)
      {
          int i;                            /* i is an index variable that indexes array items */
          int MaxIndex;                     /* MaxIndex is the location of the biggest item */
          PQItem MaxItem;                   /* MaxItem is the value of the biggest item */
55
          if ( ! Empty(PQ)) {                           /* result undefined if PQ empty */
              MaxItem = PQ–>ItemArray[0]; /* initially, let the zeroth item be the */
              MaxIndex = 0;                             /* biggest item found so far */
              for ( i = 1; i < PQ–>Count; ++i ) {       /* scan the rest of the items */
60                if (PQ–>ItemAray[i] > MaxItem ) {     /* and replace the current */
                      MaxItem = PQ–>ItemArray[i];               /* biggest with any */
                      MaxIndex = i;                     /* bigger ones that are found */
                  }
              }
65            PQ–>Count – – ;                           /* finally, decrease the item count */
              PQ–>ItemArray[MaxIndex] = PQ–>ItemArray[PQ–>Count];  /* and */
              return (MaxItem);             /* put the last item in the hole vacated by */
          }                                 /* removing and returning the biggest item */
      }
70
      /*-----------------------------------------------------------------------*/
```

Inserting a new item is simple, since all we have to do is append it to the end of *PQ's* **ItemArray** (see lines 39:45 of Program 4.8).

Removing an item of highest priority takes a bit more work, since we have to scan *PQ's* **ItemArray** to find it first (see lines 57:64). When we have located its position, we take the last item in the array and move it into the hole created by the deletion of the highest priority item, after which we return the highest priority item which was already saved as the value of the variable **MaxItem** (see lines 65:67). The remaining details of Programs 4.7 and 4.8 are nearly identical.

using a single common module interface file

Note that the module interface header file, **PQInterface.h**, is included in two important but distinct cases. First, it is included at the beginning of programs that need to gain access to the external module services declared in the interface file (e.g., see the beginning of Program 4.5 at line 2). Second, it is included at the beginning of the implementation files which define the (hidden) representation of the externally accessed module services (e.g., see line 11 of Program 4.7 and line 7 of Program 4.8). Thus, both the module implementation files and the files for programs using the module services share a single, common module interface header file. If you arrange to share a single interface file in this fashion, you are spared the worry of keeping two separate interface files up-to-date and synchronized.

4.3 Review Questions

1. What is a priority queue?
2. Name two ways that a priority queue can be represented, and sketch the main idea of how each representation works.
3. Which of the two representations has a more efficient insertion operation? Why? Which one has a more efficient removal operation? Why?

4.3 Exercises

1. Revise the function **Remove(PQ)** defined on lines 78:88 of Program 4.7 to apply the **free** procedure to recycle storage for the priority queue list node that is removed from the front of the list.
2. Why is **PQ–>Count** decremented (on line 65 of Program 4.8) *before* the last item in **PQ–>ItemArray[PQ–>Count]** is moved into the hole **PQ–>ItemArray[MaxIndex]**?

4.4   A Pocket Calculator Interface

Learning Objectives

1. To learn how modules can be used to help divide software project labor.
2. To learn how modules with clean, simple interfaces can simplify the structure of a software system.

The use of modules can help to provide a structure for dividing up the overall work in a software project into subprojects that can be tackled by individual teams. That is, modules can help provide what is called a *work breakdown structure* (WBS) for a software project.

A simple instance of this is illustrated by examining a possible structure for a pocket calculator program. The top-level program calls on two modules. One of these, which provides the calculator's user-interface and interacts with the user, is called the **CalculatorModule**. The second module accepts a string of characters, which is an arithmetic expression given by the user, and evaluates it to get an answer. In what follows, imagine that you have been given the job of writing this module, called **YourCalculationModule**. Figure 4.9 illustrates what the user sees when interacting with the calculator. The top-level program for the calculator, given in Program 4.10, is sometimes called a *shell*, since it is an empty structure with "holes" designed to accept two modules that must be plugged in to give meaning to its operations. The shell then organizes the operations within the topmost level of the overall program.

The plug-in module that you are supposed to write supplies only the function, **Evaluate(Expression)**, used in the assignment statement on line 14 of Program 4.10. This function is supposed to accept a pointer to a string for an arithmetic expression given by the user as input. It is supposed to parse the string and evaluate it, producing a pointer to an answer string that gives the numerical value (or notes either syntax

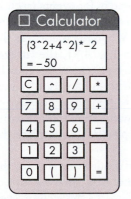

Figure 4.9 Calculator Interface

```
   |   #include <stdio.h>
   |   #include "CalculatorModuleInterface.h"
   |   #include "YourCalculationModuleInterface.h"
   |
 5 |   int main(void)
   |   {
   |       InitializeAndDisplayCalculator( );
   |
   |       do {
10 |
   |           GetAndProcessOneEvent( );
   |
   |           if ( UserSubmittedAnExpression( ) ) {      /* your module  provides */
   |               Value = Evaluate(Expression);          /* the Evaluate function */
15 |               Display(Value);
   |           }
   |
   |       } while ( ! UserWantsToQuit( ) );
   |
20 |       Shutdown( );
   |
   |   }
```

Program 4.10 Top-Level Calculator Program Shell

errors, such as unbalanced parentheses, or semantic errors, such as attempting to divide by zero). The rest of the function calls in Program 4.10 are provided by the **CalculatorModule**. Let's briefly explain what each of these is supposed to do.

The function call **InitializeAndDisplayCalculator( )**, on line 7, is supposed to initialize the system and display a window containing a picture of a calculator. The user can either click the calculator buttons (with a pointing device, such as a mouse) or press keys on the keyboard in order to specify an input expression to evaluate. The function, **GetAndProcessOneEvent( )**, on line 11, polls the system for events (such as pointing device events, keyboard events, or menu choice events) and builds up a display of the user's input expression in the calculator window. When the user clicks the "evaluate" button on the calculator (signified by "=" in Fig. 4.9), the integer (Boolean) function, **UserSubmittedAnExpression( )**, in the if-statement on line 13 evaluates to 1 (i.e., *true*), and causes the assignment statement and function call on lines 14:15 to be executed. **Evaluate(Expression)**, on line 14, computes the value of the user's expression and returns it as a pointer to a string that is stored in the string pointer variable, **Value**. On line 15, the function call, **Display(Value)**, displays the value string in the calculator window.

When the user clicks the "close box" in the calculator window, or chooses the "quit" command from a menu, the event processor sets switches that cause the integer (Boolean) function, **UserWantsToQuit( )**, on line 18 to evaluate to the value 1 (i.e.,

```
    |    /*
    |     *    the file "CalculatorModuleInterface.h"
    |     */
    |
 5  |    char *Expression, *Value;
    |
    |    extern void InitializeAndDisplayCalculator(void);
    |    extern void GetAndProcessOneEvent(void);
    |    extern int UserSubmittedAnExpression(void);
10  |    extern void Display(char *);
    |    extern int UserWantsToQuit(void);
    |    extern void Shutdown(void);
    |
```

Program 4.11 Interface File for CalculatorModule

true). This enables the **do-while** loop on lines 9:18 to terminate, after which the function, **Shutdown( )**, on line 20, is executed in order to exit the calculator program and return control to the operating system.

event-driven programs

This kind of overall program structure is called an _event-driven program_, because its behavior is determined by its reactions to the sequence of user-generated events that occur during the execution of the program.

Let's now look at Programs 4.11 and 4.12, which present the interfaces of the modules that are included in the program shell given in Program 4.10.

Programs 4.11 and 4.12 give an orderly _work breakdown structure_ for dividing up the work of building the calculator into two subprojects: (1) building the calculator's user-interface, and (2) parsing and evaluating arithmetic expressions.

In Chapter 14, where advanced recursion techniques will be discussed, we will study an implementation for **YourCalculationModule** in which we employ a _recursive descent parser_ to parse arithmetic expressions. This parser is then used inside an _infix-to-postfix_ translator, which translates a string containing an ordinary infix arithmetic expression, such as $5 * 3 - 2$, into a postfix arithmetic expression, such as $5\ 3\ * 2\ -$. The postfix arithmetic expression is then evaluated to determine its value, using a postfix stack evaluator and pushdown stack mechanisms, discussed in Chapter 7.

```
    |    /*
    |     *    the file "YourCalculationModuleInterface.h"
    |     */
    |
 5  |    extern char *Evaluate(char *);
    |
    |
```

Program 4.12 Interface File for YourCalculationModule

Note that we can organize the work of the subprojects and divide up the labor to be performed without having to know the implementation details of the modules. Only the interfaces are needed—and these tell *what* these modules do rather than *how* they work. Again, we have employed *abstraction* to separate the *what* from the *how*, and we have reaped the organizational benefits by being able to divide up the labor into separate subprojects to create separate modules that fit together cleanly through simple, well-defined interfaces that are brought together in a clean interaction by the overall program shell. Also, designing module interfaces is a useful activity during the *design phase* of a software project before coding has begun.

using abstraction to help design big systems

4.4 Review Questions

1. What is a program shell?
2. How can the use of modules help organize the work in a software project?
3. How can the use of modules help structure a software system design?

4.4 Exercises

1. Design a *program shell* for playing tic-tac-toe (also known as noughts and crosses). The program shell should call on two plug-in modules. One module provides the user interface and is called **TicTacToeUserInterfaceModule**. It interacts with the user, displays moves on the board, displays the results of the game (**X** won, **O** won, or **Draw**), and calls on the second module to get the computer to make its move.

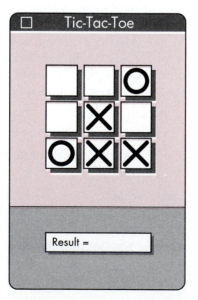

A Tic-Tac-Toe User Interface

The second module, called MoveCalculationModule, computes which move the computer makes when it is the computer's turn to make a move. In addition to giving your program shell for tic-tac-toe, you should also provide the interface files for these two plug-in modules.

4.5 How to Hide Data Representations

Learning Objectives

1. To learn additional concepts for representing abstract data types.
2. To learn how to implement representation-independent notations.
3. To learn how to structure C modules for ADTs in a general way, so that representations and item types can be changed easily.

In the module that follows, we study another important aspect of how to hide data representations so that external users don't know which representation is being used. We do this by creating what is called a *representation-independent notation*. Our example does this by creating three different modules that represent linked lists of items in three quite different ways. Nonetheless, all three modules share an identical notation for list operations because they all implement identical list operations in their interface files.

three linked-list representations

Figure 4.13 shows three representations for a list of four items (x_1, x_2, x_3, x_4). The items x_i $(1 \leq i \leq 4)$ are of unspecified type. The three representations

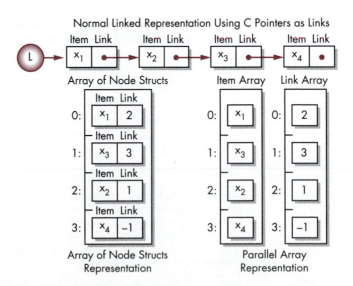

Figure 4.13 Three Representations of Linked Lists

are as follows:

> *Representation 1*: Normal linked lists using C struct nodes with pointer links.
> *Representation 2*: An array containing C structs for the list nodes.
> *Representation 3*: Parallel arrays with one array for the items, and another parallel array for the links.

In the case of the second and third representations, the links are integer indexes that access other array positions. A link of −1 represents the *null link* (and, by agreement, is outside of the index range for the arrays).

Now let's consider an interface problem. How do we arrange for the interfaces of the three modules to present the same notation to all users? Let's first make three assumptions: (1) that there is a variable or constant, null, whose value represents the *null link*; (2) that items stored in nodes of the linked lists are of type, ListItem; and (3) that pointers to nodes are of type NodePointer. The prototypes of six basic linked-list node operations are shown in Program 4.14. In short, these operations allow us to *create* and *free* nodes, and separately to access or change the *items* and *links* in nodes.

writing general
linked list programs

representation-independent
notation

Suppose we have given an include directive to access these six operations in the interface of a module (in addition to the variable or constant null which we also need). Then we are ready to write perfectly general programs that operate on linked lists. For example, Program 4.15 gives a function to reverse a list, using this general notation.

In general, when a program uses the six linked list operations given below, it does so in a notation that is *independent* of the underlying data representation and which is said to be a *representation-independent notation*.

Our next problem is to arrange for the implementation files of three different modules to give (hidden) implementations for these six interface operations, while also hiding other details of the separate underlying linked list representations.

The first module we will study is given in Program 4.16, which uses the normal C representation of linked lists, constructed from linked structs, having normal C pointers in the link fields. This module defines a symbolic constant, null, in its interface header file to be equivalent to the C pointer value, NULL (on line 9). Note also that the module uses the type of the list items, called ItemType (on line 11). It will later import this ItemType from another include file, ItemInterface.h. This ItemType is used to define the type, ListItem, in the interface of the module (on line 11), which is needed by external users of the list operation module to declare variables, parameters, and function result types, when performing operations on lists.

```
extern void SetLink(NodePointer N, NodePointer L);    /* assign L to be link of node N */
extern NodePointer GetLink(NodePointer N);            /* returns the link of node N */
extern void SetItem(NodePointer N, ListItem A);       /* change the item in node N to A */
extern void GetItem(NodePointer N, ListItem *A);      /* put node N's item in A */
extern void AllocateNewNode(NodePointer *N);          /* get a pointer to new node N */
extern void FreeNode(NodePointer N);                  /* recycle storage for node N */
```

Program 4.14 Six Basic Linked-List Node Operations

```
    |   void Reverse(NodePointer *L)          /* L's address, *L, is needed to change */
    |   {                                      /* what L contains external to this function */
    |
    |       NodePointer R;              /* R points to the first node of the reversed list */
5   |       NodePointer N;              /* N points to a node being transferred from L to R */
    |
    |       R = null;                   /* initialize R, the reversed list, to be the empty list */
    |
    |       while (*L != null) {        /* while there are still nodes remaining in L */
10  |           N = *L;                 /* let N point to L's first node */
    |           *L = GetLink(*L);       /* now, let L point to the remainder of L */
    |           SetLink(N,R);           /* link N to the rest of R */
    |           R = N;                  /* and make R point to its new first node N */
    |       }
15  |
    |       *L = R;                     /* finally, put a pointer to the reversed list R into L */
    |   }
```

Program 4.15 Reversing a Linked List, **L**

You can see that each of the four procedures on lines 42:55 in the implementation file is a rather obvious translation of a one line action that can be expressed easily using C pointer following notation (N–>), which selects members of struct nodes, given a node pointer N. The functions on lines 58:63 provide a new node allocation function based on **malloc** and provide a new name for the function **free(N)**. The only thing that these five procedures and one function do is to conceal the notation needed to operate on the underlying data types so that the use of the notation does not reveal what data representation has been used.

hiding representation-dependent notation

```
    |   /* ---------------< begin file "ListInterface.h" >--------------- */
    |
    |   /*
    |    *    The "ListInterface.h" file is included at the beginning of
5   |    *    main programs that use imported linked-list operations, and
    |    *    also at the beginning of the "ListImplementation.c" file below.
    |    */
    |
    |       #define  null              NULL;
10  |
    |       typedef  ItemType        ListItem;
    |
    |       typedef  struct NodeTag {
    |                     ListItem           Item;
15  |                     struct NodeTag  *Link;
    |               } Node;
    |
    |       typedef  Node  *NodePointer;
    |
```

Program 4.16 A Module Representing Linked Lists the Normal Way (continued)

Program 4.16 A Module Representing Linked Lists the Normal Way (continued)

```
20 |          extern void SetLink(NodePointer,NodePointer);
   |          extern NodePointer GetLink(NodePointer);
   |          extern void SetItem(NodePointer,ListItem);
   |          extern void GetItem(NodePointer, ListItem *);
   |          extern void AllocateNewNode(NodePointer *);
25 |          extern void FreeNode(NodePointer);
   |          extern void InitializationForLists(void);
   |
   |   /* ---------------< end of file "ListInterface.h" >--------------- */
   |
30 |   /* ---------------< begin file "ListImplementation.c" >--------------- */
   |
   |          /*
   |           *    Private part of module for the normal linked-list representation
   |           */
35 |
   |          #include <stdio.h>
   |          #include "ItemInterface.h"        /* import ItemType and item assignment */
   |          #include "ListInterface.h"
   |
40 |   /* ------------------------------------------------------------- */
   |
   |          void SetLink(NodePointer N, NodePointer L)
   |          {     N–>Link = L;    }
   |
45 |
   |          NodePointer GetLink(NodePointer N)
   |          {     return (N–>Link);    }
   |
   |
50 |          void SetItem(NodePointer N, ListItem A)         /* Note: AssignItem(*L,R) */
   |          {     AssignItem(&(N–>Item),A);    }            /* stores a copy of R in the */
   |                                                          /* address given by the value in L */
   |
   |          void GetItem(NodePointer N, ListItem *A)      /* AssignItem is imported */
55 |          {     AssignItem(A, N–>Item);    }             /* from the "ItemInterface.h" file */
   |
   |
   |          void AllocateNewNode(NodePointer *N)
   |          {     *N = (NodePointer) malloc(sizeof(Node));    }
60 |
   |
   |          void FreeNode(NodePointer N)
   |          {   free(N);   }
   |
65 |
   |          void InitializationForLists(void)
   |          { /* no initialization for the normal linked list representation */  }
   |
   |   /* ---------------< end of file "ListImplementation.c" >--------------- */
```

```
    |   #define MINPOINTER 0
    |   #define MAXPOINTER 100
    |   #define null −1
    |
5   |   typedef   int          NodePointer;
    |
    |   typedef   ItemType     ListItem;
    |
    |   typedef   struct {
10  |               ListItem       Item;
    |               NodePointer  Link;
    |             } Node;
    |
    |
15  |   NodePointer      Avail;
    |   Node                 ListMemory[MAXPOINTER];
```

Program 4.17 Declarations for Linked Lists Using Arrays of Node Structs

available space lists

Let's now look at how we can define a module using arrays of node structs to represent linked lists but having an interface that contains the exact same notation as the module above. The first thing we have to do is to define an array of node structs. Then we have to initialize the module by linking these node structs together into an *available space list*, Avail. Each time we allocate a new node, we take it from the front of the available space list. When we free a node, we return it to the available space list by inserting it as the new first node on Avail. Effectively, this means we have to implement our own storage allocation and management policy, since we are not using the built-in one that C already supplies.

We begin by giving the declarations of data types and variables needed to support arrays of node structs shown in Program 4.17. Our first task is to design an initialization routine that links up the node structs in the array, ListMemory, into an available space list pointed to by the pointer in the variable, Avail, as shown in Program 4.18.

```
    |   void InitializationForLists(void)
    |   {
    |       NodePointer N;
    |
5   |       for (N = MINPOINTER; N < MAXPOINTER − 1; ++N) {
    |           SetLink(N,N+1);
    |       }
    |
    |       SetLink(MAXPOINTER − 1,null);        /* SetLink will be defined below */
10  |
    |       Avail = MINPOINTER;
    |
    |   }
```

Program 4.18 Initialization Function Creating an Available Space List

```
|      void AllocateNewNode(NodePointer *N)
|      {
|          *N = Avail;                         /* let N point to the first node on the list Avail */
|          if (Avail != null) {
5  |              Avail = GetLink(Avail);        /* let Avail point to rest of Avail */
|              SetLink(*N,null);              /* set Link of N to the null link */
|          }
|      }
```

Program 4.19 Allocating a New Node

```
|      void FreeNode(NodePointer N)
|      {
|          SetLink(N, Avail);                  /* let N's link point to rest of Avail */
|          Avail = N;                          /* then, let Avail point to its new first node, N */
|      }
```

Program 4.20 Freeing a Node

This sets the link field of each node struct to contain the array index of the next node struct in the array, **ListMemory**, except for the link field of the last struct which is set to contain the *null link*. Then the variable **Avail** is set to point to the first available node on the available space list. To allocate a new node, we detach the first node from **Avail**, as shown in Program 4.19.

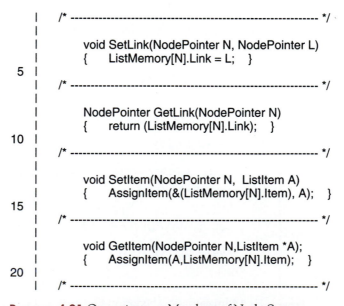

```
|      /* --------------------------------------------------------- */
|
|          void SetLink(NodePointer N, NodePointer L)
|          {    ListMemory[N].Link = L;    }
5  |
|      /* --------------------------------------------------------- */
|
|          NodePointer GetLink(NodePointer N)
|          {    return (ListMemory[N].Link);    }
10 |
|      /* --------------------------------------------------------- */
|
|          void SetItem(NodePointer N,  ListItem A)
|          {    AssignItem(&(ListMemory[N].Item), A);    }
15 |
|      /* --------------------------------------------------------- */
|
|          void GetItem(NodePointer N,ListItem *A);
|          {    AssignItem(A,ListMemory[N].Item);    }
20 |
|      /* --------------------------------------------------------- */
```

Program 4.21 Operations on Members of Node Structs

Disposing of a node, N, is just the inverse of this process. We insert N on the front of the Avail list, as shown in Program 4.20. You can see that disposing of a node actually *recycles* it by placing it back on the available space list, thus making it available for use in the future as a new node. We can now write the routines for getting and setting the Item and Link fields of the node structs in the ListMemory array. These appear in Program 4.21.

Comparing the way the six interface operations are implemented between Program 4.16 and Programs 4.18 through 4.21, we see that the prototypes of the externally available functions have stayed the same, although their implementations have changed. For example, in Program 4.16 (line 47), the link of node N is accessed using the notation, N–>Link, whereas in Program 4.21 (line 9), the link of a node N is accessed using the notation ListMemory[N].Link. It is necessary to hide this detailed link-accessing notation, using a neutral notation, such as, GetLink(N), in order to hide the underlying data representation successfully. Otherwise, the notation for link accessing and assignment would reveal the underlying representation used. Also, this underlying representation couldn't be changed without changing all instances of the link-accessing notation in all external programs using it.

the key to hiding data representations successfully

This is precisely the sort of distributed dependency that we wish to avoid in good modular programming practice, and one that is avoided by introducing the representation-independent notation we have employed.

Note that the function AssignItem(ItemType *L,ItemType R), which stores a copy of R in the address given by the value of L, is used on lines 14 and 19 of Program 4.21 and lines 51 and 55 of Program 4.16. This function is provided by some item modules we'll look at later (in Programs 4.25 and 4.26) which export integer and Airport code items and also export functions to print and assign such items.

Program 4.22 assembles the pieces given above into a module containing our array-of-node-structs representation for linked lists.

Our third and final representation for linked lists is shown in Program 4.23, which uses two parallel arrays indexed by the same range of array indices. In this representation, Item[N] and Link[N] are two separate array elements used to represent the Item and Link fields of node N.

There are several things to note about this module. First, its interface header file (on lines 1:24) is nearly identical to that of the module for the array-of-struct-nodes representation (in Program 4.22, lines 1:29). Second, its functions AllocateNewNode, FreeNode, and InitializationForLists, are identical to those in Program 4.22. Third, there are three differences: (1) the declarations for parallel arrays on lines 40:41:

```
40  |      ListItem          Item[MAXPOINTER];
    |      NodePointer       Link[MAXPOINTER];
```

differ from the declarations for the array, ListMemory, of node structs (on line 43 of Program 4.22):

```
43  |      Node              ListMemory[MAXPOINTER];
```

(2) in the actual function implementations the code to access and change the items

```
     |   /* ---------------< begin file "ListInterface.h" >--------------- */
     |
     |   /*
     |    *    The "ListInterface.h" file is included at the beginning of
 5   |    *    main programs that use imported linked-list operations, and
     |    *    also at the beginning of the "ListImplementation.c" file below.
     |    */
     |
     |       #define MINPOINTER 0
10   |       #define MAXPOINTER 100
     |       #define null −1
     |
     |       typedef   int            NodePointer;
     |       typedef   ItemType       ListItem;
15   |
     |       typedef   struct {
     |                      ListItem        Item;
     |                      NodePointer    Link;
     |                 } Node;
20   |
     |       extern void SetLink(NodePointer,NodePointer);
     |       extern NodePointer GetLink(NodePointer);
     |       extern void SetItem(NodePointer,ListItem);
     |       extern void GetItem(NodePointer, ListItem *);
25   |       extern void AllocateNewNode(NodePointer *);
     |       extern void FreeNode(NodePointer);
     |       extern void InitializationForLists(void);
     |
     |   /* ---------------< end of file "ListInterface.h" >--------------- */
30   |
     |
     |   /* ---------------< begin file "ListImplementation.c" >--------------- */
     |
     |   /*   Contains hidden implementations for externally used functions. */
35   |   /*   Also contains private ListMemory array and private Avail pointer */
     |   /*   not used external to the "ListImplementation.c" file. */
     |
     |       #include <stdio.h>
     |       #include "ItemInterface.h"
40   |       #include "ListInterface.h"
     |
     |       NodePointer      Avail;
     |       Node             ListMemory[MAXPOINTER];
     |
45   |   /* ------------------------------------------------------------ */
     |
     |       void SetLink(NodePointer N, NodePointer L)
     |       {    ListMemory[N].Link = L;    }
     |
50   |   /* ------------------------------------------------------------ */
```

Program 4.22 Module for Array of Node Structs Representation (continued)

Program 4.22 Module for Array of Node Structs Representation (continued)

```
                    NodePointer GetLink(NodePointer N)
                    {    return (ListMemory[N].Link;    }

55       /* ------------------------------------------------------------ */

                    void SetItem(NodePointer N, ListItem A)
                    {    AssignItem(&(ListMemory[N].Item),A);    }

60       /* ------------------------------------------------------------ */

                    void GetItem(NodeItem N, ListItem *A)
                    {    AssignItem(A,ListMemory[N].Item);    }

65       /* ------------------------------------------------------------ */

                    void InitializationForLists(void)
                    {
                        NodePointer N;

70
                        for (N = MINPOINTER; N < MAXPOINTER − 1; ++N) {
                            SetLink(N, N+1);
                        }

75                      SetLink(MAXPOINTER − 1,null);        /* SetLink is defined above */
                        Avail = MINPOINTER;
                    }

         /* ------------------------------------------------------------ */
80
                    void AllocateNewNode(NodePointer *N)
                    {
                        *N = Avail;               /* let N point to the first node on the list Avail */
                        if (Avail != null) {
85                          Avail = GetLink(Avail);        /* let Avail point to rest of Avail */
                            SetLink(*N,null);              /* set Link of N to the null link */
                        }
                    }

90       /* ------------------------------------------------------------ */

                    void FreeNode(NodePointer N)
                    {
                        SetLink(N, Avail);                /* let N's link point to rest of Avail */
95                      Avail = N;                /* then, let Avail point to its new first node, N */
                    }

         /* ------------------------------------------------------------ */

         /* ---------------< end of file "ListImplementation.c" >--------------- */
```

```
/* ---------------< begin file "ListInterface.h" >--------------- */

/*
 *    The "ListInterface.h" file is included at the beginning of
 *    main programs that use imported linked-list operations, and
 *    also at the beginning of the "ListImplementation.c" file below.
 */

#define MINPOINTER 0
#define MAXPOINTER 100
#define null −1

typedef   int          NodePointer;
typedef   ItemType     ListItem;

extern void SetLink(NodePointer,NodePointer);
extern NodePointer GetLink(NodePointer);
extern void SetItem(NodePointer,ListItem);
extern void GetItem(NodePointer, ListItem *);
extern void AllocateNewNode(NodePointer *);
extern void FreeNode(NodePointer);
extern void InitializationForLists(void);

/* ---------------< end of file "ListInterface.h" >--------------- */


/* ---------------< begin file "ListImplementation.c" >--------------- */

/*
 *    Contains hidden implementations for externally used functions.
 *    Also contains private Link and Item arrays and private Avail pointer
 *    not used external to the "ListImplementation.c" file.
 */

#include <stdio.h>
#include "ItemInterface.h"
#include "ListInterface.h"

NodePointer       Avail;
ListItem          Item[MAXPOINTER];
NodePointer       Link[MAXPOINTER];

/* ----------------------------------------------------------- */

void SetLink(NodePointer N, NodePointer L)
{    Link[N] = L;   }

/* ----------------------------------------------------------- */
```

Program 4.23 Unit for Parallel Array Representation (continued)

Program 4.23 Unit for Parallel Array Representation (continued)

```
50          NodePointer GetLink(NodePointer N)
            {    return (Link[N]);   }

     /* ------------------------------------------------------- */

55          void SetItem(NodePointer N, ListItem A)
            {    AssignItem(&Item[N],A);    }

     /* ------------------------------------------------------- */

60          void GetItem(NodeItem N, ListItem *A)
            {    AssignItem(A,Item[N]);    }

     /* ------------------------------------------------------- */

65          void InitializationForLists(void)
            {
                NodePointer N;

                for (N = MINPOINTER; N < MAXPOINTER − 1; ++N) {
70                  SetLink(N, N+1);
                }

                SetLink(MAXPOINTER − 1,null);      /* SetLink is defined above */
                Avail = MINPOINTER;
75          }

     /* ------------------------------------------------------- */

            void AllocateNewNode(NodePointer *N)
80          {
                *N = Avail;               /* let N point to the first node on the list Avail */
                if (Avail != null) {
                    Avail = GetLink(Avail);      /* let Avail point to rest of Avail */
                    SetLink(*N,null);            /* set Link of N to the null link */
85              }
            }

     /* ------------------------------------------------------- */

90          void FreeNode(NodePointer N)
            {
                SetLink(N, Avail);           /* let N's link point to rest of Avail */
                Avail = N;                   /* then, let Avail point to its new first node, N */
            }
95
     /* ------------------------------------------------------- */

     /* --------------< end of file "ListImplementation.c" >-------------- */
```

```
      |    /* ------------------------------------------------------- */
      |
      |         void SetLink(NodePointer N, NodePointer L)
      |         {     Link[N] = L;   }
   5  |
      |    /* ------------------------------------------------------- */
      |
      |         NodePointer GetLink(NodePointer N)
      |         {     return (Link[N]);   }
  10  |
      |    /* ------------------------------------------------------- */
      |
      |         void SetItem(NodePointer N, ListItem A)
      |         {     AssignItem(&Item[N], A);   }
  15  |
      |    /* ------------------------------------------------------- */
      |
      |         void GetItem(NodePointer N, ListItem *A)
      |         {     AssignItem(A,Item[N]);   }
  20  |
      |    /* ------------------------------------------------------- */
```

Program 4.24 Operations on Parallel Array Members of Nodes

and links in nodes is changed to operate on parallel arrays instead of on an array of node records, and (3) node structs are defined on lines 16:19 of Program 4.22. Program 4.24 shows how the parallel array implementation differs from Program 4.21.

Now that we have introduced three different underlying data representations for linked lists, all sharing a common interface with identically expressed operations, we are almost ready to write some programs that use these operations. But first, we need to ask one question: "What are the types of the items used in these linked lists of items?" As it turns out, we have written the three linked list representation modules above to import the type of the list items used from another externally defined module interface file **ItemInterface.h**. This interface file defines the type of items by defining the type, **ItemType**. The implementation file, **ItemImplementation.c**, also gives definitions of the functions **AssignItem** and **PrintItem** to assign and print items of type **ItemType**. Thus, if we want to deal with linked lists of *integers*, we could specify the module shown in Program 4.25. Alternatively, if we want to deal with linked lists of three-letter airport codes (as we did in Chapter 2), we could specify the module shown in Program 4.26.

Even though the various modules we have given can be independently compiled, they must be compiled in a certain order dictated by their *dependencies*. If Module U uses Module V (by using external entities defined in V and by including V's interface header file), we say that Module U is *dependent* on Module V. In this case, we have to compile Module V before we compile any modules dependent on it, such as Module U. Some C programming environments allow you to express the dependencies between modules in a special notation which allows the system to recompile automatically any module whose program text has been edited, and, afterward, to recompile all modules depending (either directly or indirectly) on the changed module.

defining the types of the items used in lists

```
    |   /* ---------------< begin file "ItemInterface.h" >--------------- */
    |
    |   typedef int ItemType;
    |
 5  |   extern void PrintItem(ItemType *);          /* prints an item of type ItemType */
    |   extern void AssignItem(ItemType *, ItemType);   /* assigns copy of second  */
    |                                                   /* argument to first argument */
    |   /* ---------------< end of file "ItemInterface.h" >--------------- */
    |
10  |   /* ---------------< begin file "ItemImplementation.c" >--------------- */
    |
    |   #include <stdio.h>
    |   #include "ItemInterface.h"
    |
15  |   void PrintItem(ItemType *i)                 /* needed to print integer items */
    |   {      printf("%d", *i);      }
    |
    |   void AssignItem(ItemType *Left, ItemType Right)          /* stores a copy */
    |   {      *Left = Right;      }                        /* of Right in address *Left */
20  |
    |   /* ---------------< end of file "ItemImplementation.c" >--------------- */
```

Program 4.25 A Module Exporting an Integer ItemType

```
    |   /* ---------------< begin file "ItemInterface.h" >--------------- */
    |
    |   typedef char ItemType[4];
    |
 5  |   extern void PrintItem(ItemType *);          /* prints an item of type ItemType */
    |   extern void AssignItem(ItemType *, ItemType);   /* assigns copy of second  */
    |                                                   /* argument to first argument */
    |   /* ---------------< end of file "ItemInterface.h" >--------------- */
    |
10  |   /* ---------------< begin file "ItemImplementation.c" >--------------- */
    |
    |   #include <stdio.h>
    |   #include <string.h>
    |   #include "ItemInterface.h"
15  |
    |   void PrintItem(Itemtype *i)                 /* needed to print string items */
    |   {      printf("%s", *i);      }
    |
    |   void AssignItem(ItemType *Left, ItemType Right)          /* stores a copy */
20  |   {      strcpy(*Left,Right);   }                     /* of Right in address *Left */
    |
    |   /* ---------------< end of file "ItemImplementation.c" >--------------- */
```

Program 4.26 A Module Exporting an Airport Code ItemType

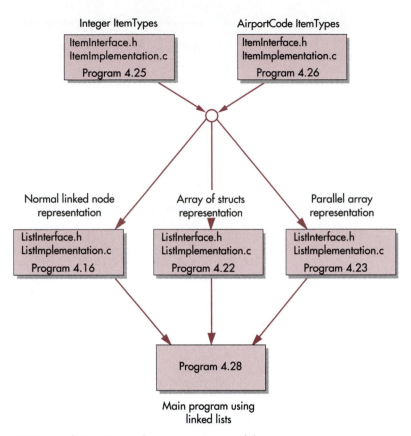

Figure 4.27 Compilation Dependencies Among Modules

Let's now write a program to manipulate linked lists using the three alternative representations for linked lists. Assume that we have compiled the modules in Fig. 4.27 in the correct order, using the integer list item type exported by the module of Program 4.25. A simple program to build up a linked list of integers, L = (23, 79, 53), print it, reverse it, and then print it again, is given in Program 4.28.

```
    |    /*
    |     *    This is an example of a "main" program which imports external
    |     *    list operations and list item types.
    |     */
 5  |
    |    #include <stdio.h>
    |    #include "ItemInterface.h"        /* the list items can be integers or Airports */
    |    #include "ListInterface.h"        /* the hidden list implementation can use */
    |                                      /* either normal linked lists, arrays of */
10  |                                      /* node structs, or parallel arrays */
```

Program 4.28 Main Linked List Program Using Module Interfaces (continued)

Program 4.28 Main Linked List Program Using Module Interfaces (continued)

```
        void PrintList(NodePointer L)
        {
            ListItem A;

15          printf("(");
            while (L != null) {
                GetItem(L,&A);
                PrintItem(&A);
                L = GetLink(L);
20              if (L != null) printf(",");
            }
            printf(")\n");
        }

25  /* ------------------------------------------------------- */

        void InsertNewFirstNode(ListItem A, NodePointer *L)
        {
            NodePointer N;
30
            AllocateNewNode(&N);
            SetItem(N,A);
            SetLink(N,*L);
            *L = N;
35      }

    /* ------------------------------------------------------- */

        void Reverse(NodePointer *L);                          /* to reverse a list L */
40      {
            NodePointer R = null;
            NodePointer N;

            while (*L != null) {
45              N = *L;                   /* let N point to L's first node */
                *L = GetLink(*L);         /* now, let L point to the remainder of L */
                SetLink(N,R);             /* link N to the rest of R */
                R = N;                    /* and make R point to its new first node N */
            }
50
            *L = R;
        }

    /* ------------------------------------------------------- */
55
    int main (void)
    {
        NodePointer L = null;         /* let L be a pointer to a list node, initially null */

60      InitializationForLists( );            /* initialize prior to list processing */
```

Program 4.28 Main Linked List Program Using Module Interfaces (continued)

```
      |          /* Create a list L pointing to (23, 79, 53) */
      |              InsertNewFirstNode(53,&L);
      |              InsertNewFirstNode(79,&L);
   65 |              InsertNewFirstNode(23,&L);
      |
      |          /* Print the List */
      |              PrintList(L);              /* prints the list (23, 79, 53) */
      |
   70 |          /* Now, reverse the list L */
      |              Reverse(&L);
      |
      |          /* Print the list L again to show the change */
      |              PrintList(L);              /* prints the list (53, 79, 23) */
   75 |      }
```

When Program 4.28 is run, it prints the list (23, 79, 53) followed by its reversal (53, 79, 23) on the next line. Now, you can note something profound: this program works with any of the three linked list representations given by Programs 4.16, 4.22, or 4.23. That is, the interface file, ListInterface.h, included on line 8 of Program 4.28 can be any of the three interface files of that name given by Programs 4.16, 4.22 or 4.23. Switching interface header files and the associated implementation files, followed by recompiling and running Program 4.28, produces the exact same behavior no matter which representation is chosen.

switching underlying data representations

Suppose now that you change the representation of list items to airport codes by changing the header file ItemInterface.h from that given by Program 4.25 to that given by Program 4.26, after which you recompile the modules in their correct order of dependency (as shown in Fig. 4.27). Also, suppose you change lines 62:65 of Program 4.28, so that they construct airport code lists instead of integer lists, as shown in the alternative main program section given in Program 4.29.

Finally, when you compile and execute Program 4.28 with the changes of Program 4.29 in its main section, it constructs and prints the airport code list (DUS, ORD, SAN), after which it prints its reversal (SAN, ORD, DUS). Substituting another choice for the interface header file, ListInterface.h, on line 8, recompiling the associated list module implementation file, and executing, yields the same results, since the program is independent of the underlying data representation chosen for linked lists.

changing to lists of airport codes

Now it's time to draw some lessons from all of this work. What have we learned?

First of all, when linked list operations are organized this way, the program using linked list services cannot tell which underlying data representation for linked lists has been chosen. In this case, we say that the data representation has been *hidden* (or *encapsulated*). Once this property has been achieved, we can switch the underlying data representation if we choose to do so. (We might wish to do this if it can improve the efficiency of the overall program, for example.) Also, when we have encapsulated the data representation, we have succeeded in creating a data abstraction, in which we know abstractly *what* the operations do, without knowing in detail

lessons learned

```
     |    int main(void)
     |    {
     |         NodePointer L = null;      /* Let L be a pointer to a list node, initially null */
     |
60   |         InitializationForLists( );          /* execute the list initialization function */
     |
     |         /* Create a list L pointing to (DUS, ORD, SAN) */
     |             InsertNewFirstNode("SAN",&L);
     |             InsertNewFirstNode("ORD",&L);
65   |             InsertNewFirstNode("DUS",&L);
     |
     |         /* Print the List */
     |             PrintList(L);                        /* prints (DUS, ORD, SAN) */
     |
70   |         /* Now, reverse the list L */
     |             Reverse(&L);
     |
     |         /* Print the list L again to show the change */
     |             PrintList(L);                        /* prints (SAN, ORD, DUS) */
75   |    }
```

Program 4.29 Alternative Main Program Section

how they are accomplished. Moreover, when we write the modules for linked list representations so that they import the list item type from another module, then we have achieved an additional dimension of abstraction—the list operations have been expressed in a manner that is independent of the kind of items used in the lists. Once this has been accomplished, all we need do is to write a few lines of code to create a new package of linked list operations that work on linked lists having a completely new type of item. In short, we have succeeded in creating a data abstraction, "linked lists of items," where the items are of a general type and where the underlying linked list representation can be changed without having to change the programs that use linked list operations. Can you begin to see why this method of structuring programs can yield important benefits for the modifiability and management of complexity of large software systems?

One slight disadvantage to what we have done is that our abstract linked list operations are a little less efficient than the use of direct linked list operations. This is because we incur the penalty of extra function calls in order to conceal the underlying notation inside function notation. This is an example of a *tradeoff* between *efficiency and generality*. Generally speaking, efficiency trades off against generality in that more generality is associated with less efficiency. This important tradeoff is another instance of one of our recurring concepts—*tradeoffs*.

Conceptually, we can now talk meaningfully about *packages of services*. We can also give just the *interface* to such a package of services, without having to know the details of the hidden representations. In short, we are able to simplify the way we deal with a layer of services by knowing only *what* the services do, without having to know *how* they are represented or programmed.

data abstraction and generalized list items

tradeoff: efficiency versus generality

4.5 Review Questions

1. What is an available space list?
2. What is information hiding?
3. How can information hiding promote ease of program modification?
4. What is a representation-independent notation?
5. Why is a representation-independent notation needed in order to hide a data representation inside a module?
6. What does it mean to say that efficiency trades off against generality? Give an example of a situation in which this happens.
7. In what way is the representation-independent notation for linked lists more general and less efficient than the representation-dependent notation used privately in the implementation files of the modules that provide linked list representations?

4.5 Exercises

1. Develop the interface for a module called **ListOperationsModule**, which provides list-processing services to its clients. The module is to have the following operations in its interface:

   ```
   extern int Size(List *L);              /* returns the number of items in list L */
   extern List *Head(List *L);            /* returns a list consisting of the first item of L */
   extern List *Tail(List *L);            /* returns a list of the items after the first item of L */
   extern List *Join(List *L1, List *L2); /* concatenates lists L1 and L2 */
   ```

   A list, **L**, is said to be *empty* if and only if **Size(L) == 0** (i.e., when it contains no items). The **Head** and **Tail** of a list **L** are not defined if **L** is empty.

2. Provide two different hidden implementations for the module, **ListOperationsModule**, whose interface you have specified in your answer to Exercise 1. The first defines the type **List** as a pointer to a linked list of node structs. [*Hint*: To do this, you may wish to use the module in Program 4.16, or modify its code in some fashion.] The second defines the type **List** to be a pointer to a struct having a **Count** member, which is an integer giving the number of items on the list, and a **Contents** member, which stores an array of **ListItems**, as in the following declarations:

   ```
   typedef  struct {
               int         Count;
               ListItem    Contents[MAXSIZE];
            } ListStruct;

   typedef  ListStruct *List;
   ```

   Your two implementations should hide the representations of lists (as much as possible in C) inside two versions of your module that provide the same list operation notation to external users. (That is, if external users use only the list operation notation in your module interfaces, they shouldn't be able to tell which underlying list representation was used—the sequential representation or the linked representation.)

3. Implement a string module that exports the following string operations:

```
extern int Length(char *S);
            /* returns an integer giving the number of characters in string S */
extern int Pos(char *Substring,char *S);
            /* gives the position of the first character of the leftmost */
            /* occurrence of the substring, Substring, in S, or gives zero */
            /* if S has no substring matching Substring */
extern char *Concat(char *S1, char *S2);
            /* returns a string consisting of the characters of S1 */
            /* followed by the characters of S2 */
extern char *Copy(char *S, int i, int j);
            /* returns the substring of S of length j starting at position i in S */
extern void Delete(char *S, int i, int j);
            /* deletes the substring of S of length j starting at position i in S */
extern void Insert(char *S1, char *S2, int i);
            /* inserts string S1 into string S2 at the i^th position. */
```

Make reasonable assumptions about what happens in abnormal cases, such as trying to delete a substring at a position that doesn't exist, or copying a substring that is too long to fit in the given string. What difficulties do you encounter in trying to implement such a string module in C while attempting to use the normal string literal notation for string constants (consisting of a sequence of characters enclosed in quote marks, "$c_1c_2...c_n$")?

4. What problems do you encounter if you try to implement strings in a module whose operations are specified in Exercise 3, using linked lists of characters as a representation?

5. Redeclare the ItemType exported by the file ItemInterface.h in Program 4.25 so that it exports the C type float as the ItemType. Then use any of the linked list modules (in Programs 4.16, 4.22, or 4.23) to provide a representation for linked lists of floats, and implement priority queues using linked lists of floats. Your priority queue implementation should be a module and should use a representation-independent notation to operate on linked lists representing priority queues (by using only the six operations given in Fig. 4.16 plus the variable or constant, null).

6. What is wrong with the following program, if anything?

```
|   #include <stdio.h>
|   #include "ItemInterface.h"      /* this module's text is given as Program 4.25 */
|   #include "ListInterface.h"      /* this module's text is given as Program 4.23 */
|
|   int main(void)
|   {
|       char *Avail = "AvailableSpaceList";
|       printf("%s\n",Avail);
|   }
```

7. Compare the efficiency of the two list reversal methods (Method 1 and Method 2) on a sample of lists in order to measure the reduction in efficiency that occurs when a representation-independent function notation is used to conceal the direct use of representation-dependent pointer following and struct member accessing notations.

```
/* For Method 1 – assume externally defined types as given in Exercises 2.5 */

     |    void Reverse1(NodePointer *L)
     |    {
     |        NodePointer R,N;
     |
  5  |        R = NULL;         /* initialize R, the reversed list, to be the empty list */
     |
     |        while (*L != NULL) {
     |            N = *L;                        /* let N point to L's first node */
     |            *L = *L–>Link;          /* now, let L point to the remainder of L */
 10  |            N–>Link = R;                      /* link N to the rest of R */
     |            R = N;                /* and make R point to its new first node N */
     |        }
     |
     |        *L = R;        /* finally, replace L by a pointer to the reversed list R */
 15  |
     |    }
```

Method 1 Representation-Dependent List Reversal

```
/*      For Method 2, assume types and operations have been provided */
/*      by an include directive */

     #include "ListInterface.h"                    /* as defined in Program 4.16 */

     |    void Reverse2(NodePointer *L)
     |    {
     |        NodePointer R,N;
     |
  5  |        R = null;         /* initialize R, the reversed list, to be the empty list */
     |
     |        while (*L != null) {
     |            N = *L;                        /* let N point to L's first node */
     |            *L = GetLink(*L);       /* now, let L point to the remainder of L */
 10  |            SetLink(N,R);                     /* link N to the rest of R */
     |            R = N;                /* and make R point to its new first node N */
     |        }
     |
     |        *L = R;        /* finally, replace L by a pointer to the reversed list R */
 15  |
     |    }
```

Method 2 Abstract Linked List Reversal

(Does it make any difference in efficiency if you compile the modules separately and link them as opposed to defining the types and functions all together in one single module?)

8. Discuss how to cope with modular program design using a version of C that does not have separate compilation of files. [*Hint:* You can prepare separate include files of definitions containing the entities in separate modules, but you won't be able to hide internal details of each module unless you follow a discipline for choosing identifiers internal to the modules that guarantees their noninterference. One possible policy is to start identifiers in separate modules with unique prefixes, such as gSet in the "g" module and pSet in the "p" module, etc.]

9. Alert readers might have noticed that the interface definition scheme we have used in this chapter does an imperfect job of hiding data representations. For instance, in Program 4.16, the types for **NodePointers** and **Nodes** (on lines 13:18) have to be given in the interface file in order for **NodePointer** parameters to be used as parameters to the extern function prototypes on lines 20:26. However, this exports too much information, since external users can then use pointer following notation (as in *X) and struct member access notation (as in R–>Item and R–>Link) to operate on variables of type **NodePointer**. It is only by agreement that external users can be constrained not to use the representation-dependent notation that is mistakenly exported by being forced to give the declarations on lines 13:18 in the interface. How could C's design be amended to overcome this deficiency by allowing the internal details of such declarations to be kept private? [*Hint:* Ada has been designed to solve this problem in its package interfaces.]

4.6 Modularity and Information Hiding in Program Design

Learning Objectives

1. To understand the general benefits of modularity and information hiding in the design of large software systems.
2. To learn about some of the philosophy and terminology in current use concerning modularity and information hiding.
3. To prepare to understand and appreciate modern software engineering concepts.

When programs get large, there is a danger that they can become highly confusing, hard to debug, and nearly impossible to modify, unless certain disciplines of structuring are rigorously followed.

good structure versus bad structure

Life in contemporary industrial societies abounds in the production and use of complex systems. Complex systems, whatever their nature, seem to share certain basic features. For instance, most large complex systems are composed of interacting subsystems.

This is true for large software systems composed of subsystems of procedures, functions, and data structures, that, in turn, ultimately translate into compositions of the primitive instructions and data available on the background computer. But because computer programming is performed in a written medium that permits a wide range of possible written expressions, the possibility for disaster is wide open. For instance, it is possible to write a large program as a disorganized mess of thousands of tiny components with numerous undisciplined and ill-understood interactions. It is also possible to write a large program using well-organized layers, each built from carefully crafted components each having carefully-defined, simple interactions (see Fig. 4.30).

In your first computer science course, you may have learned about the benefits of *procedural abstraction*. When we organize a sequence of instructions into a named procedure, $P(a_1, \ldots, a_n)$, we have created a named unit of action. Subsequently, when we can call upon and use this named unit of action, it is necessary to know only *what* the procedure does, not *how* it achieves its result. At a later time, we can go back and rewrite the procedure to substitute an improved method, which changes *how* it achieves its result, without altering *what* it computes.

Separating the *what* from the *how* (which is an act of *abstraction*), provides two benefits: (1) *ease of use*—because we need know simply *what* procedure P does, not *how* it does it, in order to use P; and (2) *ease of modification*—because we can change the details of *how* P is written, without having to make distributed changes throughout the program everywhere that P is called. In general, proper use of abstraction can help control complexity and can improve modifiability.

In your first computer science course, you may also have learned about beneficial techniques for creating and using locally declared variables and locally declared subprograms inside another outer procedure. These local entities are visible only from inside the outer procedure, and cannot be seen or used outside of it. This is an instance of *information hiding*. The local entities are hidden from outside view. Such information hiding has two benefits: (1) the use of the local entities (e.g., variables and subprograms) does not interfere with identically named entities outside the procedure, and (2) the use of outside entities cannot interfere with the local entities.

procedural abstraction

ease of use and ease of modification

information hiding

 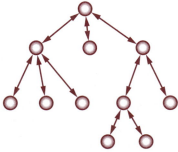

Complex tangle of
densely interacting components

Hierarchy with layers of
cleanly interacting components

Figure 4.30 Alternative Software System Organizations

A protective wall has therefore been erected around the local entities, which protects both them and the outside world from accidental (or even intentional) interference. Consequently, the region of text with which they can interact has been confined to a well-understood, local region of the overall program. This restricts and simplifies the possible interactions among program components. (In some programming languages, in which no local declarations are possible and every defined entity is visible everywhere throughout the program, the use of local name scoping is impossible, creating a disadvantage for the programmer.)

encapsulation

When we introduce devices into programming languages for building protective walls around collections of entities, we sometimes use the term *encapsulation*. The hidden local entities are said to be *encapsulated*, and we sometimes refer to the module containing them as a *capsule*.

modules, packages and units

Procedures and functions are not the only kind of program component that can benefit from the notions of information hiding and encapsulation. Sometimes we need to gather together a somewhat larger collection of interacting entities that need to be packaged into a named unit of organization and on which we need to confer the protective benefits of information hiding. *Modules*, *packages*, and *units* are three terms that are used in different contemporary programming languages for the notion of creating capsules containing collections of procedures, functions, variables, constants, and data type declarations, some of which are hidden internally and others of which are made available for external use through the interface of the capsule.

servers and clients

In attempting to create clean designs for large programs, sometimes a group of related operations and data naturally seem to belong together. Under these circumstances, it is often useful to create a module containing all the related data and operations. The module is organized specifically to provide a group of services to its users. In such a case, we speak of the module as a *server*, and we speak of the users as *clients*. In order to set up such a server module properly, it needs to have a well-defined interface. The interface contains those services and entities that can be used by the clients. Users get to see and use only what is made *visible* in the interface. The rest of the details are hidden from view in order to make them tamper-proof and in order to protect external clients from unintended accidental interference.

exporting and importing

In some modular programming languages, interface entities must be made visible explicitly by *exporting* them (i.e., by mentioning their names in explicit *export* declarations). Moreover, in some such languages, the clients wishing to use such exported services must explicitly declare which ones they intend to use by mentioning their names in explicit *import* declarations. In C, the use of **extern** declarations in a module M_1 to access entities in another module M_2 is equivalent to specifying *import* declarations.

Finally, another type of use for the information-hiding capabilities of modules is to create separate *layers* of data representations. As we have seen, it is possible to hide the details of data representations inside modules in such a way that the services available to clients in their interfaces do not reveal what data representation has been chosen. The clients get to use only the abstract data type (or ADT) exported through the interface. The data representation used is then encapsulated entirely within the hidden part of the module. By using abstraction in this fashion to create representation-independent modules, clarity, simplicity, and ease of modification are again promoted in the overall program design. Specifically, the hidden internal data representations and algorithms can be changed without changing any text in client programs—thus promoting *ease of modification*. Moreover, when properly programmed, no notational dependencies exist between the nature of the data representations used inside the module and the data access notation used by the clients, forcing the clients to change their programs whenever changes in the internal data representations used inside the module force changes in the data access notation used by clients.

4.6 Review Questions

1. Give two synonyms for the word *module*, used when referring to entities similar to modules in other contemporary programming languages (such as Pascal or Ada).
2. What is procedural abstraction?
3. What is data abstraction?
4. What is encapsulation?
5. Summarize the benefits of using C modules properly.

Pitfalls

- *Complex tangles of components*
  The structure of a software system tends to become complex and hard to debug, test, and modify, the more it exhibits a complex tangle of many components having many interactions. The use of modularity and information hiding to divide the structure into a hierarchy of a few simple components or into layers having a few simple interactions (if possible) greatly simplifies the overall structure, and increases the chances of successfully debugging, testing, and modifying the system.

Tips and Techniques

- *Use representation-independent notation to hide a data representation*
  If you are going to succeed in hiding a data representation, you need to present an interface to the users that offers a representation-independent notation. Generally, this can be done by using only function notation in the interface of a module, meanwhile hiding any instances of particular data access and update notation (such as the notations for pointer following, *X and X–>, selecting struct members, S.Member, or indexing components of arrays, A[index], all of which reveal choices of data representations to their users).

- *Use modules to help organize the work breakdown structure of your software project*

A software project can often be broken into cleanly organized subprojects by defining modules that interact through clean, simple interfaces. The interfaces can be specified first, without having to specify the implementations. The overall interaction between the modules can be given in a shell program. After this is done, separate teams can address the problems of implementing the modules.

This organizational strategy can be repeated when designing the structure of the modules, yielding a hierarchical work breakdown structure. The debugging, testing, and integration strategies for completion of the project can also benefit from this overall organization.

References for Further Study

Two influential early papers on modularity in the design of software systems were written by David Parnas.

two key papers on modularity

David L. Parnas, "On the Criteria for Decomposing Systems into Modules." *Communications of the ACM*, 15:12 (December 1972), pp. 1053–58.

David L. Parnas, "Designing Software for Ease of Extension and Contraction." *IEEE Transactions on Software Engineering*, SE-5(2) (1979), pp. 128–38.

Chapter Summary

C modules give you the capability of packaging collections of related program entities together, and of hiding the details of their implementations. These two capabilities are called modularity and information hiding. Modules can be used to provide packages of services or to provide collections of software components. Sometimes modules can be used to organize the structure of a large software system either into cleanly separated layers or into major components that have simple, well-defined interactions. Generally speaking, a software system can be given a clean organization if it can be structured using a few major components having only a few well-defined interactions. Conversely, a software system tends to exhibit a complex organization if it is a disorganized tangle of many components having a complicated pattern of interactions.

providing packages of services

providing clean software system organization

Programs are easier to modify if the modifications can be confined to a few places within well-defined boundaries and within a small local region of the total program text. If each user of a module has to be changed when the module itself is modified, then the changes are said to be distributed rather than local.

providing for ease of modification

One organizational technique helpful in promoting ease of modification is to hide the representation of data and operations inside the implementation part of a module whose interface provides a representation-independent notation. When this is done, the hidden representation inside the module's implementation part can be changed without having to change the notation in the interface. Consequently, the change is invisible to (or transparent to) the external users of the module, and their notation of use need not be changed as a consequence of changing the representation. Clarity of structure and ease of modification are both promoted by using information hiding and data abstraction in this fashion.

helping to organize work in a software project

Decomposing the organization of a software system into modules with clean interactions, and organizing the composition of the modules inside an overall shell program, can help clarify the work breakdown structure of a software project into sub-projects. This can help organize the labor of software development as well as the software system structure. Moreover, it is useful during the design phase of a project.

5

Introduction to Software Engineering Concepts

≡ **5.1** Introduction and Motivation

As mentioned earlier, software principles concerning small programs are covered in this chapter, and those concerning large software systems are covered in Chapter 16. The term *programming-in-the-small* refers to the activities that center on the creation of small programs—those consisting of a few lines or a few pages. The term *programming-in-the-large* refers to the activities that center on the creation and modification of large software systems—those that are hundreds of thousands of lines long or longer. Programming-in-the-large involves organizing and coordinating the activities of large software development teams using substantial resources. It involves considerations of software lifecycle processes and methods. These tend to be somewhat different in flavor and content from the issues that arise in programming-in-the-small.

small-scale versus large-scale programming

Although many small programs are easy to write, occasionally some small programs are quite difficult to write. The creation of such difficult small programs can then involve great subtlety of thought and can require great precision and ingenuity. In order to deal successfully with such situations, it is important for you to learn to be able to reason about small programs with clarity and mental precision.

small programs can be subtle

137

One important form of reasoning about small programs involves what are called *correctness proofs*. It is sometimes possible to prove that programs accomplish stated objectives called the *program specifications*, which can often be described in a precise, logical language. When a mathematical proof shows that a program, when executed, achieves the outcomes described by its specifications, it is said to be a correctness proof.

correctness proofs

Of course, such correctness proofs are not infallible—logical arguments that are intended to be proofs can contain mistakes. There can also be doubt that the program specifications correctly describe and capture the true goals of a program. This brings us to the subject of testing. Although testing is helpful for detecting bugs in programs, that activity too is limited. A famous adage in computer science says, "Testing can reveal the presence of bugs, but it can never prove their absence."

testing

So neither testing nor attempting to give correctness proofs are completely infallible methods for raising our confidence that programs do exactly what they are supposed to do.

One of the helpful methods for developing small programs is called *top-down programming by stepwise refinement*. In this method, we start with a top-level goal for what the program is supposed to accomplish, and we sketch a rough program strategy for how the program might go about attaining its objectives. Then, in a series of stepwise modifications, we refine the program strategy by progressively supplying more and more detail, until precise low-level details are completely filled in. We may design the top levels of the program using abstract data types—using objects and operations whose implementations are not yet known but whose expected behaviors have been precisely specified. This promotes clarity of thinking at the top level of the design, since we can write concise, lucid programs that are not contaminated with low-level details. In the later stages of refinement, we select data representations and algorithms (in parallel) to implement the top-level abstractions. This makes the whole system of parts work together cooperatively, while preserving clarity of structure in the top-level design. Such clarity of structure is important for making the program easy to understand, easy to prove correct, and easier to modify later (if the need arises).

top-down programming by stepwise refinement

Plan for the Chapter

The chapter begins by presenting a couple of examples of top-down programming with stepwise refinement. Actually, we have been using top-down programming already in the earlier parts of this book each time we refined "program strategies" into actual "programs." Given this preparation, the essential concepts should come naturally to you.

examples of top-down programming

We then study "reasoning about programs" and tackle the problem of finding the position of the largest element in an array, proving that the program that does it is correct. We introduce the idea of *assertions*—including the special kinds of assertions known as *preconditions*, *postconditions*, and *loop invariants*—and then we give a correctness proof. Following this, we show how to use the correctness proof for finding the biggest element as a step inside the proof of correctness of a selection sorting program. We then study a bit of formal logic to introduce a formal language in which we can state assertions and which we can use to reason about them precisely.

reasoning about programs

transforming and
optimizing programs

Next, we study ideas that are useful for transforming and optimizing programs to make them more efficient. We illustrate recursion removal by transforming the version of **SelectionSort** with a tail recursion (that we used in the correctness proof) into a corresponding iterative program. Then we perform a further optimization by replacing a subroutine call with its body. We compare the performance of the original and optimized versions to see how much gain in efficiency has been achieved.

program testing

Our next topic is program testing. We introduce the concepts of unit testing, integration testing, regression testing, and acceptance testing. We also introduce the concepts of stubs and drivers, and we illustrate them with examples.

measurement and tuning

We then investigate the philosophy of measurement and tuning. Oftentimes, it is surprising where the inefficiencies in programs occur, and it is hard to know in advance where programs spend their time. Frequently, over 80 percent of the execution time is spent in less than 10 percent of the code. If we can identify where the inefficiencies occur, we can often rewrite the inefficient sections to make them much more efficient. We'll compare several versions of iterative and recursive binary searching to illustrate the concepts involved.

reusable software
components

Next we turn to the topic of reusable software components. We investigate economic arguments that tell us why taking advantage of reusable components is such a good idea. In this connection, we briefly discuss the advantages of bottom-up programming.

structured programming

Finally, we discuss some concepts that help us give programs good structure so that they are easy to understand and we discuss some related concepts of what makes good program documentation.

5.2 Top-Down Programming by Stepwise Refinement

Learning Objectives

1. To learn the difference between top-down and bottom-up programming.
2. To understand the process of stepwise refinement.
3. To learn how to postpone the choice of a data representation by employing abstraction appropriately.
4. To examine how to refine choices of data structures and algorithms in parallel.

Do You Have a Winning Ticket?

winning in the lottery

In many state lotteries, you can buy a $1 ticket with an opaque coating to scratch off (see Fig. 5.1). Once you remove the coating, six numbers representing dollar amounts become visible, and you can hand in the ticket and receive the largest dollar amount repeated three or more times. If no amount is repeated three or more times, you don't win anything. Suppose your task is to write a C program that inputs the six dollar amounts from one of these scratch-off lottery tickets and prints the winning amount if there is one. If there is no winning amount $0 should be printed.

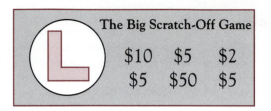

Figure 5.1 An Example of a Scratch-Off Lottery Ticket

top-down programming by
stepwise refinement

In *top-down programming by stepwise refinement*, we begin at the topmost conceptual level, by imagining a general, abstract solution. This can be expressed by sketching a program strategy in outline form before choosing any particular low-level data representations or algorithms. Then, step-by-step in progressive refinements, we make choices to fill in the details—much like the process of writing a story starting with an outline of the story's plot. Generally speaking, we choose algorithms and data structures in parallel to implement the parts of the solution sketched previously in higher-level descriptions. Eventually, we arrive at an executable C program.

investigating several
solutions

There are usually many ways to solve a problem. It's a good idea not to stop searching for solutions once a single initial solution has been sketched. Instead, it might be worthwhile to try to imagine, say, three or more solutions, and then to compare their advantages and disadvantages in order to do a thorough job of searching for a good solution.

The problem we have selected to illustrate this process is deliberately not too challenging, so that solutions will easily come to mind. Moreover, we use only one layer of refinements instead of going through several layers. Solutions to more complex problems might typically involve multiple layers of data representations and many iterations of the stepwise refinement process. By studying an easy problem with several simple, short solutions, we can compare the properties of different solutions and we can bring out some key concepts in a simple form.

At this point, the reader might take pleasure in trying to devise a solution to the problem, before reading further.

One possible solution follows the theme, "make a table and search it to find the solution." This is shown in Fig. 5.2. Another possible solution follows the theme, "sort the inputs into descending order and find the first run of three repeated amounts." This is shown in Fig. 5.3.

Let's illustrate the process of top-down programming with stepwise refinement by going through the refinement steps for the solution shown in Fig. 5.2. We can start by making a C program strategy describing the top-level goals in Fig. 5.2. This is given as Program Strategy 5.4.

To get six input amounts from the user, we might decide to use an array that can store six integers (since the whole dollar amounts given on the lottery ticket can be represented conveniently by integers). We could then write a simple input program to accept six numbers provided by the user and to store them in this array. This is our

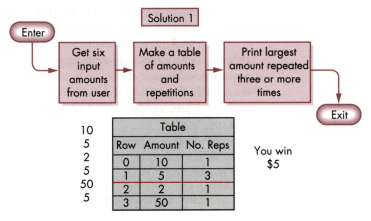

Figure 5.2 Make a Table and Search It

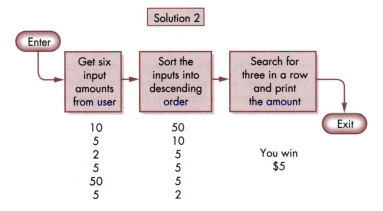

Figure 5.3 Sort the Inputs and Find a Run of Three

```
   |    void FindWinningAmount(void)
   |    {
   |
   |        (Get six input amounts from user)
 5 |
   |        (Make a Table of amounts and repetitions)
   |
   |        (Print largest amount repeated three or more times)
   |
   |    }
```

Program Strategy 5.4 Top-Level Goals for Finding Winning Amount

```
    void InsertAmount(int AmountToInsert)                    /* Insert an amount */
    {                                                         /* in the Table */

        (If one of the rows in the Table already contains the amount to insert,)
 5      (increase the number of repetitions in the row and exit the procedure)

            for (each row in the Table)  {
                if ( (the row's amount) == AmountToInsert )  {
                    (increase the row's repetition count by one)
10                  (and return from the function)
                }
            }

        (If no row's amount matched the amount to insert, then add a new row to)
15      (the table containing the amount to insert and a repetition count of one)

    }
```

Program Strategy 5.7 Inserting an Amount in the Table

```
    void FindAndPrintWinner(void)        /* Search the Table for a row having the */
    {                                    /* largest amount repeated three */
        int AmountWon;                   /* or more times and print it */

 5      (Initially establish the AmountWon to be zero.)
        (It will remain 0 unless a higher amount is discovered during the search.)

        (Search the Table to find the largest amount won among the rows)
        (having three or more repetitions)
10
            for (each row in the Table) {
                if ( (the row's number of repetitions ≥ 3) &&
                            (the row's amount  > AmountWon)  ) {
                    AmountWon = (the row's amount);
15              }
            }

        (Print AmountWon)

    }
```

Program Strategy 5.8 Printing Largest Amount Repeated Three or More Times

tion and searching operations to be used, we are in a good position to judge what kinds of representations and algorithms will work well.

Choosing a Data Representation for the Table

the advantage of postponing the choice of data representations

Note that we have given Program Strategies 5.6–5.8 for making a table, inserting new amounts into the table, and searching the table to find the largest amount won, *without having chosen the data representation for the table yet*. This means we have used abstraction to postpone the commitment to the choice of data representation for the table. Consequently, we are free to consider different table representations (such as arrays of structs representing the rows, or two-dimensional integer arrays, or linked lists of struct nodes representing the rows, or various binary tree representations that we will consider later in Chapter 11 when studying the Table ADT). And we are free to choose a representation for which there exist algorithms that efficiently implement the (insertion and searching) table operations we need to perform.

We will not get involved in the comparative advantages and disadvantages of the many possible representational choices for tables here, since we study alternative table representations thoroughly in Chapters 11, 12, and 13. However, we emphasize that this is the golden moment for selecting an advantageous data representation. The choice would be especially significant if we needed to use huge tables having efficient insertion and search times for many items. (This would be important, for instance, if we were given the problem of finding the largest amount repeated 50 or more times among 20,000 amounts. We'll see exactly how important these considerations about efficiency are in Chapter 11.) In the present case, however, the problem is so small that almost any reasonable representational choice we make for the table will be sufficient. So let's proceed to choose an array of structs for our table representation.

The following type definitions and variable declarations specify the data structures to be used in this data representation:

```
typedef  struct {
              int  Amount;              /* the dollar amount */
              int  Repetitions;         /* how many times it is repeated */
         } RowStruct;

RowStruct    Table[6];
```

Once we have made the decision to use this representation, the details of the final stepwise refinements of Program Strategies 5.6–5.8 are fairly easy to fill in.

For instance, let's now refine Program Strategy 5.6 into a detailed, executable C program. Now that we have chosen to represent the table as an array, **Table**, of up to six **RowStructs**, we can agree to keep a pointer, **LastRowUsed**, which gives the number of the last row in **Table**, used to store a **RowStruct**. We could then agree to initialize the variable **LastRowUsed** to be − 1, and then to increase it by one immediately before inserting each new row into the table. Program 5.9 contains instructions, on line 8, to perform this initialization.

We see that line 13 of Program 5.9 contains a call on a function, **InsertAmount**, which we have not written yet. Proceeding top-down, we are supposed to define the details of functions that have been called but have not yet been written. So, it is time to define the details of the function, **InsertAmount**. Program 5.10 provides these details (which refine Program Strategy 5.7).

Now that we know the details of the data representation for the table, we can fill in the details of the table searching process. To do this, we follow the outline supplied in Program Strategy 5.8, and we provide specific steps in C to accomplish its goals. The results are given as Program 5.11.

```
      void MakeTable(InputArray A)                    /* Create a Table of amounts */
      {                                                /* and their repetitions */
          int i;

5         /* To initialize the Table to be empty, we initialize */
          /* a pointer to the last row used in the Table */

              LastRowUsed = – 1;

10        /* Insert each of the six amounts into the Table */

              for (i = 0; i < 6; ++i) {
                  InsertAmount(A[i]);      /* Insert the amount A[i] into the Table */
              }
      }
```

Program 5.9 Making the Table

```
      void InsertAmount(int AmountToInsert)                    /* Insert an amount */
      {                                                        /* in the Table */

          int row;
5
          /* If one of the rows in the Table already contains */
          /* the amount to insert, then increase the number of */
          /* repetitions in that row, and return from the function. */

10            for (row = 0; row <= LastRowUsed; ++row) {

                  if (Table[row].Amount == AmountToInsert) {

                      Table[row].Repetitions++;        /* increase repetition count */
15
                      return;                  /* and return immediately afterwards */
                  }

20            }

          /* If no row's amount matched amount to insert, */
          /* then add a new row to the table containing the */
          /* amount to insert and having a repetition count */
25        /* of one */

              LastRowUsed++;

              Table[LastRowUsed].Amount = AmountToInsert;
30
              Table[LastRowUsed].Repetitions = 1;

      }
```

Program 5.10 Inserting an Amount in the Table

```
   |    void FindAndPrintWinner(void)      /* Search the Table for a row having the */
   |    {                                  /* largest amount repreated three */
   |        int row, AmountWon;                        /* or more times and print it */
   |
 5 |        /* Initially establish the AmountWon to be zero. */
   |        /* It will remain 0 unless a higher amount is */
   |        /* discovered during the search. */
   |            AmountWon = 0;
   |
10 |        /* Search the Table to find the largest amount won among the rows */
   |        /* having three or more repetitions */
   |
   |            for (row = 0; row <= LastRowUsed; ++row) {
   |                if ( (Table[row].Repetitions >= 3) &&
15 |                        (Table[row].Amount > AmountWon) ) {
   |                    AmountWon = Table[row].Amount;
   |                }
   |            }
   |
20 |        /* Print the amount won */
   |            printf("You won $ %d\n",AmountWon);
   |    }
```

Program 5.11 Printing Largest Amount Repeated Three or More Times

```
   |    void FindWinningAmount(void)
   |    {
   |        GetSixInputs(A);                    /* Get six input amounts from user */
   |        MakeTable(A);                       /* Make a Table of amounts and repetitions */
 5 |        FindAndPrintWinner( );              /* Print the largest amount repeated */
   |    }                                       /* three or more times */
```

Program 5.12 Program for Finding Winning Amount

The top-level goals given in Program Strategy 5.4 can now be refined by inserting function calls on Programs 5.5, 5.9 and 5.11. This yields Program 5.12.

Now that all the detailed, low-level functions and data representations have been completed, we can assemble them into Program 5.13, a finished program for finding a winning amount.

A Note on Program Modularity

If Program 5.13 were not a short simple program with only one instance of a table in it and having only a few simple functions, but were instead a module to be used inside a larger program, we would not let the variables **A**, **Table**, and **LastRowUsed**, declared on lines 10:12 be *global variables*, nor would we allow the functions on lines 14:19 to interact through such global variables.

Instead, we would redefine the functions to act only on their own defined function parameters (rather than acting on values of global variables), and we would bundle the rows of the **Table** together with the pointer to the **LastRowUsed** into a single

```
 1 |    /*    A Program for Finding a Lottery Winner    */
   |
   |            typedef  int  InputArray[6];
   |
 5 |            typedef  struct {
   |                         int   Amount;
   |                         int   Repetitions;
   |                    } RowStruct;
   |
10 |            InputArray        A;
   |            RowStruct         Table[6];
   |            int               LastRowUsed;
   |
   |    /* Here, insert the definitions of the functions:    */
15 |    /*    GetSixInputs          — from Program 5.5   */
   |    /*    InsertAmount          — from Program 5.10  */
   |    /*    MakeTable             — from Program 5.9   */
   |    /*    FindAndPrintWinner    — from Program 5.11  */
   |    /*    FindWinningAmount     — from Program 5.12  */
20 |
   |    int main (void)
   |    {
   |
   |        FindWinningAmount( );          /* Get inputs and print winning amount */
25 |    }
```

Program 5.13 Entire Program for Finding a Lottery Winner

composite data object, either using a struct having them as data members or using the object-oriented programming techniques discussed in Chapter 15.

An example of such data component bundling was given in the previous chapter when we defined representations for the priority queue ADT. There, a representation of a priority queue, **PQ**, was a struct having both an **ItemList** member and a **Count** member (specifying the number of items in **PQ**). Also the functions operating on priority queues carried out their actions only on their own function parameters, not on values of global variables. The "objects" defined in object-oriented programming carry this bundling process one step further by making the functions that operate on the object into "components" of the "object" so that such objects have both function components and data components.

Global variables were chosen for use in Program 5.13 in order to simplify the presentation so the reader could focus on the ideas of stepwise refinement in the absence of the clutter of extended type definitions and complex struct member selection notation required when using data object bundling to avoid the use of global variables.

A Second Refinement

Another way to find a lottery winner is to refine the second top-level strategy given in Fig. 5.3, which proposes to solve the problem by sorting the inputs in descending

```
|    void FindWinningAmount2(void)
|    {
|
|        (Get six input amounts from user)
5 |
|        (Sort the amounts into descending order)
|
|        (Search for three in a row and print it)
|
|    }
```

Program Strategy 5.14 Top-Level Goals for Finding Winning Amount

order followed by finding the first run of three adjacent identical amounts (if there is one). (In part, we perform this second refinement in order to set up an example to use in the next section on proofs of program correctness.)

First, we translate the flowchart in Fig. 5.3 into a top-level strategy, as shown in Program Strategy 5.14. To refine the goal on line 4 of that program strategy, let's agree to reuse the function, **GetSixInputs**, from Program 5.5, which gets six inputs from the user and stores them in input array **A**.

As you know, there are many ways to sort an array of numbers, **A**, into descending order. In Chapter 13, we will compare several of the most important sorting algorithms you should know about. For the purpose of performing the sorting process specified on line 6 of Program Strategy 5.14, we will use a selection sorting method. Let's make the assumption that the function call, **SelectionSort(A,0,5)**, can be used to sort the numbers in the input array, **A[0:5]**, into descending order. We will define the actual details of this selection sorting algorithm last in this section, after developing the rest of the program, so that it will be fresh on our minds when we use it as the focus for our proof of program correctness in the next section. (In other words, we assume that we can solve the sorting problem at this point in our program development, which allows us to move on to the next unsolved refinement step.)

using the selection sorting method

Let's now solve the problem of refining the goal on line 8 of Program Strategy 5.14—namely, searching for three identical numbers next to one another in an array already sorted into descending order, and printing the thrice-repeated amount, if it exists. Program 5.15 finds and prints the first amount repeated three times in succession in an array, **A**, assumed to contain numbers sorted in descending order.

The top-level Program Strategy 5.14 can now be refined by inserting the function calls that accomplish (or have been assumed to accomplish) the top-level goals. This yields Program 5.16 as our next stepwise refinement. Now we can collect all of our refined functions and place them inside a program that solves the entire problem. (We also include references to the selection sort function developed later in Program 5.19, and to its subroutine, **FindMax**, given in Program 5.20.) This yields Program 5.17, the final working program.

```
   |   void FindAndPrintWinner2(void)
   |   {
   |       int   AmountWon;                        /* the winning amount, if any */
   |       int   i;                                /* i is an index for the array A */
 5 |
   |       /* Initially establish the AmountWon to be zero, */
   |
   |           AmountWon = 0;
   |
10 |
   |       /* For each possible starting position i == 0,1,2, and 3 where a run of */
   |       /* three identical values could start in the sorted InputArray, A, check */
   |       /* to see if a run of three identical values exists, and exit if it does. */
   |
15 |           for (i = 0; i < 4; ++ i ) {
   |
   |               if ( (A[i] == A[i+1]) && (A[i+1] == A[i+2]) ) {
   |
   |                   AmountWon = A[i];       /* a winning amount A[i] was found */
20 |
   |                   break;                          /* break to exit the for loop */
   |
   |               }
   |           }
25 |
   |       /* Print the amount won */
   |           printf("You won $ %d\n",AmountWon);
   |
   |   }
```

Program 5.15 Finding the Largest Amount Repeated Three Times

```
   |   void FindWinningAmount2(void)
   |   {
   |
   |       GetSixInputs(A);                        /* Get six input amounts from user */
 5 |
   |       SelectionSort(A,0,5);            /* Sort the amounts into descending order */
   |
   |       FindAndPrintWinner2( );              /* Search for three in a row and print it */
   |
   |   }
```

Program 5.16 Top-Level Program for Finding Winning Amount

```
  |    /*     A Program for Finding a Lottery Winner    */
  |
  |    typedef        int  InputArray[6];
  |
5 |    InputArray    A;
  |
  |    /* Here, insert the definitions of the functions:          */
  |    /*    GetSixInputs           — from Program 5.5            */
  |    /*    FindMax                — from Program 5.20, below     */
10|    /*    SelectionSort          — from Program 5.19, below     */
  |    /*    FindAndPrintWinner2 — from Program 5.15              */
  |    /*    FindWinningAmount2 — from Program 5.16               */
  |
  |    int main(void)
15|    {
  |        FindWinningAmount2( );          /* Get inputs and print winning amount */
  |    }
```

Program 5.17 Second Program for Finding a Lottery Winner

We have deferred until last, the task of writing the sorting algorithm, SelectionSort(A,m,n), which sorts the subarray A[m:n] into descending order, using the method of *selection sorting*.

The idea behind selection sorting is first to *select* the largest number among the numbers in positions A[m], A[m + 1], ... , A[n], then to exchange this largest number with whatever number is in the first position A[m] (after which, A[m] is the largest number in the subarray A[m:n]), and finally to selection sort the remaining numbers in the subarray A[m+1:n]. The top-level strategy for doing this is expressed in Program Strategy 5.18. If we assume we have a function, FindMax(A,m,n), which returns the position of the largest number in the subarray A[m:n], then we can use it to refine Program Strategy 5.18 into the recursive selection sorting algorithm given in Program 5.19.

the key idea behind selection sorting

```
  |    void SelectionSort(SortingArray A, int m, int n)
  |    {
  |
  |
5 |        if (there is more than one number to sort) {
  |
  |            (Let MaxPosition be the index of the largest element in A[m:n] )
  |
  |            (Exchange A[m] ↔ A[MaxPosition] )
10|
  |            (SelectionSort the subarray A[m+1:n] )
  |
  |        }
  |
  |    }
```

Program Strategy 5.18 Selection Sorting

```
    void SelectionSort(InputArray A, int m, int n)
    {
        int   MaxPosition;          /* MaxPosition is the index of A's biggest item  */
        int   temp;                             /* temp is used to exchange items in A */
5

        if (m < n) {                              /* if there is more than one number to sort */

            /* Let MaxPosition be the index of the largest number in A[m:n] */
10              MaxPosition = FindMax(A,m,n);

            /* Exchange A[m] ↔ A[MaxPosition] */
                temp = A[m];
                A[m] = A[MaxPosition];
15              A[MaxPosition] = temp;

            /* SelectionSort the subarray A[m+1:n] */
                SelectionSort(A, m+1, n);

20      }

    }
```

Program 5.19 Selection Sorting

finding the position of
the largest

    The only remaining missing piece of our overall program that needs to be completed is to write the function, **FindMax(A,m,n)**, which finds the position of the largest integer in the subarray **A[m:n]**. This is an easy program to write, of the kind usually covered in a first programming course in C. Program 5.20 gives one solution (among many that are possible).

    In Section 5.3, we will investigate how to prove that this program does what it is

```
    int FindMax(InputArray A, int m, int n)                         /* assume m<n */
    {
        int i = m;                      /* i is an index that visits all positions from m to n */
        int j = m;                      /* j is an index that saves the position of the largest */
5                                                   /* number previously found during the search */

        do {
            i ++;                                    /* advance i to point to next number A[i] */
            if ( A[i] > A[j] ) {                       /* if A[i] > largest previous A[j] then */
10              j = i;                          /* save the position, i, of the largest number in j */
            }
        } while (i != n);                          /* stop when all i in m:n have been tested */

        return j;                                    /* return j == position of the largest */
    }                                                              /* number A[j] in A[m:n] */
```

Program 5.20 Finding the Position of the Largest Number

supposed to do. For now, we note that it is the last of the unwritten programs that needs to be defined in order to complete all the pieces needed to get the main program, Program 5.17, to work properly. Before moving on to the next section, let's pause to make two brief observations:

1. We didn't need to define another data structure while doing the second refinement, since the input array was sufficient.
2. We used *searching* in the first solution and *sorting* in the second solution. Searching and sorting are general purpose building blocks useful for solving many kinds of problems. This is why attention is given to them in computer science, in general, and in Chapter 13, in particular.

5.2 Review Questions

1. What is the difference between top-down and bottom-up programming?
2. What does it mean to postpone the choice of data representations and algorithms?
3. What is stepwise refinement? What gets refined? What are the steps in stepwise refinement?

5.2 Exercises

1. Create a different stepwise refinement of Program Strategies 5.4–5.8, using a linked list of **RowStructs** to represent the table. Each **RowStruct** in the linked list represents a row of the table, and contains: (a) a dollar amount, (b) the number of times that dollar amount is repeated in the input array, **A**, and (c) a link to the next **RowStruct** in the linked list representing the table. These items are given in the three members shown in the type definition for a **RowStruct** that follows:

```
typedef  struct RowTag {
              int              Amount;            /* the dollar amount */
              int              Repetitions;       /* how many times it is repeated */
              struct RowTag *Link;                /* pointer to next row */
        } RowStruct;

typedef  RowStruct    *RowStructPointer;
```

2. Professor van Snipe thinks the solutions produced by stepwise refinement tend to be too long. He believes that, all other things being equal, the number of program errors in an undebugged program is proportional to its size. He claims that the bigger a program becomes, the more errors it is likely to contain. He also claims shorter programs are easier to understand. He believes that for simple problems such as the lottery example, it is best to write a concise program, on the spot, without going through all the rigmarole of stepwise refinement. As evidence that a short

solution exists to the lottery problem, he offers the following program:

```
   |   int i, AmtWon = 0;
   |   int A[6];
   |
   |       int ThreeOrMore(int Amt)
 5 |       {   int j;
   |           int k = 0;
   |
   |           for (j = 0; j < 6; ++j)  if (A[j] == Amt) k++;
   |           return( k >= 3 );
10 |       }
   |
   |   int main(void)
   |   {
   |       printf("Give 6 Amounts:"); for (i = 0; i < 6; ++i) scanf("%d",&A[i]);
15 |       for (i = 0; i < 4; ++i) {
   |           if (  (A[i] > AmtWon) && ThreeOrMore(A[i]) )  {
   |               AmtWon = A[i];
   |           }
   |       }
20 |       printf("You win $ %d\n",AmtWon);
   |   }
```

Do you agree or disagree with the professor's position? Under what circumstances, if any, will clever yet obscure short solutions be undesirable in a programming project? When will concise solutions to a programming problem be advantageous, if ever?

3. A powerful programming idea is to create new programs from reusable software components. (We will explore this important idea later.) For now, suppose you had access to a C priority queue module, whose interface is given in Program 4.3, and suppose you had access to Professor van Snipe's function, **ThreeOrMore(Amt)**, given on lines 4:10 of the program in the previous exercise. Can you make use of these reusable components to refine the following program strategy into another short solution to the lottery problem?

```
   |   #include <stdio.h>
   |   #include "PQInterface.h"            /* see interface in Program 4.3 */
   |
   |   int             i, AmountWon;
 5 |   int             A[6];
   |   PriorityQueue   PQ;
   |
   |   /* Here, insert the definition of the function ThreeOrMore */
   |
10 |   int main(void)
   |   {
   |       (Initialize the priority queue, PQ, to make it empty)
   |       (Get six inputs from the user and read them into the input array, A)
   |       for (i=0; i<6; ++i) {
15 |           if ( ThreeOrMore(A[i]) ) Insert(A[i], &PQ);
   |       }
   |       AmountWon = ( Empty(&PQ)  ? 0 : Remove(&PQ) );
   |       printf("You win $ %d\n",AmountWon);
   |   }
```

4. Show that Program 5.15 can be made more efficient by replacing line 17 with the replacement line: if (A[i] == A[i+2]) { .

5.3 Proving Programs Correct

Learning Objectives

1. To understand how to annotate a program with assertions.
2. To learn about preconditions, postconditions, and loop invariants.
3. To understand the process of proving programs correct by studying some preliminary examples.
4. To learn a bit about formal logic.

the importance of reasoning about programs

Reasoning about programs is an important ability for computer scientists to master. This skill comes into play at many crucial times, such as: (a) when creating algorithms initially, (b) when debugging them, (c) when figuring out how to improve their performance, and (d) when verifying that procedures and functions inside a larger program work correctly.

In this section, we are going to walk step-by-step through an example of how to prove that a program does what it is intended to do. This process is called *program verification*.

assertions

The first problem you face in trying to prove that a program, P, does what it is *intended to do* is to come up with a precise statement of what P is intended to do. A helpful way to do this is to provide *assertions* that express the conditions both *before* and *after* P is executed. You might think of assertions as statements that can be either *true* or *false*, and that are expressed in a *precise logical language*.

preconditions and postconditions

The first assertion, called the *precondition*, describes the conditions that hold true *before* P is executed. The second assertion, called the *postcondition*, describes the conditions that hold true *after* P has been executed (assuming that the precondition was true beforehand). The general pattern is:

```
{precondition}        /* logical conditions that are true before P is executed */
P                     /* a program to execute */
{postcondition}       /* logical conditions that are true after P is executed */
```

For example, suppose we consider the function **SelectionSort(A,m,n)**, which is supposed to sort the items in the subarray, A[m:n], into descending order. To fill in this pattern in the case of **SelectionSort**, we might write:

```
{m ≤ n}               /* asserts A must have at least one item to sort */
    SelectionSort(A,m,n);     /* the sorting program to execute */
{A[m] ≥ A[m+1] ≥ ... ≥ A[n]}  /* asserts A's items are in descending order */
```

To prove that **SelectionSort(A,m,n)** sorts A[m:n] into descending order, we need to construct a proof that: if the precondition holds true and **SelectionSort(A,m,n)** is executed, then afterwards the postcondition will be true—namely, the items in A[m:n] will be rearranged into descending order: $A[m] \geq A[m+1] \geq ... \geq A[n]$.

In the process of trying to prove this final result, we may do two things: (a) place additional assertions inside the text of the **SelectionSort** program to describe intermediate conditions that arise during different phases of the computation, and (b) construct proofs of correctness of the subroutines used by **SelectionSort**, so we can use the results of the subroutines' proofs to complete the main proof.

In fact, we will start with step (b)—proving that the subroutine, **FindMax**, used by **SelectionSort**, succeeds in finding the position of the largest item in the subarray A[m:n]. Then we will use the results of this first proof inside the main proof that **SelectionSort** works properly.

The pre- and postconditions for **FindMax(A,m,n)** are as follows:

```
{m < n}                                    /* asserts A[m:n] must have more than one item */
    j = FindMax(A,m,n);                                          /* the program to execute */
{A[j] ≥ A[m:n]}                            /* asserts A[j] is the largest item in A[m:n] */
```

Here, we use the notation, $A[j] \geq A[m{:}n]$, as a synonym for asserting the truth of each of the individual assertions: $A[j] \geq A[m]$, $A[j] \geq A[m+1]$, ... , and $A[j] \geq A[n]$.

Let's now look at Program 5.21, which is a version of **FindMax** in which we have added some extra intermediate assertions. These intermediate assertions are given

```
 |     int FindMax(InputArray A, int m, int n)
 |     {
 |
 |         /* Precondition: m < n */
5|         /* Postcondition: returns position of largest item in subarray A[m:n] */
 |
 |         int i;
 |         int j;
 |
10|        i = m;
 |         j = m;
 |
 |             {♦ ( i == m) ∧ (j == m) ∧ (m < n) ♦}
 |
15|        do {
 |
 |             i++ ;
 |
 |             if ( A[i] > A[j] )  j = i;
20|
 |                 {♦ Loop Invariant: A[j] ≥ A[m:i] ∧ (i ≤ n) ♦}
 |
 |         } while ( i != n );
 |
25|            {♦ Final Assertion: A[j] ≥ A[m:n] ♦}
 |
 |         return j;                 /* return j as position of largest item in A[m:n] */
 |
 |     }
```

Program 5.21 Finding the Position of the Largest Item

inside curly braces specially marked with beginning and ending diamonds, of the general form: {♦ assertion ♦}. (In several of these assertions, the symbol, ∧, from formal logic, is used to denote the logical **and** operator.)

a step-by-step reasoning process

We will next go through a step-by-step reasoning process to show how we can reason forward from the precondition to the postcondition. Along the way, we will use the intermediate assertions together with some reasoning about the actions performed by the program's statements.

When we start to execute the program, FindMax, we can assume that the precondition (given on line 4 of Program 5.21) is true. Hence, the assertion, m < n, holds true at the moment execution begins. The first two statements to be executed are: i = m; and j = m; given on lines 10:11. After executing these two statements, the variables i and j both have the value m. Consequently, on line 13, we know that the assertion {♦ (i == m) ∧ (j == m) ∧ (m < n) ♦}, must hold true.

loop invariants

Now we come to the challenging part, which is the do-while loop, given on lines 15:23. There is only one assertion inside this loop, the loop invariant on line 21. A loop-invariant assertion is an assertion with the special property that it is always true, no matter how many times you have executed the loop.

using induction proofs

We are going to try to prove that the loop invariant always holds true using a process that resembles a proof by mathematical induction. First, we prove it holds true on the first trip through the loop. Then, assuming it holds true on the ith trip through the loop, we prove that it must hold true on the $(i+1)^{st}$ trip through the loop.

Before we enter the do-while loop for the first time, the assertion on line 13 holds true. This implies that the variable, i, has the value i == m, when the loop is entered for the first time. Executing the statement, i++; on line 17, changes the value of i to be i == m + 1. On line 19, the statement, if (A[i] > A[j]) j = i; is executed under conditions in which (j == m) and (i == m + 1). This means that in case A[m+1] is bigger than A[m], j is set equal to (m+1). Otherwise, if A[m+1] ≤ A[m], then j retains its former value, (j == m). In either case, j's value is set to the position of the larger item among the two items: A[m] and A[m+1]. This means that: A[j] ≥ A[m:m+1]. But since i == (m+1), we can rewrite this as asserting that: A[j] ≥ A[m:i], which is the first part of the loop invariant on line 21. The second part of the loop-invariant assertion, namely (i ≤ n), follows from the fact that, for any three integers, i, m, and n, if (m < n) and (i == m + 1), then (i ≤ n). (*Reason:* (m < n) means the integer m is at least 1 less than n, so adding 1 to m can make it equal to n, but can't make it greater than n.)

the induction step

Let's now tackle the hard part—reasoning inductively about what happens on the $(i+1)^{st}$ trip through the loop, assuming the loop-invariant assertion is true on the ith trip through the loop. Suppose we know that: A[j] ≥ A[m:i] ∧ (i ≤ n) is true just before we test the while-condition, while (i != n); at the end of the ith pass through the do-while loop. Suppose the while-condition (i != n) is still true, meaning we get sent around the loop one more time for the $(i+1)^{st}$ pass. Then, we need to combine two facts:

(i ≠ n)   /* from the while-condition (i != n) which was true, */
A[j] ≥ A[m:i] ∧ (i ≤ n)   /* and the loop-invariant which was true */

to get:

A[j] ≥ A[m:i] ∧ (i < n)   /* the condition that holds at the beginning */
/* of the (i+1)st trip around the loop */

We get this because (i ≠ n) and (i ≤ n) combine to yield (i < n). (*Reason:* (i ≤ n) means i was either equal to n or less than n. But i couldn't have been equal to n if (i ≠ n) was also true. Consequently, the only remaining possibility was that i had to be strictly less than n, each time we were sent back around the loop.)

On the (i+1)st trip around the loop, on line 17, we first increase i by 1, knowing beforehand that: A[j] ≥ A[m:i] ∧ (i < n). This means that after increasing i by 1, another assertion: A[j] ≥ A[m:i − 1] ∧ (i ≤ n) must hold. Now, on line 19, the statement, if (A[i] > A[j]) j = i; is executed. What this does is to compare A[j], which we know to be the largest item in A[m:i − 1], with A[i]. If A[i] is bigger, j is set to i's value, so j then points to the largest item in A[m:i], whereas if A[i] is not bigger, then even though j's value is not changed, nonetheless, j still points to the largest item in A[m:i]. In either case, after line 19 is executed, we conclude that A[j] ≥ A[m:i] must be true. Combining this with (i ≤ n), (which remained true since i's value was not changed on line 19), we conclude that after line 19 has been executed on the (i+1)st trip through the loop, the loop-invariant assertion A[j] ≥ A[m:i] ∧ (i ≤ n) still holds true. Thus we can establish that the loop-invariant assertion holds true on every trip through the loop, using an induction proof of the following form: We know the loop-invariant is true on the first trip through the loop. We also know that if it is true on any given trip, it will remain true on the next trip. Consequently, it is true on every trip through the loop.

We can finish our proof by reasoning about what happens when we exit the do-while loop on lines 15:23. Knowing the loop invariant on line 21 is true, suppose we test the while-condition in while (i != n); on line 23, and find that it is false. This causes us to exit the do-while loop. Upon exit, we can combine the knowledge that (i == n) with the conditions in the loop invariant: A[j] ≥ A[m:i] ∧ (i ≤ n). To do this, we note that (i ≤ n) simplifies to (i == n), since the alternative (i < n) couldn't have been true after we exited the loop. Moreover, we can substitute (i == n) in the first part of the condition, A[j] ≥ A[m:i], getting the result: A[j] ≥ A[m:n]. But this was the postcondition result we were hoping to establish. It asserts that A[j] is the largest item in the entire subarray A[m:n], as is stated in the final assertion, on line 25: {♦ **Final Assertion:** A[j] ≥ A[m:n] ♦}. Finally, when we return j's value as the value of the function on line 27, we can be confident j gives the position of the largest item.

finishing the proof

We're now ready to go back and prove that **SelectionSort**(A,m,n) sorts A[m:n], using the fact we just established that j = **FindMax**(A,m,n); sets j to the position of the largest item in A[m:n]. To see how to do this, we examine Program 5.22, which is a version of the **SelectionSort** program annotated with some new intermediate assertions.

The statement, MaxPosition = FindMax(A,m,n), on line 12 of Program 5.22 can be executed only when the if-condition (m < n), on line 10, is true beforehand. This means that when the function **FindMax**(A,m,n) is called on line 12, its precondition (m < n) is satisfied. We have just proven that, under these conditions, **FindMax**(A,m,n) returns the position of the largest item in A[m:n]. Consequently the variable, MaxPosition, is set to this position, and on line 14, we can assert:

```
       |     void SelectionSort(InputArray A, int m, int n)
       |     {
       |
       |         /* Precondition: m ≤ n */
   5   |         /* Postcondition: A[m:n] is sorted such that: A[m] ≥ A[m+1] ≥ ... ≥ A[n] */
       |
       |         int MaxPosition;
       |         int temp;
       |
  10   |         if (m < n) {                        /* if there is more than one item to sort */
       |
       |             MaxPosition = FindMax(A,m,n);
       |
       |                 {♦ A[MaxPosition] ≥ A[m:n] ♦}
  15   |
       |             /* exchange A[m] ↔ A[MaxPosition] */
       |                 temp = A[m]; A[m] = A[MaxPosition]; A[MaxPosition] = temp;
       |
       |                 {♦ A[m] ≥ A[m:n] ♦}
  20   |
       |             SelectionSort(A, m+1, n);  {♦ yields: A[m+1] ≥ A[m+2] ≥ ... ≥ A[n] ♦}
       |
       |                 {♦ A[m] ≥ A[m+1] ≥ ... ≥ A[n] ♦}
       |
  25   |         }
       |
       |             {♦ Final Assertion: A[m] ≥ A[m+1] ≥ ... ≥ A[n] ♦}
       |
       |     }
```

Program 5.22 Selection Sorting

{♦ A[MaxPosition] ≥ A[m:n] ♦}, meaning A[MaxPosition] is the largest item in the subarray A[m:n].

On line 17, we exchange the subarray's first item, A[m], with the subarray's largest item, A[MaxPosition]. After doing this, we assert (on line 19) that the first item, A[m], is now the largest item in A[m:n], by writing: {♦ A[m] ≥ A[m:n] ♦}.

Our final step is to sort the remaining items, A[m+1:n], into decreasing order, using the recursive call, SelectionSort(A, m+1, n), given on line 21. The effect of making this recursive call is to rearrange the items in A[m+1:n] into decreasing order, as indicated by the assertion {♦ A[m+1] ≥ A[m+2] ≥ ... ≥ A[n] ♦} on the right side of line 21. But since A[m] was not moved by the rearrangements made during the recursive call and was the largest item in the array before the recursive call was made (according to the assertion on line 19), we know that A[m] ≥ A[m+1] must also hold true after returning from the recursive call. Putting the fact, A[m] ≥ A[m+1], together with the fact, A[m+1] ≥ ... ≥ A[n], yields the final assertion: A[m] ≥ A[m+1] ≥ ... ≥ A[n], given on line 27, but only in the case that the if-statement on lines 10:25 was executed.

In the remaining case that the if-condition (m < n), on line 10, was false, combining the falsehood of (m < n) with the precondition (m ≤ n), on line 4, implies (m == n)

our final step

must have been true. In this case, A[m:n] degenerates to the subarray, A[m:m] with just one item in it, so there are no items to sort. In this case, the final assertion can be viewed as being what mathematicians call "vacuously true." Loosely translated, we could say this means that subarrays containing just one item can always be considered to be sorted in decreasing order.

Alert readers might have noticed that we used a second form of induction in constructing the proof of **SelectionSort**. This is sometimes called *recursion induction*. This method is applied by assuming that recursive calls on smaller-sized problems within the text of the main outer recursive function, correctly solve the smaller subproblems. Then the truth of the postcondition for the subproblem can be assumed inside the proof of correctness of the main recursive function. It is also necessary to prove that the postcondition holds for the base cases of the recursion.

recursion induction

(*Note:* It is furthermore necessary to prove that base cases are always encountered in a finite number of steps so that the recursion is guaranteed to stop eventually. Otherwise, an infinite regress may exist. In the case of the **SelectionSort** function, since the size of the subproblems encountered in the recursive calls goes down by one each time, and since the base case occurs when the subarray has one item in it, the **SelectionSort** function is guaranteed to terminate.)

This completes our proof that **SelectionSort** correctly rearranges the items in A[m:n] into descending order: $A[m] \geq A[m+1] \geq \ldots \geq A[n]$.

A Subtle Bug

Alert readers may have noticed a loophole in what we did. Our final postcondition, $A[m] \geq A[m+1] \geq \ldots \geq A[n]$, required only that the values in A[m:n] be in decreasing order at the conclusion of the sorting process. What if some (impish) programmer had written Program 5.23 for **SelectionSort**?

This program just replaces all the items in A[m:n] with a copy of the first item A[m]. Is this program a correct sorting algorithm?

```
  |   void ImpishSelectionSort(InputArray A, int m, int n)
  |   {
  |
  |       /* Precondition: m ≤ n */
5 |       /* Postcondition: A[m:n] is sorted such that: A[m] ≥ A[m+1] ≥ ... ≥ A[n] */
  |
  |       int i;
  |
  |       for ( i = m; i <= n; ++i ) {
10|           A[i] = A[m];
  |       }
  |           {♦ Final Assertion: A[m] ≥ A[m+1] ≥ ... ≥ A[n] ♦}
  |
  |   }
```

Program 5.23 Impish Selection Sorting

Well, according to the criteria we have been discussing, it is a correct sorting algorithm, since whenever the precondition (m ≤ n) is true, it carries out an action that makes the postcondition true. (Note that the postcondition, A[m] ≥ A[m+1] ≥ ... ≥ A[n], is true when all the items in A[m:n] are equal to A[m].)

The problem here is that the postcondition, as we have stated it, is *incomplete*. What we really intended to say was that sorting the items in A[m:n] meant rearranging them into decreasing order, without deleting or duplicating any items, or introducing any new ones. It turns out that our original selection sorting algorithm did, in fact, rearrange items without destroying any of them or adding any new ones. That this is so follows from the fact that the action of repeatedly exchanging different pairs of items (on line 17 of Program 5.22) always preserves the original items as it rearranges their order.

The flaw that we have exposed is philosophically a very deep one in software engineering. How do we know that the formal logical assertions in the preconditions and postconditions correctly and completely express the true statement of what the program is supposed to do? The answer is that we don't. We can never prove that the pre- and postconditions really capture the intentions of the program. All that a correctness proof accomplishes is to prove the correspondence between statements expressed in a language of logical assertion and the net effect of executing actions defined by the statements in the program. It can tell us that the net effect of executing those statements is to create the situation described by the postconditions, provided the preconditions held true beforehand. It cannot tell us that the formal description given by the pre- and postconditions completely captures the true meaning that the people who wrote them should have had in mind. That is, a proof of correctness won't reveal to us the fallacies that might exist when the pre- and postconditions fail to state something important that should have been captured and expressed, but was in fact left out.

This is one of the reasons why software engineers use extensive program testing in addition to techniques such as correctness proofs. Doing correctness proofs helps raise our confidence that the program will do what it is supposed to do. But testing helps raise this confidence further. In fact, thorough testing may help reveal cases where the program didn't work as intended—cases that were missed because the pre- and postconditions didn't completely capture all the possible situations in which the program was meant to work.

A Bit of Formal Logic

Reasoning about programs benefits from the use of precise thinking. Sloppy, error-prone reasoning is seldom helpful. A good way to attain precision in logical reasoning is through the correct use of formal logic.

In fact, if you have already taken a first course in C programming, you already know a lot of useful things about formal logical reasoning. Specifically, the C programming language contains logical expressions formed from things like: (1) variables, (2) relational operators (such as '>' in X > 3), and (3) logical operators (such as &&, ||, and !). Each logical expression has a value which is either 1 (for *true*) or 0 (for *false*). Logical expressions used in programming correspond to a class of propositional expressions used in what is called *propositional logic*, and the propositional expressions used in propositional logic are, in turn, a subset of an even larger set of expressions used in what is called *predicate logic*. Roughly speaking, you can think of propositional logic as using a slightly extended class of C's logical expressions, and you can think of predicate logic as adding *quantifiers* to propositional logic. Quantifiers express ideas such as, "For all x, $P(x)$ is true," symbolized as $\forall x P(x)$, or "There exists an x, such that $P(x)$ is true," symbolized as $\exists x P(x)$. (This treatment is oversimplified slightly. In particular, C's "short-circuit" operators **&&** and **||** do not correspond exactly to the logical *and* ($\wedge$) and *or* ($\vee$) operators of logic.)

For example, let's consider how to express the idea that "the array element A[j] is the biggest element among the elements in the subarray, A[m:n]." The subarray, A[m:n], consists of the individual array elements: A[m], A[m + 1], ... , A[n]. To say that A[j] is the biggest among these is the same as saying that $A[j] \geq A[m]$, $A[j] \geq A[m + 1]$, ... , and $A[j] \geq A[n]$. By using the quantifier, "for all," we can say this in another way, in English, as: "For all integers, i, if i lies in the range ($m \leq i \leq n$), then it is true that $A[j] \geq A[i]$." Using symbols in predicate logic, this could be written as, "$\forall i [(m \leq i \leq n) \supset (A[j] \geq A[i])]$." (Here, the horseshoe symbol in $A \supset B$, is a logical connective that is pronounced "A implies B," which means, "*if* A is true, *then* B must be true.")

using quantifiers

In the correctness proof given previously, we avoided using logical quantifiers ($\forall$ and $\exists$), by using two special notations. First, we used the expression, "$A[j] \geq A[m:n]$," to mean that A[j] was greater than or equal to each of the elements in the subarray A[m:n]. Second, we used the ellipsis (three dots in a row "..."). The occurrence of an ellipsis in the expression A ... B signifies that all the missing elements in the sequence between A and B are filled in. For example, to indicate that the elements in A[m:n] were arranged in decreasing order, we wrote: "$A[m] \geq A[m + 1] \geq ... \geq A[n]$." The only logical connective we used in our proof above was the "and" operator ($\wedge$). But in addition to this "and" operator, there are a few other logical operators that are worth considering. Table 5.24 presents five logical connectives commonly used in propositional calculus and the quantifiers used in first-order predicate calculus.

It is important for you to build up some skill in manipulating and stating formal logical expressions.

For example, to state that A[m:n] is sorted in decreasing order without using the ellipsis (...) as we did above, we could write: $\forall i [(m \leq i < n) \supset (A[i] \geq A[i+1])]$. In English, this is pronounced as follows: "For all i, if i is greater than or equal to m and is strictly less than n, then A[i] is greater than or equal to A[i+1]." There are many laws of logical equivalence that can be used to manipulate formal logic expressions. You probably know some of them already from your earlier study of C programming. For instance, some C courses cover deMorgan's laws: $\sim(A \wedge B) \equiv ((\sim A) \vee (\sim B))$ and $\sim(A \vee B) \equiv ((\sim A) \wedge (\sim B))$.

DeMorgan's laws can be extended to cover existential quantifiers ($\exists x P(x)$) and universal quantifiers ($\forall x P(x)$), as follows: $\sim(\forall x P(x)) \equiv (\exists x [\sim P(x)])$ and $\sim(\exists x P(x)) \equiv (\forall x [\sim P(x)])$.

Expression	Pronunciation	The expression is *true*:
~A	not A	when A is *false*
A ∧ B	A and B	when both A and B are *true*
A ∨ B	A or B	if either A or B is *true*
A ⊃ B	A implies B	if A is *true*, then B is *true* also
A ≡ B	A is equivalent to B	only if A and B are both *true* or A and B are both *false*
∀ x P(x)	for all x, P(x)	P(x) is *true* for all possible x
∃ x P(x)	there exists an x, such that P(x)	there exists an x, such that P(x) is *true*

Table 5.24 Logical Symbols and Their Meanings

There are also many logical laws that allow us to replace a subexpression inside a bigger logical expression with something that is equivalent, or to deduce that an expression Q must be true if P is true beforehand and we also know that P ⊃ Q holds true. A few of these laws are shown in Table 5.25.

Let's study just two examples of the uses of these laws to illustrate how they can be applied to the process of logical manipulation of assertions.

First, suppose you wanted to show that if the subarray A[m:n] is not sorted in decreasing order, then there exists an adjacent pair of items, A[i] and A[i+1], such that A[i] < A[i+1]. Could we possibly show this by formal logical manipulations? The answer is, yes. Here's how. We start with the logical expression, E, that defines when A[m:n] is sorted in decreasing order. Then to assert that A[m:n] is not sorted, we could assert ~E.

$$E \equiv \quad \forall i\,[(m \leq i < n) \supset (A[i] \geq A[i+1])]$$

$$\sim E \equiv \sim (\forall i\,[(m \leq i < n) \supset (A[i] \geq A[i+1])])$$

Now, we manipulate the right side of the last line by applying several exchange laws in sequence, as shown in Table 5.26.

A ⊃ B	≡	(~A) ∨ B	The definition of *implication*
A ≡ B	≡	(A ⊃ B) ∧ (B ⊃ A)	"≡" is sometimes called *coimplies*
A ∧ (A ⊃ B)	⊃	B	This law is called *modus ponens*
(A ∨ B) ∧ (~B)	⊃	A	The *modus tollendo ponens* law
~(~A)	≡	A	The double negation law

Table 5.25 Some Logical Laws

$\sim (\forall\, i\, [(m \leq i < n) \supset (A[i] \geq A[i+1])])$	The expression to manipulate
$\sim (\forall\, i\, [(\sim(m \leq i < n)) \vee (A[i] \geq A[i+1])])$	Using $[A \supset B] \equiv [\, (\sim A) \vee B]$
$\exists\, i \sim [(\sim(m \leq i < n)) \vee (A[i] \geq A[i+1])]$	DeMorgan's law for $\sim(\forall\, x\, P(x))$
$\exists\, i\, [(\sim(\sim(m \leq i < n))) \wedge \sim(A[i] \geq A[i+1])]$	DeMorgan's law for $\sim(A \vee B)$
$\exists\, i\, [(m \leq i < n) \wedge \sim(A[i] \geq A[i+1])]$	Double negation law $\sim\sim A \equiv A$
$\exists\, i\, [(m \leq i < n) \wedge (A[i] < A[i+1])]$	Since $\sim(x \geq y) \equiv (x < y)$

Table 5.26 Some Formal Logic Manipulations

translating back into English

Now we translate the last line back into English. It says, "There exists an i such that i lies in the range (m ≤ i < n) and (A[i] < A[i+1])." You can see that this is the same as saying that there exists an adjacent pair of array items A[i] and A[i+1] inside the subarray A[m:n], such that A[i] < A[i+1], which is exactly what we wanted to show.

Now you might say, "Why do we need to do all this strenuous formal manipulation, when it is intuitively obvious that if a subarray A[m:n] is not sorted in decreasing order, then there *has to be* some pair of elements that are not in decreasing order?" One possible answer to this question is that the formal manipulation can help us check our intuitive, informal reasoning when doubts arise concerning whether we are absolutely certain that we have reasoned correctly.

Our second example comes from the correctness proof of the **FindMax** function given in Program 5.21. When we were trying to prove by induction that the loop invariant on line 21, $\{\blacklozenge\ A[j] \geq A[m:i] \wedge (i \leq n)\ \blacklozenge\}$, was true each time through the do-while loop, we assumed by induction that it was true on the ith trip, and then tried to prove it true on the $(i+1)^{st}$ trip. As part of this process, we used the fact that if we evaluated the while-condition, on line 23, and found that (i != n), then we would repeat the loop again. We then combined the fact that (i != n) with the assertion that (i ≤ n), given inside the loop invariant, and we concluded that (i < n) had to hold true. Table 5.27 illustrates how we can justify using this formal logic.

formal logic helps when complexity clouds our reasoning

Few people would have any doubt about the validity of the following story. "The clay tablets were either in the King's chamber or they were on the Scribe's writing table. The Scribe determined that they weren't on his writing table. Therefore, they had to be in the King's chamber." This is a straightforward application of the law of

$(i \leq n) \wedge (i\, != n)$	To start with
$((i < n) \vee (i == n)) \wedge (i\, != n)$	Expanding $(i \leq n)$
$((i < n) \vee (i == n)) \wedge \sim (i == n)$	Replacing $(i\, != n)$ with $\sim (i == n)$
$(i < n)$	Applying the *modus tollendo ponens* law from Table 5.24

Table 5.27 Another Formal Logic Manipulation

modus tollendo ponens, at the level of common sense. But when we are reasoning about programs, intuition can sometimes become clouded by complexity. Under these circumstances, the ability to do a little formal logical expression manipulation can help raise our confidence that our reasoning is correct.

Unfortunately, space does not permit us to go much beyond this brief and sketchy introduction to the subject of formal logic. However, the experience of many computer scientists suggests that time invested in acquiring some skills in formal logic and formal reasoning pays dividends later. One immediate benefit to the practical programmer is an improved ability to reason about and simplify complex logical conditions in if-statements, while-loops, and do-while-loops in C. The last section of the "Math Reference" appendix gives a table of helpful rules for performing logical manipulation on propositional expressions (of which the logical expressions found in C programs are frequently instances).

5.3 Review Questions

1. What is an assertion inside a program?
2. What is a precondition?
3. What is a postcondition?
4. What is a correctness proof for a program?
5. What is a loop invariant?
6. What role do loop invariants play in correctness proofs?

5.3 Exercises

1. Translate the following expression from logic into English:

   $$\exists K \, [\, \exists n_0 \, [((K > 0) \wedge (n_0 > 0)) \supset \forall n \, [(n > n_0) \supset (\,|\,g(n)\,|\, < K\,|\,f(n)\,|\,)]\,]\,]$$

2. Translate the following expression from logic into English:

   $$\exists k \, [(1 \leq k) \wedge (k \leq n) \wedge \forall i \, [((1 \leq i) \wedge (i \leq n)) \supset (A[k] \geq A[i])]\,]$$

3. Translate the following expression from English to formal logic: "For any $\varepsilon > 0$, there exists a $\delta > 0$, such that if $|\,x - c\,| < \delta$, then $|\,f(x) - f(c)\,| < \varepsilon$."

4. Translate the following expression from English to formal logic: "There exists a k in the range $(1 \leq k \leq n)$ such that $A[k] \leq A[i]$ for all i in $(1 \leq i \leq n)$."

5. The logical denial of an assertion A is ~A, which is obtained by applying the logical negation operator to A. Take the logical denial of the assertion in Exercise 1 and then simplify it by applying DeMorgan's laws and other transformations from Tables 5.25 and 5.26.

6. What is the loop invariant inside the while-loop in the following program? After annotating the program with appropriate assertions, prove that it correctly computes the sum of the integers in the array A[0:n−1].

```
      int Sum(InputArray A, int n)                    /* assume n > 0 */
      {
          int i = 0, S = 0;

5         while ( i < n ) {
              S += A[i];
              i++;
          }
          return  S;
      }
```

7. Let $n!$ denote the product of the integers in the range $1{:}n$. Given the assertions annotating the following factorial program, prove that it correctly computes $n!$.

```
      int Fact(int n)
      {
          /* precondition: n is an integer such that n ≥ 0 */
          /* postcondition: Fact(n) == n! */

5
                          {♦ ( n ≥ 0 ) ♦}
          if (n > 0) {
                          {♦ ( n > 0 ) ∧ ( (n − 1) ≥ 0 ) ♦}
              Fact = n * Fact( n − 1);
10                        {♦ Fact == n! ♦}
          } else {
                          {♦ ( n == 0 ) ♦}
              return 1;
                          {♦ Fact == 1 ♦}
15        }
                          {♦ Fact == n! ♦}
      }
```

≡ **5.4** Transforming and Optimizing Programs

Learning Objectives

1. To understand program transformations.
2. To understand an example of tail recursion elimination.
3. To appreciate how applying transformations can improve program efficiency.

In this section, we are going to transform the **SelectionSort** program of the previous section, in order to improve it. Making a function call incurs a certain *overhead* consisting of extra program execution time spent: to transfer the parameters, to make the call, and to return from the call. If we can eliminate calls from a program, we can sometimes get the program to run faster.

recursion elimination   In the case of a recursive program, we can sometimes eliminate the recursive calls inside the program, by converting it to an equivalent iterative program. This is called *recursion elimination*. Usually, the equivalent iterative program is more efficient, since it avoids the overhead of making repeated recursive calls. Another way to eliminate calls that can be used sometimes is to substitute directly the body of a function in place of the function call.

Generally speaking, we can manipulate programs using what are called *program transformations*. Program transformations can be thought of as exchange laws that permit us to replace one form of a program with an equivalent form—or perhaps a subexpression inside a program with an equivalent subexpression.

program transformations

Program transformations include familiar laws of algebraic manipulation and logical expression manipulation. For instance, Program Transformation 5.28 illustrates how to perform a series of replacements inside an if-statement in a program.

It is clear why the if-condition (i < n) is simpler to compute than the original if-condition (i <= n) && (i != n) that it replaced. Also, comparing the polynomial ((x + 3)*x + 5)*x + 2 with the polynomial x*x*x + 3*x*x + 5*x + 2 that it replaced, we see that it takes three additions and five multiplications to evaluate the original polynomial, but only three additions and two multiplications to evaluate the replacement polynomial.

To generalize then, ordinary algebraic and logical manipulations can be used to transform and improve programs. But we shouldn't stop there. It might be profitable to view programs themselves (and parts of programs such as compound statements) as an extended set of expressions that can be manipulated using appropriate exchange laws. By this means, we might open up a wider range of possible program improvements than if we limited ourselves merely to rearranging logical and algebraic expressions inside programs. Some transformations of the **SelectionSort** program from the previous section illustrate these ideas.

Let's start with the text of the **SelectionSort** program, which is reproduced as

```
if ( (i <= n) && (i != n) ) {          /* original if-statement */
    y = x*x*x + 3*x*x + 5*x + 2;
}

              ⇓                         /* ⇓ means "transforms to" */

if (i < n) {                           /* first, replace condition in if-statement, */
    y = x*x*x + 3*x*x + 5*x + 2;        /* using results from Table 5.27 */
}

              ⇓

if (i < n) {                           /* second, replace the polynomial on the */
    y = ((x + 3)*x + 5)*x + 2;          /* right side of the assignment */
}
```

Program Transformation 5.28 Improving Expressions in an If-Statement

```
|    void SelectionSort(InputArray A, int m, int n)
|    {
|        int MaxPosition, temp;
|
|        if ( m < n ) {
5 |           MaxPosition = FindMax(A,m,n);
|            temp = A[m]; A[m] = A[MaxPosition]; A[MaxPosition] = temp;
|            SelectionSort(A, m+1, n);
|        }
|    }
```

Program 5.29 Recursive Selection Sorting Without Comments

Program 5.29, without comments and with fewer blank spaces (to shorten the size of the program to be transformed).

The recursive call **SelectionSort(A, m + 1, n)**, on line 7 of Program 5.29, is called a *tail recursion*, since it is a recursive call that occurs at the tail end of the program. Program Transformation 5.30 enables us to eliminate tail recursions that are given inside if-statements. Line 5 of the top program in this program transformation contains the tail-recursion call **P(e1, e2, e3)**, where **e1**, **e2**, and **e3** represent actual parameter expressions used in the function call. The formal parameters of function **P**, are represented by **a**, **b**, and **c**, on line 1.

The tail-recursion elimination transformation converts the if-statement into a while-loop and replaces the tail-recursion call with assignment statements that assign the actual parameter expressions to be values of the formal parameters of the function.

Applying Program Transformation 5.30 to Program 5.29, yields Program 5.31.

```
|    void P(a,b,c)
|    {
|        if (condition C1) {
|            (statements S1)
5 |           P(e1, e2, e3);            /* this line contains the tail recursion */
|        }
|    }

                ⇓

|    void P(a,b,c)
|    {
|        while (condition C1)  {
|            (statements S1)
5 |           a = e1; b = e2; c = e3;
|        }
|    }
```

Program Transformation 5.30 Tail-Recursion Elimination[1]

---

[1] In general, for this transformation to work, statements **S1** cannot contain recursive calls.

```
    |       void SelectionSort(InputArray A, int m, int n)
    |       {
    |           int MaxPosition, temp;
    |
5   |           while ( m < n ) {
    |               MaxPosition = FindMax(A,m,n);
    |               temp = A[m]; A[m] = A[MaxPosition]; A[MaxPosition] = temp;
    |               A = A; m = m+1; n = n;
    |           }
    |       }
```

Program 5.31 Selection Sorting after Tail-Recursion Elimination

```
    |       void SelectionSort(InputArray A, int m, int n)
    |       {
    |           int MaxPosition, temp;
    |
5   |           while ( m < n ) {
    |               MaxPosition = FindMax(A,m,n);
    |               temp = A[m]; A[m] = A[MaxPosition]; A[MaxPosition] = temp;
    |               m ++;
    |           }
    |       }
```

Program 5.32 Selection Sorting After Useless Assignment Elimination

This function is not quite in final form, since two of the three assignments created by literal application of the tail-recursion elimination transformation are useless. Specifically, on line 8 of Program 5.31, we can eliminate the useless assignments: A = A; and n = n; and we can replace m = m+1; with m++; this yields Program 5.32.

Next, we will transform Program 5.32 by replacing the function call FindMax(A,m,n) with the body of the function given in Program 5.20. It is reproduced without comments and with fewer blank spaces as Program 5.33. To replace the function call FindMax(A,m,n) in the assignment statement MaxPosition = FindMax(A,m,n); on line 6 of Program 5.32, with the text of Program 5.33, we first have to substitute

```
    |       int FindMax(InputArray A, int m, int n)          /* assume m<n */
    |       {
    |           int i, j;
    |
5   |           i = m; j = m;
    |           do {
    |               i++;
    |               if ( A[i] > A[j] )  j = i;
    |           } while (i != n );
10  |           return j;
    |       }
```

Program 5.33 Finding the Position of the Largest Number

the assignment MaxPosition = j; for the statement return j; on line 10, inside the body of Program 5.33, and we also have to add the declarations of the variables i and j to the declaration section of the resulting transformed version of Program 5.32. This transformation yields Program 5.34.

It is even possible to eliminate the variable j from lines 7:12 of Program 5.34, since j plays exactly the same role as the variable, MaxPosition. This yields Program 5.35.

Let's now compare the efficiency of the original unoptimized recursive version of SelectionSort, given in Program 5.29, with that of the optimized iterative version, given in Program 5.35. Table 5.36 compares the running times in milliseconds for these two programs on arrays of various sizes. You can see from the data in that table that recursive SelectionSort, as given in Program 5.29, has running times that are between 9.5 percent and 11.4 percent longer than those for the iterative SelectionSort, given in Program 5.35. This tells us that our program transformations bought us about a 10 percent improvement in running time. These improvements in performance resulted mostly from the elimination of the overhead involved in calling subroutines both nonrecursively (as in the case of FindMax) and recursively (as in the case of the recursive calls on SelectionSort inside itself).

what improvements did we achieve

It turns out that iterative SelectionSort takes less space during execution than recursive SelectionSort does. This is because "call-frames" for the recursive calls need to be allocated in C's run-time memory management system. For an array of size n, there are (n − 1) of these recursion call-frames. By contrast, the iterative version of SelectionSort uses only one call-frame for its (single) call. So the iterative version is more efficient both in *time* and in *space*. We will study further the manner in which C allocates space for call-frames in Chapter 7 in the section on stacks.

However, it seems more complicated to devise a correctness proof for Program 5.35 than for recursive SelectionSort. The subroutine and recursive structure of the

```
|      SelectionSort(InputArray A, int m, int n)
|      {
|           int MaxPosition, temp, i, j ;
|
5 |        while ( m < n ) {
|
|               i = m; j = m;
|               do {
|                   i++;
10 |                if ( A[i] > A[j] ) j = i;
|               } while ( i != n );
|               MaxPosition = j;
|
|               temp = A[m]; A[m] = A[MaxPosition]; A[MaxPosition] = temp;
15 |
|               m++;
|           }
|
|      }
```

Program 5.34 Almost Final Iterative Selection Sorting

```
    |     void SelectionSort(InputArray A, int m, int n)
    |     {
    |         int MaxPosition, temp, i;
    |
 5  |         while ( m < n ) {
    |
    |             i = m;
    |             MaxPosition = m;
    |
10  |             do {
    |                 i++;
    |                 if ( A[i] > A[MaxPosition] ) MaxPosition = i;
    |             } while (i != n);
    |
15  |             temp = A[m]; A[m] = A[MaxPosition]; A[MaxPosition] = temp;
    |
    |             m++;
    |         }
    |
    |     }
```

Program 5.35 Iterative Selection Sorting from Transformations

original recursive design for **SelectionSort** helped to break the overall correctness proof into simple steps. We were able to use the correctness proof of **FindMax** as a building block in the construction of the correctness proof of recursive **SelectionSort**.

Suppose we had a way of knowing that the program transformations we used preserved program correctness. Then the following philosophy of correct program development might be open to us. First, we might be able to write very concise, lucid top-level programs. Because these top-level programs would be short, simple, and clear, we might find it easy to prove them correct. Then we might be able to apply program transformations to them to optimize them and make them more efficient, perhaps at the expense of making them more detailed and less easily understood. Some of these transformations might even accomplish stepwise refinements of the original top-level programs—by selecting data representations and algorithms to refine top-level abstractions, for instance. These ideas lie at the heart of a philosophy of software development called transformational programming, which has been explored by software engineering researchers.

the method of transformational implementation

Array size n	Iterative SelectionSort	Recursive SelectionSort
125	3.5	3.9
250	13.9	15.4
500	55.4	61.1
1000	221.1	242.8
2000	884.4	968.6

Table 5.36 Iterative Versus Recursive SelectionSort Running Times (in milliseconds)

5.4 Review Questions

1. What is a program transformation?
2. Can we use exchange laws from algebra and logic to transform programs?
3. Mention two program transformations that are not simply instances of either algebraic or logical equivalence laws.

5.4 Exercise

1. Eliminate the tail recursion from the following program, which reverses a string by swapping the characters at its "edges":

```
    |    void ReverseString(char *S, int m, int n)    /* to reverse the characters */
    |    {                                            /* S[m:n] in string S */
    |        char c;
    |
 5  |        if ( m < n ) {
    |            c = S[m]; S[m] = S[n]; S[n] = c;      /* first, swap the edges */
    |            ReverseString(S, m+1, n – 1);         /* then reverse the center */
    |        }
    |    }
```

Run a timing experiment to compare the running times of the recursive and iterative versions of **ReverseString**. How much does the elimination of the tail recursion reduce the running time performance of **ReverseString**?

5.5 Testing Programs

Learning Objectives

1. To learn about unit, integration, regression, and acceptance testing.
2. To learn how to use test drivers and stubs.
3. To understand the separate roles of testing and verification.
4. To understand the difference between top-down and bottom-up testing.
5. To appreciate the value of formatted debugging aids.
6. To understand what a test plan is.

If you want to produce quality software, one of the most important skills you can learn is how to perform thorough and systematic program testing.

how do you go about testing?

Suppose you have created a detailed design for a software system, perhaps in the form of a document that gives English descriptions of the data structures and variables you'll need, plus some explicit program strategies for each of the system's functions (using, say, C containing English comments, to express your detailed design plans). You have refined your detailed design into actual C code, and now you are ready to test your overall program piece-by-piece. How should you proceed?

Bottom-Up Testing

Even though you may have used *top-down design with stepwise refinement* as a strategy for arriving at your detailed design and refining it into actual C code, it may make sense to proceed in the *opposite* order when testing. That is, it may make sense to proceed *bottom-up*. What does this mean? Suppose you first try to identify pieces of your program that are at the bottom level of your code—a set of functions, S_1, that do not call any of the other functions. These are the bottommost functions in your system (since they don't call on any lower-level ones). You begin testing these bottom-level functions thoroughly, in order to make sure they are working properly, before doing anything else. Now you have confidence that the functions in S_1 are working components, suitable for use in subsequent activities.

Next you identify another layer of functions, S_2, which make calls on the functions in S_1, but which do not call on any others. You then test the functions in S_2. Following this, you identify the next layer of functions, S_3, which make calls on functions already tested in S_1 or S_2, and you test the functions in S_3.

Proceeding in this fashion, at each stage you identify a new layer of functions, S_n, which make calls on those you have already tested, and you expand the collection of tested parts of your overall system by testing the functions in S_n. Eventually, you get to the final, topmost layer of the program—the "main program" part of your system's design—and you test that.

Figure 5.37 illustrates a possible arrangement of layers of functions that are parts of a larger software system. The downward pointing arrows represent calling relationships. For example, the node labeled A represents the main program that calls functions B, C, and D. Function B, in turn, calls functions E, F, I, and J.

The layer S_1, consisting of functions I, J, K and L, is the bottommost layer, since it consists of functions that are called by higher-level functions but do not call any lower-level functions. You would test the functions in layer S_1 first.

Layer S_2 is the second-to-bottom layer. In bottom-up testing, after testing the functions in layer S_1, you would test the functions in layer S_2. The tests of functions in layer S_2 could make calls on already tested functions in layer S_1. Likewise, the tests of functions in layer S_3 could make calls on already tested functions in layers S_1 and S_2.

In bottom-up testing, sometimes the order of testing among functions is influenced by the manner in which the functions manipulate data, as well as by the order

layers of functions

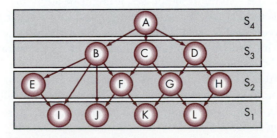

Figure 5.37 Layers of Functions in a Software System

in which they make calls on one another. For instance, you would test an initialization function that sets up the initial values in a table or a list before testing any function that operates on the table or list, assuming it had already been initialized.

mutually recursive functions

In some cases, functions are mutually recursive. For instance, given three functions X, Y, and Z, it may happen that X calls Y, Y calls Z, and Z calls X. In such cases, you have to test all three functions at the same time, in a "cluster" so-to-speak.

There is just one key idea that defines the bottom-up order of testing.

> **Bottom-Up Testing Order Principle:** Whenever possible, before testing a given function, X, test all functions that X calls or that prepare data that X uses.

Unit Testing, Formatted Debugging Aids, and Test Drivers

Suppose now that you have identified a bottom-up testing order for the functions in your software system. It's time now to answer a key question: "How are you supposed to test a given function?"

Testing a given function is called *unit testing*. (Note: The term unit testing originated with and is often used in industrial software engineering practice.)

testing boundary cases

It's important to use tests that thoroughly cover all the possible behaviors of a function, if feasible. All the different execution paths through the code in the function should be exercised, if possible. It is especially important to test "boundary cases." For example, what happens when a table or list is empty, or when a table is full? Does the function correctly handle these cases? What happens in a loop, when no iterations occur, as in the case of the following for-loop, when n == 5?

```
|     for (i = 10; i <= n; ++i) {
|          (some statements)
|     }
```

Or what happens when a sorting routine is given an array that is already in sorted order? It is important to build up your skill for imagining all the possible special cases that can occur—especially the unusual ones. Sometimes this is quite hard to do, as in the case of trying to test a user interface to see that it doesn't break when used by naive users who can do the strangest things when they don't understand how to use the system. In such cases, it might be advisable to find some actual naive users and get them to bang away at the interface in order to elicit the kinds of unusual behavior that system designers find hard to imagine (since the system designers' thinking is usually strongly influenced by expectations for how the system is supposed to behave).

checking initializations

It's also important to check that data structures are initialized properly, and that all data structures created by a function are left in well-formed condition. For example, in creating a linked list, it is important to make sure that the last cell has a null link in it.

```
|    /* print picture of D before executing R */
|         R;              /* then call function R */
|    /* and print picture of D after executing R */
```

Figure 5.38 Before-After Testing with Formatted Debugging Aid

About 30 years ago, in the dawn of the evolution of software engineering practice, it was discovered that formatted debugging aids were of special importance. A formatted debugging aid is simply a function that prints (or draws a graphical display of) a data structure. It was discovered that debugging times for a software project could often be cut in half if formatted debugging aids were implemented *first*, before implementing and testing the rest of the system.

formatted debugging aids

If you want to follow this philosophy, you should first implement and test a set of print functions that can display every possible data structure your software system uses. Then you can build up test functions that use these print functions to print the *before* and *after pictures* of each data structure that a given function changes. A test case for a function R that alters some data structures D might then assume the form shown in Fig. 5.38.

before-after pictures

Another important idea is to implement what are called *test drivers*. A test driver, T, for a function, S, is a function that enumerates test cases for S, calls S for each test case, and checks the outputs afterward to see that they are correct.

test drivers

Integration Testing

In the philosophy of bottom-up testing, unit testing is performed first to check the behavior of each function in the system. Following this, *integration testing* is performed. In integration testing, you check that combinations of the functions work together properly.

Even though you have ascertained that each of the unit functions in a system works correctly, there is still room for error. Perhaps, in your system design, you overlooked some possible conditions that arise when one function, S, creates inputs for another function, T, that function T was not designed to handle. Perhaps T's test driver has already tested T and found that it meets its specifications. But T's unit specifications may have been wrong and may not have taken into account the inputs S could create for T.

checking that things work together

When a system grows in size and complexity, things naturally get confusing. Mismatches can occur between the inputs a function is designed to handle and the inputs actually given to it by its callers. Integration testing is designed to check that the interactions between the parts of the system occur as expected, and that the parts do, in fact, cooperate successfully to achieve correct overall system behavior.

Acceptance Testing and Regression Testing

Using test drivers, a battery of tests can then be put together to exercise each of the functions in a system and to test them thoroughly. Moreover, integration tests, which exercise combinations of the parts working together, can be used to furnish additional batteries of tests. In some cases, these batteries of tests can be made to run automatically, without human intervention, and they can deliver printed test results for later inspection.

Assuming you have created a *test suite* consisting of batteries of thorough unit and integration tests that run automatically, you are in a position to accomplish two more important testing activities: *acceptance* and *regression testing*.

Acceptance tests are tests that are run before a system is released into active service. Sometimes, there is a formal development contract between the client who is acquiring the system and the system builder. Such a contract may specify that the system is not legally considered to have been "delivered" until it passes an acceptance test. The contract may even specify what the acceptance test is, or that another independent contractor will be hired to devise and conduct the acceptance test.

acceptance testing

Once the system is released into service it enters what is called the *maintenance phase* of its software lifecycle. During maintenance, software errors are discovered and fixed, and, almost inevitably, the system gets upgraded to perform new functions that are needed to ensure that it remains useful to its users under changing conditions of use. After a bug is fixed or the system is upgraded to do something new, it is of course important to test that the bug was actually removed or that the new feature actually works. Moreover, it is important to check that everything that used to work still continues to work properly. *Regression testing* thus means checking that everything that used to work before a change was made still continues to work after the change is installed.

regression testing

A discipline is usually followed when applying test suites during regression testing. It has four steps: (1) find a bug; (2) fix the bug; (3) add a test case to the test suite that tests whether or not the bug was fixed; and (4) run the test suite.

A *word to the wise*: You'd be surprised how often the elimination of a bug or the introduction of a new feature causes something else in the system to "break." Regression testing is designed to catch such problems before a new system is released into use. This practice enables software maintainers to avoid the unhappy situation in which users become predictably irate when they discover that what used to work last week in the old system release no longer works this week in the new release.

Top-Down Testing and Stubs

Bottom-up testing makes sense, since it means you always check out the behavior of the parts before testing the behavior of anything else that uses them. Nevertheless, there are circumstances in which you may want to do the reverse by testing the top levels of a system *before* testing the components that it uses. The latter order of testing is called top-down testing.

Referring again to Figure 5.37, a top-down testing order would mean testing function A before testing functions B, C, and D. In general you would test layer S_{i+1} before testing layer S_i, in top-down testing order.

Why would anyone want to do this? Wouldn't it complicate matters immensely to test function A before knowing that B, C, and D worked properly? Wouldn't it be difficult to find the cause of any misbehavior the test revealed, since any of A, B, C, and D could have caused it? By contrast, with bottom-up testing, if you are confident that B, C, and D are working properly, then when you test A, it is highly likely that

```
|    double Compound(double A, double r, int n)
|    {
|         return ( A * Power(1 + r/100, n) );
|    }
```

Program 5.39 Investment Growth under Compound Interest

any misbehavior that results is A's fault. You can see that the advantage of bottom-up testing is that it enables you to assign blame for misbehavior to different small regions of the program text when troubles arise, and to ascertain that each component in your system works, one step at a time, in a logical progression.

In top-down testing, if the first thing you do is to fire up and test the topmost function in the system, which can potentially call any other function in the system, then you may not be able easily to localize the cause if the test reveals faulty behavior.

stubs This is where the concept of *stubs* comes in. A stub is a function that stands in place of another function (that will be written later), and can *fake* its output on certain test cases. For example, suppose you decide to do top-down testing of the following function to compute the growth in an invested amount of money A, which accumulates compound interest at an interest rate of r percent over a period of n years. This is illustrated in Program 5.39.

This calls on the function, Power(1 + r/100, n), where Power(x,n) is supposed to compute the exponential quantity, x^n. Your test driver will test the function Compound(A,r,n), by making three test calls:

```
Compound(100,6.0,5);     /* $100 invested at 6% for 5 years */
Compound(100,6.0,0);     /* $100 invested at 6% for 0 years */
Compound(100,0.0,5);     /* $100 invested at 0% for 5 years */
```

These three test cases will make three respective calls on Power(x,n), which are: Power(1.06,5), Power(1.06,0) and Power(1.00,5).

Suppose now that the function Power(x,n) is not yet available for use in your top-down testing activities. In the absence of the real thing, you could write a stub that fakes the behavior of Power(x,n) in exactly the three test cases you are going to use, as shown in Program 5.40.

Now you can use your stub to fake the expected outputs for Power(x,n) in top-down tests of Compound(A,r,n) provided you stick to your intention to use only the three test cases specified above.

```
|    double Power(double x, int n)
|    {
|         if ( (x == 1.00) || (n == 0) ) {
|              return 1.00;            /* since 1^n == 1 and x^0 == 1 for any x and n */
5  |         } else if ( (x == 1.06) && (n == 5) ) {
|              return 1.3382256;                  /* since 1.06^5 == 1.3382256 */
|         }
|    }
```

Program 5.40 Stub for Power(x,n)

when to use
top-down testing

Now let's consider some circumstances in which you might want to perform top-down testing. Suppose you are working on a software project with five teammates. You have completed the design of your system and you have divided the work into five subprojects in which four of you will implement separate modules providing services for (a) the data calculations required, (b) the user interface, (c) printing reports, and (d) saving and restoring files of data. A fifth teammate has the job of writing the main part of the system that uses these four modules to (1) accept and interpret user commands and (2) execute commands to open or close files, perform computations, and print reports. Your team is on a tight schedule and each of you would like to test your section of the code before you can expect to call on tested, working software components supplied by your other teammates. By using stubs to fake the actions you expect the missing components eventually will perform, you can test your piece of the system in parallel with the development of the other pieces of the system by your teammates, or in advance of their efforts so that they can use your finished pieces in bottom-up testing of their work. You can see that top-down testing can be used to accelerate an implementation schedule that might otherwise have to be stretched out to accommodate serial dependencies.

testing mutually
dependent components

Another case in which top-down testing is useful is when the modules or components comprising a system are mutually dependent—meaning that each one uses the services of the others. In this case, using stubs to fake the expected actions of the other pieces enables the pieces to be tested independently before trying to test them together.

Test Plans

test plan documents

When software projects advance from small-scale projects to medium or large-scale ones, a helpful practice is to write a *test plan* document. A test plan enumerates the test cases, including inputs and the corresponding expected outputs, the purposes of the tests, and the exact conditions under which it can be claimed that tests succeed or fail. Test plans can be subjected to analysis for thoroughness of coverage and for whether or not they ensure that the system design specifications have been achieved.

Comparing the Roles of Testing and Verification

Testing and verification are each different activities that can help to raise our confidence that a given module works as intended. However, each activity has its weaknesses.

testing and verification
complement one another

Testing can reveal the presence of bugs, but it can never prove their absence (in all but the simplest of cases where every possible behavior can be checked). On the other hand, verification can check only the correspondence between a statement of what a program is supposed to do (expressed by some assertions in the formal language of logic) and the actions performed by the program. However, verification cannot prove that these formal logical assertions correctly and completely capture the true program intentions.

Recall, for a moment, the example stating that a program which is supposed to sort the array A[m:n] into descending order is supposed to satisfy the ordering assertion

A[m] ≥ A[m+1] ≥ ... ≥ A[n]. And recall that this assertion was incomplete because it failed to mention that sorting was supposed to be accomplished only by rearranging the order of the original items in A[m:n] without deleting any. In the absence of the complete assertion, A[m:n] could have been sorted by a nonsensical program such as for (i = m; i <= n; ++i) A[i] = A[m];. This revealed the problem of the possible incompleteness or inaccuracy of the assertions used in verification.

Consequently, the benefits of both testing and verification complement one another. Each helps to raise our confidence that a program does what it is supposed to do, but neither alone is completely sufficient to accomplish this task.

5.5 Review Questions

1. What is the difference between unit testing and integration testing?
2. Explain the concepts of regression testing and acceptance testing.
3. What is the difference between bottom-up testing and top-down testing?
4. What are stubs and test drivers?
5. Why is it wise to implement formatted debugging aids before implementing a system?

5.5 Exercises

1. Draw the calling relationships for all the functions used in Programs 4.10, 4.11 and 4.12. Draw dotted lines around the layers and label the bottommost layer S_1, the second-to-bottom layer S_2, and so on. Finally, give an ordered list of function names in bottom-up testing order.
2. Do the same for the functions in the priority queue sorting Programs 4.5 and 4.7.

5.6 The Philosophy of Measurement and Tuning

Learning Objectives

1. To understand the philosophy of measurement and tuning.
2. To learn how measurement and tuning techniques can help make a program run more efficiently.

The *philosophy of measurement and tuning* is a method for improving the efficiency of actual running programs. Experienced programmers have frequently found two things to be true about programs: (1) Oftentimes a disproportionate amount of the running time (say 80 to 90 percent) is spent in a small portion of the code (say 7 to 10 percent), and (2) Oftentimes the places where a program is inefficient are surprising and difficult to predict.

Since it is hard to predict where the inefficiencies will occur, it makes sense *first* to measure the running program and find out, and *second* to do something about it.

Once you have identified the region(s) where the program is spending most of its time, you then know the place(s) where it pays off to try to improve the program's efficiency. You then concentrate on trying to replace inefficient code with better code in these critical regions. Next, you measure the results to see how much improvement has been achieved. You might need to iterate the process of introducing trial improvements and measuring their effects. This latter process is called *tuning*.

Some modern programming environments provide tools for measuring where a program is spending its time. One type of tool for doing this is called an *execution-time profiler*. You turn on the profiler and conduct a trial run of the program you are measuring. The profiler then gives you a breakdown of what percentage of the total time was spent in different places in the code for the program. Some versions provide a pictorial histogram. Others create a file associating the names of functions with the percentage of time spent in them during the test run.

execution-time profiles

If you don't have access to a profiler, perhaps your system has access to a real-time clock. In this case, you can still gain useful information by measuring the time spent by a function, P, that is repeatedly executed inside a test driver. You can arrange to have your test driver print the difference between the starting time and stopping time of the real-time clock, divided by the total number of times function P was executed. This yields the approximate average running time for function P. (If you find that the measured average time was distorted by the fact that some overhead time, consumed by the test driver, was included in the measurement, you can often arrange to measure the time consumed by the test driver running an empty test. The test driver time can then be subtracted out to get an undistorted measure of the correct test time.)

In this section, we will provide a dramatic illustration of the point we are trying to make by comparing the running times for several versions of iterative and recursive binary searching.

Comparing Some Methods for Binary Searching

Since most introductory computer science courses and textbooks cover the process of binary searching, we will assume you know a little bit about it from your past experience. We will review the subject here, and we will compare some solutions.

The problem to be addressed in binary searching is to find the position of a search key, K, in an ordered array A[0:n−1] of distinct keys, (arranged, say, in ascending order: A[0] < A[1] < ... < A[n−1]).

The method is to choose the key in the middle of A[0:n−1], which is located at A[Middle], where Middle = (0 + (n−1)) / 2, and to compare the search key K and A[Middle]. If K == A[Middle], the search terminates successfully, since K has been found at the middle position of A[0:n−1]. On the other hand, if K < A[Middle] then further search is conducted among the keys to the left of A[Middle] (since all of the keys to the right of A[Middle] are greater than K). But if K > A[Middle], then further search is conducted among the keys to the right of A[Middle] (since all the keys to the left of A[Middle] are less than K).

a sketch of the method

In short, either we are *lucky* by finding K == A[Middle] on the first try, so that we can stop immediately, or we are *fortunate*, because we can continue searching in either

we are either lucky or fortunate

the left half array or the right half array, confining our search to a problem only half as big as the original one. By repeatedly halving the size of the search interval where we look for **K**, we rapidly converge on the solution. (Characterizing just how rapidly this works will be studied further in Chapter 6.)

but it's tricky to do it right

Actually, binary searching is one of those algorithms having a simple general plan, for which it turns out to be tricky to work out the details. In one study, more than 80 percent of a group of programmers with more than a year's programming experience got their first versions of binary search wrong when asked to write one. There are many ways to write the conventional iterative binary searching algorithm. The version given in Program 5.41 is fairly straightforward.

```
   int BinarySearch(Key K)                         /* to find the position of the search */
   {                                               /* key K in the ordered array A[0:n−1] */

       int L;                                      /* L == left boundary of search interval */
5      int Midpoint;                               /* Midpoint == midpoint of search interval */
       int R;                                      /* R == right boundary of search interval */

       /* Initializations */
           L = 0;                                  /* Initially, L is the leftmost index,  0, and */
10         R = n − 1;                              /* R is the rightmost index, n − 1 */


       /* While the interval L:R is non-empty test K against the middle key */

15         while ( L <= R ) {                      /* while the interval is non-empty */

               Midpoint = (L+R) / 2;               /* Compute midpoint of interval L:R */

               if ( K == A[Midpoint] ) {           /* if key K was found at the Midpoint, */
20                                                  /* return from the function */
                   return Midpoint;                /* with Midpoint as the result */

               } else if ( K > A[Midpoint] )  {    /* otherwise, if K is to the */
                                                   /* right of the Midpoint, search */
25                 L = Midpoint + 1;               /* next in the interval Midpoint+1:R */

               } else {                            /* whereas if K is to the */
                                                   /* left of the Midpoint, search */
                   R = Midpoint − 1;               /* next in the interval L:Midpoint−1 */
30             }

           }


35     /* If the search interval became empty, key K was not found */

           return − 1;                             /* −1 means K was not in A[0:n−1] */
   }
```

Program 5.41 Iterative Binary Search

This version of binary searching divides A[0:n−1] into a middle item, A[Middle], a left subarray A[0 : Middle − 1], and a right subarray A[Middle + 1 : n−1]. If we don't find that K == A[Middle] then we search further in the left or right subarrays, depending on whether K > A[Middle] or not.

Because it is so difficult to write a binary search program that works properly, it is helpful to illustrate briefly a technique for applying a small, thorough set of test cases. First, we initialize an array, A[10], to contain squares: 1, 4, 9, ... , 100, with the code:

```
int i, A[10];                              /* declare A[0:9] to be an array of integers */
for ( i = 0; i < 10; ++i )  A[i] = (i + 1)*(i + 1);    /* let A[i] == the square of (i+1) */
```

Not only do we test *successful searching* for each of the keys, i^2, in the array A, we also test all the cases for *unsuccessful searching* by looking for keys of the form, i^2−1 and i^2+1. In particular, when testing unsuccessful searching, we test all possible "gaps" between keys in A (including before A[0] and after A[9]).

```
for ( i = 1; i <= 10; ++i ) {                           /* test all keys and gaps in A[0:9] */
    if (BinarySearch(i*i) != (i−1) ) printf("key %d not found in A[%d]\n" ,i*i, i−1);
    if (BinarySearch(i*i + 1) != − 1 ) printf("result for key %d != −1\n",i*i+1);
    if (BinarySearch(i*i − 1) != − 1 ) printf("result for key %d != −1\n",i*i−1);
}
```

The solution to the binary searching problem can also be expressed naturally as a recursive algorithm because binary searching breaks down the overall searching problem into a combination of base cases and subproblems that are half as big and that can be solved by applying the same search method recursively. (It is instructive for the reader to try writing a recursive binary search program before looking at the solution.) Program 5.42 presents a recursive binary searching algorithm.

expressing binary search recursively

It is interesting to compare the efficiency of the recursive and iterative versions. Let's find out what happens when we measure actual running times. Table 5.43 presents some experimentally measured running times for the iterative and recursive versions of the binary search Programs 5.41 and 5.42. The numbers give *average running times* measured in microseconds. By average running times, we mean running times averaged over searches of all of the n keys in an ordered array of keys, A[0:n−1], where each of the n keys is equally likely to be used in the search. The data in this table tell us that for small numbers of keys, such as n == 10, the recursive version is 23 percent more expensive, and for larger numbers of keys, such as n == 800, the recursive version is 35 percent more expensive.

comparing the programs to see why

If you study the differences between the iterative Program 5.41 and the recursive Program 5.42, you'll conclude that the recursive program makes a recursive call each time it tries to solve a subproblem (consisting of searching in a nonempty interval of keys half as big as the original interval), whereas the iterative version simply performs one assignment (to adjust one of the endpoints of the search interval to confine it to a new search interval half as big) and then returns to perform another iteration of its main loop. The difference in running times could then be explained by the hypothesis that the time required to make recursive calls is significantly greater than that required to perform a simple assignment in order to adjust

```
     |    int BinarySearch(Key K, int L, int R)
     |    {
     |        /* To find the position of the search key K in the subarray A[L:R]. */
     |        /* Note: To search for K in A[0:n−1], the initial call is */
  5  |        /* BinarySearch(K,0,n−1). */
     |
     |        int Midpoint;
     |
     |        Midpoint = (L+R) / 2;                      /* compute midpoint of interval L:R */
 10  |
     |        if  ( L > R) {                             /* If the search interval is empty then */
     |            return −1;                             /* return −1 to signal K is not in A[L:R] */
     |        } else if ( K == A[Midpoint] ) {
     |            return Midpoint;
 15  |        } else if ( K > A[Midpoint] ) {
     |            return BinarySearch(K, Midpoint+1, R);
     |        } else {
     |            return BinarySearch(K, L, Midpoint−1);
     |        }
 20  |
     |    }
```

Program 5.42 Recursive Binary Search

the search interval size.

So far, what we have discovered isn't too surprising. We already know that, when both underlying algorithms are in the same complexity class, recursion is likely to be a little less efficient than iteration due to the fact that function calls take an amount of overhead time that is almost always greater than the times required to make simple adjustments and return to the beginning of a loop.

but, beware! often things aren't so simple

But now it is time for some surprises associated with the fact that small changes in the algorithms being measured may cause surprisingly large changes in their running times. Sometimes, what may at first seem to be a relatively trivial change, may actually cause an increase in the running time so large that it dwarfs the difference in running times between iteration and recursion. To bring this issue into sharper focus, let's look at the data in Table 5.44.

Table 5.43 Iterative Versus Recursive Binary Search Running Times (in microseconds)

Array Size	Iterative Version	Recursive Version
10	3.5	4.3
50	5.1	6.7
100	5.9	7.9
200	6.8	9.1
400	7.6	10.3
800	8.5	11.5

Table 5.44 Iterative Versus Recursive Binary Search Running Times (in microseconds)

Array Size n	Iterative Version A	Iterative Version B	Iterative Version C	Recursive Version
10	3.5	11.8	110.0	4.3
50	5.1	19.2	185.6	6.7
100	5.9	22.7	221.0	7.9
200	6.8	26.3	257.4	9.1
400	7.6	30.0	294.6	10.3
800	8.5	33.7	332.0	11.5

Table 5.44 shows running times for three versions of iterative binary searching labeled as versions A, B, and C. Version A is the same as that given in Program 5.41. Version B is the same as version A, but with the variables L, R, and Midpoint declared to be double precision integers (long ints) instead of single precision integers (on lines 4:6 of Program 5.41). Version C is the same as version A, but with the computation of the midpoint, given as Midpoint = (L+R) / 2; on line 17 of Program 5.41, replaced with Midpoint = (int) floor((L+R) / 2.0);. That is, version C replaces the integer division of (L+R) by 2 of version A with floating point division, which returns a floating point result, and then takes the floor of this floating point result by discarding its fractional part, after which it converts the result to an integer. Version C was compiled with a C compiler that did not produce code to utilize the floating point operations of the underlying computer, but instead called on floating point simulation routines. Typically, to simulate floating point operations requires from 30 to 50 non–floating point instructions.

The recursive version in the last column of Table 5.44 is the same as Program 5.42. Iterative version A and the recursive version in Table 5.44 are identical to the iterative and recursive versions compared in Table 5.43.

a not so innocent change

The apparently innocent change of declaring the three integer variables L, R, and Midpoint to be double precision integers has caused roughly a fourfold increase in running time between iterative version A and iterative version B. The new version B now takes up to three times longer to run than the recursive version, whereas iterative version A was more efficient than the recursive version. All the advantage of using iteration over recursion has been lost three times over by this one supposedly innocent change. Matters get far worse with iterative version C, which runs up to 30 times slower than the recursive version.

Moral: Things are not what they seem to be. Seemingly innocent differences in the details of an algorithm may make more of a difference in their running times than can be saved by replacing the known inefficiency of recursion by the somewhat greater efficiency of iteration.

repeatability of experiments

Repeating the experiments and measurements given above might well yield quite different results when performed with different C compilers and different computers. We live in a world where the details can make significant differences. Component costs incurred by a different computer or compiler could well yield substantially different running time results. For instance, on the same computer as used above, a C compiler that compiles code to take advantage of floating point instructions might well yield substantially reduced running times for iterative version C. And on a supercomputer that efficiently processes double precision integers, there may be no running time differences between iterative versions A and B.

That such differences could occur only emphasizes the importance of using the philosophy of measurement and tuning if you are trying to improve the efficiency of your programs.

5.6 Review Questions

1. Explain the philosophy of measurement and tuning?
2. What is an execution-time profile tool (or a profiler, for short)?
3. Does experience show that most programs consume running time approximately uniformly throughout their code, or is the distribution of time consumed often more uneven?
4. What do you do when tuning a program to make it more efficient?
5. Give some examples of cases in which small changes in a program can cause surprising differences in efficiency.

5.6 Exercises

1. Find the inefficiency in the following program, and then tune it to improve its running time.

```
       int FindMin(InputArray A, int m, int n)    /* To find the minimum integer */
       {                                            /* in the subarray A[m:n] */
           int LeftMin, RightMin, Middle;           /* where m ≤ n */

   5       if ( m == n ) {
               return A[m];
           } else {
               Middle = (int) floor( ( m + n ) / 2.0 );
               LeftMin = FindMin(A,m,Middle);
  10           RightMin = FindMin(A,Middle+1, n);
               if ( LeftMin < RightMin ) {
                   return LeftMin;
               } else {
                   return RightMin;
  15           }
           }
       }
```

2. Compile the four versions of iterative and recursive binary searching used in Table 5.44, and measure their running times on your computer. Do your results agree or disagree with those in Table 5.44? What do your results tell you about the value of the philosophy of measurement and tuning?

3. Can you rewrite Program 5.41 so that it uses only one comparison of key **K** with A[Midpoint], instead of two, in the while-loop on lines 15:32? If so, how much does this improve its efficiency? Measure your results by conducting timing experiments.

5.7   Software Reuse and Bottom-up Programming

Learning Objectives

1. To learn about software reuse and programming with reusable software components.
2. To understand the rudiments of software productivity and how productivity can be increased by making use of reusable components.

Suppose you want to build a radio. You wouldn't begin by wrapping your own capacitors starting with tin foil and wax, nor would you smelt your own iron ore to make magnets for the speakers. Instead, you might start with antennas, speakers, dials, and power supplies as ready-made components, and you might then try to put them together.

Now let's consider what you do when you build software. First, an inescapable truth is that you have to start with components at some level any time you build software—even the lowest possible level components which are individual keystrokes at your keyboard. However, if you can use higher-level components, you can build higher-level systems more easily, quickly, and reliably than if you "roll your own," starting from scratch. In many cases—for example, if you are using operating system services for file system calls, printer calls, and so on—you have no choice because you are forced to use the level of components supplied by the system you must interface with. But at other levels of system design, such as computer graphics functions, you often have a choice. For instance, you can either "roll your own" or acquire and use functions from a library.

you must always use components at some level

Oddly enough, in order to gain the understanding necessary for making sense in our later discussion of software reuse, we need to digress for a moment to consider the subject of software economics. In software economics we try to understand what determines the cost of performing various software activities in software system development. Costs can be measured in terms of resources required to accomplish a given task. For example, the costs associated with building a given software system might include (a) the number of person-months of effort needed and (b) the amount of computer resources needed (computer time, disk storage, etc.). Ultimately, the various kinds of resources used may be priced in dollars, yielding an overall dollar cost figure.

some software economics

One important equation predicting the effort required to build the most familiar class of software system comes from Barry W. Boehm's COCOMO model (the word COCOMO is an acronym for "COnstructive COst MOdel"[2]). This equation gives the

---

[2] See Boehm's book, *Software Engineering Economics*, Prentice-Hall, Englewood Cliffs, N.J. (1981). Two other classes of software projects have COCOMO equations with different constants.

number of person-months (PM) required to build a system in terms of the size of the system, as follows:

$$PM = 2.4*(KDSI)^{1.05} \qquad\qquad (5.1)$$

Effort Required to Build a Software System

The quantity KDSI refers to the *Kilo-Delivered Source Instructions* in the system. For example, if a documented, delivered software system had 37,600 lines of source code, it would have 37.6 KDSI (i.e., 37.6 thousand lines of source code). Boehm's equation predicts that 108.2 person-months would be required to build this system. (108.2 PMs are approximately nine person-years of effort).

adjusting the initial estimate

Actually, Equation 5.1 gives a *baseline* estimate, which is used only as a first approximation. To arrive at a refined estimate, this first approximation has to be adjusted, using some multipliers that depend on various characteristics of the software project. For instance, experienced software teams are much more productive than inexperienced teams, so a multiplier of 0.55 might be used to adjust the initial estimate to predict the effort required by an experienced software team. (Here, 108.2 PMs multiplied by 0.55 equals 59.5 PMs, which means that the experienced team might take only 59.5 person-months to complete the same project that an average team would take.) There are other multipliers in Boehm's model based on things like the adequacy of the computer resources available and the severity of the constraints the system being built has to meet.

software size is the biggest cost driver

However, a key fact implied by Equation 5.1 is that the effort required to build a software system is an *exponential function* of its size. This implies that size is the biggest *cost-driver* of the cost of building a software system. Consequently, all other things being equal, if you can reduce the size of the software you are required to build, you can accomplish the greatest possible reduction in the effort needed to build it.

This is where the notion of building software from reusable software components comes in. If you can acquire a set of useful software components and if you can figure out how to use them to build your system (in a fashion that meets the system requirements), then you may be able to reduce dramatically the effort required to build it, compared to writing it from scratch, starting with a blank page. The reason why is because Equation 5.1 tells you that your cost of construction is the cost of implementing the "glue" to compose the software components, rather than the cost of implementing the components themselves. The number of KDSI required to implement "glue" almost always is dramatically less than the number of instructions required to implement the components.

estimating software project costs

For example, suppose a company called Contemporary Software, Inc., is under contract to build a word processor system, called WP-2000. It can either start from scratch, or it can buy both a *system shell* and a *library of word processing routines* from two separate commercial sources. It compares two ways of building WP-2000: (1) start from scratch, using 68,546 as the estimate of the number of lines of source code required to build WP-2000, or (2) buy the system shell and library for $50,000 each and implement 34,273 additional lines of source code (consisting of glue code plus original lines of code needed to implement functions not provided in the library and the shell). *Question:* Which alternative is cheaper, if a fully burdened person-year of programmer effort costs $100,000? (The term "fully burdened" means that the cost of a person-year includes computer time, worker benefits, and company overhead costs.) Assume that Equation 5.1 has been determined to be an accurate predictor of effort under the conditions existing in the WP-2000 project at Contemporary Software.

In the case of alternative (1), we can use Equation 5.1 to predict the number of person-months needed to build WP-2000. By plugging 68.546 into Equation 5.1 we determine that 203.2 PMs are required. This translates into 16.94 person-years, which costs $1,694,000 at $100K per person-year.

In the case of alternative (2), it costs $100,000 to buy both the system shell and library, and it requires 98.15 PMs to implement the remaining 34,273 lines of code. But 98.15 PMs equals 8.18 person-years (PYs), which costs $818,000 at $100K per PY. Thus the total cost of alternative (2) is $918,000, which is only 54 percent of the cost of writing the system from scratch. If the project leaders at Contemporary Software can trust their estimating equations, these results indicate that working with reusable software components is clearly preferable to writing WP-2000 from scratch.

programming with reusable components wins

While the WP-2000 project is an example of medium-scale programming, lying somewhere between programming-in-the-small and programming-in-the-large, the ideas about software reuse and software economics that it illustrates are applicable to programming on any small or large scale.

Even before you graduate from college, you may be faced with a situation in which you alone, or you and some teammates, are assigned to build a small, yet substantial, piece of software. If you are faced with such a task, you might want to remember to consider using software component libraries, or prefabricated system shells, if any are available. The use of such components and shells can substantially cut the amount of work you need to do and can make much brighter the prospects for finishing on time (or within the amount of effort you can afford to devote). The use of table-driven software component generators is also worth considering by the same reasoning.

avoiding debugging costs

Remember, too, that debugging times are included in the estimates given by Equation 5.1. When you use components from a well-tested software component library, you are starting with reliable, proven components. If you implement your own from scratch, the debugging times needed to develop the components into reliable trustworthy condition may be quite considerable, especially if you don't entirely understand the task at the outset (and who does?). Using library components could then represent a very intelligent cost-avoidance strategy on your part.

when is bottom-up programming an advantage?

This brings us once again to the subject of bottom-up programming. In bottom-up programming the strategy is to implement general purpose software components first, and then to assemble them together into higher-level systems. Under some economic conditions—associated with developing proprietary reusable software component libraries—bottom-up programming may be preferable to top-down programming.

gaining competitive advantage

Even though it is nearly twice as expensive for Contemporary Software to implement WP-2000 starting from scratch as it is to purchase and use software components, the company may nevertheless decide to start from scratch, reasoning as follows: "If we start from scratch and implement our own set of proprietary word processor components and our own proprietary system shell, then we will finish the job of writing WP-2000 with some very important extra corporate assets. Namely, we will own proprietary reusable components (and we'll have the in-house expertise that comes from having built them). If we take care to implement our word processor components in a popular language that compiles on almost all types of computers, we will then be in a position to rehost WP-2000 on other platforms (i.e., on other kinds of computers). This will put us in a highly competitive posture in the future."

winning market share

There is much more to gaining a foothold in the commercial software market than the short glimpse of considerations mentioned here. (For example, to win market share, you may need to analyze the competition, analyze the available market niches, estimate the cost of advertising needed to capture your projected market share, and determine whether you have the capital to accomplish your objectives.) You can see how software economics begins to interact with the skills required of business executives, and how business expertise in marketing, financing, advertising, and project management all enter into the picture.

Another important consideration in developing reusable software components is to build the components so they can serve many general purposes, if possible. Object-oriented programming (OOP) techniques can help meet this goal. We will have more to say about this subject in Chapter 15.

Whether you contemplate small, medium, or large scale programming, the wisdom you can glean from thinking about the issues in this section might consist of an expanded awareness, based on two important facts:

1. The effort required to build software is an exponential function of its size.
2. Making use of reusable components can reduce the size of software you need to build.

5.7 Review Questions

1. Why does making use of reusable software components reduce the effort required to build a given software system?
2. What is Boehm's COCOMO equation relating the size of a software system to the person-months required to build it?
3. What is bottom-up programming? When might it be useful to plan to implement a software system using bottom-up programming?

5.7 Exercises

1. A software system, called *VisiPhysics*, to be used for visualizing physics data, is estimated to require 56,000 lines of source code to implement starting from scratch, but it is estimated to require only 32,000 lines of extra source code to be implemented starting with two numerical and graphics subroutine libraries. If programmer time costs $100,000 per PY and the two libraries cost $150,000 each to purchase, is it cheaper to implement *VisiPhysics* by starting from scratch, or by

buying and using the two libraries? (Assume that Equation 5.1 accurately predicts the effort needed on the *VisiPhysics* project.)

5.8 Program Structuring and Documentation

Learning Objectives

1. To review a few concepts for good program structuring.
2. To discuss some ideas that help produce good documentation.

Most beginning C courses cover elementary concepts of good program structuring. In this section, we will review a few of these structuring concepts and we will consider the characteristics of effective program documentation. We can highlight only a few of the structuring concepts here, since program structuring has been the subject of many entire books.

some general software requirements

Our starting point is to consider the properties good programs should have. Generally, software engineers try to build software to satisfy *requirements* that state what characteristics the software is supposed to have in order to meet the needs of its users. Certain requirements are common to most software: (1) it should work properly and be free of errors; (2) it should be as efficient as it needs to be; (3) it should be completed on time and within budget; and (4) it should be modifiable in the future in response to needs to upgrade it.

programming proverbs

Oftentimes advice on helpful practices is given in the form of a set of proverbs or aphorisms about programming. Table 5.45 gives a small list of some of the most common ones.

using meaningful variable names

Let's consider proverb (a) in Table 5.45. You can perform your own experiments to convince yourself that programs are hard to understand in the absence of well-chosen, meaningful variable names. To do this, take some common algorithms from one of your early programming classes, and replace the meaningful identifier names with neutral meaningless names (such as x, y, and z for variables, or F and G for function names). Then ask friends who took the class with you to figure out what the changed program does. Do they have trouble? If they do, does this suggest to you that human memory for what programs do might function so as to associate meaning with well-chosen names, as opposed to structural program features?

As an example, try to figure out what Program 5.46 does. When you succeed, go back over your solution method. Was it obvious at first what it did because you

Table 5.45 Some Programming Proverbs

(a)	Use meaningful names for your variables.
(b)	Define named constants once at the beginning of your program.
(c)	Avoid using goto's and never write spaghetti code.
(d)	Write short functions that do just one thing and do it well.
(e)	Modularize your programs so the parts interact cleanly and simply.

```
 |     float G(float x, int n)
 |     {
 |         float p;
 |
5|         if ( n == 0 ) {
 |
 |             return 1.0;
 |
 |         } else {
10|
 |             p = G(x, n / 2);
 |
 |             if ( n%2 == 0 ) {
 |                 return p * p;
15|             } else {
 |                 return x * p * p;
 |             }
 |
 |
 |         }
20|
 |     }
```

Program 5.46 Mystery Program—What Does This Do?

instantly recognized its structural features as being familiar to you? Or were you puzzled at first? Did you then attempt to try it out on various data values and make a table of inputs and outputs to see if you could find a pattern of some sort?

Now let's discuss the significance of proverb (b) in Table 5.45. Suppose you are writing a computer program that computes various geometric figures to display in a computer-graphic user interface. You discover you need to use the constant, π, in several formulas, such as the formulas for the area and circumference of a circle ($A = \pi r^2$ and $C = 2 \pi r$). Knowing the value $\pi = 3.14159$ and lamenting the lack of Greek letters on your computer, you decide to write 3.14159 everywhere that π is needed.

defining named constants

Suppose that, at some later time, your program has gotten quite big—say 9,000 lines distributed across seven separate C modules. You discover a bug that indicates the value for π you had been using didn't have quite enough numerical precision, and that you should have used the value 3.141592654 instead. If you had used defined constants at the beginning of your modules, you could have changed the definition:

```
        #define Pi   3.14159                        /* 6 digit value for Pi */
```

into:

```
        #define Pi   3.141592654                    /* 10 digit value for Pi */
```

But, alas, now you will have to search for each occurrence of 3.14159 in your 9,000 lines of code and replace it with the new value. And what if you made a typographical error, typing in one of the values of π which was accidentally typed incorrectly as 3.14195? Your text search procedure may be too literal-minded to locate such erroneous values. In fact, maybe the accuracy problems you discovered resulted from improperly typed values for π in just a few places. How can you know for sure?

If you learn to concentrate your definitions in one place (such as at the beginning of your programs or in special header files), you can always be confident that any changes you decide to make need to be made in only one place. This principle applies not only to named constants but also to named C data types, to functions, and to special values, such as strings used for formatted printing. If you concentrate these in one place, rather than spreading them all over your program and duplicating them, your program is likely (a) to be easier to modify, (b) to contain fewer errors, and (c) to be easier for a reader to understand. You can see how following this proverb could enhance the dimensions of desirable software quality such as modifiability, correctness, and ease of comprehension.

concentrating your definitions in one place

Let's skip over proverb (c) in Table 5.45 concerning the avoidance of goto's and spaghetti code, since the principles behind it are almost always covered at length in first courses in computer science. (The key idea is simple—write programs using structured features of the programming language at hand which make the structure of the text mirror the structure of the control in the program.) We also will not cover proverb (e), which was covered extensively in the last chapter.

Let's look only at proverb (d), which states, *Write short functions that do just one thing and do it well.* What could possibly be behind this prescription? Why not attempt to write functions packed with functionality, so that they do as much as possible in the shortest amount of code? Wouldn't the latter policy tend to produce highly efficient programs? Wouldn't legibility and correctness be easy to guarantee, using good documentation and program verification practices?

keep it simple,

The wisdom behind proverb (d) expresses a problem-solving strategy that says the following, in essence: "Programming is known to be a complex, error-prone cognitive activity. When human beings try to consider too many things at once, they have trouble keeping all the details straight. Consequently, to control cognitive complexity and to keep it manageable, it makes sense to try to break down complex problems into simple subproblems."

since programming is complex and error-prone

Let's take a look at a problem that has, by now, become a classic in the literature on the psychology of programming—the problem of finding the average rainfall in New Haven. The problem is to write a program that will ask the user to input values for daily rainfalls in New Haven and that will print the average rainfall at the end. The user signals the end of the data by inputting a special *sentinel* value, 99999. Negative rainfalls are illegal. The program should give an error message upon encountering a negative rainfall value, and it should not count such a negative rainfall value as being valid for purposes of counting the number of observations used to compute the average.

Program 5.47 gives a solution in C to the rainfall problem, translated from a Pascal solution given in an article by Elliot Soloway[3] in which he explained how novice programmers tend to get confused and to make mistakes when they try to

---

[3] "Learning to Program = Learning to Construct Mechanisms + Explanations," *Communications of the ACM* (September 1986), p. 853.

```
 1  |    /*      Program to compute the average rainfall in New Haven    */
    |
    |            /* a translation into C from Soloway, CACM 9-86, p. 853 */
    |
 5  |            float       sum, rainfall, average;
    |            int         count;
    |
    |    int main(void)
    |    {
10  |
    |            sum     =    0.0;
    |            count   =    0;
    |
    |            printf("Please input a rainfall: ");
15  |            scanf("%f",&rainfall);
    |
    |            while ( rainfall != 99999.0 ) {
    |
    |                    while ( rainfall < 0.0 ) {
20  |                            printf("Rainfall cannot be <0. Input again: ");
    |                            scanf("%f",&rainfall)
    |                    }
    |
    |                    sum += rainfall;
25  |                    count++;
    |                    printf("Please input a rainfall: ");
    |                    scanf("%f",&rainfall);
    |            }
    |
30  |
    |            if ( count > 0 ) {
    |                    average = sum/count;
    |                    printf("Average rainfall = %4.2f\n", average);
    |            } else {
35  |                    printf("No valid inputs. No average calculated.\n");
    |            }
    |
    |    }
```

Program 5.47 Average Rainfall with Bug (translated into C with permission of the Association for Computing Machinery, copyright © 1986.)

merge program plans to achieve several goals all at once in a given section of code. See if you can spot the bug in Program 5.47. If you found the bug, one thing you might conclude is that the author of Program 5.47 might have been trying to solve too many problems at once and didn't manage to cope with all of them successfully.

For instance, look at the while-loop on lines 19:22 of the program. This is clearly intended to screen for a legal rainfall input and to prompt the user to give another rainfall value if an illegal negative one was given. It exits only with nonnegative input values on line 22.

finding the bug

According to the program, the new rainfall values are input within a while-loop (on lines 17:28) whose while-condition screens out rainfall values that are not equal to the sentinel, 99999. The assumption appears to be made that inside this while-loop (on lines 17:28), the value of the rainfall is not equal to the sentinel, so that it can be counted and added into the running rainfall total in the variable **sum**. But this assumption can be violated by a fickle user who first gives a negative rainfall (such as –3), forcing the program to ask for a legal rainfall, using the message: "Rainfall cannot be < 0. Input again," after which the user has a sudden change of mind, and decides to give the sentinel, 99999, in order to quit. Now the sentinel becomes a legal value for the variable, **rainfall**, causing the sentinel value to be added into the running total in **sum**, on line 24, and causing the **count** to be increased on line 25. Using the sentinel value in place of a valid rainfall was not supposed to happen—and yet it did. Moreover, we see that the program fails to stop when the user inputs the sentinel, and it prints an incorrect average when it terminates.

Now you might think that mature computer scientists don't make this kind of silly error. But the interesting thing is, the original Pascal version of Program 5.47 was labeled as a correct solution to the rainfall problem, and neither the authors of the paper, nor the referees and editors who read it, noticed and corrected the bug before publication. This is not meant to be critical of these authors, referees, and editors. Rather, it is meant to remind all of us that programming is a demonstrably difficult, error-prone process, even in apparently simple circumstances. Moreover, it highlights the wisdom of proverb (d) in Table 5.45, which urges us to break things into simple components that are easy to understand and with which we can reason cleanly.

using a subroutine which does just one task

For example, the version of the rainfall program given in Program 5.48, creates a subroutine to get a valid rainfall value or sentinel from the user. This subroutine has just one simple function—to obtain one input from the user that is guaranteed not to be an illegal rainfall value. The function, declared on lines 9:22, repeatedly prompts the user and reads input values until a nonnegative value is obtained. This value must be either a legal rainfall value or the sentinel.

This function is used on lines 30 and 35 each time the main program needs to get a valid rainfall value (or sentinel). The while-loop on lines 32:36 can now assume a simple function of summing and counting valid rainfall values until a sentinel value causes it to skip to the final phase of the program, which prints the average rainfall value (on lines 38:42). Actually, there are studies of the psychology of programming that show that Pascal's looping control structures, such as while-loops and repeat-until loops, are not as good as they should be for solving some kinds of programming problems. (See the article by Soloway, Bonar, and Erlich, mentioned at the end of this chapter in References for Further Study.)

using loops that exit in the middle

In this paper, Soloway and his colleagues have shown that if you add to Pascal a looping control structure that permits an exit from its middle, then programmers find it more convenient to use this for solving problems such as the rainfall problem. For example, using a loop-exit control structure similar to the one in the programming language, Ada, Soloway *et al.* showed that programmers find it more natural to express the code on lines 30:36 of Program 5.48 as shown in Program 5.49.

In essence, this says, "Get an input from the user which is either a valid rainfall value or the sentinel. If it is the sentinel, exit from the loop and proceed to the next section of the program (to compute and print the average). Otherwise, you have a

```
1   /*    Program to compute the average rainfall in New Haven    */
    /*    with bug fixed    */

    #define SENTINEL 99999
5
    float     sum, rainfall;
    int       count;

    float GetValidInputFromUser(void)           /* a valid input is either */
10  {                                           /* a non-negative rainfall observation */
        float rainfall;                         /* or the sentinel */

        printf("Please input a rainfall or 99999 to stop: ");
        scanf("%f",&rainfall);
15
        while ( rainfall < 0.0) {
            printf("Rainfall cannot be < 0. Input again: ");
            scanf("%f",&rainfall);
        }
20
        return rainfall;
    }

    int main(void)
25  {

        sum     =   0.0;
        count   =   0;

30      rainfall = GetValidInputFromUser( );

        while ( rainfall != SENTINEL ) {
            sum += rainfall;
            count++;
35          rainfall = GetValidInputFromUser( );
        }

        if ( count > 0 ) {
            printf("Average rainfall = %4.2f\n", sum/count);
40      } else {
            printf("No valid inputs. No average calculated.\n");
        }

    }
```

Program 5.48 Average Rainfall with Bug Fixed

valid rainfall input which is not the sentinel, and which needs to be counted and added to the running rainfall total in the variable **sum**. Now loop back and do this process over and over until the user directs you to terminate it by giving the sentinel."

advantages of using
natural control structures

Soloway *et al.* discovered evidence that programmers naturally think of the main repetitive action needed to solve the rainfall problem in terms that closely mirror the

```
   |   loop
   |        rainfall := GetValidInputFromUser;
   |        exit when (rainfall = sentinel);
   |        sum := sum + rainfall;
35 |        count := count + 1;
   |   end loop;
```

Program 5.49 Loop-Exit Control Structure

```
   |   while ( 1 ) {
   |        rainfall = GetValidInputFromUser( );
   |        if ( rainfall == SENTINEL ) break;
   |        sum += rainfall;
35 |        count++;
   |   }
```

Program 5.50 A Solution in C Using a While-Loop with a Break

loop-exit control structure given in Program 5.49. Comparing the use of the while-loop on lines 30:36 of Program 5.48 to the loop-exit structure in Program 5.49, we see that the use of the while-loop forces the assignment rainfall = GetValidInputFromUser( ); to be repeated twice. In addition to being wastefully repetitive, it is unnatural, since it doesn't correspond to the way problem-solvers think about the solution, as Soloway *et al.* have shown.

Fortunately, C has powerful control structures which allow it to express the loop-exit control structure of Program 5.49 using a while-loop containing a **break** statement, as shown in Program 5.50. The **break** statement on line 33 of Program 5.50 exits the while-loop if the **rainfall** variable contains the sentinel value in exactly the same fashion as the exit statement on line 33 of the loop-exit structure of Program 5.49. (The "industrial-strength" versions of Pascal used in the contemporary software industry have been extended to include **leave** and **cycle** statements which have the same effect as C's **break** and **continue** statements.)

A useful observation to make is that the programming language you are using might not have convenient control structures to mirror the way you naturally think about expressing your solution. Under these circumstances, you may have to use awkward circumlocutions to express what you need to say. When you are forced to express your solution indirectly, and perhaps awkwardly, cognitive complexity can creep in. Thus it is best to be alert to the danger of making a conceptual mistake.

Programming Style Disciplines

If you are working on a software project (or if you are taking a computer science course), the project leader (or instructor) may require that you write programs following certain well-defined rules of programming style.

In large programming projects, following such style conventions can help make programs more comprehensible to all members of the software team than would be the case if each programmer were allowed to freelance in his or her own individual style. When the team adheres to common conventions, it helps train the eye to read programs written by others more easily and accurately. What matters is not so much what the style rules are (provided they are at least minimally sensible) but that everybody adheres to them.

advantages of following style disciplines

Documentation

Documentation is a problem-ridden topic. Have you ever tried to read a moderately intricate program that you wrote several months ago for which you didn't have time to write good descriptive comments properly? Did you find it hard to remember what you were thinking about when you wrote it, and was it difficult to figure out how it worked? Then you might well imagine the difficulty somebody other than the original author might have trying to read a poorly documented program.

a problem-ridden subject

Documentation is, of course, a form of writing, and good writing should always be performed to meet the needs of the intended audience. The trouble is, programs may have many audiences, each having different needs. One case where it is clearly recognized that documentation needs to be written for different audiences is in writing user's manuals versus system documentation. These days, commercial firms have gotten quite good at writing user's manuals for popular mass-distributed software. User's manuals are often accompanied by guided tours that use animation and on-line interactive tutorials to illustrate how the system works and to teach novices how to use it.

A difficult type of documentation to create, however, is the documentation that explains how a large software system works. Here, the problem of multiple audiences still intrudes. When you are in the thick of writing a program, and all the details are in your mind or at your fingertips, you may find that certain kinds of comments are not only obvious but are even bothersome clutter. After you have laid the program aside for a year and you are no longer current on its details, or if you are looking at somebody else's program, you constitute quite a different audience. It is thus difficult, if not impossible, to meet the needs of all possible audiences in a single set of program comments. Project managers are yet another kind of audience who require good, clear, top-level descriptions, but who don't need to make use of low-level details very often.

the problem of multiple audiences

In fact, paper may not be a very good medium in which to write program documentation. Ideally, a form of electronic paper with, say, electronic stick-on memos suited to different audiences might be much better. We might imagine two kinds of stick-on memos—yellow ones for programming experts who have all the details fresh in their minds and blue ones for novices or project leaders, who are not up on all of the subtleties and who need to gain general understanding first. Using a computer screen, such memos might be made selectively visible or invisible in response to a user's command. This way, different readers of a document could adjust the details to suit their needs of the moment (needs which may change over time as the novice grows to be an expert then perhaps reverts to being a novice again after falling out of practice over time).

paper may not be a good container for documentation

In fact, hypermedia systems have recently become available. These let you attach buttons to words in a text or to places on a page. Several kinds of actions can be attached to the buttons, so that when they are pressed (a) you can navigate to another place in the document; (b) you can show or hide a window of new explanatory text or diagrams; (c) you can play a sound (such as a spoken explanation); (d) you can initiate an animation sequence illustrating a particular point visually; or (e) you can display a video film-clip on an associated videodisc player and screen. Perhaps such hypermedia systems will eventually serve as the carriers of good system documentation in the future.

using hypermedia systems

In the meantime, however, there is at least one thing you can do to write good documentation. If you follow the method of top-down programming by stepwise refinement, you will likely first create program strategies expressing your detailed design. Let's think of these as C programs with comments giving the goals to be achieved by various sections of each function (and giving the expected behavioral characteristics of abstract data types that will eventually have to be implemented). When you refine a program strategy into an actual program, you can leave the goal comments in place, and write the actual C refinement code underneath. (Sometimes, it is convenient to place the goal comments in the right margin when refining goals in the program strategy.)

In this way, you will develop commented C programs as you write them. It may also be necessary to add additional technical comments that explain how subtle mechanisms in your refinement code work, or that describe the agreements and conventions you have used in setting up your low-level data and functions. As an example of this method, study how Program 5.19 for selection sorting was derived from Program Strategy 5.18.

developing commented programs as you write them

Two final tips for generating good documentation: (1) Remember to document your data structures and module interfaces as carefully as you document your functions, and (2) remember to put an initial comment at the beginning of each function describing the expected characteristics of the inputs and outputs (or formally giving the preconditions and postconditions of the function, if you prefer).

5.8 Review Questions

1. What is the common sense behind the programming proverb that advocates minimizing the use of global variables in a program to help communicate inputs and outputs between functions?
2. Why is it sensible to use named symbolic constants in a C program?
3. Why is it best not to complain if a software project leader imposes a sensible but unfamiliar programming style on the project teammates and instructs everyone to use it consistently?
4. Why is it impossible to write program documentation that is bound to please everybody?

5.8 Exercises

1. Figure out what the following program does, then document it by adding informative comments and by changing its variables to have meaningful variable names.

```
   |    int F(int m, int n)
   |    {
   |         if ( n == 0 ) {
   |              return m;
 5 |         } else {
   |              return F(n, m % n);
   |         }
   |    }
```

2. Figure out what the function P(n) does in the program below, then document it by adding informative comments and by changing its variables to have meaningful variable names.

```
   |    void Q(int d)
   |    {
   |         printf("%c", (char)( (int)('0') + d ) );
   |    }
 5 |
   |
   |    void P(int n)              /* assume n is a non-negative integer */
   |    {
   |         if ( n < 10 ) {
10 |              Q(n);
   |         } else {
   |              P(n / 10 );
   |              Q(n % 10);
   |         }
   |    }
```

3. Give a test case that reveals the bug in Program 5.47.

4. Develop a program transformation that will help eliminate wasteful duplication from the following program fragment.

```
   |    PlayersMove = GetMoveFromUser( );
   |
   |    while ( PlayersMove != QUITSIGNAL ) {
   |         DisplayPlayersMoveOnTheBoard( );
 5 |         MakeMachinesMove( );
   |         PlayersMove = GetMoveFromUser( );
   |    }
```

[*Hint*: In solving this problem, it may help to recall that a break statement can be used to exit from a while-loop in C.]

Pitfalls

- *Failure to implement formatted debugging aids*

   Some of the earliest studies in software engineering revealed that debugging times for software projects were cut in half by making sure to implement and use formatted debugging aids. The evidence indicates that if you fail to implement formatted debugging aids, debugging will be much tougher and will take much longer than expected. If you are interested in formulating a good software project plan, you should plan to implement and test formatted debugging aids for every data structure in your detailed system design *before* you code and test the other parts of your system. Once you can take pictures of your data structures, you can see what they look like in various stages of construction and transformation. The advantage of seeing over being blind is amazing. Errors you never dreamed could happen typically leap out at you once you begin to examine pictures of each data structure. If you don't bother to look routinely at pictures of the data your system's functions create and modify, errors will tend to propagate undetected and will usually cause symptoms to appear far from their source, making error diagnosis and debugging extremely difficult.

- *Failure to document a software system*

   Some spectacular software has been implemented by small teams, consisting of a few brilliant, talented, software geniuses. Often, though, in the passion of creation, such geniuses believe their time is better spent finishing their creations than documenting how their code works. Often after such a system is in widespread use, the original creators tire of upgrading it, and the job of maintenance is passed on to successors who must then begin to understand how the code works.

   Alas, it is rarely possible to discipline the geniuses to create documentation during their moments of spectacular creativity. So the appearance of poorly documented, yet successful software systems is likely to recur in the future. But what do you do if you are the hapless successor who is assigned the job of maintaining such a system? One intriguing answer is to get the original creators to sit in front of a video camera for an hour and just talk about how they designed the original system. Recent experience shows this to be a relatively painless way to get some high-quality information.

- *Failure to test user documentation*

   Remember to test the user's manuals and operator procedure manuals for your system on actual users and operators to make sure that all instructions are clear and effective. The user documentation should be considered as much a part of the overall system software as the computer code, and it should be granted the same project privileges as code with regard to design, testing, and debugging.

≡ ▬▬▬▬ Tips and Techniques

- *Use measurement and tuning to improve program efficiency*

    Those who are experienced in software optimization and performance enhancement advocate *measurement and tuning* as a method for improving the efficiency of actual running programs. Sometimes programming environments provide execution-time profile tools to help measure where programs are spending their time. Experience suggests (1) that oftentimes a disproportionate amount of the running time (say 80 to 90 percent) is spent in a small portion of the code (say 7 to 10 percent), and (2) that oftentimes the places where a program is inefficient are surprisingly difficult to anticipate. The philosophy of measurement and tuning holds that you should use *measurement* to find out where the program is inefficient, and then concentrate on improving the inefficient places by *tuning*—judiciously replacing possible inefficient program parts with trial versions of new parts, followed by more measurement to see if the new parts, in fact, improve the efficiency.

- *Develop documentation while refining program strategies into detailed programs*

    A good moment to develop documentation for your detailed code is during the stepwise refinement process when you are translating your top-level designs, expressed, say, in the form of program strategies, into detailed code in a particular programming language, such as C. You can often retain the goal comments in the program strategies as headers for sections of actual code that achieve those goals. Then the retained goal comments serve to announce the purpose of the code that follows. It is also good practice to place comments off to the side, explaining any intricate or unusual parts of the detailed C code. Moreover, it is good practice to place a header comment at the beginning of each function explaining its purpose, its inputs, its outputs, and any restrictions or assumptions under which it is supposed to operate. It is of especially vital importance that module interfaces have the entities in their interface header files clearly documented. Finally, it is good practice to explain the purpose and layout of the data structures, types, constants, and variables in the declaration section of your code.

- *Adhere to programming style guidelines*

    Experience shows that having your software team agree on a programming style (and then following it rigorously) helps improve efficiency and accuracy. If everybody writes in a common style, project personnel have a much easier time reading each other's code. If everybody freelances and writes code using widely different personal styles, it makes it hard on others to read code accurately and easily.

- *Use both testing and verification*

    Testing and verification should play mutually supporting roles in the quality assurance phase of your software development. Neither testing, nor verification, alone is as effective as using both together. The weakness of testing is that it can reveal the presence of bugs, but it can never prove their absence. The weakness of verification is that it is hard to know when formal logical assertions have correctly and completely captured the true intentions of the system requirements.

Moreover, many programmers have found that it is often difficult to devise formal verification proofs for many of the algorithms they develop for use in practical systems.

References for Further Study

software economics

Barry W. Boehm, *Software Engineering Economics*, Prentice-Hall, Englewood-Cliffs, N.J., (1981).
The classic reference on software economics.

structured programming

O. J. Dahl, E. W. Dijkstra, and C. A. R. Hoare, *Structured Programming*, Academic Press, New York, (1982).
An influential book on structured programming.

key paper on verification

C. A. R. Hoare, "Axiomatic Semantics for Computer Programming." *IEEE Transactions on Software Engineering* SE-5(2) (1979) pp. 128–138.
An influential paper on program verification.

programming and cognition

Elliot Soloway, "Learning to Program = Learning to Construct Mechanisms + Explanations." *CACM* 29: 9 (September 1986).

E. Soloway, J. Bonar, and K. Erlich, "Cognitive Strategies and Looping Constructs: An Empirical Study." *CACM* 26: 11 (November 1983).
Some aspects of the relation between programming and cognition are covered.

original paper on stepwise refinement

Niklaus Wirth, "Program Development by Stepwise Refinement." *CACM* 14: 4 (April 1971) pp. 221–227.
A classic paper on programming by stepwise refinement.

Chapter Summary

This book covers software engineering principles for small programs, as well as for large software systems. The first is called *programming-in-the-small*. The second is called *programming-in-the-large*. Some aspects of software engineering, applied to small programs, explored in this chapter are programming by stepwise refinement, program verification, transforming and optimizing small programs, program testing, improving program performance using measurement and tuning, programming with reusable software components, and program structuring and documentation principles.

Usually a detailed design for a program is created before undertaking the final step of producing a running implementation in a specific programming language. In this book, we have been using sketches of our programs, called *program strategies*, to serve the role of detailed designs. A program strategy describes the goals a program is supposed to achieve without prescribing the exact mechanisms or representations to be used.

top-down programming by stepwise refinement

When a program strategy is implemented, the goals in the program strategy can be achieved by filling in more specific details progressively through *stepwise refinement*. The method of starting with a top-level design and expanding its details until an actual program is developed is called *top-down programming*.

Program strategies can function as abstract program designs, and their careful use can permit the postponement of decisions regarding the selection of data structures and algorithms to use, until an advantageous moment arises.

Sometimes the creation of small programs involves great subtlety of thought and requires great precision and ingenuity. It is important to be able to reason about small programs with clarity and mental precision. Techniques from mathematical logic can sometimes be used to verify that programs are correct.

To prove that a program *P* is correct, you must first supply assertions called *preconditions* and *postconditions*. The goal is to show that if the situation described by the preconditions holds true and the program is then executed, it follows logically that the situation described by the postconditions must be true.

Proving programs correct is called *program verification*. Two weaknesses in program verification are: (1) It is often difficult to be sure that the preconditions and postconditions correctly and completely capture the true intentions of the program; and (2) It is sometimes difficult to establish a proof of correctness when programs are either complex or subtle.

It is sometimes possible to change the way a program is expressed without changing the result it computes. This can be done by applying exchange laws that replace parts of programs with different parts that are guaranteed to preserve program equivalence. *Program transformations* are the exchange laws or modification processes that accomplish such changes. Sometimes program transformations can be applied to a program to make it run faster or use less space. This is called optimizing program performance, using program transformations.

An example of a recursive program that can sometimes be optimized in this fashion is one having a *tail recursion*, which is a recursive call that occurs last in the text of a recursive function, usually inside an if-statement. Another optimizing program transformation is one that substitutes a function body in place of its call.

Programs should be tested systematically before being released into service. *Unit testing* consists of testing individual functions in isolation to see if they work on all expected classes of inputs. *Integration testing* checks the coordinated execution of functions, acting together in the context of expected conditions of actual operation. *Acceptance testing* is a practice, sometimes specified in software acquisition contracts, in which a completed software system must pass a specified test in order to be accepted for delivery by the client. *Regression testing* makes sure that everything that used to work still works in any new version of a system.

A *test plan* is a document that specifies a systematic schedule of testing activities in a software project and gives the inputs and expected correct outputs for each part of the system.

It is frequently hard to anticipate where the inefficiencies in a program lie. Often over 80 to 90 percent of the execution time is spent in 7 to 10 percent of the code. It thus pays to spend your time improving code that accounts for most of the execution time. It is important first to *measure* where a system is spending its time, and then to concentrate on *tuning* the parts that account for most of the execution time. Measurement can sometimes be performed with an *execution profile tool*. *Tuning* is a repetitive process of attempting to improve a program and then measuring it to see if the expected improvements were achieved.

---

reasoning about programs

proving programs correct

program verification

transforming and optimizing programs

program testing

measurement and tuning

reusable software
components and
software reuse

The case for advocating the use of reusable software components is based on economic arguments. The cost of building software is an exponential function of its size. Since software size is the biggest cost driver in a software project, if you can reduce the size of what you have to build you can best reduce the cost.

bottom-up programming

A software project that first attempts to build general purpose, reusable software components, and that later uses these components in system construction employs a *bottom-up* software implementation process. This contrasts with a top-down process which specifies the top-level design of a system before implementing the lower-level details.

program structuring

Experience in software development has shown that clarity and simplicity of program structure and ease of comprehension are to be prized. *Structured programming* is the name given to a set of software structuring principles that help achieve these software properties.

documentation

Program documentation is of vital importance to anyone who needs to understand how a program works. Even the programmer who wrote the original program may be in need of such documentation after a long period of time has elapsed.

6

Introduction to Analysis of Algorithms

6.1 Introduction and Motivation

the use of mathematics in the exact sciences

In the exact sciences, precise scientific laws are discovered and are expressed in the language of mathematics. In physics, for example, Newton's second law, $F = ma$, states that if you apply a force, F, to an object of mass, m, in a frictionless medium (such as outer space), it will respond to the force by accelerating at rate, a, in the direction that the force is applied.

Some areas of computer science constitute an exact mathematical science. In particular, some parts of its subject matter—within the subfield of algorithms and data structures—have been found to obey certain precisely stated mathematical laws. These laws have been formulated using techniques of mathematical analysis.

the importance of knowing about precise laws of computer science

It is important for you to know some of the major results that have been discovered by computer scientists who have analyzed algorithms and data structures over the years. In this way you will be equipped with a knowledge of the most efficient ways to solve certain widely encountered algorithmic problems and you can make use of the quantitative laws that characterize the known efficiencies. Also, knowledge of quanti-

205

tative laws will help you perform tradeoff analyses, in the event that you have to choose among several solutions to a problem.

Moreover, it is important for you to learn how to perform at least elementary and simple analyses of algorithms on your own. In developing software systems, many of the algorithms and data structures used have simple forms that are susceptible to straightforward analysis. If you can analyze the performance of even the simplest algorithms, such as those we will cover in this chapter and in the rest of this book, you will have gained a widely useful skill that can significantly improve your ability to develop high-quality software solutions.

developing your own ability to analyze algorithms

Plan for the Chapter

We begin by asking, "What do we use for a yardstick?" That is, exactly how can we characterize and measure the performance of a given algorithm, A, when this algorithm could be expressed in many different programming languages and could be executed on many different kinds of computers—some fast and some slow? Measuring the wall clock time taken by algorithm A when it executes on a given computer might not be a very meaningful way to characterize A's essential performance characteristics. So what can we do to devise a way of characterizing A's essential performance properties when hard performance measures, such as wall clock time, will vary significantly when we use different computers, compilers, and programming languages for expressing and running A?

This leads to an introduction to O-notation, pronounced "Oh-notation" (or sometimes, "Big-Oh-notation," since there is also something called "little-Oh-notation"). O-notation gives us a language for talking about the comparative efficiency of algorithms. A key goal for the chapter is to help you develop an intuition for the meaning of this language, which is commonly used by computer scientists. The objective is to master the intuition behind O-notation sufficiently so that you can understand what computer scientists mean when they say things like, "Since this search algorithm runs in time $O(\log n)$, it is better than that other one which is only an $O(n)$ algorithm." We will also learn about various common categories of possible algorithm efficiencies characterized by their O-notations.

using O-notation to compare efficiencies of algorithms

Furthermore, by the end of the chapter, you should be able to express the results of your own algorithm analyses in O-notation, so you can participate in the practical use of algorithm analysis techniques to help you identify which algorithms are of high-quality and which are of poor-quality in relation to the solution of given programming problems. We will also cover some skills for manipulating O-notation that are helpful to master.

Two skills we will employ when learning to analyze algorithms are (1) using summation notation, and (2) setting up and solving recurrence relations. We will study "beginner's examples" of sums and recurrence relations, and we will show how to apply them when analyzing a few common, yet important, kinds of algorithms. We present just a few simple methods used in algorithm analysis that mostly rely on finding sums of arithmetic and geometric progressions familiar to students of high school algebra. Nonetheless, we'll discover that even these simple techniques provide signifi-

sums and recurrence relations

cant coverage in terms of what they can accomplish. We'll also tell the story of why sums and recurrence relations are so often useful in algorithm analysis.

Much can be gained by examining a sequence of progressive examples. We start with simple algorithms for searching for an item in a list. Next, we analyze the sorting algorithm **SelectionSort** (which we proved correct in the last chapter). Then we solve the recurrence relations for the Towers of Hanoi problem and for another kind of sorting algorithm, called **MergeSort**. Finally, we progress to an analysis of binary searching in ordered arrays. Then we compare the relative efficiencies of binary searching and sequential searching, using the results of our analyses.

We close our discussion by addressing the topic, "What O-notation doesn't tell you." We learn that for small problem sizes, the conclusions based on analyses of O-notation don't hold, and we investigate what to do in such cases.

a sequence of progressive examples

some limitations

6.2   What Do We Use for a Yardstick?

Learning Objectives

1. To learn why data giving raw measurements of algorithm performance cannot be used to compare algorithms.
2. To understand how equations describing the resource consumption patterns of algorithms stay in the same family, even though computers, compilers, and languages may change.
3. To see how the dominant term of the running time equation accounts for most of an algorithm's running time for large problem sizes.

the problem of measurement

We start by posing the question, "What do we use for a yardstick?"—meaning how can we measure and compare algorithms meaningfully when the same algorithm will run at different speeds and will require different amounts of space when run on different computers or when implemented in different programming languages?

looking at selection sorting again

It helps to reason with a specific example. Consider the selection sorting algorithm given in Program 6.1. (This is a new version of the iterative selection sorting algorithm given in Program 5.35, which was derived by program transformation in the last chapter. It is rewritten slightly so it will be easier to analyze in Section 6.5, by replacing while-statements and do-while–statements with for-statements. It also finds **MinPositions** instead of **MaxPositions**.)

benchmarks

Let's now look at Table 6.2, which presents some running times that might typically be used by this algorithm to sort an array of 2000 integers on different computers. As expected, the selection sorting algorithm runs faster on more powerful computers. (In fact, running the same algorithm on different computers is sometimes used as a way of comparing the computers' relative speeds. A program used for this purpose is called a *benchmark*. Computer magazines such as *Byte* frequently run batteries of benchmark programs on new models of computers to help their readers understand the computers' performance. For example, a frequently used benchmark program is the *Sieve of Eratosthenes*, which is a program that computes prime numbers.)

```
     |     void SelectionSort(InputArray A)
     |     {
     |
     |        int   MinPosition, temp, i, j;
  5  |
     |        for (i = n − 1; i > 0; − − i) {
     |
     |           MinPosition = i;
     |
 10  |           for( j = 0; j < i; + + i) {
     |
     |              if (A[j] < A[MinPosition]) {
     |                 MinPosition = j;
     |              }
 15  |
     |           }
     |
     |           temp = A[i]; A[i] = A[MinPosition]; A[MinPosition] = temp;
     |
 20  |        }
     |     }
```

Program 6.1 Selection Sorting Algorithm for Sorting A[0:n−1]

In addition to changing according to which computer is used, running times are also affected by the programming language used to express the algorithm.

the effect of using different compilers

Even if a single programming language such as C is used, different C compilers implemented by different vendors tend to compile the same program into different sequences of machine instructions, some of which run more efficiently than others.

With all of these sources of possible variation—different computers, different programming languages, and different compilers—how can we use any of the performance numbers we measure to decide which algorithms are the best? Answer: We can't. We are forced to do something else instead.

resource consumption patterns

What we can observe is that algorithms usually consume resources (such as time and space) in some fashion that depends on the size of the problem they solve. Usually, though not always, the bigger the size of the problem that an algorithm

Type of Computer	Time
Home computer	51.915
Desktop computer	11.508
Minicomputer	2.382
Mainframe computer	0.431
Supercomputer	0.087

Table 6.2 Running Times in Seconds to Sort an Array of 2000 Integers

Array Size n	Home Computer	Desktop Computer
125	12.5	2.8
250	49.3	11.0
500	195.8	43.4
1000	780.3	172.9
2000	3114.9	690.5

Table 6.3 SelectionSort Running Times in Milliseconds on Two Types of Computers

solves, the more resources it consumes.

In what follows, let's agree to use the integer variable, n, to stand for the size of a problem. For instance, n could be the length of a list that an algorithm searches, or the number of nodes in a tree that an algorithm prints, or the number of items in an array that an algorithm sorts into descending order.

When we run a particular algorithm, A, such as **SelectionSort**, written in a particular programming language, such as C, on a particular computer using a particular compiler—and we measure the time it takes to run algorithm A on problems of various sizes, n, we usually get a set of timing measures that lie on a curve, and we can usually find an equation that fits the curve.

fitting curves to the data

For example, the **SelectionSort** algorithm, given in Program 6.1, has two sequences of running times when it is run on two different computers—a home computer and a desktop computer, as shown in Table 6.3. If we plot these numbers on a graph and try to fit curves to them, we find that they lie on two curves, each of which has the form $f(n) = an^2 + bn + c$. The difference between the two curves is that they have different constants (a, b, and c). Figure 6.4 plots these two curves. The equations for these two curves are given in Eqs. 6.1, where $f_1(n)$ fits the home computer data in

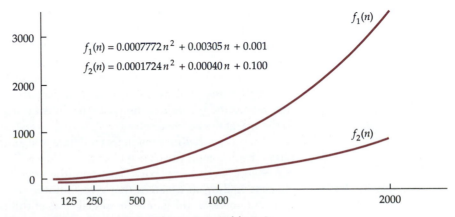

$$f_1(n) = 0.0007772\,n^2 + 0.00305\,n + 0.001$$
$$f_2(n) = 0.0001724\,n^2 + 0.00040\,n + 0.100$$

Figure 6.4 Two Curves Fitting the Data in Table 6.3

Table 6.3 and $f_2(n)$ fits the desktop computer data.

$$f_1(n) = 0.0007772\ n^2 + 0.00305\ n + 0.001$$
$$f_2(n) = 0.0001724\ n^2 + 0.00040\ n + 0.100$$

(6.1)

quadratic functions

A function of the form, $f(n) = an^2 + bn + c$, is called a *quadratic function of n* (because the highest power of n in it is n^2). What we have discovered so far is that when we run the **SelectionSort** algorithm (given in Program 6.1) on two different computers, the time taken in both cases is a quadratic function of the size, n, of the array $A[0:n-1]$ to be sorted.

a common pattern of resource consumption

It turns out that we have taken the first steps toward discovering something fundamental. If we were to continue to implement selection sorting algorithms and to measure their performance using different computers, languages, and compilers, we would discover that no matter what computer we ran the selection sorting algorithm on—whether it is a blazing fast supercomputer or a pokey home computer—the amount of time it consumed would be a quadratic function of the size of the array that is sorted.

Another way of saying this is that when you run the same selection sorting algorithm on a variety of different computers of differing speeds, or you express the algorithm in different programming languages, or you compile the program for the algorithm with different compilers—you get a family of identically shaped quadratic curves of the form, $f(n) = an^2 + bn + c$, which fit the data for the measured running times as a function of the problem size, n. Each distinct curve in this family of quadratic curves has its own special coefficients (a, b, c) associated with a particular computer, language, and compiler used.

So even though the particular running time measurements for selection sort vary under changing circumstances, what stays the same is the *shape of the curve* that expresses the running time as a function of the problem size. That is, all of the curves plotting running time versus problem size share the shape of the quadratic function, $f(n) = an^2 + bn + c$.

The generalization we are heading toward is this: When we analyze the running time of an algorithm, we will try to come up with the general shape of the curve that characterizes its running time as a function of the problem size. We won't care what the constants of proportionality are (i.e., what the coefficients such as a, b, c are), since these can change depending on the particular details of the computer, language, or compiler used. But we will care a great deal about the general shape of the curve that relates the resources consumed (such as running time or running space needed) to the size of the problem solved.

complexity classes

It turns out that running times for different algorithms fall into different *complexity classes*. Each complexity class is characterized by a different family of curves. All of the curves in a given complexity class share the same basic shape. This shared shape is characterized by an equation that gives running times as a function of problem size. Different curves in the family are special cases of this equation for the given complexity class in which only the constants (or coefficients) are different. You could say, then, that the *complexity class* for the running time of the selection sorting algorithm is *qua-*

dratic, since the function, $f(n) = an^2 + bn + c$, that gives the running time $f(n)$ as a function of the problem size, n, is a quadratic function.

In what follows, we will introduce O-notation. This notation is used by computer scientists for talking about the complexity classes of algorithms. In giving the O-notation for the quadratic function, $f(n) = an^2 + bn + c$, we will say that $f(n)$ is $O(n^2)$—pronounced "f of n is Oh of n squared." In arriving at the O-notation for $an^2 + bn + c$, we first focus on the dominant term, an^2, and ignore the lesser terms, $bn + c$. (The dominant term is the one that grows the fastest when n grows.) Then we ignore the coefficient (or constant of proportionality), a. Thus $O(an^2 + bn + c)$ simplifies first to $O(an^2)$—by throwing away all but the dominant term, an^2—and $O(an^2)$ then simplifies to $O(n^2)$—by throwing away the coefficient (or constant of proportionality) a. Thus $O(n^2)$ stands for the class of functions, $f(n)$, whose dominant terms are quadratic (of the form an^2). When we say that the running time of an algorithm is $O(n^2)$, it simply means that the dominant term in its running time equation is of the form an^2. (It may have lesser terms that grow more slowly than the quadratic term, but for large problem sizes, the running times are dominated by the effect of the quadratic term, so these lesser terms are of lesser significance, and they can be ignored for simplicity.)

introducing the language of O-notation

Let's explore, for a moment, why it might make sense to focus on the dominant term in $an^2 + bn + c$, and to ignore the lesser terms. Study the numbers in Table 6.5. You can see that, for problem sizes of n = 250 or greater, over 98 percent of the value of $f(n)$ comes from the dominant term an^2. The lesser terms, $bn + c$, contribute very little, even though the coefficient c is 250 times bigger than the coefficient b, and even though b is more than twice the coefficient a. The rationale for focusing on the dominant term, then, is that since, for big problems, the dominant term in $f(n)$ usually accounts for most of $f(n)$'s value, we can simplify our considerations without losing too much accuracy by ignoring the contribution of the lower terms.

dominant terms

In O-notation, we also ignore the constant of proportionality, a, on the dominant term, an^2, since our aim is to discover the general family of growth curves characterizing a given algorithm's resource consumption. We know that the exact resource consumption curves fitting data measured on different computers will have differing constants of proportionality, a, associated with their dominant terms, but we are trying to ignore differences in speeds of the different computers, and to identi-

ignoring the constant of proportionality

Table 6.5 Percentage Contribution of n^2 Term to the Total

$f(n) = an^2 + bn + c$ where $a = 0.0001724$, $b = 0.0004$ and $c = 0.1$			
n	$f(n)$	an^2	n^2-term as % of total
125	2.8	2.7	94.7
250	11.0	10.8	98.2
500	43.4	43.1	99.3
1000	172.9	172.4	99.7
2000	690.5	689.6	99.9

fy the common resource consumption growth pattern associated with the algorithm itself. In order to do this, we have to ignore the constant of proportionality, a.

You will see in Section 6.4 how the formal definition of O-notation is constructed so as to achieve three important properties: (1) focusing on the dominant term for large problem sizes, (2) ignoring the lesser terms and ignoring what happens on small problems, and (3) ignoring the constant of proportionality.

a road map

Now let's step back for a moment and see where we are going. We are going to introduce O-notation as the solution to the problem of finding a suitable yardstick to use to compare the efficiency of algorithms. In the next section, before defining O-notation formally, we are going to try to gain an intuitive insight into it—so you will get the "feeling" for it, so-to-speak, before you are introduced to its formal definition. Then in Section 6.4, we will present the formal definition of O-notation. We will also introduce a few rules for manipulating it, and we will give you some practice using them. Following that, we will analyze a progression of algorithms, starting with simple ones, and building up to slightly more complicated ones. In the process, we will show how to use sums and recurrence relations to find the equations characterizing the running times of the algorithms. Then we will show how to give the O-notation for the running time.

6.2 Review Questions

1. What is meant by the question, "What do we use for a yardstick?"
2. When an algorithm is written in different programming languages and is executed on different computers, what measures of the algorithm's performance can be expected to change? What facts or relations about the algorithm's performance remain unchanged?
3. What is the dominant term in the running time equation for an algorithm?
4. Why might we be justified in focusing on the behavior of the dominant term in a running time equation and in ignoring the contributions of the lesser terms?

6.2 Exercise

1. Two other algorithms for **SelectionSort** were given in Chapter 5 as Programs 5.29 and 5.35. One was recursive and the other was iterative. They both differed from the version of **SelectionSort** given as Program 6.1. Table 5.36 gave their running times. Do you suppose that these other versions of **SelectionSort** have quadratic running times characterized by the equation, $f(n) = an^2 + bn + c$, (for suitable constants a, b, and c)? Try to fit curves to the data in Table 5.36 by choosing values for the constants a, b, and c. Can you get a clean fit (say to within a tenth of a millisecond)? Compare your results with Eqs. 6.1. What does this tell you about the basic resource consumption laws governing selection sorting algorithms? Is it important whether they are expressed iteratively or recursively, or with or without the use of for-statements, while-statements, or do-while–statements in C?

6.3   The Intuition Behind O-Notation

Learning Objectives

1. To develop intuition for the meaning of O-notation by exploring patterns in some data.
2. To learn how O-notation is used by computer scientists to refer to the performance properties of algorithms.

learning a new temperature scale

Learning about O-notation is a bit like learning about a new temperature scale. For example, if you were brought up using Fahrenheit temperatures, have you ever tried to learn the Celsius temperature scale (or vice versa)? It doesn't do to memorize temperature conversion formulas between Celsius degrees (C°) and Fahrenheit degrees (F°) such as those given in Eqs. 6.2:

$$C° = \frac{5}{9}\left(F° - 32\right) \quad \text{or} \quad F° = \frac{9}{5}C° + 32 \tag{6.2}$$

Knowing the conversion formula isn't the same as knowing the intuition behind the temperature scale. Instead, to develop intuition, you have to acquaint yourself with the temperatures on the new scale you are learning for lots of familiar situations. For example, consider the temperature situations given in Table 6.6. If you spend time studying a table such as this, and you practice using it to describe temperatures on the new scale you are trying to learn, you will gradually develop confidence that you "have a feeling" for the new scale.

Table 6.6 Approximately Equal Temperature Situations in C° and F°

Common Temperature Situations	Celsius	Fahrenheit
Boiling water	100°	212°
Seriously high fever	40°	104°
Mild fever	37.3°	99.2°
Normal body temperature	37°	98.6°
Extremely hot summer day	35°	95°
Warm summer day	30°	86°
Pleasant spring day	24°	75°
Normal room temperature	22°	72°
Slightly cool room temperature	20°	68°
Cold rainy day in fall	7°	45°
Freezing (rain just turns to snow)	0°	32°
Severe cold	−18°	0°
Frostbite temperature	−28°	−18°

developing intuition for
Celsius temperatures

Let's assume you are trying to learn the Celsius scale. If you go into a room that seems a little warm and stuffy, you might try to guess the Celsius temperature by saying to yourself, "Let's see, this room temperature is about 24° C." If everybody in the room is breaking out in sweat, you might guess something like, "It's hot enough in here to be about 27° C." If you have a way of confirming your guesses and correcting them, and you practice until you can make reasonably close guesses, you will begin to feel that you have developed an intuition for Celsius temperatures.

developing intuition
for O-notation

Now let's try to learn the intuition behind a few of the common complexity classes used in analysis of algorithms. We'll also try to learn the language commonly heard among computer scientists when they use O-notation to describe algorithmic complexity. The goal, by the end of this section, is for you to begin to be confident that you have the "feeling" for what O-notation means.

As a starting point, let's look at Table 6.7, which gives some adjective names and the corresponding O-notation for seven common complexity classes. In a moment, we will study data aimed at helping you develop a feeling for what these different complexity classes imply. But before doing that, let's look at one example of the way computer scientists commonly talk about these complexity classes in everyday speech.

some eavesdropping

Dropping in on a conversation, we might overhear one computer scientist say to another, "Well, since **SelectionSort** runs in quadratic time, it ought to be fast enough for this sorting application." Suppose a second computer scientist replies, "Yes, you are probably correct, but why not be safe and use an $O(n \log n)$ sorting algorithm such as **HeapSort**? That way, your system might be free from the risk of sluggish response times, if the problem sizes get too big."

what does $O(n^2)$ mean?

Instead of using the phrase, "**SelectionSort** runs in quadratic time," the first computer scientist could equally well have said, "**SelectionSort** runs in time $O(n^2)$." (When spoken, $O(n^2)$ sounds like "Oh of en squared.") What is meant by this? The answer is that the first scientist is claiming that **SelectionSort** runs in an amount of time no greater than n^2 times some constant of proportionality, provided the problem sizes are big enough.

what does
$O(n \log n)$ mean?

When the second scientist said, "Why not be safe and use an $O(n \log n)$ sorting algorithm such as **HeapSort**?" (where $O(n \log n)$ is spoken as, "Oh of en log en"), the second scientist was asserting that, for suitably large problems, the **HeapSort** algo-

Adjective Name	O-Notation
Constant	$O(1)$
Logarithmic	$O(\log n)$
Linear	$O(n)$
$n \log n$	$O(n \log n)$
Quadratic	$O(n^2)$
Cubic	$O(n^3)$
Exponential	$O(2^n)$
Exponential	$O(10^n)$

Table 6.7 Some Common Complexity Classes

rithm runs in an amount of time bounded above by a constant times $n \log n$. We'll see in a moment why $O(n \log n)$ algorithms can be preferable to $O(n^2)$ algorithms.

Now let's look at some data derived from a hypothetical situation. Suppose we have an algorithm called algorithm A, which is being executed on a computer that can perform one step of this algorithm each microsecond. (In effect, we can imagine that this computer operates at a speed of one MIP, where a MIP = a million instructions per second, and where each instruction performs one step of algorithm A.) Suppose that the number of steps required by algorithm A to solve a problem of size n is given by $f(n)$. We might be interested in the number of microseconds it takes for algorithm A to compute its solution for various values of the problem size n and various $f(n)$. Table 6.8 gives examples of such values.

an imaginary computer

We need to translate the microsecond values in Table 6.8 into familiar time units to get a feeling for what the data are telling us. For instance, given that there are 3.15×10^{13} microseconds in a year, if algorithm A takes 2^n steps to solve a problem of size $n = 256$, then it takes $2^{256} = 1.16 \times 10^{77}$ microseconds, which translates into 3.7×10^{63} years. By the way, that's a lot of years. It is estimated that the sun will burn out in five billion years (i.e., 5×10^9 years) after it exhausts its fuel. Thus, if you start a computation to compute the answer to a problem of size $n = 256$, which is going to take 2^n steps at one microsecond per step, the sun will burn out long before your computation finishes. (Exercise 6.3.1 asks you to find the largest size problem that could be solved before the sun burns out if the problem requires 2^n microseconds to find its solution.)

translating these results into familiar time units

In Table 6.9, where it was meaningful to do so, we have translated the microsecond values given in Table 6.8 into time units that are easier to interpret. Let's draw a few conclusions from the data. First, we can conclude that if the problem size is small, say $n \leq 16$, then the complexity class of $f(n)$ might not matter very much, since algorithm A finishes in under a tenth of a second for all the different $f(n)$. However, as soon as the problem size gets medium large, say $n = 1024$, then algorithms that are no more complex than n^2 finish in a second or less and could still be considered useful. But algorithms as complex as n^3 begin to take inconveniently

drawing a few conclusions

Algorithm A stops in $f(n)$ microseconds					
$f(n)$	$n = 2$	$n = 16$	$n = 256$	$n = 1024$	$n = 1048576$
1	1	1	1	1.00×10^0	1.00×10^0
$\log_2 n$	1	4	8	1.00×10^1	2.00×10^1
n	2	1.6×10^1	2.56×10^2	1.02×10^3	1.05×10^6
$n \log_2 n$	2	6.4×10^1	2.05×10^3	1.02×10^4	2.10×10^7
n^2	4	2.56×10^2	6.55×10^4	1.05×10^6	1.10×10^{12}
n^3	8	4.10×10^3	1.68×10^7	1.07×10^9	1.15×10^{18}
2^n	4	6.55×10^4	1.16×10^{77}	1.80×10^{308}	6.74×10^{315652}

Table 6.8 Running Times for Different Complexity Classes

$f(n)$	$n = 2$	$n = 16$	$n = 256$	$n = 1024$	$n = 1048576$
1	1 μsec*	1 μsec	1 μsec	1 μsec	1 μsec
$\log_2 n$	1 μsec	4 μsecs	8 μsecs	10 μsecs	20 μsecs
n	2 μsecs	16 μsecs	256 μsecs	1.02 ms	1.05 secs
$n \log_2 n$	2 μsecs	64 μsecs	2.05 ms	10.2 ms	21 secs
n^2	4 μsecs	25.6 μsecs	65.5 ms	1.05 secs	1.8 wks
n^3	8 μsecs	4.1 ms	16.8 secs	17.9 min	36,559 yrs
2^n	4 μsecs	65.5 ms	3.7×10^{63} yrs	5.7×10^{294} yrs	2.1×10^{315639} yrs

* 1 μsec = one microsecond = one millionth of a second; 1 ms = one millisecond = one thousandth of a second; sec = one second; wk = one week; and yr = one year.

Table 6.9 Running Times for Algorithm A in Different Time Units

long, and algorithms as complex as 2^n take way too long to be of any practical use. For problems of large size, such as $n = 1,048,576$, the difference between $n \log_2 n$ algorithms, which take 21 seconds, and n^2 algorithms, which take 1.8 weeks is astonishing. (See Exercise 6.3.2 for a practical situation in which this difference is highly significant.) Another conclusion you can draw from studying Table 6.9 is that exponential algorithms, such as those that take 2^n steps, tend to take a disastrously long time for all but small problems.

Let's continue to build intuition by taking another point of view. (Changing points of view, or looking at something "from another angle" so-to-speak, is often a good way to build more intuition and understanding.) Let's do this by asking an inverse question. Suppose again that n is the problem size and that algorithm A takes exactly $f(n)$ steps, at one microsecond per step, to finish its task, where $f(n)$ is one of the functions in Table 6.8. Now we can ask: How big can n be if we expect the computation for algorithm A to terminate before a year (a week, or a day) has expired?

changing points of view

how big can n get in order to finish within a time limit?

The number of seconds in a year is $60 \times 60 \times 24 \times 365 = 31,536,000$, so the number of microseconds in a year is 3.15×10^{13}. Thus, the answer to our question is determined by finding the largest n such that $f(n) \leq 3.15 \times 10^{13}$. If $f(n) = 2^n$, then n can be at most 44 if algorithm A is to finish in less than a year. In other words, if algorithm A takes exactly 2^n steps of a microsecond each, then the largest problem that we can handle with a year's worth of computing effort is a problem of size $n = 44$. If $f(n) = 10^n$, matters are even worse—we can solve only a problem of size $n = 13$ in a year. If a year seems impossibly long to wait for our answer, or the solution seems impractical because contemporary computers cannot usually operate reliably for that long, we might see what size problem we could solve in an hour, a day, or a week. If $f(n) = 10^n$, we are still in deep trouble—the biggest n can be if the computation is to terminate in less than an hour is $n = 9$, and if we are allocated a week, the biggest n can be is $n = 11$. Thus, if the running time of our algorithm is characterized by an exponential function, we usually cannot expect to solve practical problems of very large size. Table 6.10 gives more results along these lines for functions $f(n)$ of linear or greater complexity.

Number of steps is	T = 1 min	T = 1 hr	T = 1 day	T = 1 wk	T = 1 yr
n	6×10^7	3.6×10^9	8.64×10^{10}	6.05×10^{11}	3.15×10^{13}
$n \log_2 n$	2.8×10^6	1.3×10^8	2.75×10^9	1.77×10^{10}	7.97×10^{11}
n^2	7.75×10^3	6.0×10^4	2.94×10^5	7.78×10^5	5.62×10^6
n^3	3.91×10^2	1.53×10^3	4.42×10^3	8.46×10^3	3.16×10^4
2^n	25	31	36	39	44
10^n	7	9	10	11	13

Table 6.10 Size of Largest Problem that Algorithm A Can Solve if Solution Is Computed in Time ≤ T at 1 Microsecond per Step

Thus, we see that, given an hour, we can solve a problem of size 3.6 billion if algorithm A takes n steps, but only size 60,000 if A takes n^2 steps, size 1,532 if A takes n^3 steps, and size 31 if A takes 2^n steps.

These dramatic shifts in the sizes of problems we can handle as we ascend the scale of complexity are equally dramatically reversed as we descend the scale. Thus, if *some dramatic shifts* we can replace a linear algorithm A that takes n steps by a logarithmic algorithm B that takes only $\log_2 n$ steps of equal duration, then a problem that is solved by algorithm A in one hour, would be solved by algorithm B in just 31.75 microseconds!

A Word of Caution

Our intuition-building discussion has been oversimplified a bit. While the basic theme has been correct, some of the nuances and subtleties remain to be covered. For instance, a given algorithm, such as QuickSort, does not always take the same time to run on problems of a given size, regardless of its input data. Some kinds of arrays of items we may wish to sort may take much longer for QuickSort to sort than certain other kinds of arrays (depending on various ways the original array is out of order to begin with). Consequently, it will turn out that QuickSort has an *average* running time, a *worst case* running time, and a *best case* running time. It turns out that even though the average running time for QuickSort is O($n \log n$), QuickSort's worst case running time is O(n^2).

What We'll Discover Later

Now let's take a quick peek at some of the algorithmic complexity results we will discover in the remainder of the book. This is the final intuition-building step before we study O-notation formally.

First, consider different methods of searching. One method is *sequential searching*. *sequential searching versus* Under usual conditions, this is an O(n) algorithm (i.e., an algorithm that runs in *lin-* *binary searching* *ear* time). In sequential searching of a list or an array, you look at items one after another in sequential order until you find the one you are looking for. By contrast, *binary searching* in an ordered array of items runs in *logarithmic* time (i.e., it can be performed in time O(log n)), provided the array is sorted beforehand. For searching in large tables, lists, or arrays, binary searching is incredibly more efficient than sequential searching.

Yet more efficient are techniques for searching using *hashing*. The time that hash searching takes depends on how full the hash table is. If a hash table is not filled completely with items but is instead kept no more than say 80 percent full, the average search times take no more than a *constant* amount of time, O(1). (In Section 6.4, we will give the reason why O(1) is the O-notation for a constant amount of time.) The term *constant time* means that the time required is fixed and doesn't vary when the problem size changes.

We can also use trees in searching algorithms. For instance, we can put items into binary search trees, and use binary tree searching for looking up items in the trees. If we maintain these search trees in approximately balanced condition (meaning that the left subtree of each node is made to contain about as many nodes as the right subtree does), then we can guarantee logarithmic search times, O(log n), on the average. Even though binary searching in ordered arrays also runs in average time O(log n), we can insert new items in binary search trees more efficiently than we can in ordered sequential arrays. Binary search trees therefore have some advantages (which we'll investigate in Chapter 9).

Now, let's turn to sorting. For large problem sizes, it can make a big difference which sorting method you choose (see, for example, Exercise 6.3.2). In sorting methods that compare the relative sizes of items and move them about (which are called comparison-based sorting methods), you can prove that you can't sort any faster in the average case than proportional to $n \log n$. Table 6.11 lists the complexity classes for the average sorting times of several methods. There are even some fast sorting methods that work in *linear* time, O(n). These methods work using address-calculation techniques. We will explore some of these in Chapter 13.

We have already sensed that exponential running-time algorithms are not very practical to use for any but small problems. Unfortunately, there are some kinds of algorithmic problems for which the very best solutions known to date take exponential running time. For instance, the best known algorithm for solving what is called the *traveling salesperson problem* takes exponential time. In this problem you have a map that gives cities the salesperson is supposed to visit. The map also gives the costs of traveling between various pairs of cities (for which transportation is possible). The problem is to find the route of least cost that allows the salesperson to visit each of the cities exactly once. Certain algorithms for computing moves in game-playing situations also take exponential time. These are exhaustive algo-

(margin notes)
using hashing to perform searching

using trees to perform searching

sorting methods

Table 6.11 Sorting Methods of Various Complexities

Complexity	Method Names
O(n^2)	SelectionSort, InsertionSort
O($n \log n$)	QuickSort, HeapSort, MergeSort
O(n)	Address Calculation Sorting (ProxmapSort, RadixSort)

rithms that explore the game-tree for the game in order to compare all possible moves and to select the best one.

At the opposite end of the spectrum from exponential algorithms are algorithms that run in constant time, $O(1)$. $O(1)$ algorithms are those that take no more than a fixed amount of time to run no matter how big the problem size is. An example of a constant-time algorithm is one that chooses and prints a single random array item $A[i]$ in an array, $A[0:n-1]$. It takes a fixed amount of time to compute a random number, i, lying in the index range, $0:n-1$, of the array. It takes an additional fixed amount of time to access $A[i]$ and print it. No matter how big the problem size, n, gets, it still takes the same amount of time to select and print a random array item, $A[i]$ (assuming we stay within the limits of a given computer).

constant time algorithms

If we are careful enough, many important problems can be solved with algorithms that run in linear time, $O(n)$. For instance, the parsing algorithm in your C compiler is usually a linear algorithm that runs in time proportional to the length of your C program (measured in characters). Also, string pattern matching algorithms (such as the algorithm that searches for occurrences of a given word in your word processor) can be made to run in linear time, relying on clever tricks (see Exercises 6.3.3 and 6.3.4).

linear time algorithms

Occasionally, we encounter $O(n^3)$ algorithms. An example of an $O(n^3)$ algorithm is the straightforward algorithm for multiplying two square $n \times n$ matrices. Matrices are two-dimensional tables of numbers that can be multiplied with other mathematical entities and with each other. They can be used to represent many interesting systems. For instance, if you have a computer graphics program with a three-dimensional model in it, and you want to draw a two-dimensional perspective image of what an observer would see when looking through a window at three-dimensional objects in the distance, you could use a model based on three-dimensional coordinate geometry. If you then wanted to simulate what the observer would see when moving through the model (as in making a landing on an aircraft carrier, for instance), you could use matrices to multiply the coordinates defining the lines, points, and surfaces in the model so that they would turn, expand, and shrink appropriately in order to compute the perspective view that the observer would see when moving.

cubic time algorithms

6.3 Review Questions

1. Give the O-notation corresponding to the following adjective names for various complexity classes: constant, logarithmic, linear, $n \log n$, quadratic, cubic, and exponential.
2. If you have problems of small size, does the complexity class of the algorithm make a big difference in the algorithm's running time?
3. Under what circumstances would it make a difference whether you use an $O(n^2)$ sorting algorithm or an $O(n \log n)$ sorting algorithm? Name some $O(n^2)$ sorting algorithms. Name some $O(n \log n)$ sorting algorithms.
4. Is there any restriction on the use of exponential algorithms for practical purposes?

1. What is the largest problem size, n, that could be solved before the sun burns out, if the computation requires 2^n steps at one microsecond per step? Assume the sun will burn out after 1.5768×10^{23} microseconds (which equals 5 billion years).

2. Suppose you are working for a catalog company that prints various kinds of catalogs for use by targeted industries. Your boss wants you to take a tape containing 262,144 records for the entries in the telephone book for your city, and sort it in the order of increasing telephone numbers, so your company can print a "reverse telephone book" to sell to real estate brokers (who, for business reasons, like to be able to look up the name and address of the person having a given telephone number, starting with the telephone number). For simplicity, you can think of your task as sorting 262,144 telephone numbers into increasing order. Your boss has decided to rent time on a local mainframe at $100 per minute. There are two sorting algorithms you can run on this mainframe. **SelectionSort** runs in exactly n^2 microseconds, and **QuickSort** runs in exactly $n \log_2 n$ microseconds, where n is the number of items to be sorted. How much time will **SelectionSort** and **QuickSort** take to sort the 262,144 numbers? How much will each method cost, at $100 per minute? Which method is preferable on the basis of cost?

3. If you have an option for doing "syntax checking only" on your C compiler, try timing how long it takes for your C compiler to parse programs of various lengths. Plot the parsing times (measured with a stopwatch or a wall clock) versus the program lengths (in characters) on a graph. What is the relationship? Do you conjecture that your C parsing algorithm runs in time $O(n)$?

4. Try searching for words in your word processor on documents of various lengths (measured in bytes or word counts). Plot search times versus document lengths on a graph. Do you conjecture that the search algorithm is an $O(n)$ algorithm?

6.4   O-Notation—Definition and Manipulation

Learning Objectives

1. To learn the formal definition of O-notation.
2. To learn how to prove formally that a given function $f(n)$ is $O(g(n))$.
3. To learn some useful shortcuts for manipulating O-notation.

what O-notation means

In the analysis of algorithms that we are about to explore, we will use O-notation of the form $O(g(n))$ to help characterize the time or space requirements of running algorithms. If n is a parameter that characterizes the size of the input to a given algorithm, and if we say the algorithm runs to completion in $O(g(n))$ steps, we mean that the actual number of steps executed is no more than a constant times $g(n)$, provided we deal with sufficiently large problems.

the formal definition

The preceding sections in this chapter were intended to help you develop intuition for O-notation in advance of encountering its formal definition. But now the moment has arrived to give the precise, formal definition.

> **Definition of O-Notation:** We say that $f(n)$ is $O(g(n))$ if there exist two positive constants K and n_0 such that $|f(n)| \leq K|g(n)|$ for all $n \geq n_0$.

It helps to shift our point of view by trying to interpret what this definition is trying to say in graphical terms. Figure 6.12 shows graphically the meaning of the definition of O-notation.

Assume for the moment that we are dealing with positive functions, meaning that when we plot $f(n)$ and $g(n)$, their curves both lie above the horizontal axis. Basically, Figure 6.12 says that a given function $f(n)$ can be shown to be $O(g(n))$ provided the curve, $K \times g(n)$, for some constant multiple of $g(n)$, can be made to lie *the graphical meaning* above the curve for $f(n)$ whenever we are to the right of some big enough value n_0. A *of O-notation* second way of saying this is that there is some way to choose a constant of proportionality K so that the curve for $f(n)$ is bounded above by the curve for $K \times g(n)$, whenever n is big enough (i.e., whenever $n \geq n_0$). A third way of saying this is that for all but finitely many small values of n, the curve for $f(n)$ lies below the curve for some suitably large constant multiple of $g(n)$.

An Example of a Formal Proof of O-Notation

Suppose algorithm A sorts a sequence of n numbers in an array into ascending order, and suppose it can be shown that the exact number of steps algorithm A executes is *a formal reasoning process* $f(n) = 3 + 6 + 9 + \ldots + 3n$ steps. Then it can be asserted that the algorithm runs in $O(n^2)$ steps by the following formal reasoning process.

First, we attempt to find what is called a closed-form expression for the sum $f(n) = 3 + 6 + 9 + \ldots + 3n$, meaning a formula for $f(n)$ in terms of n that does not use

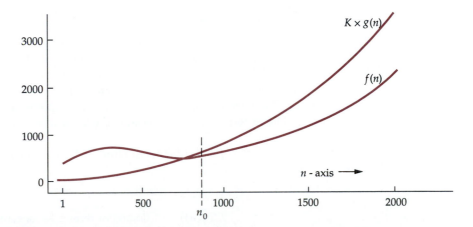

Figure 6.12 Graphical Meaning of O-Notation

the three dots (. . .) in it. To do this, we could note that $f(n) = 3 (1+ 2 + \ldots + n)$, and we could use Formula A.4 for the sum of the first n integers given in the "Math Reference" appendix, which tells us that $S = 1 + 2 + \ldots + n = n(n+1)/2$. This allows us to write:

$$f(n) = \frac{3n(n+1)}{2}.$$

the key to the formal proof

Then, choosing $K = 3$, $n_0 = 1$, and $g(n) = n^2$, and substituting in the formal definition for O-notation, we can demonstrate that $|f(n)| \leq K |g(n)|$ for all $n \geq n_0$, provided we can demonstrate that the following inequality holds true for all $n \geq 1$:

$$\frac{3n(n+1)}{2} \leq 3n^2.$$

Multiplying both sides by 2/3 and multiplying out the left side yields:

$$n^2 + n \leq 2n^2.$$

Subtracting n^2 from both sides gives:

$$n \leq n^2.$$

Dividing the latter inequality by n gives, $1 \leq n$, which clearly holds for all $n \geq 1$.

Thus we have formally proven that $f(n)$ is $O(n^2)$ by showing that $f(n)$ satisfies the formal definition of $O(n^2)$. In actual practice, there are some shortcuts we can use to make the determination of the O-notation much simpler.

Practical Shortcuts for Manipulating O-Notation

making it easy to determine O-notation

In order to prove rigorously that $f(n)$ is $O(g(n))$, we have to provide a formal proof such as the one given in the previous paragraphs. However, computer scientists have learned to apply some shortcuts that make it much easier to determine a suitable O-notation for $f(n)$, once a closed form for $f(n)$ has been obtained.

Basically, this involves separating the expression for $f(n)$ into a dominant term and lesser terms and throwing away the lesser terms. In symbols, if

$$f(n) = (\text{dominant term}) \pm (\text{lesser terms})$$

then

$$O(f(n)) = O(\text{dominant term} \pm \text{lesser terms}) = O(\text{dominant term}).$$

$$O(1) < O(\log n) < O(n) < O(n \log n) < O(n^2) < O(n^3) < O(2^n) < O(10^n).$$

Figure 6.13 Scale of Strength for O-Notation

We can rank the functions given in Table 6.7 on a scale of strength such as the one given in Fig. 6.13. Then we can use this scale to determine which among a number of terms is dominant and which are the lesser terms. Given two terms A and B on the scale in Fig. 6.13, we say A is a dominant term and B is a lesser term, if $O(B) < O(A)$ on the scale. For example, $O(n^3)$ dominates $O(n \log n)$ on the scale. This means that we could write $O(n^3 + n \log n) = O(n^3 + \cancel{n \log n}) = O(n^3)$.

using a scale to identify dominant terms

If there are coefficients (or constants of proportionality) involved, we can ignore them when determining dominant and lesser terms, and then simply cross them out in the final step. For instance, we could write:

$$
\begin{aligned}
O(6n^3 - 15n^2 + 3n \log n) &= O(6n^3 - \cancel{15n^2 + 3n \log n}) && \text{drop lesser terms} \\
&= O(\cancel{6}n^3) && \text{drop coefficient 6} \\
&= O(n^3). && \text{final result is } n^3
\end{aligned}
$$

You may have noticed that, when writing O-notation, we never used the bases of the logarithms involved, as in writing $O(\log n)$ or $O(n \log n)$. Why didn't we write logarithms with specific bases, as in writing $O(n \log_2 n)$? The answer is related to the fact that changing the bases of logarithms involves multiplying by a suitable constant. For instance, to change a base-2 logarithm into a base-10 logarithm, we can use the conversion formula:

ignoring bases of logarithms

$$\log_{10} n = \frac{\log_2 n}{\log_2 10}$$

but since

$$\frac{1}{\log_2 10}$$

is a specific constant of proportionality with the value, 0.3010, we could have written this conversion formula as:

$$\log_{10} n = 0.3010 \times \log_2 n.$$

So since changing logarithm bases only involves multiplying by new constants of proportionality, and since O-notation ignores constants of proportionality, we ignore logarithm bases inside O-notation.

A similar consideration holds for the reason we always write O(1) to denote the O-notation for constants. Suppose we could prove that algorithm A runs in a number of steps $f(n)$ that are always less than K steps, no matter what the problem size n is. Then we would have proven that $f(n) \leq K$ for all $n \geq 1$. But this is the same as proving that $f(n) \leq K \times 1$ for all $n \geq 1$, which, in turn proves $f(n)$ is O(1), or that $f(n)$ is $O(g(n))$ where $g(n) = 1$, according to the formal definition of O-notation.

why we write O(1)

To achieve mathematical rigor, we would actually have to prove that the kinds of manipulations we used above are permissible. For instance, suppose we are trying to justify $O(6\,n^2 + \cancel{5\,n\log n}) = O(\cancel{6}\,n^2) = O(n^2)$. We could start with a known inequality, such as $\log_2 n < n$, for all $n \geq 1$. Multiplying both sides of the inequality by $5n$ gives: $5\,n\log_2 n < 5n^2$, for all $n \geq 1$. Then, by adding $6\,n^2$ to both sides, we could use this last inequality to show that $6\,n^2 + 5\,n\log_2 n < 6\,n^2 + 5n^2$ for all $n \geq 1$. Now, if we take $f(n) = 6\,n^2 + 5\,n\log_2 n$ and $g(n) = n^2$, what we have shown is that $f(n) < 11 \times g(n)$, for all $n \geq 1$. But this is just a formal proof that the function $f(n) = 6\,n^2 + 5\,n\log_2 n$ is $O(n^2)$. We have succeeded in justifying our actions of cancelling lesser terms and throwing away constants of proportionality, in this one case. (Other cases are similar, and involve starting with inequalities that establish $f(n) \leq g(n)$ for $n \geq n_0$ on the scale of Fig. 6.13. Such inequalities are then multiplied by other inequalities or equalities and are added together to establish the proof of the cancellations being investigated.)

why our shortcuts are justified

In actual practice, when O-notation is used by computer scientists, there are two more implicit assumptions:

1. The bound is as tight as the speaker can make it, even though the definition of O-notation does not require a tight bound. For example, if we say that an algorithm is $O(n^2)$, then so far as we know, the algorithm is neither $O(n \log n)$, nor $O(n)$, nor in any of the classes weaker than $O(n^2)$ in Fig. 6.13. Note that, according to the formal definition of O-notation, if a function $f(n)$ is $O(n)$, then it is also $O(n^2)$, $O(n^3)$, ... , but we speak only of the tightest upper bound we know of.
2. When we speak of a function being $O(g(n))$, we make $g(n)$ as simple as possible. In particular, we make $g(n)$ a single term with a coefficient of one. For example, we would choose to say that $f(n)$ is $O(n^2)$ rather than saying that $f(n)$ is $O(3n^2 + n \log n)$, even though both statements are correct.

6.4 Review Questions

1. Give the formal definition of O-notation from memory. Compare your result with the definition given in this section to make sure you have given it correctly.
2. In your own words, describe what it means to say that $f(n)$ is $O(g(n))$.
3. In your own words, describe what you need to do to provide a formal proof that $f(n)$ is $O(g(n))$.
4. In your own words, describe some shortcuts that could allow you to conclude quickly that the O-notation for $O(18\,n\log_2 n + 19\,n + 3)$ is $O(n \log n)$.
5. Why is there no base in the logarithm notation used in the O-notation, $O(n \log n)$?
6. Why is the O-notation for a constant running time always given as O(1)?

6.4 Exercises

1. What is the simplest and best O-notation for $f(n) = 2n \log_2 n + 4n + 17 \log_2 n$?
2. What is the simplest and best O-notation for $f(n) = 5n^3 + 3n^2 + 4n + 8$?
3. Give a formal proof that $f(n) = 5n^3 + 3n^2 + 4n + 8$ is $O(n^3)$.
4. Give a formal proof that $f(n) = 7*2^n + 9*n^3$ is $O(2^n)$.
5. Give a formal proof that $\log(n + 1)$ is $O(\log n)$.

6.5   Analyzing Simple Algorithms**

Learning Objectives

1. To learn how to analyze simple yet important algorithms.
2. To see examples of algorithm analyses in each of the following complexity classes: $O(\log n)$, $O(n)$, $O(n \log n)$, $O(n^2)$ and $O(2^n)$.
3. To learn to apply the formulas for the sums of arithmetic and geometric progressions to find the closed form of sums used in algorithm analysis.
4. To learn to solve recurrence relations using unrolling and summing.

a sequence of progressive examples

Much can be gained by examining a sequence of progressive examples. We start with simple algorithms for searching for an item in a list. Next, we analyze a simple sorting algorithm, SelectionSort, which we proved correct in Chapter 5. We progress to an analysis of binary searching in ordered arrays. Then we compare the efficiencies of binary searching and sequential searching, using the results of our analysis.

why sums and recurrence relations are useful

There is a reason why sums and recurrence relations are so often useful in algorithm analysis. Basically, it is because algorithms always achieve their overall net results either (1) by composing small steps, whose stepwise costs can be summed, or (2) by decomposing the overall problem into subproblems, solving the subproblems, and combining the subproblem solutions—leading to recurrence relations that express the relation between the cost of solving the whole problem and the component costs of solving the subproblems and combining their solutions. Sums of stepwise costs often arise when analyzing iterative algorithms, and recurrence relations often arise when analyzing recursive algorithms.

Analysis of Sequential Searching

Suppose we have an array $A[0:n-1]$ that contains distinct keys, K_i, $(1 \leq i \leq n)$, where each key, K_i, is stored in the array item, $A[i-1]$ as shown in Fig. 6.14.

$$
\begin{array}{ccccc}
K_1 & K_2 & K_3 & \cdots & K_n \\
A[0] & A[1] & A[2] & \cdots & A[n-1]
\end{array}
$$

Figure 6.14 An Array $A[0:n-1]$ of n Keys

```
      |  /*
      |   *      Function to search in a SearchArray A for an occurrence of a key K
      |   */
      |
  5   |  #define   n            100                         /* or whatever */
      |  typedef   arbitrary    Key;                /* the Key's type can be arbitrary */
      |  typedef   Key          SearchArray[n];
      |
      |
 10   |  int SequentialSearch(Key K, SearchArray A)
      |  {
      |
      |      int i:                         /* i indexes successive locations, A[i], in A */
      |
 15   |      for (i = 0; i < n; + + i) {        /* enumerate successive positions A[i] */
      |
      |          if ( K == A[i] ) {                        /* if A[i] contains key K */
      |
      |              return i;              /* return i as the position of key K in array A */
 20   |          }
      |
      |      }
      |                                   /* if the entire array A was scanned and key K */
 25   |      return ( − 1);               /* was not found, then return −1 for "not found" */
      |
      |  }
```

Program 6.15 Sequential Searching

analyzing sequential
search

Suppose we are given a search key, K, and suppose our task is to find the position of the key K in A[0:n–1]—that is, we want to find the integer i in 0:n–1, such that K == A[i]. (As a precaution, let's agree to say that if K is not in A[0:n–1], it is at position –1.) Program 6.15 is a simple function to give the position of K in A[0:n–1].

We can see that the amount of work done to locate a key K depends on the position in which we find it in A[0:n–1]. For example, if K == A[0], then we have to make only one comparison of K with the key stored in A[0], after which we exit from the **SequentialSearch** function. On the other hand, if K == A[n–1], and K is not

it takes i comparisons to
determine that K = A[i]

equal to any of the earlier keys in A[0:n–2], we still have to compare K against all (n – 1) keys in A[0:n–2]—which takes (n – 1) comparisons—after which, we make the final comparison of K against A[n–1] to determine that K == A[n–1]. This is a total of n comparisons to find K in position A[n–1]. By similar reasoning, we can determine that it takes exactly i comparisons to find K in A[i–1] for any i in the range 1:n.

the best case and the
worst case

From this discussion, we can instantly determine the *best case* and the *worst case* for successful sequential searches. The best case happens when we find K in position A[0]. This takes O(1) running time. The worst case happens when we find K in the last position of the array A[0:n–1]. Since n comparisons were required, this takes an amount of work proportional to the length of the array, n, plus possibly some overhead for setting up the for-loop and for calling the function in the first place. The amount of work is therefore of the form $an + b$ for some constants a and b. The O-notation for the worst case is therefore, $O(an + \not b) = O(\not a\, n) = O(n)$. But what about the "average" case?

To reason about the average case, let's assume that each key in $A[0{:}n{-}1]$ is equally likely to be used in a search. The average can then be computed by taking the total of all the work done for finding all of the different keys and dividing by n. The work needed to find the ith key, K_i, is of the form $a\,i + b$ for the same constants a and b used in the worst case analysis. Now we have to add up the terms $a\,i + b$ for all i in the range $(1 \le i \le n)$, and then divide the total by n. First,

the average case

$$\text{Total} = \sum_{i=1}^{n}(a\,i+b) = a\sum_{i=1}^{n}i + \sum_{i=1}^{n}b.$$

Now, applying the formula for the sum

$$S = (1+2+\ldots+n) = \sum_{i=1}^{n}i = n(n+1)/2,$$

the Total simplifies to:

$$\text{Total} = a\frac{n(n+1)}{2} + bn.$$

The Average is gotten by dividing the Total by n:

$$\text{Average} = \frac{\text{Total}}{n} = a\frac{(n+1)}{2} + b$$

$$= \frac{a}{2}n + \left(\frac{a}{2}+b\right).$$

The last quantity is of the form $a'\,n + b'$ where $a' = a/2$ and $b' = (a/2 + b)$. We see that the O-notation for $O(a'\,n + b')$ is $O(n)$, using the same process as before. Consequently, **SequentialSearch** has a *linear* average running time (since it is of the form $O(n)$).

average searches take time O(n)

Analysis of SelectionSort

analyzing the inner loop first

In this subsection, we analyze the **SelectionSort** algorithm given in Program 6.1 at the beginning of the chapter. For convenience, we reproduce Program 6.1 here with less

```
   |    void SelectionSort(InputArray A)
   |    {
   |        int MinPosition, temp, i, j;
   |
5  |        for(i = n − 1; i > 0; − − i) {
   |            MinPosition = i;
   |            for( j = 0; j < i; + + j) {
   |                if (A[j] < A[MinPosition]) MinPosition = j;
   |            }
10 |            temp = A[i]; A[i] = A[MinPosition]; A[MinPosition] = temp;
   |        }
   |    }
```

Program 6.16 Selection Sorting Algorithm for Sorting A[0:n–1]

blank space as Program 6.16. In a case like this, which involves one for-loop nested inside another outer for-loop, it is helpful to begin by analyzing the inner for-loop—the one on lines 7:9 of Program 6.16. This is of the form:

```
   |        for ( j = 0; j < i; + + j) {
   |            ( Action1 )
   |        }
```

where **Action1** is the if-statement, if (A[j] < A[MinPosition]) MinPosition = j;. Looking at the cost of performing this if-statement, we see that it can have one of two time unit values: v_1 or $v_1 + v_2$, where v_1 is the cost in time units needed to perform the comparison, A[j] < A[MinPosition] and to decide whether or not to perform the assignment in the body of the if-statement, and v_2 is the cost in time units needed to perform this assignment, MinPosition = j. In the case that the comparison A[j] < A[MinPosition] is false, we do not perform the assignment, MinPosition = j, so the cost of performing the entire if-statement is just v_1. But if the comparison turns out to be true, we must perform the assignment at an additional cost v_2, making the total time to perform the if-statement $v_1 + v_2$. In either case, the cost of performing the if-statement is at most $v_1 + v_2$.

making a simplifying assumption

Here is a case where we need to make a simplifying assumption in order to continue smoothly with our algorithm analysis. We are going to consider only the maximum cost behavior, and focus on the fact that the if-statement takes at most $v_1 + v_2$ time units to perform. Since the O-notation we are aiming to derive is formally defined in terms of upper bounds, this simplifying assumption shouldn't invalidate our eventual conclusion. Moreover, since the expression, $v_1 + v_2$, is awkward to write over and over in our derivations, we will choose a simple constant, a, to stand for it. In summary, we shall assume that the if-statement in **Action1** takes at most $a = v_1 + v_2$ time units to perform, where a is a suitable constant.

Now we can figure out how much it costs to perform the for-statement in the fragment:

```
   |        for ( j = 0; j < i; + + j) {
   |            ( Action1 )
   |        }
```

This is done by noting that the for-statement performs **Action1** once for each value of the index j, where j assumes each value in the range $0{:}i-1$. A reasonable characterization for this is that it costs $i*a$ to perform this for-loop. (Here, for complete accuracy, we might want to think of including some overhead time for performing the mechanics of the for-loop, meaning the time required for initializing, incrementing, and testing the variable j. However, for simplicity, we might reasonably imagine that the cost for **Action1** is increased a bit to take these overhead costs into account, since most of these overhead costs consume a fixed amount of time on each trip through the for-loop.)

the cost of executing
the for-loop

In short, we can account for the cost of performing the for-loop by estimating that it costs $i*a$ time units consisting of i repetitions of the cost a, of performing **Action1** (where the cost a folds in some overhead costs for repeating the for-loop).

As a next step, we write down a copy of the outer for-loop in Program 6.16, in which we replace statements in its body with formulas describing their costs in time units. This is done as follows:

```
     |        for (i = n − 1; i > 0; − − i) {
  5  |
     |            Cost b₁                    /* for performing the assignment: MinPosition = i */
     |
     |            Cost i∗a                          /* for performing the inner for-loop */
     |
 10  |            Cost b₂                  /* for exchanging A[i] and A[MinPosition] */
     |
     |        }
```

Letting the constant $b = b_1 + b_2$, we can simplify this one more time to be:

```
     |        for (i = n − 1; i > 0; − − i) {
     |
     |            Cost i∗a + b             /* for performing contents of outer for-loop */
 10  |
     |        }
```

Noting that the outer for-loop lets its index variable i range downward over the values from $n-1$ to 1, we are ready to sum up the cost $a\,i + b$, for each value of the variable, i, in the range $1{:}n-1$ of the outer for-loop. This gives a sum of the form:

$$S = \sum_{i=1}^{n-1} \left(a\,i + b\right).$$

In a moment we shall need to use the formula for the sum of the first $n-1$ integers $(1 + 2 + \ldots + (n-1))$. This is a special case of formula A.4 of the *Math Reference* appendix in which $n-1$ is substituted for n. The value of the resulting sum is $((n-1)n)/2$.

And now, by manipulating the sum and substituting the value $(n{-}1)n/2$ for the sum of the arithmetic progression $(1 + 2 + ... + n{-}1)$, we get:

$$S = \sum_{i=1}^{n-1} \left(ai + b\right)$$

$$= a\sum_{i=1}^{n-1} i \; + \; \sum_{i=1}^{n-1} b$$

$$= a\frac{(n-1)n}{2} \; + \; (n-1)b$$

$$= \frac{a}{2}n^2 \; + \; \left(b - \frac{a}{2}\right)n \; - \; b.$$

concluding that the O-notation is O(n²)

The last line shows that the sum of the costs S is of the form, $f(n) = a'n^2 + b'n + c'$, where $a' = (a/2)$, $b' = (b - a/2)$, and $c' = -b$. It is now easy to determine the O-notation for S. Using the process we learned in Section 6.4 (keep the dominant term, drop the lesser terms, then drop the coefficient of the dominant term), we see that S is $O(n^2)$.

The algorithm analysis we have just completed establishes that the running time for the **SelectionSort** algorithm is $O(n^2)$. You can see that this analysis agrees well with the data in Table 6.3, the curves we plotted in Fig. 6.4, and the running time equations we gave in Eqs. 6.1.

Analysis of Recursive SelectionSort

Let's now analyze the recursive version of the **SelectionSort** algorithm, given as Program 6.17. This time we will set up and solve some simple recurrence relations in order to illustrate a second method of analysis. To use this recursive version to perform selection sorting on the array A[0:n–1], we make the function call, SelectionSort(A, n–1).

The first thing we need to do is to analyze the running time of the function, **FindMin**, given on lines 3:9 of Program 6.17. This analysis is similar to the one used to analyze the running time of the inner for-loop on lines 7:9 of Program 6.16. The result is that the cost in time units of executing the **FindMin** function to find the position of the smallest element in A[0:n] is of the form $an + b_1$, for suitable constants a and b_1. If we let $T(n)$ stand for the cost, in time units, of calling recursive selection sort on A[0:n], we can replace the contents of the if-statement given on lines 15:19 of Program 6.17, with the following:

```
15 |     if (n > 0) {
   |           Cost an + b₁        /* the cost of doing MinPosition = FindMin(A,n) */
   |           Cost b₂             /* the cost of exchanging A[n] andA[MinPosition] */
   |           Cost T(n − 1)       /* the cost of doing SelectionSort(A, n − 1) */
   |     }
```

```
    |        /* FindMin is an auxiliary function used by SelectionSort below */
    |
    |            int FindMin(InputArray A, int n)
    |            {
  5 |                int i, j = n;
    |
    |                for (i = 0; i < n; + + i) if (A[i] < A[j]) j = i;
    |                return j;
    |            }
 10 |
    |        void SelectionSort(InputArray A, int n)   /* the main SelectionSort procedure */
    |            {
    |                int MinPosition, temp;
    |
 15 |                if (n > 0) {
    |                    MinPosition = FindMin(A,n);
    |                    temp = A[n]; A[n] = A[MinPosition]; A[MinPosition] = temp;
    |                    SelectionSort(A, n – 1);
    |                }
    |            }
```

Program 6.17 Another Version of Recursive **SelectionSort**

setting up a recurrence relation

At this point, letting $b = (b_1 + b_2)$, we can write a general recurrence relation for $T(n)$ in terms of $T(n-1)$, since what the if-statement tells us is that the cost $T(n)$, for solving the whole selection sorting problem on A[0:n], is the sum of the costs on lines 16:18, as follows:

$$T(n) = a\,n + b + T(n-1), \quad \text{provided } n > 0.$$

the need for base cases

In recurrence relations, we need base cases, just as we do for recursive functions. In this case, calling, **SelectionSort**(A,0), to sort the subarray A[0:0], causes Program 6.17 to evaluate the condition $n > 0$ in the if-clause on line 15, and then to exit from the procedure. The cost of doing this is always the same, no matter how big the original problem size, n, was. So we can let $T(0) = c$, for some suitable constant, c. Recurrence Relations 6.3 can now be given completely.

$$T(0) = c$$
$$T(n) = a\,n + b + T(n-1)$$

(6.3)

Recurrence Relations

solution by the method of unrolling

To solve such recurrence relations, we can use the method of *unrolling*. We just write the general form for $T(n)$ in terms of $T(n-1)$, and then expand the formula for $T(n-1)$ in terms of $T(n-2)$, and so on. The unrolling stops when we expand the base case $T(0)$. We then examine the unrolled sum that results, and we see if we can apply some known summation formula to reduce it to a closed formula in terms of n. Let's try this approach.

$$T(n) = a\,n + b + T(n-1)$$
$$T(n) = a\,n + b + a(n-1) + b + T(n-2)$$
$$T(n) = a\,n + b + a(n-1) + b + a(n-2) + b + T(n-3)$$
$$\ldots$$
$$T(n) = a\,n + b + a(n-1) + b + a(n-2) + b + \ldots + a{*}1 + b + T(0)$$
$$T(n) = a\,n + b + a(n-1) + b + a(n-2) + b + \ldots + a{*}1 + b + c$$

Now, we can rearrange some of the terms, so all those with the coefficient a are collected together, and all those of the form b are collected together, as follows:

$$T(n) = (a\,n + a(n-1) + a(n-2) + \ldots + a{*}1) + n\,b + c$$

and from this,

$$T(n) = \sum_{i=1}^{n} (ai) + nb + c$$
$$= a\frac{n(n+1)}{2} + nb + c$$
$$= \frac{a}{2}n^2 + \left(\frac{a}{2} + b\right)n + c$$

concluding that T(n) is O(n²)

By multiplying out and collecting terms, we see that $T(n)$ can be put into the form, $T(n) = a'n^2 + b'n + c'$, where $a' = (a/2)$, $b' = (a/2 + b)$, and $c' = c$. So $T(n)$ is $O(n^2)$. Moreover, $T(n-1)$, which is the cost of calling **SelectionSort(A, n–1)** to sort A[0:n–1], can be multiplied out and simplified into the form $an^2 + bn + c$, which is also $O(n^2)$.

why recurrence relations work for recursive functions

The reason that recurrence relations work well when applied to recursive functions is that a recursive function typically solves a big problem by breaking it into smaller subproblems and combining the subproblem solutions. Following this decomposition pattern, the recurrence relation gives the cost of solving the whole problem expressed as a sum of the costs of solving the smaller subproblems and the cost of combining the subproblem solutions. This gives us a powerful method for analyzing algorithms, provided we know something about how to solve recurrence relations.

Another instance of this theme occurs when we perform the algorithm analysis for the running time of the Towers of Hanoi program. In Section 3.4 of Chapter 3, we guessed at the solution of the recurrence relations for the Towers of Hanoi, and we promised to show how to solve the recurrence later on. Now is the time to deliver on that promise.

Analysis of Towers of Hanoi

To refresh your memory, in the Towers of Hanoi puzzle we have to move a pile of n different-sized disks from a starting peg to a finishing peg, using a third peg as an intermediary. The rules of the puzzle restrict us from putting a larger disk on top of a smaller one. This forces the least wasteful solution to assume a particular form for moving piles containing n disks, whenever $n > 1$: (1) first move a pile of $n - 1$ disks from the start peg to the intermediary peg, then (2) move the bottom disk from the start peg to the finishing peg, and finally (3) move a pile of $n - 1$ disks from the intermediary peg to the finishing peg. If the pile of disks to be moved contains just one disk, we move the disk directly from the start peg to the finishing peg. The recursive algorithm expressing this policy is given as Program 3.23, and the recurrence relations that analyze the number of times disks have to be moved are given as Recurrence Relations 3.2. The recurrence relations that express the running time of the algorithm (as opposed to the number of disk moves) are similar to Recurrence Relations 3.2, and are given as Recurrence Relations 6.4.

$$T(1) = a$$
$$T(n) = b + 2\,T(n - 1)$$

(6.4)

Recurrence Relations

what the recurrence relations tell us

These recurrence relations say two things: (1) Calling the **MoveTowers** function in Program 3.23 when $n = 1$, costs a constant number of time units, a, and (2) The cost of calling **MoveTowers** for $n > 1$, costs a constant number of time units, b, plus twice the cost of calling **MoveTowers** on problems of size $n - 1$.

Let's now solve Recurrence Relations 6.4, using the technique of *unrolling plus summation*. (This technique is the main one we will develop in this section for solving recurrence relations. The "Math Reference" appendix gives one additional method based on *summing factors*.)

To unroll the equation for $T(n)$, we replace the expression for $T(n - 1)$ on its right side with the expanded version of $T(n - 1)$, as follows:

$T(n) = b + 2\,T(n - 1)$	from the original equation
$T(n) = b + 2\,(\,b + 2\,T(n - 2)\,)$	after expanding $T(n - 1)$
$T(n) = b + 2\,b + 2^2\,T(n - 2)$	multiplying through by 2

Now, as we keep unrolling, by expanding $T(n - 1)$, $T(n - 2)$, and so on, up until $T(n - i)$, we begin looking for a general pattern to emerge. Watch what happens:

$T(n) = b + 2\,b + 2^2\,(\,b + 2\,T(n - 3)\,)$	expand
$T(n) = b + 2\,b + 2^2\,b + 2^3\,T(n - 3)$	multiply out
...	keep going
$T(n) = b + 2\,b + 2^2\,b + ... + 2^{(i-1)}\,b + 2^i\,T(n - i)$	until ith expansion

You can see that as the expansions continue, the value of the parameter n in $T(n)$ keeps getting smaller and smaller. After the ith expansion, it has counted down from n to $(n - i)$. Eventually, when $i = (n - 1)$, the unrolling process must stop, because we encounter the base case, $T(1)$. In other words, when $i = (n - 1)$,

$$T(n - i) = T(n - (n - 1)) = T(n - n + 1) = T(1) = a\,.$$

stopping the
unrolling process

So we can stop the unrolling process on the $(n-1)$st expansion exactly when $i = (n-1)$ by substituting a for $T(n-i)$ and by substituting $(n-1)$ for i each place it occurs. This yields the following unrolled form for $T(n)$:

$$T(n) = 2^0\,b + 2^1\,b + 2^2\,b + \ldots + 2^{(n-2)}\,b + 2^{(n-1)}\,a \qquad \text{expansion stops}$$

spotting geometric
progressions

Note that we rewrote the coefficients of the first two terms $(b + 2\,b)$ in the new form $(2^0\,b + 2^1\,b)$ to make it easier to spot the general pattern. Can you spot the pattern? [*Hint*: If you can't see it, maybe it would be a good time to read through the "Math Reference" appendix and brush up on sums of geometric progressions.] Re-expressing the last line using the notation for sums, gives:

$$T(n) \;=\; \sum_{i=0}^{n-2} 2^i b \;+\; 2^{(n-1)} a \;=\; b \sum_{i=0}^{n-2} 2^i \;+\; 2^{(n-1)} a.$$

Now it's time to recognize that the sum

$$S \;=\; \sum_{i=0}^{n-2} 2^i$$

on the right side is just a standard geometric progression that adds up powers of 2, starting with $2^0 = 1$, ending with $2^{(n-2)}$, and having the form $S = (1 + 2 + 4 + 8 + \ldots + 2^{(n-2)})$. Applying Formula A.8 of the "Math Reference" appendix, the closed form for this sum is:

$$S \;=\; \frac{2^{(n-1)} - 1}{2 - 1} \;=\; 2^{(n-1)} - 1.$$

Consequently, we can rewrite the last equation for $T(n)$, by replacing the sum S with its closed form solution. This gives:

$$T(n) \;=\; b\left(2^{(n-1)} - 1 \right) + 2^{(n-1)} a.$$

A nearly final form for $T(n)$ now follows from collecting terms:

$$T(n) \;=\; (a + b)\, 2^{(n-1)} - b.$$

This can be expressed more cleanly in final form by multiplying $2^{(n-1)}$ by 2 to give 2^n, meanwhile dividing $(a + b)$ by 2 to compensate:

$$T(n) \;=\; \frac{(a+b)}{2} 2^n - b. \qquad\qquad (6.5)$$

checking your solution

[*Hint:* In your own work, when you have derived a solution such as this, it is a good moment to check that your solution satisfies the original recurrence relations. This is done first by checking the base case and then by checking the general case for $n > 1$. For example, $T(1) = ((a + b)/2) 2^1 - b = (a + b) - b = a$. So the base case, $T(1) = a$, is correct. Next, using your general solution, expand $T(n - 1)$ getting $T(n - 1) = ((a + b)/2) 2^{(n-1)} - b$. Then multiply it by 2 and add b, to see if it yields the solution for $T(n)$. This gives,

$$
\begin{aligned}
b + 2T(n-1) &= b + 2\left(\frac{(a+b)}{2} 2^{(n-1)} - b \right) \\
&= b + \left(\frac{(a+b)}{2} 2^n - 2b \right) \\
&= \frac{(a+b)}{2} 2^n - b \\
&= T(n).
\end{aligned}
$$

Thus you have proven that your general solution satisfies the original Recurrence Relations 6.4.]

Now we are ready to show that our solution to the number of disk moves in the Towers of Hanoi puzzle, which was $L(n) = 2^n - 1$, falls out of the general solution given in Eq. 6.5 to Recurrence Relations 6.4 when $a = b = 1$. This special case is exactly the same as that given in Recurrence Relations 3.2:

$$
\begin{aligned}
L(1) &= 1 \\
L(n) &= 2\,L(n-1) + 1 \qquad \text{for } n > 1.
\end{aligned}
$$

Consequently, by substituting $a = b = 1$ in Eq. 6.5, we get the solution to Recurrence Relations 3.2, which is:

$$
L(n) = \frac{(1+1)}{2} 2^n - 1 = 2^n - 1.
$$

If we measured some running times for executing the procedure **MoveTowers** in Program 3.23, to solve the Towers of Hanoi puzzle, we might expect the actual running times to be fit by a curve of the form, $T(n) = c\,2^n - b$, derived from Eq. 6.5 by setting $c = (a + b)/2$. (Exercise 6.5.1 asks you to collect some running time data for **MoveTowers** and to see if Eq. 6.5 fits your data.)

Using our method for determining the O-notation for $T(n) = c\,2^n - b$, we see immediately that $T(n)$ is $O(2^n)$. Thus we have proven that the Towers of Hanoi algorithm runs in exponential time.

Before considering the next algorithm to analyze, it is useful to state the solution to some recurrence relations slightly more general than Recurrence Relations 6.4. If we generalize by replacing the 2 in Recurrence Relations 6.4 with a general constant d, and if we add some terms $b\,n + c$, we get Recurrence Relations 6.6.

$$T(1) = a$$
$$T(n) = b\,n + c + d\,T(n-1)$$
(6.6)
Recurrence Relations

solving a general form of these recurrences

We can solve these recurrence relations by the same method we used above—namely, by unrolling and summing. Provided $d > 1$, the sum turns out to be a geometric progression identical to the one we saw, except that d replaces 2. The general solution is given in Table 6.18.

This solution table (along with Table 6.21 and Table A.12 of the appendix) is given in the *Math Survival Guide*, which accompanies this book. These three tables of recurrence relation solutions are handy for solving many of the elementary recurrence relations that we will encounter in analyzing algorithms.

Analysis of MergeSort

One technique that is useful for analyzing algorithms is to analyze a general program strategy instead of analyzing the detailed C program which is the refinement of that strategy. That is, you first apply abstraction to a given algorithm to express its essential actions, and then you analyze the abstract form of it.

As an example of this technique, we are going to analyze an abstract algorithm for merge sorting. We will never actually see the refined C program for merge sorting. Instead, we'll present and analyze only the program strategy.

the basic idea for merge sorting

The basic idea for merge sorting a list, such as (5, 3, 8, 6, 7, 2, 4, 1), is a three-step process: (1) *divide* the list in two halves, L = (5, 3, 8, 6) and R = (7, 2, 4, 1); (2) *sort* the two half-lists, getting L = (3, 5, 6, 8) and R = (1, 2, 4, 7); and (3) *merge* the two half-lists into the final sorted list, Merge(L, R) = (1, 2, 3, 4, 5, 6, 7, 8). The abstract program strategy for doing this is given as Program Strategy 6.19. Suppose

Table 6.18 Solutions to Recurrence Relations 6.6

Solutions to Recurrence Relations $T(n) = b\,n + c + d\,T(n-1)$, where $T(1) = a$	
Condition	General Solution
$d = 1$	$T(n) = \left(\dfrac{b}{2}\right)n^2 - \left(\dfrac{b}{2} + c\right)n + \left(a - b - c\right)$
$d \neq 1$	$T(n) = \left(\dfrac{a - b - c}{d} + \dfrac{b + c}{d - 1} + \dfrac{b}{(d-1)^2}\right)d^n - \left(\dfrac{b}{d-1}\right)n + \left(\dfrac{c - (b+c)d}{(d-1)^2}\right)$

```
 |     void MergeSort(ListType List)
 |     {
 |         if (the List has more than one item in it) {
 |             (break the List into two half-lists, L = LeftList and R = RightList)
5|             (sort the LeftList using MergeSort(L))
 |             (sort the RightList using MergeSort(R))
 |             (merge L and R into a single sorted List)
 |         } else {
 |             (do nothing, since the list is already sorted)
10|         }
 |     }
```

Program Strategy 6.19 Abstract Strategy for Merge Sorting

that the original list has n items in it. Then L and R each have $n/2$ items in them. (For simplicity, let's imagine that n is divisible evenly by 2, so that $n/2$ is an integer.)

If we think for a moment about how to merge two sorted half-lists, L and R, into a single sorted result list, SL, we can imagine that we start with an empty list, SL, and we repeatedly remove the smaller first item from the beginning of L or R and put it at the end of SL. When both L and R are empty, SL will be a merged list sorted in ascending order. This merging process involves moving all n items into SL, and may involve as

how to merge two lists

few as $n/2$ comparisons and as many as $(n - 1)$ comparisons between the first item in L and the first item in R (to see which first item is smaller so we'll know which one to move to the rear of SL). The cost of doing the work in the merging process is bounded above by the cost of moving n items and making n comparisons. If we are trying to get an upper bound for the cost of merge sorting, this means we can imagine that the cost in time units of merging is at most $b\,n$ where b is a suitable constant. (This is the same as claiming that merging is a linear algorithm requiring $O(n)$ running time.)

Now let's analyze the running time for Program Strategy 6.19. If we let $T(n)$ be the time required to merge sort a list of n items, Program Strategy 6.19 tells us two things: (1) If $n = 1$, **MergeSort** takes constant time to run, since it does nothing, and the only cost incurred is for calling and returning from a function that performs a simple test and determines there is nothing else to do. We can pick a suitable constant, say, a, to stand for the time required to do this, and we can write, $T(1) = a$. (2) If $n > 1$, then the time consumed by calling **MergeSort** is a sum of four times: (i) The time required to break the list into two half-lists, L and R. (Let's say this is a constant amount of time c, required, for example, to compute the midpoint of a list.) (ii) An amount of time $T(n/2)$, required to merge sort the left list, L. (iii) An identical amount of time $T(n/2)$, required to merge sort the right list, R, and (iv) An amount of time $b\,n$, required to merge L and R into the final sorted list. Adding up these four costs gives us, $T(n) = b\,n + c + 2T(n/2)$. This establishes Recurrence Relations 6.7 for the time required for merge sorting.

$$T(1) = a$$
$$T(n) = b\,n + c + 2\,T(n/2)$$

(6.7)

Recurrence Relations

solving by unrolling and
summing again

Let's see if we can solve these recurrence relations by our method of *unrolling and summing*. Before we begin, we can agree to restrict ourselves always to integer valued arguments, n, in these recurrence relations. If this is to be the case, then the argument n must always take the form $n = 2^k$, since the only kind of integer that can be divided repeatedly by 2 and still remain an integer is some power of 2.

Now let's start unrolling, simplifying as we go:

$T(n) = b n + c + 2\ T(n/2)$ from the general equation for $T(n)$

$T(n) = b n + c + 2\ (b(n/2) + c + 2\ T((n/2)/2))$ expanding $T(n/2)$

$T(n) = b n + c + 2\ b\ n/2 + 2\ c + 2^2\ T(n/2^2)$ multiplying through

$T(n) = b n + c + 2\ b\ n/2 + 2\ c + 2^2\ (b(n/2^2) + c +$ expanding $T(n/2^2)$
$\quad\quad 2\ T((n/2^2)/2))$

$T(n) = b n + c + 2\ b\ n/2 + 2\ c + 2^2\ b\ n/2^2 + 2^2\ c +$ multiplying through
$\quad\quad 2^3\ T(n/2^3)$

$\dots$ now make the inductive leap

$T(n) = 2^0\ b\ n/2^0 + 2^0\ c\ + 2^1\ b\ n/2^1 + 2^1\ c +$
$\quad\quad 2^2\ b\ n/2^2 + 2^2\ c + 2^3\ b\ n/2^3 + 2^3\ c +$

$\quad\quad \dots$

$\quad\quad 2^{(i-1)}\ b\ n/2^{(i-1)} + 2^{(i-1)}\ c + 2^i\ T(n/2^i\ )$ i^{th} expansion

Now, since we have assumed $n = 2^k$ for some k, the unrolling of $T(n/2^i)$ is the same as unrolling $T(2^k/2^i) = T(2^{(k-i)})$. The more we unroll, the more i increases. Eventually, $i = k$. At that moment, $T(2^k/2^i) = T(2^k/2^k) = T(1)$, and we hit the base case. This allows us to replace i with k, in the last line above, and then to replace $T(n/2^k) = T(1)$ with a (from Recurrence Relations 6.7). This stops the unrolling process. Now we can start summing up the unrolled terms:

$$T(n) = 2^0\ b\ n/2^0 + 2^0\ c\ +$$
$$2^1\ b\ n/2^1 + 2^1\ c\ +$$
$$2^2\ b\ n/2^2 + 2^2\ c\ +$$
$$2^3\ b\ n/2^3 + 2^3\ c\ +$$
$$\dots$$
$$2^{(k-1)}\ b\ n/2^{(k-1)} + 2^{(k-1)}\ c + 2^k\ a$$

By collecting like terms into summations, we get:

$$T(n) \ = \ b\,n\sum_{j=0}^{k-1}(2^j\,/\,2^j) \ + \ c\sum_{j=0}^{k-1}2^j \ + \ 2^k\,a$$

Since $(2^j/2^j) = 1$, the first sum

$$\sum_{j=0}^{k-1} (2^j / 2^j)$$

adds up k copies of 1, and has the value k. The second sum,

$$\sum_{j=0}^{k-1} 2^j,$$

is a geometric progression with sum $(2^k - 1)$. Using these facts to rewrite $T(n)$ gives:

$$T(n) = b\,n\,k + c\,(2^k - 1) + 2^k\,a,$$

which simplifies to

$$T(n) = b\,n\,k + (a + c)\,2^k - c.$$

To get the final useful form, we need to apply a substitution that gets rid of the occurrences of k and replaces them with expressions in n (since we want a solution in terms of n, not k). Recall that we assumed $n = 2^k$. Solving this equation for k yields $k = \log_2 n$. Then substituting $\log_2 n$ for k, and n for 2^k in the last line for $T(n)$ above gives:

$$T(n) = b\,n\,\log_2 n + (a + c)\,n - c. \qquad (6.8)$$

This is what we wanted. It establishes that the running time for merge sorting is $O(n \log n)$. It also provides a parameterized family of curves to use to try to fit some actual running time data for MergeSort.

Table 6.20 gives some actual and estimated running time data for a version of MergeSort that resulted from implementing a refinement of Program Strategy 6.19 in C. As you can see, by taking Eq. 6.8 and setting $b = 0.0037$, $a = 0.0024$, and $c = 0.0$, we get a remarkably good fit.

What we have shown is that analysis of an abstract algorithm (given only in the preliminary form of a program strategy) can lead to results that actually fit the observed running time data of program refinements not yet written. This may seem strange at first, but upon reflection you can see that it demonstrates the power of the algorithm analysis techniques we have been investigating. Another fact that might give you confidence in the approach we have been developing is that the different versions of SelectionSort we have presented (cf. Programs 5.29, 5.35, 6.16, and 6.17) all share the same running time equation $T(n) = a\,n^2 + b\,n + c$. We arrived at this equation in one case by direct summation and in another case by setting up and solving a recurrence relation. It might have been a lot simpler and yet still sufficient to analyze a simple abstract strategy for selection sorting. Exercise 6.5.3 asks you to do this.

analyzing an abstract
algorithm can give
accurate results

Table 6.20 Actual and Estimated Running Times for MergeSort in Milliseconds

$T(n) = 0.0037 * n * \log_2 n + 0.0024 * n - 0.0$				
Run	List size n	Observed data	Predicted data	Percent error
1	16	0.3	0.3	
2	32	0.7	0.7	
3	64	1.6	1.6	
4	128	3.6	3.6	
5	256	8.1	8.2	+ 1.2
6	512	18.4	18.3	− 0.5
7	1024	40.2	40.3	+ 0.2
8	2048	88.6	88.3	− 0.3
9	4096	191.1	191.7	+ 0.3

To conclude this subsection, we set up and solve a slightly more general class of parameterized recurrence relations than the special case given in Recurrence Relations 6.7. We then give a table of solutions for the general form depending on four special conditions. Recurrence Relations 6.9 give the parameterized version we are interested in solving.

$$T(1) = a$$
$$T(n) = b\,n + c + d\,T(n/p) \qquad \text{where } p > 1, d > 0.$$
(6.9)

Recurrence Relations

If we assume that n must always be an integer taking form $n = p^k$, we can use unrolling and summing to expand the general equation for $T(n)$ in Recurrence Relations 6.9 into the form given in Eq. 6.10:

$$T(n) = bn\sum_{j=0}^{k-1}(d^j/p^j) + c\sum_{j=0}^{k-1}d^j + d^k a$$
(6.10)

deriving more general results

Then, by applying the formula for the sum of a geometric progression in various special cases, and by noting that $n = p^k$ can be solved for k to yield $k = \log_p n$, we can produce the general-form solutions to Recurrence Relations 6.9 given in Table 6.21. (Exercise 6.5.4 asks you to derive these results for yourself.)

using the solution tables

Even though the solutions in Tables 6.21 and 6.18 often provide the key to solving the kinds of simple recurrence relations that arise when analyzing common algorithms, sometimes more advanced techniques are needed. George S. Lueker's paper in *Computing Surveys*, referenced at the end of this chapter, gives a good survey of many additional helpful techniques for solving recurrences.

Table 6.21 Solutions to Recurrence Relations 6.9

Solutions to Recurrence Relations $T(1) = a,\ and\ T(n) = b\,n + c + d\,T(n/p),\ where\ p > 1,\ d > 0$	
Condition	General Solution
$d = p$	$T(n) = bn\log_p n\ +\ \left(a + \dfrac{c}{d-1}\right)n\ -\ \left(\dfrac{c}{d-1}\right)$
$d = 1$	$T(n) = \left(\dfrac{bp}{p-1}\right)n + c\log_p n + \left(a - \dfrac{bp}{p-1}\right)$
$d = 1, b = 0$	$T(n) = c\log_p n\ +\ a$
$d \ne 1, d \ne p$	$T(n) = \left(a + \dfrac{bp}{d-p} + \dfrac{c}{d-1}\right)n^{\log_p d} - \left(\dfrac{bp}{d-p}\right)n - \left(\dfrac{c}{d-1}\right)$

Analysis of Binary Searching

In Chapter 5, Programs 5.41 and 5.42 gave iterative and recursive versions of binary searching, and Table 5.43 presented their running times on problems of various sizes. Let's now try to analyze the running time of binary search.

analyzing the worst case for successful searching

Following the technique used in the previous section, we could try to devise and then analyze an abstract strategy for binary searching. Program Strategy 6.22 gives one possible abstract strategy. We might decide first to analyze this program strategy

```
  |   int BinarySearch(Key K, SearchArray A, int L, int R)
  |   {
  |       /* search for the position of the search key K in the subarray A[L:R] */
  |       /* return the position of K as the value of the function */
5 |
  |       (compute the MidPoint of the interval L:R)
  |
  |       if (the search interval is empty) {
  |           (return −1, denoting that K was not found in array A)
10|       } else if (K equals the key at the MidPoint of A[L:R]) {
  |           (return the MidPoint, which gives the position of key K in array A)
  |       } else if (K is greater than the key at A[MidPoint]) {
  |           (return value of the function call BinarySearch(K, A, MidPoint+1, R))
  |           (which searches in the right half-interval, MidPoint+1:R)
15|       } else {
  |           (return value of the function call BinarySearch(K, A, L, Midpoint−1))
  |           (which searches in the left half-interval L:MidPoint−1)
  |       }
  |   }
```

Program Strategy 6.22 Abstract Binary Searching

for the worst case running time for successful searching. In successful searching, we consider the case where the search key K is in the array $A[0:n-1]$, so we are guaranteed to find it. In the worst case, we find K only after the search interval that results from repeated halving of the problem size gets as small as possible (namely, it shrinks to an interval of size 1 containing only one key, K).

To analyze the worst case, we can set up and solve some recurrence relations, using the following considerations. Let $T(n)$ denote the worst case running time when searching an interval with n keys in it. For the base case, if we have a search interval with one key in it, so that $n = 1$, our assumptions guarantee that key K is the only key in this search interval. So looking at Program Strategy 6.22, we would return on line 11 after testing to discover that the search interval is not empty and after finding that the search key, K, was located at the midpoint of the search interval. The time required to do this is some constant number of time units, say a. So we can write $T(1) = a$, for the base case.

Now in the general case for $n > 1$, we will find that calling the **BinarySearch** function results in (1) computing the midpoint on line 6; (2) performing the tests and comparisons on lines 8, 10, and 12, to determine that the search interval is nonempty and to determine further the new half-interval in which to continue the search; and (3) calling the **BinarySearch** function on one of the half-intervals, at a cost of at most $T(n/2)$. Since it costs a constant number of time units, say b, to compute the midpoint and to make the tests on lines 8, 10, and 12, we can write the recurrence relation for $n > 1$ as $T(n) = b + T(n/2)$.

Collecting the two equations for $T(1)$ and $T(n)$ as Recurrence Relations 6.11, we have:

$$T(1) = a$$
$$T(n) = b + T(n/2) \tag{6.11}$$

Recurrence Relations

looking up the solution in
the table

Consulting the third row of Table 6.21, and making the appropriate substitutions leads immediately to the solution, $T(n) = b \log_2 n + a$. In other words, binary searching runs in $O(\log n)$ time in the worst case. But what about the average case? How do we analyze that?

To find the solution for the average case, somehow we have to analyze the average running time for finding the search key K in each of the possible positions in the original search array $A[0:n-1]$. For example, if we find the search key K in the middle of $A[0:n-1]$ on the first try, we have to compare K against only one key in $A[0:n-1]$. This costs only one comparison (of the form $K == A[MidPoint]$). But suppose we find K on the second try in the middle of the right half-array, $A[(MidPoint + 1):n-1]$, of the original array. This takes three comparisons: (1) On the first comparison, we discover $K \neq A[MidPoint]$. (2) The second comparison, $K > A[MidPoint]$, is used to determine that further search should occur in the right half-array. Finally, (3) the third comparison successfully locates K in the middle of the right half-array.

the average case

If you study in detail how the binary searching Programs 5.41 or 5.42 work on an ordered array of search keys of size $n = 15$, where key K_i is stored in $A[i-1]$, you'll discover that the number of comparisons to locate key K_i in each position is given by the

7	5	7	3	7	5	7	1	7	5	7	3	7	5	7	number of comparisons
K_1	K_2	K_3	K_4	K_5	K_6	K_7	K_8	K_9	K_{10}	K_{11}	K_{12}	K_{13}	K_{14}	K_{15}	keys
A[0]	A[1]	A[2]	A[3]	A[4]	A[5]	A[6]	A[7]	A[8]	A[9]	A[10]	A[11]	A[12]	A[13]	A[14]	positions

Figure 6.23 Number of Comparisons Made During Binary Searching

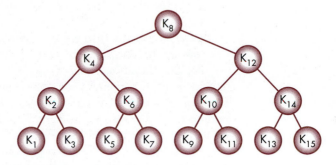

Figure 6.24 Order of Inspection of Keys K_i in Binary Searching

top row of numbers in Fig. 6.23. In fact, the order in which keys K_i are inspected during binary searching can be pictured using the tree in Figure 6.24.

For example, you first compare the search key K with the key K_8 in the middle of the array A[0:14]. If $K == K_8$, you are finished (having used one comparison). If you compare K with K_8 and you find that $K < K_8$ (using a second comparison), then you next compare K with K_4. If $K == K_4$, you are finished (having used three comparisons). But if $K != K_4$, and the fourth comparison, $K < K_4$, is false, you next compare K with K_6. If $K == K_6$, you are finished (having used a total of five comparisons). And so on.

the number of comparisons used in binary searching

[*Note:* In this discussion, we will treat only the limited special cases in which n is of the form $n = 2^k - 1$. (For example, $n = 1, 3, 5, 7, 15, ..., 2^k - 1$.) Later, we will discuss how to generalize the result to hold for any possible value of n.]

Figure 6.25 gives the number of comparisons needed to locate key K_i in Fig. 6.24

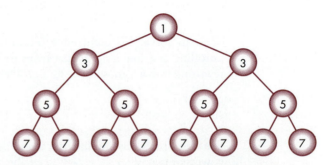

Figure 6.25 Numbers of Comparisons Needed in Binary Searching

inside the node occupied by K_i. If we could find a closed formula for the sum, $T(n)$, of the numbers of comparisons inside all n nodes of Figure 6.25, we could divide $T(n)$ by the number of nodes n, to get the average number of comparisons used in binary searching.

setting up a recurrence relation for T(n)

We will now set up and solve a recurrence relation to determine the sum, $T(n)$. First, the numbers in each row of the tree in Fig. 6.25 are two greater than the numbers in the row directly above. In the special cases we are concerned with, in which $n = 2^k - 1$, each comparison tree, such as the one illustrated in Fig. 6.25, has n nodes and k rows.

First, for the *base case*, if $n = 1$, then $T(1) = 1$, since a comparison tree with only one row in it has the number 1 at its root node.

For the *general case*, suppose we have a comparison tree with $(k - 1)$ rows in it, and we want to perform operations on it to get a new comparison tree with k rows. How might we proceed? For example, given a comparison tree with three rows in it (which looks like the one in Fig. 6.25 with the bottom row deleted), how could we create the tree with four rows in Fig. 6.25?

a construction method

The answer is (1) take two copies of the tree with $(k - 1)$ rows in it; (2) add 2 to the number in each node in both copies; (3) create a new root node with the number 1 in it; and (4) install the two copies (whose node numbers have already been increased by 2) as the left and right subtrees of this new root node.

finding the general recurrence

The mathematics that imitates these four operations gives us our general recurrence relation for $T(n)$, as follows: (1) Take two copies of comparison trees with $(k - 1)$ rows (and therefore having $n = 2^{(k-1)} - 1$ nodes each); (2) add 2 to each node in both copies, which adds 2 to each of the $2*(2^{(k-1)} - 1)$ nodes in the two copies, resulting in a contribution equal to $2*(2^k - 2)$ to be added to the equation we shall create for $T(n)$; (3) create a new node with the number 1 in it (which will contribute 1 to the total in the equation for $T(n)$); and (4) install the two copies (which must have had original comparison totals of $T(2^{(k-1)} - 1)$ for each copy) as the left and right subtrees of the new root node. The equation for $T(n)$ is gotten by adding the contributions from steps 2, 3, and 4. We therefore have Recurrence Relations 6.12:

$$T(1) = 1$$
$$T(2^k - 1) = 1 + 2\,(2^k - 2) + 2\,T(2^{(k-1)} - 1) \qquad \text{where } n = 2^k - 1 \qquad \text{(6.12)}$$

Recurrence Relations

We can solve this recurrence relation by our (by now) trustworthy method of unrolling and summing. It first helps to tidy up the equation for $T(2^k - 1)$ a bit, by rewriting it in a form suitable for unrolling. Multiplying and collecting terms gives:

$$T(2^k - 1) = 2^{k+1} - 3 + 2\,T(2^{(k-1)} - 1).$$

We now unroll this and sum the terms, using the sum of the geometric progression for powers of two $(2^0 + 2^1 + 2^2 + \ldots + 2^{(k-2)})$. (By now, you should be able to do this, so we'll leave the details out.) This gives,

$$T\left(2^k - 1\right) = (k-1)2^{k+1} - 3\left(\frac{2^{k-1} - 1}{2 - 1}\right) + 2^{(k-1)}.$$

By applying several simplification steps not shown here, this can be converted to a nearly final solution in the form,

$$T(2^k - 1) = 2k + (2k - 3)(2^k - 1).$$

converting to a solution in terms of n

It is now useful to convert this last equation into an equation for $T(n)$. If we solve the equation, $n = 2^k - 1$, for k, we get $k = \log_2(n + 1)$. Consequently, we can get rid of the occurrences of k in the last line above, first by replacing $2^k - 1$ with n, and then by replacing k with $\log_2(n + 1)$. This gives,

$$T(n) = 2 \log_2(n + 1) + (2 \log_2(n + 1) - 3) * n.$$

By multiplying out the right side of the last line and collecting terms, we get Eq. 6.13, which gives the solution to Recurrence Relations 6.12.

$$T(n) = 2 (n + 1) \log_2(n + 1) - 3n. \tag{6.13}$$

Now we have our solution, $T(n)$, giving the total number of comparisons. To get the average number of comparisons, we need to find $C(n) = T(n)/n$. This yields Eq. 6.14, which gives the average number of comparisons used in binary searching assuming each key is equally likely to be used.

$$C(n) = 2 \log_2(n + 1) - 3 + 2 \log_2(n + 1)/n. \tag{6.14}$$

Let's now give the O-notation for Eq. 6.14. Our usual method of cancellation shows that the directly derived O-notation is just $O(\log(n + 1))$. However, it is usual in the literature on binary searching to replace this with $O(\log n)$, in order to conclude that the average search time used in binary searching is logarithmic in the problem size n. Exercise 6.5.7 outlines how you can establish this fact.

how well does the solution fit actual data?

Finally, let's ask how we might use our equation for the average number of comparisons, $C(n)$, given in Eq. 6.14, to predict actual running time data for binary searching. We might reasonably estimate that the average running times, $R(n)$, needed for binary searching are proportional to the number of comparisons used, $C(n)$, plus a small constant for overhead. That is, we could predict that $R(n) = k_1 C(n) + k_2$. Table 6.26 repeats the data measured from running the binary search Programs 5.41 and 5.42 given previously in Table 5.43.

Table 6.26 Average
Iterative and Recursive
Binary Search Running
Times in Microseconds

Array Size	Iterative Version	Recursive Version
10	3.5	4.3
50	5.1	6.7
100	5.9	7.9
200	6.8	9.1
400	7.6	10.3
800	8.5	11.5

The data in Table 6.26 are fit by Eqs. 6.15 to within a tenth of a microsecond after rounding to the nearest tenth of a microsecond.

$$R(n) = 0.43\ C(n) + 1.37 \qquad \text{for the iterative version}$$
$$R(n) = 0.62\ C(n) + 1.30 \qquad \text{for the recursive version}$$

(6.15)

our methods yield very
good fits

Thus our abstract methods of analysis, based on counting comparisons, turn out to generate very good predictions of actual measured binary searching data, even though the underlying programs for binary searching are organized differently (one being iterative and the other being recursive). This should give us confidence that our algorithm analysis techniques have actual scientific validity.

In Chapter 9, we will give another analysis of binary searching that does not depend on using arrays or comparison trees with exactly $2^k - 1$ items in them, but instead works for "ragged" trees with some nodes in the bottom row missing, and for binary searching in arrays A[0:n−1] of any possible size n. Even though the analysis above gave results that fit the data quite well, it was restricted to arrays with sizes in the special series of sizes: 1, 3, 7, 15, ... , $2^k - 1$.

In the more general case, when n is not of the special form $n = 2^k - 1$, but instead can take any positive integer value, $n \geq 1$, the derivation of the average number of comparisons requires a slightly more advanced analysis. (This analysis relies on a formula for the sum of the floors of the base two logarithms of the numbers from 1 to n.) The analysis is presented in Chapter 9, and leads to Equation 9.3, which is identical to Eq. 6.14. Thus the analysis given here generalizes nicely, and its result can be shown to hold in the more general case of arbitrary n.

6.5 Review Questions

1. Give the names of five separate algorithms whose analysis reveals that their running times are in the following respective five classes: $O(\log n)$, $O(n)$, $O(n \log n)$, $O(n^2)$ and $O(2^n)$.

2. What technique could you use to solve the recurrence relations $T(1) = 2$, $T(n) = 3n + 2\ T(n/2)$?

3. Describe what you do to solve a recurrence relation by unrolling and summation.

6.5 Exercises

1. Try running the procedure **MoveTowers** from Program 3.23 to solve the Towers of Hanoi puzzle for various problem sizes, n, and measure the running times. Are your running times matched by a curve of the form $T(n) = c\,2^n - b$, where b and c are constants? [*Hint*: Remember to keep the values of n that you try very small, or you may have to wait a long time for your experiment to stop.]

2. Using the method of unrolling and summing, and applying the formulas for the sums of arithmetic and geometric progressions, derive the solutions in Table 6.18 for Recurrence Relations 6.6. [*Hint*: It helps to know that $\sum_{(1 \leq i \leq n)} i*d^i = [d/(d-1)^2]*[(n*d-n-1)d^n + 1].$]

3. Analyze the following abstract program strategy for selection sorting. Give both the running time equation and the O-notation that results from your analysis.

```
void SelectionSort(SortingArray A, int n)          /* To sort A[0:n–1] */
{
    if (n > 1) {                       /* if the array A[0:n–1] has more than one item */
        (Find the position, p, of the smallest item in A[0:n–1])
        (Exchange A[p] and A[n–1] to make A[n–1] the smallest item in A[0:n–1])
        (Sort the rest of the array A[0:n–2] by calling SelectionSort(A,n – 1))
    }
}
```

4. Using the method of unrolling and summation, and applying the formula for the sum of a geometric progression, derive the general-form solutions to Recurrence Relations 6.9 given in Table 6.21. A good starting point is to apply the conditions in the left column of Table 6.21 to Eq. 6.10.

5. Give the O-notation for each of the four general solutions listed in Table 6.21.

6. Show how Equation 6.8 for merge sorting falls out as a special case of the first line of Table 6.21.

7. Prove that the average number of comparisons used in binary searching is $O(\log n)$ by first proving the inequality, $\log_2(n + 1) < \log_2(n) + 1$, for all $n > 1$, and then by applying this inequality to Eq. 6.14.

6.6 What O-Notation Doesn't Tell You

Learning Objectives

1. To learn about circumstances in which O-notation analysis does not apply.
2. To learn what to do to find optimal algorithms under these circumstances.

O-notation may give invalid results for small-sized problems

We have seen that the definition of O-notation applies only to problem sizes that are sufficiently large for the O-notation condition to hold. For small problem sizes, the constants in the running-time equations that fit the actual running-time data may dominate the running times observed. Consequently, the conclusions that hold for large problem sizes, based on O-notation, may not hold at all for small problem sizes.

For example, we have to be quite careful in using O-notation comparisons between functions in the classes O(log log n), O(log n), and O(n), because the constants used in the running-time equations for different algorithms often differ, sometimes by large multiples. (We haven't discussed the complexity class O(log log n) yet in this chapter, but there is such a class, which we will now mention for the first time.)

To pursue this example a bit further, we have seen that if we use straightforward *sequential search* to try to find an item in an ordered list, we must inspect $(n+1)/2$ (or O(n)) items on the average, assuming each item searched for is equally likely to be chosen. We have also seen that if we use *binary search*, the number of comparisons needed to locate the item searched for is O(log n). There is a third kind of search, not studied in this book, called *interpolation search*. It works by estimating where a search key K is likely to be located in a range of keys, much like the way you would search for a name beginning with "V" starting in the back of a phone book, whereas you would search for a name beginning with "B" starting near the front, and a name beginning with "L" starting near the middle. If we use *interpolation search*, then, under proper conditions, we need make only O(log log n) comparisons, on the average.

comparing three methods for searching

As you might imagine, O(log log n) beats O(log n) handsomely for large n. For example, if $n = 2^{64} = 1.84 \times 10^{19}$, then $\log_2 n = 64$, and $\log_2 \log_2(n) = 6$. However, we cannot conclude too hastily that interpolation search is superior to the other methods. In fact, it is more costly to execute a step of a program for interpolation search than it is to execute the corresponding steps in binary search and sequential search. This is because the calculation of the "interpolation point" used in deciding where to search is more costly than calculating the midpoint used in binary searching, or in calculating how to move to the next item in sequential searching.

Thus one set of empirical data comparing the measured performances of these three searching methods showed that interpolation search was faster for searching tables of more than 500 items, whereas binary search was faster for searching tables of between 20 and 500 items, and sequential search was fastest for tables of up to 20 items. Another set of empirical data showed interpolation search was faster only for tables of more than 5000 items. (These boundaries are rough, of course, and depend on details of the implementations.)

the O(n) method is fastest for very small problem sizes

If you are trying to write an extremely efficient searching algorithm to use on problems of very small size, say less than 20 items, it might be best to write a very tight sequential searching loop (possibly even writing it in assembly language so that it counts down toward zero and takes advantage of a test for zero in the machine instruction set, thus avoiding a memory access to retrieve the lower bound used in the test for loop termination).

The method of measurement and tuning, which was recommended in Chapter 5 might be the best way to optimize the performance of algorithms for small problem sizes, given that the conclusions based on O-notation cannot be trusted to apply to small problems.

6.6 Review Questions

1. When is it inappropriate to apply the conclusions normally derived from O-notation analysis to an algorithm's running-time equation?
2. What can you do to find optimal algorithms to run on small-sized problems?

6.6 Exercises

1. Measure the difference in average running times for sequential searching and binary searching in an ordered array of integers, $A[0:n-1]$, for a range of small problem sizes $1 \leq n \leq 100$. Take care to use the most efficient form of sequential searching you can devise. Do your data show that binary searching is always more efficient than sequential searching, no matter what size problem is being considered?

 Pitfalls

- *Using algorithms of the wrong complexity*

    It is important to be sensitive to issues of algorithmic complexity. It is often possible, through carelessness or ignorance, to implement an algorithm in the wrong complexity class, when, in fact, much more efficient algorithms are known or are possible to implement. Such an oversight may not matter very much, or even at all, if the problem size is very small. But if the problem size is large, it may matter a great deal.

    For example, Exercise 6.3.2 describes a problem in which you are asked to compare the costs of sorting 262,144 numbers by two different methods. One method runs in time $O(n^2)$ and the other method runs in time $O(n \log n)$. You are asked to use a fast computer that can be rented for $100 per minute. Using the $O(n \log n)$ technique takes under five seconds of computer time and costs $7.86, but using the $O(n^2)$ technique takes over 19 hours, and costs $114,532.46—a fairly dramatic difference!

    Especially to be avoided, if possible, are exponential algorithms, which are not practical to use unless the problem sizes are very small. One circumstance in which it is easy to implement an exponential algorithm inadvertently is when converting recurrence relations directly into a recursive algorithm. Under these circumstances, the resulting algorithm may do significant useless work needlessly recomputing answers to subproblems over and over. Sometimes it is possible to reimplement such algorithms in a dramatically lower complexity class. On the other hand, some problems are known to be hard, in the sense that the best known algorithms are exponential and no algorithms of lower than exponential complexity are known. The conclusion is that it pays to be well-informed about the computational complexity classes of algorithms.

- *For small problem sizes not paying attention to the constants*
  The conclusions about algorithm running time that can be reached by developing an algorithm's O-notation hold only for large problem sizes. For small problem sizes, O-notation usually fails to describe what happens, and the comparative performance of algorithms depends on the constants in the running-time equations that fit the actual running-time data. If you are trying to find a blazing-fast, highly optimized algorithm that is supposed to run only on problems of small size, use measurement and tuning to select your candidate solutions and optimize them. Don't rely on conclusions based on O-notation.

Tips and Techniques

- *Use abstraction to analyze general cases of algorithms*
  If you need to analyze an algorithm and you are having difficulty analyzing its actual detailed implementation, it sometimes helps to back off and analyze the abstract program strategy from which the algorithm was derived. It may be more readily apparent how to go about analyzing an abstract form of an algorithm that is free from contamination with lots of special details, since the problem to be solved is often simpler. One may make certain simplifying assumptions in carrying out this approach, yet it may be the case that the simplifying assumptions do not harm the accuracy of the results obtained. As we have seen with the analysis of **SelectionSort**, for instance, it didn't matter whether we analyzed the recursive version, the iterative version, or the abstract version. We always arrived at the same quadratic running-time equation.

- *Try transforming algorithms that are hard to analyze*
  Another technique that sometimes helps when confronting an algorithm that is hard to analyze is to transform the algorithm from an iterative form to a recursive form (or vice versa). Oftentimes, the recursive and iterative forms share the same running-time equation (because they solve subproblems of identical sizes in the same order). Analyzing the recursive version may enable you to set up and solve a recurrence relation, whereas analyzing the iterative version may enable you to set up a formula for a sum of piecewise contributions and then to find the closed form for the sum. One of these two approaches (solving the recurrences or finding the closed formula for the sum) may be easier than the other. If you get stuck, changing your point of view or your problem representation is often a good way to make progress.

References for Further Study

two books covering algorithms analysis

Alfred V. Aho, John E. Hopcroft, and Jeffrey D. Ullman, *The Design and Analysis of Computer Algorithms*, Addison-Wesley, Reading, Mass., (1974).
A book covering techniques in algorithm analysis.

more on
recurrence relations

Sara Baase, *Computer Algorithms—Introduction to Design and Analysis*, Addison-Wesley, Reading, Mass., (1988).

A book covering techniques in algorithm analysis.

George S. Lueker, "Some Techniques for Solving Recurrences." *Computing Surveys* 12: 4 (December 1980) pp. 419–36.

A good survey paper covering techniques for solving recurrence relations.

Chapter Summary

precise analysis of algorithms is possible

Computer algorithms are precise mathematical objects that are susceptible to precise analysis using techniques of mathematical investigation. Quantitative analysis of many algorithms has resulted in the development of an extensive body of results which tell us a great deal about how well or how poorly various algorithms perform.

Initially, it might seem like an impossible chore to compare the performance of various algorithms when the performance data we can measure are so hard to untangle from the distorting influence of different computers, programming languages, and compilers used to implement and run the algorithms. However, it has been discovered that we can often associate with each algorithm a family of similarly shaped curves that characterize their resource consumption pattern (by giving the time or space they consume) as a function of the problem size. These resource consumption curves can be put into different complexity classes, provided (1) we ignore what happens for small problem sizes, and (2) we ignore constants of proportionality. Computer scientists commonly use O-notation to refer to the different complexity classes. O-notation is defined to work only for suitably large problem sizes, and only as an upper bound. But in giving the O-notation for $O(f(n))$, it is common practice to choose $f(n)$ to be as simple as possible and as tight an upper bound as possible.

algorithm performance can be compared using shapes of resource consumption curves

It is important to develop an intuition for the language of O-notation—especially for what it means and for how computer scientists commonly use it. Developing such intuition is a bit like learning an unfamiliar temperature scale. It pays to learn the O-notation names of several specific complexity classes and to develop an appreciation for the properties of each such complexity class.

developing intuition for the various complexity classes

For instance, the *exponential* complexity class, associated with O-notation of the form $O(c^n)$, for some constant c, describes algorithms that cannot be used practically for any but fairly small-sized problems. You can develop the intuition for why this is true by studying examples that show that an $O(2^n)$ algorithm cannot solve problems of size $n > 77$ before the sun burns out, even when the algorithm is executed on a fast computer at speeds of up to a million steps per second. The same intuition-building process might lead you to learn that, all other things being equal, $O(\log n)$ algorithms execute much faster on large-sized problems than $O(n)$ algorithms. For instance, on large problems, binary searching, which is an $O(\log n)$ algorithm, handsomely beats sequential searching, which is an $O(n)$ algorithm. There are significant performance differences between various sorting algorithms, too. $O(n \log n)$ sorting algorithms have very significant performance advantages over $O(n^2)$ sorting techniques for large problem sizes.

learning how to define and
manipulate O-notation

Having decided that O-notation is a good language to use for characterizing the comparative performance of algorithms (independently of varying characteristics of computers, compilers, and languages), and having developed an intuition for what O-notation means, the next step is to learn a bit about how to define and manipulate O-notation formally. The formal definition of the O-notation for a function $f(n)$, says that $f(n)$ is $O(g(n))$ provided the curve for $f(n)$ is bounded above by some constant multiple of $g(n)$ for sufficiently large problem sizes, n. To manipulate O-notation, using shortcuts, the first step is to establish a scale of increasing complexity classes, such as $O(1) < O(\log n) < O(n) < O(n \log n) < O(n^2) < O(n^3) < O(2^n) < O(10^n)$. The shortcut for determining the O-notation for a sum or difference of multiples of functions on this scale involves first identifying the dominant term D and the lesser terms L, according to this scale, then dropping the lesser terms, L, and finally dropping the constant of proportionality on the dominant term. For example, $O(3n^2 + 2\, n \log n + 5n + 3) = O(3n^2 + \cancel{2\,n\log n + 5n + 3}) = O(\cancel{3}\, n^2) = O(n^2)$.

methods for analyzing
simple algorithms

When attempting to analyze the simple algorithms commonly encountered in software systems, it often suffices to analyze iterative algorithms by summing up the contributions of the individual stages of the computation, and to analyze recursive algorithms by setting up and solving *recurrence relations*. Simple techniques for finding *closed formulas* for sums, such as using the formulas for the sums of *arithmetic and geometric progressions*, are often helpful. Also, many recurrence relations commonly encountered can be solved by the technique of *unrolling and summing*. Unrolling expands the formula for a recurrence relation into a sum of individual terms. The closed formula for such sums can often be determined by the same simple methods used in the analysis of iterative algorithms. Sometimes you can solve recurrences by looking up the solutions in tables of general solutions. In this chapter, two tables were given for two common types of recurrence relations encountered in practice.

examples of algorithms in
different complexity classes

The algorithm analyses covered in this chapter include analyses of algorithms in several of the principal complexity classes. For instance, sequential searching was found to have $O(n)$ running time. Selection sorting was discovered to run in time $O(n^2)$. Merge sorting, however, was found to run in time $O(n \log n)$. The Towers of Hanoi puzzle was found to be an example of an exponential running-time algorithm, having an $O(2^n)$ running time. Binary searching in ordered arrays was found to have an $O(\log n)$ running time.

when O-notation can't
be trusted

Finally, it is important to know that O-notation should not be used to draw general conclusions for problems of small size, in which the constants in the actual running-time equations may, and usually do, dominate the observed running times. Consequently, it is important to use the method of measurement and tuning to identify optimal algorithms for solving small-sized problems.

7

Linear Data Structures— Stacks and Queues

7.1 Introduction and Motivation

Linear data structures are collections of components arranged in a straight line. When we add or remove components of linear data structures, they grow or shrink. If we obey certain restrictions on the places where we add or remove elements, we obtain two important special cases of linear data structures—*stacks* and *queues*.

stacks and queues

If we restrict the growth of a linear data structure so that new components can be added and removed only at one end, we have a *stack*. If new components can be added at one end but removal of components must take place at the opposite end, we have a *queue*.

Stacks and queues can be thought of as abstract data structures obeying certain well-defined growth and decay laws, which can be represented in several ways by lower-level representations. For example, stacks and queues can each have either linked or sequential representations.

In this chapter, we will introduce and define the abstract data types (ADTs) for stacks and queues. Then we will study a few of the ways they can be represented using linked or sequential data structures.

253

Stacks are useful for processing nested structures or for managing algorithms in which processes call subprocesses. A nested structure is one that can contain instances of itself embedded within itself. For example, algebraic expressions can be *nested* because a subexpression of an algebraic expression can be another algebraic expression. Other examples of nested structures are levels of outlines for a term paper, function calls containing other function calls as arguments, and nested sets—sets containing other sets as elements. Stacks are used to implement function calls and returns when a C program is executed. Stacks are natural to use because function calls are nested inside one another during program execution whenever functions call other functions.

Within the realm of algorithms, stacks are used to implement *parsing*, *evaluation*, and *backtracking* algorithms. Parsing algorithms are used by compilers to detect the structure of computer programs being compiled. Because the structure of such programs often contains nested program parts (such as blocks within blocks, loops within loops, and subexpressions inside expressions), stacks are natural to use.

Stacks can be used to perform expression evaluation. Such evaluation is inherently nested because one needs to obtain the values of subexpressions before combining the subexpression values with an operator. Finally, stacks can be used to implement backtracking algorithms. When searching for solutions, backtracking algorithms typically organize themselves to search several subspaces of possible solutions in some order. If a solution is found when searching the first subspace, it is reported. But if no solution is found, the backtracking algorithm backs up to a previous choice point in the search, where it branched into the most recent subspace, and then branches into another subspace to continue the search. Backtracking is the process of backing up to a previous branch point in order to search a different new subspace along a different branch.

If you are searching a maze, suppose you leave a thread on the floor behind you as you travel. When you hit a dead-end (or *cul-de-sac*) you can retrace your thread to the nearest intersection and try some unexplored directions. You would thus be using the method of *backtracking*.

Queues can be used for regulating the processing of tasks in a system so as to ensure "fair" treatment. A queue is sometimes also called a *waiting line*. If a system consists of clients and servers, it may be the case that clients must "line up" to await service from various servers. After successfully obtaining service from one server, a client may need to obtain service from another server. When clients are placed in queues to await service, a first-come-first-served policy is in effect.

Many operating systems use queues of tasks to regulate the work performed by a computer. In this case, task records (representing users' jobs) are placed in queues to await service by various components of the system, such as the printer, the CPU (central processing unit), or various storage devices (such as disk and tape drives).

Queuing disciplines are also used in simulation and modeling. For example, to simulate the behavior of an air traffic control system, task records for airplanes can be placed in queues representing various states: (a) waiting to take off, (b) approaching to land, and (c) flying a particular route segment, and so on. When the system simulates a plane taking off, it removes its task record from the queue of planes awaiting takeoff and places it in the queue of planes in flight. Such task records are periodically

using stacks to process nested structures

parsing, evaluation, and backtracking

evaluation

backtracking

queues, clients, and servers

queues in operating systems

simulation and modeling

updated. As a simulated flight progresses, its task record migrates from one queue to the next along its route of flight.

predicting performance

Computer simulations can thus be useful for understanding how a proposed system will function under various loads and processing capacities. For instance, we can gain insight into how telephone systems or urban transportation systems will function under forecasted future demands for service.

By separating the design of stacks and queues into an abstract layer and several supporting underlying representation layers, we can organize our software design around the use of ADTs at the highest levels. The underlying representations can be hidden and can be implemented as interchangeable modules. Such techniques enable us to gain clarity and brevity of the top-level design, modularity and substitutability of the underlying representations, and enhanced conditions for establishing the correctness, reliability, and efficiency of a software system. In short, using ADTs can help achieve several of the important software engineering goals covered in Chapter 5.

Plan for the Chapter

In Section 7.2 our goal is to develop an intuition for stacks and to become acquainted informally with some of the important roles they play elsewhere in computer science.

In Section 7.3 we introduce the ADTs for stacks and queues. The interface specifications for C stacks and queues are presented, and the meanings of the stack and queue operations are discussed. Then we relate this method for presenting ADTs to the discussion on modularity and information hiding in Chapter 4.

Sections 7.4 and 7.5 present two applications of the stack ADT. The idea is to show how we can develop applications using only the operations in the stack ADT interface *before* giving low-level implementations of stacks. This way, we can be assured that applications using stacks do not use any low-level representational features, and that they use only abstract stack operations available in the stack ADT interface. Section 7.4 studies a use of stacks to check for properly balanced parentheses in algebraic expressions. Section 7.5 presents a way to evaluate postfix expressions using stacks. Section 7.6 presents both sequential and linked representations for stacks. Section 7.7 studies an additional application of stacks by discussing how stacks are used to implement recursion in C. This helps develop understanding for what happens when C encounters infinite regresses (i.e., chains of recursive calls that are never stopped by base cases). It also helps explain how recursion can be implemented in programming languages.

Section 7.8 introduces both sequential and linked representations for the queue ADT. We discover that queues are more representationally demanding than stacks. Linked queue representations need either special header nodes or circular two-way linking to make them work well. Sequential queue representations can be made circular to confine their travel to a bounded region of memory.

Section 7.9 discusses different applications of queues. We first look at operating systems and how queues are used in print buffers and printer spoolers as well as in regulating task processing in time-shared operating systems. We then discuss how queues are used in simulation and modeling.

≡ **7.2** Some Background on Stacks

Learning Objectives

1. To learn some common terminology.
2. To become informally acquainted with a significant use of stacks in handling recursion, in the theory of push-down automata, and in the theory of parsing, translation, and compiling.

If you have a pile of objects of any kind, such as a pile of books or a pile of coins, and you add and remove objects only at the top of the pile, you have a *stack* (see Fig. 7.1).

pushing and popping

Stacks are sometimes referred to as *push-down stacks*. Adding a new object to the top of such a push-down stack is called *pushing* a new object onto the stack, and removing an object from the top of the push-down stack is called *popping* the object from the stack. Pushing and popping are *inverse* operations: If you push an object onto a stack and then pop it off immediately afterward, you leave the original stack unchanged.

spring-loaded piles in a cafeteria

Perhaps you have seen spring-loaded piles of trays in a cafeteria. As you add new trays to a spring-loaded pile of trays, the increased weight of the pile causes the supporting spring underneath to compress, and the top of the pile remains in a fixed position. Conversely, when you remove trays from the top, the weight of the pile decreases, the underlying spring decompresses, and the pile rises so that its top remains in a fixed position.

push-down automata

The image of a push-down stack with its top remaining in a fixed position, and with the whole stack being pushed down under the addition of a new item, and rising up under the removal of an item is an image associated with an idealized machine, called a *push-down automaton* (or PDA, for short). As illustrated in Fig. 7.2, a push-down automaton has a *read head* that reads symbols on an input tape. It also uses a

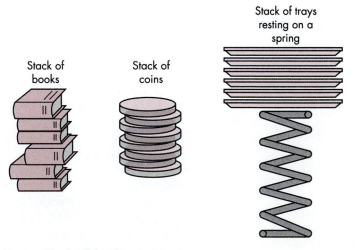

Stack of trays
resting on a
spring

Stack of
books

Stack of
coins

Figure 7.1 Various Kinds of Stacks

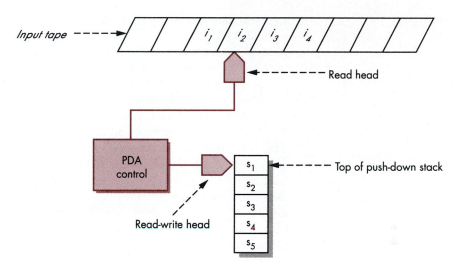

Figure 7.2 Schematic Diagram of a Push-Down Automaton

push-down stack for an internal memory. A read-write head sits next to the top symbol of the PDA's push-down stack, and it is able to push and pop symbols on this stack as well as being able to read the topmost symbol on the stack. The PDA's control unit is a "finite state control unit." This means it has a finite number of different *states* it can be in. In a given state, when the PDA is looking at a particular input symbol i_k on its input tape and sees a particular symbol s_j on top of its push-down stack, it can specify an action to perform that involves (a) entering a new state, (b) reading the next symbol on its input tape, and (c) pushing or popping a symbol from its push-down stack.

Push-down automata play a key role in the theory of formal languages and in the theory of parsing, translation, and compiling used in programming language translators (i.e., compilers). In formal language theory, a *language* is just a set of strings spelled from the letters in a given alphabet. The languages that PDAs can recognize are exactly those that are described by a commonly occurring kind of programming language grammar called a *context-free grammar*. Context-free grammars are often used to give formal definitions of the syntax of programming languages. You may have seen such grammars used in various C textbooks to define C's syntax. We will study parsers for these grammars in Chapter 14.

To summarize, stacks are used as the memory structure in push-down automata that play a key role in formal language theory as the automata that serve as the recognizers for context-free languages (which are the languages generated by context-free grammars). As a consequence, syntax analyzers for programming languages often employ push-down stacks to accomplish recognition of the structure of computer programs during compilation.

stack representations   Of course, even though we imagine that the entire stack moves *down* when a new item is pushed onto it, or *up* when the topmost item is popped, the underlying data representations we use for stacks do not behave this way. For instance, if we use arrays to hold stack items, the growth end of the stack travels through memory, and the items in the stack remain fixed in place—rather than having the growth end remaining fixed and moving all items in the stack.

Stacks are often used in ingenious ways in various algorithms to hold information about postponed obligations for further processing. We use a stack of *activation records* to keep track of a sequence of function calls during program execution. Each time a function call is made, an activation record for the call is pushed on a stack. This activation record contains space for information needed during the time the function call is being processed, and it contains information for how to resume the execution of its caller after its own execution is finished. The stack is the perfect data structure to use for this purpose, since function calls are always dynamically nested—that is, at program execution time, when one function calls another, the caller's activity is suspended while the callee is executed. The time span for the callee's execution is therefore nested inside the time span for its caller.

Sometimes the space for stack items can be found in unused fields of structs in a larger data structure. For example, some algorithms for traversing the nodes of trees in a linked tree representation (such as that shown in Fig. 2.23 in Chapter 2) make use of empty pointer fields in the tree to encode the information for a stack of postponed obligations for further traversal of the tree. This leads to algorithms that do not need external auxiliary stacks in order to traverse trees. Such algorithms can become quite important to use for garbage collection (i.e., storage reclamation) in list structure memory, since garbage collection tends to occur at the very moment that there is no more space to allocate. In particular, it occurs when there is no space for allocating a stack to use to enable traversal of list structures that need to be marked as being in use, so that they will not be swept up during garbage collection.

Stacks are sometimes called LIFO lists, where LIFO stands for "last-in, first-out," and queues are sometimes called FIFO ("first-in, first-out") lists.

using stacks to hold postponed obligations (margin note)

LIFO versus FIFO (margin note)

7.2 Review Questions

1. Why are stacks useful for processing nested structures?
2. Give four examples of nested structures.
3. What can push-down automata accomplish according to the theory of formal languages?
4. Can stacks be used to process function calls?

7.2 Exercises

1. According to a law of physics, known as Hookes' Law, the displacement, d, in a spring due to compression when an additional load, L, is added, is directly proportional to L, $d = \alpha L$. Given a stack of trays (where each tray is of weight L and thickness d) riding on a compressed spring, having a "spring constant" α, and obeying Hookes' Law, $d = \alpha L$, show that the top of the stack stays in a fixed position as trays are pushed or popped from the stack.

2. If you have two stacks, S_1 and S_2, and a single array A[0:n−1] to use for holding the stack items for both stacks, how should you arrange to represent S_1 and S_2 so that they each have the greatest possible room for growth before no more space remains inside A[0:n−1]?

7.3   ADTs for Stacks and Queues

Learning Objectives

1. To learn about data structuring methods and how they differ from ADTs.
2. To learn about abstract sequences as a data structuring method.
3. To understand the view of ADTs as data structures + operations.
4. To learn about the abstract operations and interfaces for stack and queue ADTs.

An *abstract data type* (ADT) consists of a collection of data structures together with a set of operations defined on those data structures. The data structures are usually *composite* data structures obtained by applying a *structuring method* to a collection of *components*.

You are no doubt already familiar with several structuring methods from studying C in your first course in computer science. The formation of structs, arrays, and strings using various types of components illustrate three structuring methods used in C. In addition, using pointers to components and embedding pointers inside other data structures (such as structs or arrays) enables us to create linked data structures—a fourth structuring method that C offers.

structuring methods

Speaking abstractly, the formation of linear *sequences* of components is a structuring method that many data structures share. For example, strings, arrays, lists, stacks, and queues each consist of linear sequences of components. Each of these sequential data structures has a different set of operations defined on it. Differences in the allowable operations and in the types of components distinguish these different data structures from one another.

sequences

Although the sequences generally used in mathematics can be infinite in length, we usually use finite length sequences in computer science. A finite length sequence $S = (s_1, s_2, s_3, \ldots, s_n)$ is just an ordered arrangement of finitely many components, s_i, $(1 \leq i \leq n)$. We sometimes include the empty sequence, symbolized by the Greek letter Λ in our considerations. We say that the *length* of a sequence S is the number of components in it. The length of the empty sequence is 0.

Having defined sequences in this manner, we could say that we had applied the structuring method of forming sequences to the set of elements {1,2,3,4,5} to create a sequence such as $S = (5, 3, 4, 3, 1, 2)$. [*Note:* In a *set*, the elements are considered to be unordered and have no repetitions, whereas in a *sequence*, the elements appear in a specific order and occurrences of elements may be repeated.]

ADTs = sequences + operations

To define an ADT, in addition to defining a set of data structures, we need to define *operations* on those structures. Thus, starting with sequences as the basic data structure, we can define *Stacks*, and *Queues*, by defining two separate sets of operations on sequences.

Stacks

A *Stack*, *S*, of items of type *T* is a sequence of items of type *T* on which the following operations are defined:

1. Initialize the stack *S* to be the *empty stack*.
2. Determine whether or not the stack, *S*, is *empty*.
3. Determine whether or not the stack, *S*, is *full*.
4. *Push* a new item onto the top of the stack, *S*.
5. If *S* is nonempty, *pop* an item from the top of stack, *S*.

Queues

A *Queue*, *Q*, of items of type *T* is a sequence of items of type *T* on which the following operations are defined:

1. Initialize the queue, *Q*, to be the *empty queue*.
2. Determine whether or not the queue, *Q*, is *empty*.
3. Determine whether or not the queue, *Q*, is *full*.
4. *Insert* a new item onto the rear of the queue, *Q*.
5. Provided *Q* is nonempty, *remove* an item from the front of *Q*.

As you can see, the differences between the stacks and queues consist only of differences in the operations that are defined on them—*not* in differences between the structuring method that is applied to their components to bundle the components into an aggregate structure.

A similar situation occurs in mathematics. For instance, points in the two-dimensional plane can be specified using either Cartesian or polar coordinates. In either system, pairs of real numbers are used for the coordinates. But you can't tell, just by looking at a pair of real numbers, such as (1.6, 2.5), whether it represents a point in polar or Cartesian coordinates. What distinguishes Cartesian and polar coordinates is the set of operations we apply to them to determine various known results. For instance, the distance from the origin of the coordinate system of a point (r, θ) in polar coordinates is given by r, whereas if the point (x, y) is given in Cartesian coordinates, this distance is given by

$$\sqrt{x^2 + y^2}.$$

differences in the operations sometimes define the distinction between ADTs

The definitions of the Stack and Queue ADTs deliberately do *not* mention any required underlying data representation that must be used. As we shall see presently, either linked data representations or sequential data representations can be used. In forming the linked representations, we can use structs to hold the individual items and we can link these structs to one another in a linear linked list, using pointers in the usual fashion. It may seem strange to talk about using low-level sequential data representations to represent abstract sequences at a higher level, but this is exactly what we do when we use an array or a string as the underlying representation for an abstract stack or queue.

underlying representations for abstract sequences

In short, data structures that are viewed abstractly as *sequences* at the level of ADTs can be represented in an underlying memory medium using either *linked representations* or *sequential representations*. (In fact, these are not the only two possibilities. For instance, if we had a language that offered a general-purpose set representation, we could even represent abstract stacks and queues using sets of ordered pairs constructed in an appropriate fashion. We choose to study only some of the frequently used common representations in this book, however.)

Interfaces for Stack and Queue Operations

ADT interfaces using C modules

Using separately compiled C files, we can define C modules that specify the underlying representation for stacks or queues and that implement the required abstract stack or queue operations. The stack or queue module interfaces can be invoked by an appropriate **include** directive at the beginning of a program using stacks or queues. A given stack or queue module itself may import an **ItemType** specifying the type of items that can be used inside the stacks or queues.

the way to use stack and queue ADTs in C programs

We shall structure the use of Stack and Queue ADTs following the pattern set up in Chapter 4. Specifically, Programs 7.3 and 7.4 define the respective interface header files for stack and queue operations, "StackInterface.h" and "QueueInterface.h". These interface files, in turn, include respective header files importing the data type definitions of stacks and queues, "StackTypes.h" and "QueueTypes.h". For convenience of presentation, these data type definition header files are given at the beginning of the respective implementation files for the sequential and linked representations of stacks and queues (in order to keep the typedefs for various structs and arrays close to the implementation code that uses them, thus easing the burden on the reader). For example, Program 7.8 gives an implementation of the sequential representation of the Stack ADT. Lines 1:12 of Program 7.8 specify the "StackTypes.h" header file, and lines 13:64 specify the "StackImplementation.c" file, which directly uses the typedefs for the sequential stack representation defined in "StackTypes.h" a few lines earlier on lines 1:12.

We deliberately postpone giving implementations for these stack and queue operations until after we have given some examples of applications. This way, when we write application programs, we are guaranteed that we will use only the features of stacks and queues revealed in the interface, and that we cannot build in any features that depend on hidden details of a particular low-level representation or implementation.

Later, we will give both linked and sequential representations for stacks and queues that share the same interfaces given on the following page. This way, we will again demonstrate (a) substitutability of different underlying data representations and (b) proper modular programming discipline by separating cleanly the representational details of abstract data types from their uses.

```
     |   /*      ------------< begin file "StackInterface.h" >------------     */
     |
     |        #include "StackTypes.h"          /* imports the data type definitions of */
     |                                          /* ItemType and Stack */
  5  |
     |   /* defined operations */
     |
     |        extern void InitializeStack(Stack *S);
     |             /* Initialize the stack S to be the empty stack */
 10  |
     |        extern int Empty(Stack *S);
     |             /* Returns TRUE == 1 if and only if the stack S is empty */
     |
     |        extern int Full(Stack *S);
 15  |             /* Returns TRUE == 1 if and only if the stack S is full */
     |
     |        extern void Push(ItemType X, Stack *S);
     |             /* If S is not full, push a new item X onto the top of S */
     |
 20  |        extern void Pop(Stack *S, ItemType *X);
     |             /* If S is non-empty, pop an item off the top of S and put it in X */
     |
     |   /*      ------------< end-of-file "StackInterface.h" >------------     */
```

Program 7.3 Stack ADT Interface "StackInterface.h"

```
     |   /*      ------------< begin file "QueueInterface.h" >------------     */
     |
     |        #include "QueueTypes.h"          /* imports the data type definitions of */
     |                                          /* ItemType and Queue */
  5  |
     |   /* defined operations */
     |
     |        extern void InitializeQueue(Queue *Q);
     |             /* Initialize the queue Q to be the empty queue */
 10  |
     |        extern int Empty(Queue *Q);
     |             /* Returns TRUE == 1 if and only if the queue Q is empty */
     |
     |        extern int Full(Queue *Q);
 15  |             /* Returns TRUE == 1 if and only if the queue Q is full */
     |
     |        extern void Insert(ItemType R, Queue *Q);
     |             /* If Q is not full, insert a new item R onto the rear of Q */
     |
 20  |        extern void Remove(Queue *Q, ItemType *F);
     |             /* If Q is non-empty, remove the frontmost item of Q and put it in F */
     |
     |   /*      ------------< end-of-file "QueueInterface.h" >------------     */
```

Program 7.4 Queue ADT Interface "QueueInterface.h"

1. C supplies users with several structuring methods for forming composite data structures from components. Name some of C's structuring methods.
2. What is a convenient way to package the types and operations of an ADT using C modules?
3. How can you be sure that you have used proper modular programming practices when defining and using an ADT?
4. Is there any visible indication in Programs 7.3 and 7.4 of whether the underlying representations for stacks and queues are sequential or linked?

7.3 Exercises

1. Suppose you have a programming language (more powerful than C) that permits you to define unordered sets of items of any type. How could you represent a sequence of real numbers using sets of ordered pairs as the underlying representation?
2. Would the representation you devised as your answer to Exercise 1 be efficient to use if you wanted to add or delete a new last item in your sequence? Would it be efficient if you wanted both to add a new last item and remove the first item? Would it therefore be a good representation to use for stacks or queues, or both?

7.4 Using the Stack ADT to Check for Balanced Parentheses

Learning Objectives

1. To see how the Stack ADT can be used to support an application even though the stack implementation is not yet known.
2. To lay the groundwork for defining two substitutable representations of the Stack ADT.

The first application of the Stack ADT that we will study involves a small program to determine whether parentheses and brackets are balanced properly in algebraic expressions.

In mathematics, we sometimes use parentheses, brackets, and braces of various sizes to indicate the boundaries of subexpressions. In properly formed algebraic expressions, the various types of parentheses must occur in properly matching pairs.

For example, consider the algebraic expression:

$$\{a^2 - [(b+c)^2 - (d + e)^2]*[\sin(x - y)]\} - \cos(x + y)$$

This expression incorporates parentheses ( ), square brackets [ ], and braces { }, in balanced pairs according to the pattern { [( ) ( )] [( )] } ( ).

pushing and popping to
keep track of
matching pairs

We can use stacks to check whether such algebraic expressions have properly balanced parentheses or not. To do this, we start with an empty stack and scan a string representing the algebraic expression from left to right. Whenever we encounter a left parenthesis (, a left bracket [, or a left brace {, we push it onto the stack. Whenever we encounter a right parenthesis), a right bracket], or a right brace }, we pop the top item off the stack and check to see that its type matches the type of right parenthesis, bracket, or brace encountered.

If the stack is empty by the time we get to the end of the expression string and if all pairs of matched parentheses were of the same type, the expression has properly balanced parentheses. Otherwise, the parentheses are not balanced properly.

Program 7.5 asks the user to give an input expression string and checks it to see if it has balanced parentheses. It assumes that the type of item used in stacks is a character (i.e., ItemType == char in the module interface header file for stack operations "StackInterface.h" given in Program 7.3).

As an example, if the procedure ParenMatch in Program 7.5 processes an input expression such as $\{a^2 - [(c-d)^2 + (e-f)^2]\} * \sin(x-y)$, which has a parenthesis structure of the form $\{ [( ) ( )] \} ( )$, ParenMatch first pushes the left paren-

```
     |   /*    Parenthesis Matching Using Stacks    */
     |
     |   #include <stdio.h>
     |   #include <stdlib.h>
  5  |   #include <string.h>
     |   #include "StackInterface.h"        /* Here, assume char is the ItemType */
     |
     |   char *InputExpression;             /* an arithmetic expression string */
     |
 10  |
     |   int Match(char c, char d)                              /* this function */
     |   {                                          /* returns TRUE if and only if */
     |        switch (c) {                          /* c and d are matching pairs */
     |                                                 /* of parentheses ( ) */
 15  |            case    '('   : return  d == ')' ;     /* square brackets [ ] */
     |                            break;                      /* or braces { } */
     |
     |            case    '['   : return  d == ']' ;
     |                            break;
 20  |
     |            case    '{'   : return  d == '}' ;
     |                            break;
     |
     |            default       : return (0);
 25  |                            break;
     |        }
     |   }
```

Program 7.5 Checking for Balanced Parentheses (continued)

Program 7.5 Checking for Balanced Parentheses (continued)

```c
      void ParenMatch(void)
      {
30        int      n, i = 0;
          char     c,d;
          Stack    ParenStack;

          InitializeStack(&ParenStack);    /* let the ParenStack be an empty stack */
35        n = strlen(InputExpression);              /* n == length of InputExpression */

          while ( i < n ) {

              d = InputExpression[i];                    /* d == the ith character */
40
              if (  d == '('   ||  d == '['  ||  d == '{'  ) {

                  Push(d,&ParenStack)             /* push left paren on the stack */

45            } else if (  d == ')'  ||  d == ']'  ||  d == '}'  ) {

                  if ( Empty(&ParenStack) ) {
                      printf("More right parentheses than left parentheses\n");
                      return;
50                } else {
                      Pop(&ParenStack,&c);         /* get last left paren from stack */
                      if ( !Match(c,d) ) {                  /* if not match right paren */
                          printf("Mismatched Parentheses: %c and %c\n",c,d);
                          return;
55                    }
                  }
              }

              ++i;                    /* increase index i to scan next input character */
60        }

          if ( Empty(&ParenStack) ) {
              printf("Parentheses are balanced properly\n");
          } else {
65            printf("More left parentheses than right parentheses\n");
          }
      }

      int main(void)
70    {
          InputExpression = (char *) malloc(100);      /* allocate space for a string */

          printf("Give Input Expression without blanks: ");  /* get input expression */

75        scanf("%s",InputExpression);                              /* from user */

          ParenMatch( );       /* check for balanced parentheses and print result */

      }
```

theses { [(onto the ParenStack, yielding a ParenStack with (on its top, of the following form:

$$\text{ParenStack} = \begin{array}{|c|} \hline (\\ [\\ \{ \\ \hline \end{array}.$$

When ParenMatch then encounters the first instance of a right parenthesis), it pops the left parenthesis (from the top of the stack and matches it against the right parenthesis, leaving a ParenStack of the form:

$$\text{ParenStack} = \begin{array}{|c|} \hline [\\ \{ \\ \hline \end{array}.$$

ParenMatch then processes the next parenthesis pair ( ), by pushing (on the stack and immediately popping it off again to match the right parenthesis). Upon encountering] and }, ParenMatch pops [and { off the ParenStack to match them. Finally, ParenMatch pushes (on the stack and then pops it off to match the final). At the end, the ParenStack is empty.

7.4 Review Questions

1. Is the "last-in, first-out" property of stacks crucial for detecting matching pairs of parentheses? Would it be possible to use a queue, having a "first-in, first-out" property to replace the role played by the stack in Program 7.5?
2. What property of Program 7.5 guarantees that separately defined linked and sequential representations of the Stack ADT can be used interchangeably, and thus that the property of "substitutability of representations" will be achievable?

7.4 Exercises

1. Run Program 7.5 on the following expressions having both balanced and unbalanced parentheses. Check the results for correctness.

$\{ a\wedge2 - [(b+c)\wedge2 - (d+e)\wedge2]*[\sin(x-y)] \} - \cos(x+y)$	balanced
$\{ a - [(b+c))) - (d+e)] \}$	too many right parens
$\{ a - [[[(b+c) - (d+e)] \}$	too many left parens
$\{ a - [(b+c) - (d+e) \}]$	unmatched paren types

2. Modify Program 7.5 to check for stack overflow, using the stack operation Full(ParenStack). If the ParenStack is full, then before pushing a new left paren-

thesis onto it, abort the program and print a message announcing that the results are inconclusive because of stack overflow during the parenthesis check.

3. Alan Aardvark decides he doesn't need to use a stack in order to check for properly balanced parentheses. Instead, he decides to keep three integers called ParenCount, BracketCount, and BraceCount. Each of these counts is set initially to zero. When scanning an input expression, if he encounters (, [, or {, he increments the respective ParenCount, BracketCount, or BraceCount by one. If he encounters),], or }, he decrements the respective ParenCount, BracketCount, or BraceCount by one. At the end of the input expression, if the three counts are zero, he decides all types of parentheses are balanced properly. Will his method work? If so, why? If not, say why not and give a counterexample.

7.5 Using the Stack ADT to Evaluate Postfix Expressions

Learning Objectives

1. To learn how stacks can be used to evaluate postfix expressions.
2. To see another example of modular programming techniques illustrating postponed choice of the underlying representation for stacks.

Ordinarily, for human use, algebraic expressions are given in *infix notation* in which a binary operator β is placed between left and right operands, L and R, as in the expression (L β R). Parentheses are used to specify the order of operations.

Postfix expressions can be used to specify algebraic operations using a parenthesis-free notation. The postfix expression, L R β, corresponds to the infix expression (L β R). To translate an infix expression, (L β R), into postfix, you write the postfix expression for L, followed by the postfix expression for R, followed by the operator β. Table 7.6 gives examples of infix expressions and their corresponding translations into postfix. Note that the caret operator (^) is used in postfix expressions in this table to denote exponentiation, so that the square of a, denoted a^2 in infix, is translated as $a\ 2\ \wedge$ in postfix.

postfix evaluation method It is convenient to use stacks to evaluate postfix expressions. To evaluate a postfix expression, P, you scan P from left-to-right. When you encounter an operand, X, while scanning P, you push it onto an evaluation stack, S. When you encounter an

Infix Expression	Postfix Expression
$(a + b)$	$a\ b +$
$(x - y - z)$	$x\ y - z -$
$(x - y - z)/(u + v)$	$x\ y - z - u\ v + /$
$(a^2 + b^2)*(m - n)$	$a\ 2\ \wedge\ b\ 2\ \wedge\ +\ m\ n - *$

Table 7.6 Translations of Infix Expressions into Corresponding Postfix Expressions

operator, β, while scanning P, you pop the topmost operand stacked on S into a variable R (which denotes the right operand), then you pop another topmost operand stacked on S into a variable L (which denotes the left operand). Finally, you perform the operation β on L and R, getting the value of the expression $(L \beta R)$, and you push this value back onto the stack, S. When you are finished scanning P, the value of P is the only item remaining on the stack S.

Some early computers and some recent pocket calculators use postfix instructions for evaluating arithmetic expressions. The pocket calculator program explored in Chapter 14 (on advanced topics in recursion) uses a recursive descent parser to translate infix expressions into postfix, and then evaluates the postfix to calculate and print the result, using Program 7.7.

Program 7.7 presents a simplified evaluator for postfix instructions. It assumes that a postfix string is given as input using only single digit integers as operands, and using any of the binary operators: (+) for addition, (–) for subtraction, (∗) for multiplication, (/) for division, and (^) for exponentiation.

Let's trace through a simple example of the operation of Program 7.7. Suppose a postfix string "6 7 ∗ 2 –" is given as the value of the variable, **PostfixString**. The function call on line 18 initializes an **EvalStack**, to be used during evaluation. The for-statement on lines 20:47 is used to scan through the **PostfixString** from left to right. First the digit **6** is scanned and becomes the value of the character variable **c** on line 22. (The variable **c** is used to hold the character of the **PostfixString** currently scanned.)

tracing through an example

On line 24, a determination is made whether or not the character in **c** is a digit character in the range 0:9, using the test **isdigit(c)**. In this case, since **6** is a digit character, its value is pushed onto the **EvalStack**, using the function call on line 26: **Push((float)atof(s), &EvalStack)**. The value of the digit **c** is computed by applying the conversion function **atof(s)** to a null-terminated string **s** after setting **s[0] = c**. The value of **atof(s)** is typecast to a floating point number by applying the operator **(float)**. The **EvalStack** now has the left operand **6** pushed onto it as follows:

$$\text{EvalStack} = \boxed{6.0}.$$

(Note that the operand on the **EvalStack** has been pictured as 6.0 to denote the fact that it is stored as a **float** in C.)

Control now returns to the for-statement, where the next operand, **7**, in the postfix string is scanned. By a process identical to that just explained, the value of this right operand, **7**, is stacked on top of the **EvalStack** as the new value **7.0**:

$$\text{EvalStack} = \boxed{\begin{matrix} 7.0 \\ 6.0 \end{matrix}}.$$

The next character in the postfix string is the multiplication operator, **c == '∗'**. The value of **c** is tested in the if-clause on line 28 to see if it is one of the operators:

```
   |   #include <stdio.h>
   |   #include <stdlib.h>              /* contains the conversion function atof */
   |   #include <math.h>                /* contains the exp and log functions */
   |   #include <ctype.h>               /* contains the function, isdigit(d) */
 5 |   #include <string.h>
   |   #include "StackInterface.h"          /* Here, assume float is the ItemType */
   |
   |        Stack      EvalStack;                    /* let EvalStack be a stack */
   |        char       *PostfixString;           /* the input string to evaluate */
10 |
   |   void InterpretPostfix(void)
   |   {
   |        float      LeftOperand, RightOperand, Result;
   |        int        i;          /* the index of the ith character in the PostfixString */
15 |        char       c;                  /* c = the ith character of the input string */
   |        char       *s = "x";           /* s is a string used to convert c to a float */
   |
   |     InitializeStack(&EvalStack);               /* let EvalStack be empty initially */
   |
20 |     for (i = 0; i < strlen(PostfixString); ++i ) {
   |
   |          s[0] = c = PostfixString[i];      /* set both s[0] and c to the ith character */
   |                                            /* of the input string */
   |          if ( isdigit(c) ) {            /* if c is a digit character, then push c's floating*/
25 |                                         /*  point value onto the stack, where s must be a */
   |               Push( (float)atof(s),&EvalStack);     /* null-terminated string for atof */
   |
   |          } else if ( c == '+'  ||  c == '–'  ||  c == '*'  ||  c == '/'  ||  c == '^'  ) {
   |
30 |               Pop(&EvalStack, &RightOperand);          /* but if c is an operator */
   |               Pop(&EvalStack, &LeftOperand );       /* then perform the operation */
   |
   |               switch (c) {
   |               case '+' : Push(LeftOperand + RightOperand, &EvalStack);
35 |                               break;
   |               case '–' : Push(LeftOperand – RightOperand, &EvalStack);
   |                               break;
   |               case '*' : Push(LeftOperand * RightOperand, &EvalStack);
   |                               break;
40 |               case '/' : Push(LeftOperand / RightOperand, &EvalStack);
   |                               break;
   |               case '^' : Push(exp(log(LeftOperand)*RightOperand), &EvalStack);
   |                               break;
   |               default  : break;
45 |               }
   |          }
   |     }
   |
   |     Pop(&EvalStack,&Result);                    /* remove final result from stack */
50 |     printf("Value of postfix expression = %f\n", Result);         /* and print it */
   |
   |   }
```

Program 7.7 Interpreting a Postfix String

'+', '−', '∗', '/', or '^'. Since this test succeeds, statements 30:44 are performed. First the topmost item on the **EvalStack** is popped and becomes the value of the variable **RightOperand**, using the pop procedure on line 30. Following this, the **EvalStack** is popped again, and its topmost item becomes the value of the variable **LeftOperand**. The **EvalStack** is now empty, and the left and right operands to be used have been transferred into the values of the variables **LeftOperand** and **RightOperand**, respectively. The switch-statement now performs the multiplication operation on the operands and pushes the product back onto the **EvalStack**, using the push function call on line 38. The resulting **EvalStack** now has the following appearance:

$$\text{EvalStack} = \boxed{42.0}.$$

As the scan of the postfix input string continues, the operand 2 is scanned and its value is pushed on the **EvalStack**:

$$\text{EvalStack} = \boxed{\begin{matrix} 2.0 \\ 42.0 \end{matrix}}.$$

Following this, the final operator in the postfix input string is scanned, and this operation is performed on the top two operands on the **EvalStack**. The resulting difference (42.0 − 2.0) is pushed back onto the **EvalStack**:

$$\text{EvalStack} = \boxed{40.0}.$$

Finally, the result, **40.0**, is popped from the **EvalStack**, and it is printed using the statements on lines 49:50.

7.5 Review Questions

1. Translate the following infix expression into postfix: $((a * b - c) / 5)^{1/3}$.
2. Translate the following postfix expression into infix: $x\ y\ z + - a\ b * / 2$ ^.
3. Why are parentheses needed to specify the order of operations in infix expressions but not in postfix expressions?
4. Why is a stack useful for evaluating postfix expressions? Would a queue work just as well?

7.5 Exercises

1. What does Program 7.7 print if the postfix input string is: $6\ 7 * 2 - 5 / 1\ 3 / \char`\^$?
2. Program 7.7 could fail if its stack overflows, or if an attempt is made to divide by zero, or if a malformed postfix expression is encountered, causing an empty **EvalStack** to be popped (as in evaluating the postfix expression: 8 9 ∗ ∗). Extend Program 7.7 to handle these error conditions.

7.6 Implementing the Stack ADT

Learning Objectives

1. To understand how to implement stacks in two different but substitutable ways.
2. To finish learning how to separate implementation details from abstract operations in an ADT interface.
3. To understand features of sequential and linked representations.

Our goal in this section is to show how to implement the Stack ADT in two different but behaviorally equivalent ways. These representations can be used interchangeably to implement the applications given in Programs 7.5 and 7.7. One of the implementations uses a sequential representation and the other uses a linked representation.

After having accomplished this, we can then use either representation to implement the applications of the Stack ADT used in sections 7.4 and 7.5. This accomplishes, finally, (a) substitutability of representations and (b) clean separation of the implementation details from Stack ADT usage notation.

The Sequential Stack Representation

Stacks (having bounded capacity) can be represented by sequentially arranged arrays of stack items. The stack implementation given in Program 7.8 is fairly straightforward. Stacks are of bounded capacity and can contain no more items than specified by the constant, MAXSTACKSIZE. Each stack is represented by a struct that contains (a) the number of items currently in the stack as the value of its Count member and (b) an array of stack items as its Items member.

A stack is defined to be *empty* if its Count member is zero (in which case the stack is said to contain zero items). A stack is defined to be *full* if its Count member is the MAXSTACKSIZE.

To push an item X onto a non-full stack S, you first store X in the item array at the position designated by the value in the Count member, and then you increment the Count member by one.

```
  |   /*    ------------< begin file "StackTypes.h" >------------    */
  |
  |   #define MAXSTACKSIZE 100
  |
5 |   typedef  arbitrary      ItemType;              /* the type "arbitrary" is */
  |                                                  /* defined as "char" for Program 7.5 */
  |   typedef  struct {                              /* and "float" for Program 7.7 */
  |                int        Count;
  |                ItemType   Items[MAXSTACKSIZE];
10|           } Stack;
  |
  |   /*    ------------< end-of-file "StackTypes.h" >------------    */
```

Program 7.8 Sequential Stack Implementation (continued)

Program 7.8 Sequential Stack Implementation (continued)

```
 |    /*    --------------< begin file "StackImplementation.c" >-------------    */
 |
15 |    #include <stdio.h>
 |    #include <stdlib.h>                              /* the file "StackInterface.h" comes */
 |    #include "StackInterface.h"                      /* from Program 7.3 which includes  */
 |                                                     /* "StackTypes.h" on lines 1:12 above */
 |    /* -------------------- */
20 |
 |        void InitializeStack(Stack *S);                      /* S–>Count gives  */
 |        {                                                    /* the number of items in S. */
 |            S–>Count = 0;                            /* An empty stack S has 0 items in it. */
 |        }
25 |
 |    /* -------------------- */
 |
 |        int Empty(Stack *S);
 |        {
30 | —        return ( S–>Count  ==  0  );
 |        }
 |
 |    /* -------------------- */
 |
35 |        int Full(Stack *S);
 |        {
 |            return ( S–>Count  ==  MAXSTACKSIZE );
 |        }
 |
40 |    /* -------------------- */
 |
 |        void Pop(Stack *S, ItemType *X);
 |        {
 |            if ( S–>Count == 0 ) {
45 |                SystemError("attempt to pop the empty stack");
 |            } else {
 |                – – (S–>Count) ;
 |                *X = S–>Items[S–>Count];
 |            }
50 |        }
 |
 |    /* -------------------- */
 |
 |        void Push(ItemType X, Stack *S);
55 |        {
 |            if ( S–>Count  ==  MAXSTACKSIZE )  {
 |                SystemError("attempt to push new item onto a full stack");
 |            } else {
 |                S–>Items[S–>Count] = X;
60 |                + + (S–>Count);
 |            }
 |        }
 |
 |    /*    --------------< end-of-file "StackImplementation.c" >-------------    */
```

To pop an item **X** off of a nonempty stack **S**, you first decrement the **Count** member by one and then you remove **X** from the item array at the position designated by the value in the **Count** member.

The Linked Stack Representation

A stack can be represented by a struct having an **ItemList** member pointing to a linear linked list of stack nodes in which each node contains a stack item. The first node in the **ItemList** represents the top of the stack. An empty stack is represented by **NULL**.

To push an item **X** onto a linked stack, **S**, you allocate a new stack node, **N**, place **X** in **N**'s **Item** field, set **N**'s **Link** field to point to **S**'s **ItemList**, and then let **S**'s **ItemList** pointer point to its new top node, **N**.

To pop the topmost item, **X**, from a nonempty stack, **S**, you set **X** to contain the item in the **Item** field of the first node of **S**'s **ItemList**, and then set **S**'s **ItemList** to the pointer in the **Link** field of the **ItemList**'s first node. The details are given in Program

```
     |    /*      ------------< begin file "StackTypes.h" >------------    */
     |
     |        typedef   arbitrary        ItemType;              /* the type "arbitrary" is */
     |                                                  /* defined as "char" for Program 7.5 */
  5  |        typedef   struct StackNodeTag  {           /* and "float" for Program 7.7 */
     |                    ItemType                    Item;
     |                    struct      StackNodeTag  *Link;
     |                } StackNode;
     |
 10  |        typedef   struct {
     |                    StackNode    *ItemList;
     |                } Stack;
     |
     |    /*      ------------< end-of-file "StackTypes.h" >------------    */
 15  |
     |
     |    /*      ------------< begin file "StackImplementation.c" >------------    */
     |
     |        #include <stdio.h>
 20  |        #include <stdlib.h>                    /* the file "StackInterface.h" comes  */
     |        #include "StackInterface.h"            /* from Program 7.3 which includes   */
     |                                               /* "StackTypes.h" on lines 1:14 above */
     |
     |        void InitializeStack(Stack *S)
 25  |        {
     |            S->ItemList = NULL;
     |        }
     |
     |        int Empty(Stack *S)
 30  |        {
     |            return ( S->ItemList == NULL );
     |        }
```

Program 7.9 Linked Stack Implementation (continued)

Program 7.9 Linked Stack Implementation (continued)

```
           int Full(Stack *S)
           {                           /* we assume an already constructed stack, S, is */
 35            return 0;                          /* not full, since it could potentially */
           }                                         /* grow as a linked structure */

           void Push(ItemType X, Stack *S)
           {
 40            StackNode *Temp;
                                                   /* attempt to allocate a new stack */
               Temp = (StackNode *) malloc(sizeof(StackNode));        /* node */

               if (Temp == NULL) {         /* allocation failed if Temp == NULL */
 45                SystemError("system storage is exhausted");
               } else {                            /* set Temp's link to point to the */
                   Temp–>Link = S–>ItemList;      /* remainder of the ItemList. */
                   Temp–>Item = X;                      /* set its item to be X */
                   S–>ItemList = Temp;                /* let S's ItemList  point to */
 50            }                                 /* the new topmost stack node */
           }

           void Pop(Stack *S, ItemType *X)
           {
 55            StackNode *Temp;

               if (S–>ItemList == NULL) {
                   SystemError("attempt to pop the empty stack");
               } else {                                   /* put a pointer to the */
 60                Temp = S–>ItemList;          /* top node of S's ItemList in Temp. */
                   *X = Temp–>Item;                      /* put top stack Item in X. */
                   S–>ItemList = Temp–>Link;           /* make S's ItemList point */
                   free(Temp);                        /* to the next node on the list, then */
               }                                 /* free the storage for the former top node. */
 65        }

    /*     -----< end-of-file "StackImplementation.c"  linked stacks >------   */
```

7.9. When trying to push an item, **X**, onto a stack, **S**, it may not be possible to allocate a new stack node if the system memory is exhausted. Allocation failure at this moment can force program termination (see line 45 of Program 7.9). However, there is often less risk of exhausting system storage with linked stacks than there is of running out of stack space in some individual stack if you store stacks in fixed-size arrays.

7.6 Review Questions

1. What is meant by substitutability of representations of an ADT?
2. What is meant by saying that a Stack ADT has a representation-independent notation for use of its operations?
3. Discuss the aspects of modular programming, and the lack thereof, exhibited by Programs 7.5, 7.7, 7.8, and 7.9.

7.6 Exercises

1. Try substituting both the sequential and linked representations given in Programs 7.8 and 7.9 into the postfix interpreter in Program 7.7 and the balanced parentheses checker in Program 7.5. Verify that Programs 7.5 and 7.7 work identically when the underlying stack representations are switched.

Exercises 2 and 3 call for you to conceptualize and then to implement a representation for stacks using priority queues.

2. Suppose you are given a C function TimeNow(&T), that sets the integer variable T, to the value of a real-time clock in microseconds since the year 1900. It is always guaranteed that if you make two calls TimeNow(&T) and TimeNow(&S), in which the second call occurs later than the first, then the value in S is an integer that is larger than the value in T. The integer values returned by TimeNow(&T), can therefore be used as "time stamps" to associate with data being entered into a priority queue. When you retrieve a time-stamped item from a priority queue, you can arrange to remove the item having the largest value of its time stamp as the item of highest priority. Describe how you can set up a priority queue PQ, to behave like a stack, by entering and retrieving time-stamped items into PQ.

3. Give an implementation of the Stack ADT for stacks of floating point numbers, using the abstract operations for priority queues defined in Section 4.3 and implementing these priority queue operations with time-stamped items according to your solution to Ex. 3.

4. The "*abc* mirror image language" M, is a special language of strings formed from the letters {'a', 'b', 'c', 'm'} in which each string is of the form LmR, where L is a string of one or more *abc*s, where 'm' is a special middle marker, and where R is the reverse of the string L. For example, "*abbacmcabba*" is a member of language M, since the string $L ==$ "*abbac*" to the left of m is a mirror image of the string $R ==$ "*cabba*" to the right of m. Implement a recognizer for the language M, which decides whether or not a given string S belongs to the language M, using only the abstract operations in a Stack ADT implementing stacks of C characters.

7.7 How C Implements Recursive Function Calls Using Stacks

Learning Objectives

1. To understand how C can use stacks to execute recursive function calls.
2. To learn some terminology concerning stack frames (or activation records).
3. To learn key background information.

How does the C run-time system arrange to get a recursive function to call itself? Some earlier languages, such as the original FORTRAN, did not permit recursive functions. How is it that C can accommodate recursion?

using run-time stacks

When calling an instance of a function $F(a_1, a_2, \ldots, a_n)$ with actual parameters a_i (for $1 \leq i \leq n$), C uses a run-time stack. A collection of information, sometimes

```
  |   double Factorial(int n)
  |   {
  |       if ( n <= 1 ) {
  |           return  1.0;
5 |       } else {
  |           return  n * Factorial(n – 1);
  |       }
  |   }
```

Program 7.10 Recursive Factorial Again

called a *stack frame* (or a *call frame* or an *activation record*), is prepared to correspond to the call, $F(a_1, a_2, \ldots, a_n)$, and it is placed on top of a stack of other previously generated *stack frames*.

The information in a stack frame consists of (1) space to hold the value, V, returned by the function; (2) a pointer to the base of the previous stack frame in the stack; (3) a return address, which is the address of an instruction to execute in order to resume execution of F's caller after the execution of F has terminated; (4) parameter storage sufficient to hold the actual parameter values, $a_1, a_2, \ldots, a_n$, used in the call of F; and (5) a set of storage locations sufficient to hold the values of variables declared locally within F.

> the contents of stack frames

In C, when a function call $F(a_1, a_2, \ldots, a_n)$ is used as a statement, the function value V in the stack frame is discarded after returning from the function. (*Note*: A function call used in place of a statement is not expected to return a function value).

Let's consider a simple model of what might happen when we execute the assignment, $x = \text{Factorial}(3)$, given that a recursive factorial function has been declared as shown in Program 7.10. We first calculate and place $\psi == \&x$ (the address of x) on the stack. On top of that we place a stack frame for the call **Factorial(3)**. This gives the diagram shown in Fig. 7.11. Note that the space for locally declared variables is not used in the function **Factorial(n)**, since no local variables are declared. But if local

> a simple model

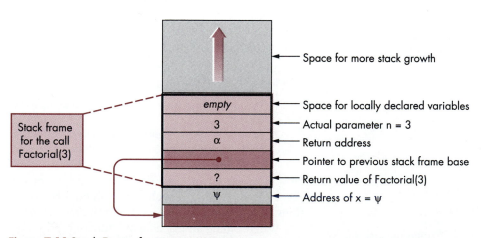

Figure 7.11 Stack Frame for Factorial(3)

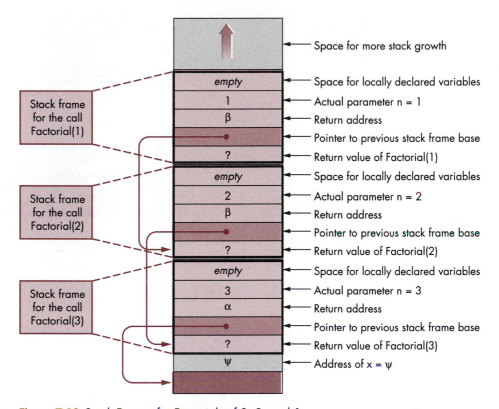

Figure 7.12 Stack Frames for Factorials of 3, 2, and 1

variables had been declared in **Factorial(n)**, space for them would have been reserved in the space marked *empty* in Fig. 7.11.

The computation of **Factorial(3)** in Fig. 7.11 is free to use more stack space on top of the stack frame for the call of **Factorial(3)**. It can use this stack space for temporary storage of intermediate values that have been computed and that await later use. It can also interrupt its execution of the call of **Factorial(3)** and place a new stack frame on the stack in order to make a recursive call. This is exactly what happens next, since the computation in **Factorial(3)** results in making a call on **Factorial(2)**. This in turn results in making a further recursive call on **Factorial(1)**. So two more stack frames get added to the top of the stack in Fig. 7.11, as shown in Fig. 7.12.

Since no values have yet been returned by any of the nest of recursive calls on **Factorial(n)**, the return value positions in these stack frames are shown as having the value "?" indicating that nothing has yet been assigned to them.

However, when the computation in the call **Factorial(1)** takes place, it determines that the condition (n <= 1) on line 3 of Program 7.10 is true, so the return statement on line 4 of Program 7.10 is executed. The value 1.0 is returned by this statement causing the floating point value 1.0 to be placed in the space for the return

unknown return values

unwinding the stack of calls

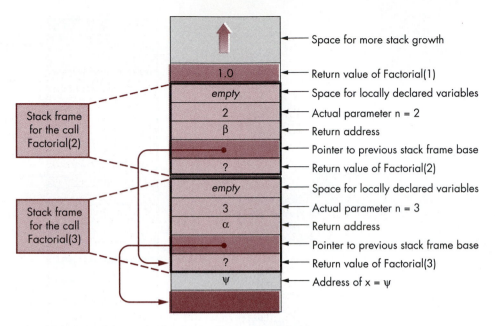

Figure 7.13 Stack Frames after Return from Factorial(1)

value of the stack frame for the call **Factorial(1)**. Following this, the call of **Factorial(1)** terminates by (a) resetting the current stack frame pointer to point to the base of the previous frame, using the pointer saved in the stack frame for **Factorial(1)** and (b) resuming execution at the address β in the code for the **Factorial** function, this being the place immediately after the call of **Factorial(1)**, which is about to use the value returned by the call of **Factorial(1)**. Figure 7.13 illustrates what happens immediately after the return from **Factorial(1)** and immediately upon resuming the computation in **Factorial(2)**.

Now the code beginning at address β is executed and consumes the return value for **Factorial(1)**, which it finds sitting on the stack immediately above its own stack frame. It multiplies this value for **Factorial(1)**, which is **1.0**, by the value of its own actual parameter, which is **2**, in order to compute the value of the expression, n * **Factorial**(n − 1), on line 6 of Program 7.10, and it places the result, which is **2.0**, in the space for the return value in its own stack frame. It then returns from its own call by resetting the stack frame pointer to the previous frame and resuming execution again at address β. This produces Fig. 7.14.

In the same fashion, the computation of **Factorial(3)** resumes. It consumes the result left by **Factorial(2)** on the stack, which is **2.0**, by multiplying it by its own copy of the actual parameter n == **3**, getting **6.0**, and it places this result in the space for the return value in its own stack frame. Finally, it returns from its own call by resetting the stack pointer to the saved pointer for the previous stack base, and by resuming execution at address α, which is the place in the code where execution needs to resume in order to finish the interrupted computation of the assignment statement,

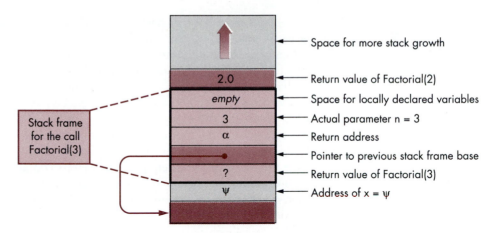

Figure 7.14 Stack Frame after Return from Factorial(2)

x = **Factorial(3)**. The resulting diagram after returning from the call of **Factorial(3)** is shown in Fig. 7.15. The code to complete this assignment can now take the value **6.0** from the stack, just where it expected to find it upon return from the call of **Factorial(3)**, and it can place this value into the address ψ, which was the address for **x** saved on the stack previous to the call of **Factorial(3)**.

finishing the job

A *word of caution*: There are many ways to implement recursive function calls using stacks. Different C compilers use different arrangements, and languages other than C may use still other arrangements. The scenario we have sketched above is only one possibility, and it omits several subtleties (such as how to ensure that the proper lexical scope for access to nonlocal variables is maintained). Courses in the theory and construction of compilers cover such subtleties, and they constitute the proper place to learn about the many important remaining details. Our purpose here was to help the reader to imagine a possible mechanical basis for how C can implement recursive function calls. By providing one model, the process is demystified, and the reader is prepared to understand explanations such as those dealing with why infinite regresses can cause C to exceed its "stack space."

some subtleties have not been covered

Even though our example was specific and lacking in additional detailed considerations, the stage is now set for being able to reach some important general conclusions, the main one being that *stacks* + *iteration* can implement *recursion*.

stacks + iteration = recursion

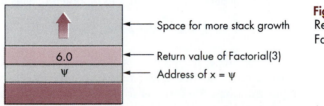

Figure 7.15 Stack after Return from the Call Factorial(3)

As mentioned in the chapter introduction, stacks can be used to process any kind of *nested structure*, in which things are contained in themselves in a nested fashion. When processing nested structures, we can start processing the outermost level of the structure, and if we encounter a nested substructure, we can interrupt the processing of the outer layer to begin processing an inner layer by putting a record of the interrupted status of the outer layer's processing on top of a stack. Later, when we have finished processing the inner layer and have returned with the results, we can resume processing the outer layer after the point of interruption, using the information saved on the stack. The stack therefore contains *postponed obligations* to resume and complete the processing of interrupted outer layers containing the current level at which we are working at any given moment. An important generalization we can reach is that stacks of structs of postponed obligations can help process nested structures to any depth of nesting.

Since calls on recursive functions are nested inside one another, and since processing the callee interrupts the processing of the caller, it is natural that stacks of recursive function stack frames can handle this nested processing of recursive calls.

7.7 Review Questions

1. Why will a nonterminating recursive C function cause a C run-time system to run out of stack space at program execution time?

7.7 Exercise

1. Explain how the C run-time stack model discussed in this section can stack the value returned by a function call in the same fashion that it can stack the value resulting from evaluation of a subexpression of a larger expression.

7.8   Implementations of the Queue ADT

Learning Objectives

1. To learn how to confine the travel of a sequentially represented queue to a circular track.
2. To understand some ways to represent queues using linked representations.
3. To learn how to implement the Queue ADT.

Not surprisingly, queues can have either sequential or linked representations. However, it turns out that queue representations involve a bit more subtlety than stack representations. We consider sequential representations of queues first.

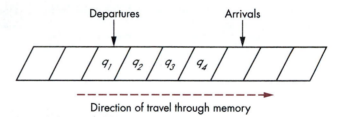

Figure 7.16 Rearward Marching Queue

Sequential Queue Representations

Suppose we place several queue items next to one another in an array. We insert new queue items at the rear and remove items from the front. As these insertions and removals take place, the queue travels through the array in the rearward direction. Eventually it bumps up against the size limit of the array, after which it can travel no further (see Fig. 7.16).

Queue representations that march through memory in a single direction, overwriting what is underneath as they go, are not very handy. Instead, it makes sense to confine the motion of a queue to a bounded region of memory. We can do this if we put a sequential queue representation on a circular track, and let it wind around and around as it moves rearward, as illustrated in Fig. 7.17.

It is easy to simulate the effect of a circular track in a linear array, using modular arithmetic. Modular arithmetic uses expressions of the form $(X \% N)$ to keep the values of X in the range $0:N - 1$. The expression $(X \% N)$ has this effect, since it computes the remainder of X after division by N, and this remainder is always less than N. Thus, as we add new items to a circular queue, we place them in the location given by the queue index, **Rear**, and then we let the rear of the queue grow by incrementing **Rear**. But whenever **Rear** is incremented so that its value becomes equal to the capacity of the queue, N, we set it to be zero—which has the effect of causing it to "wrap around" after it falls off the high end of the array so that it points to the first position at the opposite end of the array.

A similar consideration holds, when we remove items from the front of a queue. A queue index, **Front**, is used to designate the item that can next be removed at the front of the queue. After we remove an item, we increment the **Front** index so that it

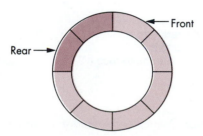

Figure 7.17 Queue on a Circular Track

Front　　=　　(Front + 1) % N;

Rear　　=　　(Rear + 1) % N;

Figure 7.18 Incrementing Indices Using Modular Arithmetic

designates the next position. But if this index falls off the high end of the array (by becoming equal to N), we wrap it around, by setting it equal to zero.

To summarize, given an array Items[0:N − 1], consisting of N items in positions 0:N − 1, and given two indices, Front and Rear, that can designate positions in the Items array, we can use the assignments shown in Fig. 7.18 to increment the pointers so that they always wrap around after falling off the high end of the array.

In the sequential queue implementation given in Program 7.19, a queue is represented by a struct that has (1) a counter, Count, which keeps track of the number of items in the queue; (2) an array index, Front, which keeps track of the index of the item that can next be removed from the queue; (3) an array index, Rear, that designates the place to insert the next queue item; and (4) an array of queue items used to hold the contents of the queue.

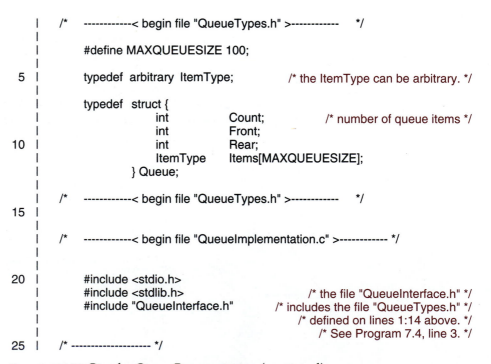

```
    |   /*    ------------< begin file "QueueTypes.h" >------------    */
    |
    |         #define MAXQUEUESIZE 100;
    |
 5  |         typedef  arbitrary  ItemType;              /* the ItemType can be arbitrary. */
    |
    |         typedef   struct {
    |                       int          Count;              /* number of queue items */
    |                       int          Front;
10  |                       int          Rear;
    |                       ItemType     Items[MAXQUEUESIZE];
    |                 } Queue;
    |
    |   /*    ------------< begin file "QueueTypes.h" >------------    */
15  |
    |
    |   /*    ------------< begin file "QueueImplementation.c" >------------ */
    |
    |
20  |         #include <stdio.h>
    |         #include <stdlib.h>                           /* the file "QueueInterface.h" */
    |         #include "QueueInterface.h"           /* includes the file "QueueTypes.h" */
    |                                                    /* defined on lines 1:14 above. */
    |                                                      /* See Program 7.4, line 3. */
25  |   /* -------------------- */
```

Program 7.19 Circular Queue Representation (continued)

Program 7.19 Circular Queue Representation (continued)

```c
        void InitializeQueue(Queue *Q)
        {
            Q->Count = 0;          /* Count == number of items in the queue */
            Q->Front = 0;          /* Front == location of item to remove next */
            Q->Rear = 0;                /* Rear == place to insert next item */
        }

  /* ------------------- */

        int Empty(Queue *Q)
        {
            return ( Q->Count == 0 );
        }

  /* ------------------- */

        int Full(Queue *Q)
        {
            return (Q->Count == MAXQUEUESIZE );
        }

  /* ------------------- */

        void Insert(ItemType R, Queue *Q)
        {
            if ( Q->Count == MAXQUEUESIZE ) {
                SystemError("attempt to insert item into a full Queue");
            } else {
                Q->Items[Q->Rear] = R;
                Q->Rear = (Q->Rear + 1) % MAXQUEUESIZE;
                + + (Q->Count);
            }
        }

  /* ------------------- */

        void Remove(Queue *Q, ItemType *F)
        {
            if ( Q->Count == 0 ) {
                SystemError("attempt to remove item from empty Queue");
            } else {
                *F = Q->Items[Q->Front];
                Q->Front = (Q->Front + 1) % MAXQUEUESIZE;
                - - (Q->Count);
            }
        }

  /* ------------------- */

  /* ------------< end-of-file "QueueImplementation.c" >------------ */
```

Linked Queue Representations

Linked queue representations come in many varieties. We present only one here, and mention a few of the others in the exercises.

The version given here represents a queue using a struct containing pointers to the *front* and *rear* of a linked list of nodes. Each node contains a queue item as its Item member, and links to the next node in the list, using a pointer in its Link member.

The linked implementations of the Queue ADT operations are given in Program 7.20. In the linked queue representation given in this program, a queue is a struct with pointers to the Front and Rear of a linear linked list of queue nodes. The Front pointer points to the first item node in the linked list, and the Rear pointer points to the last item node in the list. This is illustrated in Fig. 7.21.

The empty queue is a special case and is represented by a queue struct whose

```
 1 |    /*    ------------< begin file "QueueTypes.h" >------------    */
   |
   |    typedef  arbitrary      ItemType;           /* the ItemType can be arbitrary. */
   |
 5 |    typedef  struct  QueueNodeTag {
   |             ItemType                Item;
   |             struct QueueNodeTag     *Link;
   |          } QueueNode;
   |
10 |    typedef  struct {                           /* a queue is empty iff */
   |             QueueNode  *Front;                 /* its Front == NULL */
   |             QueueNode  *Rear;
   |          } Queue;
   |
15 |    /*    ------------< end-of-file "QueueTypes.h" >------------    */
   |
   |    /*    ------------< begin file "QueueImplementation.c" >------------    */
   |
   |        #include <stdio.h>                      /* the "QueueTypes.h" file, */
20 |        #include <stdlib.h>                     /* given above on lines 1:15, is */
   |        #include "QueueInterface.h"             /* included in "QueueInterface.h" */
   |                                                /* on line 3 of Program 7.4. */
   |        void InitializeQueue(Queue *Q)
   |        {
25 |             Q->Front  = NULL;
   |             Q->Rear   = NULL;
   |        }
   |
   |    /* -------------------- */
30 |
   |        int Empty(Queue *Q);
   |        {
   |             return ( Q->Front == NULL );
   |        }
```

Program 7.20 Linked Queue Representation (continued)

Program 7.20 Linked Queue Representation (continued)

```
35 |    /* -------------------- */
   |
   |         int Full(Queue *Q)
   |         {                               /* we assume an already constructed queue, Q, is */
   |             return 0;                       /* not full, since it could potentially grow */
40 |         }                                                /* as a linked structure */
   |
   |    /* -------------------- */
   |
   |         void Insert(ItemType R, Queue *Q)
45 |         {
   |             QueueNode *Temp;
   |                                                                  /* attempt to allocate */
   |             Temp = (QueueNode *) malloc(sizeof(QueueNode));/* a new node */
   |
50 |             if (Temp == NULL) {                 /* Temp = NULL signals allocation */
   |                 SystemError("system storage is exhausted");        /* failure */
   |             } else {
   |                 Temp–>Item = R;
   |                 Temp–>Link = NULL;
55 |                 if ( Q–>Rear == NULL ) {
   |                     Q–>Front = Temp;
   |                     Q–>Rear = Temp;
   |                 } else {
   |                     Q–>Rear–>Link = Temp;
60 |                     Q–>Rear = Temp;
   |                 }
   |             }
   |         }
   |
65 |    /* -------------------- */
   |
   |         void Remove(Queue *Q, ItemType *F)
   |         {
   |             QueueNode *Temp;
70 |
   |             if ( Q–>Front == NULL ) {
   |                 SystemError("attempt to remove item from empty Queue");
   |             } else {
   |                 *F = Q–>Front–>Item;
75 |                 Temp = Q–>Front;
   |                 Q–>Front = Temp–>Link;
   |                 free(Temp);
   |                 if ( Q–>Front == NULL ) Q–>Rear = NULL;
   |             }
80 |         }
   |
   |    /* -------------------- */
   |
   |    /* ------------< end-of-file "QueueImplementation.c" >------------   */
85 |
```

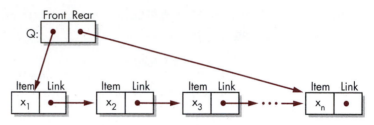

Figure 7.21 Linked Representation of Nonempty Queue

Front and **Rear** pointers are each **NULL** (see Fig. 7.22). To insert a new item, **R**, at the rear of a linked queue, you allocate a new **QueueNode**, set its **Item** member to contain **R**, and link it as the new last node of the linked list of queue nodes. Finally, you adjust the **Rear** pointer to point to this new last node.

To remove an item, **F**, at the front of the queue, you extract the item from the **Item** member of the first node in the linked list, and then delete the first node of the list. The **Front** pointer in the queue struct has to be adjusted to point to the second node in the list of queue nodes, which then becomes the new first node. Care must be taken to handle the empty queue as a special case.

Comparing Linked and Sequential Queue Representations

Sometimes before running a program it can be known how big queues can get. In order to set the stage for our comparison, we briefly illustrate the use of some queues in a *time-shared operating system*.

In a time-shared operating system, various jobs being processed have associated job status structs called *task records* that are placed in various queues to await processing. For instance, there may be an *I/O Wait Queue*, which contains records of tasks waiting to perform output (say on a printer or a screen), or to receive input from a user (perhaps from the user's keyboard). There may also be a *High-Priority Run Queue* and a *Low-Priority Run Queue*. When a task comes out of the I/O Wait Queue, it is put into the High-Priority Run Queue. When tasks advance to the front of either of the run queues, they are executed for a period of time called a *time-slice*. A time-slice in a typical operating system might be a sixtieth of a second. A task may not be able to run to completion in only one time-slice. If its time-slice is exhausted and the task still needs to run some more, it is placed in the Low-Priority Run Queue. But if a task runs to completion, it is placed into the I/O Wait Queue in order to output its results.

The reason there is a High-Priority Run Queue is to allow the operating system to exhibit a key property of good interactive computing systems—namely, *fast response to trivial requests for computation*. If you ask an interactive, time-shared system

task records in time-shared operating systems

ensuring rapid response to trivial requests

Figure 7.22 Linked Representation of Empty Queue

to evaluate and print "2 + 2," you would like to see the answer "4" instantly. If you type "2 + 2" and press the return key on the keyboard, your task, which has been sitting in the I/O Wait Queue, waiting for a completed line of input from your keyboard, is taken out of the I/O Wait Queue, and is placed in the High-Priority Run Queue. Every task in the High-Priority Run Queue gets to execute for up to one time-slice before any tasks in the Low-Priority Run Queue are executed for their respective time-slices.

What happens, then, is that your task, coming out of I/O Wait, gets an immediate small amount of execution time. If it can compute a result and get ready to print it within one time-slice, the task migrates back into the I/O Wait Queue, where it prints the result "4" on your terminal. It then seems to you as if you have gotten immediate service.

In a time-shared system with only one run queue, when your task comes out of I/O Wait and joins the rear of the run queue, it may have to wait until every task ahead of it in the run queue has received a time-slice of service before it gets to run (even though its demand for computation is negligible). If this happens, you may experience sluggish response at your terminal when you present trivial requests for computation (such as: "tell me the date," or "show me my file directory," or "compute 2 + 2," or whatever).

Experience suggests that users get annoyed if they have to wait a variable amount of time for responses to trivial requests. For example, you will get frustrated if you don't know whether you might get an instant reply or a delayed reply. Consequently, you are left hanging—do you have time just for a sip of coffee or should you go off and read a book for a while? Experience has shown that fast responses to trivial requests are psychologically important for users.

Many time-shared operating systems are designed to handle only a certain maximum number of jobs simultaneously. This maximum number is set so as not to risk overloading the system and making computation proceed slowly for all users. Consequently, the number of jobs is bounded (i.e., it can't exceed a certain maximum number). Under these circumstances, the queues used by the system to regulate the processing of tasks cannot get bigger than the known maximum, since each task record (representing a job) can be in only one of the queues at any one time. In this case it makes sense to use the sequential representation of queues because queue sizes are bounded. This representation is efficient, so long as queue overflow is impossible.

By contrast, in some queue applications, it is hard to predict how long queues will become. For example, some systems handle transactions (such as phone calls, or electronic funds transfers). If the rate of incoming transactions temporarily exceeds the capacity of the system to service them, transactions are often placed in a queue (or waiting line) to await service. Such a waiting line could grow without limit in periods where the arrival rate of transactions exceeds the service rate of the system. Under such circumstances, it makes sense to use a linked representation for queues, since the queue can grow in length so long as there is memory remaining in the system to use to allocate new nodes for queue items. At least the system won't come to a grinding halt with a queue overflow, when an insufficiently large predeclared queue-size limit gets exceeded accidentally, as can happen with sequential representation of queues.

limiting the maximum number of jobs

applications for which linked queue representations work best

7.8 Review Questions

1. What would be the disadvantage of having a linked queue representation in which there is only one pointer that points to the **Front** of the queue?
2. Is it possible to have a queue representation using a one-way linked list of queue item structs and having only a pointer to the **Rear** of the queue? If it is impossible, explain why. If it is possible, explain whether it is efficient. If it isn't efficient, what abstract queue operation(s) would be expected to take too much time?

7.8 Exercises

1. The members, **Count**, **Front**, and **Rear**, of the circular queue representation contain redundant information, since the relationship:

$$Rear == (Front + Count) \% MAXQUEUESIZE$$

   is always true. Show how to implement circular queues by modifying Program 7.19 so that the field **Rear** is eliminated, and the value for **Rear** is computed whenever it is needed. What kind of a trade-off does this modification make in comparison to the original Program 7.19?
2. If we agree to give up one location in a circular queue representation and not to use it to store any queue items, so that a queue of **N** item locations is said to be *full* when it contains **N − 1** items, then we need use only the **Front** and **Rear** fields, and the condition **Front == Rear** can be used to determine whether the queue is full or empty. Show how this can be done by modifying Program 7.19. [*Hint:* Establish conventions for setting up the **Front** and **Rear** fields so that when we attempt to insert an item, we do **Rear = (Rear + 1) % N**. If **Front == Rear**, then the queue has overflowed, but when we attempt to remove an item, if **Front == Rear**, then the queue has underflowed.]
3. Let Q be a nonempty queue, and let S be an empty Stack. Using only the abstract operations for the Queue and Stack ADTs, write a program to reverse the order of the items in Q.
4. An alternative linked queue representation uses a circular list of item nodes together with a single pointer to the **Rear** node of the queue (somewhere in the linked circular list of item nodes). Explain how this can work. How would you represent the empty queue in this method? Write a program to implement the Queue ADT operations using this circular linked representation.
5. Write an implementation of the abstract Queue ADT operations using two-way linked lists as a representation.
6. From an efficiency standpoint, what is wrong with a sequential queue representation that implements the operation **Remove(&Q,&F)** by moving the item in **Items[Front]** into F, and then shifting each of **Items[Front+1:Rear]** down one space into the locations **Items[Front:Rear − 1]** ?

7.9 More Queue Applications

Learning Objectives

1. To learn practical background information on how queues are used.
2. To learn about print buffers and printer spoolers.
3. To learn about synchronization problems using print buffers.
4. To learn about uses of queues in simulation and modeling.

In the last section we discussed how queues were used in operating systems to regulate the processing of tasks. We will now discuss more queue applications in operating systems, networks, simulation, and modeling.

Queues in Operating Systems

Queues can be used in operating systems to act as *buffers* that help synchronize the interaction between two processes that run at different speeds. For example, a queue may be used as a *print buffer* that sits between a central processing unit (CPU) and a printer. A computation running in the CPU may produce output to be printed much faster than the printer can print it. The printer gets lines to print, one at a time, from the front of a queue of lines to be printed, which are stored in the print buffer. The CPU adds new lines to be printed to the rear of the queue in the print buffer, provided the print buffer queue is not full. If the print buffer is full and the CPU needs to add more lines to the print buffer, the CPU must wait until the print buffer has room for more lines (i.e., it must wait until the printer empties the print buffer a bit by printing some lines, rendering the print buffer *not full*.) The two tasks acting on the print buffer are illustrated in Program 7.23.

```
     void WriteLineToBePrinted(void);                      /* the CPU's task */
     {
         if ( there is a line L to print) &&
5               (the print buffer is neither full nor busy) {
             Insert(L, &PrintBufferQueue);
         }
     }

10   void ReadLineToBePrinted(void)                         /* the Printer's task */
     {
         if  (the print buffer is neither empty nor busy) {
             Remove(&PrintBufferQueue, &L);
             (Print line &L on the Printer)
15       }
     }
```

Program 7.23 Reading and Writing Print Buffer Lines

Generally, the CPU and the printer execute the two tasks in Program 7.23 concurrently. If they both try to access the *print buffer* simultaneously, there is a possibility of interfering with each other. Consequently, there needs to be a mechanism for each to use to seize control of the print buffer and to lock it out from access by the other for the duration of its access. After the print buffer access is completed, the print buffer needs to be unlocked so the next task needing to access it can gain control of it. This basic problem is called *the problem of synchronizing concurrent tasks*, and the particular form of it mentioned here is sometimes called *the readers and writers problem*.

the readers and
writers problem

Two more uses of queues in connection with printing occur in operating systems and networks. A *printer spooler* is a queue that accepts a queue of lines to be printed and stores this queue as a *spooled-file*, while notifying the printer server that the spooled-file is ready to print. When the printer server is free, it starts to print the spooled-file by removing and printing lines from the front of the queue of lines in the spooled-file.

printer spoolers

As a second example, a network of computers may contain a shared printer server (such as a laser printer). The server associated with the printer may accept files to be printed. These files may be shipped to it by workstations or other computers on the network. When the files to be printed arrive at the printer server, they are placed in a queue on a first-come, first-served basis to await printing. Users sitting at workstations may be able to interrogate the status of the printer queue by executing an appropriate operating system command (such as the **interrogate printer queue** or **ipq** command available in some Unix network systems).

The advantage of printer spooling systems over the use of simple print buffers is that a task running on a CPU need not get blocked while waiting for a slow printer to print the lines in a full print buffer. For example, aircraft pilots have an aviation weather service called DUAT (which stands for Direct User Access Terminal). A pilot using this service calls a central aviation weather computer using a desktop computer and a dial-in modem. [A modem is a device which allows two computers to communicate over a phone line.] Pilots using DUAT service are allowed only twenty minutes of on-line contact before their session is shut off automatically.

using spoolers to make best
use of limited access time

When getting a thorough preflight briefing, pilots sometimes need to access many screens of information, such as current weather reports at various weather stations along the planned flight route, weather forecasts at various stations, winds aloft forecasts, significant weather alerts, and notices concerning unusual conditions (such as an area where parachute jumping is going on or where flight is prohibited because of a presidential visit, etc.).

It is convenient for pilots to print the key preflight briefing data on paper to take with them during the flight. If the DUAT access computer does not have a print spooler, but has only a print buffer, then the pilot may have to wait for the printer to print a full screen of data (usually 24 lines of 80 characters per line) before giving another command to the DUAT system to access the next screenful of information. If the printer is slow, it may be difficult for the pilot to print all the information needed before the 20 minute session cutoff occurs. On the other hand, if the system has a printer spooler, the screens of information to be printed can be placed in the printer

how pilots can beat the
twenty minute system
cutoff time

spool queue to be printed later at the printer's pace, and the pilot can go ahead and enter more commands into the DUAT system to collect the rest of the preflight briefing information without having to wait for the printer to finish printing the current screen.

added convenience for
word processor users

A similar increase in convenience is available to users of ordinary word processors who would like to print one document at the same time they continue to revise another document on their workstations. Simultaneous printing and word processor operation are available on the latest generation of workstations that have concurrent operating systems. A concurrent operating system is one that can process more than one job (or task) at the same time. Earlier types of simple home computers seldom had concurrent operating systems, forcing word processor users to wait until a print task ran to completion before resuming work on a word processor task. In such circumstances, the user could do nothing but wait for the printer to finish printing before resuming work in the word processor.

using queues as
memory buffers

More generally, queues can be used as I/O buffers in operating systems between many different kinds of devices. For example, in a time-shared operating system having virtual memory, queues are used to regulate the flow of memory pages being swapped into and out of the main memory over a swapping channel connecting the main memory to a large secondary memory (which contains the extra memory pages implementing the virtual addresses in a task's virtual memory address space). Also, queues are used to regulate the processing of read/write requests serviced by large file storage devices, such as external disks or tapes.

Queues in Simulation Experiments

Sometimes we need to study the behavior of models of a system we are trying to understand. Simulating such system behavior using a computer model is often a good way to gain insight. Computer simulations are particularly useful when dealing with systems that are sufficiently complex that it is hard to construct accurate mathematical models, but for which computer models can maintain descriptive accuracy.

our world abounds
in queues

Many systems used in everyday life incorporate queues. In fact, in highly-populated urban areas, many people may spend more time in waiting-lines than they might prefer. It seems that waiting-lines are everywhere to be seen: (a) at supermarket checkout counters, (b) at bank teller windows, (c) at ticket windows in ski areas and sports arenas, (d) at gas station pumps and car washes, (e) at the library information desk, (f) at the entrance for rides in amusement parks, (g) waiting to take off at the local airport, (h) at freeway, beltway, or autobahn on-ramps, (i) at the drive-up windows of fast food outlets, and (j) even waiting to see Santa Claus in a department store in December.

clients and servers

Each of these systems shares common features. There are queues of *clients* waiting in a first-come, first-served order for service. There are *servers* who dispense the service. Clients arrive and queue-up according to some arrival time discipline. The time a server needs to serve a client is called a *service-time interval*. These service-time intervals may be of fixed duration, or they may vary. If they vary, they may be described by a *service-time distribution*. Such a distribution may have an *average* value and a *variance* (where the variance is a measure of how broadly or narrowly the various likely service times are spread out around the average time).

Sometimes there are multiple queues and multiple servers. When a client has gone to the front of one queue and advances to a server and obtains service, the client may then join another queue to obtain another part of the total service needed. (Getting your driver's license renewed may involve a system of several queues—a queue to get your eyes examined, a queue to get your picture taken, a queue to get your exam questions graded, a queue to get your new license issued, and a queue to pay the renewal fee.)

When we use a queuing system simulation to model an actual system, we try to model each queue in the real-world system with a queue in the simulation model. We try to model the arrival rate of clients entering the system and queuing up for service. We try to model accurately the service times taken by clients obtaining service from the servers, and we try to collect statistics that measure how well the overall system performs. For example, we may be interested in measuring (a) the average waiting time to obtain service, (b) the variance in the waiting times (i.e., how dispersed or spread out the waiting times are), (c) the length of the queues, and (d) the *throughput* of the system (i.e., how many clients are served per hour). We might want to run simulation experiments under different conditions—for example, by adding or removing servers, while holding the arrival rate of clients constant—to see what happens to the measures of system performance.

For example, some supermarkets are aware that their popularity among customers is influenced by the time customers spend waiting in lines at the checkout counters. If a supermarket wants to attract more customers, it might attempt to keep checkout lines short by having a policy of opening a new checkout counter anytime a checkout line has more than three customers waiting in it. If they advertise this feature on radio and television, they may attract new customers or retain customers who might otherwise go shop at a competing supermarket. On the other hand, since profit margins in the supermarket business are thin (sometimes under 2 percent), supermarket managers need to be conscious about cost control. If too many checkout counters are open at once, and if there is slight demand, then it may cost too much. Perhaps a supermarket chain could gain insight into how some proposed policies would work by performing a computer simulation. First it would be important to collect some real data on service times and arrival rates at the checkout counter lines. These data could then be used to set up a realistic simulation. Various alternative policies could be modeled and simulated, and results could be collected to compare their differing performances.

Here are some examples of questions that might be settled by queuing system simulations in various settings:

1. Do you get better service at an airline ticket counter (or at bank teller or sports arena ticket windows) if all customers feed from a single queue, or from separate queues for each ticket agent (or bank teller)?
2. During a gasoline shortage, do drivers spend more time in line on the average if each driver can wait in line to get 4 gallons (16 liters) on any day, or if drivers with license plates ending in even digits (or the letters A:L) can get 8 gallons (32 liters) on even numbered days, and drivers with license plates ending

important aspects of queuing and simulation models

simulating supermarket checkout lines

in odd digits (or the letters M:Z) can get 8 gallons (32 liters) on odd numbered days?

3. How much does it help alleviate freeway (or autobahn, or beltway, or interstate) traffic congestion to install on-ramp metering systems which force drivers to queue-up to await a traffic signal that lets them enter the freeway?

4. In a time-shared operating system, how much does it improve response times for trivial requests if a high-priority run queue is used (according to the description at the end of the previous section), versus having a single run queue for all jobs?

the origins of
queuing theory

In the 1940s, a branch of mathematics called *queuing theory* was developed at Bell Laboratories to help predict how to build the telephone system to accommodate expected increases in telephone traffic. The objective was to find out how much copper wire to lay, and in what places around the country, so that future demand for phone service could be accommodated. The Bell Labs mathematicians needed a system of mathematics that enabled them to predict the probability that a customer might try to make a phone call and would find all circuits busy, under different conditions of telephone system loading. Statistical models for arrival rates, service time intervals, and the growth of queues were developed. It is said that the resulting models were so successful that the telephone company was saved millions of dollars in wasted copper wire. There is a story, perhaps apocryphal, that says, "So great were the savings, that Bell Labs paid for its entire future operating costs by virtue of the results of applying this queuing theory."

The mathematics of closed queuing systems has had particularly beneficial effects in the development of the theory of operating systems. A closed queuing system is one in which a fixed number of clients migrate around the system joining various queues to wait for service from various servers. Jobs in an operating system follow this discipline. It is possible to use the theory of closed queuing systems to *balance* an operating system by ensuring that the various servers (such as printers, swapping channels, CPUs, and disks) have enough capacity to service a particular expected job mix without developing *bottlenecks* (which show up as long queues where jobs are taken out of action awaiting service from a server of inadequate capacity).

7.9 Review Questions

1. Describe several uses of queues in time-shared operating systems and computer networks.
2. What kinds of systems can be modeled by queuing simulations, and what kinds of questions can be answered by the results?

7.9 Exercises

1. Develop a simulation program to investigate queuing policies for gasoline shortages, as described in situation (2) above.

Pitfalls

- *Not being careful about boundary conditions*

  When implementing linked or sequential representations for stacks and queues (and especially for queues) be careful to check that the special cases are handled properly. In particular, empty and full stacks and queues should be thoroughly checked to ensure they work properly for all prescribed ADT operations.

- *Not checking modular arithmetic for circular queues*

  Be cautious when implementing circular queues that remainders computed by modular arithmetic (using expressions such as X % N) or computed by conditional logic (using statements such as X++; if (X == N) X = 0;) lie within the proper numeric ranges, and that the index ranges of arrays used to store items are matched properly to the numeric ranges of these remainders.

Tips and Techniques

- *Use ADTs to achieve clean modular program designs*

  The use of Stack and Queue ADTs promotes clean modular program designs. The many benefits, covered in Chapter 4, accrue to the system designer who follows this advice. Among other things, top-level applications will not be contaminated with details of low-level representation choices, and inefficient implementations can be eliminated by substituting behaviorally equivalent representations having improved efficiency.

- *Use simulation and modeling to explore the behavior of proposed new designs*

  It is often helpful to use simulation and modeling techniques to explore the behavior of alternative designs for a proposed new system. If realistic data on arrival times and service times can be collected, alternative designs of a proposed new system can be simulated, and data can be collected that yield insight into system performance and efficiency. Such results can be helpful in choosing which design to implement.

- *Use queues to regulate tasks and to synchronize processes*

  Queues are useful for regulating the flow of tasks among servers in a system having multiple servers, and in which it is desirable to guarantee "first-come, first-served" service disciplines. Queues are also useful to synchronize the interaction of two concurrent processes running at different speeds that must exchange data.

- *Use stacks to process nested structures and to evaluate expressions*

  Stacks are ideal to use to process data structures that are inherently nested to any arbitrary degree of depth. They are also useful for expression evaluation in interpreters and calculators.

References for Further Study

queuing theory

William Feller, *An Introduction to Probability Theory and Its Applications*, 2nd ed., Wiley, New York, (1957).

Covers aspects of probability theory useful in setting up queuing simulations.

Chapter Summary

An abstract model for a linear data structure is the *sequence*—a finite, ordered arrangement of data items. A sequence can be thought of as one of the possible structuring methods for arranging data structure components into aggregates. Other data structuring methods include the formation of arrays, structs, sets, and linked structures.

Abstract data types based on sequences can be defined by starting with sequences of items and adding sets of allowed operations. When we confine the growth of sequences to occur at their endpoints in certain designated ways, we get *stacks* and *queues*.

stacks

Stacks are sequences of items that are allowed to grow and shrink only at one end, called the *top*. Adding a new item, X, to the top of a stack, S, is called *pushing* X *onto* S. Removing an item, X, from the top of a stack is called *popping* X *from* S.

queues

A *queue* is a sequence of items that grows at one end, called its *rear*, and shrinks at its other end, called its *front*.

uses for stacks

Stacks are useful for processing nested structures of arbitrary depth, for evaluating arithmetic or algebraic expressions, and for parsing programs written in most programming languages. They can also be used for searching in search spaces using the method of backtracking. Stacks in the C run-time system support the use of recursive functions as well as nested function calls.

uses for queues

Queues are useful for regulating the flow of tasks within a system, especially when tasks must be processed by several kinds of servers. Queues are commonly used in operating systems for this purpose. Additionally, queues are used to synchronize the exchange of data between two concurrent processes running at different speeds. Print buffers and printer spoolers offer two common examples of this use. Queues are also useful in setting up simulations and models of systems in which clients arrive and are given service.

Stacks and queues can have both sequential and linked representations. The sequential and linked representations of queues encompass a few subtleties that must be carefully considered, especially when considering the representations of full and empty queues.

The use of Stack and Queue ADTs is recommended as a good programming practice giving access to the benefits of modular programming. Low-level representation details can be hidden from use in the high-level system design, representations are made substitutable, and program clarity, simplicity, and reliability can be enhanced.

8

Lists, Strings, and Dynamic Memory Allocation

≡ **8.1** Introduction and Motivation

In Chapter 7, we studied two special cases of linear data structures. We started by applying a structuring method to collections of items—namely, we formed *sequences* of items. Sequences were just finite, linear, ordered arrangements of items. Then we added operations. When we allowed items to be removed and inserted at only one end of a sequence, we got *stacks*. When we allowed items to be removed at one end of a sequence and inserted at the opposite end, we got *queues*.

We are now ready to investigate two more linear data structures based on sequences of items—namely, *lists* and *strings*. Moreover, in this chapter, we will also cover dynamic memory allocation techniques and generalized lists, which are simply lists whose individual items are permitted to be sublists of items.

However, our emphasis in this chapter is less on packaging lists and strings into abstract data types (ADTs) and more on exploring various significant underlying representations. By now, the advantages of modular programming

lists, strings and generalized lists

296

and the use of data abstraction should be clear, and the techniques for achieving such advantages should be well-understood. Consequently, we do not place more than minor emphasis on how lists and strings can be presented as ADTs and how applications can be built from these ADTs. Instead, we emphasize the exploration of alternative data representations, and the crafting of these representations to yield various advantages from the perspectives of *efficiency* and *tradeoffs*.

In this context, several alternative representations of lists are explored—such as circular lists, doubly linked lists, and lists accessed via special header nodes.

For strings, two popular string representations are investigated: C strings and Pascal strings. We also look at how strings are represented in text files and in word processors.

dynamic memory allocation

With respect to dynamic memory allocation, we cover pointers and handles, allocation strategies for blocks of memory in heaps (such as the first-fit and best-fit strategies), and the concepts of fragmentation, coalescing, and compacting. We also explore garbage collection, marking algorithms, and the use of reference counts in incremental storage reclamation techniques.

Plan for the Chapter

list representations

In Section 8.2, we begin by exploring list representations. We first discover that ordinary sequential representations, such as those that pack list items contiguously in arrays, have disadvantages when trying to represent certain kinds of list operations, such as insertion or deletion of items in arbitrary positions. We then explore several alternative linked list representations that overcome the disadvantages of the sequential representations.

generalized lists

In Section 8.3, we explore generalized lists—that is, lists having sublists. We differentiate between generalized lists having shared sublists and those having separate copies of sublists, and we give an algorithm for printing generalized lists. A short discussion of applications of generalized lists follows in Section 8.4.

strings

Section 8.5 introduces a String ADT and compares two popular string representations in widespread use: C *strings* and *Pascal strings*. We also comment on the kinds of string representations used in contemporary word processors and in text files containing sequences of characters.

dynamic memory allocation techniques

In Section 8.6, we investigate the underlying memory allocation problems that need to be solved to support linked data structures and data structures formed from applying structuring methods to blocks of memory of differing size. We cover the difference between pointers and handles when used to reference variable size blocks of memory in heaps, and we study heap compaction algorithms. We compare two different dynamic storage allocation strategies—first-fit and best-fit. We also study garbage collection policies, including the marking and gathering method and the reference-count method.

A *List* (*L*) of items of type (*T*) is a sequence of items of type *T* on which the following operations are defined:

1. *Initialize* the list *L* to be the *empty list*.
2. Determine whether or not the list *L* is *empty*.
3. Find the *length* of a list *L* (where the *length* of *L* is the number of items in *L*, and the *length* of the *empty list* is zero).
4. *Select* the ith item of a list *L*, where $1 \leq i \leq length(L)$.
5. *Replace* the ith item, *X*, of a list, *L*, with a new item, *Y*, where $1 \leq i \leq length(L)$.
6. *Delete* any item, *X*, from a nonempty list, *L*.
7. *Insert* a new item, *X*, into a list, *L*, in any arbitrary position (such as *before* the first item of *L*, *after* the last item of *L*, or *between* any two items of *L*).

Figure 8.1 List Operations Defining a List ADT

8.2 Lists

Learning Objectives

1. To understand the advantages and disadvantages of sequential and linked representations of lists.
2. To become acquainted with one-way, two-way, and circular list representations.
3. To understand the role of list header nodes.
4. To understand that many varieties of list representations are possible.

A list is simply a sequence of items. The usual operations permitted on lists are insertions and deletions of items in arbitrary places, finding the length of a list, and determining whether or not a list is empty. (The *empty list* is a list having no items in it.)

A List ADT

An ADT for lists might be defined by specifying an appropriate set of list operations. One possible List ADT uses the list operations given in Fig. 8.1.

When we can insert and delete list items in arbitrary places, we get a class of sequential structures with more general growth and combining laws than those for stacks and queues. Lists are therefore more elastic general containers for items than either stacks or queues. They tend to be used in applications where this added generality is needed.

Sequential List Representations

the contiguous, sequential list representation

fast access to the ith item

One way to represent lists is to pack the list items next to one another in a sequential structure such as an array. When list items are stored next to one another (with no gaps in between), we say they are stored *contiguously*. Figure 8.2 illustrates the use of an array A[0:MaxSize − 1] to hold a sequential, contiguous representation of the items of the abstract list $L == (x_1, x_2, x_3, x_4)$. To complete the sequential representation of

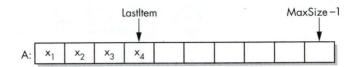

Figure 8.2 An Array Holding List Items Sequentially

lists using arrays, we also need to save the length of the list (or, perhaps instead, the array index of the last item). This aspect of the sequential representation of lists using arrays is illustrated by the index, LastItem, in Fig. 8.2. The sequential representation in this figure permits fast access to the ith item of a list, since we can use the underlying array indexing capability to select or replace the ith array item.

However, to insert a new item or to delete some item, we may need to shift all the items beyond the point of insertion or deletion, in order to maintain the contiguous sequential arrangement of items in the underlying array. This is inherently inefficient and on the average requires $O(n)$ time, where n is the length of the list (see Exercises 8.2.1 and 8.2.2).

slow insertion and deletion of all items except the last item

Another potential difficulty is that if we use declared arrays in a language such as C, we must allocate them in predetermined sizes. If an array, A[0:n−1], is used to represent a list $L == (x_1, x_2, \ldots, x_n)$, then the array is *full*, and we cannot insert another item in it without having the array *overflow*. Yet, lists are often used in circumstances where we want to handle unpredictable amounts of growth in our data, and it is inconvenient if they overflow. Rather, we need a representation of lists that can stretch to handle unforecast growth that might occur during the running of a program.

the risk of overflow

Note that there is no operation specified in the List ADT operations given in Fig. 8.1, which determines when a list is *full*, nor is there a restriction on the insertion operation to apply to non-full lists only. Consequently, the use of underlying array representations to hold sequential arrangements of list items is subject to failure from unanticipated overflow conditions. If we preallocate arrays that are too small, the chances of accidental overflow are increased. But if we preallocate arrays that are too big, we are in danger of wasting a considerable amount of space. Therefore sequential list representations have several disadvantages.

Some of these disadvantages can be overcome by using the linked representations that we recall in the next section. However, these linked representations have disadvantages of their own, such as inefficient access to the ith list item, and storage penalties for the space needed to store the links.

The One-Way Linked List Representation

In Chapter 2, we introduced simple one-way, linked list representations using chains of linked nodes. According to this technique, the way to represent the list $L ==$

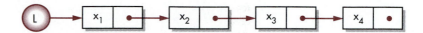

Figure 8.3 Simple One-Way Linked List

(x_1, x_2, x_3, x_4), is shown in Fig. 8.3. Recall that the empty list is represented by the null pointer, NULL.

To access the ith item of a linked list, L, we start with the pointer value in L and dereference it to access the first node of the linked list. We then repeatedly follow the pointers in the Link fields of nodes, as necessary, in order to access the ith node. Finally, we can access the Item field of the ith node. For example, to print the value of the ith item of a linked list, L, we can use an algorithm such as the one given in Program 8.4. Starting with the pointer in the variable, L, the procedure PrintItem(i,L) follows exactly i pointers to access the ith item of the list L.

Suppose that list L has exactly n items. If it is equally likely that each of these n items can be printed, then the average number of pointers followed to access the ith item is given by:

$$\text{Average} = (1 + 2 + \ldots + n)/n = \frac{n(n+1)}{2}/n = \frac{n}{2} + \frac{1}{2}.$$

accessing the ith item is expensive in linked lists

Consequently, the average time to access the ith item is O(n). By contrast, the average time needed to access the ith item in a sequential array representation of a list L (as illustrated in Fig. 8.2) is O(1), since it takes a constant amount of time to access an array item A[i], starting with the array index, i.

We can generalize slightly by observing that any process that needs to access the ith node of a one-way linked list, L, of length n, starting with a pointer to the first

```
    |   void PrintItem(int i, NodeType *L);
    |   {
    |
    |       while ( ( i > 1 ) && ( L != NULL) ) {        /* set L to point to */
 5  |           L = L->Link;                             /* the ith item of the list */
    |           i − − ;
    |       }
    |
    |
10  |       if ( ( i == 1) && (L != NULL ) ) {
    |           printf("%s", L->Item);          /* print the ith item provided it exists */
    |       } else {
    |           printf("Error—attempt to print an item that is not on the list.\n");
    |       }
15  |
    |   }
```

Program 8.4 Printing the ith Item of a Linked List

Table 8.5 Comparing Average Running Times of Various List Operations Using Sequential and Linked List Representations

List Operation	Sequential Representation	Linked Representation
Finding the length of L	O(1)	O(n)
Inserting a new first item	O(n)	O(1)
Deleting the last item	O(1)	O(n)
Replacing the ith item	O(1)	O(n)
Deleting the ith item	O(n)	O(n)

node of the list, takes $O(n)$ time, whenever each of the nodes of L is equally likely to be accessed. For example, processes such as accessing, deleting, or replacing the ith node, or inserting a new node before or after the ith node, each take time $O(n)$.

Comparing Sequential and Linked List Representations

Let $L == (x_1, x_2, \ldots, x_n)$ be an abstract list of length n. Let's compare the average running times for doing several kinds of operations on the sequential array representation of L (as illustrated in Fig. 8.2) and the simple, one-way linked representation of L (as illustrated in Fig. 8.3). Table 8.5 gives the comparison.

Running time is not the only dimension on which we might wish to compare the efficiency of list representations. Space can also be an important resource to consider in some applications. The one-way, linked representation of a list requires space for one link in each node of the linked list representation. By contrast, the sequential array representation of a list requires no space for links, but it may waste unused space for items inside an array of preallocated size.

comparing space costs

For a simple comparison, suppose that the space required by list items and the space required for pointers is identical. For example, the items might be floating point numbers each requiring 4 bytes of storage, and pointers might also take 4 bytes of storage each. Consider a list, L, of length n. The linked representation of L requires n nodes each requiring 8 bytes of storage, for a total of $8n$ bytes, to represent the entire list L. If we use an array A[0:MaxSize − 1] to hold the items of L sequentially, it takes $4n$ bytes to hold the n items of L inside A, but there is wasted space in the subarray A[n:MaxSize − 1], since this space is unused to hold items of L. The total space required for the sequential representation of L, is equal to $4n + 4(\text{MaxSize} - n)$, which simplifies to $4 * \text{MaxSize}$.

finding the tradeoff point

We can find the tradeoff point for storage utilization efficiency between the sequential and linked list representations by setting the storage used by the linked representation, $8n$, equal to the storage used by the sequential representation, which is $4 * \text{MaxSize}$, and by solving for n. Solving for n in $8n = 4 * \text{MaxSize}$ yields the solution:

$$n = \frac{\text{MaxSize}}{2}.$$

In other words, assuming that list items and pointers each take the same number of bytes of storage, the sequential representation is more space-efficient whenever the average list is longer than half the size of the arrays used to store items in the sequential list representation. The tradeoff point shifts if list items and links take differing amounts of storage. For instance, if pointers require p bytes of storage and items require q bytes of storage, then the tradeoff point is given by:

$$n = \frac{q}{(p+q)} * \text{MaxSize.} \tag{8.1}$$

In particular, the cost in space of using linked list representations is low when list item representations take a large amount of storage in comparison to the storage required for pointers. For example, suppose we want to represent a list of employee structs (each containing an employee's name, address, employee number, and department). Suppose each employee struct takes 256 bytes, and each pointer takes 4 bytes. Then the storage efficiency tradeoff point according to Eq. 8.1 is $n = 256/260 *$ MaxSize, which is the same as $n = 0.9846 *$ MaxSize. In other words, you would have to operate sequential array-based list representations at better than 98 percent of capacity to gain a space efficiency advantage over the linked list representation. But attempting to operate at over 98 percent of capacity runs the risk of list overflow in the array-based representation.

Consequently, if space efficiency is not the principal design constraint that needs to be met, and the efficiency of operations is instead of equal or greater importance, then one might choose to use either the linked or sequential list representation based on the average *time* consumed to perform an average mix of list operations (where the average mix could be measured by sampling the actual running application). The results in Table 8.5 show that the sequential representation will perform better if there is a preponderance of random accesses to list items (as in updating employee structs when the positions of the structs are known in advance). On the other hand, if we often insert new employee structs as the new first item on a list, and we occasionally print a report enumerating the whole list, then the linked list representation is preferable (from the perspective of *time* efficiency not *space* efficiency).

when efficiency in time outweighs efficiency in space

(Actually, lists are not the most efficient way to store collections of employee structs in a database that we intend to use for querying, updating, and occasional report printing. Instead, structures such as trees, hash tables, and large external file organizations give us much better solutions for many important mixes of different operations and many ranges of database sizes used in practice. We will explore the story of how different data structures have significant different advantages and drawbacks in the remaining chapters of this book. The remarks comparing linked and sequential list representations given in this subsection are just the beginning of a more extensive and thorough exploration of the possibilities.)

other representations that give better solutions

Other Linked List Representations

Linked list representations come in almost limitless varieties. Eventually, you may want to craft your own special linked list representation for a particular purpose. In

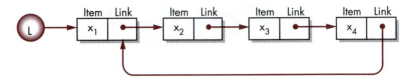

Figure 8.6 A Circular Linked List

this subsection, we cover just three of the more common varieties of linked list representations above and beyond simple one-way, linked lists. These are (a) circular lists, (b) two-way linked lists, and (c) linked lists with special header nodes.

Circular Linked Lists

A circular linked list is formed by having the link in the last node of a one-way linked list point back to the first node. Figure 8.6 shows an example of a circular linked list. A circular linked list has the advantage that any node on it is accessible from any other node. That is, given a pointer to an arbitrary node, **N**, on a circular linked list **L**, we can follow links from node **N** to access any other node, **M**, on list **L**.

Exercise 8.2.5 explores the proper way to use a circular linked list to represent a queue.

Two-Way Linked Lists

Two-way linked lists are formed from nodes that have pointers to both their left and right neighbors in the list. Figure 8.7 gives an example of such a list. In this figure **LLink** is the title of a field holding a *left link* pointing to the left neighbor node of the given node, and **RLink** is the title of a field holding a *right link* pointing to the right neighbor of the given node. Sometimes a two-way linked list is called a *symmetrically linked list*.

Given a pointer to any node, **N**, in a two-way list, **L**, you can follow links in either direction to access other nodes. Moreover, you can delete node **N**, and you can insert a new node, **M**, either before or after **N**, starting only with the information given by the pointer in **N**. It is not possible to perform these same operations starting with a pointer **N** to a node in a one-way linked list.

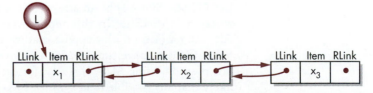

Figure 8.7 A Two-Way Linked List

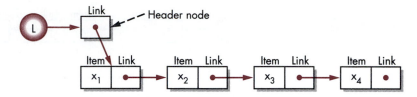

Figure 8.8 A Linked List with a Header Node

Linked Lists with Header Nodes

Sometimes it is convenient to have a special *header node* that points to the first node in a linked list of item nodes (see Fig. 8.8). The use of a header node can be combined with the use of circular or two-way lists. Header nodes can also be set up to contain additional information about the list, such as the number of nodes in the list, or a reference count (used in garbage collection and explained later in Section 8.6).

Some examples of the use of header nodes from the published literature include the following:

1. To provide a stopping place on circular lists, or to provide a unique starting place.
2. To point to both ends of a two-way list (for fast insertion of all the list's items between two items in another two-way list, or for fast storage deallocation of the nodes in the list).
3. To permit ease of deletion of the first node on a list when the list is referenced by more than one external pointer.

8.2 Review Questions

1. What is a list?
2. What are some disadvantages of using packed arrays of list items to represent lists sequentially?
3. When would it be advantageous to use a sequential array list representation instead of a linked list representation?
4. Under what circumstances would it pay to use a circular linked list instead of a one-way linked list?

8.2 Exercises

1. Let A[0:MaxSize − 1] be an array holding items in the list $L == (x_1, x_2, \ldots, x_n)$, where $n <$ MaxSize. In this representation, we store list item x_i in position A[i − 1], for $(1 \leq i \leq n)$. Suppose that we want to delete an arbitrary list item, x_i. What is the average time needed to move all the items x_j, $(i + 1 \leq j \leq n)$ down one position, using A[j − 1] = A[j] for each j in $(i \leq j < n)$, assuming it is equally likely that any possible item x_i in list L is chosen to be deleted? Give the O-notation for this average deletion time.

2. Give the O-notation for the average time to insert a new item in the ith position of a list L using the array representation in Exercise 1. Assume that insertions in any possible position are equally likely.

3. Prove the results given in Table 8.5.

4. Derive the result given in Eq. 8.1.

5. Mr. Alf Witt decides to use circular linked lists to represent queues. He lets a pointer variable **Q** point to the node on the circular list, **L**, containing the item at the front of the queue. Ms. Daisee Chayne thinks that a better design would be to have **Q** point to the node on the circular linked list **L** containing the rear item in the queue. Which queue representation is better, Alf's or Daisee's? Why?

6. Write a program module implementing all of the operations given in Fig. 8.1 on circular, one-way linked lists. Let the empty circular linked list be represented by **NULL**. Be especially careful to handle the special cases involving the empty list.

7. Suppose you are given a pointer to a node **N** in a one-way linked list, **L**, and suppose you know **N** is neither **NULL** nor a pointer to the last node of **L**. How could you delete node **N** from list **L** without being able to access the predecessor node on **L** pointing to **N**?

8.3 Generalized Lists

Learning Objectives

1. To learn how generalized lists differ from simple linear lists.
2. To understand how to represent and manipulate generalized lists.
3. To understand the difference between shared and copied sublists.

What are generalized lists?

A *generalized list* is a list in which the individual list items are permitted to be sublists. (Sometimes a generalized list is called a *list structure*.) For example, consider the generalized list $L == (a_1, a_2, (b_1, (c_1, c_2), b_3), a_4, (d_1, d_2), a_6)$. The first two items on L are a_1 and a_2, but the third item is the sublist $(b_1, (c_1, c_2), b_3)$. This sublist has another sublist (c_1, c_2) as its second item. If a list item is not a sublist, it is said to be an *atomic item* (or, more simply, it is said to be an *atom*).

In the sequential representation of a generalized list, we need to use balanced pairs of special markers (such as balanced pairs of parentheses) to delineate the boundaries of the sublists. If we store either atoms or special sublist parenthesis markers sequentially as the packed items in an array, we get a contiguous sequential array representation for a generalized list. But direct use of integer indexes to access the ith item is no longer possible when sublists are present. A string of characters in which sublists are bounded by balanced parenthesis pairs, and in which items are separated by commas, is another example of a sequential representation of a generalized list having atoms that are characters.

linked representations

To devise a linked representation of a generalized list, we need to use two different kinds of nodes: those containing atomic list items and those containing pointers to

```
   |   #define   TRUE   1
   |   #define   FALSE  0
   |
   |   typedef   struct    GenListTag {
5  |                             struct GenListTag *Link;
   |                             int Atom;
   |                             union SubNodeTag {
   |                                 ItemType            Item;
   |                                 struct GenListTag   *SubList;
10 |                             } SubNode;
   |                   } GenListNode;
   |
```

Program 8.9 Generalized List Nodes

sublists. Program 8.9 uses C's union types to define the structure of these nodes.

Using these type definitions we can write C programs to construct, manipulate, and print linked representations of generalized lists. Figure 8.10 presents a linked representation of the generalized list (((1, 2, 3), 4), 5, 6, (7)). In this case, each of the sublists is referenced by only one pointer elsewhere in the structure. Under these circumstances, we say the sublists are *not shared*.

shared sublists

On the other hand, Fig. 8.11 presents a picture of a linked representation of a generalized list having shared sublists. The shared sublists are those referenced by more than one pointer elsewhere in the structure.

printing generalized lists

Program 8.12 is designed to print generalized lists, no matter whether they have shared sublists or not. It uses a recursive call on line 11 to print each sublist. It is assumed that there is no path in the structure that forms a cycle of pointers. (A cycle is a path formed from pointers that starts at a given node and returns to itself.) If a linked representation, L, has a cycle of pointers in it, Program 8.12 will not terminate when it tries to print L.

When Program 8.12 is given the generalized list, L, of Fig. 8.11 to print, it prints: (((1, 2, 3), (1, 2, 3), (2, 3), 6), 4, 5, ((2, 3), 6)). Can you see why?

a property of shared sublists

Whenever a generalized list contains several pointers to a shared sublist, the information accessed by all pointers sharing the sublist is updated whenever the information in the shared sublist changes.

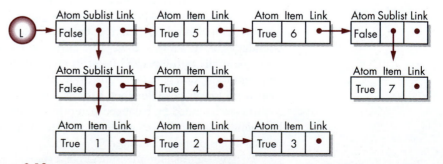

Figure 8.10 Linked Representation of Generalized List

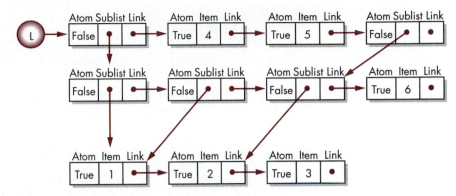

Figure 8.11 Generalized List with Shared Sublists

This property of shared sublists can be either a useful feature or an annoying bug. In many applications, it is convenient to keep one shared copy of a record, R, that will be updated periodically, and to keep references to R in every structure that needs access to the latest updated version of R. In some contemporary operating systems, one application can furnish a "hot link" to some information, such as a spreadsheet, a drawing, or a paragraph of text that can be incorporated into another application's data. When the original application updates the information in the data to which hot links refer, the users of the hot links are notified and can substitute the newly updated versions.

On the other hand, it can be a pesky source of errors if you need to maintain your own separate copy of some information, but instead you unintentionally use a reference to shared information that gets updated by somebody else. It is important, in designing generalized lists, therefore, to pay close attention to whether you want sublists to be shared, or to act as separate copies.

```
        |     void PrintList(GenListNode *L)
        |     {
        |         GenListNode *G;
        |
    5   |         printf( "(" );
        |         G = L;                             /* G points to successive nodes of L */
        |         while ( G != NULL ) {              /* then the atomic item or sublist in */
        |             if ( G–>Atom ) {               /* node G is printed */
        |                 printf("%d",G–>SubNode.Item);
   10   |             } else {                       /* sublists are */
        |                 PrintList(G–>SubNode.SubList);   /* printed recursively */
        |             }
        |             if (G–>Link != NULL) printf(" , ");   /* commas follow each item */
        |             G = G–>Link;                   /* except the last item */
   15   |         }
        |         printf( ")" );
        |     }
```

Program 8.12 Printing Generalized Lists

8.3 Review Questions

1. How is a generalized list distinguished from an ordinary list?
2. How can you use C structs and unions to declare nodes for constructing generalized lists?
3. What condition in the pointers of a linked generalized list, L, would cause Program 8.12 to get into an endless loop when it tried to print L?

8.3 Exercises

1. Write a program to reverse a generalized list and all of its sublists. Make sure your program works whether or not the sublists are shared. (*Note:* You may need to add a new field to the list nodes to designate whether they have been reversed already.)
2. Write a program to "flatten" a generalized list by creating a single linear list consisting of all the items that would be printed in sequence when printing the generalized list with Program 8.12, but having no sublists. For example, (1, 2, 3, 4, 5, 6, 7) is the flattened version of the list (1, (2, 3), 4, (5, (6, 7))).
3. Write a program to copy a linked representation of a generalized list, L. Make sure the result shares all of the sublists in exactly the same way as the original does. (*Note:* You may need to add new fields of information to the list nodes to help solve this problem.)

8.4 Applications of Generalized Lists

Learning Objectives

1. To gain some practical background knowledge about list processing.
2. To learn about one of the most important tradeoffs in computer science.
3. To understand the difference between typeless and hard-typed programming languages.

early list processing languages

The use of generalized lists in computer science has been especially important in connection with artificial intelligence applications (among others). Some early programming languages, such as LISP and IPL IV (among many others), introduced list processing at the programming language level. These languages permitted users to write programs to construct and manipulate generalized lists.

typeless languages

The lists available in LISP and IPL IV are slightly more general than the linked representations of generalized lists illustrated in Section 8.3, which were based on linking C structs together. That is because LISP and IPL IV are what are called *typeless languages*. In a typeless language, you can have variables, such as X and Y, which can take values of any type, such as integers, floating point numbers, characters, strings, or lists. Also, generalized lists can be constructed having many different types of atomic items, as in the list, L == (3.0, "string2",(26, 'c'), 3.14159). This is difficult to arrange in most C implementations without wasting space. In short, in LISP and IPL IV, lists can be of any length, they can contain any type of value as list items, and sublists are permitted to an arbitrary depth of nesting.

These general lists provide applications with a highly flexible kind of data structure that can come in many possible shapes and sizes and can contain atomic data of many sorts. Procedures and functions can be written to give these general lists highly useful combining and growth laws. The result is a programming medium of considerable flexibility and generality that can meet the difficult requirements of applications having highly unpredictable demands for supporting information structures.

supporting highly flexible
data structures

In artificial intelligence applications in particular, it is often required to support data representations whose size and shape cannot be easily forecast before the running of a program. For example, a chess playing program might need to explore many sequences of possible moves and replies. Each move and reply might have to be evaluated for its strategic significance. This can produce a highly branching network of possible imaginary situations.

examples from artificial
intelligence

Again, in a natural language processing program, the parsing of input sentences and the assignment of meaning to them, can require structural descriptors and attached data representing analyzed meaning that can grow unpredictably large and can grow into arbitrary shapes.

Finally, in symbolic mathematics systems, certain tasks often produce long chains of intermediate results, using expressions that can swell to unpredictably large sizes. There is a phenomenon called *intermediate expression swell* in algebraic manipulation systems that is often encountered. For instance, suppose we are trying to multiply two polynomials $(x - 1)$ and $(x^2 + x + 1)$. We desire to have a result in simplified form.

intermediate expression
swell

A typical algebraic manipulation system might first try to multiply out all the terms, obtaining:

$$(x - 1) * (x^2 + x + 1) = (x^3 + x^2 + x - x^2 - x - 1),$$

after which, it collects terms of like degree, getting:

$$(1\ x^3 + (1 - 1)\ x^2 + (1 - 1)\ x - 1).$$

Following this, it needs to perform arithmetic where possible, enabling it to substitute zero for the two occurrences of the expressions $(1 - 1)$, getting:

$$(1\ x^3 + (0)\ x^2 + (0)\ x - 1).$$

It then applies once the simplification law, $1 * y \Rightarrow y$, and it applies twice the simplification law, $0 * y \Rightarrow 0$, getting:

$$(x^3 + 0 + 0 - 1).$$

Finally, it performs arithmetic on constants again, simplifying $(0 + 0 - 1)$ to -1, getting the final result:

$$(x^3 - 1).$$

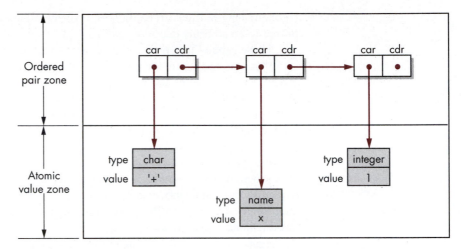

Figure 8.13 List Representation Used in Some Early LISP Systems

In this small derivation, you can see how the intermediate expressions used swelled up to a large size before simplification laws were applied to reduce them back down to a smaller final size.

In contrast to the postfix expressions used for stack evaluators in the previous chapter, symbolic algebraic manipulation systems often use prefix operator expressions inside generalized lists. For example, the expression $(x - 1)$ would be represented by the list $(-, x, 1)$ whose first item is the minus operator, and whose second and third items are the left and right operands to be subtracted. Similarly, the polynomial $(x^2 + x + 1)$ might be represented by $(+, (\wedge, x, 2), x, 1)$. Here, the addition operator $(+)$ can take arbitrarily many operands to be added together in the list that follows. (This is similar to C's printf function which can take arbitrarily many operands to be printed.)

using prefix operator expression lists

In some early implementations of the LISP programming language, memory was divided into two zones. One zone contained representations of atoms, to be used as list items, and the other zone contained ordered pairs of pointers. The left pointer in a pointer pair was stored in a field named the **car** field, and the right pointer was stored in the **cdr** field, as shown in Fig. 8.13. This figure contains the representation of the prefix expression list $(+, x, 1)$ representing the infix algebraic expression $(x + 1)$.

background on how LISP works

You can see that in the *atomic value zone* in Fig. 8.13, each atom is a struct having a **type** field and a **value** field. The **type** field contains a tag specifying the type of the value in the value field. For instance, if the **type** is *char*, the value in the value field represents a character value, and if the **type** is *integer*, the value in the value field represents an integer. This system is called a *tagged type system*, since each value is *tagged* with its type. When we operate on tagged values during program execution, we need to read the tags to decide which operation to perform. For example, if we try to add a value tagged as the integer 1 to another value tagged as the floating point number 6.0, we have to select some code to execute that applies a floating point conversion to the integer 1, getting the floating point constant, 1.0, and then we have to perform float-

> Efficiency Trades Off Against Generality

Figure 8.14 An Important Tradeoff in Computer Science

ing point addition on 1.0 and 6.0, to get 7.0. Finally, we have to package the result 7.0, into another struct with a tag "real" to denote that it is a floating point value, and we have to find space in which to store this result in the atomic value zone. This kind of mechanics is called doing "interpreted arithmetic at run time," because it is similar to what a language interpreter would do during program execution (such as an interpreter for the BASIC programming language).

hard-typed languages

By contrast, using a hard-typed language, such as C, the compiler always knows the types of all of the operands of an operator at compile time and can compile code that directly executes the required type conversions and operations without having to examine type-tags to select which variation of the operation to perform. Consequently, compiled code for hard-typed languages runs faster than the interpreted type-switching code for typeless languages such as LISP.

an important tradeoff

This discussion reemphasizes one of the famous tradeoffs in computer science that we have noted before in this book. In this case, when we use a typeless language like LISP, we purchase increased flexibility in the kinds of data structures we can construct and manipulate during the running of a program. However, this increased flexibility is purchased in the coinage of reduced execution-time efficiency. Often in computer science, we find that the more general we make a language or a system, the less efficient it becomes, whereas the more limited we make a system, the more efficiently it can be made to run. Figure 8.14 restates the important underlying tradeoff that applies in this case.

The unused pointer pairs in the *ordered pair zone* in Fig. 8.13 can be linked together into a single one-way list, using links in their **cdr** fields. This list of unused pairs is called an *available space list*.

When new lists are being formed, new pointer pairs are detached from the front of the available space list for use in construction of the new list. If the available space list becomes empty, a process needs to be invoked to identify and collect any unused pointer pairs that may have become detached during other manipulations and are no longer in use. A marking process is used to trace all pointer pairs that are in use in the system. Following this marking process, a sweep is made to gather and link all pairs marked as unused into a new available space list. This marking and gathering process is called *garbage collection*. We will study more about garbage collection in Section 8.6.

the LISP language

The LISP programming language is still in widespread use at the moment and is especially popular for artificial intelligence applications. Many generations of ingenious computer scientists have developed the early LISP systems into their current highly evolved forms. To overcome the inefficiency of interpretive run-time execution and tagged-type systems, many LISP systems today offer optional hard-type declarations with fully efficient compilation and run-time execution. They also have many ingenious storage management enhancements that overcome, to a considerable degree, the inefficiencies of linked representations and garbage collection methods. Some LISP systems can even shift automatically to sequential (nonlinked) list representations (using what is called *cdr-direction linearization*) when efficiency considerations reveal it to be advantageous. (There is much more to this story than can be sketched here, and interested readers are urged to pursue the literature which contains a gold mine of ingenious techniques which can often be applied in other circumstances.)

8.4 Review Questions

1. How does a typeless language differ from a hard-typed language?
2. What flexibility and generality do typeless list processing languages provide that is difficult to achieve in hard-typed languages such as C?
3. What price is paid for the generality of typeless list processing languages?
4. What is intermediate expression swell in an algebraic manipulation system?

8.4 Exercises

1. (Project) Write a C program that multiplies polynomials and reduces them to simplest form.
2. (Project) Write a C program to add, subtract, multiply, and divide symbolic fractions, and to reduce the results to a single cleared fraction with a single numerator and denominator. (Implement laws such as: $a/b + c/d = (ad + bc)/bd$, $(a/b)/(c/d) = (ad/bc)$, and $(a/1) = a$, etc.)

8.5 Strings

Learning Objectives

1. To gain additional understanding of string operations and string representations beyond what is offered in first courses in computer science.
2. To learn about advantages and disadvantages of some popular string representations.
3. To gain an initial impression of how strings can be represented in text files and word processors.

Strings are sequences of characters. To name just a few of their many applications, strings are used in word processors, in fields of records used in databases, and in electronic mail systems as the text of messages that are exchanged. Many different kinds of string operations are defined on strings in these various contexts. Moreover, many different representations of strings are used.

A String ADT

In C's Standard Library you can access a collection of useful string operations by including the header file <string.h> at the beginning of your source file. It is reasonable to view these C string functions as providing a predefined String ADT. Some of the operations in <string.h> are shown in Fig. 8.15. (Here, let S and T be string variables defined to be of type (char *) in the usual fashion, and let i and n be integers.)

examples using string operations

For example, suppose we had initialized the string variables S and T using the declarations char *T = "lieutenant"; and char *S = "ten"; Then, since S is a substring of T, strstr(S, T) is a pointer to the first character 't' in the substring "tenant" of string T.

Likewise, if we give the initializing declarations char *Digits = "0123456789"; and char *Number = "1359.4625e−7"; then 4 is the value returned by the function call strspn(Number,Digits) because there is a four digit prefix "1359" that begins the string "1359.4625e−7". (A *prefix* of a string S is a (possibly empty) subsequence of the characters at the beginning of S.)

strlen(S) = the number of characters in string S. Here, if S == "$c_1 c_2 c_3 \ldots c_n$", then strlen(S) == n.

strstr(S, T) = a pointer to the first occurrence of string S in string T (or NULL if there is no occurrence of string S in string T).

strcat(S, T) = concatenate (i.e., append) a copy of the string T to the end of string S and return a pointer to the beginning of the (newly enlarged) string S.

strcpy(S, T) = make a copy of the string T including a terminating null character '\0', and store it starting at the location pointed to by the character pointer S (which is of type char *).

strspn(S, T) = return the length of the prefix of S consisting of characters in the string T. (Here, provided that strspn(S, T) > 0, a *prefix* of S is an initial substring of S consisting of the first character of S and as many characters following the first character of S as are also found in string T. If strspn(S, T) == 0, then the prefix of S is the empty string.)

strpbrk(S, T) = returns a pointer to the first occurrence in string S of any character of string T, except that, if no characters of string T are found in string S, the value returned is the NULL pointer.

Figure 8.15 Predefined String Operations for a String ADT

Some String Representations

In this subsection, we discuss two string representations used in currently popular programming languages: C strings and Pascal strings.

A C string is a string representation of indefinite length whose end is marked by the occurrence of a special *null* character (represented by the byte '\0'). To represent the string S == "canine" as a C string, we first allocate a block of memory, B, at least seven bytes long, and we place the characters of S == "canine" in bytes B[0:5]. Finally we set byte B[6] to contain the null byte, '\0'. This is illustrated in Fig. 8.16.

Program 8.17 shows how to concatenate (or join together) two C strings, S and T. Line 11 allocates space for a character array of length 1 + strlen(S) + strlen(T), which is long enough to hold strlen(S) characters of S followed by strlen(T) characters of T followed by a terminating null byte. The pointer P returned by malloc on line 11 is typecast to a character pointer (using (char *)). Pointer P is used to point to successive characters of the concatenation of S and T while it is "under construction."

On lines 17:18, the while-statement, while ((*P++ = *S++) != '\0'); transfers copies of string S's characters into the initial positions of the concatenation. The assignment (*P++ = *S++) deserves study. Because of C's operator precedence rules, the pointer dereferencing operator (*) in *S++ is applied to S before the pointer incrementing operator (++). Thus, the character referenced by the character pointer S is copied into the position referenced by the character pointer P before both character pointers S and P are incremented to point to the next characters in succession. The character that was copied becomes the value of the assignment expression (*P++ = *S++). After the null byte('\0') at the end of S has been transferred, the character pointer P has been incremented to point one character position past the transferred null byte. Consequently, the pointer P is decremented on line 21 to point to the null byte transferred immediately beforehand from S, in order that the transfer of characters from string T can begin in the position immediately following the characters of S.

Finally, on lines 24:25, the characters of T (including its terminating null byte) are transferred into the positions following the characters of S. The value returned by the function on line 28 is the initial value of P furnished by malloc that points to the beginning of the concatenated sequence of characters. Note that this value had been saved in a temporary variable, temp, on line 14, beforehand.

Many versions of Pascal have been augmented to manipulate strings. In many of these extended versions of Pascal, strings are represented using fixed-length character arrays as containers. Typically, a Pascal string, S, can be up to 255 characters long, and the characters of S are stored sequentially in positions 1:255 of a packed 256-byte character array, A[256]. The zeroth byte, A[0], of array A is called the *length-byte*, and it is used to store the length of the string stored in A.

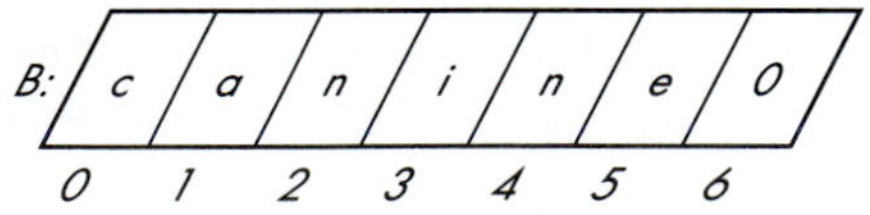

Figure 8.16 A C String Representation

```
      |   char *Concat(char *S, char *T);
      |   {
      |       char *P;
      |       char *temp
    5 |
      |       /* P is a pointer used in the concatenation of S and T during */
      |       /* the time that the concatenation is "under construction."  */
      |       /* The pointer temp remembers the starting position of P. */
      |
   10 |       /* Allocate space for the concatenation of S and T, plus 1.  */
      |           P = (char *)malloc( 1 + strlen(S) + strlen(T) );
      |
      |       /* Let temp remember the starting position of P. */
      |           temp = P;
   15 |
      |       /* Copy the contents of S into P up until the end-of-string null char. */
      |           while ( ( *P++ = *S++ ) != '\0' )
      |               ;
      |
   20 |       /* Move back one character to overwrite the end-of-string null char. */
      |           P – – ;
      |
      |       /* Copy the contents of T into P immediately after the copy of S in P. */
      |           while ( ( *P++ = *T++ ) != '\0' )
   25 |               ;
      |
      |       /* Return the starting position of P as the pointer to the result. */
      |           return temp;
      |   }
```

Program 8.17 Concatenating Two C Strings

Let's look at an example. Suppose the string S == "canine". Let A[0:255] be an array of 256 bytes. To store the string S in A, we set A[0] to 6, and we store the characters of "canine" in A[1:6]. This is shown in Fig. 8.18. You can see that having strings whose lengths are easily retrievable using their length bytes makes it easy to perform certain kinds of operations efficiently. For example, if we want to join the strings S == "canine" and T == "friends" to get the string Concat(S,T) == "caninefriends", we could first make a copy, say C, of the array A holding S, then we could copy the characters of T into the 7th through 13th positions of C, and finally we could set the length byte, C[0], to 13 to indicate the length of the newly formed concatenated string.

drawbacks of Pascal strings

As you might imagine, the Pascal string representation has some drawbacks. First of all, since Pascal strings are of bounded length, overflows cannot be accommodated conveniently. Typically, string concatenation and insertion operations defined in Pascal ignore overflows. That is, if the result of concatenating two strings or of inserting one string in another is longer than 255 characters, the excess characters beyond 255 are dropped (without even notifying the user that anything was lost).

Another drawback relates to waste of space. All Pascal strings consume 256 bytes of space, regardless of their length. Unused space inside the arrays holding these Pascal string representations is wasted. This can be a hazard for unsuspecting Pascal

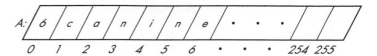

Figure 8.18 A Pascal String Representation

programmers who are working with tight memory constraints. The hazard can often be alleviated by declaring shorter types of Pascal strings. For instance, the type declaration, **type** ShortString = String[7]; can be used in some Pascal systems to declare a string type, ShortString, each instance of which consumes only eight bytes of storage (one length byte plus seven bytes to hold up to seven characters of strings whose maximum length is seven).

comparing C strings and Pascal strings

You can see that C strings do not have the drawback that they waste unused space inside character arrays of predetermined fixed size. Also, in principle, they do not overflow (because we can supposedly allocate new blocks of characters big enough to accommodate their growth to any new size, provided the underlying memory allocation system can find space). On the other hand, finding the length of a C string involves scanning the underlying character sequence looking for the terminating null byte. This takes time proportional to the string's length, O(strlen(S)), whereas finding the length of a Pascal string takes time O(1).

String Representations in Text Files and Word Processors

In this subsection, we briefly sketch limited examples of how strings can be represented in text files and in word processors. These examples come from a system used by one computer vendor, whose operating system furnishes basic building blocks for operating on files of text. You can think of these files of text as long strings of characters broken into individual lines of text by the occurrence of end-of-line characters. When a text file is read into main memory, a special representation is set up to make it convenient to operate on the text line-by-line. Here's how it works.

a few practical examples

A text file stored on an external memory medium (such as a floppy disk, a hard disk, or a tape) has both a *logical structure* and a *physical structure*. The logical file structure specifies the *logical length*, L, of the text in characters and provides a file *position counter*, P. Given a text file, T, which is L characters long, the position counter, P, can assume any value in the range $0{:}L$. When $P == 0$, the position counter is positioned *before* the first character of the file, and when P assumes any value n in the range $(1 \leq n \leq L)$, the position of P is *after* the nth character in T and *before* the $(n+1)^{\text{st}}$ character in T. Thus P always designates a position that is *between* two characters (or *before* the first character or *after* the last character) in the file T.

physical file lengths

The *physical length*, L_{phys}, of the file T is a separate length number giving the total number of available character positions in a linked list of blocks of file space that hold the actual text of the file. Different media (such as floppy disks, hard disks, or tapes) are divided up into different size blocks. For example, a floppy disk may be divided up

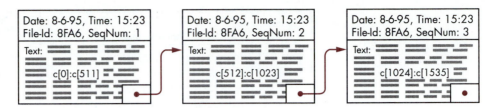

Figure 8.19 Linked Character Blocks in a Text File

into storage blocks of 512 bytes each, and a hard disk may be divided up into blocks of 4096 bytes each.

Suppose that a text file T has a logical length $L == 562$ characters (meaning that its text is 562 characters long). On a floppy disk with 512-character blocks, one block is not long enough to hold the entire text, so two blocks would have to be used. The first block would contain the first 512 characters, and it would be linked to a second block containing the remaining 50 characters. In this case, the physical length of the text file would be $L_{phys} == 1024$, since there are a total of 1024 physical character positions available in the two linked blocks holding the 562 characters in the logical file structure. The same 562 character text file would require only one 4096-character block on a hard disk, in which case $L_{phys} == 4096$.

extra information in the
physical text file structure

The physical structure of the file also contains some extra information hidden from the logical structure. Such information can be used to check on the accuracy of the storage media holding the file and to recover lost files. In addition to holding the text characters of the file, each block in the physical file representation is stamped with the date and time of its creation, a special unique file Id-number (different from the Id-numbers of all other files), and a block sequence number. Moreover, the first block of the file stores a "cyclical check sum," which is the sum of the integer values of all the characters in the file. In the event that the file directory on a given disk (or other storage medium) is lost or damaged, the information in the physical blocks can be used to help recover the lost files (by linking all blocks stamped with the same file Id-number into a linked list in the order given by their block sequence numbers).

Figure 8.19 shows some of the information in the physical representation of a text file which is stored in a medium (such as a floppy disk) using 512-byte blocks.

the representation of text in
main memory

When a text file, T, is read into main memory to be operated on, another different text representation is created. This text representation has two parts: (a) a single large block, B, of text characters representing the text of the file, and (b) an array, A, of *line starts*. Each array entry, $A[i]$, gives the position of the beginning of the ith line of text in the text file (where lines are terminated by end-of-line characters, and where positions lie between two adjacent characters). Figure 8.20 illustrates the structure of a text file, T, in main memory.

The operating system supplies primitive operations enabling programmers to select the text between two positions, and to delete it or copy it, as well as permitting new text to be inserted at a given position. (This is how the text operations *Cut*, *Copy*, and *Paste*, are implemented.) The line start information in the array A is useful for fast display and scrolling of lines of text inside a text window on the user's workstation.

Line starts	Character text
0:	Forescore and seven
21:	years ago our fathers
43:	brought forth on this
65:	continent, a new nation,
90:	conceived in Liberty,
112:	and dedicated to the
133:	proposition that all
154:	men are created equal.
177:	Now we are engaged in
201:	a great civil war,
220:	testing whether that
241:	nation or any nation so
265:	conceived and so
282:	dedicated, can long
302:	endure.

Figure 8.20 A Text File in Main Memory

more advanced text representations

More advanced professional word processors need to use text representations that are even more complicated than the simple one described here. Some word processors permit users to designate whether they want to have the entire text file reside in main memory (assuming their computer has lots of main memory) or whether they want only a few pages of text to be in main memory at a time (in case their computer has only a limited amount of main memory). Depending on which option the user chooses, the word processor may attempt to read either the full file or only a few pages of it into main memory. Having the entire file in main memory reduces the time required to perform certain operations (such as searching for a keyword or doing spelling correction). But this advantage cannot be gained unless the user's computer has enough main memory.

Also, in advanced word processors, the raw characters of text in the text file are usually augmented with special invisible code characters that designate style and formatting features such as fonts, tabs, indents, paragraphing, and underlining. Finally, links can be planted in the text to link in pictures or special graphics. Moreover, new blocks of text to be inserted can be linked into a given block at an insertion point instead of being directly inserted in the sequential character sequence. These links can be eliminated when the text is transferred to an external file or is reorganized during operations such as repagination (in which an altered text is divided into pages).

8.5 Review Questions

1. What is the C string representation for the empty string (of length zero)?
2. How do C and Pascal strings differ?

3. Describe a method for storing a file of text on an external memory medium, such as a floppy disk.

4. Discuss how text can be represented in main memory for use by a word processor. Discuss some possible roles for "invisible text codes" in this text representation.

8.5 Exercises

1. Write a C function to implement the string operation **strlen(S)** described in Figure 8.15.

2. Write a C function to implement the string operation **strstr(S, T)** described in Figure 8.15.

3. Write a C function to implement the string operation **strcpy(S, T)** described in Figure 8.15.

4. Write a C function to implement the string operation **strspn(S, T)** described in Figure 8.15.

8.6   Dynamic Memory Allocation

Learning Objectives

1. To understand the difference between static and dynamic memory allocation.
2. To learn about available space lists and garbage collection.
3. To learn how heaps can be used to support dynamic memory allocation.
4. To learn about fragmentation and coalescing.
5. To learn about handles and heap compaction.
6. To learn how reference counts can be used to support incremental storage reclamation.

static versus dynamic allocation

We begin by reviewing the difference between *static* and *dynamic* memory allocation. Suppose we have a C program, *P*, that (1) defines general list nodes using the node types defined in Program 8.9, and (2) that declares two variables: (a) a global integer array **A**, and (b) a variable **L** which is of type **GenListNode***, (see Program 8.21). Now suppose that later in the text of *P*, we encounter the statements in Program 8.22.

As you can see, when the statements in Program 8.22 are executed, they cause a new general list node to be allocated, they cause the node's **Item** member to be set to the integer value **A[99]**, and they cause its **Link** member to be set to **NULL**.

```
      |     /* Insert Program 8.9 declaring the type GenListNode. */
      |
      |     int A[100];
      |
    5 |     GenListNode *L;
      |
```

Program 8.21 Two Global Variables in a C Program

```
     |   L = (GenListNode *)malloc(sizeof(GenListNode));        /* allocate a new */
     |                                                    /* list node and put a pointer to it in L */
20   |   L–>SubNode.Item = A[99];      /* set L's Item member to the integer A[99] */
     |   L–>Link = NULL;                               /* set L's Link member to NULL */
```

Program 8.22 Some Statements in Program *P*

Let's now compare the times at which storage is allocated for the array **A** and at which storage is allocated for the node referenced by the pointer in **L**. The space for array **A** can be allocated before the execution of program *P* begins. That is, the compiler that compiles the code for program *P* can analyze the information in the declaration of **A**, and it can compile code that, when executed, will access and update the array items **A[0:99]**. The locations of these array items are fixed in advance of the running of program *P*, and the space for them is reserved in advance of the running of program *P*. In this case, we say that the array **A** has been *statically* allocated. The word *static* means "not in motion." Program *P* is not in motion at the time this *static* storage allocation takes place, because *P* has not been executed yet. (*Note:* There is a **static** storage class in C in which variables local to a function retain their values between calls and which can be used to make names of variables and functions invisible outside a given source file. We are using the adjective *static* in a different sense from the reserved word **static** in C.)

static memory allocation

By contrast, let's examine the time when storage is allocated for the general list node referenced by the pointer in the variable, **L**. The space for this node is allocated at the time the statement **L = (GenListNode *)malloc(sizeof(GenListNode));** is executed (on line 18 of Program 8.22). We say that storage for this node is *dynamically* allocated, because it gets allocated only when the program is executed. The word *dynamic* can be taken to mean "in motion," and it describes an action that is taken during program execution.

dynamic memory allocation

Static memory allocation can take place for all global variables declared at the beginning of a C program. This is because C's rules compel us to provide enough information, when declaring global types and variables, that their exact size and memory requirements can be calculated from analyzing the text of the C program at compile time.

On the other hand, when we execute a C program that calls functions, the number of calls cannot be predicted in advance of the running of the program. Rather, as each call is encountered during program execution, we can allocate new space on a run-time stack to accommodate the call's storage requirements. Such stack-based allocation is one form of dynamic memory allocation.

Another kind of dynamic memory allocation occurs when we execute a statement, such as **L = (GenListNode *)malloc(sizeof(GenListNode));** in a C program. The space for the node referenced by **L**, that gets allocated when we execute this statement, cannot be placed on a run-time stack, since this space may need to remain in existence regardless of whether we call or return from various subroutines. If we reserved space for the node referenced by **L**'s pointer on the run-time stack, then the space would have to disappear the moment we returned from any currently executing function. To guarantee the persistence of the storage for node **L** independently of sub-

dynamic allocation
in heaps

routine calls and returns, we can use a separate region of memory, and we can allocate blocks of memory of various sizes from this region whenever the need arises. Dynamic memory allocation can then take place using blocks allocated from this region anytime during the running of a program. We refer to such a region of memory as a *heap*.

In addition to using stacks and heaps to support dynamic memory allocation, it is also possible to base dynamic memory allocation on the use of a list of available space—a form of dynamic allocation useful for lists formed by linking together nodes of identical size.

In the subsections that follow, we will discuss the kind of dynamic memory allocation that occurs when we organize a region of memory into an available space list and the techniques for dynamic memory allocation in heaps.

Available Space Lists and Garbage Collection

the available space list

In Fig. 8.13 we saw how to divide memory up into two zones for use in list processing applications. One zone of memory held nodes containing pairs of pointers, and the second zone held representations of atomic values tagged with their types. In such a scheme, before execution of the main program begins, the zone of memory holding nodes for pairs of pointers is initialized by organizing it into a single one-way linked list called the *available space list*. The available space list is a pool of free memory containing nodes that can be allocated on demand whenever the need arises. Generalized lists can be constructed from building blocks removed from the front of this available space list. Thus the available space list turns memory into a flexible commodity that can be allocated on demand during the running of a program.

Now we consider two policies for recycling used list nodes. These are called *storage reclamation policies* since they reclaim space for nodes that are no longer in use. Policy 1 places deallocation of list nodes under direct programmer control. Policy 2 automatically collects deallocated nodes when they are needed.

explicit deallocation

- *Policy 1—Explicit Deallocation by the Programmer*

    In some list processing systems, when a list node is no longer needed, it is the direct responsibility of the programmer to return it to the available space list (by linking it back onto the available space list, either at the beginning or the end of the available space list). The early list processing language IPL IV used this policy for recycling unused list nodes for further use.

automatic reclamation

- *Policy 2—Automatic Storage Reclamation*

    In other list processing systems, while list nodes are removed from the front of the available space list when needed, the programmer is not responsible for returning unused nodes back to the available space list. When the available space list runs out of nodes to allocate (i.e., when it becomes empty), an automatic storage reclamation process, called *garbage collection*, is invoked. For example, the LISP programming language uses automatic storage reclamation policies.

how garbage collection works

Let's look for a moment at how the garbage collection process works. First of all, it is assumed that each list node has a special bit allocated in it, called the *mark bit*. This mark bit can be set to one of two values, *free* or *reserved* (where, for example, *free* is represented by the bit value "0" and *reserved* is represented by the bit value "1"). The process proceeds in three phases. In the first phase, called the *initialization phase*, a pass is made through the list memory region setting the mark bits on each node to *free*. In the second phase, called the *marking phase*, all list nodes currently in use are identified and are marked by having their mark bits set to *reserved*. The idea is to mark all the nodes in current use to prevent them from being collected during the final phase. In the third phase, called the *gathering phase*, another sweep is made through the list space, and all nodes marked *free* are linked together into a new available space list. The available space list now consists of all the inaccessible nodes that were not previously incorporated into structures in use. These inaccessible nodes are sometimes called *garbage*, and the process of identifying them and linking them together into a new available space list is called *garbage collection*.

Program Strategy 8.23 outlines the main steps in the "mark and gather" strategy for garbage collection. On line 8 of this program strategy, there is an **Item** member in the struct for a **ListNode** that contains a **ListNode** pointer. However, we assume that the **Item** pointer in a list node containing a pointer pair can point either to another list node in the *ordered pair zone* or to an atomic value node in the *atomic value zone*. (See Fig. 8.13 for an illustration of these two zones in the case of a LISP-like list processing system.) An *address range discrimination* can be used at the assembly language level to distinguish whether a pointer points to an address inside the ordered pair zone or the atomic value zone. An assembly language test can thus distinguish which kind of operations to apply to a node, depending on whether the node resides in the ordered pair zone or the atomic value zone. One way to store pointers to objects of two or more types in C is to store pointers to objects of type **void** (using **void *** as the type) and then to typecast the **void** pointers to pointers of the appropriate type after fetching them. Union types can also solve this problem.

An unfinished piece in Program Strategy 8.23 is the marking function **MarkListNodesInUse**, which is called on line 31. Let's investigate how to organize a marking process. Program Strategy 8.24 provides a sketch. We assume that we start with a single **ListNode** pointer, as the value of the variable **L**, and our task is to trace out and mark all **ListNodes** accessible from **L** via any path of pointers starting with either the **Item** member or the **Link** member of **L**'s referent.

You can see that Program Strategy 8.24 makes two recursive calls (on lines 10 and 14). These recursive calls apply the node marking process to the nodes referenced by the **Item** and **Link** pointers of the node referenced by the pointer in **L**. When the function **MarkListNodesInUse** looks at the node referenced by the pointer in **L**, it immediately tests to see if the node is already marked as **RESERVED**. If a node is already marked as **RESERVED**, it has already been visited by the marking process along some other path of pointers, and it does not need to be considered further. However, if the node is not yet marked as **RESERVED**, its **MarkBit** member is immediately marked as **RESERVED**, and the marking process proceeds further to examine the nodes referenced by the **Item** and **Link** pointers. If the pointer in the **Item** member points to a **ListNode**, then the marking process is applied to the node it references. In any event, the marking process is applied to the node referenced by the pointer in the **Link** member. The process eventually terminates when every **ListNode** accessible via a path of pointers from the initial pointer in **L** is marked as **RESERVED**.

using recursive calls to mark all accessible nodes

```
    |   #define FREE          0
    |   #define RESERVED      1
    |
    |   /*  Each ListNode has a MarkBit which is either FREE or RESERVED  */
 5  |
    |       typedef  struct NodeTag {
    |                        short            MarkBit;      /* FREE or RESERVED */
    |                        struct NodeTag   *Item;
    |                        struct NodeTag   *Link;
10  |            } ListNode;
    |
    |   /* Assume further that all ListNodes are allocated inside a region of */
    |   /* memory as an array of nodes called the ListNodeArray, as follows: */
    |
15  |       ListNode ListNodeArray[ListNodeArraySize];
    |       ListNode *Avail;                 /* Avail will point to the available space list */
    |
    |   void GarbageCollection(void)
    |   {
20  |       int i;               /* i is a local variable which indexes the ListNodeArray */
    |
    |       /* Phase 1—Initialization Phase—mark all ListNodes FREE */
    |
    |           for ( i = 0; i < ListNodeArraySize; ++i ) {
25  |               ListNodeArray[i].MarkBit = FREE;
    |           }
    |
    |
    |       /* Phase 2—Marking Phase—mark all ListNodes in use RESERVED */
30  |
    |           (Use the function MarkListNodesInUse of Program Strategy 8.24)
    |           (to mark all list nodes in use)
    |
    |       /* Phase 3—Gathering Phase—link all FREE ListNodes together */
35  |
    |           Avail = NULL;
    |           for ( i = 0; i < ListNodeArraySize; ++i ) {
    |               if ( ListNodeArray[i].MarkBit == FREE ) {
    |                   ListNodeArray[i].Link = Avail;
40  |                   Avail = (ListNode *)(&ListNodeArray[i]);
    |               }
    |           }             /* at the conclusion, Avail is the new available space list */
    |
    |       }
```

Program Strategy 8.23 Garbage Collection by Marking and Gathering

Heaps and Dynamic Memory Allocation

allocating blocks of
different sizes

To support dynamic memory allocation for C structs of different sizes we cannot use the available space list technique discussed in the previous subsection. This is because the available space list contains linked blocks of *identical* sizes, whereas what we need to provide is a means for allocating blocks of memory of *differing* sizes.

```
 |     void MarkListNodesInUse(ListNode *L)
 |     {
 |
 |         if ( ( L != NULL ) && ( L->MarkBit != RESERVED ) ) {
 5 |            L->MarkBit = RESERVED;
 |
 |
 |            if (L->Item is a pointer to a ListNode) {
10 |                MarkListNodesInUse(L->Item);
 |            }
 |
 |
 |            MarkListNodesInUse(L->Link);
15 |        }
 |
 |     }
```

Program Strategy 8.24 Marking List Nodes in Use

The problem we face is this. Given a request size, n, for a block of memory of n bytes, how can we allocate a block of size n? More generally, how can we organize a region of memory to allow us to allocate and free blocks of memory of various different sizes, given a sequence of requests to do so?

Figure 8.25 shows a region of memory called a *heap*. It contains blocks of memory of various sizes that have been reserved in response to allocation requests. The shaded region represents unallocated memory.

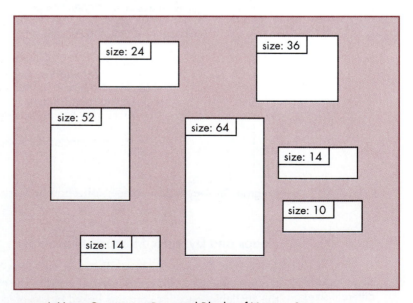

Figure 8.25 A Heap Containing Reserved Blocks of Various Sizes

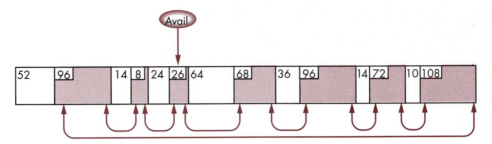

Figure 8.26 The Two-Way Linked List of Free Blocks in a Heap

The question now arises: How can we organize the unallocated space sitting between the reserved blocks so that future allocation requests can be satisfied? Two of the allocation policies we shall examine use a circular, two-way linked list of unallocated blocks. Figure 8.26 gives us another picture of the heap shown in Fig. 8.25. It shows the heap as being arranged in one linear zone of memory (with memory addresses increasing, say, from left to right), with shaded blocks of free memory containing their sizes and arranged into a two-way linked list using double-headed arrows to symbolize the two-way links. Since this two-way list is circular, we will call it a *ring*, in what follows. (*Note:* Even though Fig. 8.26 shows the two-way linked list as linking the free blocks together in increasing order of their addresses, in general, this will not be the case in actual applications. Instead, the free blocks can be linked into a ring in any order.)

using circular two-way lists of unallocated blocks

Suppose we are given a pointer, *Avail*, to one of the free blocks on the ring of free blocks. Starting from any block on the ring, we can move either left or right to neighboring blocks. We can also search the ring in either direction to find a block, B, of suitable size to satisfy a memory allocation request. We can also remove block B from the ring by linking B's left and right neighbors to one another, and we can mark B as being reserved, in order to put it in service to satisfy a request.

Let's now take a look at two different policies for allocating a new block of memory, given a request for a block of size *n*.

First-Fit

In the *first-fit* policy, we travel around the ring of free blocks starting at the block referenced by the pointer, *Avail*, until we find the first block B such that $Size(B) \geq n$, and we use B to satisfy the request. If $Size(B) > n$, then we break B into two blocks, B_1 of size *n* and B_2 of size $(Size(B) - n)$. We use B_1 to satisfy the request, and we link B_2 back into the ring of free blocks. If $Size(B) == n$, then we have what is called an *exact fit*, and we detach B from the ring of free blocks and use it directly to satisfy the request. In this second *exact fit* case, there exists no remaining unused block B_2 to link back into the ring of free blocks.

For example, in Fig. 8.26, suppose the request size is 72. We start at the block whose size is 26, which is referenced by the pointer *Avail*, and we compare the request size 72 with the block size 26. Since the block of size 26 is not big enough to satisfy

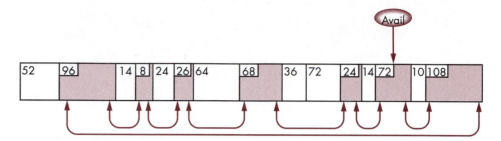

Figure 8.27 First-Fit Allocation of a Block of Size 72

the request, we advance around the ring (moving, let us say, in the rightward direction), and we consider next the block of size 68. This block is not big enough either, so we again move to the right to the block of size 96. This time, the block of size 96 is big enough. So we divide it into a block of size 72 and a block of size 24. We use the block of size 72 to satisfy the request, and we link the remaining block of size 24 back onto the ring of free blocks. The result of doing this is shown in Fig. 8.27. Note that the *Avail* pointer has been reset to point to the block of size 72 to the right of the original block of size 96 that we split in order to satisfy the request.

Best-Fit

Under the *best-fit policy*, we travel around the ring attempting to find a block that is the "best fit" for the request size n, as follows. Starting at the block, B, referenced by the pointer *Avail*, we compare $Size(B)$ to the request size n. If $Size(B) == n$, we have an *exact fit*, so we use block B to satisfy the request immediately by detaching it from the ring of free blocks and marking it as reserved. But if $Size(B) \neq n$, then we continue to search around the ring. We stop whenever we find an exact fit. But if we travel all the way around the ring without having found an exact fit, we use the closest fit we discovered on our trip around the ring. The closest fit is the block B on the ring having the property that $(Size(B) - n)$ is as small as possible. Again, we split the block B into a block B_1 of size n and a block B_2 of size $(Size(B) - n)$. We mark B_1 as reserved, and we link B_2 back into the ring of free blocks.

Figure 8.28 shows the result of using the best-fit policy to allocate a block of size 72, starting with the situation given in Fig. 8.26. Starting with the situation in Fig. 8.28, if we use the best-fit policy to satisfy a request to allocate a block of size 64, the block of size 68 would be selected (since it is the tightest fit, having the least excess storage of any of the blocks on the ring of sizes 108, 96, 68, and 96 that are large enough to satisfy a request of size 64).

Fragmentation and Coalescing

fragmentation   If we operate a heap storage allocation system for a while, using either the first-fit policy or the best-fit policy, the ring of free blocks will tend to contain smaller and small-

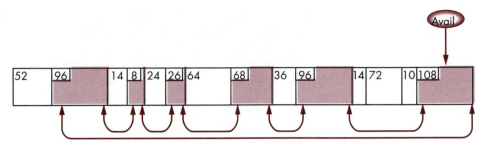

Figure 8.28 Best-Fit Allocation of a Block of Size 72

er blocks. This happens because we keep splitting larger blocks to satisfy requests for more storage. This tendency is called *fragmentation*.

The problem with fragmentation is that if the free blocks on the ring keep getting divided up into smaller and smaller size blocks, there may come a time when we encounter a request to allocate a block of size n that cannot be satisfied because all the free blocks are too small. This is called *allocation failure*.

In order to reduce the chances of encountering allocation failure, we can perform what is called *coalescing*. When we *coalesce* two blocks that are sitting next to one another in memory, we join them into a single larger block. A good moment to try coalescing is when we free the storage for a block, B, and attempt to return it to the ring of free blocks. Instead of just linking B into the ring of free blocks, we can look at B's immediate left and right neighbor blocks (in address order, not ring order) and if either of these neighbors is free, we can join it to B to make a larger coalesced block before putting this larger block back on the ring of free blocks.

For example, if we attempted to dispose of the block of size 36 in Fig. 8.28, we could coalesce it with its two neighbors of sizes 68 and 96, getting a new large co-alesced block of size 200 **==** (68 + 36 + 96) to return to the ring of free blocks. (In order to make this coalescing policy work efficiently, we need to store each free block's *size* and a mark bit designating it as *free* not only at the top of each block but also at its bottom boundary.)

We say that a storage allocation policy is operating under *equilibrium* when, over time, the average amount of space in new blocks being reserved is equal to the aver-age amount of space in blocks being freed, and when, in addition, the distribution of block sizes in the system remains the same. We need to use a coalescing policy to combat the tendency toward storage fragmentation, since, in most cases, without using a coalescing policy, the system will not achieve equilibrium over time (since the distribution of block sizes will keep getting smaller and smaller and the risk of alloca-tion failure will increase).

One more detail is worth mentioning in connection with the use of the first-fit and best-fit policies. This concerns the importance of using a *roving pointer*, *Avail*, to point to blocks on the ring of free blocks. In the roving pointer technique, we let *Avail* point to the successive blocks on the ring of free blocks when we search for a block B to satisfy a request, and after B has been located, we make *Avail* point to the block immediately beyond B on the ring. (By contrast, in a nonroving pointer tech-

allocation failure

coalescing

equilibrium

using roving pointers

nique, we always start our search for block B starting at a fixed initial block referenced by *Avail*.) The result of using the roving pointer technique is that *Avail* keeps circulating around and around the ring of free blocks, and immediately ahead of it, the blocks have had the longest time among any others to coalesce and form bigger new blocks due to the return of freed blocks. If we keep scanning along the ring of free blocks from a fixed initial starting point (as we do in the nonroving pointer technique), then small fragments will tend to concentrate in the initial part of the search path, increasing the time required to satisfy larger requests. This inefficiency is quite noticeable and severe in some cases.

Compacting to Deal with Allocation Failures

When we make a request to allocate a block of size n, and the system finds that no block on the ring of free blocks is large enough to satisfy the request, it may still be the case that the sum of the block sizes on the ring of free blocks is larger than n. In this case, allocation failure could be said to have occurred because of the fragmentation of free blocks on the ring of free blocks. In particular, if we had a way of coalescing all the free blocks together into a single large block, we could proceed to satisfy the original request.

compacting the heap

The process of moving all the reserved blocks into one end of the heap, while moving all the free blocks into the opposite end and coalescing them all into one large free block is called *compacting the heap* (or *heap compaction*). But in order to accomplish this, we need to make it possible not only for the reserved blocks to shift position but also for all external pointers to these blocks to be updated to point to the new addresses to which the blocks have been moved.

handles

One technique for making this process easy is to use what are called *handles*. Handles are *double pointers*—or pointers to pointers. To create handles, we set aside a region of the heap to contain a zone of *master pointers*. These master pointers point to reserved blocks. Then we use a pointer to a block B's master pointer as the *handle* to B. We always use handles to provide external access to blocks from outside the heap, and to allow blocks to contain pointers to point to one another inside the heap. Figure 8.29 shows a heap divided into a normal block allocation heap zone and a master pointer zone.

moving blocks in the heap and updating their master pointers

If we agree always to access reserved blocks in the normal heap zone using their handles, then the stage is set to make it easy to move the blocks around in the heap. All we have to do when we move a block, B, is to change B's master pointer to point to the new location to which B has been moved. After B has been moved to a new location, external access to B through its handle still works. In order to make it easy to update B's master pointer when we move B, we can agree to store a copy of B's handle inside B (along with B's *size* and its *mark bit* telling whether B is *free* or *reserved*).

Compacting the heap then consists of scanning the heap zone from bottom to top, moving each reserved block down as far as possible and updating the block's master pointer to point to its new location. Finally, the free space at the top is joined into one large free block. The heap is then said to be *compacted*. Figure 8.30 shows the result of compacting the heap illustrated in Fig. 8.29.

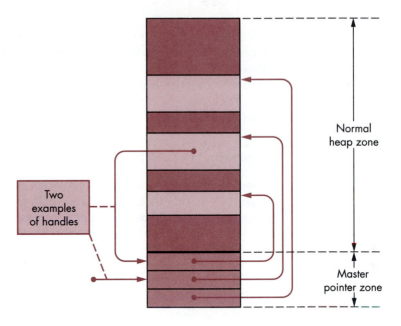

Figure 8.29 A Heap with a Master Pointer Zone and Handles

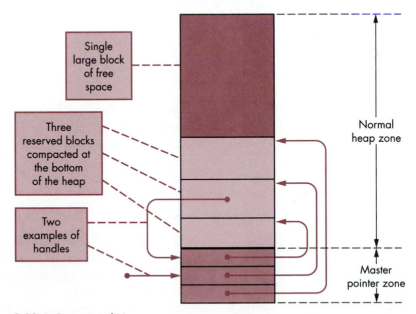

Figure 8.30 A Compacted Heap

double dereferencing

If H is a variable in a C program that contains a handle, then the notation for accessing the block to which H points uses what is called *double dereferencing* (or sometimes *double indirect addressing*). Suppose a handle H references a block *B* containing a struct having a **Size** member. Then a C expression that has the value *Size(B)* starting with H is (*H)–>**Size**. An assignment statement that sets *B*'s **Size** to be N is (*H)–>**Size** = N.

Comparing Uses of Heaps in Applications

handles versus
single pointers

Comparing the use of single pointers with use of handles, we observe that it costs more both in *space* (to store two pointers instead of just one) and in *time* (to perform double dereferencing instead of single dereferencing) when we use handles instead of pointers. What we gain, however, is convenience in arranging for the underlying storage allocation scheme to be able to accommodate a range of allocation request sizes and to be able to compact memory easily so we can coalesce all fragmented blocks of free space into one large free space block.

applications of heaps

It is perhaps not surprising then that the use of heaps containing blocks referenced by handles is a popular way to organize memory in some contemporary computing systems. One vendor's operating system divides a computer memory into a *system heap* (to contain operating system data structures) and various *application heaps*, each supporting given software applications. Software vendors can write software (such as spreadsheets, word processors, painting and drawing programs, electronic mail programs, and so forth) relying on the availability of such heaps to support their applications. Application software typically uses blocks in an application heap to contain representations of data supporting menus, windows, pictures, text, file control blocks, device control blocks, buttons, scroll bars, and all manner of application support data structures.

Some modern object-oriented programming languages allocate data structures representing *objects* in heaps and automatically assume that these objects are referenced by handles, so the programmer never needs to use double-dereferencing notation in a program to refer to objects. We address this issue when we study C++ object-oriented programming techniques in Chapter 15.

Reference Counts

There is one more concept worth mentioning before we close this section on dynamic memory allocation techniques. This is the idea of *reference counts*.

pausing for storage
reclamation

One of the troubles with the storage reclamation techniques we have discussed so far is that they cause a program to pause while they reorganize memory. The garbage collection technique uses a three pass algorithm to sweep memory setting mark bits to free, then to mark all list nodes in use, and finally to link all unused list nodes into a reconstituted available space list. The heap compaction algorithm also requires making a sweep of the heap zone during which reserved blocks get moved and their master pointers get updated. Each of these processes requires time $O(N)$, where N is the size of the memory being reorganized.

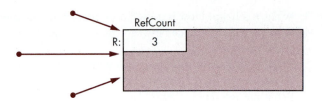

Figure 8.31 A Struct, R, with a Reference Count of Three

If we have a *real-time application*, requiring a system to respond quickly—within a fraction of a second, let's say, to incoming stimulus events (as is the case in systems such as robots used in manufacturing assembly lines or in collision avoidance systems in airline aircraft)—then we have to guarantee that the system will not be taken off-line for a period of time longer than the required real-time response interval. Garbage collection and heap compaction algorithms both have two unfortunate features: (a) it is unpredictable when the moment to execute them will arise, and (b) they take a considerable amount of time to run to completion (often more than a few fractions of a second when a system has a huge list or heap memory, especially on slower computers). Consequently, it is important to know about alternative *storage reclamation techniques* that work *incrementally* instead of all at once. (An *incremental* technique is one that performs its work in tiny increments, doing its job bit by bit every now and then.)

responding in real time

The use of *reference counts* can provide an incremental storage reclamation technique under suitable circumstances. A *reference count member* in a struct, R, is a member containing a number that counts the number of pointers that reference R. Figure 8.31 illustrates a struct R having three pointers that point to it and having a reference count of three as its RefCount member.

incremental storage reclamation

Each time we create and use a new pointer that references R, we increase R's RefCount by one. And each time we destroy a pointer to R, we decrease R's RefCount member by one. Whenever R's RefCount member reaches zero, we know that no more pointers in the system refer to R, so we can return the block of storage used to hold R to the available space list (or to the ring of free blocks in the heap, whichever is appropriate to the storage allocation technique we are using). This policy accomplishes something important. Namely, it automatically frees the storage for R the instant R's storage is no longer in use. Free storage in the system is therefore reclaimed incrementally (instead of all at once, as is the case for mark-and-gather garbage collection or heap compaction). If a real-time system needs to use dynamic memory allocation techniques, the reference count technique may provide a solution that helps the system meet its real-time response constraints.

8.6 Review Questions

1. What is the difference between static and dynamic memory allocation?
2. Explain what is done in each of the three phases of garbage collection using the marking and gathering technique.

3. What is a heap? How is it used to support dynamic memory allocation?
4. What is the difference between the first-fit and best-fit policies for dynamic memory allocation?
5. What do fragmentation and coalescing refer to in the case of heaps?
6. What are handles? How are they affected by heap compaction?
7. What are reference counts? How do they provide for incremental storage reclamation?

8.6 Exercises

1. Why is it the case that, in order to make the free block coalescing policy work efficiently, we need to store each free block's size and a mark bit designating it as free not only at the top of each block but also at its bottom boundary?
2. Can you draw a picture of several nodes with nonzero reference counts that are linked to one another but are not referenced from the outside? What defect does this imply in the reference count method for incremental storage reclamation?

 Pitfalls

- *Improper initialization of your data representations*

    Did you remember to initialize all data structures properly? When creating data representations for lists, strings, or dynamic memory allocation support packages, it is easy to overlook proper initialization. Does each one-way, linked list terminate with a **NULL** link? Is each string marked properly with a terminating *null* byte? Did you properly initialize all the links, sizes, tags, master pointers, and boundary markers in your heap?

    The use of formatted debugging aids is highly useful in detecting deficiencies in your implementations. If you can see a printed representation of each of your structures, your errors, especially those errors related to improper initialization, will tend to leap out at you. In fact, a good policy is to implement the formatted debugging aids before implementing the algorithms for the operations. That way, you will be ready to check out the operation of each newly implemented algorithm thoroughly.

- *Unannounced overflows and allocation failures*

    When using sequential representations that can overflow, such as Pascal strings, some implementations do not give any overflow warnings. The remainder of a string beyond 255 characters may simply be lost without warning. This is similar to an overflow in integer arithmetic when, say, an integer sum becomes greater than C's maximum integer value **INT_MAX**, and wraps around unannounced to an unintended negative number without warning. In many dynamic memory allocation systems using heaps, allocation failure can also happen unannounced. One policy used to signal an allocation failure in a heap is to return a **NULL** handle as the reply to an allocation request to allocate a block of size *n*. (For example, see the definition of **malloc** in C's Standard Library <stdlib.h>.)

In order to develop production-quality, commercial software applications, you will need to develop a style of programming that detects and overcomes overflows and allocation failures, and which anticipates running out of storage by offering the user the option to save files and data before a system crash occurs due to insufficient memory or file space.

Tips and Techniques

- *Look at operations before choosing representations*

    It is helpful to become informed about the intended operations you need to perform on your data before choosing a low-level representation. An ideal way to proceed is as follows: First, define your intended operations abstractly (by, for instance, thoroughly specifying an ADT for your data and operations at the abstract level). Second, if possible, collect size measurements for the data structures you will need to use in your application and obtain frequency counts for the mix of operations you will need to perform on your data. Third, identify the constraints on your implementation devices and media (and determine whether space efficiency or time efficiency or both will be important to achieve). Fourth, select your data representations and algorithms to meet the implementation constraints and to optimize the performance measures (such as efficiency in time or efficiency in space) that you have selected.

    For example, in choosing a list representation to implement the List ADT operations given in Fig. 8.1, linked list representations will generally provide more flexibility (and will protect better against accidental overflow) than sequential list representations. They will also accommodate insertions, deletions, and rearrangements more efficiently. But they will not be as efficient when accessing and updating list items randomly, starting with an item's position in the list. Storage allocation efficiency in linked lists will generally be good when the space required to hold links is small in comparison to the amount of space required to hold the rest of the information in list nodes. Sequential list representations will generally pay off when random list item access by position is frequently required, and when the risk of list overflow is absent or minimal (which can arise, for instance, if list sizes are known in advance to be bounded).

- *Supporting dynamic memory allocation*

    It is not always the case that a programmer gets to choose which dynamic memory allocation technique to use to support an application being programmed. Often the programmer is stuck with whatever methods are offered by the underlying implementation medium selected for a project. For instance, a version of C might provide C strings, and dynamic memory allocation based on heaps (using unknown implementations for **malloc** and **free**). A list processing language, such as LISP, might provide dynamic memory allocation techniques supporting the construction of generalized lists using available space lists and automatic garbage collection, but it may suffer efficiency penalties for being a typeless language and for not being able efficiently to allocate and update packed sequential data structures containing items of identical type. A version of Pascal might provide Pascal strings and methods (of unknown efficiency) for allocating blocks of memory in a heap. A vendor's operating system might provide heap operations at the microcode level, but they might have been implemented inefficiently.

It is important to measure the performance and efficiency of an externally supplied dynamic memory allocation package in order to make an informed decision about whether to use it or not, provided you have the choice.

If you are faced with implementing your own dynamic memory allocation support package, it would be useful to study some of the advanced techniques available in the literature (which are beyond the scope of this book), before plunging ahead and implementing a technique by trial-and-error.

References for Further Study

classic paper on list processing

John McCarthy, "Recursive Functions of Symbolic Expressions and Their Computation by Machine, Part I," *Communications of the ACM* 3: 4 (April 1960), pp. 184–95.

A classic paper introducing list processing ideas.

comparing policies

Thomas A. Standish, *Data Structure Techniques*, Addison-Wesley, Reading, Mass., (1980).

If you are curious to know how the performance of the *first-fit* and *best-fit* policies compare, some information is given in a more advanced book by the author.

Chapter Summary

lists

Lists are finite, ordered sequences of items. We can represent lists by packing their items contiguously in arrays—getting the *sequential representation of lists*, or by putting the items in individual nodes and linking these nodes into chains—getting the *linked representation of lists*. The many varieties of linked list representations include one-way linked lists, circular linked lists, two-way linked lists, and linked lists having special header nodes.

linked versus sequential representations

Sequential list representations provide fast access to arbitrary items by position, but, in comparison to linked lists, it may be more costly to delete or insert items in the middle of sequential list representations, and they run the risk of overflowing or of wasting space not used to store items. Linked lists provide for fast insertion and deletion of items, but accessing items by position is slower than is the case for sequential lists, and linked lists can exhibit poor storage utilization efficiency.

generalized lists

Generalized lists are lists whose items are permitted to be sublists. As with ordinary lists, generalized lists have both sequential and linked representations. Sublists of generalized lists can either be shared, or they can exist as separate copies.

Generalized lists are used in important applications in artificial intelligence and are the main data structuring method available in various list processing languages. Such list processing languages are often said to be *typeless*, because they allow the use of variables that can have values of any type and because items of any type can be stored in the generalized lists that these languages provide. Unfortunately, there is a price to be paid for the generality and flexibility that such typeless languages offer, since their generality is often purchased in the coinage of reduced efficiency.

string representations

Two string representations currently in popular use are *C strings* and *Pascal strings*. A C string is a packed sequence of characters of arbitrary length whose end is marked by a special *null* character. A Pascal string is stored as a fixed-length packed character array, starting with a length byte specifying the length of the string.

text files

Text files are files that contain strings representing text. In one example studied in this chapter, text files are represented on external storage media as linked blocks in which each block contains a packed array of characters holding a portion of the text. Each of these linked blocks is stamped with (a) a unique file identifier, (b) the date and time of the text file's creation, and (c) a block sequence number. In the event of a read-write failure on the storage medium, or in the event of the loss of file directory information, such a text file can be recreated using the information stamped on each block, by linking all blocks having a given unique file identifier in the order specified by their block sequence numbers.

When text files are read into main memory, the text is coalesced into a single large block, containing the sequence of characters in the text, and a separate array of *line starts* is created (which is useful for quickly displaying the text in a window on the user's workstation, and for rapidly scrolling this text up and down in the window).

static versus dynamic storage allocation

Static storage allocation takes place before a program is executed, and it involves setting up storage areas whose size and arrangement can be calculated from declarations in the text of the program before the program is run. Dynamic storage allocation takes place during program execution. Three kinds of dynamic allocation are (1) stack-based dynamic allocation used to support subroutine calls and returns; (2) organizing memory into an available space list, in order to perform dynamic allocation of list nodes on demand at run-time; and (3) organizing memory into a heap that can be used to allocate blocks of different sizes on demand during program execution.

garbage collection

When an available space list containing list nodes becomes empty, storage reclamation can be attempted by an *automatic garbage collection* process. The marking and gathering method for garbage collection is a three-phase process. In the initialization phase, all list nodes are marked as *free*. In the marking phase, all list nodes in current use are marked as *reserved*. In the gathering phase, all *free* list nodes are linked into a new available space list.

heaps

A heap is a zone of memory organized to support dynamic memory allocation of blocks of storage of differing sizes. Two methods for allocating a block of size n in a heap are the *first-fit* method and the *best-fit* method. The first-fit method scans a two-way linked ring of free blocks and allocates the first block big enough to satisfy the request. The best-fit policy scans the entire ring of free blocks to find the block that is the tightest possible fit satisfying the request, where the tightest possible fit is the one having the least excess size beyond the size requested.

fragmentation and
coalescing

Fragmentation occurs during the use of the first-fit and best-fit policies when free blocks are split into smaller blocks. *Coalescing* is a method used to counteract the tendency toward fragmentation. When a block is freed and can be returned to the ring of free blocks, it is possible to *coalesce* it with any of its neighbors that are also free, in order to form larger free blocks.

allocation failure

Allocation failure occurs in a heap when a request to allocate a block of size n cannot be accommodated either because there is not enough free space left, or because all the blocks on the ring of free blocks are too small to satisfy the request. *Compacting* is a strategy that can be used for storage reclamation when allocation failure occurs in a heap. When a heap is compacted, all reserved blocks are moved to one end of the heap, allowing all free blocks to be moved to the opposite end and to be coalesced into one large free block. Handles are used to make heap compacting easy. A *handle* is a *pointer to a pointer*. Each reserved block in a heap is referenced by a *master pointer* in a special master pointer region. A handle to a block is a pointer to the block's master pointer. When a block is moved during heap compacting, its master pointer is updated to point to the block's new location. References to the block, using double dereferencing of the block's handle, are unaffected by the act of moving a block and updating its master pointer.

reference counts and
incremental storage
reclamation

Garbage collection and heap compaction have the disadvantage that the system must pause to perform storage reclamation. These pauses may occur at unpredictable moments since it is difficult to forecast when allocation failures will occur. In real-time systems, which must be able to guarantee responses to external events within specified time limits, it may be unacceptable to pause for storage reclamation. An incremental technique for storage reclamation that can be used to overcome this deficiency is one based on the use of *reference counts*, in which each node contains a number equal to the number of external pointers in use to reference the node. When pointers to a node are destroyed, the node's reference count is decreased. When the node's reference count becomes zero, its storage can be returned to the pool of available space. Since this can be done incrementally, long pauses for the execution of multipass storage reclamation algorithms can be avoided.

applications of heaps

Heaps are used in many contemporary applications to support data representations used by operating systems and by application software. Data structures supporting windows, menus, spreadsheets, pictures, drawn objects, word processor text, file and device control blocks, scroll bars, buttons, and many other sorts of objects used in programming are commonly stored in heaps, and space for them is commonly allocated using dynamic storage allocation methods, such as those explained in this chapter.

9

Trees

trees are important and useful

Trees are one of the most important data structures in computer science. They come in many forms. They provide natural representations for many kinds of data that occur in applications, and they are useful for solving a wide variety of algorithmic problems.

Sometimes trees are *static*, in the sense that their shape is determined before the running of an algorithm, and they do not change shape while the algorithm runs. In other cases, trees are *dynamic*, meaning that they undergo shape changes during the running of an algorithm. Tree shape can change as a result of the insertion and deletion of nodes. There are also shape-changing operations that alter the structure of a tree locally without inserting or deleting any nodes. Trees can also change shape when they are combined with one another. An example of a combining operation is the substitution of one expression tree for a node inside another expression tree (where expression trees are used to represent algebraic expressions, such as: $x^2 + 2\,x\,y + y^2$).

static and dynamic trees

337

game trees

Another kind of dynamic tree is one that is generated during the solution of a problem. For example, a *game tree* is a tree representing the possible moves of the players at each stage of a game. A given node in a game tree represents a specific game situation, and the branches leading from this node represent possible moves a player can make in this situation.

search trees

A *search tree* is a tree used to help search for prestored information that is often associated with *search keys*. Each node in the search tree may represent a test that is performed on the search key being used. The outcome of the test may determine which branch to follow in the tree to narrow the search. Search trees can be used to organize efficiently the search index to the information in a large file or database.

priority queues and heaps

Trees can also be used to create specially efficient representations for various algorithmic tasks. For example, priority queues were defined in Chapter 4 as an ADT specifying a type of queue that holds prioritized items. Items can be put into a priority queue in any order, but they are removed in the order of highest-to-lowest priority. One of the efficient ways to represent a priority queue is to create a special kind of binary tree called a *heap*. (*Note:* This is a different use of the word "heap." In Chapter 8, another kind of heap was used to organize dynamic memory allocation strategies.)

sequential and linked representations

Sometimes trees can be represented efficiently using sequential representations. In other cases, linked tree representations offer advantages. Some tree representations are even implicit in the operation of an algorithm. For example, the call trees we examined in Chapter 3, in order to study recursion, are not trees that are explicitly represented as data structures when a particular program executes a pattern of recursive calls.

Plan for the Chapter

concepts and terminology

Section 9.2 introduces some basic concepts and terminology pertaining to trees. The basic anatomy of trees—such as roots, leaves, and internal nodes—is discussed.

binary trees

Section 9.3 begins to explore *binary trees*. These are trees that are either empty or have nodes with two children that must in turn be binary trees. Section 9.4 examines representations of binary trees. One such representation is the sequential representation, in which the nodes of a binary tree are packed next to one another in an array so that there are no gaps between the nodes. Not only does this provide quick random access to the kth node of the tree, it also enables us to move around the tree using efficient operations on integer array indexes. The sequential representation is much more efficient in space than the linked representation, but it does not tolerate some kinds of changes in shape very well.

representing priority queues using heaps

Section 9.5 presents an application of the sequential representation of binary trees to the task of representing priority queues. By arranging the values in nodes of a sequential representation of a binary tree in a special way, we obtain a *heap*. When heaps are used to represent priority queues, we can obtain good performance of the insertion and deletion operations in the Priority Queue ADT. Section 9.5 presents algorithms for implementing the Priority Queue ADT using heaps.

binary tree traversals

In Section 9.6, we study some techniques for traversing binary trees. A traversal of a binary tree is a process that visits each node in the tree exactly once in some specified order. Different orders for visiting the nodes yield different traversals. One particular traversal of interest is the *postorder traversal* of an expression tree representing an algebraic expression. The postorder traversal of such an expression tree yields a postfix instruction sequence that can be used by a postfix interpreter (such as that given in Program 7.7) to calculate the value of the expression. We also present several significant techniques for traversing linked representations of binary trees using recursion, stacks, and queues.

Section 9.7 explores binary search trees. Linked binary trees were first introduced in Fig. 2.23, where their linked representations were illustrated. The coverage in Section 9.7 takes the basic idea much further by analyzing performance characteristics of binary search trees. We discover that, in the worst case, searching a binary tree of n nodes can take time $O(n)$. However, in the average case, search times are shown to be $O(\log n)$.

binary search trees

This discovery sets the stage for the exploration of AVL trees in Section 9.8. AVL trees are binary search trees that are kept in nearly balanced—although not perfectly balanced—condition. They overcome the $O(n)$ worst case performance of unbalanced binary search trees, and they can be shown to have $O(\log n)$ performance for all significant operations, such as searching for a node with a given key, inserting a new node, and deleting a node. One can even give an implementation of the List ADT, using AVL trees, that overcomes the principal disadvantages of the sequential and linked representations of lists.

AVL trees

Section 9.9 presents another useful kind of search tree, called a 2–3 tree. These are trees that can have nodes with either two or three children and that have all leaves on a single bottom row. These trees exhibit good performance properties similar to those of AVL trees.

2–3 trees

Section 9.10 introduces briefly another kind of search tree, called a *trie*, which is organized according to a "discrimination net" principle different from that used to organize binary search trees and 2–3 trees. Tries have remarkably good search tree performance, and their shape is insensitive to the order in which new keys are inserted (a property not enjoyed by binary search trees and 2–3 trees).

tries

Finally, in Section 9.11, we see how binary trees can be applied to the process of establishing a minimal-length encoding for messages spelled with letters in an alphabet, where the frequency of use of the letters is known. This is called a Huffman code, and the binary tree constructed to yield the code is called a Huffman coding tree.

Huffman codes

9.2   Basic Concepts and Terminology

Learning Objectives

1. To learn how to refer to various parts of trees.
2. To learn about some relationships that are always true in trees.

Let's begin by reviewing some of the basic concepts and terminology related to trees, starting with "basic tree anatomy." Figure 9.1 illustrates a tree.

three sources of tree terminology

Tree diagrams are formed from nodes and line segments. The line segments are called either *edges* or *branches*. We draw on three sources of terminology when talking

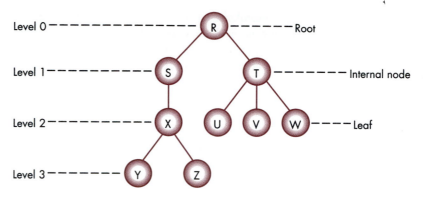

Figure 9.1 Basic Tree Anatomy

about trees: (1) *family relationships* (such as parents or children), (2) *geometric relationships* (such as left and right, or bottom and top), and (3) *biological names* for parts of trees (such as roots and leaves).

For example, in Fig. 9.1, node R is the *root* node of the tree. If we travel downward along the edges that start at R, we arrive at R's two *children*, which are the nodes S and T. Traveling upward in the tree, we say that node R is the *parent* of node S. The *descendants* of a node consist of the nodes that can be reached by traveling downward along any path starting at the node. For example, the descendants of node S are the nodes X, Y, and Z.

roots, children, and descendants

If you start at a node in the tree and travel upward along the path toward the root, you encounter the ancestors of the node. For example, the ancestors of node Y are nodes X, S, and R. Of these ancestors, only X is the *parent* of node Y.

ancestors and parents

The *leaves* of the tree are the nodes that have no children. In Fig. 9.1, the leaves are the five nodes: Y, Z, U, V, and W. If a node has children, it is called an *internal node*. For example, node T is an internal node, since it has three children.

leaves

The nodes of a tree can be arranged into numbered *levels*. The topmost level, which contains only the root node, is called *level 0*. *Level 1* contains all the children of the root node. *Level 2* consists of the grandchildren of the root node. In general, any node, N, can be reached by traveling downward along a path, p, starting at the root. If path p has n edges in it, then node N is said to belong to level n, and the *length* of path p is said to be n. For example, in Fig. 9.1, if we start at the root, R, and travel downward to node X, we travel along a path with two edges in it (consisting of the edge from R to S and the edge from S to X). Consequently, we have traveled over a path of length 2, and node X is therefore on level 2.

levels

In a tree, there is exactly one path from the root R to each descendant of R. (If there is *more than one path* from the root to some node N, then you do not have a tree. In particular, diagrams containing paths that are cycles are not tree diagrams, and diagrams having two paths that separate at a node and then come back together later at some other node are also not tree diagrams.)

geometric terms

We will use *geometric terms* to refer to parts of trees, also. For example, we could talk about the bottommost row of nodes in the tree in Fig. 9.1. This would refer to the leaves Y and Z at level 3 of the tree. We could also say that U is the *left child* of T, W is the *right child* of T, and V is the *middle child* of T.

Geometrically speaking, the root of a tree is its *topmost* node. It is traditional in computer science to draw diagrams of trees *upside-down*, with the root of a tree at the top and with the leaves of the tree at the bottom. Many algorithms process the nodes of a tree in an order that starts at the root and progresses to additional nodes on the lower levels. By drawing trees with their roots at the top and the descendants of the root lower down on the page, the normal order of reading of a page (from top to bottom) reflects the order in which nodes get processed in these algorithms. Consequently, the upside-down way of drawing trees makes sense in connection with the consideration of these kinds of tree-processing algorithms.

In some situations, it is convenient to define and use the *empty tree*—a tree having no nodes and no edges.

9.2 Review Questions

1. Referring to Fig. 9.1, give a list of each of the following: (a) the ancestors of node U, (b) the children of node S, (c) the descendants of node S, (d) the parent of node V.
2. How many nodes in a tree have no ancestors?
3. What is the name for a node in a tree that has no descendants?
4. Given a particular node N in a tree, how many paths are there that connect the root node of the tree to node N?

9.2 Exercises

1. Count the number of edges, e, and the number of nodes, n, in the tree in Fig. 9.1. Draw some other trees, and count their nodes and edges. Is there a relationship that you notice between the number of nodes and the number of edges? Can you prove that this relationship is always true for any tree, T?
2. Suppose each node in a tree T has either exactly two children or has no children. In other words, each node is either a leaf or it has exactly two *nonempty* children. We call such a tree a *full binary tree*. What is the relationship between the number of leaves and the number of internal nodes in tree T? Prove that this relationship holds true for any full binary tree.

9.3   Binary Trees

A *binary tree* is a tree in which each node has exactly two children. Either or both of these children is permitted to be *empty*. If a node has two empty children, it is said to be a *leaf*. It is convenient to define a binary tree using a recursive definition.

> A **binary tree** is either the *empty tree* or a node that has *left* and *right* subtrees that are binary trees.

left and right children

Figure 9.2 provides a diagram of a binary tree. Node R is the root node of this binary tree. The leaf nodes are X, Z, U, and W. Nodes Y and V each have only one nonempty child. Node Y has an empty left child and has a right child Z. Node V has a left child W and has an empty right child.

Note that, in a binary tree, *every* node has both a left and a right child. Whether or not such left and right children are *nonempty* or *empty* can *vary* from node to node, but what is always *invariant* about each node in a binary tree is that each node has a left and right child.

extended binary trees

Sometimes we explicitly picture occurrences of empty binary trees. A small square, □, is used to indicate each occurrence of an empty binary tree. An *extended binary tree* is a binary tree having its empty binary subtrees explicitly represented by square symbols (□). Figure 9.3 illustrates the extended binary tree that results from explicitly representing the empty binary trees in Figure 9.2.

Figure 9.2 A Binary Tree

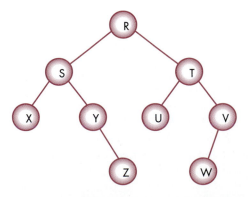

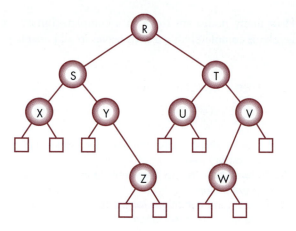

Figure 9.3 An Extended Binary Tree

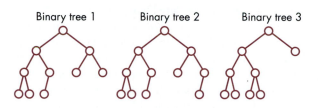

Figure 9.4 Complete and Incomplete Binary Trees

Binary tree 1   Binary tree 2   Binary tree 3

Let's define just one more type of binary tree before moving on to consider binary tree representations and various binary tree operations. A *complete binary tree* is a binary tree with leaves on either a single level or on two adjacent levels such that the leaves on the bottommost level are placed as far left as possible. Figure 9.4 illustrates three binary trees. The first is a complete binary tree. The second fails to be complete because the leaves on its bottommost level are not placed as far left as possible. The third fails to be a complete binary tree because even though its leaves are on two levels, they are not on two *adjacent* levels.

We will see in a moment how complete binary trees form the basis for an efficient sequential binary-tree representation.

9.3 Review Questions

1. Give the definition of a binary tree.
2. What is an extended binary tree?
3. Define the concept of a complete binary tree.
4. Does there exist a binary tree whose leaves are the same as its root?

9.3 Exercises

1. What is the relationship between the number of empty binary trees in an extended binary tree (symbolized by squares) and the number of internal (nonempty) nodes (symbolized by circles)?

2. How many nodes are there in a complete binary tree with levels 0:n, in which level n is completely filled with leaves in all possible positions.

9.4   A Sequential Binary Tree Representation

Suppose we take a complete binary tree such as the one shown in Fig. 9.5 and number the nodes level-by-level. That is, we start at the topmost level and number the root node, H, as node number 1. Then we move down to the next level containing the children, D and K, of the root node, and we number these nodes from left to right, as nodes 2 and 3. On the next level, we number the nodes B, F, J, and L, from left to right as nodes 4, 5, 6, and 7. Finally, on the bottom row, we number the nodes A, C, E, G, and I as nodes 8 through 12.

numbering nodes level-by-level

Note: A tree need not be a binary tree to have its nodes numbered level-by-level in this fashion, since we can always number the nodes of a tree level-by-level from top to bottom, and left to right within each level. The ordering of nodes produced by this process is called the *level order* of the nodes.

level order

Let's now create an array A[0:12] containing the information in the nodes of the binary tree of Fig. 9.5 in level order. Figure 9.6 shows such an array, A, which is called the *contiguous sequential representation* of the complete binary tree of Fig. 9.5. (The word "contiguous" means "touching" and means that there are no "gaps" between the items in the sequential representation in the array A. Also A[0] remains empty.)

the contiguous sequential representation

To travel around the binary tree in the contiguous sequential representation, we can use some arithmetic operations on the array index *i*, in A[*i*], as indicated in Table

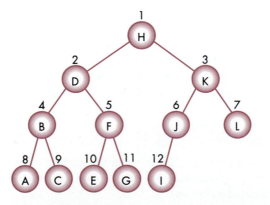

Figure 9.5 A Complete Binary Tree with Numbered Nodes

Figure 9.6 Sequential Representation of a Complete Binary Tree (with A[0] Empty)

Table 9.7 How to Find Nodes in a Contiguous Sequential Representation of a Complete Binary Tree, A[1:n]

To Find:	Use:	Provided:
The left child of A[i]	A[2 i]	$2\,i \leq n$
The right child of A[i]	A[2 i + 1]	$2\,i + 1 \leq n$
The parent of A[i]	A[i / 2]	$i > 1$
The root	A[1]	A is nonempty
Whether A[i] is a leaf	True	$2\,i > n$

9.7. In this table we consider a more general case in which we are dealing only with array positions A[1:n] containing information for a complete binary tree of n nodes.

Now let's apply some of the relationships in Table 9.7 to the array in Fig. 9.6 containing the sequential representation of the complete binary tree in Fig. 9.5. For example, what is the parent of node C? Since node C == A[9] in the array A of Fig. 9.6, its parent is located at A[9/2] == A[4]. Since A[4] == B, the parent of C is B. Referring to Fig. 9.5, we see that the parent of node C is also B.

locating parents

Now let's calculate the right child of node F. Since F == A[5], its right child is located at A[2*5 + 1] == A[11], where A[11] contains G. We see that G is the right child of node F in the tree of Fig. 9.5 also. Similarly, the left child of F is located at A[2*5] == A[10], where A[10] contains E.

locating children

Let's now look at the test for whether node A[i] is a leaf. Table 9.7 asserts that A[i] is a leaf if and only if 2*i > n. In Fig. 9.6 there are 12 nonempty nodes in the array A, so that n == 12. Consequently, A[i] is a leaf if and only if 2*i > 12, which is the same as the condition i > 6. This implies that nodes A[7:12] must be leaves, and that nodes A[1:6] must be internal nodes. Checking this assertion against the tree in Fig. 9.5, we see that nodes A[7] through A[12] are the leaves.

the leaf test

9.4 Review Questions

1. What is the contiguous sequential representation of a complete binary tree? How is it defined mathematically?
2. How do you find the parent of node A[i] in the contiguous sequential representation of a binary tree? What node has no parent?
3. How do you find the left child of node A[i] in the contiguous sequential representation of a binary tree? What nodes have no left children?
4. How do you find the right child of node A[i] in the contiguous sequential representation of a binary tree? What nodes have no right children?

9.4 Exercises

1. Why is it the case that $A[i]$ is a leaf in a complete binary tree of n nodes, if and only if $2i > n$?
2. Given that there are n nodes in a complete binary tree, T, how many levels does T have as a function of n?
3. On what level of a complete binary tree T does node $A[i]$ reside?

9.5 An Application—Heaps and Priority Queues

Learning Objectives

1. To learn how to represent a heap using a contiguous sequential representation.
2. To learn how heaps can serve as efficient representations for priority queues.
3. To discover some important mathematical properties of heaps that will be used later.

a new meaning for the word "heap"

In Chapter 8, we used the word *heap* to refer to a region of memory organized to provide dynamic memory allocation. In this section, we will discuss a separate, new meaning for the word heap, which refers to a complete binary tree with values at its nodes arranged in a certain way.

> A **heap** is a complete binary tree with values stored in its nodes such that no child has a value bigger than the value of its parent.

using heaps to represent priority queues

Figure 9.8 shows a diagram of a heap with integer values stored in its nodes. Note that these integers decrease in value along any path, starting at the root and traveling

Figure 9.8 An Example of a Heap

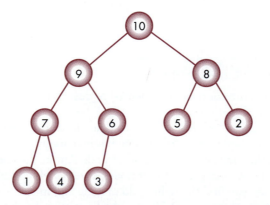

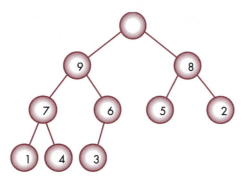

Figure 9.9 An Arrangement of Nodes with No Root Value

downward. A heap provides a representation for a *priority queue*. Recall from Section 4.3 that a priority queue was defined as an ADT having the property that items are removed in the order of highest-to-lowest priority, regardless of the order in which they were inserted.

If a heap is used to represent a priority queue, it is easy to find the item of highest priority, since it sits at the root of the tree. (Exercise 9.5.1 asks you to prove this fact by considering whether values would decrease along all paths if the largest value resided in some node other than the root.) However, if we remove the value at the root, we must restructure the tree to be a heap again.

In Fig. 9.8, suppose we remove the largest value, 10, from the root node of the heap. This produces the arrangement of nodes in Fig. 9.9 that is not a heap since the root node has no value. In order to convert Fig. 9.9 back into a heap again, we use the following process. First, we delete the rightmost leaf on the bottom row, which is the node containing the value 3. (*Note:* The rightmost leaf on the bottom row is the *last leaf in level order*.) Then we place this deleted node's value, 3, into the root node. This gives the diagram in Fig. 9.10.

Next, we restore the heap property among the remaining nodes in Figure 9.10 by starting at the root node and repeatedly exchanging its value with the *larger* of the values of its children, until no more exchanges are possible. Let's trace how this works.

In Figure 9.10, starting at the root node with value 3, we see that the left and right children of the root have the values 9 and 8, respectively. We exchange the

deleting the last leaf in level order

restoring the heap property

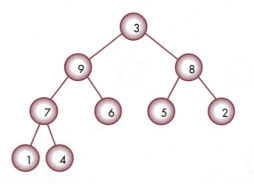

Figure 9.10 Tree with Root Value Replaced and Last Leaf Deleted

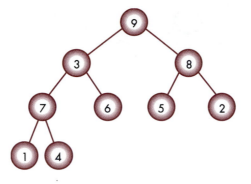

Figure 9.11 Tree with Root Value Exchanged with Larger Child Value

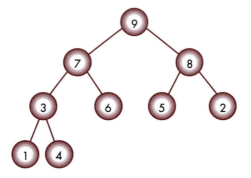

Figure 9.12 Intermediate Tree That Is Not Yet a Heap

value 3 in the root node with the value 9 in the left child of the root, since 9 is the *larger* value among the two values (8 and 9) of the two children of the root. This yields the tree in Fig. 9.11, which still fails to be a heap since the node containing 3 has two children containing bigger values 7 and 6. So we again exchange the value 3 with the larger of the children's values, 7, yielding the tree in Fig. 9.12.

Again, since the node containing 3 has a right child with a bigger value, 4, we do not have a heap, so we make a final exchange of 3 and 4, which yields the tree in Fig. 9.13. Although the process illustrated in this example moved the value 3 from the root in Fig. 9.10 all the way down to a leaf in Fig. 9.13, it is not always the case that a

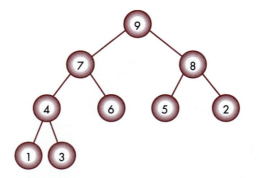

Figure 9.13 Tree with Heap Property Restored

new value in the root will move all the way into a leaf position. In general, the downward-moving value will stop at the first internal node having children with smaller values than the downward moving value.

To formulate the reheapifying process as a general procedure, suppose that H is a heap, that L is the last node of H in level order, and that node L contains the value V. (Again note: The last leaf in level order is the same as the rightmost leaf on the bottom row of H.) We must replace the value at the root of H with value V, we must then delete node L, and we must finally reheapify H in order to restore its heap property. Program Strategy 9.14 gives a sketch of the general process for doing this.

The process for restoring the heap property by repeatedly exchanging the value at the root with the larger of its children's values, until no more exchanges are possible, is sketched in Program Strategy 9.15.

To organize the values in the nodes of an initially unorganized complete binary tree, H, into a heap, we can apply Program Strategy 9.15 to each of the internal nodes of H in reverse level order. Program Strategy 9.16 sketches the method for doing this.

Let's now consider an example of an initial configuration of nodes and values in a complete binary tree that is not a heap. Figure 9.17 illustrates such an initial configuration.

We now illustrate how to apply the process of Program Strategy 9.16 to the configuration of nodes and values in Fig. 9.17, in order to convert it into a heap. We

```
 |     ItemType Remove(Heap *H)
 |     {
 |         NodeType   L;                    /* let L be the last node of H in level order */
 |         NodeType   R;                    /* R is used to refer to the root node of H */
5|         ItemType   ItemToRemove;         /* temporarily stores item to remove */
 |
 |         if  (*H is not empty)  {
 |
 |             /* Remove the highest priority item which is stored in */
10|            /* H's root node, R */
 |                 ItemToRemove = (the value stored in the root node, R, of H);
 |
 |             /* Move L's value into the root of H, and delete L */
 |                 (R's value) = (the value in leaf L);
15|                 (delete node L);
 |
 |             /* Reheapify the values in the remaining nodes of H starting at */
 |             /* the root, R, by applying the algorithm in Program Strategy 9.15 */
 |             /* to the root node, R, in heap H */
20|                 if  (H is not empty)  {
 |                     (Reheapify the heap H starting at node R);
 |                 }
 |
 |             return (ItemToRemove);
25|        }
 |     }
```

Program Strategy 9.14 Removing an Item from a Heap

```
     |    void (Reheapify the heap *H starting at node N)
     |    {
     |        NodeType    N, M;
     |        ItemType    V1,V2;
  5  |
     |        (let V1 refer to N's value)
     |
     |        while (node N still has children)  {
 10  |
     |            (Let M be the child of node N having the larger value, V2)
     |
     |            if ( V1 ≥ V2 ) {
     |                return;
 15  |            } else {
     |                (exchange the values in nodes N and M);
     |                (let N refer to node M and let V1 refer to N's value);
     |            }
     |
 20  |        }
     |
     |    }
```

Program Strategy 9.15 Reheapifying a Heap Starting at Node N

```
     |    void Heapify(Heap *H)
     |    {
     |        NodeType    N;
     |
  5  |        for (N = the internal nodes of H in reverse level-order)  {
     |
     |            (Reheapify the heap H starting at node N);
     |
     |        }
 10  |
     |    }
```

Program Strategy 9.16 Heapifying a Complete Binary Tree

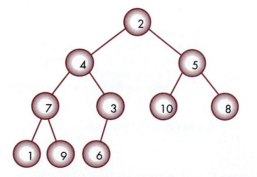

Figure 9.17 An Initial Complete Tree That Is Not a Heap

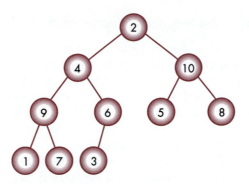

Figure 9.18 The Configuration After Three Exchanges

enumerate the internal nodes of Fig. 9.17 in reverse level order. The internal nodes in level order are the nodes containing the values 2, 4, 5, 7, and 3. Therefore, in reverse level order, the internal nodes are the nodes containing the values 3, 7, 5, 4, and 2.

Hence we start with the subtree in Fig. 9.17 rooted at the node containing 3. Since this node has a child containing a larger value 6, we exchange the 3 and the 6. Let's denote this exchange by the notation (3 ↔ 6). We next consider the subtree rooted at 7, and we exchange 7 with the larger of the values of its children, 9, using the exchange (7 ↔ 9). We then move up to the right end of the row above to consider the node containing 5. We exchange 5 with the larger of its children's values, 10, using the exchange (5 ↔ 10). Figure 9.18 illustrates the composite effect of these three exchanges (3 ↔ 6), (7 ↔ 9), and (5 ↔ 10).

performing exchanges

The next node to be considered in reverse level order contains the value 4. After exchanging 4 with the larger of its children's values, 9, using the exchange (4 ↔ 9), we must continue exchanging 4 with 7, using (4 ↔ 7) in order to reheapify the subtree rooted originally at the node containing 4. This yields the tree of Fig. 9.19.

Finally, we consider the root node, containing 2, which is the last node in reverse level order. Figure 9.19 requires only two more exchanges (2 ↔ 10) and (2 ↔ 8) to convert it to a heap. The heap that results is identical to the one we started with earlier in Figure 9.8 (before removing the root value 10 and reheapifying).

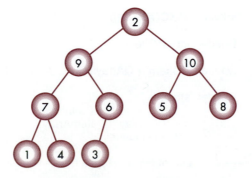

Figure 9.19 Almost Final Tree During Conversion to a Heap

Converting to the Sequential Representation

In the previous discussion, we performed operations on the nodes of binary trees without committing ourselves to a particular underlying tree representation, such as a sequential representation or a linked representation. Let's now see what happens when we represent heaps by the contiguous sequential representation of complete binary trees. A useful way to illustrate this is to provide a third implementation for the Priority Queue ADT, which was originally introduced in Section 4.3 of Chapter 4. (Recall that two other implementations for priority queues were presented in Section 4.3.)

Program 9.20 gives the type definitions for **PQItems** and **PriorityQueues** used by Program 9.21. These are similar to those given in Section 4.3 except that **PQArrays** contain an extra empty zeroth item.

Let's now define a C module that implements priority queues using heaps. Recall that we need to implement the following Priority Queue ADT operations: Initialize(&PQ), Empty(&PQ), Full(&PQ), Insert(PQItem,&PQ), and Remove(&PQ), (see Program 4.3 in Chapter 4). Program 9.21 uses the operations and relationships given in Table 9.7 to represent heaps in item arrays. The interface and implementation files defined in Program 9.21 can be substituted for the other priority queue modules that use the Priority Queue ADT in Section 4.3. For example, when this substitution is performed on Program 4.5, which defined a method for sorting using priority queues, a version of *heapsort* is obtained.

obtaining a version of heapsort

Heapsort is a sorting method that first converts an array of items to be sorted into a heap (using the **Heapify** algorithm given in Program Strategy 9.16), and then, treating the heap as a priority queue, removes items from the heap one by one (using the algorithm in the **Remove** function of Program 9.21) to arrange them in sorted order. While the variations of priority queue sorting studied in Section 4.3 worked in time

```
    |   /*
    |    *    The Priority Queue Types Header File "PQTypes.h"
    |    */
    |
 5  |   /* ------------< begin file "PQTypes.h" >------------    */
    |
    |
    |        #define MAXCOUNT 10
    |
10  |        typedef  int   PQItem;
    |
    |        typedef  PQItem  PQArray[MAXCOUNT + 1];
    |
    |        typedef  struct {
15  |                      int          Count;
    |                      PQArray      ItemArray;
    |                 } PriorityQueue;
    |
    |   /* ------------< end-of-file "PQTypes.h" >------------    */
```

Program 9.20 Priority Queue Types Header File for the Heap Representation

```
    /*  ------------< begin file "PQInterface.h" >------------     */

    #include "PQTypes.h"                /* defines types: PQItem and PriorityQueue */

    extern void Initialize(PriorityQueue *PQ);            /* sets PQ to be empty */
    extern int Empty(PriorityQueue *PQ);                  /* true if PQ is empty */
    extern int Full(PriorityQueue *PQ);                     /* true if PQ is full */
    extern void Insert(PQItem Item, PriorityQueue *PQ);    /* puts Item into PQ */
    extern PQItem Remove(PriorityQueue *PQ);            /* removes Item from PQ */

    /*  ------------< end-of-file "PQInterface.h" >------------     */

    /*  ------------< begin file "PQImplementation.c" >------------     */

    #include "PQInterface.h"

    /*-----------------------------------------------*/

        void Initialize(PriorityQueue *PQ)
        {
            PQ->Count = 0;
        }

    /*-----------------------------------------------*/

        int Empty(PriorityQueue *PQ)
        {
            return (PQ->Count == 0);
        }

    /*-----------------------------------------------*/

        int Full(PriorityQueue *PQ)
        {
            return (PQ->Count == MAXCOUNT);
        }

    /*-----------------------------------------------*/

        void Insert(PQItem Item, PriorityQueue *PQ)
        {
            int   ChildLoc;                          /* location of current child */
            int   ParentLoc;                        /* parent of current child */

            (PQ->Count)++;                          /* caution: insertion does not */
            ChildLoc = PQ->Count;                   /* guard against overflow */
            ParentLoc = ChildLoc/2;
```

Program 9.21 Implementation of Priority Queues Using Heaps (continued)

Program 9.21 Implementation of Priority Queues Using Heaps (continued)

```
50              while (ParentLoc != 0) {                    /* while a parent still exists */
                    if ( Item <= PQ–>ItemArray[ParentLoc] ) {
                        PQ–>ItemArray[ChildLoc] = Item;              /* store Item */
                        return;                                      /* and return */
                    } else {                    /* here, Item > PQ–>ItemArray[ParentLoc] */
55                      PQ–>ItemArray[ChildLoc] = PQ–>ItemArray[ParentLoc];
                        ChildLoc = ParentLoc;
                        ParentLoc = ParentLoc/2;
                    }
                }

60
                PQ–>ItemArray[ChildLoc] = Item;  /* Put Item in final resting place */

            }

65      /*-----------------------------------------------*/

        PQItem Remove(PriorityQueue *PQ)
        {
            int      CurrentLoc;              /* location currently being examined */
70          int      ChildLoc;                          /* a child of CurrentLoc */
            PQItem   ItemToPlace;              /* an Item value to relocate */
            PQItem   ItemToReturn;            /* the removed Item value to return */


75          if (Empty(PQ)) return;           /* result is undefined if PQ was empty */

            /* Initializations */
                ItemToReturn = PQ–>ItemArray[1];        /* value to return later */
                ItemToPlace = PQ–>ItemArray[PQ–>Count];/* last leaf's value */
80              (PQ–>Count) – –;                    /* delete last leaf in level order */
                CurrentLoc = 1;                         /* CurrentLoc starts at root */
                ChildLoc = 2*CurrentLoc;  /* ChildLoc starts at root's left child */


85          while (ChildLoc <= PQ–>Count) {          /* while a child still exists */

                /* Set ChildLoc to location of larger child of CurrentLoc */
                    if (ChildLoc < PQ–>Count) {          /* if right child exists */
                        if ( PQ–>ItemArray[ChildLoc+1] >
90                              PQ–>ItemArray[ChildLoc]) {
                            ChildLoc++;
                        }
                    }
95
```

Program 9.21 Implementation of Priority Queues Using Heaps (continued)

```
    |                        /* If item at ChildLoc is larger than ItemToPlace, */
    |                        /* move this larger item to CurrentLoc, and move */
    |                        /* CurrentLoc down. */
    |                            if (PQ–>ItemArray[ChildLoc] <= ItemToPlace) {
100 |                                PQ–>ItemArray[CurrentLoc] = ItemToPlace;
    |                                return (ItemToReturn);
    |                            } else {
    |                                PQ–>ItemArray[CurrentLoc]=PQ–>ItemArray[ChildLoc];
    |                                CurrentLoc = ChildLoc;
105 |                                ChildLoc = 2 * CurrentLoc;
    |                            }
    |                    }
    |
    |                    /* final placement of ItemToPlace */
110 |                        PQ–>ItemArray[CurrentLoc] = ItemToPlace;
    |
    |                    /* return the Item originally at the root */
    |                        return (ItemToReturn);
    |                }
115 |
    |        /*------------------------------------------------*/
    |
    |        /*  ------------< end-of-file "PQImplementation.c" >------------   */
```

O(n^2), it can be shown that heapsort does better, by working in time O($n \log n$). The efficiency of heapsort is studied in Chapter 13, which covers sorting.

It is worth mentioning that a subtle optimization was used in implementing the **Remove** function in Program 9.21—one that was not used in Program Strategy 9.14 for removing an item from a heap. You might have noticed, while studying the examples in Figs. 9.8 through 9.13, which show how to restore the heap property after removing the item at the root, that the value 3 was repeatedly exchanged with the larger values 9, 7, and 4 in child nodes as the value 3 was moved downward toward its final resting place. Instead of doing pairwise exchanges of values to accomplish this motion, we could instead have moved the values 9, 7, and 4 upward, while making a hole at the bottom for the final resting place in which to store 3. The **Remove** function in Program 9.21 uses this more efficient latter strategy (which amounts to a cyclical shift) instead of using less efficient pairwise exchanges. The **Insert** procedure in Program 9.21 uses a similar strategy for the upward motion of a new item being inserted in a heap.

a subtle optimization

A Few Mathematical Facts About Heaps**

Suppose we have a heap containing *n* items. We might inquire how much time it takes to establish the heap property in the sequential heap representation, starting with an initially unorganized array of *n* items, and how much time it takes to insert and remove heap items. Let's start by studying the times for removal and insertion first.

We know that to remove an item from a heap, H, we must delete the last leaf, L, in level order, and then reheapify the tree that results from replacing the root's value with L's value, V. During this reheapification process we repeatedly exchange the value V with the larger of the values of the children nodes on some path from the root downward toward V's final resting place. The longest possible path for these pairwise exchanges is a path from the root to some leaf on the bottommost row of H. To determine the worst case time for item removal, we need to determine the length of a path from the root to any of the leaves on the bottommost row of H.

the worst case times for
item removal and insertion

Assuming that H has n items in it when we reheapify it after removal of the root value, we need to calculate the level number of the bottom row in H. This will be the length of the longest path from the root to a bottom leaf in H, and it will also give the number of pairwise exchanges needed to move V to the bottom row of H during reheapification. If you make a table in which you draw complete binary trees of n nodes (for $n \geq 1$) and you write down the level number of the bottom row of each tree, you will be able to conclude that the level number of the bottom row of H is always given by $\lfloor \lg n \rfloor$. Consequently, removal of an item from a heap, using the process given in Program Strategy 9.14, requires time $O(\log n)$.

Since insertion of a new heap item can cause pairwise exchanges of node values to occur along a path from a leaf in the bottom row upward all the way to the root, similar considerations allow us to conclude that the worst case time for insertion of a new value into a heap takes time $O(\log n)$ also.

the cost of making a heap

We now turn to the problem of calculating the cost of making a heap out of an initially unorganized complete tree of items, using the heapification process given in Program Strategy 9.16. Suppose the tree we are considering has l levels. Figure 9.22 illustrates such a tree in which the nodes have been numbered in level order. An item in a node at level i could be exchanged with children along any downward path at most $(l - i)$ times before coming to rest—since, in the worst case, it would come to rest in a leaf at the bottommost level l. Now note that Fig. 9.22 contains 2^i nodes on

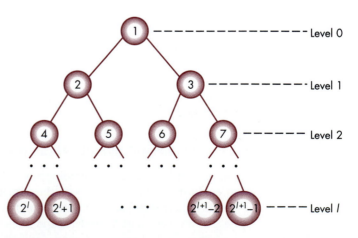

Figure 9.22 Node Numbers in Level Order in a Complete Binary Tree

level i. For example, there is $2^0 = 1$ node on level 0. There are $2^1 = 2$ nodes on level 1. There are $2^2 = 4$ nodes on level 2, and so forth. Since each of the 2^i nodes on level i could be exchanged downward at most $(l - i)$ times, the cost of processing the nodes on level i is at most $(l - i) * 2^i$. Consequently, the total number of exchanges needed to apply the heapifying process to all nodes on all levels except the bottom level could not exceed the sum, S, obtained by adding the costs for levels $0{:}l - 1$ as follows:

$$S = \sum_{i=0}^{(l-1)} (l-i) * 2^i.$$

By exchanging $(l - i)$ and i, the sum S can be rewritten as:

$$S = \sum_{i=1}^{l} i * 2^{(l-i)}.$$

In the latter sum, we can factor out 2^l, leaving us with:

$$S = 2^l * \sum_{i=1}^{l} \frac{i}{2^i}.$$

It can be shown that

$$\sum_{i=1}^{l} \frac{i}{2^i} < 2$$

(see Exercise 9.5.4). Hence, $S < 2^{(l + 1)}$. Now, if n is any number of nodes sufficient for at least one node to reside on level l, then n lies in the range $2^l \le n \le 2^{(l + 1)} - 1$. But $2^l \le n$ implies that $2^{(l + 1)} \le 2n$. Putting these facts together, we see that:

$$S < 2\,n.$$

heapifying can be done in linear time

In other words, it takes at most $O(n)$ pairwise exchanges of values to convert an unorganized complete binary tree into a heap. Since the time to heapify a complete tree is dominated by the time to perform these exchanges, we conclude that it is possible to heapify a complete tree in time $O(n)$.

This is a significant finding. It implies that we can heapify an array of values in *linear time*, using the contiguous sequential representation of complete binary trees.

Let's combine the facts we have discovered with the facts we already know about the running times of priority queue operations for the other two representations we studied in Section 4.3. The results are presented as Table 9.23. We see that the heap representation for a priority queue does not have the worst running time in any row of the table. Moreover, since a heap can be initialized in linear time and subsequently can accommodate insertions and deletions in logarithmic time, it is a potentially

Priority Queue Operation	Heap Representation	Sorted List Representation	Unsorted Array Representation
Organize a priority queue	$O(n)$	$O(n^2)$	$O(1)$
Remove highest priority item	$O(\log n)$	$O(1)$	$O(n)$
Insert a new item	$O(\log n)$	$O(n)$	$O(1)$

Table 9.23 Comparing Running Times of Priority Queue Operations for Three Representations

superior representation for priority queues, possessing good performance characteristics. The facts summarized here will come in handy in Chapter 13 when we analyze the running time for **HeapSort**.

9.5 Review Questions

1. Give the definition of a heap as it is used in this section (not as it is discussed in Chapter 8 in connection with dynamic memory allocation).
2. How can a heap be used to represent a priority queue? Discuss how to perform the operations of item insertion and removal in heaps used to represent priority queues?
3. How do you go about organizing the items in an initially unorganized complete binary tree into a heap? How long does it take to do this efficiently?
4. How long does it take to insert and remove items from a heap containing n items?

9.5 Exercises

1. Prove that if H is a heap, its largest value must be found at the root of H. [*Hint:* Consider what would happen if the largest value were in some node, N, other than the root. In this case N's parent would have a smaller value than N's value. Could the heap property then hold true for H?]
2. Let H be a heap with n nodes in it. How many of these nodes are internal nodes? How many are leaf nodes?
3. Give a refinement of Program Strategy 9.16 as it applies to the contiguous sequential representation of heaps. Apply the for-statement on lines 5:9 of Program Strategy 9.16 only to the internal nodes of the array containing the heap items, using a decreasing sequence of values (for (N = U; N >= 1; – – N)) whose initial value U is determined by the answer to Exercise 2.
4. Prove that

$$\sum_{i=1}^{l} \frac{i}{2^i} < 2.$$

[*Hint*: Write each of the terms $i/2^i$ vertically beneath one another, and expand each one into a row of i copies of $1/2^i$. Now add up each column, using the formula for the sum of a geometric progression. The sums of the respective columns in left-to-right order are no more than 1, 1/2, 1/4, 1/8, etc., and the sum of these is no more than 2.]

5. Demonstrate that Program 9.21 can be used interchangeably to implement priority queues by invoking it in Program 4.5 and executing Program 4.5 to perform priority queue sorting. Measure the running times for arrays of different sizes, and compare them to the corresponding running times for the use of the sorted list and unsorted array representations of priority queues. What do you conclude about the relative efficiencies of these three representations for this task?

9.6 Traversing Binary Trees

Learning Objectives

1. To learn about four types of traversal orders commonly applied to the nodes of binary trees.
2. To understand how to write programs to perform these traversals on the linked representation of binary trees.
3. To learn how stacks and queues can be used to perform nonrecursive traversals of linked binary tree representations.

Expression trees are binary trees used to represent algebraic expressions formed with binary operators. For example, Fig. 9.24 gives the expression tree corresponding to the algebraic expression, $(b\verb|^|2 - 4*a*c)/(2*a)$.

In Figure 9.24, we have used the caret operator (^) to indicate exponentiation (meaning that $b\verb|^|2$ stands for b^2), and we have assumed that the normal operator precedence rules for algebraic expressions have been used. In particular, in the

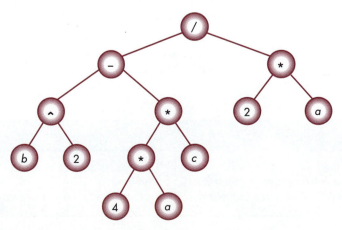

Figure 9.24 The Expression Tree for $(b\verb|^|2 - 4 * a * c) / (2 * a)$

using operator
precedence rules to form
expression trees

absence of parentheses to indicate otherwise, we assume exponentiation ($\wedge$) is performed before multiplication and division ($*$ and $/$), which are, in turn, performed before addition and subtraction ($+$ and $-$). Moreover, among operators of equal precedence, such as ($+$ and $-$) or ($*$ and $/$), we assume association is to the left, so that $4 * a * c$ means $((4 * a) * c)$. Here, we performed the left multiplication $(4 * a)$ first. Similarly, had we not put parentheses around the denominator $(2 * a)$ to indicate multiplication was to be performed with 2 and a, and had we casually written: $(b\wedge 2 - 4 * a * c) / 2 * a$, it would have signified the same as $((b\wedge 2 - 4 * a * c) / 2) * a$, since, by the left association rule, any expression of the form $x / y * z$ signifies, $((x / y) * z)$, and not $(x / (y * z))$.

Using various parsing algorithms, it is possible to read in an algebraic expression expressed in linear form as a string of characters, and to parse the expression to determine the boundaries of its various subexpressions according to the rules of operator precedence. An intermediate expression representation, called a parse tree, can then be constructed to represent the results of parsing the input expression. An expression tree is one of the forms that such a parse tree could take. Such expression trees can then be converted into assembly code by code generators, or they can be converted to postfix instructions for interpretation by postfix interpreters.

In this section, we explore some traversal techniques for visiting the nodes of a binary tree, which can be used, among other purposes, for conversion of expression trees into postfix or prefix operation code sequences.

A traversal of a tree is a process that visits each node in the tree exactly once in some particular order. Three popular traversal orders for binary trees are *PreOrder*, *InOrder*, and *PostOrder*. Table 9.25 defines how to traverse the nodes of a binary tree in each of these three orders. Let's assume that each node of an expression tree contains a single character, and that what it means to *visit a node* in such a tree is to print the character contained in that node.

three traversal orders

Let's take a simple case first. Consider the expression tree in Fig. 9.26 for the expression $(a - b)$.

If we perform the three traversals of Table 9.25 on the expression tree in Fig. 9.26, we get the following results:

PreOrder:	$- a\, b$
InOrder:	$a - b$
PostOrder:	$a\, b -$

PreOrder	InOrder	PostOrder
Visit the root Traverse left subtree in PreOrder Traverse right subtree in PreOrder	Traverse left subtree in InOrder Visit the root Traverse right subtree in InOrder	Traverse left subtree in PostOrder Traverse right subtree in PostOrder Visit the root

Table 9.25 Traversal Orders for Binary Trees

Figure 9.26 Expression Tree for (*a* − *b*)

If we perform the three traversals of Table 9.25 on the somewhat more complicated expression tree of Figure 9.24, we get the following results:

PreOrder: $/ - \wedge b\, 2 * * 4\, a\, c * 2\, a$
InOrder: $b \wedge 2 - 4 * a * c / 2 * a$
PostOrder: $b\, 2 \wedge 4\, a * c * - 2\, a * /$

Using the postorder traversal of an expression tree gives us the postfix string representing the original expression. If we have a postfix interpreter, such as the one given in Program 7.7 in Chapter 7, we can evaluate the postfix string to obtain its value.

A common strategy used in early language processors was to parse the input into an expression tree and then to convert the expression tree into a postfix operator expression sequence suitable for subsequent interpretation by a run-time interpreter.

Traversals Using the Linked Representation of Binary Trees

A convenient representation of binary trees to use in connection with traversal algorithms is the *linked representation* of binary trees. We first discussed this representation in Section 2.6 in Chapter 2 and illustrated it in Fig. 2.23.

To declare the types for tree nodes to use in linked binary tree representations of expression trees, we can provide a C **typedef** such as the following:

```
typedef  struct NodeTag {
            char            Symbol;
            struct NodeTag  *LLink;
            struct NodeTag  *RLink;
         } TreeNode;
```

Here, the **LLink** and **RLink** members of a **TreeNode** contain pointers to the respective left and right subtrees of a node. If a subtree is empty, its corresponding node pointer is **NULL**. For example, Fig. 9.27 shows both the expression tree for the expression ($x - y + z$), and its linked representation using the **TreeNodes** defined above.

It is easy to write a general recursive function to perform traversals in the various traversal orders given in Table 9.25, starting with the linked representation of binary trees. In order to make the function general, we first define an enumeration for three symbolic constants, giving names for the three traversal orders. We then use a second parameter in the general traversal procedure to specify which traversal order to use.

a general recursive traversal function

```
typedef enum {PreOrder, InOrder, PostOrder} OrderOfTraversal;
```

Program 9.28 gives the general recursive function for visiting nodes of a linked representation of a binary tree, where the second parameter is a symbolic enumeration constant specifying the particular traversal order to be followed.

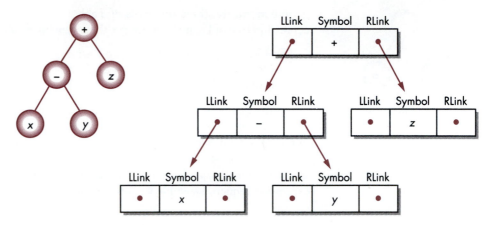

Figure 9.27 An Expression Tree and Its Linked Representation

```
  |    void Traverse(TreeNode *T, OrderOfTraversal TraversalOrder)
  |    {
  |        /* to visit T's nodes in the order specified by the */
  |        /* TraversalOrder parameter */
5 |
  |        if (T != NULL) {                              /* if T == NULL, do nothing */
  |
  |            if ( TraversalOrder == PreOrder ) {
  |
10|                Visit(T);
  |                Traverse(T–>LLink,PreOrder);
  |                Traverse(T–>RLink,PreOrder);
  |
  |            } else if ( TraversalOrder == InOrder ) {
15|
  |                Traverse(T–>LLink,InOrder);
  |                Visit(T);
  |                Traverse(T–>RLink,InOrder);
  |
20|            } else if ( TraversalOrder == PostOrder ) {
  |
  |                Traverse(T–>LLink,PostOrder);
  |                Traverse(T–>RLink,PostOrder);
  |                Visit(T);
25|            }
  |        }
  |    }
```

Program 9.28 Generalized Recursive Traversal Function[1]

---

[1] A powerful generalization of Program 9.28 results from passing a pointer to the **Visit** function as an additional parameter to **Traverse**.

```
    |    #include <stdio.h>
    |    #include "StackInterface.h"                    /* to use the operations of */
    |                                                   /* Program 7.3 in Chapter 7 */
    |    void PreOrderTraversal(TreeNode *T)
  5 |    {
    |        Stack  S;
    |        TreeNode  *N;
    |
    |        InitializeStack(&S);              /* initialize the stack S to be the empty stack */
 10 |        Push(T,&S);                                 /* push the pointer T onto stack S */
    |
    |        while ( !Empty(&S) ) {
    |
    |            Pop(&S,&N);                             /* pop top pointer of S into N */
 15 |
    |            if (N != NULL) {
    |                printf("%c", N–>Symbol);            /* when visiting N, print its symbol */
    |                Push(N–>RLink,&S);                  /* push right pointer onto S */
    |                Push(N–>LLink,&S);                  /* push left pointer onto S */
 20 |            }
    |
    |        }
    |    }
```

Program 9.29 PreOrder Traversal of an Expression Tree Using a Stack

using stacks for nonrecursive traversals

Using the Stack ADT and using the linked representation of binary trees, we can write nonrecursive traversal functions in which a stack is used to hold pointers to subtrees awaiting further traversal. For example, Program 9.29 uses a stack to perform an iterative preorder traversal of an expression tree, writing out the symbols in the nodes as it visits each node in preorder.

using stacks to hold postponed obligations

We can view the stack, **S**, in Program 9.29 as being used to hold *postponed obligations* for further processing. During the preorder traversal process, when we come to each node, **N**, we first print the symbol in node **N**. Next, we stack first the right link of **N** and then the left link of **N**. The stack now holds two postponed obligations to process first the left subtree of **N** and later the right subtree of node **N**. Since we pushed **N**'s right link first and its left link second, the left link will be processed before the right link (since stacks always use the *last-in-first-out* order of processing).

Now suppose we change the type of container used to hold the postponed obligations for further processing, by using a queue instead of a stack. Suppose that after visiting a node, **N**, and printing its symbol, we insert its left and right links (in that order) into a queue, **Q**. Now **Q** holds postponed obligations to process the left and right subtrees. When we remove pointers from **Q** and process the non-null ones, we first print the symbols in the nodes referenced by the pointers, and then we insert the left and right links of these nodes on the rear of **Q**. What happens when we do this is that we print the symbols in the nodes of the original tree in level order. Program 9.30 gives an explicit example of this process for printing the symbols in expression

```
   |   #include <stdio.h>
   |   #include "QueueInterface.h"          /* to use the operations of Program 7.4 */
   |
   |   void LevelOrderTraversal(TreeNode *T)
 5 |   {
   |       Queue Q; TreeNode *N;
   |
   |       InitializeQueue(&Q);        /* initialize the queue Q to be the empty queue */
   |       Insert(T,&Q);                         /* insert the pointer T into queue Q */
10 |       while ( ! Empty(&Q) ) {
   |           Remove(&Q,&N);          /* remove first pointer of Q and put it into N */
   |           if (N != NULL ) {
   |               printf("%c",N–>Symbol);
   |               Insert(N–>LLink,&Q);            /* insert left pointer on rear of Q */
15 |               Insert(N–>RLink,&Q);           /* insert right pointer on rear of Q */
   |           }
   |       }
   |   }
```

Program 9.30 LevelOrder Binary Tree Traversal Using Queues

trees in level order. For example, the level order traversal of the linked representation of the binary expression tree given in Figure 9.24 is: $/ - * \wedge * 2\, a\, b\, 2 * c\, 4\, a$.

9.6 Review Questions

1. What are the names for three traversal orders of binary trees given in Table 9.25?
2. How do you define these three traversal orders?
3. Is a level order traversal of a binary tree equivalent to any of the three traversal orders given in Table 9.25? If so, which one is it? If not, why not?
4. Describe how stacks and queues can be used to define nonrecursive binary tree traversals. What different kinds of traversals can be defined naturally using stacks and queues?

9.6 Exercises

1. Give the PreOrder, InOrder, PostOrder, and LevelOrder traversals of the nodes in the tree of Figure 9.2.
2. Construct the expression tree whose PostOrder traversal is $a\, 2 \wedge 2\, a * b * - b\, 2 \wedge + a\, b - /$.
3. Write a program to construct an expression tree, given a character string specifying its preorder traversal.
4. Given an expression tree, T, write a program to print the infix expression corresponding to T in which parentheses are printed only when required by operator precedence or right associativity among operators of equal precedence. For example, if T is the expression tree corresponding to $((a * (b + c)) * d)$, your program should print: $a * (b + c) * d$. If T is the expression tree corresponding to $((b \wedge 2) / (2*a))$, your program should print: $b^\wedge 2 / (2*a)$.

9.7 Binary Search Trees

1. To learn how to search for a key K in a binary search tree.
2. To learn what shapes binary search trees must take to yield the best and worst search performance.
3. To learn how binary search trees perform in the average case.

the binary search tree property

In Chapter 2, we briefly introduced the linked representation of binary trees (see Fig. 2.23). In a *binary search tree*, a node N with key K is inserted so that the keys in the left subtree of N are less than K, and such that the keys in the right subtree of N are greater than K. To summarize, for each node N in a binary search tree:

Keys in left subtree of N < Key K in node N < Keys in right subtree of N.

We assume it is possible to compare any two keys K_1 and K_2 and to determine which one of the following three possible relations holds: $K_1 < K_2$, $K_1 == K_2$, or $K_1 > K_2$. Since numerical and alphabetical order have this property, we can use numerical keys compared in numerical order or alphabetic keys compared in alphabetical order.

how to search for a key

To search for a key, K, in a binary search tree, T, we compare K to the key, K_r, in the root of T. If $K == K_r$, the search terminates successfully. If $K < K_r$, the search continues in the left subtree of T, and if $K > K_r$, the search continues in the right subtree of T. If T is the empty tree, the search fails.

For example, to search for the key ORD in the binary search tree of Fig. 9.31, we compare the search key ORD to the key ORY in the root. Since ORD < ORY, we continue searching in the left subtree of the root. ORD is next compared to JFK. Since ORD > JFK, the search continues in the right subtree of JFK. Since ORD > MEX, the search continues in the right subtree of MEX. Finally, ORD

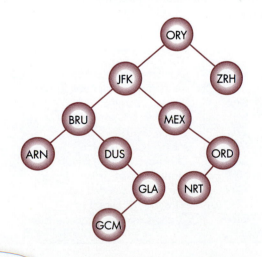

Figure 9.31 A Binary Search Tree

matches the key in the root of the right subtree of MEX, so the search terminates successfully.

If we search the tree of Fig. 9.31 for the key DCA (the airport code for Washington, D.C.'s National Airport), the search fails and we conclude DCA is not present, since the search path traced out by the comparisons DCA < ORY, DCA < JFK, DCA > BRU, and DCA < DUS leads to the empty left subtree of DUS. If we insert a new node for DCA as the left subtree of DUS, we obtain a new binary search tree of twelve nodes. In fact, the binary search tree of Fig. 9.31 was built up in this fashion by inserting the airport codes of Table 9.32 in top-to-bottom order, starting with an empty tree. Thus, ORY was considered first and was placed at the root of a new binary search tree. JFK was considered second and was inserted as the new left subtree of ORY. BRU was considered third and was inserted as the new left subtree of JFK. DUS was considered fourth and was inserted as the new right subtree of BRU. ZRH was considered fifth and was inserted as the new right subtree of the root ORY, and so on. This is called the *insertion method*.

using failed searches to locate insertion points

the insertion method

Analyzing Performance Characteristics**

determining performance advantages

Binary search trees are interesting, in part, because they yield important performance advantages. It will turn out that searching for keys takes logarithmic time in a tree of n keys, provided the tree is balanced, but that it takes linear time if the tree is deep and skinny. We can gain more precise insight into the nature of these phenomena by performing a little mathematical analysis.

the best, worst, and average cases

To get a handle on the issues, we will try to develop formulas for the number of comparisons needed to locate keys in a binary search tree in the *best case*, the *worst case*, and the *average case*. Moreover, we will assume that each of the keys in a binary search tree is equally likely to be chosen for use in a successful search. Furthermore, we will assume that the binary trees used to characterize the "average" binary search tree of n nodes were chosen with equal likelihood from the set of all trees constructed using the insertion method, by inserting keys $K_1, K_2, \ldots, K_n$ in each of their possible different orders.

Table 9.32 Airport Codes Used to Construct Fig. 9.31

1.	ORY	Orly Field, Paris, France
2.	JFK	Kennedy Airport, New York
3.	BRU	Brussels, Belgium
4.	DUS	Düsseldorf, Germany
5.	ZRH	Zürich, Switzerland
6.	MEX	Mexico City, Mexico
7.	ORD	O'Hare, Chicago, Illinois
8.	NRT	Narita Airport, Tokyo, Japan
9.	ARN	Stockholm, Sweden
10.	GLA	Glasgow, Scotland
11.	GCM	Grand Cayman, Cayman Islands

(*Review:* Different orderings of keys are called *permutations*. For example, there are six different permutations of the keys K_1, K_2, and K_3. These are $K_1 K_2 K_3$, $K_1 K_3 K_2$, $K_2 K_1 K_3$, $K_2 K_3 K_1$, $K_3 K_1 K_2$, and $K_3 K_2 K_1$. In general, the n keys, $K_1 : K_n$, have $n!$ different permutations, where $n!$ signifies the factorial of n. Thus the "average" tree containing n keys that we shall consider is an average one chosen from the population of all trees constructed by taking each distinct permutation of n keys and building up a tree using the insertion method by inserting the keys into the empty tree in the order given by the permutation.)

counting comparisons

Now suppose we want to count the comparisons used by a binary tree searching program. The work needed to find a particular key, K, in a binary search tree, T, could be measured by counting the number of comparisons needed to locate K in T. If K is located at level l in T, the number of comparisons is just $C = 2*l + 1$. (Recall: The level l containing key K is the length of the path from the root of tree T to the node containing K. For example, the level l containing the key ORD in Fig. 9.31 is $l = 3$, since the length of the path from the root node ORY to the node containing ORD is 3. Also recall that length of a path is the number of edges in it. There are three separate edges in the path from ORY to ORD in Fig. 9.31.) Accordingly, $C = 7$ comparisons are needed to find ORD in Fig. 9.31, since substituting $l = 3$ in the formula $C = 2*l + 1$ yields $7 = 2*3 + 1$.

the distinction between comparisons and decisions

You might initially think that only *four* comparisons are needed to locate ORD in Fig. 9.31 since there are four decisions needed to trace out the search path from the root containing ORY to the node containing ORD. These four decisions are (ORD < ORY), (ORD > JFK), (ORD > MEX) and (ORD = ORD). However, the binary search algorithm performing these comparisons always first tests a key K to see if it is *equal* to the key K_i in a node N_i, and only if $K \neq K_i$, does the algorithm perform the further test $K < K_i$ in order to decide whether to search further in the left or right subtree of node N_i. This implies that it takes one comparison ($K = K_i$) to find key K at node N_i, but that it takes two comparisons to decide whether to search further in the left or right subtree of N_i. Consequently, the number of comparisons needed to find a key successfully at level l is $2*l + 1$, since it takes one comparison to locate K on level l, and $2*l$ comparisons to descend from the root to the node containing K.

the internal path length

What these observations reveal is that the length, l, of the path from the root to a given node, N, provides a number from which we can calculate the actual number of comparisons used. If we are trying to calculate the *average* number of comparisons used to locate a key, K, in binary search tree T, (where keys are chosen with equal likelihood), it is convenient to define a quantity, I, called the *internal path length* of the tree T. The internal path length is just the sum of all of the path lengths to the individual nodes in T. For example, the internal path length of the tree in Fig. 9.31 is $I = 28$, since:

$$28 = (0 + 1 + 1 + 2 + 2 + 3 + 3 + 3 + 4 + 4 + 5).$$

the average number of comparisons in a successful search

If search for each of the keys, K, in a binary search tree of n nodes is equally likely, and if I is the internal path length of the tree, then the number of comparisons required by an average successful search is $C_n = (2*I + n) / n$. For example, the average number of comparisons used in a search for a key K in Fig. 9.31 is $(2*28 + 11)/11 = 67/11 = 6.09$.

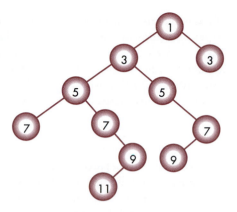

Figure 9.33 Comparisons Needed to
Locate Keys in Nodes of Fig. 9.31

Figure 9.33 is a version of Fig. 9.31 in which each node contains the number of comparisons needed to find the key in that node. There are eleven nodes in Fig. 9.33. By adding up numbers of comparisons in all of the nodes of this figure ($1 + 3 + 3 + 5 + 5 + 7 + 7 + 7 + 9 + 9 + 11 = 67$) and dividing by 11 ($67/11 = 6.09$), we confirm that the average number of comparisons needed in binary searching of Figure 9.31 is 6.09.

external path lengths

For unsuccessful searches, it turns out to be convenient to examine properties of the extended binary trees we defined earlier (as illustrated in Fig. 9.3). The extended binary tree corresponding to the binary search tree of Figure 9.31 is shown in Fig. 9.34. Recall that the square boxes (□) explicitly indicate the empty subtrees in an extended binary tree. We can now define the *external path length*, E, of an extended binary tree to be the sum of the path lengths from the root to each of the square boxes. Thus the external path length of the tree in Fig. 9.34 is $E = 50$, since

$$50 = (4 + 4 + 4 + 6 + 6 + 5 + 3 + 5 + 5 + 4 + 2 + 2).$$

average comparisons used in unsuccessful searches

If an unsuccessful search for a key K occurs in an extended binary tree, T, then the search lands in one of the square boxes of the extended tree. Moreover, if a particular

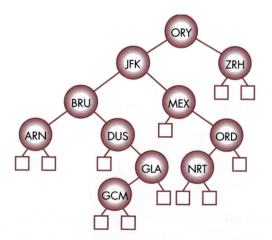

Figure 9.34 Extended Binary
Search Tree

box is at level l in the extended tree, it takes exactly $2*l$ comparisons to determine that the search is unsuccessful. If the extended tree, T, has n internal nodes, then it has $(n + 1)$ boxes as leaves (see the answer to Exercise 9.3.1 for the reason why the number of leaves is always one greater than the number of internal nodes.) Therefore, if each of the boxes in T is an equally likely target for an unsuccessful search, then the total number of comparisons required for an average unsuccessful search is $C'_n = 2*E/(n + 1)$. For example, an average unsuccessful search of the tree in Fig. 9.34 requires $C'_n = 2*50/12 = 100/12 = 8.33$ comparisons.

There is a useful relationship between the internal and external path lengths of a binary tree that we shall need to use in a moment in order to calculate the average number of comparisons needed for searching. This is given by Eq. 9.1. Let T be a binary tree with n internal nodes. Then,

$$E = I + 2n. \tag{9.1}$$

Relationship Between Internal and External Path Lengths

This formula can be proved by induction, starting with an empty tree ($\square$). (Exercise 9.7.5 asks you to provide this proof.)

Now, we are ready to ask, "What are the shapes of binary trees having minimum and maximum average search times, assuming each key in the tree is equally likely to be chosen?"

The Best Case

It can be proven that an extended binary search tree of n nodes can have a minimum internal path length only if its leaves ($\square$) are on at most two adjacent levels. Figure 9.35 illustrates some shapes of trees having minimal internal path lengths. Two of these (the first and the third) are complete binary trees, since all the leaves on the bottommost row of trees 1 and 3 are in the leftmost possible positions. However, binary tree 2 is not a complete tree, even though its leaves are on two adjacent levels. The minimal internal path lengths of trees of n nodes, such as those shown in this figure, are calculated by taking the sum of the floors of the base-2 logarithms of the integers from 1 to n. If you assign an integer to each node giving its position in level order in such a tree, the root node is numbered 1, the nodes on the next level are numbered 2 and 3, the nodes on the next level are numbered 4, 5, 6, and 7, and so on. Figure 9.22, given earlier, illustrates this numbering system for a complete binary tree. The path length, l, from the root to node i in this ordering is just the floor of the base two logarithm of i, $l = \lfloor \lg i \rfloor$. Study the numbers in Table 9.36 to see why the path lengths to each node i in level order are given by $\lfloor \lg i \rfloor$.

If we could find a way to calculate the sum of the floors of the base-2 logarithms of the numbers from 1 to n,

$$L_n = \sum_{i=1}^{n} \left\lfloor \lg i \right\rfloor,$$

tree shapes that minimize path lengths

calculating minimal path lengths

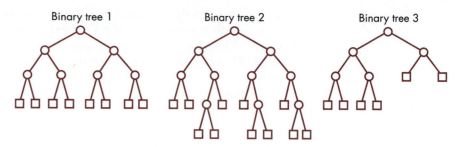

Figure 9.35 Some Tree Shapes with Minimum Internal Path Lengths

we would have a formula for the internal path length, I, that we are seeking. Unfortunately, finding a formula for L_n requires techniques beyond the scope of this book. However, this sum is known to be given by Eq. 9.2.

$$L_n = \sum_{i=1}^{n}\left\lfloor \lg i \right\rfloor = (n+1)q - 2^{(q+1)} + 2, \text{ where } q = \left\lfloor \lg(n+1) \right\rfloor \qquad (9.2)$$

Sum of the Floors of the Base-2 Logarithms

approximating the best case

Hence, in the best case, the average number of comparisons needed in a successful search of a binary search tree, T, of n nodes, is given by $C_n = (2*L_n + n)/n$, which can be approximated, for large n, by

$$C_n = (2*L_n + n)/n \approx 2\left(1 + \frac{1}{n}\right)\lg(n+1) - 3 \approx 2\lg n - 3. \qquad (9.3)$$

The Worst Case

maximum internal path lengths

The maximum internal path length is exhibited by trees that are as deep and skinny as possible. It can be proven that any tree with exactly one internal node on each

i	$\lg i$	$\lfloor \lg i \rfloor$
1	0.000	0
2	1.000	1
3	1.585	1
4	2.000	2
5	2.322	2
6	2.585	2
7	2.807	2
8	3.000	3
9	3.170	3

Table 9.36 The Relationship Between the ith Node in Level Order and the Length of the Path from the Root to Node i

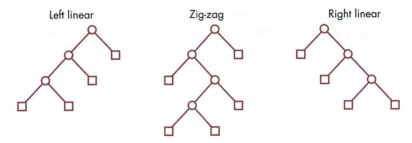

Figure 9.37 Some Tree Shapes with Maximum Internal Path Lengths

level has a maximum possible internal path length. Figure 9.37 illustrates three trees that maximize internal path length, each having exactly one internal node on each level. The internal path length for any such tree having n internal nodes takes the form $I = (0 + 1 + 2 + \ldots + (n-1))$.

Thus $I = n(n-1)/2$, from which we can observe that the average number of comparisons needed to locate keys successfully in binary search trees of the worst possible shape, takes the simple form, $C_n = n$, as illustrated in Eq. 9.4:

$$C_n = (2I + n)/n = \left(\frac{2n(n-1)/2 + n}{n}\right) = n. \tag{9.4}$$

The Average Case

Now for the challenging case. What happens in the average case with equally likely choice of each tree in the set of binary search trees built-up using all the different permutations of n keys, and with equally likely choice of each of the search keys in such a tree?

defining what "average" means

In what follows, C_n stands for the average number of comparisons required for a *successful* search in such an average tree, and C'_n stands for the average number of comparisons used in an *unsuccessful* search in such an average tree.

We already know the following three facts:

$$E = I + 2n$$

$$C_n = \frac{2I + n}{n}$$

$$C'_n = \frac{2E}{(n+1)}$$

Putting these facts together, we can solve for a relation between C_n and C'_n as follows:

$$C'_n = \left(\frac{n}{n+1}\right)(C_n + 3). \tag{9.5}$$

It turns out to be convenient to consider what happens in the case of unsuccessful searching in order to develop a recurrence relation that yields the formula for the average number of comparisons that we are seeking.

In particular, we argue as follows. Suppose we have an average binary search tree, T, of n nodes. For this tree, we know that C'_n gives the average number of comparisons required in an unsuccessful search. How can we develop the formula for C'_{n+1}? Suppose we insert another new key into tree T. We do so by replacing an empty tree (□) at average depth with a new nonempty internal node having two empty subtrees (♣). The new tree has $(n + 1)$ nodes. Now, what changed?

1. We replaced one box (□) which cost C'_n comparisons to reach. Thus C'_n comparisons must be subtracted from the original number $(n+1)C'_n$ required to reach all of the $(n+1)$ boxes in the original tree. This leaves $n\,C'_n$ comparisons.
2. Then we added two new boxes as children of the new internal node that replaced the box we just subtracted. It takes two more comparisons to reach each of these two new boxes than it did to reach the box that got replaced. So we must add $2 + C'_n$ comparisons to reach each of these two new boxes for an additional contribution of $2(2 + C'_n)$ comparisons.
3. Now we need to add up all the comparisons needed to reach all of the boxes in this new tree with $(n + 2)$ boxes, and we need to divide this total by $(n + 2)$ to get the average number of comparisons for the unsuccessful search, C'_{n+1}. This yields,

$$C'_{n+1} = \frac{nC'_n + 2(2 + C'_n)}{n+2}.$$

A little simplification of this latter formula yields the following recurrence relation:

$$C'_{n+1} = C'_n + \frac{4}{n+2}.$$

By substituting $(n - 1)$ for n in this latter result, and also noting that $C'_1 = 2$, we can obtain a useful form of the recurrence relations for C'_n which we seek. These are as follows:

$$C'_1 = 2$$

$$C'_n = C'_{n-1} + \frac{4}{n+1}.$$
(9.6)

Recurrence Relations

Using the technique of unrolling these recurrence relations, we can expand the formula for C'_n as follows:

$$C'_n = \frac{4}{n+1} + \frac{4}{n} + \frac{4}{n-1} + \dots + \frac{4}{3} + C'_1$$

Using the fact that $C_1' = 2$, and adding and subtracting the quantity $(4/2 + 4/1)$, yields:

$$C_n' = \left(\frac{4}{n+1} + \frac{4}{n} + \frac{4}{n-1} + \ldots + \frac{4}{3} + \frac{4}{2} + \frac{4}{1}\right) - \frac{4}{2} - \frac{4}{1} + 2.$$

Now, we use some knowledge concerning Harmonic numbers, H_n. The nth Harmonic number is defined by the equation, $H_n = 1 + 1/2 + 1/3 + \ldots + 1/n$. Hence, $H_{n+1} = 1 + 1/2 + 1/3 + \ldots + 1/n + 1/(n + 1)$. Therefore the last formula above simplifies to:

$$C_n' = 4H_{n+1} - 4. \tag{9.7}$$

If we now combine this result with Eq. 9.5,

$$C_n' = \left(\frac{n}{n+1}\right)(C_n + 3)$$

and simplify, using the fact that $H_{n+1} = 1/(n + 1) + H_n$, we can obtain an exact result:

$$C_n = 4\left(1 + \frac{1}{n}\right)H_n - 7. \tag{9.8}$$

finding a simpler approximate result

We can now use an approximation for the nth harmonic number to obtain a simpler approximate result. It is known that $H_n = \ln n + \gamma + O(1/n)$, where γ is called Euler's constant and has the value $\gamma = 0.57721566$. Therefore we can approximate C_n in Eq. 9.8 by approximating H_n with $\ln n + \gamma$, by approximating $(1 + 1/n)$ with 1, and by converting $\ln n$ to a base-2 logarithm using $\ln n = \ln 2 * \lg n$, where $\ln 2 = 0.69314718$. This yields:

$$C_n = 2.77 \lg n - 4.7. \tag{9.9}$$

Comparison and Summary of Results

Now compare Eq. 9.9 for the average number of comparisons in an average tree with Eq. 9.3 giving the average number of comparisons in the best possible tree. For large enough n, the constants 3 and 4.7 in these formulas will be small in relation to their first terms. Consequently, we discover that, in the average case, the number of comparisons for a successful search is about 38.6 percent greater than in the best case. This implies that, on the average, deep unbalanced trees are relatively rare, and that most trees constructed by inserting keys in a random order are reasonably well balanced.

average trees are reasonably well balanced

Once we know the results for the best, worst, and average cases for C_n, we can use Eq. 9.5 to obtain the results for C_n'. After performing this conversion, we can summarize our conclusions in Tables 9.38, 9.39, and 9.40.

Table 9.38 The Shape That a Binary Search Tree Takes in the Best, Worst, and Average Cases

Case	Tree Shape
Best case	Leaves on at most two adjacent levels
Worst case	Exactly one internal node on each level
Average case	Reasonably balanced, only occasionally deep

Table 9.39 Exact Formulas for Number of Comparisons Used When Searching for a Key in the Best, Worst, and Average Cases, where

$$H_n = H_n = \sum_{i=1}^{n} 1/i \text{ and}$$

$$L_n = L_n = \sum_{i=1}^{n} \lfloor \lg i \rfloor$$

Case	$C_n =$	$C_n' =$
Best case	$(2 L_n + n) / n$	$(2 L_n + 4n) / (n + 1)$
Worst case	n	$n + 2 - 2 / (n + 1)$
Average case	$4\left(1+\frac{1}{n}\right)H_n - 7$	$4 H_{n+1} - 4$

Table 9.40 Approximate Average Numbers of Comparisons for Successful Searches (C_n) and Unsuccessful Searches (C_n') in the Best, Worst, and Average Binary Search Trees

Case	$C_n \approx$	$C_n' \approx$
Best case	$2 \lg n - 3$	$2 \lg n$
Worst case	n	$n + 2$
Average case	$2.77 \lg n - 4.7$	$2.77 \lg n - 1.7$

9.7 Review Questions

1. What is a binary search tree?
2. How do you search for a key in a binary search tree?
3. Define the external and internal path lengths of a binary search tree? How are they related?
4. Give the O-notation for the number of comparisons required in an average successful search for a key, K, in a binary search tree of n keys, assuming each key, K, in the tree is equally likely to be chosen: (a) in the best case, when the tree has the shape that minimizes the average search time; (b) in the worst case, when the tree has the shape that maximizes the average search time; and (c) in the average case when trees being searched are drawn with equal likelihood from the set of trees constructed by inserting keys in the order given by each permutation of the keys in the set of all permutations of keys.

9.7 Exercises

1. Leff Wright wrote the following program to perform search for AirportCodes in binary search trees. (See Exercises 2.5 on p. 53 for the typedef of AirportCode.) Is the program correct or incorrect?

```
     |     typedef  struct TreeNodeTag {
     |                  AirportCode           Airport;
     |                  struct TreeNodeTag   *LeftLink;
     |                  struct TreeNodeTag   *RightLink;
  5  |              } TreeNode;
     |
     |     TreeNode *BinaryTreeSearch(AirportCode A, TreeNode *T)
     |     {
     |          TreeNode *N;  int result;
 10  |
     |          N = T;
     |          while (N != NULL) {
     |              if ( (result = strcmp(A,N–>Airport)) == 0) {
     |                  return(N);              /* N points to the node containing A */
 15  |              } else if (result < 0) {
     |                  N = N–>LeftLink;      /* let N point to the left subtree's root */
     |              } else {
     |                  N = N–>RightLink; /* let N point to the right subtree's root */
     |              }
 20  |          }
     |          return (N);
     |     }
```

2. Write a recursive version of the program in Exercise 1 that works correctly.

3. Write a recursive function, TreeInsert(KeyType K, TreeNode **T), to insert a new key, K, into a binary search tree whose root node is referenced by the tree node pointer in *T.

4. Verify that the binary search tree of Fig. 9.31 can be constructed by inserting the nodes of Table 9.32 into an initially empty binary tree, using your solution to Exercise 3. The nodes should be inserted in the order given in Table 9.32.

5. Using induction, and starting with an empty tree ($\square$) as a base case, prove that the relationship between the internal and external path length of a binary tree with n nodes is $E = I + 2n$.

6. Derive the formula, $C_n = (2r - 3) + 2r/n$, as a special case of the exact formula for the best case in Table 9.39, when n takes the special form, $n = 2^r - 1$, where r = the number of rows in the tree. (*Note:* The number of rows, $r = \log_2(n+1)$, is one greater than the number of the deepest level.) Use Eq. 9.2, and note that $q = r$ in that formula. (*Note:* When you substitute $r = \log_2(n+1)$ into the formula $C_n = (2r - 3) + 2r/n$, you get Eq. 6.14 in Chapter 6, for the number of comparisons binary searching takes in a sorted table of n keys. This generalizes the results obtained only for the particular case, $n = 2^r - 1$, given by Eq. 6.14, and shows what happens when tables of any possible size are used in binary searching.)

7. Write a computer program to calculate and compare the results obtained by the exact and approximate formulas in Tables 9.39 and 9.40 for the average case. Compare the results computed for $n = 510$, $n = 511$, and $n = 1023$. Is there any constant k, such that for $n \geq k$, the exact and approximate formulas agree to within 2 percent?
8. Write a program to verify that the formulas for the exact and approximate values of C_n for the best case in Tables 9.39 and 9.40 differ by less than 2 percent for any $n \geq 197$.
9. Write a program to delete a node in a binary search tree. Can you devise an algorithm that gives a result that does not have deeper leaves than the input tree?

9.8 AVL Trees and Their Performance

Learning Objectives

1. To learn the definition of AVL trees.
2. To learn about some tree transformations that keep AVL trees balanced.
3. To understand the performance advantages of AVL trees.

From the results in Table 9.40, we see that balanced binary search trees have the best search times. If trees get out of balance or have deep search paths, their search performance deteriorates. In the worst case, instead of having $O(\log n)$ search times, the performance degrades to $O(n)$ search times.

Suppose we decide to keep a given binary search tree, T, as completely balanced as possible by rebalancing it each time a new key is inserted. Then it would be guaranteed that T would always have $O(\log n)$ search times.

There is only one trouble with this idea. That is that the cost of rebalancing the tree can sometimes take $O(n)$ operations. To see why, consider the binary search trees in Fig. 9.41, which use integers as keys. In this figure, a new key, 1, has been inserted into the left tree to yield the middle tree, and this middle tree has been rebalanced to

the trouble with
complete balancing

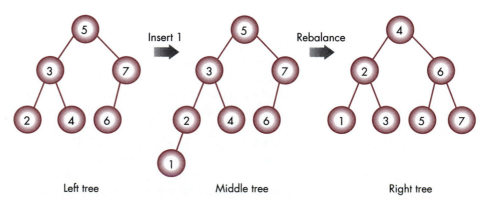

Left tree   Middle tree   Right tree

Figure 9.41 Completely Rebalancing After Inserting a New Key

yield the right tree. Note that every key in the left tree was moved to a new node when the right tree was constructed by balancing the middle tree. This demonstrates that rebalancing can take time O(n) in the worst case.

If restoring complete balance is made a part of the key insertion operation, then even though searching will be guaranteed to take O(log n) time, the insertion operation can take time O(n). We are therefore led to ask, "Is there some way of achieving O(log n) search times while also achieving O(log n) insertion times?"

using trees that are almost balanced

It turns out that the answer is *yes*. The main idea is to define a class of binary search trees that are almost balanced, but not completely balanced. These almost-balanced trees can be shown to have O(log n) search times and also O(log n) insertion times for new keys. They were discovered by two Russian mathematicians, Adelson-Velskii and Landis, after whom they are named, and they are commonly known as AVL trees in the computer science literature.

definition of AVL trees

Here is the key idea. We define the *height* of a binary tree to be the length of the longest path from the root to some leaf. (As a special case, we define the height of the empty tree to be –1.) If N is a node in a binary tree, T, we say that node N has the *AVL property* if the heights of the left and right subtrees of node N are either equal or if they differ by 1. An *AVL tree* is defined to be a binary tree in which each of its nodes has the AVL property.

It helps to look at a few examples in order to make the concept of AVL trees clear. Figure 9.42 shows some AVL trees, and Fig. 9.43 illustrates some trees that are not AVL trees.

looking at examples of AVL trees

Let's take a closer look at some of the properties of the AVL trees in Fig. 9.42. First, let's get the concept of the *height* of a tree clear in our minds. The three trees in Fig. 9.42 have heights of 2, 3, and 4 respectively, since the length of the longest paths from the root to some leaf in these trees is 2, 3, and 4. Focusing now on AVL tree 1, we see that the height of the left subtree of the root is 1, and the height of the right subtree of the root is zero (since the right subtree is a single node having no nonempty subtrees). Consequently, the heights of the left and right subtrees of the root of AVL tree 1 differ by at most 1, and therefore the root of this tree has the AVL property. All the other nodes in AVL tree 1 also have the AVL property. For example, the node that is the root of the left subtree in AVL tree 1 has an empty right subtree, whose height is –1 (by definition) and has a left subtree of height 0

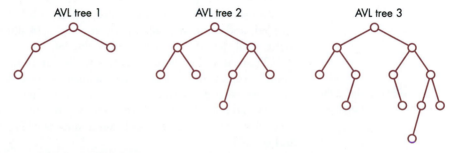

Figure 9.42 Some AVL Trees

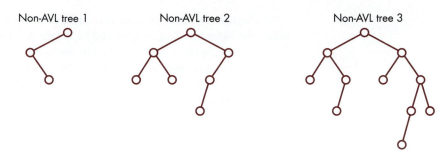

Figure 9.43 Trees That Are Not AVL Trees

(since a single leaf is a subtree of height 0). Consequently, the root of the left subtree has the AVL property.

A quicker way to tell whether a node, N, in a tree has the AVL property is to compare the lengths of the longest left and right paths starting at N and traveling downward. For example, the root of AVL tree 3 in Fig. 9.42 has a longest left path of 3 and a longest right path of 4. Since these left and right path lengths differ by at most one, AVL tree 3 has the AVL property at its root node. (For practice, you should verify that each node of each tree in Fig. 9.42 has the AVL property by checking that their longest left and right paths differ in length by at most one.)

a quicker way to check

Figure 9.43 illustrates some trees that are not AVL trees. The root of the first tree fails to have the AVL property since the left subtree of the root has height 1, and the right subtree of the root, being the empty tree, has height -1. These two heights (1 and -1) differ by 2, violating the AVL property. (Alternatively, since the longest left path starting at the root has length 2 and the longest right path has length 0, the root fails to have the AVL property.) In non-AVL tree 2 of Fig. 9.43, the right subtree of the root is not an AVL tree. In non-AVL tree 3, the right subtree of the root again fails to have the AVL property since the left path starting at its root has length 1 whereas the right path has length 3.

using rotation to restore the AVL property

When we are building up a binary search tree using the insertion method, it is possible that the AVL property will be lost at some point. For example, starting with the empty tree, if we insert the three airport codes, JFK, DCA, and GCM in the order given, we get a binary search tree whose shape is that of non-AVL tree 1 in Fig. 9.43. When the AVL property is lost at a node, we can apply some shape-changing tree transformations to restore the AVL property. Only four different transformations are needed, and these are called *rotations*. Fig. 9.44 illustrates the four rotations: single right, single left, double right, and double left.

relationship to the associative law of algebra

There is a close analogy between the rotations depicted in Fig. 9.44 and some applications of the associative law of algebra. If we imagine that the trees in Fig. 9.44 are expression trees (such as those given earlier in Fig. 9.24) in which the nodes Ⓐ, Ⓑ, and Ⓒ play the role of operators and the subtrees T_1, T_2, T_3, and T_4 play the role of operands, then the AVL tree rotations of Fig. 9.44 can be expressed as shown in Fig. 9.45.

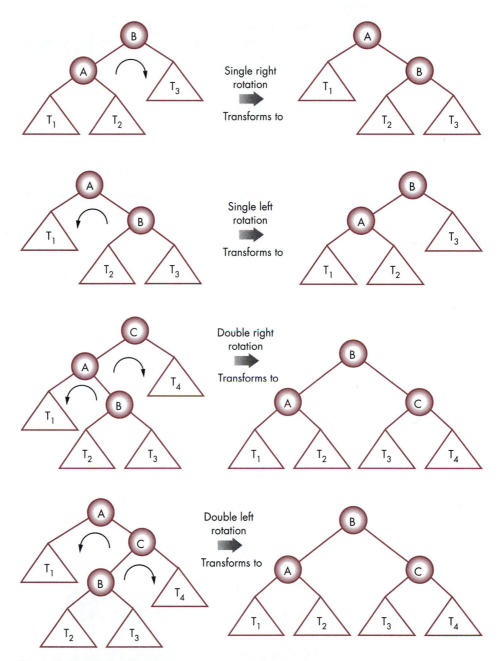

Figure 9.44 AVL Tree Rotations

Single right rotation:

$$((T_1 \text{ Ⓐ } T_2) \text{ Ⓑ } T_3) \Rightarrow (T_1 \text{ Ⓐ } (T_2 \text{ Ⓑ } T_3))$$

Single left rotation:

$$(T_1 \text{ Ⓐ } (T_2 \text{ Ⓑ } T_3)) \Rightarrow ((T_1 \text{ Ⓐ } T_2) \text{ Ⓑ } T_3)$$

Double right rotation:

$$((T_1 \text{ Ⓐ } (T_2 \text{ Ⓑ } T_3)) \text{ Ⓒ } T_4) \Rightarrow ((T_1 \text{ Ⓐ } T_2) \text{ Ⓑ } (T_3 \text{ Ⓒ } T_4))$$

Double left rotation:

$$(T_1 \text{ Ⓐ } ((T_2 \text{ Ⓑ } T_3) \text{ Ⓒ } T_4)) \Rightarrow ((T_1 \text{ Ⓐ } T_2) \text{ Ⓑ } (T_3 \text{ Ⓒ } T_4))$$

Figure 9.45 AVL Rotations Expressed Using the Associative Law

You may be wondering why the last two transformations in Fig. 9.45 are called "double" rotations. The reason is that each of the double rotations can be achieved by composing two single rotations.

For example, starting with $((T_1 \text{ Ⓐ } (T_2 \text{ Ⓑ } T_3)) \text{ Ⓒ } T_4)$, a double right rotation can be accomplished first by doing a single left rotation on the left subtree of Ⓒ rooted at Ⓐ,

$$(T_1 \text{ Ⓐ } (T_2 \text{ Ⓑ } T_3)) \Rightarrow ((T_1 \text{ Ⓐ } T_2) \text{ Ⓑ } T_3)$$

which gives $(((T_1 \text{ Ⓐ } T_2) \text{ Ⓑ } T_3) \text{ Ⓒ } T_4)$. This can be followed by a single right rotation applied to the root Ⓒ, which yields, $((T_1 \text{ Ⓐ } T_2) \text{ Ⓑ } (T_3 \text{ Ⓒ } T_4))$.

The semicircular arrows in Figure 9.44 indicate the directions in which the single rotations are applied in order to yield the double rotations.

Building an AVL Tree Using Insertions and Rotations

Let's watch what happens when we build up a binary search tree, using the keys of Table 9.32, and applying AVL rotations as necessary to maintain the AVL tree property at all times. We will use the keys in Table 9.32 in the order that they were given: ORY, JFK, BRU, DUS, ZRH, MEX, ORD, NRT, ARN, GLA, and GCM. The first node is ORY.

We can insert the next node, JFK, without destroying the AVL property:

But adding the next node BRU creates an unbalanced tree which fails to have the AVL property at its root.

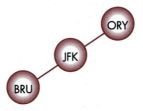

We apply a single right rotation to the root, ORY, to remove the imbalance, getting:

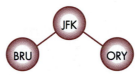

The next four airport codes can be inserted in the sequence DUS, ZRH, MEX, and ORD without requiring any rotations:

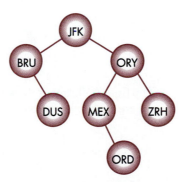

However, when we try to add NRT, the subtree rooted at MEX becomes unbalanced and requires a double left rotation to restore the AVL property:

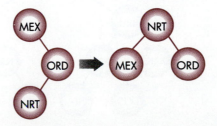

The next two airports, ARN and GLA, can be added without requiring any rotations to yield:

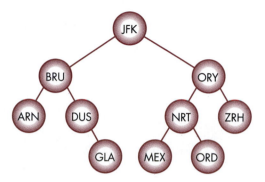

However, the attempt to insert the final airport code GCM produces an unbalanced subtree rooted at DUS. Another double left rotation is needed to remove this imbalance.

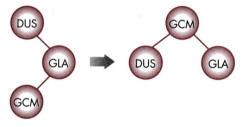

The final AVL tree is shown in Figure 9.46. Assuming that the search keys in this figure are equally likely to be used, the average successful search requires

$$C_n = \frac{(1+3+3+5+5+5+5+7+7+7+7)}{11} = \frac{55}{11} = 5.00 \text{ comparisons.}$$

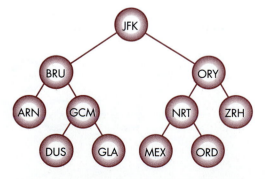

Figure 9.46 AVL Tree After Inserting All Keys

This is an improvement over the binary search tree of Figure 9.31 (using the same insertion order but no rebalancing), since the average number of comparisons required to search the tree of Fig. 9.31 was 6.09.

Balance Factors and Comments on Rotation Algorithms

By adding a new member to each node of an AVL tree, we can keep track of whether the left and right subtrees are of equal height, or whether one is higher than the other. Let a new C enumeration **typedef** be specified as follows:

```
typedef enum {LeftHeavy, Balanced, RightHeavy} BalanceFactor;
```

Then let nodes of AVL trees be declared using the following C struct definition:

```
typedef  struct AVLTreeNodeTag {
             BalanceFactor           BF;
             KeyType                 Key;
             struct AVLTreeNodeTag   *LLink;
             struct AVLTreeNodeTag   *RLink;
         } AVLTreeNode;
```

An analysis of various possibilities can reveal the different cases when it is necessary to apply one of the four AVL tree rotations (of Fig. 9.44) when inserting new nodes to build up an AVL Tree.

For instance, let the symbols, $\oslash$, $\ominus$, and $\oslash$, denote the situations where subtrees of a node make the node left heavy, balanced, or right heavy, respectively. (The symbols $\oslash$, $\ominus$, and $\oslash$ are simply visible representations of the balance factors of the nodes.)

Now suppose that subtrees T_1, T_2, and T_3 each have height h. Suppose that a new node is inserted that makes T_1 into a new AVL subtree T_1' of height $h + 1$. Then if the balance factors before changing T_1 into T_1' are indicated by

$$((T_1 \ominus T_2) \oslash T_3)$$

then after changing T_1 into T_1', the tree loses the AVL property at the root. But applying a single right rotation to the root restores the AVL property, by producing the new tree

$$(T_1' \ominus (T_2 \ominus T_3)).$$

local rotations restore the AVL property in the whole tree

Note that, beforehand, if the height of a subtree ($((T_1 \ominus T_2) \oslash T_3)$ is $h + 2$, then after changing T_1 into T_1' and rotating, the height of $(T_1' \ominus (T_2 \ominus T_3))$ is also $h + 2$. Consequently, none of the balance factors need to be changed in the entire tree above the subtree where the insertion and rotation took place. In other words, the single local rotation was sufficient to restore the AVL property to the entire tree.

In the case of double rotations, similar considerations apply. For instance, if subtrees T_1 and T_4 have height h, subtrees T_2 and T_3 have height $h - 1$, and these subtrees are arranged into a larger tree of the form

$$(T_1 \oslash ((T_2 \ominus T_3) \ominus T_4)),$$

then any insertion that unbalances the tree by increasing the height of either T_2 or T_3 by one (creating, say, T_2' or T_3' in the process) can have this imbalance removed by applying a double left rotation to create a tree of the form

$$((T_1 \ominus T_2') \ominus (T_3' \ominus T_4)).$$

Again, if the height of

$$(T_1 \oslash ((T_2 \ominus T_3) \ominus T_4))$$

before insertion was $h + 2$, then after insertion of the new node to create T_2' or T_3' followed by double rotation to restore the AVL property, the subtree

$$((T_1 \ominus T_2') \ominus (T_3' \ominus T_4))$$

also has height $h + 2$. Thus none of the nodes above this subtree needs to have its balance factor changed, and one double rotation suffices to restore the AVL property everywhere in the tree.

By analyzing all the possible combinations of subtree heights and balance factors, such as those illustrated in the two cases considered above, it is possible to write an algorithm that searches for a node N in an AVL tree T having a search key K, and if the search is unsuccessful, inserts a new node with key K, adjusts balance factors and applies a rotation to remove imbalances if necessary.

The reader is invited to work out the details in Exercise 9.8.3. This is a challenging set of algorithms to devise successfully—perhaps the most challenging in this entire book. Almost every upper-division data structures book covers the solution of this problem in detail. Therefore if the reader gets stuck, a variety of published solutions will be readily available.

Analysis of Performance**

It is informative to ask how many comparisons are needed to locate a search key K in an AVL tree T having n nodes.

a lower bound for the maximum number of comparisons

The minimum number of comparisons in an extended binary search tree having n internal nodes occurs in a tree balanced so that all external nodes (where all external nodes are leaves) are either on one level or on two adjacent levels. An extended binary search tree of height h has at most 2^h external nodes (just when all leaves appear at the same bottommost level in a complete tree). Since the number of internal nodes n is always one less than the number of leaves in an extended tree (see Exercise 9.3.1), we have $n \le 2^h - 1$. Solving for h in this last inequality gives us a constraint on

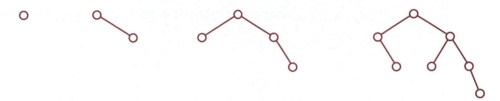

Figure 9.47 Fibonacci AVL Trees

h, namely, $h \geq \lceil \lg(n + 1) \rceil$. Therefore, since the maximum number of comparisons, C, needed in a completely balanced tree is $2h + 1$, we know that this maximum number of comparisons is bounded below by $2 \lceil \lg(n + 1) \rceil + 1$ in the case of the optimum shaped tree,

$$C > 2 \lceil \lg(n + 1) \rceil + 1.$$

Now let's investigate what happens in the worst case. In order to determine the answer, we need to find out how high we can make an AVL tree using the fewest number of nodes. In other words, given n internal nodes, how can we arrange them to create the AVL tree of greatest possible height? The solution is obtained by, say, systematically favoring the right subtree by using the least possible number of nodes to create a left subtree of height h, and then using the least possible number of nodes to create a right subtree of height $h + 1$. Since the AVL property must hold for all subtrees of an AVL tree, similar conditions must hold recursively for the left and right subtrees. Figure 9.47 shows a sequence of such right heavy AVL trees of greatest height for n internal nodes. If we then make a table of the number of internal nodes in the left and right subtrees of this figure, we get the results shown in Table 9.48.

analyzing the worst case

It is easy to see that the recurrence relation, $G_h = 1 + G_{h-1} + G_{h-2}$, characterizes the numbers of nodes, G_h, in the last column of this table. The reason is that each tree of height h is formed by taking a subtree of height $h - 1$ on its right (containing G_{h-1} nodes), a subtree on its left of height $h - 2$ (containing G_{h-2} nodes), and a new root (containing one node).

Table 9.48 Numbers of Nodes in Fibonacci AVL Subtrees

height	number of nodes in left subtree	number of nodes in right subtree	number of nodes in whole tree
0	0	0	1
1	0	1	2
2	1	2	4
3	2	4	7
4	4	7	12

If we use the initial conditions $G_0 = 1$ and $G_1 = 2$, we get Recurrence Relations 9.10.

$$G_0 = 1,$$
$$G_1 = 2,$$
$$G_h = 1 + G_{h-1} + G_{h-2}$$
Recurrence Relations

(9.10)

The Fibonacci numbers[2] are a famous sequence of numbers of the form:

$$0, 1, 1, 2, 3, 5, 8, 13, \dots, \text{ and so on,}$$

in which each number is the sum of the preceding two numbers. For example, $8 = 3 + 5$, and $13 = 5 + 8$. The recurrence relations for the Fibonacci numbers are: $F_0 = 0$ and $F_1 = 1$, and $F_n = F_{n-1} + F_{n-2}$, for $n \geq 2$.

Comparing these Fibonacci numbers with the numbers in the columns of Table 9.48, we can conjecture that G_h is just one less than some corresponding Fibonacci number. In fact, the relationship, $G_h = F_{h+3} - 1$, can be easily proven by induction. For this reason, the trees in Figure 9.47 are called *Fibonacci AVL trees*.

Since the Fibonacci AVL Trees of height h have the fewest nodes among all possible AVL trees of height h, we know that the number of internal nodes, n, in any AVL tree of height h obeys the relationship $n \geq G_h$. Consequently,

$$n \geq F_{h+3} - 1.$$

To make further progress, we have to use some advanced mathematical facts about Fibonacci numbers that are beyond the scope of this book (and which result from using *generating functions* to solve the Fibonacci recurrence relations—a technique beyond the techniques we have been using). In particular, it is known that the kth Fibonacci number F_k is bounded below by a power of the inverse of the golden ratio, denoted by the Greek letter phi, $\phi = (1 + \sqrt{5})/2$. Specifically, it is known that $F_k > \phi^k/\sqrt{5} - 1$. Putting this together with $n \geq F_{h+3} - 1$, we see that

$$n > \phi^{h+3}/\sqrt{5} - 2.$$

By adding 2 to both sides of this latter inequality and then by taking base ϕ logarithms, we observe that

$$\log_\phi(n+2) > \log_\phi(\phi^{h+3}/\sqrt{5}) = (h+3) - \log_\phi\sqrt{5}.$$

----

[2] Leonardo Fibonacci introduced these numbers in the year 1202. They have been studied extensively by mathematicians.

Solving the latter inequality for h yields,

$$h < \log_\phi (n+2) + \log_\phi \sqrt{5} - 3.$$

Now, using the fact that, numerically, $\phi = 1.618034$, and applying a logarithm base conversion $\log_\phi x = (\lg x / \lg \phi)$, we get,

$$h < 1.44042 \lg (n+2) - 1.327724.$$

Recall now that the relationship between the length, h, of a search path in a binary search tree and the number of comparisons, C, used in a successful search along that path was $C = 2h + 1$. From this, the most that the number of comparisons can be in the deepest possible Fibonacci AVL tree of n nodes is:

$$C < 2.88 \lg (n+2) - 1.66.$$

AVL trees are no more than 44 percent worse than optimal trees

Comparing this result with the result given earlier that the smallest C can get in a deepest search of an optimum shaped tree was given by $C > 2 \lceil \lg(n+1) \rceil + 1$, we can conclude that, in the worst case, AVL tree searches can require no more than about 44 percent more comparisons than required in the most costly search of an optimum shaped AVL tree.

By conducting empirical tests, it has been shown that the average search in an AVL tree takes about $2 \lg n + c$ comparisons for some small constant c (where $c \approx 1.5$ for large n). So the worst case AVL tree search is no more than about 44 percent more expensive than the average search.

Since path lengths in AVL trees of n nodes are bounded above by $1.44 \lg(n+2)$, it can be shown that searches, insertions, and deletions are each $O(\log n)$ in the worst possible cases. (Essentially, the amount of work involved can be no more than proportional to the work needed for processing each of the nodes in the search path from the root to the node containing the search key, or to the node where insertion or deletion will take place, plus a small constant additional amount of work.)

As Exercise 9.8.1 shows, by adding a field to each node in an AVL tree that contains one more than the number of nodes in the node's left subtree, the time needed to find the kth item given k, becomes $O(\log n)$. Thus using AVL trees to represent a List ADT can have several advantages—namely, one can perform rapid insertion (overcoming the drawback of using sequentially allocated linear list representations), and one can perform rapid random access (overcoming the drawback of using one-way, linked list representations).

9.8 Review Questions

1. Define the *height* of a binary tree.
2. What does it mean for a node N in a binary search tree T to have the AVL property? Then define what it means for tree T to be an AVL tree.

3. Draw diagrams illustrating four types of rotations that can be used to restore the AVL property in a binary search tree.
4. What is the O-notation for the worst case search time for a key K in an AVL tree of n nodes?

9.8 Exercises

1. (Using AVL trees to represent a List ADT.) Show that AVL trees can be used to provide a representation for the List ADT defined in Fig. 8.1 so that each list operation takes no more than O(log n) time for a list representation containing n items. [*Hint:* Add to each node of an AVL tree a field containing 1 + the number of nodes in the left subtree of the node. Use this field to compute the list length and to find the kth item in O(log n) time.]
2. (TreeSort) It is possible to sort n keys by inserting them one-by-one into a binary search tree and then reading them off using an **InOrder** traversal. Implement a **TreeSort** algorithm. Does it help to use AVL trees? How?
3. (AVL rotation algorithms) Implement the AVL tree rotation programs using the sketch given in the text as a hint.
4. Implement an algorithm to delete a node containing a given key K in an AVL tree T.
5. (Efficient dynamic memory allocation) Chapter 8 described two algorithms, **FirstFit** and **BestFit**, which are commonly used to allocate blocks of storage in dynamic memory allocation schemes. These two methods are linear time algorithms in the worst case. (Since they must search the entire list of n free blocks, they can each take time at most O(n).) Can AVL trees be used to organize the free blocks in a dynamic memory allocation scheme so that block allocation takes O(log n) time instead of time O(n)? [*Hint:* Take all free blocks of a given size, S, and link them into a two-way ring. This partitions free memory into a collection of rings, where each ring contains blocks of the same size. Now take one block on each ring and treat it as the *representative* of that ring. Organize these representatives into an AVL tree using block sizes as search keys. To locate a best-fit block in this AVL tree, given a request size, N, search the AVL tree for a block of size N. Either an exact-fit block of size N is found, or the last node from which a left descent was made along the search path will give the best fit for N.]

9.9 Two–Three Trees**

Learning Objectives

1. To learn another effective method for implementing dynamic search trees.
2. To understand how to insert new nodes and to search for keys.
3. To understand the performance characteristics of these trees.

As we noted in the previous discussion, maintaining perfect balance in binary trees yields shortest average search paths, but the attempt to maintain perfect balance

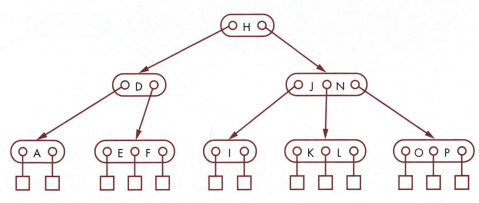

Figure 9.49 A 2–3 Tree

when we insert or delete nodes can incur costly rebalancing in which every node of the tree has to be rearranged. AVL trees presented a method in which we agreed to abandon the goal of trying to maintain perfect balance and to adopt the goal of keeping the subtrees of nodes "almost balanced." We discovered that we could get good performance in searches, insertions, and deletions by adopting this slight compromise from the maintenance of perfect balance.

the idea behind 2–3 trees

Another way to compromise on the goal of maintaining perfect balance is to arrange for all subtrees to be perfectly balanced with respect to their heights, but to permit the number of search keys stored in nodes to vary. This is the main idea behind 2–3 trees. Each node in a 2–3 tree is permitted to contain either one or two search keys, and to have either two or three descendants. All leaves of the tree are empty trees that lie on exactly one bottom level.

Figure 9.49 illustrates a 2–3 tree in which we have used letters of the alphabet as search keys. Note that all leaves of the tree, denoted by small square boxes (□), lie on the bottommost level.

how to search for a key

To search for the key L, for example, we start at the root and note that L > H, so we follow the pointer to the right subtree of the root node. Now we note that the key L lies *between* the keys J and N in alphabetical order, since J < L and L < N, so we follow the *middle* pointer between J and N to the node containing the keys K and L where the search terminates successfully by locating the key L.

Now let's look at the process of inserting new keys. In the simplest case, we will attempt to add a new key to a node containing only one key already and which has room to expand in order to contain two keys. For instance, suppose we want to insert the new key B into the tree of Fig. 9.49. Since B < H, we follow the left pointer from the root node to the node containing D in the second row. Again, we follow the left pointer of D's node to the node containing A. The node containing A has room for one more key, so we plant B in this node. The leftmost node on the bottom row of internal nodes in Fig. 9.50 shows the result of this insertion, starting with the tree of Fig. 9.49.

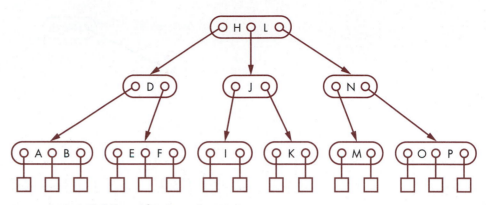

Figure 9.50 A 2–3 Tree After Some Insertions

A more challenging case occurs when we try to insert a new key into a node that already contains two keys. In this case, the node would overflow (by containing three keys), so we need a policy for insertion that maintains the 2–3 tree property. The method is this: "*Split the overflowed node into two nodes and pass the middle key up to the parent.*" This could cause a sequence of further splits, leading possibly to splitting the root, adding a new root, and deepening the 2–3 tree by one more level.

To see how this works, let's consider inserting more keys into the 2–3 tree of Fig. 9.49. First, let's insert the key M. This leads to the attempt to add M to the node (○ K ○ L ○).

However, if we did this, we would get an overflowed node of the form (○ K ○ L ○ M ○) having four children and three keys, in violation of the 2–3 tree property. Hence, we split (○ K ○ L ○ M ○) into two new nodes (○ K ○) and (○ M ○), and we pass the middle key L up to the parent node (○ J ○ N ○). The attempt to add L to this parent node yields another overflowed node in which the key L lies between the keys J and N, (○ J ○ L ○ N ○).

So we split this parent into two new nodes (○ J ○) and (○ N ○), and we pass the middle key L up to the root. The root has room for L, so we change it from (○ H ○) to (○ H ○ L ○). These changes are illustrated in Fig. 9.50.

If we were to attempt to add the new keys Q, R, and S to the tree of Fig. 9.50, the root of the tree (○ H ○ L ○) would split when P was passed up from below, and we would pass L up to form a new root with two children. This would deepen the tree by one more level.

You might think that the number of node splits on insertion could become excessive and could hinder the performance of 2–3 trees. However, since each split produces exactly one new node, the total number of splits to create a tree is just one less than the number of nodes in the tree. Moreover, if a split starts at level k, it could progress upward toward the root and could split the root, so, in the worst case, $(k + 1)$-splits are needed when we insert a new key at level k. But a 2–3 tree containing n keys with the maximum number of levels takes the form of a binary tree in which each internal node has one key and two children. In such a tree $n = 2^{k+1} - 1$, where k is the number of the lowest level. This implies that $(k + 1) = \lg (n + 1)$, from which we see that the number of splits per insertion is at worst O(log *n*). Similar considerations yield the result that searches and deletions are also O(log *n*) in the worst cases.

In summary, 2–3 trees have O(log *n*) search, insertion, and deletion times, and can be recommended for reasons similar to those connected with the advantages of using AVL trees.

B–Trees—A Generalization of 2–3 Trees**

The basic principle of operation of 2–3 trees is used extensively in practical circumstances to handle indexes to large files containing many records. A generalized version of 2–3 trees, called B–trees, is used for this purpose.

increasing the number of children

If we increase the number of children allowed in a nonroot node of a 2–3 tree to be some number in the range, say, from 128 to 256, then we have a B–tree of order 256. In general, in a B–tree of order *m*, each internal node except the root and the leaves must have between $\lceil m/2 \rceil$ and *m* children. The root can either be a leaf or it can contain from 2 to *m* children. All leaves lie on the same bottommost level and are empty.

Roughly speaking, a B–tree of order *m* has nodes that have some number of children between half of *m* and *m*. When we insert a new key, *K*, into a node, and the node overflows by containing *m* keys, and requiring it to have *m* + 1 children, we split the node. To do this, we line the keys up in increasing order, pass the middle key up to the parent, and form two new nodes containing the remaining bottom and top halves of the ordered key sequence in the overflowed node.

branching factors

Suppose we have a B–tree, *T*, of order *m* in which each internal node is as full as possible and has *m* children. The number *m* is called the *branching factor* of the tree. If *T* contains *n* keys and *p* nodes, then *p* = *n*/(*m* – 1), since each node of *T* contains *m* – 1 keys. We can now ask how many levels tree *T* has. In general, there is one node (the root) on level 0, and there are *m* nodes on level 1, m^2 nodes on level 2, ... , and m^k nodes on level *k*. The total number of nodes, *p*, is therefore just the sum of a geometric progression $p = 1 + m + m^2 + ... + m^k$. Hence, $p = (m^{k+1} - 1)/(m - 1)$.

We can combine the result that *p* = *n*/(*m* – 1), with the last result to eliminate *p* and solve for *k* in terms of *n*. This yields,

$$k = \log_m (n + 1) - 1.$$

For example, if *m* = 256 and *n* = 16,777,215, $k = \log_{256} (16777216) - 1 = 3 - 1 = 2$. Consequently, a full B–tree of order 256 can store 16 million records in just three levels (numbered level 0, level 1, and level 2), and it requires accessing just three nodes to find a given search key.

By contrast, if we store the same 16,777,215 keys in a completely balanced binary tree, the bottom level is given by $k = \log_2(16777216) - 1 = 23$, so it could take up to 24 accesses of nodes on different levels to find a key. In general, the larger the branching factor *m*, the smaller the number of levels needed to store a given fixed number *n* of keys in a completely balanced tree. (Another way of saying this is that a balanced tree of *n* nodes has $\log_m(n+1)$ rows, and the larger we make the base of the logarithm, the smaller the logarithm will be.)

The use of trees with high branching factors makes sense when we store the tree nodes on external memory devices with slow access times, such as disks or drums. Storing 16 million records on an external disk as a binary tree could require up to 24 separate disk accesses, whereas storing it as a B–tree of order 256 could require at most 5 accesses to separate nodes. Consequently, binary trees may be efficient when used in fast internal primary memory, but trees with higher branching factors are substantially more efficient when storing and accessing tree nodes on slow, rotating external memory. (*Note*: For efficiency, we usually read the entire ordered key sequence in a B–tree node into internal memory all at once. Then we use fast binary searching in internal memory to search for a key in this ordered sequence.) We will explore this subject in greater detail in Chapter 12 when discussing techniques for handling large external collections of data.

using trees with high branching factors

9.9 Review Questions

1. Define what it means for a tree *T* to be a 2–3 tree.
2. What is the advantage of using 2–3 trees rather than trees that are completely balanced?
3. What is the branching factor of a tree?
4. When is it advantageous to use trees with high branching factors?

9.9 Exercises

1. Draw the 2–3 tree that results from inserting the keys Q, R, and S into the 2–3 tree of Fig. 9.50. Perform node splits as necessary to maintain the 2–3 tree property at all times.
2. Derive a formula giving the height *k* of the tallest B–tree, *T*, of order *m*, such that *T* contains *n* keys.

9.10 Tries

Learning Objectives

1. Learning another efficient storage and retrieval method based on trees.
2. Learning how to construct and use Tries.

A *Trie* is a special kind of information access tree whose name comes from the word Re*trie*val. It is a common convention to pronounce the word "trie" as if it rhymed with "*try*" or "*pie*," in order to distinguish it from the word "*tree*" when spoken.

special pronunciation

In constructing a *trie* from a collection of search keys, we use the initial alphabetic prefixes of the keys to construct a *discrimination net* such as the one shown in Fig. 9.51. In this figure a trie is constructed from the airport code search keys given in

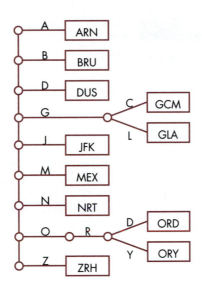

Figure 9.51 A Trie Using Airport Codes

how to search in a trie

Table 9.32. These keys, in alphabetic order are ARN, BRU, DUS, GCM, GLA, JFK, MEX, NRT, ORD, ORY, and ZRH.

At the root of the tree, we use the first letter of each airport code to distinguish which branch to pursue further. In many cases, the first letter alone is sufficient to distinguish a given airport code from all others in the tree. For example, in Figure 9.51, ARN and BRU are the only airport codes beginning with A and B, respectively. Therefore a test on the first letter of ARN and BRU is sufficient to lead to two separate branches of the tree having ARN and BRU as the only leaves. No further analysis needs to be performed to find ARN or BRU.

By contrast, GCM and GLA share the same first letter, G. Analyzing the first letter, and following the "G" branch of the trie leads to a second node at which a second discrimination is made on the second letter of GCM and GLA. Here, the second letters "C" and "L" are sufficient to differentiate between GCM and GLA, and so a test on the second letter leads to the separate leaves containing GCM and GLA respectively. In the final case of interest, both ORD and ORY begin with the same two letters "OR." Consequently, we have to use their third letters, "D" and "Y" to distinguish them. Hence, the trie in Fig. 9.51 does not discriminate between ORD and ORY until testing their third letters.

Tries have surprisingly good search times. If we use "random" keys, K (such as base m fractional numbers evenly distributed in the interval $0 \leq K \leq 1$), then the number of characters examined during a random average search (with each of the keys considered equally likely to be used) is approximately $\log_m N$, for nodes with m links and for N random keys stored in the trie.

Tries are insensitive to the order of insertion of the keys, but they are sensitive to clustering in the spelling of prefixes of the keys.

9.10 Review Questions

1. How do you pronounce the word "*trie*"?
2. Explain how a trie works.
3. What are the advantages and disadvantages of tries when used for searching?

9.10 Exercises

1. Discuss how you could represent a trie efficiently when search keys are (a) three letter airport codes, and (b) words in a dictionary containing 65,000 words with a longest word length of 33.

9.11 An Application—Huffman Codes**

Learning Objectives

1. Learning how to employ binary trees to construct minimal length encodings of strings based on known letter frequencies.
2. Learning how to construct and use Huffman trees.
3. Understanding why Huffman trees minimize the weighted path lengths of coding trees.

Binary trees can be used in an interesting way to construct minimal length encodings for messages when the frequency of letters used in the messages is known. A special kind of binary tree, called a *Huffman coding tree*, is used to accomplish this.

For example, we might take some samples of free-running English text, such as might be found in a newspaper, and we might try to count the frequencies of the letters of the alphabet used in these text samples. After analyzing several samples of such text, we might discover that the numbers of times each letter was used have the same relative proportions as the numbers given in Table 9.52.

using shorter codes to represent more frequent letters

The numbers in Table 9.52 are called *frequencies*, since each number gives the frequency of occurrence of its corresponding letter in the samples analyzed. If the frequencies in the sample are representative of the frequencies that will be encountered

E — 1231	L — 403	B — 162
T — 959	D — 365	G — 161
A — 805	C — 320	V — 93
O — 794	U — 310	K — 52
N — 719	P — 229	Q — 20
I — 718	F — 228	X — 20
S — 659	M — 225	J — 10
R — 603	W — 203	Z — 9
H — 514	Y — 188	

Table 9.52 Some Frequencies of Letters Typical for English Text

E — 29
T — 10
N — 9
I — 5
S — 4

Table 9.53 Five Letters and Their Frequencies

in future samples of text, we can use such frequencies to construct an encoding of the letters that will minimize the length of the encodings. The idea is to use bit-sequences of differing lengths to encode the various letters, with short bit-sequences being used to represent the frequent letters, and longer bit-sequences to represent less frequently used letters. But how can we proceed so as to achieve the minimum possible length encodings?

Let's consider a small example to illustrate the process of building and using a Huffman coding tree. Suppose we are given only the five letters and five corresponding frequencies shown in Table 9.53.

We start with the frequency values and sort them into increasing order, getting (4, 5, 9, 10, 29). Then we choose the two smallest values 4 and 5, and we construct a binary tree with labeled edges using these two smallest values,

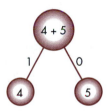

Here, 4 and 5 are placed inside the leaves, and the root contains the sum of the values in the leaves, 4 + 5. The left branch is labeled "1" and the right branch is labeled "0."

Next we return to the sequence of values (4, 5, 9, 10, 29) and we replace the two smallest values 4 and 5 with their sum 9, getting a new sequence (9, 9, 10, 29), which we must rearrange to be in increasing order (if it is not that way already). We again take the two new smallest values, 9 and 9, in this sequence, and we construct a labeled binary tree:

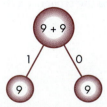

The root again contains the sum of the values of the leaves. Now, we substitute the first tree above into the second tree to get a composed tree:

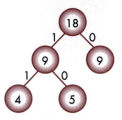

Continuing in this fashion, we return to the sequence (9, 9, 10, 29). We replace the first two frequencies, 9 and 9, with their sum 18, to get (18, 10, 29) and we rearrange the new sequence into ascending order, (10, 18, 29). We again build a tree from the two lowest frequencies:

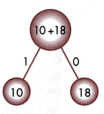

and we again compose the second to last tree above with the last tree above so as to substitute the root 18 for a leaf having the matching value 18, getting:

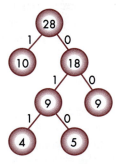

The final step is to replace the two smallest terms in (10, 18, 29) with their sum, getting the sequence (28, 29) and to build the tree:

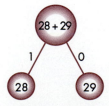

This tree can be composed with the next to last tree by substituting the root with value 28 for the leaf with value 28, getting the final composed tree:

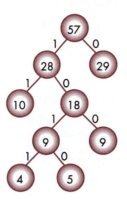

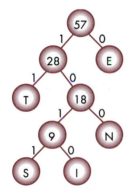

Figure 9.54 Huffman Coding Tree for Letters in Table 9.53

We now convert the final composed tree into a Huffman coding tree by making a one-for-one replacement of the frequencies of the leaves with letters from Table 9.53 having those frequencies. This gives the tree in Fig. 9.54, which is used to encode and decode strings in the alphabet $A = (E, T, N, I, S)$. The code assigned to each letter is found by following the path from the root of the coding tree to the leaf containing the letter and by reading the labels on the edges in the path in succession. This results in the assignment of the codes given in Table 9.55. Note that the most frequent letters in this table have the shortest codes assigned and that the least frequent letters have the longest codes assigned.

To encode a string, we replace each letter with its corresponding bit code, using the correspondence in Table 9.55. Some examples are:

String	Encoded String
SENT	1011010011
TENNIS	11010010010101011
NEST	1000101111
SIT	1011101011

To decode a bit-string S, we use the successive bits of S to find a path through the coding tree of Fig. 9.54, starting at the root. A "1" means descend to the left, and a "0" means descend to the right. Each time we reach a leaf in the coding tree, we emit

Table 9.55 Huffman Codes Assigned to Letters of Table 9.53

Letter	Bit code	Frequency
E	0	29
T	11	10
N	100	9
I	1010	5
S	1011	4

the letter that the leaf contains, and we return to the root of the coding tree to start a fresh path using the next bit of the encoded sequence. For example, the encoded string,

1 1 0 1 0 0 1 1 1 0 1 1,

decodes as "TENTS" because the initial 1 1 leads to a T, the next 0 leads to an E, the succeeding 1 0 0 leads to an N, the following 1 1 leads to a T, and the final 1 0 1 1 leads to an S.

It is actually possible to prove that a Huffman code minimizes the length assigned to coded messages that use letters with the same frequency as the frequency in the sample from which the Huffman code was constructed.

The critical measure to minimize is a quantity called the *weighted path length* of the Huffman tree. Looking at Table 9.55, for the alphabet A = (E, T, N, I, S), if we multiply each number in the Frequency column, f_i, by the length, l_i, of the corresponding Huffman code in the Bit code column, we would get the total number of bits needed to represent f_i of the letters in the Letter column. By adding up all the products of frequencies and bit code lengths, $\sum_{(1 \le i \le n)} f_i * l_i$, for all n letters in the alphabet, we get the length of the bit code for an encoded message that uses each letter in the alphabet exactly as many times as its frequency specifies. This sum, $W = \sum_{(1 \le i \le n)} f_i * l_i$, is called the weighted path length because it represents the sum of the path lengths in Figure 9.54 weighted by their frequencies, in the following sense: (a) multiply the length, l_i, of the path from the root to a leaf by the frequency, f_i, of the letter, L_i, at that leaf, and (b) add up all such individual path lengths in the tree weighted by their frequencies to obtain the weighted path length, $W = \sum_{(1 \le i \le n)} f_i * l_i$. The average number of bits per letter needed to encode a message is then given by, Average = $W / \sum_{(1 \le i \le n)} f_i$, since the average consists of the total number of bits used to encode all letters in the sample divided by the total number of letters in the sample.

It is possible to prove that W is minimized among all possible coding trees by a Huffman coding tree. A rough sketch of an induction proof that establishes this fact is as follows: The base case in the induction can start with any two letters, L_1 and L_2, having frequencies f_1 and f_2. Here, the only tree that can be constructed is

the weighted path length

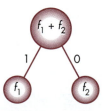

and this tree has weighted path length, $f_1 + f_2$.

The idea for the induction step is to choose a tree, T, among all coding trees on n letters, such that T has minimum weighted path length. Since there are only a finite number of trees that can be constructed for n letters, such a minimal weighted path length tree surely exists. Next, choose an internal node, N, at greatest distance from the root of T. If N does not have the two smallest frequencies, f_1 and f_2, as leaves, then whatever leaves, f_j and f_k, that N has can be exchanged with occurrences of leaves containing f_1 and f_2 elsewhere in the tree T without increasing T's weighted path length. (If this weren't the case, the assumed minimality of T's weighted path length would be contradicted.)

Finally, you can show that T is minimal if and only if a new tree T' is minimal, where T' is constructed from T by deleting f_1 and f_2 and making N into a new leaf containing the frequency $(f_1 + f_2)$. Here tree T' is the tree with minimal weighted path length over the set of $n - 1$ frequencies $(f_1 + f_2, f_3, \ldots, f_n)$. The reason this must be so is because T and T' have weighted path lengths that differ by a constant because of the way T' was constructed from T. (To see why the weighted path lengths of T and T' differ by a constant, note that f_i is a summand of every internal node on the path from the leaf containing f_i to the root.) This completes the induction step.

9.11 Review Questions

1. What is a Huffman code?
2. What is a Huffman coding tree and how do you use it to encode and decode strings?
3. Why is a Huffman code advantageous in comparison to codes that assign fixed-length bit codes to the characters in an alphabet?

9.11 Exercises

1. Using the Huffman coding tree in Figure 9.54, encode the strings **STINT** and **SINE**.
2. Using the Huffman coding tree in Figure 9.54, decode the bit strings **100101010001011** and **101010011010011**.
3. Write a program to build a Huffman coding tree, starting with a set of letters and their corresponding frequencies. Build the Huffman coding tree using the letters and frequencies given in Table 9.52.

 Pitfalls

- *Not treating empty trees carefully during tree traversals*

  When designing tree traversals both recursive and nonrecursive techniques come readily to mind. The nonrecursive techniques can often profit from the systematic use of stacks and queues. One pitfall that seems to be encountered frequently is failure to consider the case of empty trees properly. If tests for empty trees are absent in key places, it can cause nonrecursive traversal algorithms to attempt to dereference the null pointer, and recursive traversal algorithms can fail to terminate with the proper base cases. As an illustration, can you discover what is wrong with the following version of Program 9.28?

```
       |    void Traverse(TreeNode *T, int TraversalOrder)
       |    {
       |        if ( TraversalOrder == PreOrder )  {
       |
    5  |            Visit(N);                 /* if N == NULL, Visit(N) does nothing */
       |            Traverse(N->LLink,PreOrder);
       |            Traverse(N->RLink,PreOrder);
       |
       |        } else if ( TraversalOrder == InOrder ) {
   10  |
       |            Traverse(N->LLink,InOrder);
       |            Visit(N);
       |            Traverse(N->RLink,InOrder);
       |
   15  |        } else if ( TraversalOrder == PostOrder ) {
       |
       |            Traverse(N->LLink,PostOrder);
       |            Traverse(N->RLink,PostOrder);
       |            Visit(N);
   20  |        }
       |    }
```

- *The hidden expense of dynamic memory allocation*

   When implementing certain kinds of search trees, such as 2–3 trees, one often uses an underlying dynamic memory allocation scheme of unknown expense to allocate nodes of different sizes (such as nodes having either two or three children). Not all underlying dynamic memory allocation schemes operate with peak efficiency. Some use costly linear search algorithms to find new free blocks to allocate. If performance is critical, it might be best to apply the philosophy of *measurement and tuning* by measuring the performance of the underlying dynamic memory system, and comparing it, if necessary, to one that you implement from scratch using arrays of node types of identical size having available space lists of free nodes under your own direct control.

Tips and Techniques

- *Be prepared to use binary search tree representations to achieve performance*

   Binary search trees can often supply representations that yield substantial performance advantages when representing List ADTs or tables. If the mix of operations involves insertions and deletions, as well as searches, then AVL trees can provide substantial performance advantages over linked list or sequential list representations. The trick of adding an extra field, **F**, to each node, **N**, of an AVL tree, such that **F** contains one plus the number of nodes in **N**'s left subtree, can be used as a basis for algorithms giving rapid random access to the kth node, given k, and for calculating the total number of nodes in the tree (in order to represent the length function of a List ADT). Look-up tables that associate structs with search keys can also profit from the use of binary search tree representations when the table is expected to undergo changes resulting from insertions and deletions of new rows.

- *Know when to use AVL trees instead of ordinary binary search trees*

  The use of AVL trees incurs a substantial programming expense, so it may not be appropriate to use them when it suffices to use ordinary binary search trees. If keys arrive for insertion in an ordinary binary search tree in fairly random order, then it may not be necessary to implement AVL trees to maintain reasonable balance. However, if keys tend to arrive in sorted order, or in runs or bursts of a given order (such as descending or ascending order), then trees constructed from them will tend to become deep and skinny (these being the binary search trees with poor performance). Under such circumstances, it may pay to convert to the use of AVL trees.

- *Use heaps to implement priority queues when appropriate*

  If you have an application that needs to use priority queues, using the heap representation for priority queues could yield important payoffs. Priority queues can occur in many contexts. Some examples are (a) event-driven simulation systems (in which events are time-stamped and the next event to simulate is the one closest in time to the current time); (b) searches in game-trees in which the next move to explore is the one starting from the node in the game-tree having the highest strategic score; (c) priority scheduling algorithms in operating systems, in which the task to schedule for execution next is the one having highest priority; and (d) various "best-first" algorithms, where the next step in the algorithm involves choosing the best candidate among the available candidates at the moment.

References for Further Study

a thorough reference

Donald E. Knuth, *The Art of Computer Programming, Searching and Sorting,* vol. 3, 2nd ed., Addison-Wesley, Reading, Mass., (1973).

A classical, thorough reference that develops the performance characteristics of many kinds of trees.

a useful survey

J. Nievergelt, "Binary Search Trees and File Organization," *Computing Surveys* 6: 3 (September 1974), pp. 195–207.

A survey article, which explores balanced binary trees a bit further than the discussion in this book.

Chapter Summary

basic tree anatomy

In computer science, it is traditional to draw diagrams of trees *upside-down* with the *root* at the top and the *leaves* at the bottom. The *leaves* of a tree are the nodes having no *descendants*, and the *root* is the node having no *parent*. There is always exactly one path from the root of a tree to a given node. Nodes that are not leaves are called *internal nodes*.

binary trees

A *binary tree* is either the empty tree or a node having left and right subtrees that are binary trees. A *full binary tree* is one in which each node is either a leaf or else has two nonempty children. In a full binary tree the number of leaves, L, is always one more than the number of internal nodes, N (i.e., L = N + 1).

complete binary trees

A *complete binary tree* is one having leaves either on a single level or on two adjacent levels, such that the leaves on the bottommost level are in the leftmost positions. A complete binary tree of n nodes has an efficient contiguous sequential representation in which the nodes are placed in level order into an array A[1:n]. In this representation, A[1] contains the root, and the children of A[i], if they exist, are in A[2*i] and A[2*i + 1]. A node A[i] is a leaf just when 2*i > n (since, to the contrary, if A[i] were not a leaf, it would then have a left child at position 2*i, which would have to be less than or equal to the position, n, of the last node A[n]).

heaps

Heaps are complete binary trees having values at the nodes such that the values are arranged in descending order along any path from the root toward the leaves. In a heap, the highest value always sits at the root. Heaps provide efficient representations for *priority queues*. A complete tree of n items can be arranged into a heap in time O(n) and items can be removed and inserted into heaps in time O(log n). Consequently, heaps provide a more efficient representation for priority queues than alternatives such as linked lists, or arrays of items kept in sorted or random order.

tree traversals

A *traversal* of a binary tree is a process that systematically visits each node in the tree exactly once. Three common traversal orders for binary trees are *PreOrder*, *InOrder*, and *PostOrder*. If a binary tree for an algebraic expression is traversed in postorder and the symbols at its nodes are emitted when the nodes are visited, a postfix instruction string results. The value of this postfix string can be calculated by a postfix interpreter, using a stack to hold intermediate values of subexpressions. This idea served as the basis for many early programming language processors, which translated source programs into postfix, and used stack-based, run-time interpreters to execute the postfix instructions.

Traversals of linked representations of binary trees can be accomplished easily using recursive functions. Traversals can also be accomplished by nonrecursive functions that use stacks or queues to hold pointers to subtrees awaiting further traversal. When a stack is used, if, after visiting node N, the pointers to the right and left subtrees of N are pushed onto the stack, a preorder traversal occurs by processing subtrees in the order that results from popping subtree pointers from the stack. Using a queue, and inserting subtree pointers on the rear of the queue, while removing subtree pointers from the front of the queue, yields a *level order* tree traversal.

binary search trees

Binary search trees are binary trees with keys stored in the nodes, such that, for each node, N, the keys in the left subtree of N are less than the key in node N, and the keys in the right subtree of N are greater than the key in node N. If you traverse a binary search tree using InOrder, the keys in the nodes are visited in ascending order. A sorting method called **TreeSort** consists of inserting keys into a binary search tree in the order originally given, and then in reading off the keys in the resulting binary search tree using an InOrder traversal.

In a binary search tree, the *level* of a node, N, is the length of the path from the root to node N (where the *length* of a path is the number of edges in it). The *height* of a binary search tree is the length of the longest path from its root to some leaf (where the *height* of an *empty tree* is defined to be -1 as a special case).

Among binary search trees built up by inserting keys into an initially empty tree in random order, the worst case search times occur in trees that are deep and skinny—those having only one internal node on each level. In this worst case, with keys in a tree of n nodes chosen with equal likelihood for use in the search, the average search time is $O(n)$. The best case search times occur in trees that are as balanced as possible—those having leaves on one level or on two adjacent levels. In this case, average search times are $O(\log n)$, where, again, each key in such a tree is equally likely to be chosen for use in the search. If trees are randomly constructed, using with equal likelihood any of the possible permutations of keys for building up the tree by the insertion method, then deep skinny trees are relatively rare and reasonably balanced trees are fairly common. In such trees, on the average, a search for a randomly chosen key takes only 38.6 percent more time than it does in the best case, using balanced trees with leaves on at most two levels.

the performance of binary search trees

An *AVL tree* is a binary search tree in which each node, N, has the property that the height of N's left and right subtrees differ by at most one. If insertion of a new node should cause an AVL tree to lose the AVL property at a given node, four shape-changing tree transformations, called *rotations*, can be applied to a local portion of the tree to restore the AVL property. AVL trees have good performance, in that searches, insertions, and deletions require at most $O(\log n)$ time. This overcomes the worst case $O(n)$ performance possible with randomly constructed binary search trees.

AVL trees

Theoretically, the worst case performance of an AVL tree can be at most 44 percent worse than that of the best case binary search tree (with leaves on at most two levels). Moreover, empirical studies indicate that the *average* performance of AVL trees is remarkably close to that of the best case binary search trees. AVL trees can therefore be warmly recommended for use any time a binary search tree representation is advantageous. For example, using AVL trees to represent a List ADT provides $O(\log n)$ performance, overcoming the disadvantage of linked list representations (which require time $O(n)$ to locate the kth item, given k) and overcoming the disadvantage of contiguous sequential representations (which require time $O(n)$ to perform insertions).

2–3 trees

2–3 trees are an alternative data structure useful for providing representations of search trees. In a 2–3 tree, nodes other than the leaves have either two or three children, and all leaves are on the same bottom level. Each node in a 2–3 tree contains either one or two keys. To insert a new key in a 2–3 tree, if adding a key to a node causes the node to overflow, the overflowed node is split into two new nodes, each containing a single key, and the middle key (among the three that caused the overflow) is passed up to be inserted into the parent node. 2–3 trees enjoy $O(\log n)$ performance properties similar to those exhibited by AVL trees.

Tries

A *trie* is another kind of search tree based on the idea of a *discrimination net*. At the root of a trie, the initial letter of a search key is used to determine which subtree to use for further search. If the initial letter in a key distinguishes the key from all others in the trie, no further discrimination is needed, and the key resides in a leaf that is a subtree of the root accessed by a branch labeled with the key's first letter. If two or more keys share a common prefix, p (i.e., if the first few initial letters, p, of a group of keys is identical) then a search path starting at the root and labeled with the successive letters of p, leads to a node at which a discrimination is made, using the different letters following the prefix p in the various keys. Unlike AVL trees and 2–3 trees, the shape of a trie is insensitive to the order in which the trie was built up, using insertions of keys. However, a trie's shape is sensitive to bunching in the prefixes of keys. Tries have remarkably good logarithmic search times.

Huffman coding trees

Binary trees can be applied to determine minimal length encodings for messages whose letters occur with known frequency. To achieve this result, a *Huffman coding tree* is constructed. This tree assigns bit codes of differing lengths to the various letters. In general, Huffman coding trees assign shorter length bit codes to more frequent letters, and longer length bit codes to less frequent letters in a fashion that minimizes the total expected length of encoded messages.

10

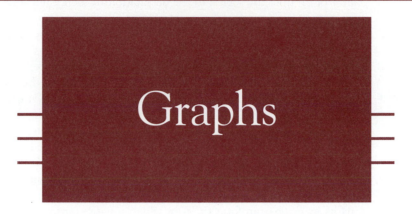

Graphs

≡ 10.1 Introduction and Motivation

what are graphs?

Graphs are collections of nodes in which various pairs of nodes are connected by line segments. The nodes are usually called *vertices* and the line segments are called *edges*.

The vertices and edges in a graph can be augmented by additional information. For example, vertices may be numbered or labeled, and edges may have numbers attached to them. Such augmented graphs are useful in a variety of contexts for modeling information encountered in computer applications. For instance, a graph in which the vertices represent cities and the edges represent the distances between those cities (or the cost of an airline ticket between those cities), can be used as a "transportation network" to study the total distances (or costs) of trips that make multiple stops at several cities. One might ask, "What is the path with one or more stops of shortest overall distance (or least overall cost) connecting a starting city and a destination city in such a transportation network?" This is an instance of a *shortest path problem* in a graph.

graphs are useful in computer applications

flow graphs

Again, one might have a graph whose edges represent a network of oil pipelines and whose vertices represent oil pumping stations. Oil might be pumped from a source through pipes in the network and might leave the network at a specific destination. If the edges in the graph are marked with the maximum oil flows that the corresponding oil pipes can carry, we might ask, "What is the maximum possible overall flow of oil from the source to the destination in such a network of oil pipes?" This is an instance of a *maximal flow problem* in a flow graph.

searching in graphs

We might also search in a graph for a vertex having a particular property. When creating a computer program to play a board game such as chess or checkers, a game graph results when particular board configurations are represented by vertices and when edges between those vertices represent moves in the game that change one board configuration into another. A computer algorithm might search such a game graph to attempt to find a sequence of *forcing moves* leading to a *win*. (Here, a *forcing move* is one for which the opponent has only one legal reply, and a *win* is a board configuration, such as a checkmate in chess, in which a player is defined to have won the game according to the game's rules.)

graphs are more general than trees

Even though every tree is a graph (since trees are built from vertices in which pairs of vertices are joined by edges), graphs are more general than trees. For instance, paths in graphs can form *cycles* in which a path starting at a given vertex follows a sequence of successive edges that eventually return to the starting vertex (by making a "round trip" so-to-speak). Trees can never contain cycles. Also, a graph can consist of one or more *connected components*. A connected component is a portion of a graph in which there is a path connecting any two vertices in the component. If a graph has several separate connected components, there is no path from a vertex in one component to a vertex in a separate component. A tree always has exactly one connected component.

generality trades off against simplicity

There are two important consequences of the fact that graphs are more general than trees: (1) graphs are useful in a broader variety of problem representations and (2) the algorithms for processing graphs are more complex. This reveals another kind of tradeoff that we often see in computer science—the tradeoff between generality and algorithmic simplicity. The more complex and flexible that a representation becomes, the less simple are the algorithms that are used to perform fundamental operations on it (such as traversal and searching). For instance, depth-first and breadth-first searching algorithms are defined both for trees and graphs. However, these algorithms are more complicated for graphs than for trees. In the case of graphs, the algorithms must take into account the possibility that nodes being searched have already been visited before along another path in the graph, whereas, in the case of trees, a node can be reached only along one path starting at the root of the tree.

Plan for the Chapter

concepts and terminology

Section 10.2 introduces some basic concepts and terminology pertaining to graphs. We cover the basic anatomy of graphs by describing their parts, such as vertices, edges, and components, and by introducing fundamental concepts, such as paths, cycles, and connectedness.

graph representations

Section 10.3 explores *graph representations*. There are a variety of ways we can represent graphs using computer data structures. For example, we can use a matrix (i.e., a table) that contains ones and zeros to specify which edges connect which vertices. We can use an array of linked lists, in which each position in the array represents a distinct vertex, and the list stored in that position gives the other vertices to which the given vertex is connected by an edge. We can also use various set representations, since a graph can be viewed as a set of pairs of vertices in which each pair of vertices corresponds to an edge.

graph searching algorithms

Graph searching algorithms are explored in Section 10.4. Two well-known methods are depth-first searching and breadth-first searching. The algorithms for these two methods are similar to the corresponding depth-first and breadth-first searching algorithms for trees, in that stacks are used to implement depth-first searching and queues are used to implement breadth-first searching. The only difference is that graph algorithms must be augmented to handle situations involving several connected components as well as multiple paths that may form cycles—two situations that do not arise in trees, since trees cannot have cycles and have only one connected component. We use abstract program strategies to express these graph searching algorithms in order not to be tied down to a particular data representation. In this sense, we use the mathematical definition of graphs as an ADT, and we leave particular choices of representational details to the reader. The same policy holds true for the remaining graph algorithms considered in this chapter in order to maintain maximum clarity and flexibility.

topological ordering

Section 10.5 presents a method for discovering a *topological ordering* of the vertices in a graph. Suppose that the edges in a graph define an ordering between pairs of vertices. For example, if vertices represent college courses, and vertices A and B are two such courses, then the edge from A to B might express the relationship that course A is a *prerequisite* for taking course B. In this case, a topological ordering of the courses is simply a list of the courses in which the prerequisites for every course X are listed before X itself is listed.

shortest path algorithms

Section 10.6 investigates a *shortest path algorithm*. When edges in a graph are annotated by distances, a shortest path connecting a starting point A and a destination B is a path from A to B of shortest total distance, possibly traveling through other intermediary vertices. Such a shortest path is not guaranteed to be unique. There may be more than one shortest path. If there is more than one, all of them have an identical total distance. This shortest total distance is shorter than the distance of other paths from A to B that are not in the set of shortest paths.

task networks

Section 10.7 introduces *task networks*—graphs whose vertices represent tasks and whose edges represent prerequisite relations among the tasks. The vertices are augmented to contain task durations. We are not allowed to begin a given task until we have completed all the predecessor tasks that are found at the origins of the edges that terminate on the given task's vertex. A question we might ask of such a task network is, "What is the earliest time that we could complete the entire project, given that we start the first task in the project on a specific starting date?" We also define a *critical path* in a task network to be a sequence of tasks that cannot have their completion times delayed without delaying the completion time for the entire project, and we investigate how to compute the critical path.

some general background

Section 10.8 discusses some useful background information on additional graph problems. Even though this information is presented informally, it is nonetheless helpful for literacy in computer science. Among the problems discussed are spanning tree problems, maximum flows in flow networks, the four-color problem, and several NP-complete graph problems such as finding k-cliques and Hamiltonian circuits.

≡ **10.2** Basic Concepts and Terminology

Learning Objectives

1. To establish a basic vocabulary of graph concepts.
2. To introduce concepts such as paths, components, and connectedness that are essential for understanding graph algorithms.

an informal description

Let's start with an informal description. A *graph* is a collection of points in which some pairs of points are connected by line segments. If the line segments have arrowheads on them, which indicate a direction of travel, we have a *directed graph* (which is sometimes called a *digraph*, for short). In an *undirected graph*, the line segments have no arrowheads on them. In both kinds of graphs, the points are usually referred to as *vertices*, and the line segments or arrows connecting pairs of vertices are usually referred to as *edges*. Figure 10.1 shows examples of both directed and undirected graphs.

paths, cycles, and adjacency

Two different vertices, x and y, in a graph are said to be *adjacent* if an edge connects x to y. A *path* is a sequence of vertices in which each vertex is adjacent to the next one. The *length* of a path is the number of edges in it. A *cycle* is a path of length greater than one that begins and ends at the same vertex. In an undirected graph, a *simple cycle* is a cycle formed from three or more distinct vertices in which no vertex is visited more than once along the simple cycle's path (except for the starting and ending vertex, which must be identical in order for the cycle to close and form a loop as it is supposed to do.)

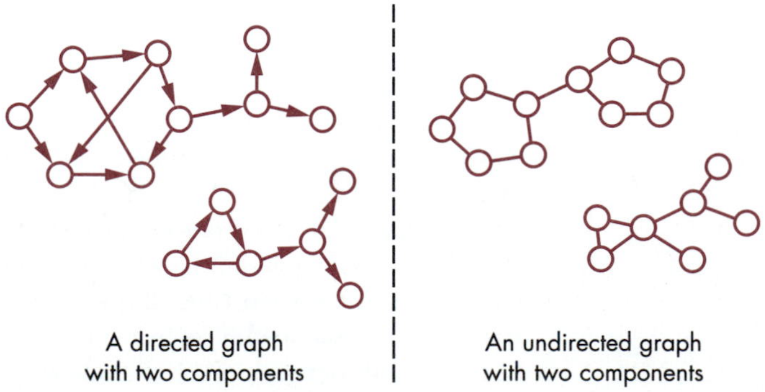

A directed graph
with two components

An undirected graph
with two components

Figure 10.1 Directed and Undirected Graphs

In an undirected graph, two distinct vertices, x and y, are *connected*, if there is a path between them. Also, a subset of the vertices, S, is said to be *connected* if there is a path from each vertex x of S to any other distinct vertex y of S. An undirected graph can always be divided into separate *connected components*. Each connected component consists of a subset of vertices that are all connected to each other (in the sense that any two distinct vertices are connected by some path lying inside the component). However, if an undirected graph consists of one or more separate components, there is never a path from a vertex in one component to some vertex in another separate component.

A free tree is a special kind of undirected graph consisting of exactly one connected component having no simple cycles.

Let's now give some slightly more formal definitions of these informal concepts in order to establish a notation useful for developing the graph algorithms studied later in the chapter.

connectivity and components (margin note)

free trees (margin note)

Some Formal Definitions

Formally speaking, a *graph* $G = (V, E)$, consists of a set of vertices, V, together with a set of edges, E, where the edges in E are formed from pairs of distinct vertices in V. In an *undirected graph*, each edge $e = \{v_1, v_2\}$ is an *unordered pair* of distinct vertices, which connects the two vertices v_1 and v_2, without prescribing a direction from v_1 to v_2 or from v_2 to v_1. By contrast, in a *directed graph* (or *digraph*, for short), each edge $e = (v_1, v_2)$ is an *ordered pair* of vertices, which connects the pair of vertices v_1 and v_2, in the direction *from v_1 to v_2*. In this case, we say v_1 is the *origin* of the edge $e = (v_1, v_2)$ and v_2 is the *terminus* of the edge e.

Note: When we use the word *graph* without a modifier, we shall usually mean an *undirected graph*, and we shall reserve the terms *digraph* and *directed graph* for graphs whose edges are directed.

Paths, Cycles, and Adjacency

Two vertices v_i and v_j in a graph $G = (V, E)$ are *adjacent* if there exists an edge $e \in E$ such that $e = (v_i, v_j)$. A *path* p in a graph $G = (V, E)$ is a sequence of vertices of V of the form, $p = v_1 v_2 \ldots v_n$, $(n \geq 2)$, in which each vertex v_i is adjacent to the next one, v_{i+1} (for $1 \leq i \leq n - 1$). A *cycle* is a path $p = v_1 v_2 \ldots v_n$, such that $v_1 = v_n$ (so that p starts and ends at the same vertex and forms a loop). Figure 10.2 illustrates paths and cycles in a graph.

In an undirected graph, a simple cycle is a path that travels through three or more distinct vertices and connects them into a loop. Formally speaking, this means that if p is a path of the form, $p = v_1 v_2 \ldots v_n$, then p is a *simple cycle* if and only if $(n > 3)$, $v_1 = v_n$, and $v_i \neq v_j$ for distinct i and j in the range $(1 \leq i, j \leq n - 1)$. Put differently, when you travel around the loop in a simple cycle, you must visit at least three different vertices, and you cannot travel through any vertex more than once.

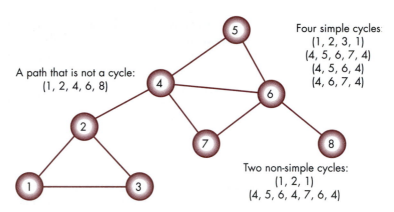

A path that is not a cycle:
(1, 2, 4, 6, 8)

Four simple cycles:
(1, 2, 3, 1)
(4, 5, 6, 7, 4)
(4, 5, 6, 4)
(4, 6, 7, 4)

Two non-simple cycles:
(1, 2, 1)
(4, 5, 6, 4, 7, 6, 4)

Figure 10.2 Paths and Cycles in Graphs

Connectivity and Components

Two vertices in a graph $G = (V, E)$ are said to be *connected* if there is a path from the first to the second in G. Formally, this means that if $x \in V$ and $y \in V$, where $x \neq y$, then x and y are *connected* if there exists a path, $p = v_1 v_2 \ldots v_n$, in G, such that $x = v_1$ and $y = v_n$.

In the graph $G = (V, E)$, a *connected component* is a subset, S, of the vertices V that are all connected to one another. Formally, S is a *connected component* of G if, for any two distinct vertices, $x \in S$ and $y \in S$, x is connected to y. A connected component S of G is a *maximal connected component* provided there is no bigger subset, T, of vertices in V, such that T properly contains the vertices of S (i.e., $T \supset S$), and such that T itself is a connected component of G. Informally, this means that S is a maximal connected component of G if you cannot enlarge S by adding new vertices not already in S that are connected to other vertices in S. An undirected graph G can always be separated into distinct maximal connected components, $S_1, S_2, \ldots, S_k$, such that $S_i \cap S_j = \varnothing$ whenever $i \neq j$. The considerations for directed graphs are slightly different.

In a directed graph, suppose there is a path from vertex v_1 to vertex v_2, but that there is no path from v_2 back to v_1. Then, according to the definition of connectivity given previously, v_1 is connected to v_2, but v_2 is not connected to v_1. This implies that we need to define a slightly different version of connectivity for components in directed graphs than we did for those in undirected graphs. We say that a subset S of vertices in a directed graph G is *strongly connected* if for each pair of distinct vertices (v_i, v_j) in S, v_i is connected to v_j and v_j is connected to v_i. By contrast, we say that a subset S of vertices in a directed graph G is *weakly connected* if for each pair of distinct vertices (v_i, v_j) in S, *either* v_i is connected to v_j *or* v_j is connected to v_i. Figure 10.3 gives two examples of directed graphs, one of which is strongly connected and one of which is weakly connected.

Adjacency Sets and Degrees

Another way to define a graph $G = (V, E)$ that is equivalent to the definition using G's vertex set V and its edge set E, is to specify *adjacency sets* for each vertex in V. Let

connectivity

connected components

adjacency sets

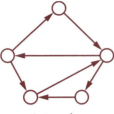
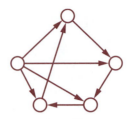

Figure 10.3 Strongly and Weakly Connected Digraphs

A strongly
connected digraph

A weakly
connected digraph

V_x stand for the set of all vertices adjacent to x in the graph G. Formally, we define V_x to be the set of all vertices y such that (x,y) is an edge in E. $V_x = \{y \mid (x,y) \in E\}$ in symbols. If we give both the vertex set V and the collection $A = \{V_x \mid x \in V\}$ of adjacency sets for each vertex in V, we have given enough information to specify the graph G. In an undirected graph G, the *degree* of a vertex x is the number of edges e in which x is one of the endpoints of edge e.

in-degrees and out-degrees

If x is a vertex in a directed graph $G = (V, E)$, we can speak of the *predecessors* of x and the *successors* of x. The predecessors of x, denoted Pred(x), is the set of vertices $y \in V$ such that (y,x) is an edge in E. The successors of x, denoted Succ(x), is the set of vertices $y \in V$ such that (x,y) is an edge in E. The *in-degree* of a vertex x is the number of predecessors of x, and the out-degree of x is the number of successors of x.

Some of the data representations for graphs that we shall discuss in the next section directly use representations of the adjacency sets for each vertex in the graph.

10.2 Review Questions

1. Give the formal definition of a *directed graph* and of an *undirected graph*.
2. How do directed and undirected graphs differ?
3. What is a *path* in a graph? What is a *cycle* in a graph?
4. Define the concept of a *simple cycle*.
5. When are two vertices in a graph connected?
6. What is a connected component of a graph?
7. What is an *adjacency set* for a vertex x in a graph G?
8. Define the *in-degree* and the *out-degree* of a vertex in a directed graph G.

10.2 Exercises

1. List the vertices of degree 3 in the graph of Fig. 10.2.
2. List the adjacency sets for each vertex in the graph of Fig. 10.2.
3. You are given an undirected graph G consisting of the vertices $V = \{a, b, c, d, e, f, g, h, i\}$ and having the following adjacency sets $V_a = \{b,c\}$, $V_b = \{a,c\}$, $V_c = \{a,b,d\}$, $V_d = \{c,e,f\}$, $V_e = \{d\}$, $V_f = \{d\}$, $V_g = \{h,i\}$, $V_h = \{g,i\}$ and $V_i = \{g,h\}$. Draw a diagram of the graph G. How many separate connected components does G have? Give the vertices in each of the two simple cycles of G.

≡ **10.3** Graph Representations

Learning Objectives

1. To learn about adjacency matrices and edge lists.
2. To understand how to use both sequential and linked allocation techniques to represent graphs.
3. To understand the range of possible data representations for graphs.

Let $G = (V, E)$ be a graph. Suppose we number the vertices in V, as $v_1, v_2, \ldots, v_n$ (for some integer n). Now let's make a table $T[i,j]$ having n rows and n columns, such that row i corresponds to v_i and column j corresponds to v_j, ($1 \leq i, j \leq n$). We will fill table T with ones and zeros by putting a 1 in row i and column j exactly when there is an edge $e = (v_i, v_j)$ in E, and by putting a zero in $T[i,j]$ otherwise. Formally, $T[i,j] = 1$ iff[1] there exists $e \in E$, such that $e = (v_i, v_j)$ and $T[i,j] = 0$ iff there *does not* exist an edge $e \in E$, such that $e = (v_i, v_j)$. Such a table, T, is called an *edge matrix*, or an *adjacency matrix* for the graph G. Fig. 10.4 shows a graph and its corresponding *adjacency matrix*.

adjacency matrices

Let's focus for a moment on a row R_i corresponding to a vertex v_i in the adjacency matrix, T, for a graph G. Row R_i has a one in each column j for which an edge $e = (v_i, v_j)$ exists in the edge set E of graph G. We could represent the information in row R_i using a bit vector in C. A bit vector representing row R_i would consist of a sequence of n bits packed together, $R_i = b_1 b_2 \ldots b_n$, such that bit $b_j = T[i,j]$. In C, we could support this representation by a *bit vector representation of sets* as follows. Let **SetSize** be the number of elements in a set, and assume that the set elements are represented by the non-negative integers in the range **0:SetSize – 1**. Let **ByteSize** represent the number of bits in a byte. We will represent a set by a contiguous array of bytes large enough to hold one bit for each element in the set. In what follows, we assume for convenience that the **SetSize** is an exact multiple of the **ByteSize**.

```
#define ByteSize 8          /* assuming that a byte has the same size as a char */
#define SetSize 6*ByteSize   /* assume SetSize is an exact multiple of ByteSize */

typedef char Set[SetSize/ByteSize];
typedef Set AdjacencyMatrix[SetSize];
```

---

[1] The symbol "iff" means "if and only if."

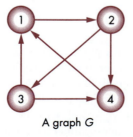

A graph G

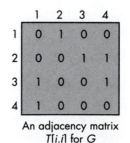

An adjacency matrix
$T[i,j]$ for G

Figure 10.4 A Graph G and Its Adjacency Matrix

To determine the value of the ith bit in a set **S**, we can use the function Member(i,S) defined as follows (where the shift operator **a >> b** shifts byte **a** right by **b** bit positions and where **x & 1** extracts the rightmost bit of **x**):

```
int Member(int i, Set S)              /* to return the value (0 or 1) of the ith bit */
{                                      /* in the bit vector */
    return ( S[ i / ByteSize ] >> (i % ByteSize) ) & 1;    /* representing set S */
}
                    /* Note: The bits in each byte of S are stored in right-to-left order */
```

using C bit vectors to represent edge sets

Row R_i of adjacency matrix T can be represented by a C bit vector specifying which vertices belong to row R_i and which do not belong, where vertex v_j at the top of column j is defined to belong to row R_i iff $T[i,j] = 1$. You can see that this bit vector representation for R_i is identical to the adjacency set for vertex v_i, because the vertices v_j that belong to it are exactly those that are adjacent to vertex v_i.

using lists to represent adjacency sets

Another family of representations for a graph uses list representations of the adjacency sets V_x for the vertices x in the graph. For instance, we could replace each row R_i of the adjacency matrix T with a list of the numbers j of the vertices v_j corresponding to the 1's in row R_i. Such adjacency lists are just another representation for the adjacency sets mentioned above, and these adjacency lists could be represented either with sequential or linked representations as shown in Fig. 10.5. Here, the length of each sequentially represented adjacency list is given in the *degree* column. Recall that, in an undirected graph the *degree* of a vertex v is the number of edges that touch v,

degrees versus in-degrees and out-degrees

whereas, in a directed graph each vertex has two kinds of degrees. The *in-degree* of v is the number of arrows that terminate on v. The *out-degree* of v is the number of arrows that start at vertex v. Consequently, the *degree* column in the sequentially represented adjacency list table actually gives the out-degree of each vertex in Fig. 10.5.

undirected graphs and symmetric adjacency matrices

You can see that the adjacency matrix T corresponding to an *undirected graph* is a *symmetric matrix*. In particular, $T[i,j] = T[j,i]$ for all i and j in the range ($1 \leq i, j \leq n$). This means that the top half of the matrix T above the diagonal d (which runs from the top-left corner to the bottom-right corner of T) is a mirror image of the bottom half of matrix T that lies below the diagonal d. Also, the diagonal entries of d are

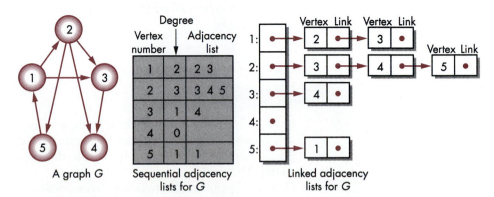

Vertex number	Degree	Adjacency list
1	2	2 3
2	3	3 4 5
3	1	4
4	0	
5	1	1

A graph G   Sequential adjacency lists for G   Linked adjacency lists for G

Figure 10.5 Sequential and Linked Adjacency Lists

themselves zero—i.e., $T[i,i] = 0$ for i in $(1 \leq i \leq n)$, since graphs as we have defined them are not permitted to have looping self-referential edges that connect a vertex to itself.

The adjacency matrix T for a directed graph need not be a symmetric matrix, since it is permissible for a directed edge to go from v_i to v_j without there being an edge from v_j to v_i traveling in the reverse direction. In such a case we would have $T[i,j] = 1$ and $T[j,i] = 0$. The adjacency matrix in Fig. 10.4 is an example of such an unsymmetric matrix.

accessing all vertices from
a starting vertex

In considering search or traversal algorithms for graphs, in which we would like to visit the vertices of a graph G in some systematic order, it is useful to distinguish two separate cases. If G is an undirected graph consisting of a single big connected component, or G is a directed graph consisting of a single strongly connected component, then we can start at any arbitrary vertex of G and we can reach all the other vertices of G by following various paths in G. That is, all vertices of G are accessible, starting from any arbitrary vertex in G.

On the other hand, if G is a directed graph with a single weakly connected component, or if it is either an undirected or a directed graph with several separate components, then we cannot start at any arbitrary vertex v of G and expect to reach all the other vertices of G by following paths starting at v. In the search algorithms explored in the next section, the algorithms we study will take into account this more difficult situation where we may possibly start at a vertex v in G from which it is not possible to access all vertices of G.

10.3 Review Questions

1. What is the adjacency matrix for a graph G? How do the adjacency matrices for directed and undirected graphs differ?
2. Describe how to use C bit vectors to represent a graph, G.
3. What do adjacency sets represent in a graph representation that uses them?
4. What is the difference between the in-degree and the out-degree of a vertex in a directed graph?

10.3 Exercises

1. In Fig. 10.5, the adjacency lists actually list the vertices in the successor vertex sets, Succ(x) for each vertex x in the graph G. Describe how to compute lists of the predecessor vertices, Pred(x) for each x in the graph G, starting with an adjacency matrix, $T[i,j]$ for G.
2. Give an algorithm for converting a representation of a directed graph G, given as an array of linked lists of successor vertices, into a representation of G that uses C bit vectors to represent the adjacency sets.

≡ **10.4** Graph Searching

Learning Objectives

1. To learn about abstract algorithms for depth-first and breadth-first searching in graphs.
2. To learn about the roles stacks and queues can play in organizing searches in graphs.

the basic idea

Let's start with some preliminaries. To search a graph G, we need to visit all of G's vertices in some systematic order. To do this, we usually proceed by identifying some vertex v in G as a starting point. We then systematically enumerate all the other vertices accessible from v along paths in G. Program Strategy 10.6 presents this basic idea.

visiting accessible vertices

We next develop some ideas for enumerating and visiting all vertices w in V that are accessible from an initial starting vertex v in V. First, because the graph we are searching may contain cycles, we need some way for marking a vertex as having been visited so that we do not travel around cycles in an endless loop visiting vertices we have already seen before.

Given that we have defined an enumeration: **typedef enum {false, true} Boolean;** let's assume that each vertex v is a struct having a **Boolean**-valued member v.Visited, which is initially set to **false** for all vertices in G (which are all initially unvisited) and which later gets set to **true**, immediately after we have visited v.

Now we need a way to enumerate the vertices accessible from some vertex x. To do this, we can assume we have an adjacency list V_x (or an equivalent representation for x's adjacency set chosen from the possibilities we discussed in the last section). If vertex x has not been visited before, we mark it as having been visited, by setting **x.Visited = true;**. Then we access the adjacency list V_x and we enter all the unvisited vertices on the list V_x into some sort of storage container, C, which holds unvisited vertices we need to visit in the future.

continuing the search

To continue the search process, provided that container C is not empty, we remove a new vertex x from C, mark x as having been visited, and then enter all the unvisited vertices on V_x into C. This process is repeated until C becomes empty.

two kinds of containers

Let's now write this as Program Strategy 10.7, which is a refinement of Program Strategy 10.6, and see what happens in two separate cases: (1) when the container C is a *stack*, and (2) when the container C is a *queue*.

```
   |    void GraphSearch(G,v)              /* Search graph G starting at vertex v */
   |    {
   |         (let G = (V,E) and let v ∈ V be a vertex of G.)
   |
 5 |         for (each vertex w ∈ V that is accessible from v) {
   |              Visit(w);
   |         }
   |    }
```

Program Strategy 10.6 Preliminary Graph Searching Strategy

```
     |   typedef enum {false, true} Boolean;
     |
     |   void GraphSearch(G,v)                /* Search graph G beginning at vertex v */
     |   {
   5 |       (Let G = (V,E) be a graph.)
     |       (Let C be an empty container.)
     |
     |           for (each vertex x ∈ V) {
     |               x.Visited = false; /* mark each vertex x ∈ V as being unvisited */
  10 |           }
     |
     |       /* Use vertex v ∈ V as a starting point, and put v in container C */
     |           (Put v into C);
     |
  15 |           while (C is non-empty) {
     |
     |               (Remove a vertex x from container C);
     |
     |               if ( !(x.Visited) ) {          /* if vertex hasn't been visited already */
  20 |                   Visit(x);                              /* visit x, and then */
     |                   x.Visited = true;            /* mark x as having been visited */
     |                   for (each vertex w ∈ Vₓ) {    /* Enter all unvisited vertices */
     |                       if ( !(w.Visited) )  (Put w into C);        /* of Vₓ into C */
     |                   }
  25 |               }
     |           }
     |
     |   }
```

Program Strategy 10.7 First Refinement

the stack

When C is a stack, let's suppose that the meaning of the operation (Put v into C) means "push the vertex v onto the top of stack C." Let's also suppose that the operation (Remove a vertex x from container C) means "pop the topmost vertex from C and put it in x."

Let's now try executing this stack-container version of Program Strategy 10.7 on the tree in Fig. 10.8, using vertex 1 at the root of the tree as a starting point.

First, we push vertex 1 onto the top of an initially empty stack C, getting C = (1). Then we repeatedly pop vertices from C, mark them visited, and push their unvisited neighbors on C, until C becomes empty. Let's trace this through.

Figure 10.8 A Tree to Search

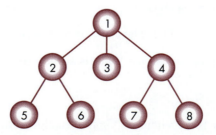

First C = (1). Then we pop 1 from C and put it in x, after which C = () and $x = 1$. We then visit x, and mark it as visited, denoting this, say, by changing $x = 1$ into $x = \underline{1}$. Following this, we push the unvisited vertices on $V_1 = (2,3,4)$ onto C, which gives C = (2,3,4). (Here, we suppose that we push the vertices onto C in the order 4, 3, 2.)

Since C is not empty, we perform the statements in the while-loop on lines 15:26 of Program Strategy 10.7. First, we pop C into x, giving C = (3,4) and $x = 2$. We mark x visited, giving $x = \underline{2}$, and we push the unmarked vertices on $V_2 = (5,6)$ onto C, again in the order: 6, 5. This gives C = (5,6,3,4).

Since C is again nonempty, we pop 5 from C, mark it as $\underline{5}$, and push its unmarked neighbors (of which there are none) onto C. This makes C = (6,3,4). Similarly, 6 and 3 are popped from C and are marked as $\underline{6}$ and $\underline{3}$. Since neither $\underline{6}$ nor $\underline{3}$ have any unmarked neighbors, C now becomes C = (4). After removing 4 from C and marking it as $\underline{4}$, we push 4's unmarked neighbors (7,8) onto C. These are in turn popped from C, and marked as $\underline{7}$ and $\underline{8}$. But since neither 7 nor 8 had any unmarked neighbors, C became empty and remained empty after the removal of $\underline{7}$ and $\underline{8}$. Consequently, the while-loop on lines 15:26 terminates the next time the while-condition on line 15 is tested, immediately after the iteration on which 8 got marked as $\underline{8}$.

You can see that the order in which the nodes of Fig. 10.8 got visited was 1, 2, 5, 6, 3, 4, 7, and 8. This is called a *depth-first order* since any unvisited descendants of a given node x were always visited before any unvisited right brothers or sisters in the tree. In short in any tree, given a choice, depth-first searching always goes *down* (by visiting unvisited children) before going *across* (by visiting unvisited brothers and sisters of a previous parent vertex). If you go down before going across, you are performing depth-first search.

In generalized graphs, however, the directions *down* and *across* lose their meanings. Instead, what happens when depth-first searching is used is that immediate unvisited neighbors of a given vertex v are always visited before any unvisited neighbors of the vertex w, which was visited immediately before v. If you look at the (di)graph of Fig. 10.9, which turns the graph of Fig. 10.8 on its side and adds directed edges to it, you'll see that depth-first search of Fig. 10.9, beginning at vertex 1, still visits the same numbered vertices in the same order.

tracing the operation of the search algorithm

depth-first order in trees

generalized depth-first order

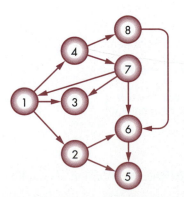

Figure 10.9 Another Graph to Search

Now let's change the container C used in Program Strategy 10.7 from a stack into a queue. Given that C is a queue, let's suppose that the meaning of the operation (Put v into C) means "insert the vertex v onto the rear of queue C," and let's also suppose that the operation (Remove a vertex x from container C) means "remove the first vertex from the front of queue C and put it in x."

Let's again trace the execution of Program Strategy 10.7 on the tree of Fig. 10.8 under these new conditions using a queue C. Suppose that we again start with C = (1).

We first remove the vertex 1 from the front of queue C and put it in x, giving C = () and $x = 1$. After marking $x = \underline{1}$ as visited, we enter the unvisited neighbors of vertex $\underline{1}$ onto the rear of queue C, giving C = (2,3,4). (However, this time, we enter the vertices 2, 3, and 4 in left-to-right order: 2, 3, 4.) We again remove the first vertex 2 from the *front* of queue C and mark it as $\underline{2}$, after which we insert its unmarked neighbors (5,6) onto the *rear* of queue C, giving C = (3,4,5,6). Removing and marking 3 from C leaves C = (4,5,6). Since $\underline{3}$ had no unvisited neighbors, C's rear did not grow as a result of processing $\underline{3}$. After removing 4 and processing it, $\underline{4}$'s unvisited neighbors (7,8) are added to the rear of C, which yields C = (5,6,7,8). These final vertices in C are removed and processed in order, after which C becomes empty and the process terminates.

The order in which the vertices of Fig. 10.8 were visited in this version of graph searching was 1, 2, 3, 4, 5, 6, 7, and 8. You can see that the vertices of the tree in Fig. 10.8 have been visited in level order. We call this process *breadth-first searching*,

since we process all unvisited immediate neighbors of a given vertex x *before* processing any neighbors of x's neighbors—meaning that we go *broad* in the search before we go *deep*. Again, if you perform breadth-first search on the graph of Fig. 10.9, you visit the nodes in the order 1:8, even though there are additional directed edges in the graph when it is compared to the simple tree of Fig. 10.8.

Either the stack version or the queue version of Program Strategy 10.7 will visit every vertex in a graph G provided G is a directed graph with a single strongly connected component or an undirected graph with a single connected component. However, under other circumstances in which some vertices of G are not accessible via paths starting at the initially chosen vertex v in the search, Program Strategy 10.7 will not visit all vertices of G. In such cases, we can embed Program Strategy 10.7

```
 |    void ExhaustiveGraphSearch(G)
 |    {
 |         (Let G = (V,E) be a graph.)
 |
5|         for (each vertex v ∈ V) {            /* perform Program Strategy 10.7 */
 |              GraphSearch(G,v);                         /* for each v ∈ V */
 |         }
 |
 |    }
```

Program Strategy 10.10 Exhaustive Version of Graph Searching

inside an enumeration of vertices of G to ensure all vertices of G will eventually be visited, as shown in Program Strategy 10.10.

If you know whether or not every vertex in G is accessible from any arbitrary starting vertex v in G, you'll have the information you need to choose whether to use the simpler Program Strategy 10.7 or the stronger version given in Program Strategy 10.10.

10.4 Review Questions

1. Describe the difference between depth-first searching and breadth-first searching in a tree, then describe the difference between depth-first and breadth-first searching in a general graph.
2. What are the differences between using stacks and using queues to hold unvisited vertices that need to be visited in the future during graph searching?
3. How can we ensure that a graph searching process will visit all possible vertices, even though the graph being searched is not a single connected component?

10.4 Exercises

1. Trace the operation of Program Strategy 10.7, using a queue as the container C, on the graph of Fig. 10.9, and show both the order in which the vertices are visited and the contents of the queue C at each stage.
2. Implement a refinement of Program Strategy 10.7 in which adjacency sets V_x are represented using linked lists.
3. Implement a new version of Program Strategy 10.7 that performs depth-first searching using recursion instead of using a stack container C.
4. Implement new versions of Program Strategies 10.7 and 10.10 that are guaranteed to visit each vertex of a graph once and only once.

≡ 10.5 Topological Ordering

Learning Objectives

1. To understand the concept of a topological order.
2. To learn an algorithm for producing a topological order.

topological order   Suppose we have a directed graph G that contains no cycles. For example, G might be a graph in which the vertices represent college courses to take and in which an edge is

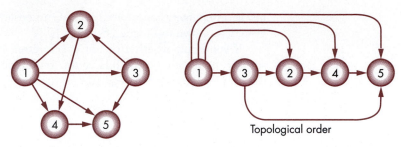

Figure 10.11 A Directed Acyclic Graph and Its Vertices in Topological Order

directed from the vertex for course A to the vertex for course B if course A is a prerequisite for course B. A *topological ordering* for the vertices in graph G is a sequential list L of G's vertices such that if there is a directed path from vertex A to vertex B in G, then A comes before B in the list L. In the case of the prerequisite graph G for college courses, L would list courses in an order such that all prerequisites of each course C are listed before C itself occurs in the list L.

Figure 10.11 shows a directed graph G containing no cycles and gives a topological order for the vertices in G. (If a graph G contains no cycles, it is said to be an *acyclic graph*. The abbreviation *DAG* is sometimes used for a *directed acyclic graph*.)

Let G be a DAG. Let's see if we can think through a rough general strategy for discovering a topological order for the vertices of G. We know that we cannot place a particular vertex v in G on the list L until all of v's predecessors have been listed in L. Suppose we have an array $D[v]$ which gives the in-degree of each vertex v in G. The vertices v in G that have no predecessors in G are the ones in array D having zero for in-degrees. That is, if $D[v] == 0$, it means v has no predecessors, since the in-degree counts the number of predecessors. So to start the list L, we could initially list all vertices v of G that have no predecessors, which consists of those vertices v such that $D[v] == 0$. A step of an abstract program strategy to accomplish this might read

initializing the list L

(Initially let L be the list of all vertices v, such that $D[v] == 0$).

Now, suppose we decide to make the array entry $D[v]$ keep track of the number of remaining predecessors of v that have not already been listed in L. That is, we decide to change the meaning of $D[v]$ from

$$D[v] == \text{(the number of predecessors of vertex } v \text{ in graph G)}$$

to become

$$D[v] \; == \; (\text{the number of predecessors } p \text{ of vertex } v \text{ in graph G, such that } p \notin L).$$

To update the array D to keep track only of the number of predecessors that have *not been listed* in list L, we need to change the counts in D at the moment we add a new vertex v to the end of list L. To do this, we can enumerate the successors of v and decrease each of their remaining in-degree counts by 1. Some steps of a program strategy to do this would be

```
/* Add vertex v to the end of list L */
    for (each successor w ∈ Succ(v) in the graph G) {
        D[w] – –;
    }
```

When the successors $w \in \text{Succ}(v)$ have their in-degree counts decreased, as a result of putting v on the end of list L, some of them may reach a condition in which their in-degrees have diminished to zero, $D[w] == 0$. This signifies that all of their predecessors have already been listed in L. Consequently, there is an opportunity to put w on the end of list L, since it now has no predecessors that have not been listed already. If we maintain a queue of vertices with in-degree 0 to be added to the end of list L, we can place w on this queue immediately after its in-degree decreases to zero. Let Q be a queue of vertices with in-degree 0 awaiting processing. We can then rewrite the above program fragment as

```
/* Add vertex v to the end of list L */
    for (each successor w ∈ Succ(v) in the graph G) {
        D[w] – –;
        if ( D[w] == 0 ) (insert w in queue Q);
    }
```

We can agree to let the role of the queue, Q, be the same as that for the queue used in breadth-first searching of a graph G. Namely, Q can contain vertices that remain to be visited in breadth-first order. Essentially, we can modify the algorithm for performing a breadth-first search, using the queue Q, so that it repeatedly removes a new vertex v from the front of queue Q, puts v on the end of list L, decreases the in-degrees of the successors of v, and inserts on the end of Q any such successors of v whose in-degrees have decreased to zero. By this means, a queue-driven, breadth-first searching process enumerates vertices in topological order and adds them to the end of the list L.

A complete strategy for accomplishing this is presented as Program Strategy 10.12. Exercise 10.5.1 asks you to implement this program strategy in C using an array of pointers to linked representations of adjacency lists as the representation for the directed graph G.

```
        |    void TopologicalOrder(Graph G,  List *L)
        |    {
        |        (Let G = (V,E) be a graph.)
        |        (Let L be a list of vertices.)                    /* see Program 7.4 */
    5   |        (Let Q be a queue of vertices.)                   /* for queue operations */
        |        (Let D[V] be an array of integers indexed by vertices in V.)
        |
        |        /* Compute the in-degrees D[x] of the vertices x in G */
        |            for (each vertex x ∈ V) D[x] = 0;             /* initialize D[x] to zero */
   10   |            for (each vertex x ∈ V) {
        |                for (each successor w ∈ Succ(x)) D[w]++;
        |            }
        |
        |        /* Initialize the queue Q to contain all vertices having zero in-degrees */
   15   |            Initialize(&Q);                    /* initialize Q to be the empty queue */
        |            for (each vertex x ∈ V) {                         /* insert x on the */
        |                if (D[x] == 0) Insert(x,&Q);              /* rear of Q if D[x] == 0 */
        |            }
        |
   20   |        /* Initialize the list L to be the empty list */
        |            InitializeList(&L);
        |
        |        /* Process vertices in the queue Q until the queue becomes empty */
        |            while ( !Empty(&Q) ) {
   25   |                Remove(&Q,x);          /* Remove vertex x from the front of Q */
        |                AddToList(x,&L);                  /* Insert x on the rear of list L */
        |                for (each successor w ∈ Succ(x)) {
        |                    D[w] − −;                  /* decrease predecessor count of w */
        |                    if (D[w] == 0) Insert(w,&Q);       /* insert w on the rear of Q */
   30   |                }
        |            }
        |
        |        /* The list L now contains the vertices of G in topological order. */
        |
        |    }
```

Program Strategy 10.12 Topological Ordering

10.5 Review Questions

1. What is a DAG (i.e., a directed acyclic graph)?
2. Define the concept of a topological order for the vertices of a DAG.
3. Sketch a process for finding a topological order for the vertices of a DAG.

10.5 Exercises

1. Implement Program Strategy 10.12 in C using an array of pointers to linked representations of adjacency lists as the representation for the directed acyclic graph G.
2. How could you augment Program Strategy 10.12 to detect illegal cycles in the graph G?

3. Can you give a second abstract strategy for producing a topological ordering of the vertices in a directed, acyclic graph using a modification of the recursive strategy for performing a depth-first search of G?
4. Analyze the running time of your implementation of Program Strategy 10.12. Can you show that it is O($e + n$), where n is the number of vertices in G and e is the number of edges in G?

≡ **10.6** Shortest Paths

Learning Objectives

1. To learn about the concept of weighted graphs.
2. To learn how to find shortest paths in such graphs.

Weighted graphs are digraphs in which numbers called *weights* are attached to the directed edges. The weights attached to edges could be used to represent quantities such as distances, costs, or times. For instance, if the vertices of a graph represent cities on a map, the weight on an edge connecting city A to city B could represent the travel distance from A to B, the cost of an airline ticket to fly from A to B, or the time required to travel from A to B. Suppose for the moment that such a graph gives distances between cities. Then, given two cities X and Y, we might want to know the path of shortest distance from X to Y. Such a shortest path might travel through intermediate cities along the way from X to Y.

weighted graphs

Figure 10.13 gives a weighted graph showing distances between cities. A shortest path from 1 to 5 is shown by the thickened edges in this graph. To represent a weighted directed graph G, suppose we use an adjacency matrix $T[i,j]$ in which, $T[i,j] = w_{ij}$ if there exists an edge $e = (v_i, v_j)$ of weight w_{ij}, in which $T[i,i] = 0$, and in which $T[i,j] = \infty$ if there is no edge from v_i to v_j. Suppose further that all edge weights are positive numbers, $w_{ij} > 0$. The matrix T for the graph in Fig. 10.13 is given as Table 10.14.

weighted adjacency matrices

Suppose we are trying to find the shortest path from vertex 1 to vertex 5 in the graph in Fig. 10.13. We start with a vertex set $W = \{1\}$ containing only the origin vertex of the path, 1. We will progressively enlarge W by adding one new vertex at a time, until W includes all vertices of V, where $V = \{1, 2, 3, 4, 5, 6\}$, and consists of all vertices in the vertex set V of graph G.

enlarging the vertex set W in stages

Figure 10.13 The Shortest Path in a Graph

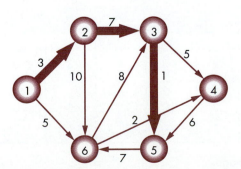

—	1	2	3	4	5	6
1	0	3	∞	∞	∞	5
2	∞	0	7	∞	∞	10
3	∞	∞	0	5	1	∞
4	∞	∞	∞	0	6	∞
5	∞	∞	∞	∞	0	7
6	∞	∞	8	2	∞	0

Table 10.14 Adjacency Matrix, T, for the Graph in Fig. 10.13

The vertex we add at each stage is the vertex w in $V - W$, which is at a minimum distance from the origin x among all vertices in $V - W$ that have not yet been added to W. The way we keep track of the "minimum distance from x" at each stage is to use an array, ShortestDistance[u], which keeps track of the shortest distance from x to each vertex in $u \in W$ and also to each vertex u in $V - W$ using a path p starting at x, such that all vertices of path p lie in W, except the last vertex u, which lies outside W. Every time we add a new vertex to W, we update the array, ShortestDistance[u] to keep its values "up-to-date."

Table 10.15 presents a step-by-step example of how this works for the graph G in Fig. 10.13. In the row corresponding to the start stage, $W = \{1\}$, the shortest distance from vertex 1 to some vertex in $V - W = \{2, 3, 4, 5, 6\}$ is chosen by finding the smallest number among the values of ShortestDistance[u] in the columns for $\{2, 3, 4, 5, 6\}$ on the right side of Table 10.15. The column for vertex 2 has a distance of 3, and the column for vertex 6 has a distance of 5. This is because vertex 1 connects to vertices 2 and 6 via edges of length 3 and 5 in Figure 10.13. Here the path of smallest distance connecting vertex 1 to some vertex outside the set $W = \{1\}$ is just the edge from vertex 1 to vertex 2, so we choose $w = 2$ for the second stage of the process.

choosing a new vertex in the second stage

In the second stage (corresponding to row 2 of Table 10.15), we see that $w = 2$ and the shortest distance from 1 to w is given in the $\Delta(w)$ column as $\Delta(w) = 3$. Also, we have enlarged W, by adding the vertex 2, so that, now, $W = \{1, 2\}$. In turn, this makes $V - W$ shrink, because of the loss of 2, so that $V - W = \{3, 4, 5, 6\}$, as shown

Stage	W	$V-W$	w	$\Delta(w)$	$\Delta(1)$	$\Delta(2)$	$\Delta(3)$	$\Delta(4)$	$\Delta(5)$	$\Delta(6)$
					Values of ShortestDistance[u] = $\Delta(u)$					
Start	$\{1\}$	$\{2,3,4,5,6\}$	—	—	0	3	∞	∞	∞	5
2	$\{1,2\}$	$\{3,4,5,6\}$	2	3	0	3	10	∞	∞	5
3	$\{1,2,6\}$	$\{3,4,5\}$	6	5	0	3	10	7	∞	5
4	$\{1,2,6,4\}$	$\{3,5\}$	4	7	0	3	10	7	13	5
5	$\{1,2,6,4,3\}$	$\{5\}$	3	10	0	3	10	7	11	5
6	$\{1,2,6,4,3,5\}$	$\{\ \}$	5	11	0	3	10	7	11	5

Table 10.15 Expanding the Vertex Set W in Stages

in row 2. We now need to update the array, **ShortestDistance[u]**, by recomputing shortest distances to vertices in $V - W$, accessible via paths starting at vertex 1, and using intermediary vertices in W, except for the last vertex $u \notin W$. We see that we can get to vertex 3, starting at 1, via the two paths $(1, 2, 3)$ and $(1, 6, 3)$. Of these two paths, the path $(1, 2, 3)$ has the shorter distance 10, and the path $(1, 6, 3)$ has the longer distance 13. So we put 10, for the shortest distance from 1 to 3, in the $\Delta(3)$ column of row 2 of Table 10.15 to show that 10 is the shortest distance to vertex 3 from vertex 1 via a path traveling entirely along vertices in W except for the path's last vertex. Note that we cannot access vertices 4 or 5, via any possible path starting at vertex 1, and traveling via vertices in $W = \{1, 2\}$, so the shortest distances $\Delta(4) = \Delta(5) = \infty$ in row 2, to denote that vertices 4 and 5 are inaccessible via paths through W. Also, even though a new path $(1, 2, 6)$ opened up to access vertex 6 starting at vertex 1, its distance was 13, which is not shorter than the original direct distance 5, so we do not need to update the distance in the $\Delta(6)$ column in row 2. Had it been the case that path $(1, 2, 6)$ opened up a shorter route to vertex 6 than the direct route of length 5, we would have updated the $\Delta(6)$ entry by substituting this new shorter distance.

We are now ready to begin stage three of the process, by choosing a new vertex w in $V - W = \{3, 4, 5, 6\}$ of least distance from the origin vertex, 1. To do this we scan row 2 under the columns $\Delta(3)$, $\Delta(4)$, $\Delta(5)$, and $\Delta(6)$ to find the entry of least distance, and we choose $w = 6$, since $\Delta(6) = 5$ is smaller than $\Delta(3) = 10$ and also smaller than $\Delta(4) = \Delta(5) = \infty$. Thus, we add vertex 6 to W, which now becomes $W = \{1, 2, 6\}$. Then, we proceed to fill in more entries in row 3, by setting $V - W = \{3, 4, 5\}$, $w = 6$, and $\Delta(w) = 5$.

Finally, we need to recompute shortest distances to vertices in $V - W = \{3, 4, 5\}$, by examining G to see if new paths of shorter distance have opened up that travel through vertices in the newly enlarged W to vertices in $V - W$. We see that we can now access vertices 3 and 4, via the new paths $(1, 6, 3)$ and $(1, 6, 4)$. The first of these paths $(1, 6, 3)$ takes us to vertex 3 along a path of length 13, which is not shorter than the old distance 10 we already had established via the path $(1, 2, 3)$. So no update is performed in the $\Delta(3)$ column in row 3. However, the path $(1, 6, 4)$ takes us to vertex 4 along a path of length 7, so we can put a 7 in the $\Delta(4)$ column in row 3, to signify that the minimum distance to vertex 4, starting at vertex 1, along a path lying wholly within W except for vertex 4 itself, has now become 7. Again, vertex 5 is still inaccessible via paths using vertices in W, so its entry remains $\Delta(5) = \infty$, to signify that it is still inaccessible via paths through W.

We are now ready to proceed to stage four. The entry of shortest distance among the vertices in $V - W = \{3, 4, 5\}$ of row 3 is vertex 4. Its distance is 7, which is shorter than the others. So we begin to fill in the row for stage four. First, we enlarge W by adding vertex 4, making $W = \{1, 2, 6, 4\}$. This diminishes $V - W$ to become $\{3, 5\}$. Then we set $w = 4$, and its distance $\Delta(w)$ to be equal to 7. Finally, we update the shortest distances to vertices in $V - W = \{3, 5\}$ by entering the new distance 13 in the $\Delta(5)$ column in the row for stage four, since vertex 5 has now become accessible via the shortest path $(1, 6, 4, 5)$ of length 13.

Now, in the fifth stage, we choose the next closest vertex $w = 3$, among the vertices $\{3, 5\}$ in the set $V - W$, since $\Delta(3) = 10$ and $\Delta(5) = 13$. We enlarge W to become

starting stage three of the process

stage four

stage five

{1, 2, 6, 4, 3} and then fill in the other columns in the row for stage five. When we update the shortest distances in row 5, the entry in the $\Delta(5)$ column changes from $\Delta(5) = 13$ to $\Delta(5) = 11$. This is because a new path (1, 2, 3, 5) of length 11 opened up traveling via vertices in $W = \{1, 2, 6, 4, 3\}$ that was shorter than the best former path (1, 6, 4, 5) of length 13 which traveled through the former smaller W, which excluded vertex 3.

the last stage
In the sixth and final stage, we choose $w = 5$, since 5 is the only remaining unchosen vertex in $V - W$, and we conclude that its shortest distance is 11. The thickened path in graph G of Figure 10.13, shows this shortest path.

We are now ready to move from consideration of one specific example to a general description of the shortest path algorithm, and to a proof that the algorithm, indeed, finds the correct result.

Let's look at Program Strategy 10.16 for the algorithm, which is called Dijkstra's Algorithm, after its discoverer, Edsger W. Dijkstra. In this **ShortestPath** algorithm, we assume $G = (V, E)$ is a weighted directed graph. We let $T[i,j] \geq 0$ give the weight on the edge from vertex i to vertex j, where $T[i,i] = 0$, where $T[i,j] > 0$ if there exists an edge from i to j in the edge set E, and where $T[i,j] = \infty$ if there is no edge from i to j in

```
     void ShortestPath(void)
     {

  5      (Let MinDistance be a variable that contains edge weights as values)
         (and let Minimum(x,y) be a function whose value is the lesser of x and y.)

         /* Let v₁ ∈ V be the origin vertex at which the shortest path starts. */
         /* Initialize W and ShortestDistance[u] as follows: */
            W = {v₁};
 10         ShortestDistance[v₁] = 0;
            for (each u in V − {v₁} ) ShortestDistance[u] = T[v₁][u];

         /* Now repeatedly enlarge W until W includes all vertices in V */
            while (W != V) {
 15            /* find the vertex w ∈ V − W at the minimum distance from v₁ */
               MinDistance = ∞;
               for (each v ∈ V − W) {
                  if (ShortestDistance[v] < MinDistance) {
                     MinDistance = ShortestDistance[v];
 20                  w = v;
                  }
               }
            /* add w to W */
               W = W ∪ {w};
 25         /* update the shortest distances to vertices in V − W */
               for (each u ∈ V − W) {
                  ShortestDistance[u] =
                     Minimum(ShortestDistance[u],
                        ShortestDistance[w] +T[w][u]);
 30            }
            }
     }
```

Program Strategy 10.16 Dijkstra's Shortest Path Algorithm

E. We assume every vertex in V is accessible via a weighted directed path from some origin vertex v_1 in V, and we are trying to find a shortest path from v_1 to every other vertex in G.

You can see that, at each stage of this process, we enlarge W by one new vertex w and update the shortest distances from v_1 to every vertex in V − W via paths with intermediary vertices lying in W. Eventually, W grows to encompass all the vertices V of the graph G that are accessible via a path starting at v_1. Provided that the destination vertex y is accessible by at least one path in G starting at v_1, y will eventually be included in W, and the shortest distance to y will be known.

Now, we might ask, "What gives us confidence that this process actually works correctly?" That is, why do we have a right to assume that this process for stepwise enlargement of the vertex set W, followed by updating of the array ShortestDistance[u], will succeed in finding the shortest path?

proving Dijkstra's Algorithm

Thus we need to prove that our process for adding a new vertex w to W and updating ShortestDistance[u] for $u \in$ V − W will, in fact, preserve the invariant property that, after W is enlarged by the addition of w, ShortestDistance[u] gives the distance of the shortest path from v_1 to every vertex $u \in$ V − W via intermediaries lying wholly in W. We proceed to prove this by induction on the size of the vertex set, W.

base case

For the *base case*, suppose W = $\{v_1\}$. Since ShortestDistance[u] is initialized to give the length of the edge from v_1 to u for every $u \in$ V − $\{v_1\}$, it must give the shortest distance from v_1 to u via intermediaries lying in W, since there is only one such intermediary, namely, v_1 itself.

induction step

Now for the *induction step*. Let's say that we are ready to enlarge the vertex set W by choosing a new vertex, w, to add to it. We choose $w \in$ V − W so that ShortestDistance[w] is the minimum for all vertices not in W (using lines 15:22 of Program Strategy 10.16).

If ShortestDistance[w] is not the length of the shortest path from v_1 to w, there must exist some shorter path p, which starts at v_1 and contains a vertex in V − W, other than w. We can start at the origin v_1 and proceed along path p, passing through vertices in W, until we come to the first vertex, r, that is not in W. But the length of the initial portion of the path p from v_1 to r is shorter than the length of the entire path p from v_1 to w (since all edges in the path p have positive weights, and we are only adding up the values of some of them, not all of them, to get the length of the path from v_1 to r). Since we assumed the length of path p was shorter than ShortestDistance[w], the length of the path from v_1 to r is shorter than ShortestDistance[w] also. Moreover, the path from v_1 to r has all of its vertices except for r lying in W. Thus we would have had ShortestDistance[r] < ShortestDistance[w] at the time w was chosen as the next vertex to add to W. But this contradicts the choice of w and would have meant that we would have chosen r instead (since r's distance was less than w's, and since we were choosing the vertex u in V − W of least distance given by ShortestDistance[u] as the next vertex to add to W). Because the assumption that a shorter path p existed led to this contradiction, we see that no such shorter path p could exist. So ShortestDistance[u] is the length of the shortest path from v_1 to u.

the final part of the induction step

In order to prove the final part of the induction step we need to verify that ShortestDistance[u] gives the shortest distance from v_1 to every vertex $u \in$ V −W traveling via intermediaries in W after the new vertex w has been added to W. The updating process on lines 25:30 of Program Strategy 10.16 guarantees that this condition is maintained after we add the new vertex w to W. This is because of the fact that if any new paths from v_1 to u traveling through the new vertex w are opened up after vertex w is added to W, the new shortest distances available via these new shorter paths will replace the older shortest distances existing in the array ShortestDistance[u] before the update occurred.

Program Strategy 10.16 runs in time $O(n^2)$, where n is the number of vertices in V, and computes the length of the shortest path from vertex v_1 to each vertex in V. To see why this is so, the initialization on line 11 runs through $(n - 1)$ vertices and takes time $O(n)$. The while-loop on lines 14:31 runs through the $(n - 1)$ vertices of $V - \{v_1\}$ one at a time, and for each such vertex, the selection of the new vertex at minimum distance, on lines 17:22, as well as the updating process on lines 25:30, takes time proportional to the number of vertices in $V - W$. If for each i in the range 2:n you do an operation, $(n + 1 - i)$ times, that costs each time at most a constant time, C, the dominant cost is of the form $\sum_{(2 \leq i \leq n)} \sum_{(1 \leq j \leq (n+1-i))} C$, which is $O(n^2)$. (Exercise 10.6.2 asks you to find a proof for this fact.)

10.6 Review Questions

1. What is a weighted graph? How do you define a shortest path in it?
2. Describe informally how Dijkstra's Shortest Path Algorithm works.

10.6 Exercises

1. Implement Program Strategy 10.16 using the graph in Figure 10.13. Confirm that your implementation finds the shortest path length, 11, for the path from vertex 1 to vertex 5.
2. Given a constant, C, show that $S = \sum_{(2 \leq i \leq n)} \sum_{(1 \leq j \leq (n+1-i))} C$ is $O(n^2)$ by showing that $S = C*n(n - 1)/2$.

10.7 Task Networks

Learning Objectives

1. To gain an intuitive understanding of critical path problems and their solutions presented as PERT Charts and Milestone Charts.
2. To learn about task networks using graphs whose vertices are weighted with task durations.
3. To learn about algorithms for computing critical paths and earliest project completion times.

critical path problems

In this section we investigate *critical path problems* in the overall setting of a project consisting of a network-like organization of various activities.

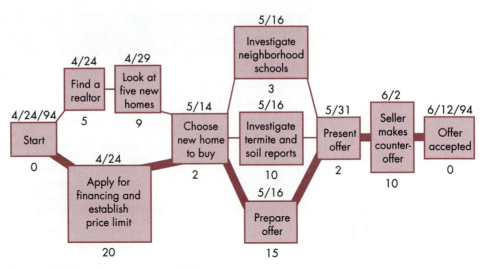

Figure 10.17 An Example of a PERT Chart for a Project

We imagine that each *project* has a number of component activities called *tasks*. Each task has a *duration*, which is the amount of time required to complete the task. Each task is linked into a network that specifies which other *predecessor tasks* must be accomplished before it can be started, and which *successor tasks* cannot be started until the given task is finished. An example of such a network is given in Fig. 10.17, where the date at the top of each task box is the start date for the task, and the number at the bottom is its duration in days.

The network in Fig. 10.17 is an example of a *PERT chart*. PERT stands for *Project Evaluation and Review Technique*. PERT charts have been used in large, serious applications to help project managers detect which activities are falling behind schedule. It is reported that the PERT chart for the Apollo Moon Project encompassed over 10,000 tasks whose task status reports were updated daily prior to the launching of the first manned rocket to the moon.

A key concept in a PERT chart is the notion of a *critical path*. A critical path has the property that each task on it is *critical* in the following sense: If the completion time of any task on the critical path slips by an amount of time ΔT, then the completion time for the whole project slips by ΔT. A critical path in Fig. 10.17 is shown as a thick line that goes from the "Start" node to the "Offer accepted" node.

Noncritical tasks not lying on the critical path may have what is called *slack time*. If such noncritical tasks have their completion times slip by an amount of time not exceeding their slack time, the project can still finish at its current completion time. In other words, such slack time represents an extra time allowance for slippage of a task's individual completion time that can occur without delaying the entire project. Consequently, another property of the critical path is that no task on the critical path can have slack time.

Some types of project management software enable managers to enter a network of individual tasks, by describing each task's duration, predecessors, and successors,

projects and tasks

PERT charts

defining the critical path

slack time

milestone charts

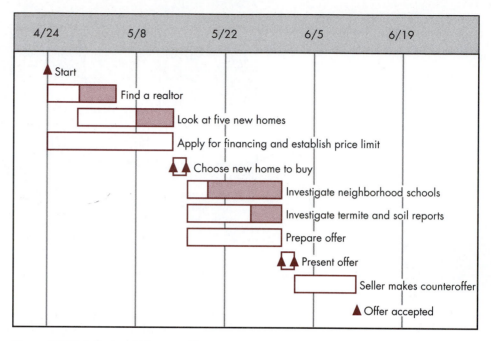

Figure 10.18 A Project Milestone Chart

and then to discover the critical path and the estimated project completion date. The PERT chart for the project can be displayed graphically, and other *views* of the project data such as *milestone charts* and *resource consumption estimates* can be computed. For example, Fig. 10.18 shows a milestone chart for the project in Fig. 10.17.

The solid triangle labeled "Start" is the beginning *milestone* on this chart. The next milestone is "Choose new home to buy." In between these two milestones are the three tasks: "Find a realtor," "Look at 5 new homes," and "Apply for financing and establish price limit." The task "Apply for financing and establish price limit" (which takes 20 days and is on the critical path of Fig. 10.17) has no slack time, as indicated by its clear rectangle in the milestone chart. However, the task "Find a realtor" (which takes 5 days and is not on the critical path) has 6 days of slack time, as indicated by the shaded area of its rectangle. "Find a realtor" has slack time because when its 5-day duration is added to the 9 days it takes to perform its successor task "Look at 5 new homes," giving a total of 14 days, there are still 6 days left before the start of the next task "Choose new home to buy," whose start date is forced to be 20 days after the start date of the whole project by the 20 day duration of the task "Apply for financing and establish price limit."

To develop algorithms for finding critical paths in task networks, we can use graphs as a formal representation. Such graphs are just directed graphs containing no cycles, in which tasks are represented by numbered vertices and in which task durations have been attached below the vertices. For example, the PERT chart in Fig. 10.17 is represented by the graph in Fig. 10.19. Each such graph must be a DAG.

interpreting a milestone chart

using graphs to represent task networks

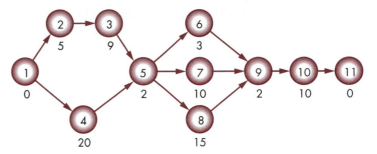

Figure 10.19 Directed Acyclic Graph with Durations Below Vertices

(Recall that graphs with no cycles are called *acyclic*, and directed acyclic graphs are abbreviated as DAGs.)

using arrays to represent task networks

We could also represent the PERT chart in Fig. 10.17 or the DAG in Fig. 10.19 using the array in Table 10.20. Each row of the array could be represented by a struct. The last two members of the struct representing each row could contain representations of the *successor list* and *predecessor list* for the vertex corresponding to the row.

We are now ready to develop the algorithms that determine critical paths, and the earliest and latest starting and finishing times for each task in a DAG representing the tasks, task durations, and task dependencies of a project. We will agree to use the term *task network* to refer to such a DAG with task durations attached to the vertices.

Critical Path Algorithms

Let's agree to keep task durations in an array D[1:MaxVertex], indexed by vertex numbers, where vertex numbers start at 1 and increase to the largest vertex number,

Vertex Number	Title of Task	Start Date	Duration	Successor List	Predecessor List
1	Start	4/24/94	0	(2,4)	( )
2	Find a realtor	4/24/94	5	(3)	(1)
3	Look at 5 new homes	4/29/94	9	(5)	(2)
4	Apply for financing and establish price limit	4/24/94	20	(5)	(1)
5	Choose new home to buy	5/14/94	2	(6,7,8)	(3,4)
6	Investigate neighborhood schools	5/16/94	3	(9)	(5)
7	Investigate termite and soil reports	5/16/94	10	(9)	(5)
8	Prepare offer	5/16/94	15	(9)	(5)
9	Present offer	5/31/94	2	(10)	(6,7,8)
10	Seller makes counteroffer	6/2/94	10	(11)	(9)
11	Offer accepted	6/12/94	0	( )	(10)

Table 10.20 Array Representation of PERT Chart

MaxVertex. We shall proceed by computing several times associated with each vertex in the graph, and we shall store these times in various arrays, also indexed by vertex numbers. In particular, let

$$\text{EFT}[v] = \text{the Earliest Finish Time for vertex } v$$
$$\text{LFT}[v] = \text{the Latest Finish Time for vertex } v$$
$$\text{EST}[v] = \text{the Earliest Starting Time for vertex } v$$
$$\text{LST}[v] = \text{the Latest Starting Time for vertex } v$$

and let's also define a quantity, PFT, as follows:

$$\text{PFT} = \text{the Project Finishing Time.}$$

We now discuss some additional rules we agree to follow when dealing with task networks. In any task network, we agree that we can never begin work on a given task until all of the task's predecessors have been completed. We assume there is a clock that starts at time 0. At the start time for the entire project, we can start working on any of the tasks having no predecessors, and we can start working on them at time 0—the *project starting time*.

For a given task, t, having predecessor tasks in the list $\text{Pred}(t) = (t_1, t_2, \ldots, t_k)$ we can begin working on task t only after all the tasks $(t_1, t_2, \ldots, t_k)$ have been completed. For example, in Table 10.20, task 5 has predecessors, $\text{Pred}(5) = (3,4)$, so we can begin working on task 5, only after tasks 3 and 4 have both been completed.

We now desire to compute several important times for the entire task network and for the vertices in this network. For example, we would like to know PFT, the *project finishing time*, which gives the earliest time on the clock (which started ticking at time 0) at which the entire project could finish. Also, for each vertex v, we would

computing several
important times
for the task network

like to know the earliest time, $\text{EST}[v]$, at which we can start work on the task represented by vertex v, as well as the latest time, $\text{LST}[v]$, at which we can start working on v, *without delaying the completion time for the entire project*. We would like to know the earliest and latest finishing times for v, as well, where $\text{EFT}[v]$ gives the earliest possible time at which v could be completed, and where $\text{LFT}[v]$ gives the latest time at which v could be finished without delaying the completion time for the entire project.

It turns out that there is an easy way to compute all of these times, once we have computed a *topological order* for the vertices of the task network, G. Recall, from Section 10.5, that a topological order for the vertices in G is just a sequential order for

using topological order

G's vertices in which all predecessors of each vertex v are listed before v itself. Suppose we execute the algorithm in Program Strategy 10.12 on the task network shown in Figure 10.19. Suppose that the result is a list represented by an array, **TopoOrderArray[1:MaxVertex]**, which gives a topological ordering for the vertices of Fig. 10.19. In particular, Table 10.21 gives one possible result for this topological order.

computing earliest
finishing times

Suppose that we are trying to compute the earliest finish times, $\text{EFT}[v]$, for each vertex v, in the task network. We could start by identifying the vertices having no predecessors, since these are the ones corresponding to tasks that can be started at the

	Values of TopoOrderArray[i]										
array index i =	1	2	3	4	5	6	7	8	9	10	11
vertex in TopoOrderArray[i] =	1	2	4	3	5	6	7	8	9	10	11

Table 10.21 Topological Order for Vertices in Fig. 10.19

moment the clock begins to tick, at time 0. The earliest time on the project clock that such a v can finish is just its duration, $D[v]$, since it starts at time 0, and finishes after time $D[v]$ has elapsed.

Now suppose we have a task v with predecessors $w \in \text{Pred}(v)$, for which the earliest finishing times, $EFT[w]$, are known for each $w \in \text{Pred}(v)$. When is the earliest time on the project's clock that task v itself can finish? Since work on task v cannot begin until all of v's predecessor tasks have been completed, the *latest* of the completion times for v's predecessors defines the earliest time at which work on v can begin. That is, the *earliest starting time* for v, $EST[v] = maximum(EFT[w])$ where the *maximum* is taken over all $w \in \text{Pred}(v)$. (Here, the *maximum* operation, when applied to clock times, $EFT[w]$, finds the *latest* such time, since the latest time on the project clock is the one with the biggest time value on that clock.) Then, to find the *earliest finishing time* for v, $EFT[v]$, all we have to do is add v's duration $D[v]$ to its earliest starting time, $EST[v]$. Figure 10.22 expresses these observations in symbols.

Once we know the earliest finishing times for all vertices v, we can calculate, PFT, the earliest time at which the entire project can finish. PFT is simply the latest among the times $EFT[v]$, for all vertices v in the task network. That is, the earliest time on the project clock that the entire project can finish is the earliest time at which all tasks in the project are completed, which, in turn, is the latest among the times $EFT[v]$, at which the individual tasks can be completed. Figure 10.23 expresses this in symbols.

Fortunately, when we need to compute the times $EFT[v]$ and $EST[v]$, we can consider the vertices of the graph G in topological order. The reason why this works is that we can compute $EFT[v]$ according to Fig. 10.22, whenever the EFTs of all of v's predecessors are already known. But if, when computing such EFTs, we process ver-

computing the project finishing time

If task v has no predecessors (i.e., if $\text{Pred}(v) = \varnothing$, the empty list) then
  $EFT[v] = D[v]$.

Otherwise, if task v has predecessors, $w \in \text{Pred}(v)$
    $EST[v] = maximum(EFT[w])$ for all $w \in \text{Pred}(v)$
  and
    $EFT[v] = EST[v] + D[v]$.

Figure 10.22 Earliest Starting and Finishing Times

> The project finishing time (PFT) is defined by
> PFT = maximum(EFT[v]) for all v ∈ the graph G.

Figure 10.23 The Project Finishing Time

tices of G in topological order, we are guaranteed to have computed the EFTs for all of v's predecessors before we attempt to compute the EFT for v itself. So our algorithm for computing EFTs needs only to apply the formulas of Fig. 10.22 to the vertices of G in topological order. It's that simple. Program Strategy 10.24 expresses how to do this. Here we assume that we have already first computed a topological ordering for the vertices, and that we have stored a list of such vertices in topological order in the array TopoOrderArray[1:MaxVertex] (as illustrated in Table 10.21).

the algorithm for the project finish time

Once we have computed the earliest starting and finishing times for each of the tasks in the project, we are prepared to compute the project finishing time (PFT), the

```
     void EarliestStartingAndFinishingTimes(void)
     {

         (Let TopoOrderArray[1:MaxVertex] give a topological order for the)
 5       (vertices of the graph, G = (V, E), and let D[v] give the duration of)
         (the task represented by vertex v for each v in the range 1:MaxVertex.)

         (Let Pred(v) be a list of the vertices which are predecessors of v in)
         (the graph G, and let Pred(v) == ∅ if and only if v has no predecessors.)
10

         /* Process the vertices of G in topological order */

         for (i = 1;  i <= MaxVertex;  ++i ) {
15
             v = TopoOrderArray[i];  /* let v be the ith vertex in topological order */

             if (Pred(v) == ∅) {                    /* if v has no predecessors, then */
                 EST[v] = 0;                         /* v can start at time 0, and */
20               EFT[v] = D[v];         /* v's duration is its earliest finishing time */
             } else {
                 EST[v] = 0;
                 for (each w ∈ Pred(v)) {                    /* find the latest among the */
                     if (EFT[w] > EST[v]) {                  /* finishing times of */
25                       EST[v] = EFT[w];                    /* v's predecessors to */
                     }                               /* determine v's earliest starting time */
                 }
                 EFT[v] = EST[v] + D[v];    /* then v's earliest starting time plus */
             }                           /* its duration is its earliest finishing time */
30       }
     }
```

Program Strategy 10.24 Computing Earliest Starting and Finishing Times

```
|    void ComputeProjectFinishingTime(void)
|    {
|         (Let v be a vertex of the graph G)
|         (We wish to compute, PFT, the earliest time)
5   |         (at which the project can finish.)
|
|         /* Initialize PFT to zero for the latest possible finishing time found so far */
|
|         PFT = 0;
10  |
|         /* Find the latest among the finishing times of all vertices in the graph */
|
|         for (v = 1; v <= MaxVertex; + + v) {
|              if ( EFT[v] > PFT) {                          /* update PFT to latest  */
15  |                  PFT = EFT[v];                          /* finishing time found so far */
|              }
|         }
|    }
```

Program Strategy 10.25 Computing the Project Finishing Time

earliest time at which the entire project can finish. This is just the latest of the earliest finishing times of all of the individual tasks in the project. Program Strategy 10.25 gives the procedure for determining the PFT.

Now that we know the PFT, we are in a position to calculate the latest starting (and finishing) times at which tasks can be begun (and completed) without delaying the completion time for the entire project. To calculate these times, we enumerate the vertices of the graph in the reverse of topological order. When we do this, each vertex, v, of the graph G is considered after its successors have been processed and after these successors have had their LST's and LFT's computed.

For example, suppose a vertex v has no successors (i.e., suppose $Succ(v) = \varnothing$, where $Succ(v)$ gives the list of successor vertices of vertex v and where $\varnothing$ is the symbol for the empty list of successors). For example, see the vertex lists in the next to last column of Table 10.20 for the values of the successor lists of the vertices in the graph in Fig. 10.19.

Now, if $Succ(v) = \varnothing$, then v's latest finishing time, LFT[v], is simply the project finishing time, PFT. In other words, if v is a task with no successor tasks that come after it, the latest that v's finishing time can be is the finishing time for the entire project, since if v's finishing time were any later, the finishing time for the entire project would slip past its current value, which is the time given by PFT.

Once we know v's latest finishing time, LFT[v], we can easily compute v's latest starting time, since LST[v] = LFT[v] − D[v], meaning that the latest time v can start without delaying the entire project completion time is simply v's latest completion time minus its duration.

Suppose, now, that for each w that is a successor of v, we know both LFT[w] and LST[w]. Then the latest that task v can itself finish must be the *earliest* of the starting times given by LST[w], for $w \in Succ(v)$. This is computed by taking the *minimum* among the set of numbers, LST[w], for $w \in Succ(v)$, since the earliest of a set of times

computing latest start and finish times

If task v has no successors (i.e., if Succ(v) = ∅, the empty list), then
            LFT[v] = PFT
    and
            LST[v] = LFT[v] − D[v].

Otherwise, if task v has successors, $w \in$ Succ(v), then
            LFT[v] = *minimum*(LST[w]) for all $w \in$ Succ(v)
    and
            LST[v] = LFT[v] − D[v].

Figure 10.26 Latest Starting and Finishing Times

on the project clock is obtained by taking the minimum of the numbers representing those times. Figure 10.26 expresses these considerations in symbols.

Program Strategy 10.27 gives the algorithm for computing the LFT[v] and the

```
     |   void LatestStartingAndFinishingTimes(void)
     |   {
     |       (Let TopoOrderArray[1:MaxVertex] give a topological order for the)
     |       (vertices of the graph, G = (V, E), and let D[v] give the duration of)
  5  |       (the task represented by vertex v for each v in the range 1:MaxVertex.)
     |
     |       (Let Succ(v) be a list of the vertices which are successors of v in)
     |       (the graph G, and let Succ(v) == ∅ if and only if v has no successors.)
     |
 10  |
     |       /* Process the vertices of G in the reverse of topological order */
     |
     |       for (i = MaxVertex; i >= 1; − − i ) {
     |           v = TopoOrderArray[i];    /* let v be the iᵗʰ vertex in topological order */
 15  |           if (Succ(v) == ∅) {                      /* if v has no successors, then */
     |
     |               LFT[v] = PFT;                    /* PFT is the latest v can finish, and */
     |               LST[v] = LFT[v] − D[v];               /* v's LST must precede */
     |                                                     /* its LFT by its duration */
 20  |           } else {
     |
     |               LFT[v] = PFT;
     |               for (each w ∈ Succ(v) ) {          /* find the earliest among the */
     |                   if ( LST[w] < LFT[v] ) {            /* starting times of */
 25  |                       LFT[v] = LST[w];               /* v's successors to */
     |                   }                          /* determine v's latest finishing time */
     |               }
     |               LST[v] = LFT[v] − D[v];     /* then v's latest finishing time minus */
     |           }                                    /* its duration is its latest starting time */
 30  |       }
     |   }
```

Program Strategy 10.27 Computing Latest Starting and Finishing Times

```
|   void ComputeCriticalPath(void)
|   {
|       /* This algorithm computes a list, CP, of vertices on the critical path. */
|
5  |
|       (Let CP be an initially empty list of vertices.)
|
|           InitializeToEmptyList(&CP);
|
10 |   /* Process the vertices of G in topological order */
|
|       for (i = 1; i <= MaxVertex; ++i) {
|           v = TopoOrderArray[i];  /* let v be the ith vertex in topological order */
|           if (LST[v] == EST[v]) {      /* if v's latest and earliest start times are */
15 |               InsertOnList(v,&CP);  /* identical, then v is on the critical path. */
|           }
|       }
|   }
```

Program Strategy 10.28 Computing the Critical Path

$LST[v]$ for all v in the graph G, assuming the PFT has already been computed using Program Strategy 10.25.

computing slack times and the critical path

The slack times of each task v can now be determined by noting the differences between the earliest and latest starting times, $SlackTime[v] = LST[v] - EST[v]$. Moreover, if any task, v, has a slack time of zero, then v is on the critical path (since critical tasks are those having no slack time, which means that they have no time available with which to delay their start times without delaying the entire project's completion time). This leads to Program Strategy 10.28 for computing the vertices on the critical path (or critical paths, if there is more than one critical path).

matching the results

If we execute Program Strategies 10.24, 10.25, 10.27, and 10.28 (in that order) on the graph in Fig. 10.19, we obtain the results shown in Table 10.29. Converting days into dates, you can see that the results in this table match the results shown in Figs. 10.17 and 10.18, where for example, task number 3 (entitled, "Look at 5 new homes") has an earliest start date of 4/29/94, which is five days after the project start date of 4/24/94. Moreover, its slack time of 6 days, shown as a shaded area in

Vertex number i =	1	2	3	4	5	6	7	8	9	10	11
Vertex in TopoOrderArray[i] =	1	2	4	3	5	6	7	8	9	10	11
Earliest start time, EST[i] =	0	0	5	0	20	22	22	22	37	39	49
Earliest finish time, EFT[i] =	0	5	14	20	22	25	32	37	39	49	49
Project finish time, PFT =	49										
Latest finish time, LFT[i] =	0	11	20	20	22	37	37	37	39	49	49
Latest start time, LST[i] =	0	6	11	0	20	34	27	22	37	39	49
Vertices on critical path =	1	4	5	8	9	10	11				

Table 10.29 Critical Path Results for the Graph in Fig. 10.19

Fig. 10.18, is the same as that resulting from differencing task 3's earliest and latest start times in Table 10.29 (since LST[3] – EST[3] = 11 – 5 = 6 days).

Also, the project finish time is 49 days after the project start date of 4/24/94, which puts it at 6/12/94. To see this, note that there are 6 days remaining in April after the start date 4/24/94. This uses up 6 of the 49 total days, leaving 43 more. Then the month of May uses up 31 of the remaining 43 days, leaving 12 days in June. The project therefore finishes on June 12, 1994.

The PERT chart in Fig. 10.17 was actually computed by using some project management software for a popular desktop computer, which required PERT charts to have a single start node and a single finish node. You can see that this restriction does not reduce the generality of the software, since any project network with multiple start nodes (those having no predecessors) can be changed to have a single start node of zero duration, leading to the former start nodes as successors. Likewise, if a project network has multiple finish nodes (each of which has no successors), they can all be joined to a single new finish node of zero duration. The configuration shown in Fig. 10.17, having only single start and finish nodes, is therefore general enough to handle project networks with multiple start and finish nodes.

using commercial project management software

You can easily see how the algorithms presented in the program strategies in this section could be used to perform the calculations at the heart of a project management software package that could generate diagrams such as those shown in Figs. 10.17 and 10.18 (both taken from an actual commercial software project management package). To implement such a package, you would need to add a user interface that would allow the user to enter task nodes together with their durations and their predecessors and successors. Then you would need to implement commands for computing the critical paths and displaying the results in various views, such as PERT charts and milestone charts.

10.7 Review Questions

1. Explain the following terms: task network, PERT chart, and milestone chart.
2. Given a task network, G, how do you define a critical path in G?
3. What is slack time? How is it defined?
4. Why do tasks on a critical path have no slack time?

10.7 Exercises

1. Refine Program Strategies 10.24, 10.25, 10.27, and 10.28 into running programs in C and verify that they produce the results given in Table 10.29 for the task network given in Fig. 10.19. Use arrays in C indexed by array indices in the range **0:MaxVertex – 1** instead of the range **1:MaxVertex** used in the Program Strategies.
2. When do two noncritical tasks *share* the same slack time in a task network and when do they have *independent* slack times that do not need to be shared? For example, compare the pairs of tasks {2,3} and {6,7} in the graph in Fig. 10.19.

☰ 10.8 Useful Background on Graphs

Learning Objectives

1. To learn about additional important graph problems whose solutions are known.
2. To understand that some graph problems can be solved using reasonable computing resources and that others require more resources than are usually available in practice.
3. To acquire an appreciation for the range of difficulty of graph problems.
4. To become aware that the most difficult ones are impractical to solve unless they are of small size.
5. To acquire modest informal understanding of NP-complete problems.

In this book, we have had time only to scratch the surface of the extensive body of knowledge about graphs, graph algorithms, and graph data representations. Entire courses are given on the subjects of graph algorithms in computer science and on mathematical graph theory in mathematics.

In this section, we sketch informally some important things that are known about graphs. It is helpful to be well-informed about this subject so that you will be aware of circumstances where it pays to look further before you leap.

Minimal Spanning Trees

spanning trees

Suppose we have an undirected graph, G, with weighted edges, and that G is connected, meaning that there is a path in G between any two distinct vertices. A tree, T, using edges in G, that contains all the vertices of G is called a *spanning tree* for G. We say that T spans all the vertices in G.

If we define the cost of a spanning tree T to be the sum of the weights on its edges, we might then seek to find the spanning tree, T, of minimal cost that spans all the vertices in G. This is called a *minimal spanning tree*.

Let's consider two practical applications. Suppose we have an electrical circuit, and we wish to tie together a number of separate electrical terminals so that they all have the same voltage level. We might use wires to connect pairs of terminals. If the cost of connecting two terminals is the cost of the wire between them, we might want

applications of minimal spanning trees

to know the least costly way to connect them all together to establish the common voltage level. It is sufficient to tie them all together using a tree of wires connecting pairs of terminals, since any circuit containing a cycle can have one of its edges removed, and yet the same voltage level will be maintained, since all the terminals in the broken cycle are still connected. In this case, if we could find a minimal spanning tree for our circuit, we would have a solution to the problem.

As another example, telephone companies used to provide a service called a "multidrop line" which would connect telephones of a single customer in several

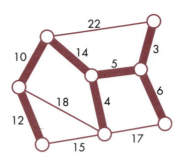

Figure 10.30 A Weighted Graph with a Minimal Spanning Tree

cities into a common telephone circuit. Telephone companies would charge for the multidrop line on the basis of a minimal spanning tree connecting the cities in the multidrop line's telephone circuit. Figure 10.30 shows a graph with weighted edges. A minimal spanning tree is indicated by the thicker lines in the graph.

Efficient algorithms are known for finding minimal spanning trees in graphs. One of these is called Prim's Algorithm. Suppose we agree to use the word "distance" to refer to the weight of an edge in a weighted graph G. In Prim's Algorithm, you start by picking any vertex v in G. Next you find the new vertex w that is connected to v by the edge of least distance in G, and you add w and the edge $e = (v,w)$ that connects them to the minimal spanning tree T you are starting to grow. Proceeding in this fashion, at each stage of the process, you add one new vertex, w, that has not already been chosen. The way that you identify which vertex to add to T is to choose that vertex w that is not already in the tree T such that the closest distance from w to some vertex in T is less than or equal to the closest distance of all the other vertices v that are not yet in T. Then you add to T both w and the edge of least distance connecting w to some vertex in T. You stop when T includes all vertices of G.

Prim's Algorithm

It can be shown that Prim's Algorithm can be made to run in time $O(n \log n)$, where n is the number of edges in graph G, using suitable data representations for the edges and vertices in the graph.

Prim's Algorithm is called a *greedy algorithm*, because it succeeds in finding a global optimum by making a sequence of locally greedy choices. A locally greedy choice is a choice of the best among several local alternatives at a particular stage of the solution process. In the case of Prim's Algorithm, the greedy choice is to add a new vertex w to T that is closest to the vertices already in T. When such a sequence of locally opportunistic choices leads to the overall best solution, the algorithm is said to be a greedy algorithm.

greedy algorithms

Not all search processes can succeed by making locally opportunistic choices. For example, take hill-climbing problems. When climbing a hill, you begin at some starting position on a map and you try to climb to the top of the tallest hill. If there is only one hill on the map and the terrain slopes upward from every point on the map toward the top of the only hill, then you can get to the top of this hill by taking local steps in the local direction that increases your altitude the most at each step. However, if you have two hills, A and B, where A is taller than B, and your starting position is on the slope leading up to the top of B, then if you climb in a locally opportunistic direction so as to increase your altitude the most at each local step, you

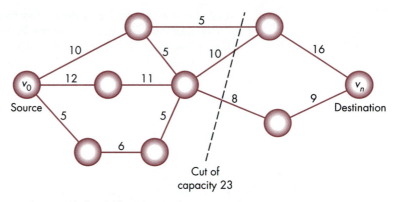

Figure 10.31 A Graph for a Flow Network

will soon find yourself at the top of hill B, and not at the top of hill A. To get to the top of hill A, you must first make locally unopportunistic choices for a while (by descending for a bit into the valley between hills A and B) before starting your climb up hill A. In this case, locally unopportunistic choices are needed at first in order eventually to locate the global optimum.

Flow Networks

graphs representing flows on networks

Suppose we have a graph whose vertices represent pumping stations and whose edges represent oil pipelines. There is a single source vertex, v_0, from which oil flows into the system, and there is a single destination vertex, v_n, at which all oil arrives and is taken out of the system (say, to be put into storage tanks). The intermediate vertices between v_0 and v_n are relay stations that take oil from their input pipelines and transfer it into their output pipelines. Suppose further that each edge in the graph is assigned a weight representing the capacity of its corresponding pipeline, where the capacity is a number representing the oil flow, say, in barrels per minute, that the pipe is capable of carrying.

We may wish to know the maximum flow of oil that such a pipeline network can accommodate. Figure 10.31 illustrates a graph for a flow network.

A solution to the maximum flow problem in a flow network is as follows. Suppose you make a cut that divides such a network into two parts, where one part contains the source and the other part contains the destination. The dashed line in Fig. 10.31 shows such a cut. You can think of a cut as a set of edges which, when removed, separate the graph into two disconnected components, one containing the source vertex v_0 and the other containing the destination vertex v_n. Informally, a cut is a set of pipes connecting adjacent vertices which, if removed, will completely stop oil from flowing from the source part to the destination part of the network. The capacity of a cut is the sum of the capacities of the edges in it. (You can think of the capacity of a cut as the sum of the flows through all pipes in the cut that were removed when the cut was made.)

It can be proven that the *maximum flow* in a flow network is equal to the capacity of the *minimum cut*. This means that the best flow in a network is determined by a "bottleneck" of sorts. The bottleneck is the set of pipes of least total capacity that connect a source part of the network to a destination part. An algorithm has been developed for determining the minimum cut, and hence the maximum flow in any such network, called the *max-flow, min-cut algorithm*.

the max-flow, min-cut theorem

The Four-Color Problem

Cartographers have believed for ages that you need only four colors to color the countries on a map so that each two countries that are adjacent to one another use different colors. (Here, when two countries are adjacent, it means they share a common border. It does not mean that they touch only at a single point, or at several single points.)

coloring maps with just four colors

If you represent the countries in a map by vertices in an undirected graph, and you draw an edge between any two countries that are adjacent, you get what is called a *planar graph*, which represents the map. A planar graph is a graph that lies in a two-dimensional plane without any of its edges crossing over one another.

planar graphs

The four-color problem can be formulated as a graph problem in the following sense. Given any planar graph $G = (V, E)$, is it possible to assign at most four colors (c_1, c_2, c_3, c_4) to the vertices V, using a function $c(v) = c_i$, where the function $c(v)$ sends vertices $v \in V$ into the four colors c_i, $(1 \le i \le 4)$, such that if (v,w) is an edge in E, then $c(v) \ne c(w)$? Figure 10.32 shows a map of some southern states in the USA and a planar graph representing adjacent states in this map.

A graph G is called *k-colorable*, if each of its vertices can be assigned one of k different colors such that adjacent vertices have different colors. An algorithm which tries to assign one of k different colors to each vertex in a graph G so that adjacent vertices are assigned different colors is called a *k-coloring algorithm*.

coloring algorithms

The four-color problem teased mathematicians for many years. It was a famous example of a conjecture that many mathematicians intuitively believed was true but

Appel and Haken's proof

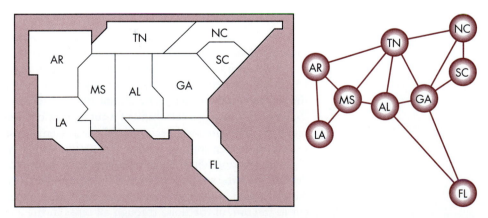

Figure 10.32 A Four-Colorable Map of Some Southern States

had great difficulty proving. In 1977 two mathematicians, Appel and Haken, discovered a proof (see the reference at the end of this chapter). Their proof was long and it involved identifying many hundreds of basic 4-colorable building block "patterns" that could be combined to form any possible planar graph.

In general, the best known algorithms for k-colorability take exponential running time. In fact, k-colorability has been shown to be an NP-complete problem, a subject we will discuss in the next section.

NP-Complete Graph Problems

One of the big mysteries in contemporary computer science is whether P = NP. Roughly speaking, P stands for the class of problems that can be solved in polynomial time on a deterministic computer, and NP stands for the class of problems that can be *a big mystery* solved in polynomial time on a nondeterministic computer. If you have a problem of size n, you can think of polynomial time as being an amount of time that is $O(n^k)$ for some integer k. The difference between deterministic and nondeterministic computers is more subtle.

Informally speaking, a deterministic computer is one that makes exactly one completely determined choice at each choice point when it runs a program. That is, given an if-statement, "if (condition C) {statement A} else {statement B}," or given a *deterministic computers* switch statement, "switch (n) { <n-cases> }," a deterministic computer evaluates the value of C or n, and chooses exactly one among the alternatives to pursue next. You are familiar with deterministic computers, since those are the only kind you actually use in the real world.

A *nondeterministic computer* is one that can make *nondeterministic choices* at a choice point. One way to think of this is that, when confronted with a choice among a number of alternatives, a nondeterministic computer is endowed with a magic fore- *nondeterministic computers* sight that enables it to choose only the correct alternative that leads to a solution to the problem (if there is one). It never chooses to pursue an incorrect alternative that leads down a blind alley and forces it to abandon its search and to backtrack to a previous choice point to try the next available alternative.

Another way to think of a nondeterministic computer is to imagine that, when presented with a choice point, the computer can reproduce itself (like a biological cell undergoing cell division) by dividing into as many separate offspring computers as there are alternatives, whereupon each of the new offspring computers pursues exactly one of the separate alternatives. If one of these offspring computers eventually reaches a solution in time $O(n^k)$, we can say that the problem it solved belonged to NP, since its solution was found in polynomial time by a nondeterministic machine. In this formulation, we can think of a nondeterministic computer as one that is capable of exploring a tree of alternatives to a depth d in time $O(d)$.

At the present time, computer scientists and mathematicians have not been able to settle whether or not P = NP. But some very remarkable discoveries have been made regarding the class of problems, NP.

In particular there is a class of problems called *NP-complete problems*. Each of these problems is in the class NP, meaning that they can each be solved in time

$O(n^k)$ on a nondeterministic machine. But more than this, there exist translations between NP problems and the NP-complete problems such that any one of the NP problems can be translated to any of the NP-complete problems in polynomial time. This implies that if you can solve any NP-complete problem in polynomial time, then you can solve every NP problem in polynomial time also. In particular, if you could find a way to solve just one of these NP-complete problems in time $O(n^k)$ on a deterministic machine, then any NP problem could be solved in time $O(n^k)$ on a deterministic machine also. Yet nobody has been able to solve any of these NP-complete problems in less than *exponential time* on a deterministic machine. This leads many computer scientists to the suspicion that P $\neq$ NP, only they have not yet been able to prove it.

NP-complete problems

It turns out that there are many graph problems that are NP-complete. If you can discover an algorithm for solving any of these problems that runs in time $O(n^k)$ on a deterministic computer (meaning any computer in ordinary everyday use) then you will be very famous, since you will have discovered how to solve an NP-complete problem in polynomial time on a deterministic machine. This will imply that all the other NP problems can be solved in time $O(n^k)$ on a deterministic machine, as well. This would be a big breakthrough, if it were possible, since you would have succeeded in knocking down the current best-known running times of the best-known solutions from exponential time to polynomial time. Many seasoned computer scientists do not think this breakthrough will ever be possible, since they do not believe that P = NP.

a few NP-complete
graph problems

Let's briefly mention a few graph problems that are known to be NP-complete. The first one is the problem of k-colorability of graphs. If a graph is not planar, it may require more than four colors to color. For example, a *complete graph* is one in which every vertex is connected via an edge to every other vertex. If you have a complete graph of k-vertices, you need k distinct colors to color it so that no two adjacent vertices have the same color assigned. Actually, it is known that it is NP-complete to determine whether a planar graph is 3-colorable.

finding k-cliques

In an undirected graph, a *clique of size n*, is a set of n vertices each of which is connected to every other by an edge in the graph. (In other words, a clique of size n is just a complete subgraph of the graph.) Given an integer k and a graph G, we may want to decide whether or not G contains a clique of size k. It is known that this k-clique decision problem is NP-complete.

finding vertex covers

Another NP-complete graph problem is the *vertex-cover problem*. If k is an integer, $G = (V, E)$ is an undirected graph, and W is a subset of k vertices chosen from V, we say that W is a k-cover for V, provided that for every edge $e = (v,w)$ in E, either $v \in W$ or $w \in W$. The problem of deciding whether there is a k-cover for a graph G is NP-complete.

Hamiltonian circuits and
the traveling salesperson
problem

The last two NP-complete graph problems that we shall mention are related to finding cycles in graphs. A *Hamiltonian circuit* is a cycle in a directed graph of n vertices that travels through each of the vertices exactly once and returns to its starting vertex. The problem of finding a Hamiltonian circuit in a directed graph is NP-complete. The final NP-complete problem we shall discuss is the *traveling salesperson problem*. Suppose we have a directed graph with weighted edges. You can think of such a graph as having vertices that represent cities, and having edges connecting pairs of cities whose weights give the cost of traveling between those cities. The problem is to find a circuit of least cost that visits all the cities in the graph exactly once and returns to its starting point. This is the route that a traveling salesperson might follow to visit all of the cities at the least possible expense.

Nobody has ever found an $O(n^k)$ algorithm to solve any of these NP-complete graph problems on a deterministic machine. All the best-known solutions require exponential running time. In practice this means two things. First, unless somebody proves someday that P = NP, you should not expect to solve NP-complete problems exactly if they are of more than modest size. (Remember from Chapter 6 that exponential running-time algorithms cannot find exact solutions for big problems in a practical amount of time.) Second, if you need to solve a big problem that is known to be in NP, you should think about settling for an approximate solution instead of an exact solution. For example, an approximate solution might guarantee to give you a solution to within, say, 3 percent of the exact solution, if you are willing to invest a polynomial amount of time finding it. Polynomial running-time algorithms are known for many NP-complete problems that will yield an approximate solution rather than an exact solution.

some sage advice

Concluding Remarks

Graphs present a framework of great generality and flexibility for representing many kinds of problems that can be solved by computers. The algorithms required to solve such problems can occasionally be simple and efficient. At other times, the best-known algorithms that determine exact solutions require exponential running time and thus are not practical to use to find exact solutions for any but fairly small-sized problems. Nevertheless, there are sometimes restricted versions of difficult general graph problems that are known to have efficient solutions. For example, finding k-cliques in planar graphs can sometimes be performed efficiently (e.g., you can find a 4-clique in a planar graph in quadratic time by enumerating all 4-sets).

The moral is that it pays to be well-informed about graph problems and their solutions in order to know what kinds of problems are soluble within the limits of available computing resources. If you decide not to make the investment of time and energy to learn more about graph problems later in your career, you can at least decide that, when confronted with a graph problem of importance, you could remember that it might be worthwhile to consult an expert in order to determine whether what you need to do is possible within the limits of what is known about graph problem solutions and within the resources available to you.

10.8 Review Questions

1. How do you define a *spanning tree* of a connected, undirected graph? If you have a weighted, connected, undirected graph, what is a *minimal spanning tree*?
2. What is a *flow network*? How do you find the *maximum flow* from a source to a destination in a flow network?

3. What is the *four-color problem*? Has it been solved yet?
4. What does it mean to say that a problem is in NP? What does it mean to say that a problem is NP-complete? What is the meaning of the question, "Does P = NP?"
5. What is the O-notation for the best-known time anyone has ever discovered for solving any NP-complete problem?
6. What would become possible if somebody were to prove someday that P = NP?
7. What is a *Hamiltonian circuit*?
8. What is the *traveling salesperson problem* (often abbreviated TSP)?

10.8 Exercises

1. Using four colors, red(*r*), green(*g*), blue(*b*), and yellow(*y*), assign colors to the vertices of the graph in Fig. 10.32 (by annotating the vertices with the letters *r*, *g*, *b*, or *y*) such that no two adjacent vertices have the same color.
2. What is the maximum flow on the graph of Fig. 10.31?

Pitfalls

- *Choosing the wrong data representations for graphs*

    If you are a bit rushed when implementing graph algorithms, it is easy to choose data representations that are inefficient either in time or space or both. For example, a large adjacency matrix, mostly filled with zeros and only sparsely occupied by ones, can consume a lot of memory space. It may be possible, for instance, to save a lot of space by using packed bit vectors for the rows, because single bits consume a a lot less memory than full integer representations of the zeroes and ones.

    Some algorithms, which need to use the predecessor list of vertices for each vertex, will not be well-served by using data representations that give only the successor lists for the graph's vertices, and so on.

    The moral of the story is to make sure to design an efficient data representation for a graph problem by explicitly enumerating the characteristics and constraints of the problem and the algorithms for solving it, and then to choose the characteristics of the data representation so as best to optimize the programs and data used in the solution.

Tips and Techniques

- *Be aware of graph problems and their known solutions*

    The greatest single barrier to your being able to devise efficient solutions to graph problems may be a lack of knowledge about graph problems and their solution methods. In a book such as this one it is possible only to open the door a bit to the more extensive knowledge of graph problems available in advanced books and courses. However, even a little awareness of the subject will assist you in knowing when to seek deeper knowledge.

References for Further Study

four-color problem

K. Appel and W. Haken, "Every Planar Map is 4 Colourable," *Illinois Journal of Mathematics* 21: 3 (1977), pp. 429–90, 491–567.
The proof that a solution to the four-color problem exists is given.

graph theory

C. Berge, *The Theory of Graphs and Its Applications*, John Wiley, New York, (1968).
A classical reference on the mathematical theory of graphs.

graph algorithms

Shimon Even, *Graph Algorithms*, Computer Science Press, Rockville, Md., (1979).
A good book on graph algorithms has been written by Shimon Even.

Chapter Summary

basic anatomy of graphs

A *graph* is a collection of *vertices* in which some or all of the pairs of vertices are connected by line segments called *edges*. If directions are prescribed on the edges, we have a *directed graph*. If no directions are prescribed on the edges, we have an *undirected graph*. A *path* in a graph is a sequence of vertices in which each vertex in the sequence, except the last, is connected to its successor in the sequence by an edge in the graph. If the starting and ending vertices in a path are the same, the path forms a *cycle*.

connected components

Undirected graphs can be divided into connected components. A *connected component* is a maximal subset of the vertices in which any two vertices are connected by a path. Any two separate components are disconnected in the sense that there is no path joining a vertex in one to a vertex in the other.

free trees

A *free tree* is an undirected graph that is connected but has no cycles. A *directed acyclic graph* (DAG) is a directed graph having no cycles.

data representations for graphs

There are many ways to represent graphs using computer data structures. For example, an adjacency matrix, T, with rows and columns representing the vertices, can have entries, $T[i,j]$, which are either 0 or 1. If $T[i,j] = 1$, then the edge from vertex v_i to vertex v_j is in the graph, whereas if $T[i,j] = 0$, then the edge from vertex v_i to vertex v_j is not in the graph. Rows of the adjacency matrix, T, can be represented compactly, using bit vectors. One can also give an array, A, of adjacency lists, where the array entry $A[i]$ corresponds to the ith vertex, v_i, and provides a list of the other vertices to which v_i is connected by an edge in the graph. Such adjacency lists can be represented in either sequential or linked form. Another possibility is to use set representations of various kinds. For instance, a graph can be represented by a set of the pairs of vertices that form edges of the graph. Also, the rows of the adjacency matrix, T, can be represented by sets of vertices.

graph searching

Graphs can be searched to find vertices having particular properties. Two methods are *depth-first search* and *breadth-first search*. When a vertex is enumerated in a search, it is marked as having been *visited*. This way, if the vertex is encountered a second or succeeding time during the search and is marked already visited, it need not be visited again. Multiple encounters of a given vertex in a graph search are possible if the vertex is accessible by more than one path from the starting point in the search. In graphs this can happen when paths form cycles or provide alternative routes from the starting vertex to a given destination vertex. In depth-first searching, when we arrive at a vertex v along an edge from a predecessor vertex w, we search the unvisited successors of v before searching the unvisited successors of w. By contrast in breadth-first searching, we search the unvisited successors of w before searching the unvisited successors of v.

topological orders

If G is a DAG, then it is possible to provide a sequential list, L, of the vertices of G in which each vertex v of G appears on the list L before any of its successors appear on L. Such an order is called a *topological order*. For example, if G gives the prerequisite relations among college courses, then a topological ordering in L lists all prerequisites of each course before listing the course itself. Topological orderings for a given graph G are not unique and there are several algorithms for producing them.

finding shortest paths

A *weighted graph* is one in which positive numbers, called *weights*, are attached to the edges. For example, the weights might represent distances between pairs of cities on a map, or the cost of travel between pairs of cities. In such a graph, it might be useful to compute a shortest path from a given origin vertex to some destination vertex. The shortest path might then yield the shortest travel distance or the least costly way to travel from the origin to the destination. Dijkstra's Shortest Path Algorithm gives a way to compute the shortest paths from a single origin vertex to every other vertex in a weighted directed graph.

task networks and
critical paths

Graphs can be used to represent networks of tasks comprising parts of an overall project. Each task is represented by a vertex in the graph to which the task's duration is attached. Also, directed edges in the graph represent prerequisite relationships among the tasks. It is agreed that work on a given task cannot begin until all of its prerequisite tasks have been completed. Under these circumstances, it is useful to be able to compute the earliest time that the entire project can be completed, and also which tasks in the project lie on the project's *critical path*, a path connecting tasks whose completion times cannot be delayed without delaying the entire project's completion time.

some additional useful
background on graphs

The graph computations explored in this chapter constitute only a tiny portion of the extensive list of topics in graph theory that have been investigated by computer scientists and mathematicians. It is useful for you to gain a bit of background literacy about various other topics in graph theory, and about which kinds of graph problems are efficiently soluble versus which kinds of graph problems are computationally very difficult and inefficient to solve. For example, there exist reasonably efficient algorithms to find minimal spanning trees in weighted undirected graphs, and maximal flows in flow networks whose edges are weighted with numbers giving flow capacities of pipes connecting vertices in the network. On the other hand, the general problem of coloring graphs with k-colors, and the problem of finding a least cost circuit for visiting every vertex in a graph exactly once, are known to be difficult problems to solve efficiently. In particular, the best known solutions for these problems take exponential time, and they are known to lie in the class of NP-complete problems. There is a suspicion among computer scientists that NP-complete problems will eventually be found to require exponential time to solve, but nobody has been able to prove it yet.

avoiding entrapment

An informal acquaintance with these unusual discoveries will enable you to be aware that there is a vast range of possible efficiencies for graph algorithms, with some being acceptable for use in practical problem-solving applications, and others being unacceptable for solving any but very small-sized problems. Such an awareness on your part may help you to avoid future entrapments in which a lack of awareness could lead you to act on the belief that various graph problems are efficiently soluble, when, in fact, the opposite is true.

11

Hashing and the Table ADT

In this chapter, we can think of a *table* as an abstract storage device that contains *table entries*. Moreover, we'll agree that each table entry contains a unique key, K. That is, we agree that different table entries always have different keys. This implies that the key in a given table entry uniquely identifies that entry and distinguishes it from all other separate table entries. A table entry may also contain some information, I, associated with its key. Abstractly, then, we can think of a table entry as an ordered pair (K,I), consisting of a unique key, K, and its associated information, I.

what are tables?

Given a table, T, *table searching* is an activity in which, given a search key, K, we attempt to find the table entry (K,I) in T containing the key K. Once we have found such an entry, we may wish to *retrieve* or *update* its information, I, or we may wish to *delete* the entire table entry (K,I), by removing it from the table. If no entry with key K exists in table T, we may wish to *insert* a new table entry having K as its key. Occasionally, we may wish to *enumerate* all entries in table T—for example, to print a report of the contents of the table. If an ordering is defined on the keys, we may wish

some table operations

450

to perform this enumeration in, say, ascending order of the keys in the table entries. (This would be useful, for instance, if we wanted to print a report listing all table entries in the alphabetical or numerical order defined by their keys.)

By now, you can easily imagine that there are numerous ways to represent an abstract table, T, and to implement abstract table operations such as *retrieve*, *update*, *delete*, *insert*, or *enumerate*. For example, you could represent a table entry by a C struct having various members in which to store its key and its information items. Then you could use an array of such structs, stored sequentially in ascending order of their keys, to represent table T. On the other hand, you could add additional members to the structs for the table entries to contain links and balance factors, and you could link them into an AVL tree.

some table representations

In this chapter, we will investigate another class of representations for abstract tables relying on a technique called *hashing*. If you have never been introduced to the concepts underlying hashing before, this chapter should have great value for you, because it will expand your repertoire of useful techniques quite significantly. That is because hashing is an extraordinary discovery in computer science that provides methods yielding truly amazing performance advantages.

hashing, an
amazing discovery

In some cases, in which there are only a small number of possible keys, K, that can be used in table entries, it is possible to reserve one table entry in advance for each possible key. For example, suppose we have a card game in which there are 52 cards being used. Suppose, further, that we wish to keep some information associated with each possible card, such as whether or not it has been seen in play during the game so far. Under these circumstances, it would be possible to keep a table, T, of 52 entries, and to reserve one entry for each possible card. We would then need a mapping to send a key, K, identifying a particular card (such as the 7 of spades: 7 ♠) onto one of the table addresses. These table addresses might be the integers in the range, 0:51, for example.

In other cases, although we might have a very large number of possible keys, K, only a fraction of all of these possible keys would be used in an actual table. For example, suppose we want to keep a table of employee structs for a firm that employs 5000 people. If the firm is located in the United States, we might decide to use nine-digit social security numbers, in order to identify each employee struct. Or we might decide to issue our own employee-identification numbers chosen so as to encode information about the corporate division and department in which the employee works. For instance, on my campus of the University of California (UC), employee numbers are nine-digit numbers in which the first two digits provide a code specifying one of the nine UC campuses where the employee works. Since there are one billion (10^9) different nine-digit numbers, if we have 5000 employees in a given firm, only five ten-thousandths of one percent (0.0005%) of all possible keys are needed to provide a set of unique keys such that each employee struct in the table is guaranteed to have a unique key.

of the many possible keys,
only a few are used

Now let's consider the problem of how to retrieve employee structs efficiently in this context. Given a search key, K, consisting of a particular employee number, and given a table, T, consisting of 5000 employee structs, how shall we organize table T so that retrieval of the employee struct containing key K is as efficient as

retrieving structs in
this situation

possible? One technique we could use is to place the structs into an array in ascending (numerical) order of the keys and to use binary search to locate the struct. From Equation 6.14, we know this takes approximately $(2*\log_2 5001 - 3)$ comparisons (or ≈ 21.6 comparisons), on the average, if each key is equally likely to be used. Another possibility is to arrange the employee structs into an AVL tree, according to the (numerical) order of the employee numbers used as keys. In this case, on the average, searching in an AVL tree takes $(2*\log_2 5000 + 1.5)$ comparisons (or ≈ 26.1 comparisons).

why hashing wins

On the other hand, we might use a technique called *double hashing*, which we will introduce later in this chapter. If we were to store the 5000 employee structs in a table T that had space for 6000 structs, we could reduce the average number of comparisons needed to locate an employee struct to fewer than 2.15 comparisons! In other words, using hashing techniques in this case enables us to perform retrieval more than ten times more efficiently.

Now let's consider, for a moment, how we map keys into table addresses. A *hash function* is a mapping, $h(K)$, that sends a key K onto the address of a table entry in table T. Ordinarily, we try to store the table entry (K,I) containing the key K at the table address given by $h(K)$, but it may not always be possible to do so because of *collisions*. Almost always, we use hashing techniques in cases in which there are many more distinct keys K than there are table addresses, and so we can encounter a situation in which two distinct keys, $K_1 \neq K_2$, map to the same table address (meaning that $h(K_1) = h(K_2)$). In this case, we cannot store both table entries (K_1,I_1) and (K_2,I_2) at the same table address, since there is not room for both of them, and we have what is called a *collision*. Under these circumstances, we need to invoke and use some sort of *collision resolution policy* to find additional storage in which to store one of the two table entries that cannot be stored directly at the table address given by the hash address of its key.

collision resolution policies

Three such collision resolution policies that we will mention in this chapter are collision resolution by: (1) *chaining*, (2) *open addressing*, and (3) *buckets*. We will study the first two of these policies in this chapter, and we will study the third policy in Chapter 12. In the case of open addressing, we will find that some collision resolution methods that are initially appealing, because they are so simple to understand and implement, in fact have some performance drawbacks. However, we will discover that there exist some alternative techniques, such as double hashing, that have extraordinarily good performance, and which, nonetheless, are not too difficult to understand and implement.

We will also study a couple of different ways to compute hash functions, $h(K)$, given some set of keys, K, that we wish to hash into table addresses. One of these methods relies simply on *division* of one integer by another.

comparing representations
of abstract tables

Finally, we will compare three ways to represent abstract tables using (1) arrays of structs kept in ascending sequential order of their keys, (2) AVL trees, and (3) hash tables using double hashing. Of special significance is the comparison between the efficiencies of the table operations for searching and enumeration using these three separate representations. This comparison will reveal the advantages and drawbacks of hashing in relation to the other representations.

Plan for the Chapter

abstract tables and the
Table ADT

Section 11.2 introduces the concept of the Table ADT, which provides an abstract model of a table as a storage device. Table ADTs can be represented by various actual data representations, three of which are (a) hash tables, (b) AVL trees, and (c) arrays of table entries sorted in the ascending order of their keys. The Table ADT supports abstract table operations such as retrieving, updating, inserting, and deleting table entries, as well as enumeration of all entries in the table in increasing order of their keys. In Section 11.7, the performance of these three Table ADT representations is compared.

simple examples

Section 11.3 introduces hashing concepts by means of a series of simple examples. The goal is to provide a clear notion of how hashing works, while simultaneously introducing concepts such as collisions and probe sequences.

collisions, clusters, and
load factors

Section 11.4 defines the concepts of collisions, load factors and clustering more formally, and develops their properties. It is shown that even in sparsely occupied hash tables, collisions are relatively frequent. Primary clustering is defined, and data are presented to show that the use of linear probing leads to the formation of primary clusters, whereas the use of double hashing does not lead to primary clustering.

algorithms for hashing and
their performance

Section 11.5 introduces algorithms for hashing by open addressing. It then presents two examples that use hash insertion algorithms to illustrate the formation of primary clusters when linear probing is used, but which avoid primary clustering when double hashing is used. Also, in Section 11.5, it is proven that the probe sequences used by the hashing algorithms completely cover all table addresses during search and insertion. Near the end of Section 11.5, performance formulas are presented that cover the average number of probes used in hashing, and some of these formulas are derived. Finally, theoretical results from the performance formulas are compared with actual measured results from hashing experiments in order to help develop insight into when hashing methods perform well and when they do not.

choosing hash functions

Section 11.6 investigates how to choose hashing functions so that they work well, and how to avoid several pitfalls that are known to produce hashing functions that do not work well.

11.2 The Table ADT

Learning Objectives

1. To introduce a model for a table, seen as an abstract storage device with several useful table operations.
2. To lay the groundwork for a later comparison of three actual data representations of the Table ADT in Section 11.7.
3. To present an abstraction of a table useful in modular programming using clean interfaces and deferred choice of the actual data representation to be used.

A *table*, T, is an abstract storage device that contains *table entries* that are either *empty* or are pairs of the form (K,I), where K is a key and I is some information associated

1. *Initialize* the table, T, to be the *empty table*. The *empty table* is filled with *empty table entries*, (K_0, I_0), where K_0 is a special *empty key*, distinct from all other nonempty keys.
2. *Determine* whether or not the table, T, is *full*.
3. *Insert* a new table entry (K, I), having key, K, and information, I, into the table, T, provided T is not already full.
4. *Delete* the table entry (K, I) from table T.
5. Given a search key, K, *retrieve* the information, I, from the table entry (K, I) in table, T.
6. *Update* the table entry (K, I) in table, T, by replacing it with a new table entry (K, I'), which associates new information, I', with key K in table T.
7. *Enumerate* the table entries (K, I) in table, T, in increasing order of their keys, K.

Figure 11.1 Table Operations Defining a Table ADT

with key K. Distinct table entries have distinct keys. Figure 11.1 presents the operations defining a Table ADT.

As an example of an abstract table ADT, consider Table 11.2, which has three-letter airport identifier codes as keys and has, as information items, the names of the associated cities where the airports are located. Each row represents a table entry, (K, I), which contains a key, K, and some associated information, I, where the key, K, is a three-letter airport code, and the associated information, I, is the name of the city where the corresponding airport, designated by key K, is located.

In this chapter, we will explore some new ways of representing the Table ADT based on hashing. But from your knowledge of previous chapters, you can already imagine how to represent a Table ADT using techniques such as binary search trees (including AVL trees), arrays of structs stored in ascending order of their keys, linked lists of structs containing keys, and so forth.

Table 11.2 Airport Codes and Names

Key K = Airport Code	Associated Information I = City
AKL	Auckland, New Zealand
DCA	Washington, D.C.
FRA	Frankfurt, Germany
GCM	Grand Cayman, Cayman Islands
GLA	Glasgow, Scotland
HKG	Hong Kong, China
LAX	Los Angeles, California
ORY	Paris, France
PHL	Philadelphia, Pennsylvania

11.2 Review Questions

1. What is a Table ADT?
2. What operations are defined on a Table ADT?
3. Name some possible data representations for a Table ADT.

11.2 Exercises

1. Sketch how you would implement the Table ADT operations if the Table ADT were represented using arrays of table entry structs, sorted in the ascending order of their keys.
2. Sketch how you would implement the Table ADT operations if the Table ADT were represented using AVL trees of table entry structs.

11.3 Introduction to Hashing by Simple Examples

Learning Objectives

1. To gain an intuitive understanding of hashing concepts using simple examples.
2. To become familiar with hash functions, collisions, collision resolution policies, open addressing, probe sequences, chaining, and buckets.
3. To lay the groundwork for the analysis of hashing algorithms.

some simple examples

A good way to introduce basic concepts of hashing is to consider some simple examples. Once these are fresh in our minds, it will be easy to understand the more general principles of hashing.

In these simple examples, we will use, as keys, letters of the alphabet having subscripts, such as A_1, B_2, C_3, R_{18} and Z_{26}. Each letter's subscript is an integer giving the letter's position in alphabetical order. For instance, since the letter "A" is the first letter in the alphabet, its subscript is "1," yielding A_1 as a key. Similarly, since Z is the last of the 26 letters in the alphabet, its key is Z_{26}. Again, from the key, R_{18}, we can verify that the letter "R" is the 18th letter in the alphabet.

keys with subscripts

The table, T, that we will use is deliberately chosen to be very small. In fact, table T contains space for only seven entries, numbered from 0 to 6.

Figure 11.3 shows an example of table T, with the keys J_{10}, B_2, and S_{19} inserted. (For simplicity, no associated information has been shown along with the keys in table T. In other words, we are considering only where to store the keys in T, and we are ignoring the associated information, for the sake of simplicity.)

The locations in table T used for storing the keys J_{10}, B_2, and S_{19}, were computed by dividing 7 into the value of the key's subscript and determining the *remainder* after division by 7. For example, to find where to try to insert the key J_{10} into an initially empty table T we divide the subscript 10 by 7, getting a quotient of 1 and a remainder of 3. So we try to insert J_{10} into location 3 in table T.

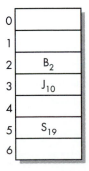

Figure 11.3 Table T

Likewise, to insert B_2 into table T, we divide the subscript 2 by 7, getting a quotient of 0 and a remainder of 2. So we try to insert B_2 into location 2 in table T. Finally, to place the key S_{19} into table T, we divide the subscript 19 by 7, getting a quotient of 2 and a remainder of 5. So we try to insert S_{19} into location 5 in table T.

the definition of $h(L_n)$

In general, to find where in table T to try initially to place a key, L_n, consisting of the letter "L" and the subscript "n," we take the remainder of n after division by 7 (which is computed by evaluating n % 7). The function, $h(L_n)$ which computes this location is given in symbols by

$$h(L_n) = n \text{ % } 7. \tag{11.1}$$

We refer to $h(L_n)$ as a *hash function* of the key, L_n. A good hash function, $h(L_n)$, will map keys, L_n, uniformly and randomly onto the full range of possible locations (0:6) in table T.

Now let's try inserting the new keys N_{14}, X_{24}, and W_{23} into the table T shown in Fig. 11.3. If we try placing the key N_{14} into the table location, $h(N_{14}) = 0$, we are lucky to find an empty slot. So N_{14} can be inserted directly into position 0 in table T. This gives the configuration of table T shown in Fig. 11.4. However, when we try to place key X_{24} into position $h(X_{24}) = 3$, we are not so lucky, since position 3 of table T already contains the key J_{10}. This is called a *collision*, because the keys X_{24} and J_{10} collide at the same *hash address*, $3 = h(J_{10}) = h(X_{24})$, when we try to insert them both into table T. Now we need a policy for resolving the collision.

The simple collision resolution policy we shall use for our first example is to look in table T to find the first empty entry at a lower location than the location of the collision and to insert the colliding key into that empty location. (If all the lower numbered locations below the collision location are already filled, we "wrap around" and start searching for empty locations at the highest numbered location in the table.)

For example, since $h(X_{24}) = 3$, and location 3 in table T in Fig. 11.4 is already occupied by the key J_{10} we look at the next lower table location, location 2, to see if it is empty. Since location 2 is occupied by the key B_2, we look next at location 1 and

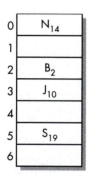

Figure 11.4 Table T

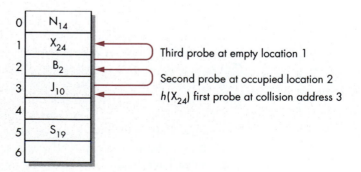

Figure 11.5 Table T

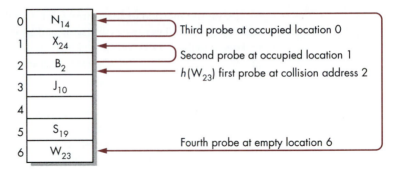

Figure 11.6 Table T

we find that location 1 is empty. Therefore we place the key X_{24} in location 1. This gives the configuration of table T shown in Fig. 11.5.

Finally, let's try to insert the new key, W_{23}. When we first try to insert W_{23} at its hash address, $h(W_{23}) = 2$, we find location 2 is already occupied by the key B_2. Consequently, we search consecutive lower numbered locations 1 and 0 to try to find **wrapping around** an empty location. Since locations 1 and 0 are already occupied, we *wrap around* and **during search** start searching at the highest numbered location in T, which is location 6. Because location 6 is empty, we insert W_{23} in location 6. This yields the configuration of table T shown in Fig. 11.6.

The locations that we examine when we attempt to insert a new key, L_n, into table T are called a *probe sequence*, since we "probe" each location in the probe sequence to see if we can find an empty location in which to insert the new key. The first location in the probe sequence is the hash address, $h(L_n)$. The second and **probe sequences** succeeding locations in the probe sequence are determined by the *collision resolution policy*. In the case of Fig. 11.6, the probe sequence for the key W_{23} starts at location 2, since $h(W_{23}) = 2$, and it continues with locations 1, 0, 6, 5, 4, and 3. The probe sequence is arranged so that it examines every different location in table T exactly once.

In order to guarantee that we will always find an empty location in every probe sequence, we define a "full" table, T, to be a table having exactly one empty table entry. This way, when we search for an empty entry along the route given by the probe sequence, we need not count the number of locations visited to see if the total count equals the table size in order to determine when to stop searching. Instead, we can always expect to find an empty location somewhere along the probe sequence path, in order to stop the search.

In the example given above, the probe sequence for a key, L_n, is determined by a simple downward count, starting at the hash address, $h(L_n)$, counting downward in decrements of 1, and wrapping around to the top of table T when we "fall off" the **linear probing** bottom. In this case, we say the *probe decrement* is 1, since 1 is used to decrease the current probe location each time we need to find the next probe location in the probe sequence. We also refer to such a probing process as *linear probing*, because the sequence of table locations that are consecutively probed forms a straight line.

Also, the method of inserting keys into empty locations in table T is called *open addressing*. A bit later, we will discover that the method of *open addressing with linear probing*, which we have illustrated in Figs. 11.3 to 11.6, has some serious performance drawbacks, especially when the table becomes nearly full.

In fact, there are other open addressing methods that perform much better than open addressing with linear probing. One of these methods, called *double hashing*, uses nonlinear probing by computing different probe decrements for different keys. Let's now give a second simple example by showing how double hashing works for the same empty table, T, and for the same keys we inserted in T previously.

First, however, we need to define the probe decrement function, $p(L_n)$, which computes the *probe decrement* for the key L_n. For our simple illustration, we let the value of $p(L_n)$ be the quotient of n after division by 7, except that if the quotient is zero, we define the value to be 1 instead (since using a probe decrement of 0 would not accomplish the goal of ensuring that the probe sequence probes all of the table locations). The way we can express this idea mathematically is to say that $p(L_n)$ is defined to be the maximum value of the pair of quantities $(1, n / 7)$, since if $n / 7$ has the value 0, the maximum of $(1,0)$ is equal to 1, whereas if $n / 7$ has a value of 1 or greater, the maximum value of $(1, n / 7)$ is the same as $n / 7$. Equation 11.2 defines the probe decrement function.

double hashing

using quotients for the probe decrements

$$p(L_n) = \max(1, n / 7). \tag{11.2}$$

For example, $p(W_{23}) = 3$, since the quotient of 23 divided by 7 equals 3 (with the remainder of 2 discarded).

Here, when we divide 23 by 7, we use the remainder 2 as the value of the hash function $h(W_{23})$, and we use the quotient 3 as the value of the probe decrement function $p(W_{23})$.

As another example, $p(B_2) = 1$, because, even though 2 divided by 7 has a quotient of 0, (i.e., $2 / 7 = 0$), we choose the maximum of $(1,0)$ to obtain the value 1 for $p(B_2)$.

Table 11.7 summarizes the values of $h(L_n)$ and $p(L_n)$ for each of the keys to be inserted into table T. Now, let's start by inserting the first four keys, J_{10}, B_2, S_{19}, and N_{14} into the empty table T. Again, we use the value of the hash function, $h(L_n)$, to determine the hash location where we first try to insert these keys. Since there are no

Key = L_n	$h(L_n)$	$p(L_n)$
J_{10}	3	1
B_2	2	1
S_{19}	5	2
N_{14}	0	2
X_{24}	3	3
W_{23}	2	3

Table 11.7 Values of $h(L_n)$ and $p(L_n)$

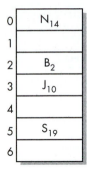

Figure 11.8 Table T

inserting the last key

collisions when we try to insert these keys at their hash addresses in T, we obtain the configuration of table T shown in Fig. 11.8.

Up until this moment, the key insertions are identical to those for open addressing with linear probing illustrated before, since only the probe sequences used for collision resolution differ between the linear probing and double hashing methods.

Next, we try to insert the key X_{24} at location $3 = h(X_{24})$ in the table shown in Fig. 11.8. This produces a collision at location 3, which is already occupied by the key J_{10}. This time, however, we use a probe decrement of $3 = p(X_{24})$ to determine the probe sequence to be used to resolve the collision. Consequently, the next table location to be probed is 0, which is determined by subtracting the probe decrement of 3 from the starting hash address 3. Since location 0 is occupied by the key N_{14}, we need to determine the next location in the probe sequence. This requires us to "wrap around" from the other end of table T (by counting 6, 5, 4) to arrive at the location 3 less than location 0 after wrapping around. Consequently, we probe location 4, and, after finding it empty, we insert X_{24} there. This yields the configuration of table T shown in Fig. 11.9.

Finally, we attempt to insert the key W_{23} into table T. We start by trying to insert W_{23} at its hash address, $2 = h(W_{23})$. But this yields a collision with the key B_2, already occupying location 2. So, using the probe decrement $3 = p(W_{23})$, we try to find the next empty location in the probe sequence for W_{23}. Starting at location 2 and counting down 3 takes us past the lowest location in table T, and causes us to wrap around, starting at the highest numbered location in T, which is 6. Since location 6 is empty, we can place W_{23} in location 6 in T. This yields the final configuration for table T, as shown in Fig. 11.10.

In double hashing, when two keys collide at the same initial hash address, they usually follow different probe sequences when a search is made for the first available empty table location. For instance, the keys J_{10} and X_{24} both collide at hash address 3 in table T. But, since $p(J_{10}) = 1$ and $p(X_{24}) = 3$, we see that the two colliding keys have different probe decrements, even though they have identical hash addresses (which caused the initial collision). When colliding keys trace out *different* search paths by following their probe sequences after a collision, they will tend to find empty locations more quickly than in the case when all keys colliding at a given initial hash

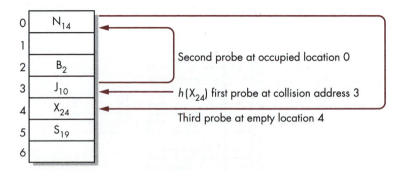

Second probe at occupied location 0

$h(X_{24})$ first probe at collision address 3

Third probe at empty location 4

Figure 11.9 Table T

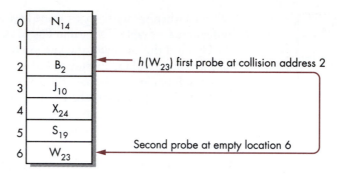

Figure 11.10 Table T

address follow *identical* search paths. In open addressing with linear probing, all keys colliding at a given address follow the same probe sequence. But in open addressing with double hashing, colliding keys tend to follow different probe sequences. Consequently, double hashing tends to perform better than linear probing. Later we will give the performance formulas that characterize just how much better double hashing is than linear probing.

separate chaining

Let's now give another in our series of simple examples by showing a third method for resolving collisions in a hash table, T: *collision resolution by separate chaining*. The idea is simply to place all keys that collide at a single hash address on a linked list starting at that address.

For instance, if we had entered the keys J_{10}, B_2, S_{19}, N_{14}, X_{24}, and W_{23} into an initially empty table T, using collision resolution by chaining (and using hash addresses given by $h(L_n) = n \% 7$, the same as those shown in Table 11.7), then the resulting table configuration would be that shown in Fig. 11.11.

hashing with buckets

To complete our series of examples, we will mention briefly one additional hashing method called *hashing with buckets*, which will be explored further in the next chapter. Suppose we had a big hash table, T, with, say, 20,000 empty entries. We could divide this big table into 200 smaller subtables each containing 100 empty entries, and we could call each such small subtable a "bucket." We could agree to store keys in each bucket sequentially in increasing order of their keys. Initially, we would hash a key, K, into one of the 200 different buckets. That is, $h(K)$ would be an

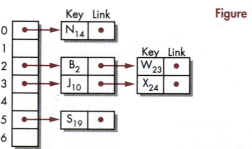

Figure 11.11 Table T

integer in the range 0:199, specifying one of the 200 smaller subtables (each of size 100). Then we could use binary search to locate key K in the ordered sequence of entries in the bucket designated by the hash address $h(K)$. While this technique does not give superior performance if table T is stored in primary memory, it turns out to give quite good performance when T is stored on relatively slow rotating external memory (such as disks). For this reason, we will study hashing with buckets in the next chapter when we explore techniques that work well on large collections of data.

11.3 Review Questions

1. Explain how linear probing differs from double hashing.
2. Explain how collision resolution with separate chaining works.
3. Describe the method of hashing with buckets.

11.3 Exercises

1. Give the final configuration of table, T, that results from inserting the keys in Table 11.7 into an initially empty table T, using linear probing, if the order of insertion of the keys is X_{24}, W_{23}, J_{10}, B_2, N_{14}, and S_{19}.
2. Repeat Exercise 1, with double hashing used in place of linear probing. What is the final configuration of table T?
3. Implement algorithms to insert and search for table entries using the method of separate chaining, as illustrated in Fig. 11.11.
4. How could you redesign the hash search algorithm in order to reduce the time for unsuccessful searching using the method of separate chaining, given an implementation of chaining that initially keeps keys on each chain in the order they were inserted?

11.4 Collisions, Load Factors, and Clusters

Learning Objectives

1. To be able to define collisions, load factors, and clustering.
2. To discover that collisions are frequent, even in sparsely occupied tables.
3. To discover how primary clusters form when using linear probing, and how they do not form when using double hashing.

In order to extend our understanding of hashing ideas a bit further we need to introduce and define a few terms, and we need to explore the performance properties of the hashing methods introduced in the previous section.

First, let's talk a bit about hashing functions themselves. Suppose T is a hash

uniform random hashing

table having M table entries whose addresses lie in the range 0:M – 1. (You might think of this as a one-dimensional C array of the form $T[0:M – 1]$.) An ideal hashing function, $h(K)$, maps keys, K, onto table addresses in the range 0:M − 1 in a *uniform and random* fashion. The words "uniform and random" mean that for any arbitrarily chosen key K, any of the possible table addresses in the range 0:M − 1 is *equally likely* to be chosen (at random) by the function, h, which sends key K onto its hash address $h(K)$.

It is actually a bit tricky to select good hashing functions. We will have more to say on this subject later in Section 11.6, which deals with choosing hashing functions. For now, simply think of a hashing function as something akin to tossing numbered balls into a row of numbered slots. Each numbered slot corresponds to a table location in table T, and each numbered ball corresponds to a key, K. If the person or device that tosses the balls into the slots randomly selects the target slot from the table with each slot having equal probability to be selected, it models the characteristic of a good hashing function that we will assume in the following discussion.

Collisions

Let's now discuss the phenomenon of collisions. A collision happens when two separate keys, K and K', map onto the same hash address in table T.

> A **collision** between two keys, K and K', occurs if, when we try to store both keys in a hash table, T, both keys have the same hash address, $h(K) = h(K')$.

collision resolution policies

A *collision resolution policy* is a method for finding an empty table entry in which to store a key, K', if, after trying to store key K' in a hash table, T, we find the table location given by the hash address $h(K')$ already occupied by another key, K, which has been entered into table T previously.

One of the remarkable facts about collisions that is contrary to most peoples' intuition is that collisions are relatively frequent, even in sparsely occupied hash tables. There is a famous "paradox," called the *von Mises Birthday Paradox*,[1] that helps us to understand the issue. According to this paradox, if there are 23 or more people in a room, the chance is greater than 50 percent that two or more of them will have the same birthday. (Another variant of this says that if there are 88 or more people in a room, the chance that three or more will have the same birthday is greater than 50 percent.)

collisions are likely, even in sparsely occupied tables

When you think about the von Mises paradox in terms of the model we described above, in which we toss balls into numbered slots, it seems, at first, to be unlikely to be true. In terms of the ball-tossing model, the von Mises paradox says that, given a table T with 365 numbered slots (where each slot corresponds to a different day of the

---

[1] See R. von Mises, Über Aufteilungs-und Besetzungs-Wahrscheinlichkeiten, *Revue de la Faculté des Sciences de l'Université d'Istanbul*, N.S. 4. 1938–39, pp. 145–63.

year on which a person could have a birthday—ignoring leap years, for the moment), if we toss 23 balls at random into these 365 slots (with each toss selecting a slot independently and randomly among the 365 possible slots), the chance is greater than 50 percent that we will toss two or more balls into the same slot. Most people initially have the opinion that this result is inaccurate, since when 23 balls are placed in a table with 365 positions, the table is only 6.3 percent full (since 23/365 = 0.063), and we are asserting that there is better than a 50–50 chance of a collision when the table is only 6.3 percent occupied. How can that be? The answer comes from an argument in probability theory, which we discuss next, and which nonmathematically oriented readers may wish to skip.

The von Mises Probability Argument[**]

We can compute the probability of one or more collisions when we randomly toss 23 balls into 365 slots as follows. Let $Q(n)$ be the probability that when we randomly toss n balls into a table, T, with 365 slots, then none of the n balls collide, and let $P(n)$ be the probability that there is at least one collision when we randomly toss n balls into a table with 365 slots. We see that $P(n)$ and $Q(n)$ are related by the formula

$$P(n) = 1 - Q(n),$$

since 1 minus the probability of no collisions equals the probability of one or more collisions.

Now, it is easy to compute $Q(n)$ by the following argument. $Q(1) = 1$, since whenever we toss one ball into an empty table, the probability is 1 (i.e., it is totally certain) that there will be no collisions. When we toss the second ball into the table, the chance of hitting an unoccupied slot is now 364 out of 365, since there are only 364 unoccupied slots left in a table having one ball already occupying one slot. So $Q(2) = Q(1)*(^{364}/_{365})$. When we toss the third ball into the table, the chance of hitting an unoccupied slot now drops to 363 out of 365, since we have to miss the two slots occupied by the two balls already in the table. This means that $Q(3) = Q(2)*(^{363}/_{365}) = Q(1)*(^{364}/_{365})*(^{363}/_{365})$.

Continuing in this fashion, we get two recurrence relations:

computing the probability of no collisions

$$Q(1) = 1 \text{ and}$$
$$Q(n) = Q(n-1) * (365 - n + 1)/ 365$$

Recurrence Relations

(11.3)

Using $Q(1) = 1 = (^{365}/_{365})$ and unrolling these recurrence relations, we get

$$Q(n) = \frac{365 * 364 * \ldots * (365 - n + 1)}{365^n}.$$

The last equation can be rewritten in terms of factorials, as follows:

$$Q(n) = \frac{365!}{365^n \, (365-n)!}.$$

Substituting this for $Q(n)$ in the equation $P(n) = 1 - Q(n)$ gives

von Mises birthday paradox
collision probability

$$P(n) = 1 - \frac{365!}{365^n \, (365-n)!}. \tag{11.4}$$

Exercise 11.4.1 challenges you to write a C program to compute values of $P(n)$ for various n. Table 11.12 gives some of these values. Figure 11.13 plots $P(n)$ on the y-axis versus n on the x-axis. As you can see, the von Mises probability (i.e., the probability of two or more people in a room having the same birthday) rises rapidly and passes 50 percent when 23 or more people are in the room. Moreover, as soon as 47 or more people are in the room, the chances are better than 19 out of 20 that two or more people will have the same birthday. In terms of a hash table with 365 entries, this means that as soon as the table is 12.9 percent full, there is greater than a 95 percent chance that at least two keys will have collided. This investigation con-

Table 11.12 Values of P(n) for Various n

n	P(n)
5	0.02713557
10	0.11694818
15	0.25290132
20	0.41143838
22	0.47569531
23	0.50729723
25	0.56869970
30	0.70631624
35	0.81438324
40	0.89123181
45	0.94097590
50	0.97037358
55	0.98626229
60	0.99412266
65	0.99768311
70	0.99915958
75	0.99971988
80	0.99991433
85	0.99997600
90	0.99999385
95	0.99999856
100	0.99999969

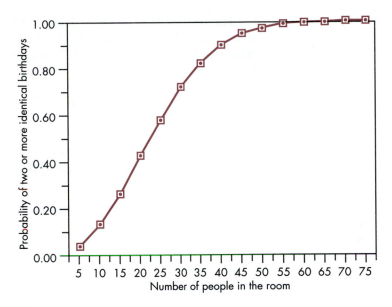

Figure 11.13 von Mises Probability Curve

firms the statement that, "Even in sparsely occupied hash tables, collisions are relatively common."

Actually, the word "paradox" is misapplied in the strict sense of mathematical logic, when referring to the von Mises paradox. In mathematics, the word "paradox" refers to a statement that is self-contradictory. In the von Mises paradox, the word "paradox" refers to a situation that is contrary to common sense, or "counter-intuitive." It is not actually a self-contradiction in the mathematical sense. (See Exercise 11.4.2 for an example of a paradox in the sense of mathematical logic.)

Load Factors and Clustering

In this subsection, let's focus our attention only on open addressing methods (and let's put aside, for the moment, considerations of hashing using separate chaining and buckets).

the load factor

In this context, a useful term to define is the *load factor* of a hash table T. Suppose that table T is of size M, meaning that it has space for M table entries, and suppose that N of these M entries are *occupied* (whereas M – N entries are *empty*). We define the load factor, α, of table T to be the ratio of N to M.

> The **load factor**, α, of a hash table of size M with N occupied entries is defined by
>
> $$\alpha = \frac{N}{M}.$$

For example, if a hash table T of size 100 has 75 occupied entries and 25 empty entries, then T's load factor is 0.75. The load factor, α, is always a fraction lying between zero and one, $0 \le \alpha < 1$. (The reason that the load factor can never be exactly equal to 1 is because, in open addressing, we define a *full* table to be a table with exactly one empty entry. Later, we will see that it is important to guarantee that there is at least one empty entry so that the algorithms for searching for a key and for inserting a new key in a table will terminate efficiently.)

You can also think of the load factor as being related to the percentage of entries in table T that are occupied. For instance, a table with a load factor of 0.25 is 25 percent full, and a table that is 50 percent full has a load factor of 0.50. We will see later that the load factor determines how efficient searching and insertion are in open addressing hash tables.

Let's now turn to the subject of clustering. A *cluster* is a sequence of adjacent occupied entries in a hash table. Clusters have no empty keys in them, and consist of contiguous runs of occupied entries. It turns out that the method of linear probing is subject to something called *primary clustering*. We can see that, when a number of keys collide at a given location, and when we use linear probing to resolve the collisions, the colliding keys are inserted into empty locations immediately below the collision location (because, linear probing looks for empty table locations at the immediately lower addresses starting at the collision location). This can cause a small puddle of keys to form at the collision location.

primary clustering

Roughly speaking, what happens in primary clustering is as follows. The small puddles of keys grow larger, and the larger they get the faster they grow, since they are wider targets for new keys that are being inserted. Whenever we try to insert a new key into the middle of a puddle, linear probing always makes us look to the bottom edge of the puddle in order to find the first empty location in which to insert the new key. Consequently bigger puddles collect more "hits" of new keys being inserted, and they grow rapidly at their lower edges (where "lower" refers to the direction of low table addresses, and "higher" refers to the direction of high table addresses). Moreover, during growth, small puddles join together to form bigger puddles, and the bigger puddles formed by such mergers grow even faster. This phenomenon of puddle formation, puddle growth, and puddle mergers is called primary clustering.

how primary clusters grow

By contrast, when we perform collision resolution by *double hashing*, instead of by linear probing, there is no primary clustering. It will turn out that double hashing performs much better than linear probing because of the absence of clustering in double hashing.

You can get a slight appreciation of the phenomenon of primary clustering by examining and comparing Figs. 11.14 and 11.15, although you have to be a keen observer to see what is going on.

Figure 11.14 illustrates a hash table being filled by open addressing with linear probing at increments of 10 percent full. The black bands in this figure represent clusters (or "puddles" of adjacent keys, as we described them metaphorically in the informal description just given). Figure 11.15 illustrates the same table being filled by double hashing in increments of 10 percent full.

You can see that primary clustering has taken place in Fig. 11.14 by the fact that the clusters are larger on the average and that there are fewer of them than is the case

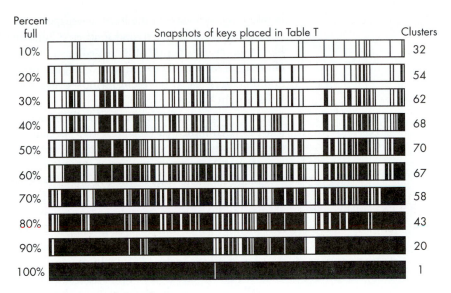

Figure 11.14 Linear Probing Clusters

in Fig. 11.15, which has no primary clustering. (The clusters in Fig. 11.15 occur because of random placement of keys into adjacent table locations, illustrating that random placement generates a certain amount of natural clustering. As an aside, the author is writing this in California at a time when the state has just experienced several earthquakes above magnitude 6.0 in a period of a few days. There is a debate

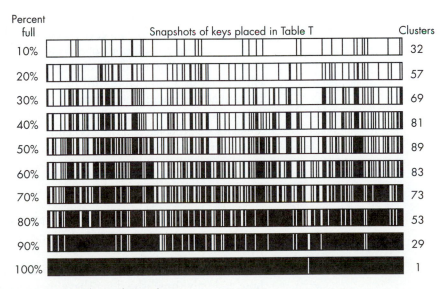

Figure 11.15 Double Hashing Clusters

between seismologists in the local newspaper. One seismologist argues that the cluster of earthquakes in northern and southern California are possibly related and are possibly symptoms of a period of increased seismic activity, while another argues that such clusters are most likely to be purely random since it is the nature of collections of random occurrences to have clustering—otherwise, the occurrences are not random. Who is right?)

In the rightmost column of Figs. 11.14 and 11.15 the number of clusters in each row has been indicated (assuming that, because of "wrap around," the clusters at the opposite ends of the table are part of the same cluster and do not count as two separate clusters.)

comparing cluster counts

Examining the rows of each figure corresponding to 70 percent full, we see that linear probing has generated 58 clusters, whereas double hashing has generated 73 clusters. In other words, there are 26 percent more clusters (which are, on the average, smaller) when using double hashing at 70 percent full than there are when using linear probing. This is because of primary clustering.

Again, if you look at Fig. 11.14 starting, say, in the row corresponding to 60 percent full, and you scan downward from the biggest clusters in the 60 percent full row, you will see primary clusters growing at their left ends (or low table address ends), and you will see clusters join to form bigger clusters that grow even faster, as you move downward from row to row.

When you try to find this phenomenon in Fig. 11.15, you discover that it does not work the same way. Clusters do not tend to grow fastest only at their left edges, nor do nearby clusters tend to join together so readily. This is symptomatic of the absence of primary clustering.

11.4 Review Questions

1. Define what it means for two keys to collide in a hash table.
2. What is a collision resolution policy?
3. Under what conditions will the chances be greater than 50 percent that a collision will happen in a hash table with room for 365 table entries, assuming the hash function $h(K)$ is uniform and random?
4. Define the load factor of a hash table, T, having room for M table entries of which N entries are occupied and (M − N) entries are empty.
5. What is primary clustering? How and when does it occur?

11.4 Exercises

1. Write a C program to compute values of P(n), as given in Eq. 11.4 for various values of n. Determine the value of n for which P(n) ≥ 0.5 and for which P(n − 1) < 0.5.
2. (The Barber of Seville paradox) There is a Barber in Seville, Spain, who shaves those and only those who don't shave themselves. Can he shave himself? (This is

called a paradox of self-reference.) Investigate the logical consequences of two initial assumptions: (a) the Barber of Seville shaves himself, (b) the Barber of Seville does not shave himself.

≡ 11.5 Algorithms for Hashing by Open Addressing

Learning Objectives

1. To learn how the actual algorithms work for hashing with open addressing.
2. To illustrate how the use of these algorithms leads to the formation of primary clusters for linear probing but not for double hashing.
3. To learn why probe sequences in these algorithms are guaranteed to inspect all possible hash table locations.
4. To learn how to derive some of the performance formulas characterizing how well hashing works.
5. To compare the theoretical and actual measured experimental performance of hashing techniques and to develop intuition for when they work well and when they don't.

In order to develop some algorithms for hashing with open addressing, let's assume we have a hash table T of size M, and let's assume we are using integers as keys with the understanding that there exists a special EmptyKey having a value of 0. (It is easy to generalize the algorithms so that the keys are not integers, such as those used in subsequent examples, where we use strings representing three-letter airport codes as keys.)

Thus we can declare some constants for use in our algorithms, as follows:

```
/* Assume that the following constants are defined for use in the hash table */
/* Programs 11.16 and 11.17 given later */


    #define  M   TableSize        /* where TableSize is a suitable integer that */
                                  /* must be chosen carefully according */
                                  /* to considerations explored later */


    #define  EmptyKey  0              /* initially we use positive integers for */
                                  /* nonempty keys and zero as the empty key */
```

Specifically, we intend that table T have M entries, numbered starting at 0 and ending at M − 1, where M − 1 is the maximum table address.

We then search for the table entry in table T containing the search key K. If we find key K in the table entry $T[i]$, we will return the location i as the result of a successful search. However, if the search is unsuccessful, we will agree to return the special value, −1, to denote that the search was unsuccessful.

We can also define some other C types to portray the structure of tables and table entries, as follows:

```
typedef   int   KeyType        /* although, initially, the KeyType is an integer, it */
                               /* could be specified otherwise, as shown later */

typedef   struct {
               /* some members of various types giving */
               /* information associated with search keys */
          } InfoType;

typedef   struct {
               KeyType      Key;
               InfoType     Info;
          } TableEntry;

typedef   TableEntry   Table[M];        /* a Table contains M table entries */
```

The only other preparatory declaration we need is to declare a variable representing the hash table T itself. This is done as follows:

```
Table T;                               /* the hash table, T, contains table entries */
```

Before we start inserting entries into table T, we need to initialize T to be the empty table. We can do this by storing the **EmptyKey** in every entry of T using a for-statement, such as:

```
|          for (i = 0; i < M; ++i ) {
|                   T[i].Key = EmptyKey;
|          }
```

Now, suppose we want to insert a key, K, and some associated information, I, into table T. Let's assume that we have defined a hash function $h(K)$ and a probe decrement function $p(K)$. How could we proceed? Program 11.16 gives a hash insertion algorithm. Next, we need to specify the algorithm for searching for the table entry $T[i]$ containing a given search key, K. This is performed by Program 11.17.

You can see that if the probe decrement function $p(K) = 1$, then Program 11.16 performs *linear probing*, whereas if $p(K)$ is a secondary hash function that computes different probe decrements for different keys K, then Program 11.16 performs *double hashing*.

Two Examples of Primary Clustering and Its Absence

We now study two small examples that have been carefully chosen to illustrate how primary clusters form when we use linear probing, and how such clusters do not form when we use double hashing. Since the table size used is so small, the examples have been chosen to play the role of caricatures of what happens in larger tables.

To do this, we will execute Programs 11.16 and 11.17 on a hash table, T, of size $M = 11$, with entries numbered 0:10, and will use three-letter airport codes as search

```
            void HashInsert(KeyType K, InfoType I)
            {
                int   i;
                int   ProbeDecrement;

                i = h(K);                           /* let i be the first hash location */
                ProbeDecrement = p(K);              /* compute the probe decrement */

                while (T[i].Key != EmptyKey) {
                    i -= ProbeDecrement;            /* compute next probe location */
                    if (i < 0) {
                        i += M;                     /* wrap around if needed */
                    }
                }

                T[i].Key = K;                       /* insert new key K in table T, and then */
                T[i].Info = I;                      /* insert new Info I in table T */
            }
```

Program 11.16 Inserting a New Table Entry into a Hash Table

```
            int HashSearch(KeyType K)
            {
                int        i;
                int        ProbeDecrement;
                KeyType    ProbeKey;


                /* Initializations */
                i = h(K);                           /* let i be the first hash location */
                ProbeDecrement = p(K);              /* compute probe decrement */
                ProbeKey = T[i].Key;                /* extract first probe key from table */



                /* Search loop */
                while ( (K != ProbeKey) && (ProbeKey != EmptyKey) ) {
                    i -= ProbeDecrement;            /* compute next probe location */
                    if (i < 0) {
                        i += M;                     /* wrap around if needed */
                    }
                    ProbeKey = T[i].Key;            /* extract next probe key */
                }

                /* Determine success or failure */
                if (ProbeKey == EmptyKey) {
                    return -1;                      /* return -1 to signify that K was not found */
                } else {
                    return i;                       /* return location, i, of key K in table T */
                }
            }
```

Program 11.17 Searching for a Table Entry with Search Key K

Table 11.18 Hash Function and Probe Decrement Values

Key K = Airport Code	Hash Function h(K)	p(K) for Double Hashing	p(K) for Linear Probing
PHL	4	4	1
ORY	8	1	1
GCM	6	1	1
HKG	4	3	1
GLA	8	9	1
AKL	7	2	1
FRA	5	6	1
LAX	1	7	1
DCA	1	2	1

keys. Table 11.18 gives the values of the hash function, $h(K)$, and gives two separate probe decrement functions $p(K)$, one of which will be used for linear probing and the other of which will be used for double hashing.

The hash function $h(K)$, used in Table 11.18, was computed by considering the keys to represent base-26 integer values and by reducing these integer values modulo the table size, 11. When we let a three-letter airport code, $X_2X_1X_0$, represent a base-26 integer, we let the letter "A" represent the digit-value 0, the letter "B" represent the digit-value 1, the letter "C" represent the digit-value 2, the letter "D" represent the digit-value 3, and so on, up until the letter "Z," which represents the digit-value 25.

Then the three-letter airport code, $K = X_2X_1X_0$, can be converted from a base-26 number into a decimal integer, using the formula

$$Base26ValueOf(K) = X_2*26^2 + X_1*26^1 + X_0*26^0.$$

For example, if K = "DCA," then, since the digit values of "D," "C," and "A" are 3, 2, and 0, respectively, we have

$$Base26ValueOf(\text{``DCA''}) = 3*26^2 + 2*26^1 + 0*26^0$$
$$= 3*676 + 2*26 + 0*1$$
$$= 2028 + 52$$
$$= 2080.$$

We then define the value of the hash function $h(K)$ to be the remainder of $Base26ValueOf(K)$ after division by 11, which is computed by

$$h(K) = Base26ValueOf(K) \% 11. \tag{11.5}$$

For example, $h(\text{``DCA''}) = 2080 \% 11 = 1$, since $2080 = 11*189 + 1$. The hash function values in the second column of Table 11.18 are each computed using Eq. 11.5.

The values of the double hashing probe decrement function, $p(K)$, used in the third column of Table 11.18 are computed using the formula

$$p(K) = max(1, (Base26ValueOf(K) / 11) \% 11)).\qquad(11.6)$$

In other words, to compute the probe decrement $p(K)$ to use for double hashing, you take the quotient of $Base26ValueOf(K)$ after division by 11, and you reduce that quotient to a number in the range 0:10, by taking its remainder modulo 11. Then if the result turns out to be 0, you use 1 instead, to ensure that the probe decrement will always have a value of 1 or greater. Equation 11.6 is used to determine the values in the third column of Table 11.18.

computing probe decrements

Finally, the probe decrement function $p(K)$ used for linear probing is defined by the formula $p(K) = 1$, since linear probing always decrements the current probe location by 1 in order to get the next probe location. This fact is reflected in the fourth column of Table 11.18, which gives probe decrements of 1 for every possible key.

Now that we have determined values of $h(K)$ and $p(K)$, we are ready to insert some airport code keys into an initially empty table, T. Let's use the method of open addressing with linear probing first. This means, we will use $p(K) = 1$ for all keys K. We proceed to insert keys in the order given by the first column of Table 11.18, using the hash insertion algorithm Program 11.16 for hash insertion. After inserting the first three keys, PHL, ORY, and GCM, we get the table configuration shown in the leftmost (or first) column of Fig. 11.19.

linear probing is tried first

After inserting the next two keys, HKG and GLA, we get the configuration shown in column two of Fig. 11.19. When we try to insert the key HKG, we find that it collides at location 4 with the key PHL already in the table, and we probe downward in increments of one location to try to find an empty table location. The first empty table location below 4 is location 3, so we insert HKG into location 3. The arrows to the right of column two illustrate the probe sequence followed during insertion. Similarly, when we try to insert GLA, it collides with the key ORY already

primary clusters begin to form

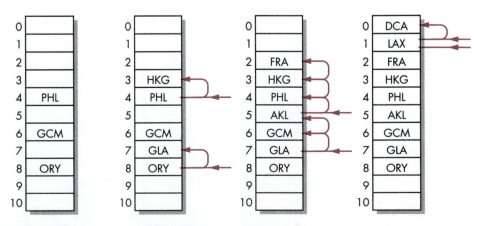

Figure 11.19 Table T with Linear Probing

in location 8, and we search downward to find the first empty location, which is location 7. So we place GLA in location 7. Note that the two colliding keys PHL and HKG have formed a small, two-key primary cluster at the point of collision. Note also that inserting GLA has caused a three-key cluster to form by joining two nearby one-key clusters. Primary clusters have already begun to form, even in this simple example.

When we next insert the keys AKL and FRA, we get the configuration shown in the third column of Fig. 11.19. First, AKL collides with the key GLA already in location 7. Downward searching in probe decrements of 1 locates the first empty table entry at location 5. So AKL is placed in location 5. This joins the previous two primary clusters together into one big primary cluster. Next, when we try to insert the key FRA at location 5, we find it is occupied, and, after probing downward, we find the first empty table entry at location 2. So we insert FRA in location 2.

When we try to insert the last two keys, LAX and DCA, we find LAX goes into an empty entry at location 1 on the first probe. DCA then collides with LAX and is inserted below location 1 at location 0.

If we try to search for the key AKL, using Program 11.17, we find that we first attempt to find AKL at its hash location $h(AKL) = 7$, and, not finding it there, we trace along the probe sequence in decrements of 1, until finding AKL at location 5. Similarly, if we search for a key, such as MIA, which is not in table T, where $h(MIA) = 4$, we first probe at location 4, and trace out the probe sequence 4, 3, 2, 1, 0, 10, looking for a table entry containing MIA or for the first empty table entry. Since we encounter an empty entry at location 10 before finding an entry containing MIA, we conclude that MIA is not in table T, and we return the special table address, –1, to signal that MIA is not in table T.

now we try double hashing

Let's now switch from linear probing to double hashing and let's see what happens when we fill table T with the keys in Table 11.18 in the same order as before. This time we will use values of $p(K)$ from column three of Table 11.18. Figure 11.20 gives four snapshots of the insertion process.

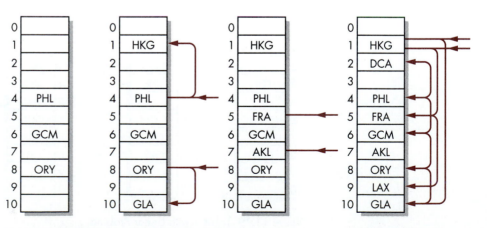

Figure 11.20 Table T with Double Hashing

how double hashing differs
from linear probing

In the first column of Fig. 11.20, we have inserted the keys PHL, ORY, and GCM. We are again inserting keys in the order given by Table 11.18. Since there are no collisions, these first three keys are inserted in their first hash locations. Consequently, the first column of Fig. 11.20 looks exactly like the first column of Fig. 11.19. However, when we insert the next two keys, HKG and GLA, to produce the configuration shown in the second column of Fig. 11.20, we begin to see how collision resolution by double hashing differs from collision resolution by linear probing.

First, we attempt to insert HKG at its hash location, 4, but we find location 4 is already occupied by the key PHL. To resolve this collision, we look up the probe decrement, $p(HKG)$, in Table 11.18, and we find $p(HKG) = 3$. So we subtract 3 from the initial probe location 4 to find the next probe location in the probe sequence for HKG, which is location 1. Here we find an empty location, so we insert HKG in location 1. In the second column of Fig. 11.20, the straight arrow pointing at location 4 shows the first probe at the hash address, $h(HKG) = 4$, and the curved arrow starting at location 4 and ending at location 1 shows the second probe in the probe sequence. By a similar process, the key GLA collides with ORY at table location 8, and lands in location 10. Comparing the second columns of Figs. 11.19 and 11.20, we see that double hashing has avoided creating the primary clusters associated with linear probing.

Next we insert the keys AKL and FRA to get the configuration of table T shown in the third column of Fig. 11.20. Here we are lucky, because both AKL and FRA go directly into empty locations at their hash addresses without encountering any collisions, as is shown by the straight arrows to the right of column three.

Finally, we attempt to insert the last two keys, LAX and DCA. When we attempt to insert LAX at the location $h(LAX) = 1$, we encounter a collision with HKG. So we compute the probe decrement $p(LAX) = 7$, and we start counting down 7 locations from location 1 to find the next location in the probe sequence. After counting down one location out of the seven we have to travel, we fall off the bottom of the table, so we wrap around to the top, and continue counting down six more locations from location 10, the topmost location. This brings us to location 5, which is already occupied by the key, FRA. Consequently, we need to count down seven more locations, starting at location 5, to find the next location in the probe sequence. Again we fall off the bottom of the table and wrap around to location 9. Since location 9 is empty, we insert LAX in location 9.

Finally, we attempt to insert the key DCA. DCA's initial hash address is also location 1, which is occupied by HKG. So we use $p(DCA) = 2$, as the probe decrement to compute locations in DCA's probe sequence. After wrap around, this leads us to examine locations 10, 8, 6, 4, and 2, in sequence. We find that location 2 is the first empty table entry in this probe sequence, so we can place DCA in location 2.

the two keys trace out
separate probe sequences

Note here that even though the two keys LAX and DCA collide initially at the same occupied hash address, 1, they trace out separate probe sequences after their first point of collision. Thus double hashing often leads initially colliding keys to search for empty locations along *separate* probe sequence paths. This is more efficient than linear probing, which causes all keys colliding at the same initial location to trace out identical search paths when looking for an empty table entry. Because colliding keys (usually) trace out separate probe sequences in the double-hashing method, there is no primary clustering in double hashing.

Now let's look at what happens when we try to search for the key, MIA, which is not in the table given in the fourth column of Fig. 11.20. The key MIA has an initial hash location of $h(\text{MIA}) = 4$ and has a probe decrement of $p(\text{MIA}) = 8$. Program 11.17 directs us to look first at location 4, where we have a collision with the key, PHL. We then trace out locations on the probe sequence starting at location 4 and decrementing by 8 locations each time. (It turns out that decrementing by 8 and wrapping around from bottom-to-top is identical to incrementing by 3 and wrapping around from top-to-bottom.) So we investigate locations 4, 7, 10, 2, 5, 8, and 0. We find that location 0 is empty, so we conclude that MIA is not in table T, and we return the special table address, –1, to signal that MIA is not in table T.

Ensuring That Probe Sequences Cover the Table**

In order for the open addressing hash insertion and hash searching algorithms to work properly, we have to guarantee that every probe sequence used can probe all locations in the hash table. Otherwise, the hash insertion algorithm would not be guaranteed to find a new empty table entry in which to insert a new key, and the hash search algorithm would not be guaranteed to find an empty entry to signal it to stop, when searching for a key that is not in the table.

linear probing obviously covers the table

It is rather obvious that the linear probing method generates a probe sequence that covers all possible table locations, since, starting at the initial collision location, linear probing moves downward, systematically enumerating a contiguous linear sequence of table addresses, until it falls off the bottom of the table and then wraps around to the top to continue its downward march—returning eventually to the original collision location in an unbroken wrap-around cycle.

It is not so obvious that the differing probe decrements, $p(K)$, used for double hashing will always cover all table locations in some order in the probe sequences they generate. Let's start with an example. Choose any key from Table 11.18 and retrieve its hash address, $h(K)$ and its probe decrement (for double hashing), $p(K)$. For instance, choosing the key, HKG, we have $h(\text{HKG}) = 4$, and $p(\text{HKG}) = 3$. This means we initially probe at the hash address 4. Then we probe in decrements of 3, at location 1, and, after a first wrap-around, at locations 9, 6, 3, 0. After a second wrap-around, we continue probing at locations 8, 5, and 2. After a third wrap-around, we probe at locations 10 and 7, before returning to the original hash location, 4. You can see that all 11 table locations were covered exactly once in the probe sequence

$$4, 1, 9, 6, 3, 0, 8, 5, 2, 10, 7.$$

Moreover, no table location was enumerated twice before all original locations were covered once.

a clever design principle

If you try the same experiment for any other key in Table 11.18, you will discover that the probe sequence for double hashing covers all table locations exactly once, no matter what the initial hash address is, and no matter what the probe decrement is. Evidently, there is some sort of clever design principle lurking beneath the example we have been using that guarantees this aspect of double hashing's performance. It's now time to investigate what this design principle is.

It so happens that the table sizes, 7 and 11, for both examples we have used so far in this chapter have been prime numbers. Our first example in Section 11.3 used a table size of M = 7 locations with keys of the form L_n, where L was a letter of the alphabet, and n was its ordinal position in the alphabet. Our second example used a table size of M = 11 locations and used three-letter airport codes as keys. The values of the probe decrements, $p(K)$, were chosen to be positive integers in the range $1 \leq p(K) < M$. The locations visited by the probe sequences were therefore of the form

$$[h(K) - i*p(K)] \% M, \quad \text{for } i \text{ in the range } 0 \leq i \leq (M - 1).$$

Here, the use of "% M" is a mathematical way of capturing the wrap-around behavior of the probe sequence. In particular, for the ith location in the probe sequence, we calculate $h(K) - i*p(K)$ (which is equal to the original hash location $h(K)$, minus i copies of the probe decrement $p(K)$), and we reduce it modulo M, to wrap it into a table address in the range 0:M − 1.

Now, let's prove that the probe sequence locations, $[h(K) - i*p(K)] \% M$, cover all table addresses in the range 0:M − 1 exactly once. To do this, suppose there are two distinct integers j and k in the range, 0:M − 1, which generate the same probe location. That is suppose, $j \neq k$, and suppose

$$[h(K) - j*p(K)] \% M = [h(K) - k*p(K)] \% M .$$

Suppose also that it is known that M is a prime number. Now we can apply some of the manipulation rules from Section A.5 of the "Math Reference" appendix covering modular arithmetic.

First, recalling the definition of *congruence*, "if (a mod m) = (b mod m) then, by definition, $a \equiv b$ (*modulo m*)," (and noting that % represents mod in C) we have

$$\{[h(K) - j*p(K)] \equiv [h(K) - k*p(K)]\} \ (\textit{modulo M}).$$

Then, applying Eq. A.26 in the appendix, we can subtract $h(K)$ from both sides of this congruence, and we can multiply through by −1, to get

$$[j*p(K) \equiv k*p(K)] \ (\textit{modulo M}).$$

Now applying Eq. A.27 of the appendix, we are allowed to divide out $p(K)$ from both sides of the latter congruence, provided $p(K)$ and the modulus M are relatively prime. (Recall that two numbers a and b are relatively prime if they have no common divisors other than 1.) Since we have chosen the table size, M, as a prime number, M has no divisors other than itself and 1, so M and $p(K)$ are relatively prime. Accordingly, we can apply Eq. A.27, and cancel $p(K)$ from both sides of the congruence, leaving

$$j \equiv k \ (\textit{modulo M}).$$

Again, using the definition of congruence, we can expand this last line into

$$(j \text{ \% } M) = (k \text{ \% } M).$$

Now recall that both j and k are integers in the range $0:M - 1$. This means that when j and k are reduced % M to numbers in the range $0:M - 1$, they are equal to themselves—i.e., $(j \text{ \% } M) = j$, and $(k \text{ \% } M) = k$. Consequently, the above equality reduces to

$$j = k.$$

all table locations are
covered exactly once

But this contradicts the original assumption that $j \neq k$. Therefore it is impossible to have two different probes in the original probe sequence mapping to the same table location. Since all M of the locations in the probe sequence lie in the range of table addresses, $0:M - 1$, and since all M of these probe locations are different, the entire range of table addresses, $0:M - 1$, must be covered exactly once in the set of locations enumerated by the probe sequence, which is what we wanted to prove.

Note that in the proof above, the only requirement on the probe decrement, $p(K)$, was that it had to be *relatively prime* to the table size, M. Because of this fact, we could, for instance choose the table size, M, to be a power of two, and we could choose $p(K)$ to be any odd number. Then we would still be guaranteed to have the probe sequences cover the entire range of table addresses.

For example, suppose $M = 2^3 = 8$, and we choose $p(K) \in \{ 1, 3, 5, 7 \}$. Then, starting at any initial hash address, $h(K)$, in the range of table addresses, $0:7$, and using any odd probe decrement, the probe sequence covers all addresses in $0:7$ exactly once before repeating. For example, if $h(K) = 5$ and $p(K) = 3$, the probe sequence is: 5, 2, 7, 4, 1, 6, 3, 0.

In summary, two popular and effective ways to set up double hashing tables are (a) to choose a prime number, such as 997, as the table size M, and to choose as probe decrements, any integer in the range, $1:M - 1$, and (b) to choose a power of two, such as $2^{10} = 1024$, as the table size M, and to choose as probe decrements, any odd integer in the range, $1:M - 1$.

Performance Formulas

Now let's turn to the subject of characterizing the efficiency of performance of open addressing methods using both linear probing and double hashing.

You can imagine that, as the load factor α of a hash table T increases, the efficiency of inserting new keys K, decreases. This is because, as table T gets more and more full, when we attempt to insert a new key K, there is less and less chance that we will accidentally hit an empty location on the first hash, and in the event of a collision, it will take more and more time to enumerate the sequence of table locations in the probe sequence before finding the first empty table location in which to insert the new key, K.

If we search for a key K already known to be in table T, the number of probes required to locate it will be exactly the same as the number of probes required when it was inserted in the first place. This is because the exact same probe sequence is followed both during a successful search and when it was inserted originally. Recall that when we inserted key K originally, we were either lucky and found an empty table location at its hash address $h(K)$ where we inserted it with just one probe, or we used a collision resolution policy by following successive locations in the probe sequence until finding the first empty location in the probe sequence. We then inserted key K at this first empty location. So when we search for K, we again follow the identical probe sequence used when inserting it, and we locate it at the former empty location at the last address visited in the same probe sequence used for inserting it.

Suppose hash table T of size M has exactly N occupied entries, so that its load factor, α, is N/M. Let's now define two quantities, C_N and C_N', where C_N is the average number of probe addresses examined during a successful search, and where C_N' is the average number of probe addresses examined during an unsuccessful search (or, what is identical, during the insertion of a new key, K).

For open addressing with linear probing, we have the two performance formulas:

efficiency of linear probing

$$C_N \approx \frac{1}{2}\left(1 + \frac{1}{1-\alpha}\right) \qquad \text{for successful search}$$

$$C_N' \approx \frac{1}{2}\left(1 + \left(\frac{1}{1-\alpha}\right)^2\right) \qquad \text{for unsuccessful search}$$

(11.7)

These formulas are known to apply when table T is up to 70 percent full (i.e., when the load factor, α, obeys the inequality, $\alpha \leq 0.7$).

For open addressing with *double hashing*, the two corresponding performance formulas are

efficiency of double hashing

$$C_N \approx \frac{1}{\alpha} \ln\left(\frac{1}{1-\alpha}\right) \qquad \text{for successful search}$$

$$C_N' \approx \left(\frac{1}{1-\alpha}\right) \qquad \text{for unsuccessful search}$$

(11.8)

Finally, for collision resolution by *separate chaining* (in which you keep all keys colliding at a given hash location on a linked list starting at that location, as in Fig. 11.11), the two corresponding performance formulas are

efficiency of separate chaining

$$C_N \approx 1 + \frac{1}{2}\alpha \qquad \text{for successful search}$$

$$C_N' \approx \alpha \qquad \text{for unsuccessful search}$$

(11.9)

Derivations for Half of the Performance Formulas**

Although we do not have time or space to derive all of these formulas, it is possible to derive half of them using reasonably short arguments.

For instance, suppose we are performing collision resolution by separate chaining. Let's consider, first, the case of unsuccessful searching. When we hash a key, K, into table T, we find a chain (i.e., a linked list) at location $h(K)$, which contains, let us say, j keys. (Here, it is possible that $j = 0$, if the chain at location $h(K)$ is the empty chain). Under the assumption that the hash function, $h(K)$, is uniform and random, all of the N keys previously stored in table T are distributed uniformly over all of the M table locations, forming M separate chains (some of which are empty, and some of which contain one or more keys). Thus the average chain length equals the number of keys, N, in all of the chains, divided by the total number of chains, which is M— i.e., the average chain length is $\alpha = N/M$. Since on the average, an unsuccessful search must compare the search key K with all of the keys in a chain, the average number of comparisons, C'_N, for unsuccessful searching is just α.

For the case of successful searching, suppose we compare the search key K against keys in a chain with j keys in it. From our analysis of searching in linked lists, we know that the average number of comparisons required to find a key in a linked list with j keys in it is $(j + 1)/2$. But this time, we cannot assert that the average length of such a chain is α. Since the chain we are searching must have at least one key in it, during a successful search, we must have selected a chain already containing the search key K. Consequently, the expected number of keys on the chain containing the search key K must be $1 + (N - 1)/M$, since the remaining $(N - 1)$ keys other than the search key must be distributed uniformly over all M locations in table T. In all cases except those of small hash tables having small load factors, we can approximate $(N - 1)/M$ by $N/M = \alpha$. That is, the exact average chain length, $1 + (N - 1)/M$, in successful searching can be approximated by $1 + \alpha$. Now setting $j = 1 + \alpha$, in the expression $(j + 1)/2$, gives $((1 + \alpha) + 1)/2$ as the approximation for C_N. So, $C_N \approx ((1 + \alpha) + 1)/2 = 1 + \frac{1}{2} \alpha$, which is the formula for successful searching given in Eqs. 11.9 above.

Finally, let's derive the formula for unsuccessful searching in the case of open addressing with double hashing. To analyze double hashing, we make the assumption that probes in the probe sequence are all uniform and random. (It turns out to be incredibly challenging to prove that this assumption is valid, and after a long history of investigation by clever and prominent computer scientists, this fact has only recently been proven for the full range of possible load factors by two of my colleagues in the Irvine Computer Science Department, George Lueker and Mariko Molodowitch.)

Now suppose the load factor of table T is α. If we probe at the first hash address, $h(K)$, and find an empty address, the unsuccessful search terminates immediately. Thus the probability that the search stops after the first probe is $(1 - \alpha)$, since α is the chance that a randomly chosen location is occupied, and $(1 - \alpha)$ is the probability that a randomly chosen location is unoccupied. On the other hand, the chance that an unsuccessful search will terminate after two probes is the product of the chance α

(margin note) deriving the formulas for separate chaining

(margin note) the formula for unsuccessful search with double hashing

that the first location probed will be occupied, times the chance $(1 - \alpha)$ that the second probe will find an empty location. Similarly, the probability that an unsuccessful search will terminate after 3 probes is $\alpha^2(1 - \alpha)$, since the chance is α that each of the first two probes will hit occupied locations and the chance that the third probe will hit an empty location is $(1 - \alpha)$. Continuing in this fashion, the probability that an unsuccessful search will terminate after j probes is $\alpha^{j-1}(1 - \alpha)$. The average number of probes used in an unsuccessful search is obtained by evaluating the formula for the expected value

$$C_N' = \sum_{(1 \leq j < M)} j * \alpha^{j-1}(1 - \alpha).$$

By moving the factor $(1 - \alpha)$ outside the summation, and by multiplying inside and dividing outside by α, we can rewrite the above formula as

$$C_N' = \frac{(1 - \alpha)}{\alpha} \sum_{(1 \leq j < M)} j * \alpha^j.$$

Then, we can apply Eq. A.33, from the "Math Reference" appendix, to evaluate the sum, $\sum_{(1 \leq j < M)} j * \alpha^j$. Equation A.33 is

$$\sum_{1 \leq i \leq n} i d^i = \left(\frac{d}{(d-1)^2} \right) [(nd - n - 1)d^n + 1].$$

Substituting α for d, j for i, and $(M - 1)$ for n, in this formula gives

$$\sum_{1 \leq j < M} j \alpha^j = \left(\frac{\alpha}{(1-\alpha)^2} \right) [((M-1)\alpha - (M-1) - 1)\alpha^{(M-1)} + 1].$$

But whenever we have hash tables of reasonable size M, the quantity $\alpha^{(M-1)}$, will be nearly zero, since raising any number $\alpha < 1$ to a high power results in a quantity very close to zero. For instance, $(0.9)^{100} = 0.000026561$ and $(0.99)^{500} = 0.00657$. Consequently, we can use 1 to approximate

$$[((M-1)\alpha - (M-1) - 1)\alpha^{(M-1)} + 1].$$

This allows us to approximate the sum above by

$$\sum_{1 \leq j < M} j \alpha^j \approx \left(\frac{\alpha}{(1-\alpha)^2} \right).$$

And substituting this last result in

$$C_N' = \frac{(1-\alpha)}{\alpha} \sum_{(1 \le j < M)} j * \alpha^j,$$

yields the result

$$C_N' \approx \frac{(1-\alpha)}{\alpha} \left(\frac{\alpha}{(1-\alpha)^2} \right).$$

After appropriate cancellations, we get the final result

$$C_N' \approx \left(\frac{1}{1-\alpha} \right).$$

The other hashing performance formulas are a bit more challenging to derive. The derivations can be found in several advanced textbooks on algorithms and data structures.

Comparing Theoretical and Empirical Results

It is now of critical importance to build some intuition for what these theoretical results mean, and to compare both theoretical results and actual measurements from experiments for a range of load factors.

Table 11.21 gives the theoretical results for several load factors. Table 11.22 gives some actual measured results for hash tables of size 997. The experimental results in

Load Factors						
	0.10	0.25	0.50	0.75	0.90	0.99
Successful Search						
Separate chaining	1.05	1.12	1.25	1.37	1.45	1.49
Open/linear probing	1.06	1.17	1.50	2.50	5.50	50.5
Open/double hashing	1.05	1.15	1.39	1.85	2.56	4.65
Unsuccessful Search						
Separate chaining	0.10	0.25	0.50	0.75	0.90	0.99
Open/linear probing	1.12	1.39	2.50	8.50	50.5	5000
Open/double hashing	1.11	1.33	2.00	4.00	10.0	100.0

Table 11.21 Theoretical Results for Number of Probes

Load Factors						
	0.10	0.25	0.50	0.75	0.90	0.99
Successful Search						
Separate chaining	1.04	1.12	1.25	1.36	1.44	1.49
Open/linear probing	1.05	1.16	1.46	2.42	4.94	16.4
Open/double hashing	1.05	1.15	1.37	1.85	2.63	4.79
Unsuccessful Search						
Separate chaining	0.10	0.21	0.47	0.80	0.93	0.97
Open/linear probing	1.11	1.37	2.38	8.36	39.1	360.9
Open/double hashing	1.11	1.33	2.00	4.10	10.9	98.5

Table 11.22 Measured Experimental Results for Number of Probes

Table 11.22 come from averaging the number of probes in the two open addressing methods over 50 trials, and the results for chaining come from averaging the number of key comparisons over 3 trials. Comparing the two open addressing methods, note how primary clustering damages the actual measured performance of linear probing as compared to that of double hashing for load factors of 0.75 or greater.

Also observe that the performance of these hashing techniques is not dependent on the total number of keys stored in a hash table. Instead, the performance is dependent on how full the hash table is. For example, if 897 keys are stored in a hash table with 997 locations (so that $\alpha \approx 0.9$), double hashing was measured to take 2.63 probes for an average successful search and 10.9 probes for an average unsuccessful search. But if those same 897 keys are stored in a table roughly twice as big with 1801 hash table locations (so that $\alpha \approx 0.5$), measurements (averaged over 50 trials) show that an average successful search took 1.37 probes, and an average unsuccessful search took 2.01 probes.

11.5 Review Questions

1. Sketch the method by which Program 11.16 inserts a new table entry with key K into a hash table using open addressing with double hashing.
2. What happens when Program 11.17 searches for a key K in a table T, which has no table entry containing key K, using open addressing with linear probing?
3. What is a probe sequence? How do the probe sequences used in linear probing and in double hashing differ?
4. Name some conditions under which it can be guaranteed that the probe sequences used in double hashing will enumerate all of the table locations exactly once without duplications.

5. Which of the following methods theoretically takes the least average number of probes (or key comparisons) to locate a key successfully in a hash table with a load factor of 0.9: (a) separate chaining, (b) open addressing with linear probing, or (c) open addressing with double hashing?

11.5 Exercises

1. If you have access to a computer graphics device such as a plotter or a bit-mapped computer display screen, set up and run some experiments that use Program 11.16 to insert keys into a hash table using open addressing with linear probing and double hashing. Generate experimentally produced diagrams, such as those given in Figs. 11.14 and 11.15 which illustrate primary clustering and its absence when linear probing and double hashing are used.

2. Set up and run experiments that measure the number of probes (or key comparisons) used for open addressing with linear probing and double hashing, and for separate chaining. Do your experimental results confirm or reject the theoretical results given in Table 11.21?

3. (Triangle Number Hashing) Another class of open addressing methods explored in the computer science literature is the class of methods that use what is called *quadratic probing*. One such quadratic probing method is called triangle number hashing. In this method the probe decrements used for collision resolution are chosen to be the sequence of decrements 0, 1, 3, 6, 10, and so on, where the probe decrement 0 is considered to have been used up when the hash address $h(K)$ is first probed. The numbers in this probe decrement sequence are called triangle numbers since they give the number of dots in triangles of the form:

↑ the hollow dot (∘) signifies the empty triangle

Since all keys colliding at a given initial hash location, $h(K)$, trace out the same probe sequence, quadratic hashing methods are said to be affected by *secondary clustering* (even though they are not affected by the primary clustering evident in linear probing).

For hashing methods affected by secondary clustering, the theoretical performance formulas for a hash table with load factor α are

$$C_N \approx 1 - \ln(1-\alpha) - \frac{\alpha}{2} \qquad \text{for successful search}$$

$$C_N' \approx \left(\frac{1}{1-\alpha}\right) - \alpha - \ln(1-\alpha) \qquad \text{for unsuccessful search}$$

Implement the following algorithms for triangle number hashing and measure their performance on tables having a table size that is a power of two (e.g., $M = 2^{10} = 1024$). Show that the probe sequence covers the table. Compare the theoretical and actual measured experimental results. Do they agree reasonably well, averaged over a suitable number of trials? Is quadratic hashing superior in performance to either linear probing or double hashing?

```
/*-----------------------------------------------------------------------------*/

        |       void HashInsert(KeyType K, InfoType I)
        |       {
        |               int          i, j;
        |               KeyType      ProbeKey;
     5  |
        |
        |               /* initializations */
        |                   i = h(K);                                           /* first hash */
        |                   j = 0;                   /* initialize counter for triangle number hashing */
    10  |                   ProbeKey = T[i].Key;
        |
        |               /* find first empty slot */
        |                   while (ProbeKey != EmptyKey) {
        |                       j++;                      /* increment triangle number hashing counter */
    15  |                       i -= j;                            /* compute next probe location */
        |                       if (i < 0) {
        |                           i += M;                                /* wrap around if needed */
        |                       }
        |                       ProbeKey = T[i].Key;
    20  |                   }
        |
        |               /* insert new key K and info I into table T */
        |                   T[i].Key = K;
        |                   T[i].Info = I;
        |       }

/*-----------------------------------------------------------------------------*/


/*-----------------------------------------------------------------------------*/

        |       int HashSearch(KeyType K)
        |       {
        |
        |               int          i, j;
     5  |               KeyType      ProbeKey;
        |
        |
        |
        |               /* initializations */
    10  |                   i = h(K);                                           /* first hash */
        |                   j = 0;                   /* initialize counter for triangle number hashing */
        |                   ProbeKey = T[i].Key;
        |
```

```
      |        /* find either an entry with key, K, or the first empty entry */
15    |            while ( (K != ProbeKey) && (ProbeKey != EmptyKey) ) {
      |                j++;                /* increment triangle number hashing counter */
      |                i -= j;                  /* decrement probe location by the amount j */
      |                if (i < 0) i += M;                      /* wrap around if needed */
      |                ProbeKey = T[i].Key
20    |            }
      |
      |        /* return the position of key K in table T, or return −1 if K not in T */
      |            if (ProbeKey == EmptyKey) {
      |                return −1;                /* return −1 to signify K was not found */
25    |            } else {
      |                return i;                /* return location, i, of key K in table T */
      |            }
      |
      |        }
      |
/*-------------------------------------------------------------------------------*/
```

≡ 11.6 Choosing a Hash Function

Learning Objectives

1. To learn how an ideal hash function is supposed to perform.
2. To learn about the division method for choosing a hash function and about how to avoid pitfalls in its design.
3. To learn about other methods for designing a good hash function.

ideal hash functions are uniform and random

In order for the hashing methods analyzed in the preceding sections to work well, the hash function $h(K)$, which maps keys K into hash table locations, must be chosen properly. Ideally, $h(K)$ will map keys uniformly and randomly onto the entire range of hash table locations with each location being equally likely to be the target of $h(K)$ for a randomly chosen key, K. A poorly chosen hash function might map keys nonuniformly into table locations, or might map contiguous clusters of keys into clusters of hash table locations.

As an example of a pitfall in the design of hash functions, suppose we are using the method of open addressing with double hashing, and suppose we select a table size that is a power of two, such as $M = 2^8 = 256$. We decide to define our hash function by the equation, $h(K) = K$ % 256, where the keys K are variables up to three characters long in a particular assembly language using 8-bit ASCII characters. Thus, we can represent each key K, by a 24-bit integer that is divided into three equal 8-bit sections, each representing a single ASCII character.

The trouble with this policy is that it has the effect of selecting the low-order character of the three-character key, K, as the value of $h(K)$. (This is because the three-character key, $C_3C_2C_1$, when considered as a 24-bit integer, has the numerical value, $C_3*256^2 + C_2*256^1 + C_1*256^0$, and when this is reduced % 256, it has the value C_1.)

Now consider what happens when we hash the six keys, X1, X2, X3, and Y1, Y2, Y3, using $h(K)$. Since only the last character is selected by $h(K)$, we have

$$h(X1) = h(Y1) = \text{'1'}$$
$$h(X2) = h(Y2) = \text{'2'}$$
$$h(X3) = h(Y3) = \text{'3'}$$

(In fact, the integer values of the ASCII codes for '1', '2', and '3' will be the actual values of the table locations selected by $h(K)$. These values are 50, 51, and 52 respectively.) Consequently, the six original keys will be mapped into a common cluster of three contiguous table addresses. Moreover, contiguous runs of keys in the key space will map into contiguous runs of table locations, so it could be said that $h(K)$ preserves clusters, which is poor. A well-designed $h(K)$ will *spread* clusters of keys instead of preserving them or clustering them even more tightly.

The Division Method

One method for choosing a hash function $h(K)$ that can be made to work well for double hashing applications is to choose a prime number as the table size M, and, interpreting the keys, K, as integers, to divide K by M getting a quotient Q and a remainder R. The remainder R is used as the value of $h(K)$, and the quotient Q can be used as the value of the probe decrement for double hashing (except that if Q = 0, then 1 must be used instead, since all probe decrements must be nonzero). In symbols, we take

double hashing by the
division method

$$h(K) = K \% M, \quad \text{and}$$
$$p(K) = \max(1, K / M).$$

(11.10)

In practice, it is useful to reduce $p(K)$ to a number in the range 1:M − 1, by replacing $p(K) > M$ with $\max(1, p(K) \% M)$, if necessary.

However, there are some precautions we need to take in choosing the prime number, M, to use in conjunction with the division method. In particular, if r is the radix of the character set for the keys, K, and k and a are small integers, then we should not choose a prime of the form $M = r^k \pm a$.

For example, suppose we again consider three character keys, $C_3C_2C_1$, in 8-bit ASCII, where the radix of the character set is again, $r = 256$. Suppose we then choose a table size M = 65537, which is known to be a number called a Fermat prime, with the value $2^{16} + 1$. If we then compute $h(C_3C_2C_1)$, we get the result

$$h(C_3C_2C_1) = (C_2C_1 - C_3)_{256}.$$

Thus, as a base-256 number, the value of $h(C_3C_2C_1)$ is simply a difference of products of the characters. Generally, if M is of the form, $r^k \pm a$, the value of $h(K)$ will tend to be simple sums and differences of products of the characters C_i. Such a hash function will not spread clusters of keys, nor will it map keys uniformly and randomly onto the space of hash table locations.

Other Hash Function Methods

Three other methods of choosing a hash function are: *folding*, *middle-squaring*, and *truncation*.

In *folding*, the key is divided into sections, and the sections are added together. For example, if we had 9-digit keys, such as the key K = 013402122, we could divide K into three sections: 013, 402, and 122, and we could add them together getting 537 for the value of $h(K)$. (We could also use multiplication, subtraction, and addition in some fashion to combine the sections into the final value.)

In *middle-squaring*, if we again had the 9-digit key, K = 013402122, we could take the middle digits, 402, and square them, getting $h(K)$ = 402^2 = 161604. If 161604 exceeded the table size, M, we could choose, say, the middle four digits of the result, getting $h(K)$ = 6160.

In *truncation*, we simply delete part of the key and use the remaining digits (or bits or characters). For example, if K = 013402122, we could ignore all but the last three digits, getting $h(K)$ = 122. While truncation takes hardly any time to compute, it tends not to spread the keys randomly and uniformly into the space of hash table locations. For this reason, it is often used in conjunction with the other methods mentioned above, but it is seldom used alone.

11.6 Review Questions

1. When can we say that a hash function $h(K)$ performs well, and when can we say that it performs poorly?
2. What is the division method of hashing in reference to open addressing with collision resolution by double hashing? What does the term "double hashing" refer to?
3. Give an example of a pitfall when choosing a hash function.

11.6 Exercises

1. Mr. Alf Witt decides to use $h(K)$ = (K % M) for his hash function. He selects M = 4096 as a table size, and uses keys that are 24-bit integers representing three character keys in an assembly language that represents characters in 8-bit ASCII. Did Witt choose a good hash function?
2. (Multiplicative Hash Functions) Suppose we choose a hash table size M = 2^n, which is a power of two (such as M = 2^{12} = 4096). Suppose we are using keys, K, which are 16-bit C integers in the range 0:32767. Let w = 32768, let θ = 0.6125423371, and choose an integer A such that $\theta \approx A/w$. Now compute $h(K)$ by taking the leftmost n bits of (($A*K$) % w). Run an experiment to show how $h(K)$ maps the keys K = 1, 2, 3, 4, etc. into a table, T, whose size M is a power of 2 (such as M = 2^{12}). Does $h(K)$ disperse the keys reasonably uniformly and randomly? In this exercise, $h(K)$ is called a multiplicative hashing function.
3. (Perfect Hash Functions) A *perfect hash function* is one that maps a finite set of n distinct keys onto a finite hash table of size M = n, such that $h(K)$ is a 1–1, onto

function. Can you find a perfect hash function for the set of 32 C reserved words: {auto, break, case, char, const, continue, default, do, double, else, enum, extern, float, for, goto, if, int, long, register, return, short, signed, sizeof, static, struct, switch, typedef, union, unsigned, void, volatile, while}?

▤ **11.7** Comparison of Searching Methods Using the Table ADT

Learning Objectives

1. To compare the performance of three actual data representations that can be used to represent Table ADTs.
2. To understand which of these three representations performs the best.

recalling the features of the Table ADT

Consider the Table ADT introduced earlier in Section 11.2. Recall that an abstract table, T, was defined to be a collection of pairs of the form (K,I), where K was an identifying key, and I was some information associated with key K, such that no two distinct pairs in the collection had identical keys, and such that seven operations were defined to *initialize* T, to determine if T were *full*, to *enumerate* the entries in T, and to *insert*, *delete*, *retrieve*, and *update* table entries.

It is clear that we can choose a variety of different underlying data representations for the Table ADT. Figure 11.23 presents three interesting possible representations to compare. Let's analyze the relative efficiencies of these three representations. Suppose there are n table entries in table T.

using sorted arrays of structs

Consider first representation 1—using a *sorted array* of table-entry structs. We can search for a struct containing a given key, K, in time $O(\log n)$, using binary search. We can enumerate the entries of T in time $O(n)$, since they are already in the proper order for enumeration (i.e., the ascending order of their keys, K). Inserting and deleting entries can be done in time $O(n)$, since, on the average, we need to move half of the table entries when we insert or delete a new entry. Retrieving and updating take the same time as searching, $O(\log n)$.

using AVL trees

Now consider representation 2—using *AVL trees* of table-entry structs. We can search for a struct containing a given key, K, in time $O(\log n)$, using AVL tree search. We can enumerate the entries of T in time $O(n)$ by using an InOrder traversal of the nodes of the AVL tree. Inserting and deleting nodes in AVL trees can be done in time $O(\log n)$, and retrieving and updating take the same time as searching, $O(\log n)$.

using hash tables

Finally, consider representation 3—using *hash tables*. In a hash table, we can search for a struct containing a given key, K, in time $O(1)$. It may seem strange to characterize hash table search as occurring in time $O(1)$, so consider why we might make this claim. Suppose we agree to use a hash table that is never more than half-

1. Representing T by an *array of structs* sorted in increasing order of their keys, K.
2. Representing T by a *hash table*.
3. Representing T by an *AVL-tree* organized using keys, K, from the table entries.

Figure 11.23 Three Table ADT Representations

full. (If the table ever gets more than half-full, we can expand the table by choosing a new table twice as big, and by rehashing the entries of the original table so they reside in the new, larger table.) In summary, suppose we are guaranteed that the load factor of our table obeys the constraint, $\alpha \leq 0.50$. Suppose, also, that we elect to use double hashing as our hashing method (similar arguments can be made for the other hashing methods).

Then, from Tables 11.21 and 11.22, or, equally, from Eqs. 11.8, we know that the average number of key comparisons used in a successful search will be at most 1.39 and that the average number of key comparisons used in an unsuccessful search will be at most 2.00, regardless of the size, n, of the table. Consequently, the number of comparisons is independent of the table size and independent of the number of keys stored in the table. As long as we agree to use hash tables that are no more than half full, the average number of key comparisons is bounded above by 2. Speaking more generally, if we agree to obey some predetermined limit on the percentage of the hash table that contains occupied table entries, we can be guaranteed that the average number of comparisons will not exceed some given, fixed, predetermined constant number. So, being a constant independent of both the table size and the number of keys, hash table search is O(1).

To enumerate the entries of a hash table, T, we must first sort the entries into ascending order of their keys. This requires time $O(n \log n)$, if we use a suitably efficient comparison-based sorting technique. Hence, the table enumeration operation is $O(n \log n)$. Because insertion of a new table entry in a hash table takes the same number of key comparisons as unsuccessful search, insertion takes time O(1). Finally, retrieving and updating in a hash table take the same time as searching, O(1).

Deletion in some hash table representations is easy, but in the open addressing methods, deletion poses troublesome problems. For instance, if we are using the chaining method, deletion of a table entry containing a given key requires only that we delete a node from a linked list, which is straightforward. However, if we try physically to delete a particular table entry, E, from a hash table using open addressing, leaving a table entry with an empty key in place of E, we destroy the validity of the searching operations for subsequent keys. The reason is that search always terminates when it finds an empty table entry in the probe sequence being examined. If we artificially introduce an empty entry, it could interrupt the original probe sequence starting at the initial hash address, $h(K)$, and ending at the location where another key K is to be found.

deletion can be troublesome

Consequently, in open addressing techniques, when we need to delete a given table entry, what is normally done is to mark the entry as deleted with a special bit, while leaving it physically present in the table. The searching algorithms then probe past entries marked as deleted, treating them as if they had not been deleted. But the insertion algorithms can insert new entries in place of any entry that is marked as deleted. In short, insertion algorithms treat deleted entries as if they were empty entries, and search algorithms treat deleted entries as if they were nonempty entries. Unfortunately, under this policy, a hash table can fill up and can become clogged with entries marked as deleted. If this happens, it is possible to rehash the table entries so that only the ones not marked as deleted are retained, and actually to delete the ones marked as deleted. In any event, the time required to delete a table entry

Operations ⇒ Representations ⇓	Initialize	Determine if full	Search Retrieve Update	Insert	Delete	Enumerate
Sorted array of structs	$O(n)$	$O(1)$	$O(\log n)$	$O(n)$	$O(n)$	$O(n)$
AVL tree of structs	$O(1)$	$O(1)$	$O(\log n)$	$O(\log n)$	$O(\log n)$	$O(n)$
Hash table	$O(n)$	$O(1)$	$O(1)$	$O(1)$	$O(1)$	$O(n \log n)$

Table 11.24 Comparative Performance of Table ADT Representations

with a given search key, K, is still $O(1)$, no matter which of the hash table methods we are using.

We now put these results together into Table 11.24 so we can make some comparisons. Some observers express the opinion that such comparisons lead them often to recommend AVL trees as a good representation, since the operation times for AVL trees are uniformly not the worst in any column of the table.

Other observers sometimes express the opinion that which representation best suits a given application depends on the frequency of the different operations to be performed. For instance, suppose we have both an AVL tree and a double-hashing table, each containing $2^{12} = 4096$ structs. Suppose the load factor of the hash table is $\alpha = 1/2$, because we are using a hash table with 8192 table entries.

Then an average successful search takes 1.39 key comparisons in the hash table, but takes 25.5 key comparisons in the AVL tree (using the formula, $2 \lg n + 1.5$). If searches are much more frequent than, say, deletions or enumerations, the hash table representation offers an enormous efficiency advantage.

11.7 Review Questions

1. Name three possible data representations for a Table ADT.
2. Sketch how the Table ADT operations would be implemented in the case of a hash table representation.

11.7 Exercises

1. Under what circumstances will a hash table representation of a Table ADT be superior?
2. Under what circumstances will an AVL tree representation of a Table ADT be superior?
3. (Interpolation Search) This exercise asks you to do a mini research project on a new kind of searching called *interpolation search*. Suppose you are given a Table ADT representation using an array of M table entry structs sorted in ascending order of their keys. Interpolation searching is a search technique that finds a table

entry containing the search key K in time O(log log M). Roughly speaking it works by predicting where to locate a key K in table T by predicting where to look for K in its current search interval using a calculated *interpolation point*. By analogy with telephone-book searching, suppose you are looking for the name "Adams." You might start searching for this name right near the beginning of the phone book. But if you were searching for "Williams," you would look near the end, and for "Miller" near the middle. In general, if the search key K is a name that is, say, X percent of the way through the alphabet in alphabetical order, you would start searching for K at a point X percent through the phone book. Interpolation searching works similar to binary searching in selecting a sequence of increasingly smaller search intervals in which to search for a key, K. But it computes the endpoints of those search intervals using interpolated estimates, instead of using the half-way division points that binary searching uses. Given this hint, can you implement your own version of interpolation searching? After trying to do it yourself, go search the literature for an explanation of how it works and for the algorithm analysis showing that it runs in time O(log log M). Then compare the theoretical and actual search times of your algorithm with hashing techniques? Which ones perform better on tables of various sizes?

Pitfalls

- *Choosing a poor hash function*

    If you are careless, it is easy to choose a hash function, $h(K)$, that does not work very well. A common mistake is to choose a table size, M, as a power of 2, say 2^n, and to choose $h(K) = K \% M$, which has the effect of truncating the key by selecting its last n bits. Since this is equivalent to the truncation method, it suffers the same disadvantages. A more subtle pitfall is to choose to use the division method with the table size chosen to be a prime number M of the form $r^k \pm a$, where r is the radix of the character set used for forming keys, and where k and a are small integers. In this case, the hash function tends to superimpose sums and differences of products of the characters used in the keys, which is not very effective.

- *Choosing a probe decrement that fails to enumerate all table locations*

    In double hashing, it is easy to make a mistake by choosing a probe decrement function, $p(K)$ that fails to enumerate all table locations. An easy, but frequently made mistake, is to forget that $p(K)$ must always be defined to have a value of 1 or greater. If $p(K)$ is defined to be zero for some key K, then Programs 11.16 and 11.17 will get into endless loops. Another precaution to observe is to ensure that $p(K)$ is relatively prime to the hash table size, M. For example, if M is a prime, then any $p(K) \geq 1$ is suitable. But if M is a power of 2, such as $M = 2^{14}$, then $p(K)$ must be chosen to be an odd integer for double hashing to work properly.

Tips and Techniques

- *Postpone selection of your table data representations*

  A good programming technique is to design your program to use an abstract table and to employ the Table ADT operations in a module interface to be used by the rest of your program. Later, you can chose a good representation for your Table ADT when you develop information about the frequency of operations to be performed on your table, and when you know if any of the operations must be performed efficiently enough to meet real-time or total-processing-time constraints.

  Hash tables are enthusiastically to be recommended if you need to perform numerous table searches with the highest possible efficiency. AVL trees can be recommended if table deletions, insertions, and enumerations must be performed relatively often, and if the efficiency of searching is not at a premium.

- *Always check the performance of your hashing method*

  A careful programmer will always do some experiments and performance measurements to check that an implementation of a particular hashing method is working properly. The use of formatted debugging aids to picture what is going on is strongly encouraged, since any anomalies or misperformances of hashing implementations tend to leap out when presented visually. For example, a poorly designed hash function, which preserves clustering of the keys or which does not cover the table address space evenly will be quickly revealed when visual data on its performance for a set of typical keys is examined. Also, if probe sequences fail to cover all table addresses, visual inspection can frequently reveal the presence of the problem.

References for Further Study

Almost every data structure and algorithms book covers hashing. In this chapter, we have been able to cover only a few of the rudiments of hashing techniques. The reader may wish to pursue additional topics such as multiplicative hashing functions (which was only sketched in Exercise 11.6.2), extendible hashing (which can be used to expand hash tables that are too full for good performance), and ordered hashing (which gives an efficiency improvement for unsuccessful search, by ordering the keys along a probe sequence).

E. Horowitz and S. Sahni, *Fundamentals of Data Structures in Pascal*, Computer Science Press, New York, (1990).

recent developments

Covers some of the more recent developments in hashing discovered during the last decade.

Donald E. Knuth, *The Art of Computer Programming*, vol. 3: *Searching and Sorting*, Addison-Wesley, Reading, Mass., (1973), pp. 506–49.

more on hashing

A classical reference which covers multiplicative hashing and ordered hashing.

Chapter Summary

the basic idea of hashing

Hashing is a method for storing and retrieving information in tables. Individual items of information, I, are stored in table entries of the form (K, I), identified by unique keys, K. Given a key, K, to find the table entry, (K, I), containing K, a hash function, $h(K)$, is computed. The value of $h(K)$ is a table location where we can start searching for the table entry (K, I). If we do not find the table entry (K, I) immediately at the location given by $h(K)$, we invoke a collision resolution policy that enables us to search systematically through the remaining locations in the table in order to find (K, I), if it exists, or to conclude that there is no table entry having the key K.

the Table ADT

A *Table ADT* is an abstract storage device that models the storage and retrieval properties of tables. We can think of a Table ADT, T, as a collection of table entries, (K,I), where K is a key, and I is some information associated with K, such that no two distinct table entries have the same key. The operations we can perform on table T include initializing T to be the empty table, determining whether or not T is full, enumerating the table entries in T in increasing order of their keys, and retrieving, updating, inserting, and deleting table entries in T. Table ADTs can be represented by hash tables, AVL trees, and sorted arrays of structs.

collisions and collision resolution policies

When we attempt to store two distinct keys, $K_1 \neq K_2$, with the same hash address, $h(K_1) = h(K_2)$, in a given hash table, T, a *collision* is said to occur. When this happens, a *collision resolution policy* is needed to resolve the collision. Three different collision resolution methods are (a) the separate chaining method, (b) hash bucket methods, and (c) open addressing methods. Even though, at first, you might think that collisions would be relatively rare, in fact, collisions are relatively frequent, even in sparsely occupied tables. For example, in a table of 365 locations, the chance of having a collision is greater than fifty-fifty as soon as the table is more than 6.3 percent full (i.e., as soon as there are 23 or more table entries). So it is important to have effective methods for resolving collisions.

separate chaining

In the method of *separate chaining*, when keys collide at a given hash address, the table entries containing them are placed on a linked list (or chain) starting at the collision address.

hash bucket methods

In *hash bucket* methods, a big hash table is divided into a number of smaller subtables called buckets. The hash function $h(K)$, maps a key K into one of the buckets where it is stored sequentially. Since these bucket methods work comparatively well with large tables stored on external memory devices, we will study them in the next chapter when we examine methods that work well for large collections of data.

open addressing methods

In *open addressing methods*, table entries containing the keys are placed in open (or empty) locations in the hash table. When a collision occurs, a systematic search is conducted among the other table locations to identify another open address (or empty entry) in which to place a new table entry containing the colliding key. Two noteworthy collision resolution policies for use with open addressing methods are (a) *linear probing*, in which you scan sequentially among the hash table locations, starting at the collision location, to find the first available empty entry, and (b) *double hashing*, in which, when a key, K, collides at a given location, you compute a second hash function, $p(K)$, to determine a *probe decrement*.

The probe decrement is used to determine a probe sequence by starting at the collision location and probing for empty entries at intervals equal to the probe decrement in the direction of decreasing table locations. Whenever you fall off the bottom of the table during this process, you "wrap around" and start examining locations starting at the top of the table. In double hashing, different probe decrements, $p(K)$, are computed for different keys, K, so even though two keys collide at the same initial hash location, they tend to trace out *different* probe sequences when searching for the first available empty table location.

clustering

When using open addressing with linear probing, colliding keys tend to occupy contiguous sequential runs of table entries called *clusters*. Linear probing is subject to a phenomenon called *primary clustering* in which, roughly speaking, colliding keys begin to form clusters, which tend to join with other clusters to make even bigger clusters. The bigger the clusters get, the wider they are as targets for collecting collisions by new keys that are being inserted. Thus, the bigger they become, the faster they grow.

By contrast, when using double hashing, primary clusters do not form since colliding keys tend to follow separate probe sequences that bounce around among the table locations when looking for an available empty entry, and which do not cause colliding keys to be inserted in clusters containing the original collision locations.

load factors

The *load factor* of a hash table is the ratio of the occupied table entries to the total number of table entries. The higher the load factor of a hash table, the worse the performance of a hashing method becomes. However, some methods are worse than others at high load factors. For example, when a hash table is three-quarters full, it takes on the average of 8.5 probes to locate an empty table entry in which to insert a new key when *linear probing* is used, but it takes only 4 probes when *double hashing* is used. At higher load factors, the performance advantage of double hashing over linear probing is even more pronounced. Double hashing works better than linear probing at high load factors because double hashing does not produce any primary clustering. At low load factors (for example, when a hash table is at most 25 percent full), linear probing and double hashing perform about the same.

ensuring complete
table search

In the open addressing methods, it is important to ensure that probe sequences used in linear probing and double hashing cover all the possible table locations, so that searches for available empty entries will be complete. This can be guaranteed for double hashing methods if the second hash function, $p(K)$, used to compute the probe decrement, is *relatively prime* to the hash table size.

comparative performance
of hashing methods

Even though clustering inhibits the performance of open addressing hash methods, still, the performance of hashing methods, in general, can be quite superior to competing techniques, such as the use of AVL trees or the use of arrays of table entries sorted in the order of their keys. For example, considering only the operation of *searching* in a table, T, for a table entry (K,I), given a search key, K, suppose table T has 4096 entries. Then searching in an AVL tree representation of table T takes on the average of 25.5 key comparisons; searching in a sorted-array representation of T, using binary search, takes 21 key comparisons; and searching in a hash table that is 50 percent full or less, using either linear probing or double hashing, takes at most 1.5 key comparisons.

It is important to choose hash functions, $h(K)$, carefully so that they map keys, K, uniformly and randomly onto table locations in the hash table. In the division method, a key K is imagined to represent a number, and it is divided by the size, M, of a hash table, T, to produce a quotient, Q, and a remainder, R. The remainder (reduced modulo M to fit in the range of table addresses, 0:M − 1), can be used for the value of the hash function, $h(K)$, and the quotient, Q, can be used to derive the value of the probe decrement, $p(K)$, to be used for double hashing. Other techniques for choosing hash functions are (a) *folding*, in which a key, K, is divided into sections that are added, subtracted, or multiplied together; (b) *middle-squaring*, in which a middle section of K, treated as a number, is squared; and (c) *truncation*, in which all but the low-order portion of key K is deleted.

choosing hash
functions carefully

Suppose T is an abstract Table ADT. Then T could be represented by a variety of data representation techniques, including hashing, AVL trees, and arrays of table entries sorted in ascending order of their keys. Which of these three representations is advantageous to use in a given application depends on the mix of operations being performed on the table T. If search and retrieval are the only operations to be performed and if speed is at a premium, then hash table techniques are the best performers. However, if searches are intermingled with frequent insertions, deletions, and ordered enumerations of the table entries in T, then AVL trees might offer the best overall performance.

finding the best Table ADT
representations

12

External Collections of Data

=12.1 ## 12.1 Introduction and Motivation

familiar algorithms work poorly on large collections of data

When processing large collections of data, we sometimes find that the algorithms that work well for small collections of data residing in primary computer memory do not work at all well for large collections of data residing in secondary memory. For example, if you have a large file of data stored on an external disk, then many of the familiar best algorithms for searching, sorting, retrieval, updating, and insertion of new items, do not work well, and an entirely new set of considerations come into play.

but what does "large" mean?

It becomes problematic, however, to define what we mean by a "large collection of data," because we are shooting at a moving target, so to speak. If we define the adjective *large* solely in terms of physical characteristics, as in the proposed definition, "a *large* collection of data is any file containing a quarter million records or more," we run afoul of the fast pace of progress in the computer hardware field.

About two decades ago, a medium to large mainframe computer might have had a primary memory of perhaps 256K to 512K words, and a file containing 512K records might well have had to reside on an external disk or drum memory. A few decades

497

before that, disk memories were much smaller than they are today, and were much more expensive. For example, CDC's model 3300 disk used to contain 4 megabytes, and IBM's model 3330 disk used to contain a little more than 100 megabytes. Today, however, it is not uncommon to find desktop computers having primary memories of 2, 4, or even 16 megabytes, and hard disks capable of containing 170 to 520 megabytes. So what was called a "large" file in former times is now perhaps not so large any more, and the capacities and speeds of former mainframe computers (which used to fill whole rooms and cost over $3 million) are now exceeded by the capacities and speeds of computers sitting on our desktops.

Consequently, what the word "large" means is not absolute, but, instead, is *relative* to the sizes and capacities of memory devices on typical computers of the times. At the moment, there is no end in sight to the astonishing trend of ever-increasing memory capacities at ever-faster speeds at ever-lower prices. So, to define what we mean by a "large collection of data," we had best use some concept that will withstand the test of time. One sensible way to accomplish this is to define a *large collection of data* as any collection that cannot reside in the fast primary memory of a computer all at once, but must be stored, instead, on relatively slower secondary memory devices. Thus, what is a large collection of data relative to the capacities of one computer may not be a large collection relative to the capacities of some other bigger computer or to many computers of the future.

(The folks who try to define what a *supercomputer* is have the same problem. They end up defining a supercomputer as the most powerful of the current generation of computers. But what is a supercomputer to one generation tends to become a desktop computer to subsequent generations, as progress in the hardware field continues to make giant strides.)

Because of these precautions, the numbers given in this book for "typical" access times and seek times for external disk-type memory should not be taken as definitive for more than a few years beyond the time of publication of this book. However, the general principles developed in this chapter should continue to be valid, as long as memory is divided into two categories: (a) fast, relatively expensive, relatively small, primary memory, directly accessible to the computer's central processor, and (b) slow, relatively inexpensive, relatively large, secondary memory stored on devices external to the primary computer, and which are accessed indirectly via controller hardware separate from the computer's central processor.

In any event, what you will learn in this chapter is that many algorithms (such as binary searching in arrays; AVL tree searching, insertion, and deletion; double hashing using open addressing; and sorting using comparisons and exchanges in primary memory) are all poor algorithms to use to process a large file of data stored on, say, an external disk. Instead, some new and different algorithms that minimize the number of separate external data accesses are needed to attain good performance.

Plan for the Chapter

Section 12.2 discusses the characteristics of external storage devices in order to learn why they are relatively slow in comparison to the speeds of primary memory. Terms such as *latency time*, *transmission time*, and *seek time* are introduced.

Margin notes

rapid progress in processor speeds and rapid declines in hardware costs

the meaning of "large" is relative

supercomputer folks have the same problem

the principles will endure even if the numbers become invalid

external device characteristics

techniques which do not
work well

Section 12.3 examines why the techniques introduced earlier in this book do not work so well when applied to large files of data on external memory devices. We will discover why binary searching in arrays, sorting relying on many pairwise exchanges of items, AVL tree algorithms, and double hashing techniques are all rather poor ideas to use when writing programs for dealing with large external data collections.

techniques which do
work well

Section 12.4 introduces new ideas and techniques that work comparatively well for large data files stored on external devices. Hashing with buckets, the use of B-trees instead of AVL trees, sorting using MergeSort in several phases, and a technique called the indexed sequential access method (ISAM) will be introduced and their performance advantages will be revealed.

information retrieval and
databases

Section 12.5 gives a brief glimpse of information retrieval systems, file queries, and databases. File-inversion techniques and query languages are briefly introduced. A definition and a short example of a database are also given, to serve as a pointer to this much broader subject.

12.2　Characteristics of External Storage Devices

Learning Objectives

1. To learn about the characteristics of external storage devices such as tapes and disks.
2. To learn about seek times, latency times, and transmission times for these devices.

external storage devices

The forms of data organization appropriate to various external storage devices depend on the accessing time, storage, and cost properties of such devices. We first explore the properties of tapes, and, later, the properties of rotating storage devices such as disks.

Tapes

A magnetic tape is a long strip of tough plastic coated with magnetic material capable of being magnetized in small local areas to hold bit encodings. For instance, tapes may be on the order of 800 to 1000 meters in length, and the bit encodings may occur along the tape at densities of from 300 to 700 bits per centimeter. Bit encodings are written across the width of the tape along, say, five to nine parallel tracks. One of the tracks is sometimes reserved for a parity bit. For example, on a 9-track tape, eight of the tracks can be reserved to hold an 8-bit byte and one of the tracks can hold a parity bit. (In turn, the 8-bit byte is sometimes used to encode a 7-bit ASCII character plus a parity bit.) Figure 12.1 illustrates a 9-track tape encoding.

bit encodings on tapes

an example tape

Of course, technology changes rapidly and there is a spectrum of tape characteristics in use at the moment that falls outside the boundaries of the "typical" tapes we are discussing. However, by studying a specific, imaginary, example tape, we can achieve a focus that will help provide insights useful for dealing with other serial storage media of low cost and slow access time. Thus we introduce a specific *example tape*, having the characteristics listed in Table 12.2.

Encoding 111010011

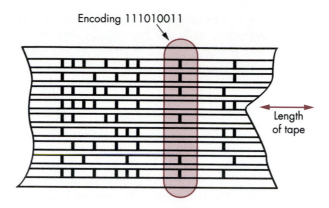

Figure 12.1 Byte Encodings on a 9-Track Tape

Length of tape

Let us compute the storage capacity of a single example tape. The recording density allows us 500 8-bit bytes per centimeter, and there are 1000 meters × 100 centimeters/meter × 500 bytes/centimeter = 50,000,000 bytes, or 400 megabits, on one tape.

Thus it costs only six cents per megabit to store data on a completely dense tape. A 300-page mystery novel requires on the order of four megabits to store so, theoretically, our example tape could store 100 such books at a cost of 24¢ each, if we could take advantage of completely dense encoding. However, because the tape drives must accelerate and decelerate the tape before and after reading and writing, gaps of unwritten tape of length 1 cm may be created. These gaps may occur between adjacent records, or between adjacent blocks of records, depending on the policy used for grouping records on the tape, but the existence of interrecord and interblock gaps reduces the storage utilization factor for the tape to less than the theoretical maximum density of 400 megabits per tape.

cheap mass storage

Let us now compute the data-transfer rate of an active tape. If an active tape moves at 300 cm/sec, and holds 500 bytes/cm, it transfers 150,000 bytes/sec, or about 1 byte every $6^2/_3$ microseconds. To make a complete pass over the tape without stopping takes about $5^1/_2$ minutes.

the tape transfer rate

Equipment manufacturers utilize a variety of policies for writing records on tapes. In one scheme, the tape is initially *calibrated* by writing sequentially ascending *block addresses* on it at regular intervals. It is then possible to search for particular block addresses and to read or write records in the associated block spaces. Such records can be grouped together into files by a combination of sequential and linked grouping. A "directory," consisting of names of files, their starting block

Table 12.2 Example Tape Characteristics

Length	1000 meters
Number of tracks	9 tracks (holding 8 data bits and 1 parity bit)
Density	500 bits per centimeter
Read/write speed	300 centimeters/second
Cost/tape	$24.00

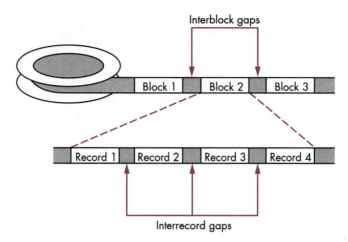

Figure 12.3 Interblock and Interrecord Gaps on a Tape

addresses, and their length in number of records, can be maintained at the beginning of the tape.

variable length blocks Another policy is to write blocks of contiguous records on tape without first assigning an address space to the tape. Such blocks can be of variable length, and they are separated by interblock gaps. Sometimes the records in each block are separated by interrecord gaps. This situation is depicted in Fig. 12.3.

Blocks of records can be read and written from tape into contiguous "buffer" areas in the main memory of a computer. In some policies, the interrecord gap is set long enough to allow the tape unit to start and stop between each record. In other policies, only the interblock gaps are long enough to permit stop and start operations, so a whole block must be read or written as a unit.

Disks

Disks come in several varieties and formats. On personal computers of the current era, users tend to be familiar with floppy disks and Winchester disks (which are often simply called hard disks).

floppy disks A *floppy disk* is constructed from a single, tough, flexible, plastic disk coated with magnetic material. When a floppy disk is inserted in a disk drive, some read/write heads are moved into position close to the upper and lower magnetic surfaces. These read/write heads can be moved in toward the central disk spindle, or out toward the disk's outer rim, stopping at each of a series of numbered positions. When stopped at any numbered position, the read/write heads can either read from or write on one track on the top of the disk and one track on the bottom of the disk. A track is a circular band of bit encodings that is, in turn, divided into *sectors*, which are angular regions of the track. A typical sector on a floppy disk might contain magnetic encodings for 512 bytes.

Winchester disks A *Winchester disk* (or a *hard disk*) is a rotating magnetic storage device constructed from a stack of circular plates coated with magnetic material. On the order of five to ten plates might be involved in a stack. Read/write heads may be placed on each disk surface using a comblike access assembly, which permits them to be moved inward or outward on top of the disk surfaces along a line from the rim toward the center of the stack (thus giving a *movable-head disk*). As with the floppy disk, the surface of each disk is divided into tracks, and sectors, each containing a fixed number of bits. Figure 12.4 shows tracks and sectors on a disk surface and also shows the movable heads of the comblike access assembly of a typical Winchester movable-head disk.

Some larger, commercial varieties of movable-head disks permit the read/write heads to be retracted completely past the outer rim of the disk stack, and the stack of disks to be removed and exchanged. These are called *exchangeable-disk packs* (or sometimes *removable-disk packs*).

removable-disk packs

A set of tracks positioned vertically above one another is called a *cylinder*. To locate a particular sector, we must first select a cylinder c, then a track t within that cylinder, and then a sector s within that track. This leads to a three-component addressing system (c, t, s) for disks. The disk address space can then be thought of as a numbered sequence of cylinders, each of which contains a sequence of tracks, each of which consists of a sequence of sectors.

cylinders

The access time for a record stored on a disk has three components, which are defined as follows:

1. **Seek time:** The time to move the read/write heads to the proper track (or cylinder).
2. **Latency time:** The rotational delay until the proper sector moves beneath the read/write head on the appropriate track.
3. **Transmission time:** The rotational delay while the portion of the track containing the record passes under the read/write head.

the seek time formula

If the cylinders are numbered from 1 to N as the read/write heads move from the outer rim toward the center, the seek time for the heads to move from cylinder i to

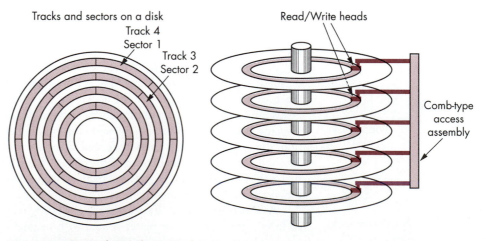

Figure 12.4 Typical Winchester Disk

cylinder j in a movable-head disk can be given by a function such as $f(i, j) = (2.5 + 0.2 \times |i - j|)$ milliseconds. (The formula for $f(i, j)$ expresses the idea that it takes a total of 2.5 ms to accelerate the read/write heads up to full speed and then, later, to slow them down to a stop over the destination track, plus 0.2 ms/track to move the read/write heads across the $|i - j|$ tracks over which they pass when moving from starting track i to destination track j.)

The average seek time, under the assumption that i and j are chosen randomly on a 128-cylinder disk, is given by $f(i, j) = 11.0 = (2.5 + 0.2 \times 42.7)$, since the average value of $|i - j|$ with i and j chosen randomly between 1 and 128, is

$$\frac{2 \times \binom{129}{3}}{128^2} \approx 42.7$$

(cf. Exercise 12.2.2). If the disk rotates at 7200 rpm, each rotation takes 8.33 ms, so the average latency time (which is the time for half a rotation) is 4.2 ms. Thus the *average random-access time*, which is the sum of the average seek and average latency times, is about 15.2 ms (where 15.2 ms = 11.0 ms + 4.2 ms).

For the purpose of further discussion, we will focus on a typical Winchester disk, a movable-head hard disk, having the characteristics listed in Table 12.5. In using disks, it is important to minimize the number of seeks, since the seek times dominate the transaction times for most random accesses.

The characteristics of a typical floppy disk are somewhat different than those of the typical Winchester disk. For example, a typical $5\frac{1}{4}$ inch floppy disk spins at 300 rpm (or 5 revolutions per second), and therefore has an average latency time of a

floppy disk characteristics

tenth of a second (or 100 ms). The average seek time is about 125 ms, so summing the average latency and seek times gives 225 ms for the average random access time. The transmission rate is 23 Kbytes/sec. A floppy might typically contain 160 tracks with 10 sectors per track and 512 bytes per sector (for a total of 819.2 Kbytes per floppy disk).

Table 12.5 Typical Winchester Disk Characteristics

Number of:	
Cylinders	128
Tracks/cylinder	10
Sectors per track	64
Bytes per sector	2048
Average seek time (average of $(2.5 + 0.2\| i - j \|)$ ms)	11.0 ms
Rotations per minute	7200 rpm
Average latency time	4.2 ms
Number of bytes per disk	167,772,160
Transmission rate	15.7 Mbytes/sec

The key thing to remember about disk memory is that the average random-access time to access a given sector is very large in relation to the transmission time per byte and to the access time of a byte in fast, primary random-access memory. For example, taking the characteristics of the typical Winchester disk from Table 12.5, and comparing them to an assumed access time of 1 microsecond (1 μsec) for access to a byte of primary, random-access memory (RAM), we observe the following:

1. It takes 15.2 milliseconds (or ≈ 15,200 μsec) to access a random byte of disk storage (where 15.2 ms = 11.0 ms seek time + 4.2 ms latency time + 0.064 μsec transmission time per byte).
2. Compared to 1 μsec to access a byte of RAM, it is 15,200 times more expensive to access a random byte on disk than to access a random byte of RAM.
3. It takes only 15.3 ms to access and read in an entire 2048 byte sector from disk, compared to 15.2 ms to access and read in one byte (since the time to read a sector is 15.3 ms = 11.0 ms seek time + 4.2 ms latency time + 0.13 ms transmission time per 2048 bytes).

So random accesses to arbitrary bytes on our typical Winchester disk are devastatingly more costly than random accesses to a byte in primary random-access memory (by a factor of 15,200). But, since it costs no more than 1 percent more time to read in an entire randomly accessed 2048 byte sector from disk than it does to read in a single randomly accessed byte, it often makes sense to read in whole sectors of data at a time from disk, and to craft solutions to data-access problems in terms of access to blocks of memory accessed from disk at a single time.

random disk access costs

12.2 Review Questions

1. Define the latency time of a disk memory.
2. Define the seek time of a disk with movable read/write heads.
3. Define the transmission time of a disk memory.

12.2 Exercises

1. If a hard disk rotates at 3600 rpm, what is its average latency time?
2. Prove that the average of $| i - j |$ for i and j chosen randomly from 1:n is

$$\frac{2 \times \binom{n+1}{3}}{n^2}.$$

3. An old adage in data processing shops is that on an average random access on a disk with movable read/write heads, the heads move a distance of *one-third* the number of tracks, n, on the average. Is this adage true (i.e., can you prove that the average of $| i - j |$ for i and j chosen randomly from 1:n is $\approx n/3$)?

≡ **12.3** Techniques That Don't Work Well

Learning Objectives

1. To understand why some techniques for searching and sorting that work well in primary random-access memory, do not work well on slow, rotating external memory.

assume we have an abstract Table ADT

For the purpose of this section, let's assume we have a collection, T, of one million records, representing a Table ADT, as defined in the previous chapter. Each record in T is identified by a unique key, K. The operations we intend to perform on T include *inserting*, *deleting*, and *updating* records, *retrieving* the information in a record associated with a search key K, and occasionally *enumerating* the records in T in increasing order of their keys.

consider AVL tree representations

In Section 11.7, we observed that AVL trees were a good representation for abstract Table ADTs, since many of the critical operations on tables, such as retrieval, updating, insertion, and deletion, could be performed in $O(\log n)$ time, and table enumeration could be performed in time $O(n)$. But is an AVL tree a good representation to use if table T is a big collection of records residing on an external disk memory? Let's reason about this situation.

Given that T contains 10^6 records, suppose we construct one node of an AVL tree for each record in T. In Chapter 9, we determined that the worst case for searching for a key, K, in an AVL tree of n nodes would take no more than 2.88 lg n comparisons (using ≈ 2 comparisons per node). This implies that if all n nodes were stored on external disk memory, no more than 1.44 lg n nodes would be accessed in the worst case. Recall, also, that in the average case, approximately lg n + 1.5 nodes are accessed to search successfully in an AVL tree. Consequently, given $n = 10^6 \approx 2^{20}$ nodes, it takes approximately 21.5 node accesses in the average case, and 29 node accesses in the worst case, to search an AVL tree on external disk.

Using the example disk characteristics from Table 12.5, an average access to an AVL tree node will take approximately 15.2 ms. Thus the time required to search successfully for a node containing a given search key, K, in an AVL tree on a disk (having the characteristics given in Table 12.5) will be 326.8 ms (which is computed by multiplying 21.5 nodes times 15.2 ms/node). So it takes roughly a third of a second, on the average, to access a node in an AVL tree of one million records stored on our example Winchester disk.

an example of poor performance

This is an example of comparatively poor performance. If the same AVL tree had been stored inside fast, random-access primary memory, and cost, say, 50 μsec per node to search, the average search time would have been 1.075 milliseconds instead of 326.8. In other words, searching the AVL tree on external disk takes over 300 times longer than searching one in primary, random-access memory (using these particular examples of performance figures).

how about binary searching?

As a second example of poor performance, let's consider how the procedure for binary searching might work on a disk. Suppose we store a representation of the abstract table T as a sorted file of 10^6 records on a disk, by storing the records in ascending order of their keys in successive sectors of successive tracks of successive cylinders on a typical movable-head disk (where the order of storage on the disk is given in increasing numbers of the respective sectors, tracks, and cylinders). How many disk accesses would it take, on the average, to search successfully for the record in T containing a given search key, K?

Recall from Eq. 6.14 that the average number of comparisons used when binary searching an array of n records was given by $C(n) = 2 \lg(n + 1) - 3 + 2 \lg (n + 1)/n$ (where two comparisons per record were needed). This means that the number of separate records accessed on a disk containing the records of T would be $C(n) \approx \lg(n + 1) - 1.5$. Given $n = 10^6 \approx 2^{20}$ records in the sequentially stored representation of T on disk, it would take $C(n) \approx \lg(2^{20} + 1) - 1.5 \approx 18.5$ disk accesses to locate a record containing a search key, K, using binary searching of records stored sequentially on the disk. Again, this is not a very inviting performance result.

As a third example, suppose we want to use hashing to search for records containing a search key K, and suppose we again have a file containing a million records stored on an external disk. Suppose we decide to use open addressing with double hashing. What happens if we perform a successful average search for a record stored in a region of the disk reserved for hash table records that was, say, 95 percent full? Recall from Eq. 11.8 that the efficiency of an average successful search for double hashing was given by the formula $C_N = (1/\alpha) \times \ln(1/(1 - \alpha))$, where α was the load factor. In this case, since $\alpha = 0.95$, we get $C_N = 3.15$. That is, we would need to perform an average of 3.15 random disk accesses to find a record containing a search key K, using double hashing on a 95 percent full table containing a million records stored on external disk.

As a fourth and final example, suppose we need to enumerate the records in the hash table we just discussed in increasing order of their keys (given that enumeration was one of the abstract Table ADT operations we said we needed to be able to perform occasionally.) We might first have to sort the records in the hash table representation of table T in order to enumerate them. How can we sort a file of a million records stored externally on a disk, given that the primary memory of our computer is too small to hold all million records at once?

In previous chapters, we have seen several sorting techniques, such as selection sorting, that use key comparisons and exchanges of records' positions in an array of records to sort an array of records. In the next chapter, many more techniques will be given that use key comparisons and exchanges to sort an array of records containing keys. If we use key comparisons and exchanges to sort the records on an external disk, we are in danger of paying the price of random disk accesses every time we want to compare-and-exchange a pair of records. Even if we use efficient $O(n \log n)$ sorting techniques, which work well in fast, primary, random-access memory, we will have to wait a long time to sort a million records if we were so foolish as to use an $O(n \log n)$ sorting method that required, say, the exchange of $n \lg n$ pairs of records on disk. For $n = 10^6 \approx 2^{20}$ records, $n \lg n = 2^{20} \times 20 \approx 10 \times 2^{21} \approx 21$ million exchanges. If it takes 60.8 ms to perform a comparison and exchange one pair of records, it would take 1.275 million seconds (or, equivalently, $14^{3}/_{4}$ days) to sort the entire file. Clearly, there has to be a better way.

what about sorting?

So we are driven to inquire whether or not there might be better ways of organizing our searching and sorting activities when performing operations on collections of data stored on external memory devices having relatively slow random-access times.

12.3 Review Questions

1. Name four examples of techniques for searching or sorting that work well in primary, random-access memory but do not work at all well when applied to large collections of records stored on external disk memory.
2. Why are AVL trees not a very good representation to use for searching large collections of records on disks?

12.3 Exercises

1. Estimate how many disk accesses it would take, on the average, to search successfully for a record containing a given key in an AVL tree containing 16.777 million nodes stored on an external disk.
2. Given a hash table stored on disk containing 16.777 million records that was 95 percent full, how many disk accesses, on the average, would it take to locate a record successfully, using double hashing? [*Hint:* Use Eq. 11.8 in Chapter 11.]

≡ 12.4   Techniques That Work Well

Learning Objectives

1. To discover searching and sorting techniques for large collections of records stored on external disks.
2. To learn why multiway trees, such as B-trees, are useful for organizing large external data collections for efficient search.
3. To learn about indexed sequential access methods.
4. To learn about using buckets for hashing.

how can we sort?

At the end of the last section, we saw an example of why sorting would take a long time if we naively applied comparison-and-exchange sorting techniques to a large collection of records stored on an external disk. What can we do to cut down sorting times when large external collections of records are involved?

Sorting Large External Files

One answer is to use a variant of merge sorting. Recall that we investigated merge sorting in Chapter 6, and that we analyzed the running time of **MergeSort** in Eq. 6.8 to be $O(n \log n)$. The predicted and actual measured running times for **MergeSort** were shown to be nearly identical in Table 6.20.

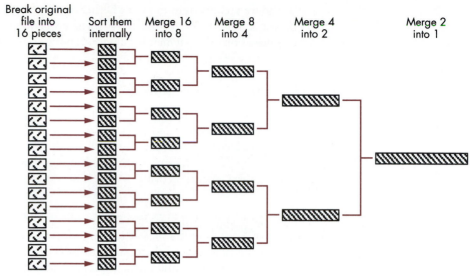

Figure 12.6 Polyphase Merge Sorting

One idea is to take a large external file, containing, say, 1,048,576 records, and to break it into, say, 16 files containing 65,536 records each. Let's say, for the sake of argument, that we can fit a file of 65,536 records in our computer's primary, random-access memory, where we can apply an efficient known sorting method (such as those we will investigate in the next chapter).

Assuming we begin by dividing our original file of a million records into 16 files of 64K records each (where 64K = 2^{16} = 65,536), we could then read in each of the 16 small files, sort them internally in primary memory, and write them back out on disk again.

We would then have 16 sorted files of 64K each. Assuming now that we have a programming language and an operating system that allow us to open two input files for reading simultaneously, and, at the same time, to open an output file for writing, we could merge pairs of sorted input files of n records each to yield new sorted output files of size $2n$ records each. We could use *buffering techniques* to read in blocks of records one at a time from our input files, and to accumulate an entire block of merged sorted records before writing it on the output file. Figure 12.6 illustrates the process, which is called *polyphase merge sorting*.

merging with buffering

If the operating system can support writing the files onto sequentially allocated disk sectors, the transfer of merged files into-and-out-of primary memory from disk can be made even more efficient. (*Note:* Some operating systems interleave the blocks of a sequential file on sectors of a hard disk, as in writing a block of the file every other sector, or every fourth sector, in order to match the disk's data-transfer rate to the operating system's data-transfer rate. The latter may, in some instances, be less than the maximum data-transfer rate of the disk.)

From Fig. 12.6, you can see that, during merge sorting, each data block of the final file gets read and written five times. Using the characteristics of the example

Winchester disk from Table 12.5, if it costs 15.3 ms to read or write a 2048 byte block, each block of the file spends 153 ms getting read and written to and from the disk and primary memory. If, for example, each record of the original file takes 64 bytes, making the original file of 2^{20} = 1,048,576 records occupy 64 Mbytes (or 67,108,864 bytes), or, equivalently, 32,768 disk sectors, then the total time spent transferring 2048 byte sectors to and from disk, during merge sorting, is (153 ms/sector) × (32,768 sectors) = 5014 seconds = 1 hour and 24 minutes. This is the dominant time required for external polyphase merge sorting. (The internal sorting and merging times using fast, primary, random-access memory are substantially smaller—e.g., on the order of 3 seconds to **QuickSort** 16 files of 2^{16} records internally on a 1 MIP[1] computer, and on the order of 2 seconds to merge two files of 2^{16} records into an output file of 2^{17} records, for a total merge cost of $5 \times 16 \times 2$ seconds, or 2 minutes and 40 seconds).

The total time of 1 hour and 24 minutes is substantially better than the $14^3/_4$ days we estimated it would take to sort the same file using naive application of a compare-and-exchange sorting method to individual pairs of records on the external disk file.

The Indexed Sequential Access Method

Let's now focus on applications for which we need to perform all of the Table ADT operations—i.e., for which we need to perform rapid random access, update, insertion, and deletion of records, as well as sequential processing of the records in ascending order of their keys. Let's suppose we are dealing with a large collection of records stored on external rotating disk memory.

In Section 12.3, we discovered that naive application of balanced search tree techniques, such as AVL trees, leads to on the order of 20 or so disk accesses for a file of a million records. If the nodes of such a search tree are placed randomly on the disk, we may incur unacceptable cumulative seek-time penalties.

the ISAM method

A popular method for organizing a file to permit both random access and sequential operations, incurring on the average fewer than four disk accesses per random retrieval, is the *Indexed Sequential Access Method* (ISAM).

The idea behind the ISAM technique is to write records of a file sequentially on portions of each successive cylinder in a disk in order of increasing keys K, and then to prepare a *cylinder surface index*, which may be used to ascertain where the record containing a particular search key K resides. The cylinder surface index has a *top-level index*, which for key K tells on which cylinder the record for K resides. On each cylinder, a *track index* is stored, which in turn indicates on which track the record containing K resides. The track index for each cylinder is stored on the lowest numbered track, say track 0. A few tracks of highest number, say M and M − 1, can be set aside for use as *overflow areas* to handle later insertions that do not fit on a given full track. Then the tracks that are not used either for holding the track index or for holding overflow records, say tracks 1 to M − 2, are called the *primary area* and are used to hold the records initially written in sequential order.

[1] One MIP equals one *million instructions per second*.

This system of indexing is roughly analogous to a card catalog in a library. Each tray of cards in the card catalog is analogous to a cylinder. The tray holds *tab cards* that divide its alphabetically arranged cards at intervals. These tab cards are analogous to the contents of the track index on track 0 of a cylinder (and are contained in the tray, just as the track index is contained in the cylinder). To locate an appropriate tray in which to search, an external tray index for the card catalog is consulted. Usually, the range of alphabetical keys held by a tray is written on the outside of the tray, and the trays are arranged in increasing order of their alphabetical ranges. If such information were placed in an index that mapped the alphabetical ranges contained by trays into tray numbers, such an index would correspond to the cylinder index of an ISAM file.

analogy with a library card catalog

Perhaps such a card catalog tray index would require a booklet of several pages of alphabetical range listings corresponding to the trays. If there were 4096 trays, such a booklet might contain 32 pages, and each page might contain 128 individual tray listings. Then the table of contents for the booklet that tells which page to use to search further for the tray number containing a given listing would be analogous to what is sometimes called a *master index* in some ISAM files. The master index enables us to locate a *cylinder index* containing key K. The cylinder index indicates which cylinder K is located on, and the *track index* on that cylinder indicates on which track the record for K is located. The track must be searched in order to locate the record containing K.

only three disk accesses needed

Thus, in the absence of overflows, an ISAM file with a master index requires at most four disk accesses if all three levels of indexes are stored on disk. In practice, however, the master index (or, more generally, the top-level index) is kept in main memory during file access, so that at most three disk accesses are required if no overflows occur.

an inventory control system example

In order to set a context for the discussion of overflow policies and to get a feeling for the specific details of how a particular instance of an ISAM technique can work, we examine an ISAM scheme for a small movable-head disk. Suppose we are operating an inventory-control system for a parts supply distributor who has 200,000 parts in stock. The inventory-control system permits on-line query, update, insertion, and deletion for operations such as purchase-order handling. Also, sequential processing is involved for reordering, price-list printing, and management reporting. Let us suppose, further, that the records in the system are each 64 characters in length, and that they are ordered on a search key K consisting of a six-digit part number (see Fig. 12.7).

Suppose we are using a disk with 200 cylinders, each of which contains 20 tracks, each track of which contains 64 sectors having 64 bytes per sector. Space on this disk is allocated as follows. Cylinder 000 is reserved for the *cylinder index* and various file maintenance statistics. Cylinders 001 through 184 are designated as *prime cylinders*, and cylinders 185 to 199 are designated as *general overflow cylinders*. On each of the

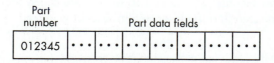

Figure 12.7 Record for a Part in a Parts Inventory System

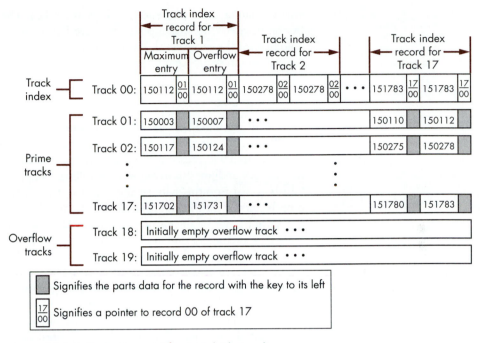

Figure 12.8 Cylinder Format After Initial File Loading

prime cylinders, track 00 is reserved for the *track index*, tracks 01 through 17 are reserved as *prime tracks*, and tracks 18 and 19 are reserved as *overflow tracks*. Each of the prime tracks contains 64 records, stored one record to a sector.

For the initial loading of the file 200,192 parts records are stored in ascending order of their part-number keys on the prime tracks of the prime cylinders in ascending order of cylinders, and of tracks within cylinders. This exactly fills all the prime tracks on the prime cylinders (since $64 \times 17 \times 184 = 200{,}192$), leaving the overflow tracks on each prime cylinder and the general overflow cylinders empty (but poised for action). The track index on track 00 of each prime cylinder is a sequence of *index records* in which there is one index record for each of the 17 prime tracks. Each index record contains two pairs of the form (key, pointer). The first pair is the *maximum track entry*, and consists of the highest-numbered key stored on the track together with a pointer to the first record of the track. The second pair is the *overflow entry* and consists of a part-number key and a pointer to an overflow record. When there are no overflows on a track, the overflow entry is identical to the maximum track entry. Figure 12.8 shows an example of a cylinder surface format after initial loading of the file in sequential order.

If, for instance, it had been determined that the search key $K = 150124$ was located on the cylinder of Fig. 12.8, the track index would be read from track 00 and searched (perhaps by binary search in main memory) for the index record with the smallest key $K' \geq K$. Thus the index record for track 02 would be selected because its associated maximum key entry $K' = 150278$ is the smallest key in the track index greater than or equal to the search key $K = 150124$. The track 02 is associated with K' by the pointer $^{02}/_{00}$ which points to record 00 of track 02. Track 2 is now read and searched for the record with key $K = 150124$. This record is found in the second sector position in sequence on track 2.

Handling Overflows

How shall we handle overflow records when records are inserted randomly? In the specific scheme pictured in Fig. 12.8, all the prime tracks are full, so the next record to be inserted will cause an overflow into the overflow area on tracks 18 and 19. One method of handling this overflow is as follows. Suppose we wish to insert a new record 150277 into the cylinder illustrated in Fig. 12.8. The record 150278 must then be moved off the end of track 02 into overflow track 18, in order to preserve the sequential order of the records on track 02. Now, however, the maximum key on track 02 has changed and must be adjusted in the index record for track 2 in the track index. Also, the overflow entry is changed in the index record for track 2 to hold the *largest* key value of any of the records that have overflowed track 2 while the associated pointer gives the address of the first record in an ordered linked list of overflow records for track 2, this list being ordered in increasing order of the keys of its elements. The last element of such an ordered linked overflow list points back to the beginning of the track whose overflows it stores. Figure 12.9 shows the status of the cylinder of Fig. 12.8 after the insertion of record 150277 , and Fig. 12.10 shows the status after the record 150120 has been inserted into the configuration of Figure 12.9. If the overflows exceed the capacity of overflow tracks 18 and 19, further overflows are placed on the reserved overflow cylinders (185 through 199). These records are linked into linked lists in ascending order on their chains. Thus the general overflow cylinders are treated as an available space list for linked lists.

The cylinder index, stored on cylinder 000, is analogous to the track index for each cylinder. It contains an ordered sequence of index records, one for each of the

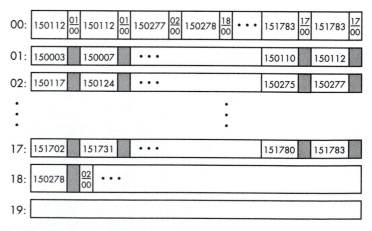

Figure 12.9 Cylinder Format After First Overflow

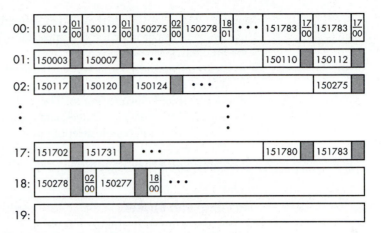

Figure 12.10 Cylinder Format After Second Overflow

prime cylinders in sequence. The highest key value stored on prime cylinder i is stored in the ith record of the cylinder index. Thus to locate the cylinder containing search key K, the cylinder index on cylinder 000 is searched for the lowest key $K' \geq K$, and further search continues on its associated cylinder.

Deletions and File Maintenance

In some ISAM techniques, deletions of records are handled by marking the records as "deleted" but not removing the deleted record physically. As with the deletion problem in open addressing techniques for hashing, this method may lead to eventual clogging of the cylinders with physically present deleted records, and to overflow chains that are long and that perhaps incur extra seek-time penalties.

Periodically, such an ISAM file can be rewritten in order to eliminate the deleted records, to readjust the overflow areas, and to compute a new index. A question arises as to how often we should perform such file reorganizations. There exist methods for choosing an optimum time such that the cost of reorganization and the cost of degraded performance in the absence of reorganization are taken into consideration.

Using B-Trees

The use of B-trees of order m to provide indexes to large external files can work well if we use a large m to ensure substantial multiway branching numbers at the nodes, providing a correspondingly shallow number of levels. B-trees also provide low-cost easy maintenance of B-tree shape under insertions and deletions. In addition, sequential enumeration of records indexed by B-trees is possible using a generalized InOrder tree traversal of the B-tree index.

It can be shown that the worst case number of nodes l we have to search in a B-tree of order m that indexes N keys is constrained by the inequality $l \leq 1 + \log_{\lceil m/2 \rceil}((N + 1)/2)$, so that, for instance, l is at most 3 if N = 1,999,998 and m = 199.

Further, it can be shown that, when splitting nodes during insertion, the average number of splits per insertion is at most $1/(\lceil m/2 \rceil - 1)$, so maintenance costs for insertion are quite low.

B-trees of order m, for $m \approx 200$, are therefore useful for representing a Table ADT of 2 million records or more, while keeping the number of disk accesses needed to access an arbitrary record down to 3 or so. This yields a substantial improvement over the performance of AVL trees or 2–3 trees, and compares favorably with the ISAM technique. Moreover, B-trees can handle deletions more effectively than the ISAM method.

When accessing a B-tree, all the keys in a node are read into primary memory at once, after which they are searched efficiently using binary search.

Hashing with Buckets

Suppose now that we drop the requirement for sequential enumeration of the records in our Table ADT, but retain the requirements for rapid random access for queries, updates, insertions, and deletions. Under these circumstances, certain hashing methods can be of use. (Sometimes, in the literature, these hashing methods are called *scatter storage* methods, when speaking of files.)

An important objective is to devise a hashing method that avoids cascades of disk seeks that might be encountered if we naively apply collision-resolution techniques, such as chaining or open addressing with double hashing, that work so well for tables in primary memory. For instance, if we use chaining, an attempt should be made to keep chains on the same cylinder, if possible.

Average Accesses in an Unsuccessful Search by Separate Chaining (% full = 100α%)							
Bucket size, b	10%	50%	60%	70%	80%	90%	95%
1	1.0048	1.1065	1.1488	1.197	1.249	1.307	1.3
5	1.0000	1.0619	1.1346	1.249	1.410	1.620	1.7
10	1.0000	1.0222	1.0773	1.201	1.426	1.773	2.0
20	1.0000	1.0028	1.0234	1.113	1.367	1.898	2.3
50	1.0000	1.0000	1.0007	1.018	1.182	1.920	2.7
Average Accesses in a Successful Search by Separate Chaining (% full = 100α%)							
Bucket size, b	10%	50%	60%	70%	80%	90%	95%
1	1.0500	1.2500	1.3000	1.350	1.400	1.450	1.5
5	1.0000	1.0358	1.0699	1.119	1.186	1.286	1.3
10	1.0000	1.0070	1.0226	1.056	1.115	1.206	1.3
20	1.0000	1.0005	1.0038	1.018	1.059	1.150	1.2
50	1.0000	1.0000	1.0000	1.001	1.015	1.083	1.2

Table 12.11 Knuth's Theoretical Data

Average Accesses in a Successful Search by Linear Probing (% full = 100α%)							
Bucket size, b	10%	50%	60%	70%	80%	90%	95%
1	1.0556	1.5000	1.7500	2.167	3.000	5.500	10.5
5	1.0000	1.0307	1.0661	1.136	1.289	1.777	2.7
10	1.0000	1.0047	1.0154	1.042	1.110	1.345	1.8
20	1.0000	1.0003	1.0020	1.010	1.036	1.144	1.4
50	1.0000	1.0000	1.0000	1.001	1.005	1.040	1.1

Table 12.12 Knuth's Theoretical Data

In actual practice, the use of buckets containing b or fewer records for each of the M hash addresses that can be computed, and the use of open addressing with linear probing, have been found effective as hashing methods to use with external direct access storage devices.

For example, Table 12.11 presents a sample of the average number of accesses given by Knuth (1973, p. 535), when we use buckets of size b and when we assume that, when a bucket overflows, we plant a link to an overflow area and keep the overflowed records on separate chains (one for each overflowed bucket) in this overflow area. It is advantageous to put the overflow areas on the same cylinder as overflowed buckets, if possible. Here the load factor $\alpha = N/bM$, where N is the number of records.

Sometimes planting links on the end of records is inconvenient when the records are all of identical size. In this case, we might consider using the open address method with linear probing. Here, however, instead of choosing a linear probe increment of one-record size, we might instead choose an increment c that minimizes drum or disk latency delays due to rotation between consecutive addresses probed. Table 12.12 presents a portion of Knuth's data (Knuth, 1973, p. 536) for such an open addressing scheme.

It is rather remarkable that at bucket size $b = 50$ and upward of 80 percent saturation, the open addressing method beats the separate chaining method for successful searches!

Table 12.13 presents a sample of empirical results obtained by Lum, Yuen, and Dodd (1971) for successful searches using the chaining and open addressing methods on actual files. The division method of calculating hash addresses was used for both tables.

In these tables, the average number of accesses for linear probing is the average of $S + 1$, where S is the number of buckets away from the key's home bucket $h(K)$, whereas in separate chaining, each record located in the home bucket $h(K)$ is said to require one access, and the average number of accesses is the average of $T + 1$, where T is the position of K along the overflow chain.

The Lum, Yuen, and Dodd empirical data were calculated for eight different sets of keys used in actual practice. As they point out, a comparison of the empirical and theoretical data in Tables 12.11, 12.12, and 12.13 reveals that the division method of calculating hash addresses works out in practice slightly better than completely ran-

Average Accesses for Successful Search by Separate Chaining (% full = 100α%)						
Bucket size, b	50%	60%	70%	80%	90%	95%
1	1.19	1.25	1.28	1.34	1.38	1.41
5	1.02	1.05	1.09	1.13	1.24	1.25
10	1.00	1.01	1.03	1.08	1.16	1.20
20	1.00	1.01	1.01	1.04	1.09	1.17
50	1.00	1.00	1.00	1.01	1.03	1.08

Average Accesses for Successful Search by Linear Probing (% full = 100α%)						
Bucket size, b	50%	60%	70%	80%	90%	95%
1	4.52	5.04	4.73	10.10	22.42	25.79
5	1.02	1.05	1.10	1.31	1.94	4.47
10	1.00	1.01	1.02	1.08	1.32	2.32
20	1.00	1.00	1.01	1.03	1.08	1.25
50	1.00	1.00	1.00	1.00	1.01	1.03

Table 12.13 Lum, Yuen, and Dodd's Empirical Data (reprinted with permission of the Association for Computing Machinery, copyright © 1971 ACM. See reference on p. 522.)

dom hash functions for the larger bucket sizes when open addressing is used, and for almost all bucket sizes when chaining is used.

12.4 Review Questions

1. Given a large file, F, on an external disk, which of the following two methods works well and which works poorly: 2–3 tree organization of the records in F or organization of the records in F using a B-tree of order $m \approx 200$? Why?
2. Given the file F in the preceding question, which of the following works well and which works poorly: sorting F using **MergeSort** or sorting F using **SelectionSort**? Why?
3. Given the file F in Question 1, which of the following works well and which works poorly: hashing F using open addressing with double hashing or hashing F using buckets of size ≈ 50? Why?

12.4 Exercises

1. Given a file, F, of 4 million records of 16 bytes each stored on a disk having the characteristics given in Table 12.5, how many disk accesses will be required to access an average random record of F if the records are organized as an AVL tree?
2. Given the file F in Exercise 1, how many disk accesses will be required on the average if F is stored as an ISAM file on the disk?

≡ **12.5** Information Retrieval and Databases

Learning Objectives

1. To learn about new forms of file organization, such as file inversion, which assist in answering queries.
2. To learn about various kinds of queries.
3. To learn what a database is.

The file organizations mentioned so far in this chapter have been those that represent the abstract Table ADT—namely, collections of records each of which is identified by a unique key. Clearly there are other possibilities for how to organize a file of information to serve other purposes than those of supporting the Table ADT operations. The purpose of this section is to sketch, very briefly, some of these other possibilities.

File Inversion Techniques

Suppose we have a file, F, consisting of a collection of records, each identified by a unique key. Suppose further that each record contains other data fields beside the key. For example, consider a file of employee records for a firm, where each employee record is identified by the employee's unique employee number, and that contains the employee's department code, age, and salary. Suppose, further, that file F is stored on an external disk.

A *table of contents* for file F might be a list of pairs of the form (n,a), giving, for each employee number n, the sector address, a, on the disk for the location of the employee record for employee n inside file F.

We could also prepare some additional information, similar to the index of a book, which could assist us in retrieving records from file F in order to make certain kinds of information retrieval efficient. For example, we could prepare several lists of the form D:$(a_1, a_2, \dots , a_k)$, giving for each department code, D, a list of the addresses, a_i, of the employee records for employees in department, D. This would make it easy and efficient to print an answer to the query, "Who are the employees in department D?" Had we not prepared the department lists in advance, then, in order to answer the query about who is in department D, we would have had to enumerate all the records in file F to identify employee records having the code D in their department code fields. If F were a big file of employees (say, too big to fit in the primary memory of the computer at hand), it might take many disk accesses and considerable time to enumerate the entire file.

We could also prepare additional lists, say, of the form, A:$(a_1, a_2, \dots , a_k)$, giving each of the employees having age, A, and of the form S:$(a_1, a_2, \dots , a_k)$, giving each of the employees having the salary, S. Such lists would enable us efficiently to answer queries about employees' ages and salaries, such as, "How many employees over age 45 have salaries above \$50,000?"

A file, F, is said to be *inverted* with respect to a field f of its records, R, if a collec-
inverted files tion of lists, L(A_1), L(A_2), $\dots$, L(A_m), is prepared, giving for each possible value, A_j,

of field f, the list, $L(A_j)$, of addresses of records whose f-field has the value A_j. (Sometimes, instead of giving addresses of records, we give the unique identifying keys of the records, instead. This way, if the records in the file are moved around during file reorganization operations, the addresses of records in the inversion lists do not have to be updated to point to the records' new locations).

For example, if we had prepared the lists of addresses of all records in each department D of the employee file F, we would say that file F was *inverted* with respect to its department code field.

A *fully inverted file* is one which is inverted with respect to every possible value in every field of its records. Had we prepared all the lists for the departments, ages, and salaries of all employee records in file F, we would say that F was a fully inverted file.

full inversion

As an application of these ideas, let's imagine that a book is an example of a file. We could view a book as a big text file that is divided into individual pages, each page of which is viewed as a text record identified by a unique key called its page number. If we wanted to prepare a really thorough index at the back of the book, we might take each word on each page and put it in the index. The index would then give an alphabetical listing of every word in the book, with each word followed by a list of the page numbers on which it was used. A book with such an index would be a fully inverted text file.

As an example of the use of this concept, the Grolier Encyclopedia has been put on a compact disk read-only memory (or CD ROM). A small CD ROM, the size of an ordinary audio compact disk, has three miles of track on it, and can contain up to 650 megabytes of information. The entire contents of the Grolier Encyclopedia, represented as a text file, occupies the first third of the CD ROM. A complete inverted index for the contents of the encyclopedia occupies the next third of the CD ROM. The final third of the CD ROM is empty. Using the inverted index on the CD ROM, a user can pose a query, such as, "What are all the occurrences of the word 'Edison' in the Grolier Encyclopedia?" If there are five occurrences of the word "Edison" in the encyclopedia, the inverted index on the CD ROM will list the page numbers of all five occurrences. This makes it easy to browse the encyclopedia looking for specific words, and it makes it vastly less costly to answer various queries.

a tradeoff law for information retrieval systems

In information retrieval systems there is always a rough law of tradeoffs that goes something like this: "The more effort you put into indexing the information in an information retrieval system, the greater the cost of storage within the system and the less the cost of processing future information retrieval requests. Conversely, the less effort you put into indexing the information in an information retrieval system, the less will be the cost of storage within the system, but the greater will be the cost of processing future information retrieval requests." This leads to a discussion of the topics in the next subsection.

Queries and Information Retrieval

queries in information retrieval systems

A difficult and challenging area of exploration is that of *information retrieval*. Oftentimes, we ask difficult and complex questions when retrieving information from large files, such as "How many married taxpayers who filed joint returns for the last three years had adjusted gross incomes between $75,000 and $100,000 in the last of these three years and, in the last of these three years, paid taxes that were less than 20 percent of their adjusted gross incomes?" and "What percentage were these of all taxpayers in the $75,000-to-$100,000 income bracket?" Sometimes queries such as these are called *multiattribute retrievals* because they involve testing several of the *attributes* (i.e., values of record fields) stored in a record for certain properties, as opposed to a simpler query such as the ones considered earlier that involved finding a unique record containing a given unique search key K.

Generally, the queries in information retrieval are formulated in a *query language*, which may possess some subset of the following capabilities:

1. *Simple random access:* Find the record containing key K.
2. *Simple value queries:* Find all records R whose A-attribute has the value V.
3. *Range queries:* Find all records R whose A-attribute has a value V such that (a) $V < k$, (b) $V > k$, or (c) $k_1 \leq V \leq k_2$.
4. *Function queries:* Find f of the values of attribute A over all records in the file, where f is a function such as the *average, minimum, maximum, sum*, etc.
5. *Boolean queries:* Using the operators *and, or,* and *not,* find some Boolean combination of answers to queries 1 through 4. For example, find all records R such that (age(R) $\leq$ 18) *and* (sex(R) = male) *or* (*not*(45 $\leq$ age(R) $\leq$ 65) *and* (occupation (R) = bricklayer)).
6. *Quantified queries:* Answer a question such as "Is it true of the airline schedule file that all flights that leave for Denver after 2 P.M. on Friday or Saturday from Boston stop in Chicago, St. Louis, or Dallas?"
7. *Covering retrievals:* Find all records having at least some subset of attribute values; for example, find all documents with keywords "hashing," "scatter storage," and "file."
8. *Similarity retrievals:* For example, find all passengers in the airline reservation file with last names similar to "Schumacher" or "Shumaker."

Various indexing and organization techniques can be used to facilitate the processing of queries composed in query languages incorporating subsets of features drawn from the above list. These techniques include methods such as file inversion, multiple indexing, multilinking, and hybrids of the simpler organization techniques involving hashing, tree-indexing, and the like.

While the brief discussion in the previous subsection gives a hint of how file inversion can make the answering of some kinds of queries more efficient, a broader discussion of other techniques is beyond the scope of this book. Our purpose here is to provide only a brief glimpse of this topic.

Databases

An even more advanced topic is that of *database systems*. A *database* is a collection of files concerned with a particular organization or enterprise. A database system consists of the database itself, together with the set of machines, people, policies, and procedures that govern its use in the context of the enterprise. For instance, one major airline has a database system that handles the following tasks:

1. Maintenance of an on-line flight reservation system for passengers on flights in its schedule and those connecting to other airlines, accessible from 4000 on-line terminals distributed across North America.
2. Crew scheduling, including resolution of bids for route assignments by pilots and flight attendants.
3. Delivery of up-to-date weather information including terminal, area, and winds-aloft data to pilots for preflight and enroute navigation planning.
4. An aircraft-maintenance scheduling service that keeps track of the time in service of every part of every aircraft, together with its complete maintenance history, and which notifies the proper service personnel whenever an aircraft or one of its subsystems requires scheduled maintenance.
5. Extensive management reporting capabilities on all phases of its operations.
6. An on-line system for assigning passenger seating at airport gates and for printing boarding passes at over a hundred airports.

In a system such as this, issues of reliability and security are important. The system operates 24 hours a day, and each fifteen minutes it is out of service imposes a loss of $3 million on the airline. For example, to guard against failure of its external commercial power source, it is equipped with an "uninterruptible power source" consisting of batteries and generators. When the commercial line voltage fails, the batteries come on line to supply continuous power until the generators can be started up. Needless to say, the data structuring and file maintenance capabilities in a system such as this must be designed to function reliably and efficiently over many years of continuous usage.

Unfortunately, the investigation of database systems is also beyond the scope of this book. However, some of the file-organization techniques we have covered in this chapter are relevant to the implementation of database systems.

12.5 Review Questions

1. What is a fully inverted file?
2. What is a query language?
3. What is a database system?

12.5 Exercises

1. Describe the kinds of data kept in the student records in a database maintained by the registrar and the admissions office in your college.
2. What kinds of database operations are performed on the database you described in Exercise 1?

Pitfalls

- *Using the wrong technique when dealing with a large file*

    If you are a bit rushed, it is natural to try to use one of the techniques for sorting or searching that work well for small files or small tables in primary memory, assuming that they will "scale-up" and work well for large files stored on slow rotating external memory. But such is often not the case because the random-access times for data on an external rotating memory can be tens of thousands of times greater than the access times for data in fast, primary random-access memory. This access-time difference can make a method that is blazing-fast when solving a small problem in primary memory turn into a method that is "slow as molasses in Antarctica."

Tips and Techniques

- *Use appropriate techniques when dealing with large data collections*

    When dealing with large files of data on external memory devices, such as disks, be sure to use techniques that are known to stand a chance of working within acceptable resource limits. For example, consider using polyphase MergeSorting, ISAM file organizations, B-trees, or hashing with buckets.

- *Don't overlook the opportunity to use simple techniques in special cases*

    Sometimes a simple, direct solution is available that is not an instance of one of the general techniques for dealing with large data collections. For example, suppose you are a company intending to issue your own credit cards. In such a case, you may have the choice of assigning your own credit-card numbers. You could choose to issue numbers of the form: *ccc-ttt-sss*, where *ccc* is a cylinder number, *ttt* is a track number, and *sss* is a sector number for a disk that will contain the credit-card holders' credit records. Using this method, you have implemented what is called a *direct-access file organization*, which has no need for using methods that search for records having given search keys at the expense of several separate disk accesses. Only one disk access suffices to locate any record, since the credit-card number is the address of the corresponding credit record.

References for Further Study

database systems

C. J. Date, *An Introduction to Database Systems*, Addison-Wesley, Reading, Mass., (1977).

A classical reference on the subject of databases.

Donald E. Knuth, *The Art of Computer Programming*, vol. 3: *Searching and Sorting*, Addison-Wesley, Reading, Mass., (1973).

V. Y. Lum, P. S. T. Yuen, and M. Dodd, "Key-to-Address Transform Techniques: A Fundamental Performance Study on Large Existing Formatted Files." *Communications of the ACM* 14: 4 (April 1971), pp. 228–39.

Chapter Summary

large data collections

This chapter focuses on techniques that apply to large collections of data, which might be defined as collections that are too large to fit all at once inside the fast, random-access internal memory of a computer but that could be stored on external memory devices of large capacity (but usually having slower access times).

tapes and disks

Two kinds of external storage media are tapes and disks. Tapes have enormous data capacity and can be used to store massive amounts of data relatively cheaply. But they have slow random-access times. Disks have faster access times than tapes, but these access times can be tens of thousands of times slower than the access times for fast, internal, random-access memory.

seek, latency, and transmission times

The access time to a randomly chosen sector on a movable-head disk is composed of three component times: (a) the *seek time*—the time to move the read/write heads from the current track to the track containing the data, (b) the *latency time*—the rotational delay encountered while the portion of the disk containing the data rotates under the read/write head, and (c) the *transmission time*—the time for the portion of the disk containing the data to pass under the read/write head.

comparing primary and secondary memory access times

Comparing a Winchester disk to a primary, random-access memory inside a computer having a 1 μsec access time, we might find that a contemporary Winchester disk takes perhaps 15 ms to access a particular record. This access time is on the order of 15,000 times greater than the time to access data in primary memory. Consequently, when dealing with large files stored on disks, the dominant costs in processing the data tend to be the times required for data access. If we plan to store a large file of data on a disk, we need to identify algorithmic techniques that minimize the number of random data accesses required if we want to use methods that perform well.

Some methods for searching and sorting, which perform well on small collections of data in fast, primary, random-access memory, do not perform at all well on large collections of data stored on relatively slow external memory devices. For instance, binary searching, double hashing using open addressing, AVL tree techniques, and sorting using comparisons and exchanges, are all methods that tend to perform particularly poorly on large external data collections stored on disks. The reason for this is that each of these methods involves many random accesses to the underlying data, which incur high performance penalties when these methods are executed on data residing on an external disk.

Needed instead are methods that minimize the number of random accesses to data but that accomplish the same objectives in a different manner. Some of the techniques that work comparatively well on large external collections of data are merge sorting, the use of B-trees of order $m \approx 200$, the use of hashing with buckets, and the indexed sequential access method.

information retrieval

Sometimes we desire to perform *information retrieval* operations on files other than simply searching for a record containing a unique search key, K. For instance, we may want to query a file of employee records to ask a question such as, "How many employees in the Accounting Department are over age 45 and have salaries greater than $50,000?"

fully inverted files

A *fully inverted file*, F, is one for which an index has been prepared giving, for each value, V, of each field inside the records of F, a list $L(V)$ of each of the records containing the value, V. Thus, speaking loosely, an inverted file index for an encyclopedia might list all pages of the encyclopedia containing references to a given word. That is, given an arbitrary word, such as "pancake," the inverted index would contain an entry for "pancake" listing all pages on which the word "pancake" appears.

queries and query languages

Sometimes information retrieval systems provide query languages that permit users to express a variety of queries that they wish to have answered in relation to the information in the system. Such queries may include (a) *range queries*, such as, "Find all employees with ages between 30 and 45;" (b) *Boolean combinations* of simple queries using Boolean operations (e.g., *and*, *or*, and *not*), such as "Find all records R in the file such that $(30 \le \text{age}(R) \le 45)$ *and* $((\text{salary}(R) < \$50,000)$ *or not* $(\text{Department}(R) = \text{Accounting Department}))$;" and (c) *similarity retrievals*, such as "Find all employees with last names similar to 'Shumaker,' or 'Schumacher.'"

database systems

Database systems can be even more complicated than information retrieval systems. A *database is* a collection of files concerned with a particular organization or enterprise. A database system consists of the database itself, together with the set of machines, people, policies, and procedures that govern its use in the context of the enterprise. Many issues arise in connection with database systems. For example: (a) How do you keep the data in a database secure from improper access and from unauthorized tampering?, (b) How do you maintain backups of the data so that recovery from a crash is possible?, and (c) How do you provide for efficient access, update, query, and report generation?

13

Sorting

13.1 Introduction and Motivation

the richness of the
sorting problem

The problem of sorting an initially unordered collection of keys to produce an ordered collection is one of the richest in computer science. The richness derives, in part from the fact that the number of different ways of solving the sorting problem is plentiful. Because the sorting problem has fascinated theoretical computer scientists, much is known about the efficiency of various solutions, and about limitations on the best possible solutions. Consequently, an investigation of various sorting algorithms makes an excellent case study for acquainting you with the kind of progress in our understanding of computer science that has been made during the last half-century.

the *n* log *n* barrier for
comparison-based methods

For instance, if an algorithm uses comparisons between keys as its means for deciding how to arrange the keys in sorted order, then it cannot sort a sequence of *n* keys in an average amount of time less than proportional to *n* log *n*. This *n* log *n* *lower bound* for comparison-based sorting does not imply that there do not exist even faster sorting methods that do not use key comparisons. In fact, there exist O(*n*) sorting algorithms relying on what are called address-calculation techniques. For some

524

strange reason, most algorithm and data structures books cover only the $O(n \log n)$ comparison-based methods, and rarely, if ever, comment on the existence of the faster $O(n)$ address-calculation techniques.

Sometimes a sorting technique that works well in primary memory does not work at all well for sorting large files contained on external memory media, such as disks or tapes. Also, among the $O(n \log n)$ techniques, even though a fast technique, such as QuickSort, can sort n keys twice as fast on the average as a competing $O(n \log n)$ technique, such as HeapSort, the worst case time for QuickSort is $O(n^2)$, whereas the worst case time for HeapSort is $O(n \log n)$.

worst case times are occasionally important

The fact that HeapSort has a much better worst case behavior than QuickSort could turn out to be important, even though HeapSort is twice as slow as QuickSort on the average. For instance, if you are applying a sorting technique to meet a time constraint under which you need to guarantee that n keys will be sorted within a specified time limit, you might choose to use HeapSort over QuickSort because HeapSort will always finish in time $O(n \log n)$.

learning how to choose the best method

Familiarity with the performance characteristics of different sorting methods could be of significant value in helping you select a sorting technique that is well-matched to the characteristics of a particular problem you need to solve. If your goal is to become a proficient software engineer, then it is essential to know how to choose the best available methods for solving important often-encountered software problems.

goal: basic knowledge + comparative performance

Although the kind of comparative study offered in this chapter is not as highly detailed as those that you might encounter in graduate or professional software engineering courses, or in advanced undergraduate courses on algorithms, it nonetheless provides you with a good start on the subject of sorting. The goal is to give you an intuitive grasp of how the various sorting methods work, how they are related to one another as common instances of unifying abstract themes (such as *divide-and-conquer* or *priority queue sorting*), and some of what is known about their comparative performance.

Plan for the Chapter

Sorting methods can be grouped in various clusters that share common themes. One way to organize them (although not the only possible way) is suggested by the diagram in Fig. 13.1. In fact, we have chosen to organize the sections in this chapter to discuss each of the different sorting themes shown in this figure.

sorting themes

Before discussing specific sorting techniques, however, Section 13.2 lays some theoretical groundwork by showing that $n \log n$ is a lower bound for the average time that comparison-based methods must take to sort n keys.

priority queue methods

Section 13.3 investigates two priority queue sorting methods: SelectionSort and HeapSort. Recall that a priority queue is a collection of items in which items can be inserted in any order, but in which only the item of top-priority can be removed. Suppose that PQ is a priority queue, and that when we remove items from PQ one after another, they are removed in largest to smallest order. If, when we remove items from PQ, we then place them on the rear of an ordinary queue, Q, their order of arrival on the rear of Q is in sorted order from largest to smallest. In both SelectionSort and HeapSort, we treat the remaining items to be sorted as a priority

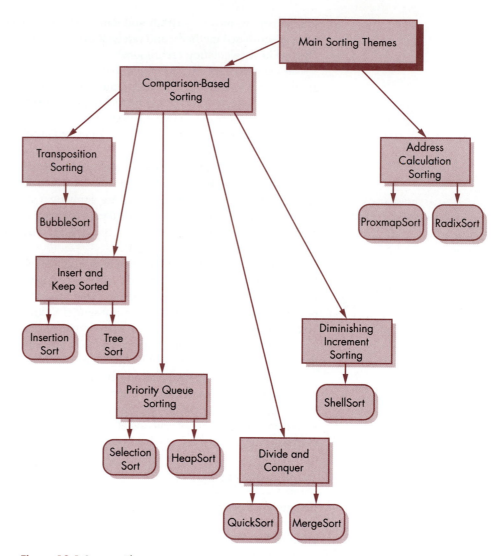

Figure 13.1 Sorting Themes

queue. In the case of **HeapSort**, these remaining unsorted items are organized into a heap, and we remove the largest item from this heap at each stage. In the case of **SelectionSort**, the remaining unsorted items are treated as an unordered sequence, and we scan the entire sequence each time we remove an item in order first to locate the position of the largest item to remove. Thus **SelectionSort** can be viewed as using the unordered-array-representation for a priority queue, whereas **HeapSort** can be viewed as using the heap representation of a priority queue.

divide-and-conquer
methods

Section 13.4 studies two *divide-and-conquer* methods: **MergeSort** and **QuickSort**. A divide-and-conquer sorting method is one that first *divides* a sequence of *n* keys into two subsequences, such as a *left subsequence* and a *right subsequence*. It then sorts these two subsequences. Finally, it combines the two sorted subsequences into a single sorted result.

insertion-based methods

Section 13.5 studies two sorting methods that use insertion: InsertionSort and TreeSort. Such methods start with an empty storage container, C, and insert new keys into the container one after another. The inserted keys are always maintained in sorted order inside C.

address-calculation methods

Section 13.6 investigates two methods, ProxmapSort and RadixSort, that use address-calculation techniques and that run in average time $O(n)$. It is of some interest that *RadixSort* was one of the methods used by early electromechanical, punched-card sorting machines that were employed in business data processing before the advent of electronic-digital computers.

Section 13.7 investigates two additional methods: ShellSort and BubbleSort. ShellSort is called a diminishing-increment sorting technique. BubbleSort makes repeated passes through an unsorted sequence of keys, and transposes any adjacent pair of keys that is not in sorted order. BubbleSort's performance is particularly poor unless the sequence of keys it is given to sort is nearly sorted already.

comparing the methods

Section 13.8 provides a discussion that attempts to compare the various methods and put them in perspective. It also covers some additional special cases not previously mentioned, such as the case in which the keys are a permutation of the integers from 0 to $n - 1$ and can be used directly as table addresses for final placement of the keys.

13.2 Laying Some Groundwork**

Learning Objectives

1. To learn how comparison trees are defined.
2. To see how to use comparison trees to prove that comparison-based sorting methods must use at least $n \log n$ comparisons on the average.
3. To understand that this $n \log n$ lower bound applies only to comparison-based methods and not to all possible sorting methods.

Many sorting methods decide how to rearrange keys into sorted order by first comparing the values of the keys. These methods are called comparison-based methods.

It turns out that, on the average, any comparison-based method must make a certain minimum number of comparisons between pairs of keys in order to gather enough information to decide how to rearrange them into sorted order. The argument that demonstrates why this must be the case depends on defining what are called *comparison trees*. A comparison tree is a binary tree in which, at each internal node, a comparison is made between two keys, and in which each external (or leaf) node contains a sorted arrangement of keys. The left descendant of each decision node represents a *yes* decision, and the right descendant represents a *no* decision. The decisions made on a path from the root to a given leaf node are sufficient to determine that the keys must be arranged in the order specified by the ordered sequence of keys given in that leaf node.

In the examples and arguments given below, we assume we are dealing with distinct keys and that the decisions comparing two keys, a and b, can have only two outcomes: $a < b$ and $a > b$. Treating the more complicated case, in which two keys, a and b, could be equal (as in $a = b$), would add more case analysis and complexity to the argument but would not reduce the minimum average number of comparisons needed to decide how to sort distinct keys. Consequently, to establish the minimum average number of comparisons, we need consider only the simpler case in which all keys are distinct from one another.

dealing only with distinct keys

Let's now consider a simple example of a comparison tree. Suppose we are trying to sort an array A[0:2] containing three distinct keys, a, b and c:

A[0]	A[1]	A[2]
a	b	c

comparison trees

Figure 13.2 illustrates a comparison tree in which we compare various pairs of keys and, based on the (*yes* or *no*) outcome of each comparison, follow a path downward through the tree that performs additional comparisons until enough information is gathered to decide upon a final sorted order for the keys.

For example, in Fig. 13.2, if the result of comparing $a < b$ is *yes*, we then descend from the root downward to the left, and compare b and c. If the result of comparing $b < c$ is *no*, we descend further to the right and compare a and c. Finally, if the result of comparing $a < c$ is *yes*, we know that the ascending sorted order for the keys must be (a, c, b). Therefore the ordered sequence of keys in the box that is the left descendant of the node containing the comparison $a < c$ is the sequence (a, c, b).

In general, a given comparison-based sorting algorithm, S, will compare pairs of keys in some order. Comparisons of pairs of keys will usually be interleaved with rearrangements of the order of various pairs of keys, as algorithm S progressively moves the keys into final sorted order. The particular comparisons that S performs at a given stage in its execution will, in general, depend on the outcomes of previous comparisons and previous rearrangements of the keys that S has already performed. In any event, each comparison-based sorting algorithm, S, must perform comparisons

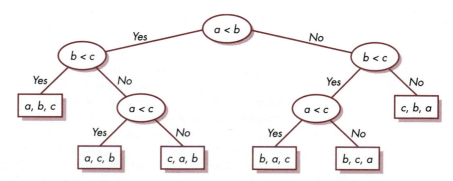

Figure 13.2 A Comparison Tree

between designated pairs of keys in *some* order, until it eventually terminates after having arranged the keys in sorted order. Let's now reason about the minimum possible number of comparisons S could use, on the average, in order to sort a collection of distinct keys successfully.

The comparison tree in Fig. 13.2 sorts only three keys. Let's now suppose that we have *n* distinct keys, instead of just three keys, and let's ask, "How many distinct sorted orders could result from sorting *n* distinct keys?"

We see that, for three keys, *a*, *b* and *c*, any one of the three could be the smallest and could appear first in sorted order. So there are three distinct ways in which a sorted sequence of three distinct keys could begin. Then, having chosen one of the three keys as the smallest, there are two remaining possibilities for choosing the next smallest key. Finally, after the second smallest is chosen, by a process of elimination, there is only one key left to be the largest. If we choose the first key any one of three ways, and then choose the second key any one of two ways, we get six total possible ways of choosing an order for the three distinct keys. These six distinct possible orderings are shown in the boxes that are the leaves of the comparison tree in Fig. 13.2.

In the special case of three distinct keys, the total number of distinct orders (6) is equal to the factorial of the number of keys (3!), since $6 = 3! = 3 * 2 * 1$. The same holds true for *n* distinct keys—namely, that the total number of distinct orderings of *n* keys is given by *n* factorial (*n*!). The reason is that any of the *n* keys could be the smallest and could appear first in sorted order. So an ordered arrangement of keys could start any one of *n* distinct ways. Second, any of the remaining $(n - 1)$ keys could occur next in sorted order. Third, any of the remaining $(n - 2)$ keys could occur in third place in sorted order, and so on until, by a process of elimination, only one key remains to place last in sorted order. The product $n * (n - 1) * (n - 2) * \ldots * 2 * 1$, which is the same as *n*!, then gives the total number of distinct sorted orders that are possible outcomes for sorting *n* distinct keys. (In mathematics, we say that each such distinct order is a *permutation* of the *n* keys, and that *n*! gives the total number of permutations of the keys.)

Now that we know that there are *n*! distinct orders for *n* keys, we can reason about the minimum average number of comparisons needed to sort *n* keys. Consider all possible comparison trees that correspond to algorithms that sort *n* keys. The boxes at the leaves of such comparison trees each contain one of the *n*! distinct permutations of the *n* keys, and there must be at least *n*! such leaves (or external nodes) in any valid comparison tree that can sort *n* keys. (Otherwise, if there were less than *n*! external nodes, one or more of the possible sorted orders could not be achieved, and the algorithm would fail to sort properly in such cases.)

If we travel down a path in a comparison tree, the number of comparisons encountered on the path from the root down to an external node (or leaf node) is identical to the number of comparisons needed to decide how to sort the original *n* keys into the particular order given in the box at the external node. Moreover, the number of comparisons is identical to the path length from the root to the external node (since there is exactly one edge in the path below each internal comparison node on the path). Therefore the average number of comparisons needed to sort *n* keys, according to the comparison tree, can be obtained by dividing the *external path length* of the tree by the number of external nodes. (Recall, from Chapter 9, that the

six possible orders for three distinct keys

n! orders for n distinct keys

$$n! \approx \sqrt{2\pi\, n}\left(\frac{n}{e}\right)^n \left(1 + \frac{1}{12n} + O\left(\frac{1}{n^2}\right)\right)$$

Stirling's Approximation for n!

$$\ln n! = \sum_{i=1}^{n} \ln i \approx \left(n + \frac{1}{2}\right)\ln n - n + \ln\sqrt{2\pi} + \frac{1}{12n} - \frac{1}{360 n^3} + O\left(\frac{1}{n^5}\right)$$

Approximation for the sum of the natural logarithms

Figure 13.3 Stirling's Approximation and the Sum of the Natural Logs

external path length is the sum of the lengths of the paths from the root to each external node.)

Consequently, the average number of comparisons will be at a minimum just when the external path length of the comparison tree is at a minimum. Again recalling the discussion of binary trees in Chapter 9, we know that among all possible binary trees, the binary trees having minimal external path lengths are those with leaves either on one level or on two adjacent levels.

the minimum average number of comparisons

If a comparison tree has k external nodes and has minimal external path length, then the length, p, of the shortest path from the root to a leaf must be constrained by the inequality, $p \geq \lfloor \lg k \rfloor$. You can see that this is so, since if r is the level number of any leaf at least distance from the root in a binary tree with leaves on at most two adjacent levels, and the number of leaves, k, lies in the range $2^r : (2^{(r+1)} - 1)$, then $r = \lfloor \lg k \rfloor$, and a path from the root to any leaf must contain at least r edges.

The minimum average number of comparisons required for comparison-based sorting of n keys can now be obtained by using a comparison tree of minimum external path length having $k = n!$ external nodes. In such a tree, the minimum average path length p must obey the inequality, $p \geq \lfloor \lg (n!) \rfloor$. Consequently, if we could obtain a good estimate for the expression $\lg (n!)$, we would have a good lower bound for the minimum average number comparisons required to sort n keys using comparison-based methods.

An estimate for $\lg (n!)$ can be derived from a famous approximation for $n!$, called Stirling's Approximation. Figure 13.3 gives both Stirling's Approximation and an approximation for the natural logarithm of $n!$ (which is also equal to the sum of the natural logarithms of the integers from 1 to n). Because the last four terms of the approximation for $\ln n!$ in Fig. 13.3 sum up to a positive contribution, we can drop them in order to obtain a lower bound for $\ln n!$

$$\ln n! > (n + \tfrac{1}{2}) \ln n - n$$

Multiplying out the first term on the right $(n + \tfrac{1}{2}) \ln n$, and further dropping the positive term $\tfrac{1}{2} \ln n$, retains $n \ln n - n$ as a simpler lower bound for $\ln n!$

$$\ln n! > n \ln n - n$$

> The minimum average number of comparisons required to sort n keys using a comparison-based sorting method is $n \log n$.

Theorem 13.4 Minimum Average Comparisons for Sorting

By splitting and regrouping $n \ln n - n$ into $(\frac{1}{2} n \ln n) + (\frac{1}{2} n \ln n - n)$ and noting that $(\frac{1}{2} n \ln n - n)$ is positive whenever $n > 7$, we can obtain an even simpler lower bound for $\ln n!$

$$\ln n! > \frac{1}{2} n \ln n$$

Dividing both sides by $\ln 2$ converts the natural logarithms to base-2 logarithms yielding

$$\lg n! > \frac{1}{2} n \lg n, \quad \text{for } n > 7.$$

[*Note:* By a more delicate argument, we can establish that $\lg n! \geq \frac{1}{2} n \lg n$ for all $n \geq 1$.] Since $2 = \lg 4$, we can convert to base-4 logarithms, getting

$$\lg n! > n \log_4 n$$

Just as we did with O-notation, we can ignore the bases of the logarithms in the lower bound by noting that, in general, $\lg n! > n \log n$, for suitably large n and for a suitable constant of proportionality expressed by a choice of an appropriate logarithm base. Our chain of reasoning is now complete. We state the conclusion as Theorem 13.4.

Many of the sorting techniques we shall investigate in the following sections are comparison-based methods. For example, **SelectionSort**, **InsertionSort**, **MergeSort**, **QuickSort**, **HeapSort**, **BubbleSort**, **ShellSort** and **TreeSort**, are all comparison-based methods. In view of Theorem 13.4, you should be prepared to confirm that all of these can sort n keys in an average amount of time no faster than that given by the complexity class $O(n \log n)$.

13.2 Review Questions

1. What is a comparison-based sorting method?
2. What is a comparison tree?
3. What is a lower bound for the minimum average time required to sort n keys using any comparison-based method?
4. What is the shape of a full binary tree having minimum external path length?

5. Why is a comparison tree with minimum external path length also a tree that represents the minimum average number of comparisons to sort n keys?

13.2 Exercises

1. If r is the level number of any leaf at least distance from the root in a full binary tree with leaves on at most two adjacent levels, and the number of leaves, k, lies in the range $2^r \leq k \leq 2^{(r+1)} - 1$, prove that $r = \lfloor \lg k \rfloor$ and a path from the root to any leaf must contain at least r edges.
2. Prove that $\lg n!$ is approximately equal to $\ln (n!)/\ln 2 + O(n)$.
3. Give the O-notation for $\sum_{(1 \leq i \leq n)} \lg i$.

≡ 13.3 Priority Queue Sorting Methods

Learning Objectives

1. To learn about abstract priority queue sorting.
2. To learn how SelectionSort and HeapSort are each refinements of abstract priority queue sorting.
3. To see how SelectionSort represents its priority queue of yet-to-be-sorted keys as an unsorted subarray.
4. To see how HeapSort represents its collection of yet-to-be-sorted keys as a heap.
5. To derive the O-notation for the sorting times for SelectionSort and HeapSort.

before we begin

Before we begin discussion of the priority queue sorting techniques covered in this section, we need to introduce some preliminary assumptions that will hold throughout the discussion of most of the sorting techniques in the remainder of the chapter.

Some Preliminary Assumptions

In what follows, we will be sorting arrays of keys. The keys can be of any type whatsoever. For instance, the keys could be integers, or strings, or floating point numbers. The important thing about keys is that any two given keys, K_1 and K_2, can be *compared*, as a result of which, one and only one of the following relationships will be true: $K_1 < K_2$, $K_1 = K_2$, or $K_1 > K_2$. Consequently, by rearranging the order of the keys in an array, A, the keys can be put into *ascending order* (where, specifically, ascending order means *nondecreasing order* such that $A[i] \leq A[i + 1]$ for all i in the range $0 \leq i < n - 1$).

In the algorithms that follow, we shall assume that we always start with an unsorted array, A, of n keys, and that the objective is to arrange the keys in A into ascending order. The array indices for A are assumed to start at 0 and to end at some largest index, $n - 1$, which is one less than the size of the array, A. The C declarations in Program 13.5 define the kinds of arrays we will use.

```
/* defined constant */

    #define n AnyArbitrarySize              /* n gives the number of items */
                                            /* in the array to be sorted */
/* type definitions */

    typedef T KeyType;                      /* where T == int, float, string, or */
                                            /* whatever your keys' type is */
    typedef   KeyType SortingArray[n] ;

/* variable declaration */

    SortingArray  A;              /* A[0:n − 1] is an array of keys to be sorted */
```

Program 13.5 Declarations Assumed for Sorting Algorithms

Priority Queue Sorting

Section 4.3 introduced the Priority Queue ADT, and Section 9.5 introduced heaps as a representation for priority queues. Then, in Table 9.23, we compared running time efficiencies of operations on three priority queue representations: (a) heaps, (b) sorted lists, and (c) unsorted arrays.

sorting based on priority queues

We can imagine a family of sorting algorithms based on the use of priority queues, as follows. First, given the initial unsorted array, A, we can imagine that we organize the keys in A into a priority queue representation, PQ. Then, we imagine that we have an output queue, Q, which is initially empty and which will accumulate new keys in arrival order as they are inserted on Q's rear end.

We then remove keys from PQ, one at a time, and insert them on the rear of Q. We repeat this process until PQ is empty. Since the keys removed from PQ were removed in largest to smallest order, and were inserted into Q in arrival order, Q will contain keys in decreasing order at the end of the process.

two refinements of abstract priority queue sorting

Let's first look at Program Strategy 13.6, which expresses this process of abstract priority queue sorting. Then we will give two specific representations of priority queue sorting. The first will represent the priority queue, PQ, as an unsorted subarray of the array A. The second will use a heap to represent the priority queue PQ. In both cases, the output queue, Q, will be represented by a subarray of array, A, lying at the highest index positions of array A, and PQ will be represented by a subarray lying at the lowest index positions of array A. In the first case, we will discover that we have implemented a variant of **SelectionSort**. In the second case, we will have implemented an algorithm called **HeapSort**.

Programs 4.4 and 4.5 gave implementations of abstract priority queue sorting using various substitutable priority queue modules (each having identical module interfaces but having different underlying data representations). Recall that these examples were given to illustrate the *substitutability* of data representations in modular programming. We shall now give two specific refinements of abstract priority queue sorting that use two separate subarrays of array A to hold the priority queue PQ and the output queue Q, and which therefore actually accomplish sorting by rearranging the order of the keys in A.

```
    |    void PriorityQueueSort(SortingArray A)
    |    {
    |         (Let Q be an initially empty output queue)
    |         (Let PQ be a priority queue)
    |         KeyType  K;
  5 |
    |
    |         (Organize the keys in A into a priority queue, PQ)
    |
    |         while (PQ is not empty) {
 10 |
    |              (Remove the largest key, K, from PQ)
    |              (Insert key, K, on the rear of output queue, Q)
    |
    |         }
 15 |
    |         (Move the keys in Q into the array A in ascending sorted order)
    |
    |    }
```

Program Strategy 13.6 Abstract Priority Queue Sorting

Figure 13.7 gives a diagram of the general situation we expect during the priority queue sorting process. Here, the sorting array, A, is divided into two subarrays, with the subarray holding the keys in *PQ* on the left, and the subarray holding the keys in *Q* on the right.

Let's imagine that we have been engaged in priority queue sorting for a while, and that the first few of the largest keys have already been placed in the subarray *Q* of array A, holding output keys in their final ascending order.

Now, let's focus on how we remove the next key from *PQ*, and place it on the rear of *Q*. We first identify the index position of the largest key in subarray *PQ*. Suppose this occurs at index position, j. Suppose also that index, i, points to the last position in the subarray *PQ*. We then exchange the keys in $A[i]$ and $A[j]$, and we move the boundary between *PQ* and *Q* one position to the left. This action is shown in Fig. 13.8.

The net effect of the actions illustrated in Fig. 13.8 is to remove the largest key in *PQ* and insert it on the rear of the output queue, *Q*. If this action is performed repeat-

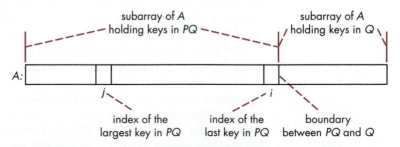

Figure 13.7 General Situation in Priority Queue Sorting

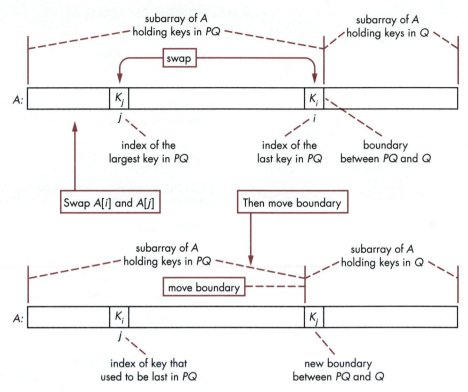

Figure 13.8 Swap $A[i] \leftrightarrow A[j]$, then Move Boundary

edly until PQ becomes empty, then Q will expand to become the entire array A, and it will contain keys in ascending order.

SelectionSort

If we now refine abstract priority queue sort by using an unsorted subarray of keys as the representation for the priority queue, PQ, we get the SelectionSort algorithm. At each stage, to identify the position of the largest key, j, in the subarray PQ, we scan all the keys in PQ, remembering the position, j, of the current maximum as we go. Then we swap $A[j]$, the largest key in PQ, with $A[i]$, the last key in PQ, and decrease i by 1 to move the boundary between PQ and Q. Program 13.9 gives the details.

In constructing Program 13.9 as a refinement of abstract priority queue sorting, as given in Program Strategy 13.6, some optimizations have been subtly introduced. First, no work is involved in organizing the keys in the unsorted array, A, into a priority queue, PQ, since A is being used directly as the representation of PQ. Second, no effort is required to move the keys from the final output queue, Q, into array A in ascending order, since Q has grown from an empty subarray of A into the entire array, A, by the time the algorithm finishes. Third, and finally, the while-loop, which

some program optimizations

```
 |        void SelectionSort(SortingArray A)
 |        {
 |
 |                int          i, j, k;
 5 |                KeyType      Temp;
 |
 |
 |                /* Initially, Q is empty, and PQ contains all keys in A, so the index, i, */
 |                /* of the last key in PQ is set to n – 1, the index of the last key in A. */
10 |
 |                i = n – 1;
 |
 |
 |                /* While PQ contains more than one key, */
15 |                /* identify and move the largest key in PQ into Q */
 |
 |                while ( i > 0 ) {
 |
 |                        /* Let j initially point to the last key in PQ */
20 |                        j = i;
 |
 |                        /* Scan remaining positions in 0:i – 1 to find largest key, A[j] */
 |                        for (k = 0; k < i; ++k) {
 |                                if (A[k] > A[j])  j = k ;
25 |                        }
 |
 |                        /* Swap the largest key, A[j], and the last key, A[i] */
 |                        Temp = A[i]; A[i] = A[j]; A[j] = Temp;
 |
30 |                        /* Move boundary between PQ and Q downward one position */
 |                        i – –;
 |
 |                }
 |
 |        }
```

Program 13.9 SelectionSort as a Refinement of Priority Queue Sort

extracts keys from PQ and puts them into Q, terminates when PQ contains one key, instead of terminating when PQ is empty, as shown in Program Strategy 13.6. It is possible to stop when PQ contains only one key, since that key must be the smallest key in A, by a process of elimination, and since that smallest key is already in its final position in A.

Analysis of SelectionSort**

SelectionSort runs in time $O(n^2)$

Since Program 13.9 exchanges $A[j]$ with $A[i]$ for each i starting at $n - 1$ and counting down to 1, SelectionSort performs $(n - 1)$ exchanges. Also, the number of key comparisons performed on line 24 of Program 13.9 is a sum of the form: $(n - 1) + (n - 2) + \ldots + 2 + 1$, which has the value $(n*(n - 1))/2$, (see Eq. A.4 of the "Math

Reference" appendix). Since **SelectionSort** does $O(n^2)$ comparisons and $O(n)$ exchanges, it is an $O(n^2)$ sorting algorithm.

HeapSort

Let's reconsider the abstract priority queue sorting algorithm given in Program Strategy 13.6. We will construct a new refinement by representing the priority queue, PQ, as a heap, using the sequential representation of the heap as a subarray $A[1:n]$ of an extended sorting array declared by: **KeyType A[n+1];**

representing the priority queue by a heap

We first consider PQ to be the entire subarray $A[1:n]$, and we organize its keys into a heap by applying the heapifying process sketched in Program Strategy 9.16 in Section 9.5. At the conclusion of this heapifying process, the largest element in the heap sits in position, $A[1]$. We can now swap the first and last keys in PQ by performing the exchange, $A[1] \leftrightarrow A[n]$, after which we can move the boundary between PQ and Q, so that Q now contains one key that is the former largest key in PQ, and so that PQ has been shortened to contain one less key.

We then have to reheapify PQ because the new key at its root may have made it lose the heap property, after which the largest among the remaining keys in PQ will have been moved into position $A[1]$. We then repeatedly swap the first and last keys in the subarray PQ, move the boundary between PQ and Q, and reheapify PQ until only one key remains in PQ.

At the conclusion of this process, PQ contains the smallest of the original keys in A, Q contains the remaining keys of A in ascending order, and A, which consists of the subarray PQ followed by the subarray Q, now contains the original keys of A in ascending order. Hence nothing needs to be done to extract the keys in Q and rearrange them in A, since A is already sorted.

Program 13.10 gives an optimized refinement of priority queue sorting, using the sequential representation of heaps.

When **HeapSort** begins, it is assumed that all keys in the subarray $A[1:n]$ are to be organized into a heap, PQ, representing a priority queue. Observe that during the initial heapification of these keys, on lines 8:10 of **HeapSort**, the subtrees of PQ are heapified in reverse level order. Moreover, only the nontrivial subtrees of PQ are heapified (meaning only those that are not single leaf nodes), and the subtree consisting of the entire tree is not heapified, since that action is deferred until executing line 17 during the first cycle through the for-loop on lines 16:19.

The procedure, **SiftUp(A,i,n)**, is an auxiliary routine which converts a tree that is almost a heap into a heap, by using a cyclical shift of keys, starting at the root node and moving downward on a path along which the largest of the keys larger than the original root key are moved upward, in order to create a hole for final placement of the root key, which in turn is moved downward. **SiftUp(A,i,n)**, is applied only to trees that depart from satisfying the heap property at their roots, if at all. Because **SiftUp** uses a cyclical shift of keys, it is more efficient than the reheapifying process illustrated in Program Strategy 9.15, which uses repeated pairwise exchanges of keys instead. (Recall that Program 9.21 also uses the efficient cyclic shift method when removing an item from a priority queue.)

```
     |     void HeapSort(SortingArray A)
     |     {
     |             int             i;
     |             KeyType     Temp;
  5  |
     |             /* Heapify all subtrees except the subtree containing the root */
     |
     |             for ( i = (n / 2); i > 1; – – i) {
     |                 SiftUp(A,i,n);
 10  |             }
     |
     |
     |             /* Reheapify starting at root, remove root, put it on output queue, and */
     |             /* replace root with last leaf in level order, until heap contains one key */
 15  |
     |             for (i = n; i > 1; – – i ) {
     |                 SiftUp(A,1,i);
     |                 Temp = A[1]; A[1] = A[i]; A[i] = Temp;          /* swap A[1] and A[i] */
     |             }
     |     }

/* ---------------------------------------------------------------------------------------------------- */

     |     void SiftUp(SortingArray A, int i, int n)
     |     {
     |             /* Let i point to the root and let n point to the last leaf in level order */
     |
  5  |             /* assume: typedef  enum  {false, true} Boolean; has been declared */
     |
     |                 int j;    KeyType RootKey;   Boolean NotFinished;
     |
     |             /* Let RootKey be the key at the root */
 10  |                 RootKey = A[i];
     |
     |             /* Let j point to the left child of i */
     |                 j = 2*i;
     |                 NotFinished = (j <= n); /* SiftUp is not finished if j exists in the tree */
 15  |
     |             /* Move any larger child that is bigger than the root key upward one */
     |             /* level in the tree */
     |                 while (NotFinished) {
     |
 20  |                     if (j < n) {                    /* if a right child of i also exists in the tree */
     |                         if (A[j+1]>A[j]) j++;        /* set j to point to the larger child */
     |                     }
     |
     |                     if (A[j] <= RootKey) {      /* if the larger child is not bigger than*/
 25  |                         NotFinished = false;   /* the root key, no more keys sift up */
```

Program 13.10 HeapSort (continued)

Program 13.10 **HeapSort** (continued)

```
   |                } else {
   |                    A[i] = A[j];         /* move larger child up one level in the tree */
   |                    i = j;               /* now, let i point to the larger child, j */
   |                    j = 2*i;             /* and let j point to the new left child of i */
30 |                    NotFinished = (j <= n);    /* SiftUp is not finished iff */
   |                }                              /* j exists in the tree */
   |
   |            }
   |
35 |        /* Final placement of the root key */
   |            A[i] = RootKey;
   |
   |    }
```

Analysis of HeapSort**

Now let's use the mathematical facts about heaps that we developed in Section 9.5 to reason about the running time of **HeapSort**. First, it was proven that the process of converting the unorganized keys in array A into a heap takes time $O(n)$. Moreover, the process of removing the root of the heap, replacing it with its last leaf in level order, and reheapifying the resulting tree containing i keys, was shown to take at most $\lfloor \lg i \rfloor$ pairwise exchanges of keys (and in the similar case of **SiftUp**, takes $\lfloor \lg i \rfloor + 2$ shifts of keys from one node or temporary variable to another, forming a cyclic shift).

HeapSort runs in time $O(n \log n)$

Consequently, the total effort to remove all keys, except the last, from PQ and to move them to the rear of Q, takes at most an amount of effort proportional to the sum of the floors of the logarithms from 2 to n, $\sum_{(2 \le i \le n)} (\lfloor \lg i \rfloor + 2)$. (The total number of key comparisons is a like sum, bounded above by $\sum (2\lfloor \lg i \rfloor + 1)$.) Equation A.31 in the "Math Reference" appendix shows the sum, $\sum \lfloor \lg i \rfloor$, to be of the form, $(n+1) q - 2^{(q+1)} + 2$, where $q = \lfloor \lg (n + 1) \rfloor$. Using some manipulation of inequalities, this latter quantity can be shown to be $O(n \log n)$. Since this is the dominant time, **HeapSort** runs in time $O(n \log n)$.

13.3 Review Questions

1. Explain how abstract priority queue sorting works.
2. Describe the representation of priority queues used in **SelectionSort**.
3. Describe the representation of priority queues used in **HeapSort**.

13.3 Exercises

1. Using Equation A.31 of Appendix A, plus some manipulation of inequalities, demonstrate that $\sum_{(2 \le i \le n)} (\lfloor \lg i \rfloor + 2)$ is $O(n \log n)$.
2. Why is **SiftUp(A,i,n)** applied only to the subtrees rooted at i in the range 2:n/2, and why are these roots, i, considered in decreasing order?

13.4 Divide-and-Conquer Methods

1. To understand the divide-and-conquer theme, as applied to sorting methods.
2. To review why MergeSort is an O(n log n) sorting method.
3. To learn how QuickSort works.
4. To establish that QuickSort runs in average time O(n log n).

the main idea   In this section, we consider two *divide-and-conquer* sorting methods, **MergeSort** and **QuickSort**. The theme behind these sorting methods is a three-step process: (1) divide the initially given unsorted array into two subarrays, (2) sort the two subarrays, and (3) combine the two sorted subarrays into the overall solution.

The abstract program strategy for divide-and-conquer sorting is given in Program Strategy 13.11. It is expressed in a form that allows it to be applied recursively to subarrays of array A.

MergeSort

We have already seen **MergeSort** in Section 6.5, where we determined its running time to be O(n log n). To help refresh your memory on the main theme behind **MergeSort**, its abstract strategy is reproduced as Program Strategy 13.12.

```
    |    void Sort(SortingArray A, int m, int n)       /*to sort the subarray A[m:n] of */
    |    {                                             /* array A into ascending order */
    |
    |        if (there is more than one item to sort in A[m:n]) {
 5  |            (Divide A[m:n] into two subarrays A[m:i] and A[j:n])
    |            (Sort the subarray A[m:i])
    |            (Sort the subarray A[j:n])
    |            (Combine the two sorted subarrays to yield the sorted original array)
    |        }
    |    }
```

Program Strategy 13.11 Divide-and-Conquer Sorting Strategy

```
    |    void MergeSort(SortingArray A, int m, int n)   /*to sort the subarray A[m:n] of */
    |    {                                              /* array A into ascending order */
    |
    |        if (there is more than one item to sort in A[m:n]) {
 5  |            (divide A[m:n] into two halves, LeftArray and RightArray)
    |            (MergeSort the LeftArray A[m:middle])
    |            (MergeSort the RightArray A[middle+1:n])
    |            (Merge LeftArray and RightArray to obtain the result)
    |        }
    |    }
```

Program Strategy 13.12 Strategy for MergeSort

```
     |    void QuickSort(SortingArray A, int m, int n)    /*to sort the subarray A[m:n] of */
     |    {                                               /* array A into ascending order */
     |
     |        if (there is more than one key to sort in A[m:n]) {
  5  |            (Partition A[m:n] into a LeftPartition and a RightPartition)
     |            (using one of the keys in A[m:n] as a pivot key.)
     |            (QuickSort the LeftPartition)
     |            (QuickSort the RightPartition)
     |        }
     |    }
```

Program Strategy 13.13 Strategy for QuickSort

QuickSort

QuickSort is another divide-and-conquer sorting method that runs in average time $O(n \log n)$.

The main theme behind QuickSort is as follows. You first choose some key in the array A as a *pivot key*. This pivot key is used to separate the keys in A into two partitions: (1) A *left partition* containing keys less than or equal to the pivot key, and (2) a *right partition* containing keys greater than or equal to the pivot key. QuickSort is then applied recursively to sort the left and right partitions. After this has been done, no further rearrangement is needed, since the original array, A, containing the two sorted left and right partitions, is now in ascending order. The main theme behind QuickSort is given in the abstract strategy shown in Program Strategy 13.13.

An actual C version of QuickSort is given as Program 13.14. As you can see, the actual procedure, QuickSort, is an executive routine that calls a subprogram, Partition(A,&i,&j), to do the actual work of creating the left and right partitions, after which it calls itself recursively to sort the left and right partitions.

The partition algorithm is given as Program 13.15. Its goal is to partition the subarray A[i:j] into a left and right partition, using the key in the middle of the subarray as a pivot key. The heart of the QuickSort algorithm, then, is the partitioning method, given by the Program 13.15, Partition(A,&i,&j). Let's examine four initial stages of the partitioning process.

the main theme used in QuickSort

```
     |    void QuickSort(SortingArray A, int m, int n)    /*to sort the subarray A[m:n] of */
     |    {                                               /* array A into ascending order */
     |        int i, j;
     |
  5  |        if (m < n) {
     |            i = m; j = n;            /* Initially i and j point to the first and last items */
     |            Partition(A,&i,&j);      /* partitions A[m:n] into A[m:j] and A[i:n] */
     |            QuickSort(A,m,j);
     |            QuickSort(A,i,n);
 10  |        }
     |    }
```

Program 13.14 QuickSort

```
|   void Partition(SortingArray A, int *i, int *j)
|   {
|       KeyType Pivot, Temp;
|
5|      Pivot = A[ ( *i + *j ) / 2 ] ;           /* choose the middle key as the pivot */
|
|       do {
|
|           while (A[*i] < Pivot) (*i)++;    /* Find leftmost i such that A[i] ≥ Pivot. */
10|
|           while (A[*j] > Pivot) (*j) − −;/* Find rightmost j such that A[j] ≤ Pivot. */
|
|           if (*i <= *j) {          /* if i and j didn't cross over one another, swap */
|               Temp = A[*i]; A[*i] = A[*j]; A[*j] = Temp;    /* A[i] and A[j] */
15|             (*i) ++;                                   /* move i one space right */
|               (*j) − −;                                   /* move j one space left */
|           }
|
|       } while (*i <= *j);            /* while the i and j pointers haven't crossed yet */
20|
|   }
```

Program 13.15 QuickSort's Partition Algorithm

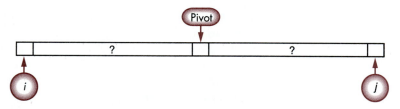

Figure 13.16 At the Start of the Partitioning Process

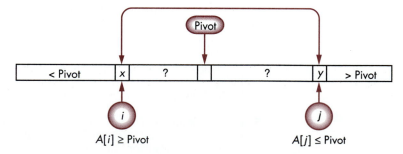

Figure 13.17 Finding Keys in the Wrong Partition

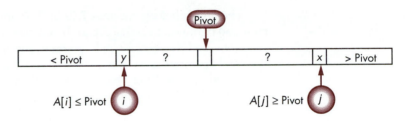

Figure 13.18 After Swapping Keys into Their Proper Partitions

At the very beginning, on line 5 of Program 13.15, we choose the middle key of the subarray, $A[i{:}j]$, as the pivot key. The variable, **Pivot**, contains the value of this key. Initially, as shown in Fig. 13.16, the array index variables, i and j, point to the leftmost and rightmost positions in the subarray, $A[i{:}j]$. Starting at index position, i, we scan rightward comparing each of the successive keys in the sequence, $A[i]$, $A[i + 1]$, $A[i + 2]$, . . . , to the pivot key, **Pivot**. We stop when i points to the first key in this sequence that is greater than or equal to the pivot key, $A[i] \geq$ **Pivot**. We could summarize this by saying that the while-statement on line 9 finds the *leftmost* key in $A[i{:}j]$ that is greater than or equal to the pivot key.

Similarly, starting at the right end of the subarray, $A[i{:}j]$, we start at index position j and compare the sequence of keys $A[j]$, $A[j - 1]$, $A[j - 2]$, . . . , to the pivot key, and we stop at the first key that is less than or equal to the pivot key, $A[j] \leq$ **Pivot**. We could summarize this by saying that the while-statement on line 11 finds the *rightmost* key in $A[i{:}j]$ which is less than or equal to the pivot key. The situation we have at this moment is illustrated in Fig. 13.17.

In a sense, what we have done so far is to choose the pivot key, and then to find the leftmost and rightmost keys in the respective left and right partitions that belong in the other partition. Since these keys are in the wrong partition, the very next thing we do is to swap them in order to place them in their correct partitions. Figure 13.18 shows the situation after we have swapped the keys $A[i]$ and $A[j]$.

Now that all keys from the left end of the subarray up through the current key in $A[i]$ are less than or equal to the pivot, and now that all keys from the right end of the subarray downward through $A[j]$ are greater than or equal to the pivot, we can move the index positions i and j one space each toward the middle of the subarray, and we can solve the remaining subproblem of partitioning the keys in the middle that have not yet been partitioned. Figure 13.19 shows what happens after we have increased i and decreased j (on lines 15:16 of Program 13.15).

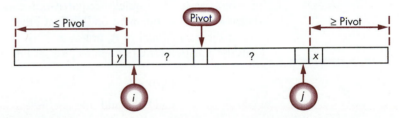

Figure 13.19 After Swapping Keys into Their Proper Partitions

The do-while loop, on lines 7:19 of Program 13.15 repeatedly identifies the leftmost and rightmost keys that are in the wrong partition, swaps them into their correct partitions, and moves the i and j pointers one space each toward the middle. When the i and j pointers cross over one another, the partitioning process is complete. This is detected on line 19 of Program 13.15 when the condition in the **while** (*i <= *j) part of the do-while loop becomes *false*.

Analysis of QuickSort**

Let's derive the O-notation for the average number of key comparisons, $C(n)$, performed by **QuickSort** to sort an average array, $A[0:n-1]$, with keys chosen randomly and uniformly from some space of possible keys. To do this, we will use the quantity, $C(n,k)$, which is defined to be the number of key comparisons performed by the partitioning algorithm when the pivot key, K, is eventually moved to reside in position $A[k-1]$ in array, A, at the end of the partitioning process.

The partitioning algorithm, given in Program 13.15, stops when the i and j pointers cross over one another (i.e., when $i > j$). But immediately before the i and j pointers cross, during the next-to-last trip through the do-while loop on lines 7:19 of Program 13.15, the i and j pointers will either be equal (i.e., $i == j$), or they will be adjacent (i.e., $i + 1 == j$). Since the pivot key, K, is compared to each $A[i]$ and each $A[j]$ for every value that i and j take during partitioning, Program 13.15 performs either exactly n key comparisons (when $i + 1 == j$ on the next-to-last trip through the loop) or exactly $n + 1$ comparisons (in the event that $i == j$ on the next-to-last trip through the loop). Therefore, in deriving the O-notation for the number of comparisons (which is an upper bound), we can use the bigger value of $(n + 1)$ to determine an upper bound on the number of key comparisons performed. Thus we can write

$$C(n,k) = (n + 1) + C(k - 1) + C(n - k)$$

to express the idea that the average number of comparisons, $C(n,k)$, used to sort the array, A, when the pivot key, K, is moved into the final position $A[k-1]$ after partitioning, and when the two partitions $A[0:k-2]$ and $A[k:n-1]$ are recursively quicksorted subsequently, is at most $(n + 1)$ comparisons used in partitioning, plus an average of $C(k-1)$ comparisons used to quicksort the left partition, plus an average of $C(n-k)$ comparisons used to quicksort the right partition.

We also have the two initial conditions, $C(0) = 0$ and $C(1) = 0$, because no comparisons are used to quicksort partitions containing either zero keys or one key (because of the if-statement on line 5 of Program 13.14, which neither partitions nor sorts a subarray $A[m:n]$ of A, unless $m < n$). Putting these initial conditions together with the equation for $C(n,k)$ above, we get Eqs. 13.1:

$$C(0) = 0,$$
$$C(1) = 0, \text{ and} \qquad\qquad (13.1)$$
$$C(n,k) = (n + 1) + C(k - 1) + C(n - k)$$

To solve these equations, we need to write down one additional fact, which is that the average number of comparisons to quicksort an array, A, containing n keys, $C(n)$, can be computed by taking the average of $C(n,k)$ for each integer k in the range $1 \le k \le n$, to express the idea that the average is taken over all possible final positions, $A[k - 1]$, of the pivot key, K, after partitioning has taken place, with equal weight given to each possible final position, $k - 1$. Thus we can write

$$C(n) = \frac{1}{n} \sum_{k=1}^{n} C(n, k).$$

The latter sum expands and simplifies as follows, when we substitute the right side of the equation for $C(n,k)$ from Eqs. 13.1:

$$C(n) = \frac{1}{n} \sum_{k=1}^{n} [(n+1) + C(k-1) + C(n-k)]$$

$$= \frac{1}{n} \sum_{k=1}^{n} (n+1) + \frac{1}{n} \sum_{k=1}^{n} C(k-1) + \frac{1}{n} \sum_{k=1}^{n} C(n-k)$$

$$= \frac{1}{n} n(n+1) +$$

$$\frac{1}{n} (C(0) + C(1) + \ldots + C(n-2) + C(n-1) +$$

$$\frac{1}{n} (C(n-1) + C(n-2) + \ldots + C(1) + C(0)).$$

The last line simplifies to

$$C(n) = (n+1) + \frac{2}{n} [C(0) + C(1) + \ldots + C(n-2) + C(n-1)].$$

The next step is to write down the last line after substituting $(n - 1)$ for n.. This gives

$$C(n-1) = n + \frac{2}{(n-1)} [C(0) + C(1) + \ldots + C(n-2)].$$

Now we multiply the line for $C(n)$ by n, and the line for $C(n - 1)$ by $(n - 1)$ and subtract the latter from the former, getting:

$$n\,C(n) = n\,(\,n + 1\,) + 2\,[\,C(0) + C(1) + \ldots + C(n - 2) + C(n - 1)]$$
$$- (n - 1)\,C(n - 1) = - (n - 1)\,n - 2\,[\,C(0) + C(1) + \ldots + C(n - 2)]$$

$$n\,C(n) - (n - 1)\,C(n - 1) = 2\,n + 2\,C(n - 1).$$

If we now collect the $C(n-1)$ terms in the last line, we get

$$n\,C(n) = 2\,n + (n+1)\,C(n-1).$$

Now, dividing both sides by, $n\,(n+1)$, gives

$$\frac{C(n)}{(n+1)} = \frac{2}{(n+1)} + \frac{C(n-1)}{n}.$$

The latter equation can be unrolled to yield

$$\frac{C(n)}{(n+1)} = \frac{2}{(n+1)} + \frac{2}{n} + \frac{2}{(n-1)} + \ldots + \frac{2}{3} + \frac{C(1)}{2}.$$

But, since $C(1) = 0$ from Eqs. 13.1, the last fraction $C(1)/2$ can be dropped, and the last line can be rearranged to yield

$$\frac{C(n)}{(n+1)} = 2\left[\frac{1}{n} + \frac{1}{(n-1)} + \ldots + \frac{1}{3} + \frac{1}{2} + \frac{1}{1}\right] + \frac{2}{(n+1)} - 2\left[\frac{1}{2} + \frac{1}{1}\right].$$

Now using the formula for the nth harmonic number, H_n, (from Equation A.32 of Appendix A), the last line simplifies to

$$\frac{C(n)}{(n+1)} = 2H_n + \frac{2}{(n+1)} - 3.$$

Multiplying both sides of the last line by $(n+1)$, and rearranging gives

$$C(n) = 2\,n\,H_n + 2\,H_n - 3\,n - 1.$$

But since H_n has the value, $\ln n + \gamma + O(1/n)$, (from Eq. A.32 of Appendix A), the last line above simplifies to

$$C(n) = 2\,n\,\ln n + O(n).$$

In the last formula, we can convert the natural logarithm, $\ln n$, to a base-2 logarithm, $\lg n$, using the conversion formula, $\ln n = (\ln 2)(\lg n) = 0.693\,\lg n$. This yields

$$C(n) \approx 1.39\,n\,\lg n + O(n). \tag{13.2}$$

Equation 13.2 allows us to infer that the O-notation for the average number of comparisons used by **QuickSort** is $O(n \log n)$, which is what we wanted to demonstrate.

The Worst Case for QuickSort

In the worst case, instead of the average case, QuickSort can take time $O(n^2)$ to sort n keys. This can happen when the pivot key for each partition is always chosen to be either the greatest or least key in the partition. In such a case, the partition process separates the original n keys in array, A, into a partition containing only one key and another partition containing $(n-1)$ keys. The $(n-1)$ keys are separated again into a partition containing one key and another containing $(n-2)$ keys, and so on. The total number of comparisons used in creating all of these partitions is a sum of the form: $2 + 3 + ... + (n-1) + n$, which is $O(n^2)$.

13.4 Review Questions

1. What does it mean to sort using a divide-and-conquer method?
2. How does the MergeSort method work?
3. Why is QuickSort an instance of a divide-and-conquer sorting method?

13.4 Exercises

1. Give an example of an array, A, that causes QuickSort to realize its worst case running time of $O(n^2)$.
2. One method of choosing the pivot key is to choose the median of the first, last, and middle keys in the array, A. (The median of three values is the middle value—for example, median(1,7,3) = 3, median(4,9,1) = 4, and median(1,3,3) = 3.) Under what conditions would it be advantageous to choose the pivot key using the "median of three" method?

13.5 Methods That Insert Keys and Keep Them Sorted

Learning Objectives

1. To learn two sorting methods, InsertionSort and TreeSort, which insert unsorted keys into an initially empty container, C, and keep them sorted at all times inside C.
2. To determine the efficiency of InsertionSort and TreeSort.

Some sorting methods are based on the idea of dividing the keys to be sorted into two collections: (a) a collection, U, of unsorted keys, yet to be sorted, and (b) a collection, S, of keys that have already been sorted and are to be maintained in sorted order.

the basic idea Initially, U is the entire set of unsorted keys, and S is empty. The idea is to remove keys, one-at-a-time, from U and to insert them in S, while maintaining the sorted order of keys in S. When the last key is removed from U and inserted into S, the process terminates.

The InsertionSort method uses subarrays of an array A to hold the sets of keys, S and U. The TreeSort method takes keys from U and inserts them one-at-a-time into a binary search tree, S. When U becomes empty, an InOrder traversal of tree S is performed to enumerate the keys in ascending order.

InsertionSort

The InsertionSort method uses the original array, A, to contain subarrays S and U, which sit side-by-side in A. In particular, S is a subarray at the left end of A, containing keys always arranged in ascending sorted order, and U is a subarray at the right end of A, containing keys yet to be sorted.

how InsertionSort works   At each stage of the InsertionSort process, a new key to insert, K, is detached from the left end of U, and is inserted into S. The way this new key is inserted is illustrated in Fig. 13.20. First, the insertion key, K, is removed from the left end of

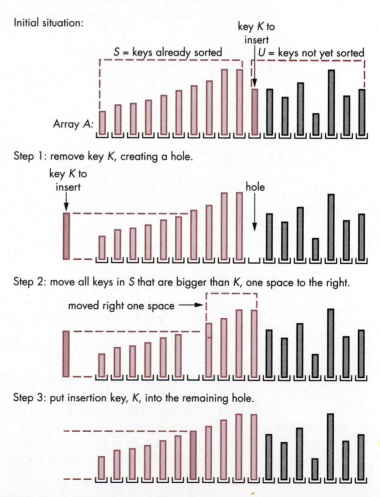

Figure 13.20 Inserting a Key During InsertionSort

```
     |    void InsertionSort(SortingArray A)
     |    {
     |        /* assume: typedef  enum  {false, true} Boolean; has been declared */
     |
5    |            int          i,j;
     |            KeyType      K;
     |            Boolean      NotFinished;
     |
     |
10   |        /* For each i in the range 1:n – 1, let key K be the key, A[i]. Then */
     |        /* insert K into the subarray A[0:i – 1] in ascending order */
     |
     |        for (i = 1;  i < n;  ++i) {
     |            /* Move each key bigger than K in A[0:i – 1] */
15   |            /* one space to the right */
     |            K = A[i];
     |            j = i;
     |            NotFinished = (A[j – 1] > K);
     |
20   |            while (NotFinished) {
     |                A[j] = A[j – 1];          /* move A[j –1] one space to the right */
     |                j – –;
     |                if (j > 0) {
     |                    NotFinished = (A[j – 1] > K);
25   |                } else {
     |                    NotFinished = false;
     |                }
     |            }
     |
30   |            /* Move key K into hole opened up by moving */
     |            /* previous keys to the right */
     |                A[j] = K;
     |        }
     |    }
```

Program 13.21 The InsertionSort Algorithm

U, creating a hole. Second, all keys in S bigger than K are moved right one space. Third, and finally, K is inserted into the remaining hole in S. This process is repeated until all keys in U are inserted in S, at which point S occupies the entire array A.

Program 13.21 gives the algorithm for InsertionSort.

Analysis of InsertionSort**

For each key $K == A[i]$, where $i = 1, 2, \ldots, n – 1$, Program 13.21 inserts K into the subarray $A[0:i – 1]$. The lengths of the respective subarrays, S, in which each K gets inserted are therefore $1, 2, \ldots, (n – 1)$. On the average, half of the keys in a given subarray, S, will be bigger than K, and half will be smaller than K. The bigger keys will have been moved to the right to allow K to be inserted, and during this process K will have been compared to each of the bigger ones, plus one additional key in S that is less than or equal to K, in order to stop the search for bigger ones to move

InsertionSort runs in time $O(n^2)$

rightward. This implies that, if there are j keys in S, then the number of comparisons, $C(j)$, will be $j/_2 + 1$.

Therefore to compute the average total number of comparisons used during the entire insertion sorting process to sort an array, A[0:$n - 1$], we need to evaluate the sum, $\Sigma_{(1 \leq j \leq (n - 1))}\ C(j) = \Sigma_{(1 \leq j \leq (n - 1))}\ (j/_2 + 1) = (^1/_2)\ \Sigma_{(1 \leq j \leq (n - 1))}\ j + (n - 1) = (^1/_4)n^2 + (^3/_4)n - 1$. Consequently, InsertionSort runs in time $O(n^2)$.

TreeSort

In TreeSort, you take the unsorted keys in the original array, A[0:$n - 1$], and insert them into an initially empty binary search tree, S, one at a time. After all keys in A have been inserted into S, you perform an InOrder traversal of S, reading S's keys off in ascending order during the traversal, and you move them back into A in ascending order.

Analysis of TreeSort**

From Table 9.40, if S is a binary search tree containing i keys, it takes approximately $2.77 \lg i - 1.7$ comparisons to insert a new key, K, into S, since the number of comparisons required for insertion is identical to the number of comparisons required for an unsuccessful search.

Consequently, to compute the average total number of comparisons, $C(n)$, used to insert all keys originally in A into S, when S has sizes, 0, 1, 2, ..., $(n - 1)$, we have to compute $\Sigma_{(1 \leq i \leq (n - 1))}\ (2.77 \lg i - 1.7)$. This is the same as

$$2.77\ \Sigma_{(1 \leq i \leq (n - 1))}\ \lg i - 1.7(n - 1).$$

TreeSort runs in time $O(n \log n)$

An approximation for the sum of the logarithms $\lg n! = \Sigma \lg i$ can be obtained by taking logarithms of both sides of Stirling's Approximation in Fig. 13.3 and converting from natural logarithms to base-2 logarithms. Thus, from the following facts

$$\ln n! \approx n \ln n + O(n), \text{ and}$$
$$\lg n! = (\ln n! / \ln 2),$$

we can deduce that $C(n)$ is $O(n \log n)$.

13.5 Review Questions

1. Give a rough description of how InsertionSort works.
2. How does TreeSort work?
3. Give the O-notations for the average running times of InsertionSort and TreeSort.

1. Can you find and fix the bug in the following incorrect version of **InsertionSort**? [*Hint:* Suppose array index range checking is turned on.]

```
   |    void InsertionSort(SortingArray A, int m, int n)
   |    {
   |        int i; KeyType C;
   |
 5 |        if (n > m) {
   |
   |            /* Insertion sort the subarray A[m:n – 1]. */
   |                InsertionSort(A,m,n – 1);
   |
10 |            /* Move each key bigger than A[n] in A[m:n – 1] */
   |            /* one space to the right */
   |                C = A[n];
   |                i = n;
   |                while ( (A[i – 1] > C) && (i > m) ) {
15 |                    A[i] = A[i – 1];
   |                    i – –;
   |                }
   |
   |            /* Move A[n] into hole opened by moving previous keys */
20 |                A[i] = C;
   |
   |        }
   |
   |    }
```

2. Analyze how many keys get moved on the average in **InsertionSort**. Is this number greater than or less than the corresponding number of times that keys are moved on the average in **SelectionSort**?

13.6 O(n) Methods—Address Calculation Sorting

Learning Objectives

1. To learn that despite the *n* log *n* barrier on comparison-based sorting methods, there exist still faster O(n) sorting methods, not based on the use of comparisons.
2. To explore two O(n) methods, ProxmapSort and RadixSort.

the basic idea

In sorting by address calculation, you define a mapping on the keys to be sorted, which sends them into a location in the output array that is expected to be close to what the final sorted position will be. Some local rearrangement in the vicinity of the final location of each key may be necessary to move keys into their actual final locations.

Since you are using a mapping on keys, instead of comparisons of keys with one another, to send keys into locations close to their final sorted locations, the techniques are not "comparison-based." Hence, the $n \log n$ barrier for comparison-based methods may not apply.

ProxmapSort

In proxmap sorting, you compute a "proximity map," or *proxmap* for short, which indicates, for each key, K, the beginning of a subarray of the array A in which K will reside in final sorted order. You then enumerate the keys in A and insertion sort them into their final subarrays. We proceed by example in order to help reveal the main ideas.

Let's suppose we have an array A of 13 keys to sort, as shown in Fig. 13.22. You can see that the keys used in A are decimal numbers ranging in value from a low of 0.4 to a high of 11.5. When we map a key, K, to an array index, i, we will use the simple mapping of rounding K down to the next lower integer by taking the floor of K. That is, MapKey(K) == $\lfloor K \rfloor$. For example, MapKey(3.7) == 3, MapKey(1.2) == 1, and MapKey(0.4) == 0. (While designed to be easy to use and easy to follow for the purposes of our simple example, this mapping is not a good one, in general. We will discuss how to design effective MapKey functions for actual examples later on in this section.)

If we were to use i == MapKey(K) to send K into a location, A[i], in array A where we kept a linked list of keys, sorted in ascending order, we could scan through the original unsorted array, A, and send its keys into a collection of sorted linked lists, as shown in Fig. 13.23.

For example, starting with the first key, A[0] == 6.7, of Fig. 13.22, we map the key, 6.7, into position 6, (using MapKey(6.7) == 6), and we insert 6.7 on an empty list in position 6. Sometime later, we encounter key, A[11] == 6.1, and map it also into position 6, (using MapKey(6.1) == 6). Here, we insert it into the linked list that already contains the key 6.7. Since each linked list is to be kept in sorted order, we

inserting keys into sorted linked lists

insert 6.1 before 6.7 on this linked list in position 6. You can see that the remaining linked lists in Fig. 13.23 were formed by inserting each key, A[i], for i in 0:12, into the linked list in position, MapKey(A[i]), and keeping the keys in each linked list in ascending order. If we now make a pass in left-to-right order along the diagram of Fig. 13.23 and enumerate the keys in each linked list in the order given by each list, we would enumerate the keys of the original array A in ascending sorted order.

insertion locations

Now, ProxmapSort does not use linked lists such as are shown in Fig. 13.23. Instead, it reserves, in advance, subarrays of the array A for the keys in each of the linked lists, and it insertion-sorts these keys into the reserved subarrays. For example, the keys in the linked list containing (1.1, 1.2, 1.8) of Fig. 13.23 would eventually be

i =	0	1	2	3	4	5	6	7	8	9	10	11	12
A[i] = [6.7,	5.9,	8.4,	1.2,	7.3,	3.7,	11.5,	1.1,	4.8,	0.4,	10.5,	6.1,	1.8]

Figure 13.22 Initial Unsorted Array, A, for Use in ProxmapSort

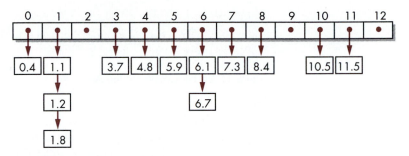

Figure 13.23 Sorted Linked Lists of Keys

inserted in the subarray $A[1:3]$ of A, and this subarray of A is reserved for each of the keys, 1.1, 1.2, and 1.8, using location $A[1]$ as the future *insertion location* for each key in (1.1, 1.2, 1.8). Similarly, the list of keys, (6.1, 6.7), will map into the future reserved subarray, $A[7:8]$, using $A[7]$ as the future insertion location for keys 6.1 and 6.7.

The actual *proxmap* (which is short for "proximity map"), is a mapping that can be used to send each key K into the beginning location of the reserved subarray of A where it will be inserted in ascending order. When all keys have been mapped into their respective reserved subarrays and have been inserted in ascending order, the array A contains the final sorted arrangement of the original keys. The **proxmap** is computed in advance of moving any keys and is based on *hit counts* derived from mapping keys, K, in A, using **MapKey**(K), during a preliminary pass through A.

hit counts

Let's now proceed, step-by-step, with our example to see how we compute (a) *hit counts*, (b) the *proxmap*, and (c) the future *insertion locations* for each key, K, in the original array, A. After computing the future insertion locations, we then begin to move keys to their reserved, final subarrays, where we insertion-sort them to complete the final phase of the **ProxmapSort** process. In short, in **ProxmapSort**, we first compute in advance where the reserved subarrays containing each final sorted key will lie. Then we move each key into its final reserved subarray where it is inserted in ascending order (using some local insertion sorting inside the reserved subarray).

First, we compute the hit counts. Suppose H is an array of 13 positions, $H[0:12]$, each of which initially contains zero ($H[i] == 0$ for i in 0:12). If we execute the for-statement

```
/* compute hit counts, H[i], for each position, i, in A */
    for (i = 0; i < 13; ++i) {
        j = MapKey(A[i]);
        H[j] ++;
    }
```

then each location $H[i]$ will contain the number of keys in A that map into location i. Figure 13.24 shows the hit counts corresponding to the keys in Fig. 13.22. You can see that the hit count in each location, $H[i]$, is identical to the number of keys on the linked list in position i of the diagram in Fig. 13.23.

```
i =   0    1    2    3    4    5    6     7    8    9    10    11   12
A[i] = [6.7,  5.9,  8.4,  1.2,  7.3,  3.7,  11.5,  1.1,  4.8,  0.4,  10.5,  6.1,  1.8]
H[i] = [ 1    3    0    1    1    1    2     1    1    0    1     1    0 ]
```

Figure 13.24 Hit Counts for the Array A

computing the proxmap

From the hit counts, $H[i]$, we compute a proxmap, $P[i]$, where each entry $P[i]$ gives the location of the beginning of the future reserved subarray of A that will contain keys, K, mapping to location, i, under the mapping MapKey(K) == i. The proxmap, $P[i]$, is shown in Fig. 13.25.

For instance, all keys, such as (6.7, 6.1), which map to $P[6]$ find that $P[6]$ == 7, meaning that 7 is the location of the beginning of the reserved subarray where (6.7, 6.1) will both be inserted in the future. A for-statement that computes the proxmap, $P[i]$, starting with the hit counts, $H[i]$, and using a running total is as follows:

```
/* convert hit counts to a proxmap */
    RunningTotal = 0;                              /* initialize a running total to 0 */
    for (i = 0; i < 13; ++i)  {
        if (H[i] > 0) {
            P[i] = RunningTotal;
            RunningTotal += H[i];
        }
    }
```

You can see how executing this for-statement on the hit counts, $H[i]$, in Fig. 13.25 produces the values of the proxmap, $P[i]$, (assuming the values of $P[i]$ were initially 0).

The final step is to compute future insertion locations, $L[i]$, for the key, K, in each position, $A[i]$, of the original unsorted array, A. A for-statement which does this is

```
/* compute insertion locations, L[i], for each key, K == A[i], in array A */
    for (i = 0; i < 13; ++i)  {
        L[i] = P[ MapKey(A[i]) ];
    }
```

Figure 13.26 gives the future insertion locations, $L[i]$, which were computed using this process. (In the ProxmapSort algorithm given later, we will actually save the locations MapKey($A[i]$) when they are first computed, so we do not have to compute them twice in case the MapKey function turns out to be expensive to compute. Thus the for-statement above is a bit oversimplified and is intended only to help convey the general flavor of what needs to be accomplished.)

```
i =   0    1    2    3    4    5    6     7    8    9    10    11   12
A[i] = [6.7,  5.9,  8.4,  1.2,  7.3,  3.7,  11.5,  1.1,  4.8,  0.4,  10.5,  6.1,  1.8]
H[i] = [ 1    3    0    1    1    1    2     1    1    0    1     1    0 ]
P[i] = [ 0    1    0    4    5    6    7     9    10    0    11    12   0 ]
```

Figure 13.25 Proxmap for Array A

$i =$	0	1	2	3	4	5	6	7	8	9	10	11	12
$A[i] = [$	6.7,	5.9,	8.4,	1.2,	7.3,	3.7,	11.5,	1.1,	4.8,	0.4,	10.5,	6.1,	1.8]
$P[i] = [$	0	1	0	4	5	6	7	9	10	0	11	12	0]
$L[i] = [$	7	6	10	1	9	4	12	1	5	0	11	7	1]

Figure 13.26 Future Insertion Locations, $L[i]$, for each Key, $A[i]$

For example, the keys 6.7 and 6.1 in positions $A[0]$ and $A[11]$ each have future inser-tion locations $L[0] == 7$ and $L[11] == 7$, since they will both be moved into the reserved subarray $A[7:8]$ for insertion into final placement in sorted order. Similarly, the keys 1.2, 1.1, and 1.8, in positions $A[3]$, $A[7]$, and $A[12]$, each have future inser-tion locations of 1 (i.e., $L[3] == L[7] == L[12] == 1$), since they will each be mapped into the beginning location $A[1]$ of the reserved subarray, $A[1:3]$, for future insertion into final sorted order.

The final phase of ProxmapSort consists in moving each key, $A[i]$, in the original unsorted array A into the location $L[i]$ at the beginning of its reserved future subarray, and in inserting it in ascending order into the sequence of keys already occupying its reserved subarray. If we had two copies of A, say A_1 and A_2, where A_1 was the original unsorted array, and A_2 was an initially empty copy of A designed to accumulate the keys of A in final sorted order as they were being inserted, then we could map each key, $A_1[i]$, into its insertion location, $L[i]$, in A_2, and insert it in ascending order into the sequence of keys beginning at $L[i]$ in A_2. For example, Fig. 13.27 shows A_1 and A_2 before the process of moving keys begins. Figure 13.28 shows A_1 and A_2 after the first 7 keys have been moved, and Fig. 13.29 shows A_1 and A_2 after the first 11 keys have been moved.

To obtain Fig. 13.28, starting with the situation shown in Fig. 13.27, we move key $A_1[0] == 6.7$ into location $L[0] == 7$ in A_2, we move 5.9 into location 6 of A_2, and so forth, until moving key $A_1[6] == 11.5$ into location 12 of A_2.

The next key to be moved is key $A_1[7] == 1.1$, which is supposed to go into loca-tion $L[7] == 1$ of array A_2. This is an interesting situation, since location $A_2[1]$ already contains the key 1.2, from a previous insertion. What happens is that the key 1.1 is insertion-sorted into the reserved subarray, $A_2[1:3]$ beginning at location $A_2[1]$. Recall that the subarray $A_2[1:3]$ has been reserved by the proxmap computation to handle the keys, 1.2, 1.1, and 1.8. At this particular moment, the second of the three final keys that will occupy $A_2[1:3]$ is being inserted. When 1.1 is inserted into the sequence of keys in ascending order beginning at $A_2[1]$, the situation that results is

$i =$	0	1	2	3	4	5	6	7	8	9	10	11	12
$A_1[i] = [$	6.7,	5.9,	8.4,	1.2,	7.3,	3.7,	11.5,	1.1,	4.8,	0.4,	10.5,	6.1,	1.8]
$L[i] = [$	7	6	10	1	9	4	12	1	5	0	11	7	1]
$A_2[i] = [$	–.–,	–.–,	–.–,	–.–,	–.–,	–.–,	–.–,	–.–,	–.–,	–.–,	–.–,	–.–,	–.–]

Figure 13.27 Before Moving any Keys into Their Reserved Subarrays

(margin note) final phase: moving the keys

(margin note) inserting keys into a common reserved subarray

$i =$	0	1	2	3	4	5	6	7	8	9	10	11	12
$A_1[i] =$ [6.7,	5.9,	8.4,	1.2,	7.3,	3.7,	11.5,	1.1,	4.8,	0.4,	10.5,	6.1,	1.8]
$L[i] =$ [7	6	10	1	9	4	12	1	5	0	11	7	1]
$A_2[i] =$ [–.–,	1.2,	–.–,	–.–,	3.7,	–.–,	5.9,	6.7,	–.–,	7.3,	8.4,	–.–,	11.5]

Figure 13.28 After Moving 7 Keys into Their Reserved Subarrays

$i =$	0	1	2	3	4	5	6	7	8	9	10	11	12
$A_1[i] =$ [6.7,	5.9,	8.4,	1.2,	7.3,	3.7,	11.5,	1.1,	4.8,	0.4,	10.5,	6.1,	1.8]
$L[i] =$ [7	6	10	1	9	4	12	1	5	0	11	7	1]
$A_2[i] =$ [0.4,	1.1,	1.2,	–.–,	3.7,	4.8,	5.9,	6.7,	–.–,	7.3,	8.4,	10.5,	11.5]

Figure 13.29 After Moving 11 Keys into Their Reserved Subarrays

shown in subarray $A_2[1:2]$ of Fig. 13.29. Note that the key 1.2 has been moved one space to the right to accommodate the newly inserted key 1.1.

When the final two keys $A_1[11] == 6.1$, and $A_1[12] == 1.8$ are inserted into A_2, at insertion locations 7 and 1 respectively, the insertion-sorting process causes 6.1 to be inserted into location $A_2[7]$ after displacing 6.7 one space to the right into $A_2[8]$ and causes 1.8 to be inserted into location $A_2[3]$. The array A_2 is now in final sorted order, as shown in Fig. 13.30.

Now, actually, the version of **ProxmapSort** given in Program 13.32 does not use two copies of the array A, as illustrated in Figs. 13.27 through 13.30. Instead, **ProxmapSort** rearranges the keys of A in place. This is called an *in situ* rearrangement (from the Latin words *in situ*, which mean "in place").

Some slight trickery is needed to accomplish this which involves marking each entry in A with a *status code* indicating whether it is *empty*, *not-yet-moved*, or already *moved*, and then playing a game resembling "musical chairs," in which when a key, K_1, is inserted into its future reserved subarray and displaces another key, K_2, which has not been moved, then K_2 is the very next key to be moved. If, however, K_1 lands in an empty slot that has been vacated by removing a key previously moved, K_1 is placed in the empty slot, and a left-to-right scan is undertaken to find some new key that has not yet been moved.

Figure 13.31 shows the placement of successive keys in A using this *in situ* rearrangement game of "musical chairs."

$i =$	0	1	2	3	4	5	6	7	8	9	10	11	12
$A_1[i] =$ [6.7,	5.9,	8.4,	1.2,	7.3,	3.7,	11.5,	1.1,	4.8,	0.4,	10.5,	6.1,	1.8]
$L[i] =$ [7	6	10	1	9	4	12	1	5	0	11	7	1]
$A_2[i] =$ [0.4,	1.1,	1.2,	1.8,	3.7,	4.8,	5.9,	6.1,	6.7,	7.3,	8.4,	10.5,	11.5]

Figure 13.30 After Moving All Keys into Their Reserved Subarrays

Original Unsorted Array A

0	1	2	3	4	5	6	7	8	9	10	11	12
[6.7 ,	5.9 ,	8.4 ,	1.2 ,	7.3 ,	3.7 ,	11.5,	1.1 ,	4.8 ,	0.4 ,	10.5,	6.1 ,	1.8]

Hit Counts

1	3	0	1	1	1	2	1	1	0	1	1	0

Proxmap

0	1	0	4	5	6	7	9	10	0	11	12	0

Insertion Locations

7	6	10	1	9	4	12	1	5	0	11	7	1

Successive Stages of Insertion at One Key per Stage

0	1	2	3	4	5	6	7	8	9	10	11	12
[--- ,	--- ,	--- ,	--- ,	--- ,	--- ,	--- ,	--- ,	--- ,	--- ,	--- ,	--- ,	---]
[--- ,	--- ,	--- ,	--- ,	--- ,	--- ,	--- ,	6.7 ,	--- ,	--- ,	--- ,	--- ,	---]
[--- ,	1.1 ,	--- ,	--- ,	--- ,	--- ,	--- ,	6.7 ,	--- ,	--- ,	--- ,	--- ,	---]
[--- ,	1.1 ,	--- ,	--- ,	--- ,	--- ,	5.9 ,	6.7 ,	--- ,	--- ,	--- ,	--- ,	---]
[--- ,	1.1 ,	--- ,	--- ,	--- ,	--- ,	5.9 ,	6.7 ,	--- ,	--- ,	--- ,	--- ,	11.5]
[--- ,	1.1 ,	1.8 ,	--- ,	--- ,	--- ,	5.9 ,	6.7 ,	--- ,	--- ,	--- ,	--- ,	11.5]
[--- ,	1.1 ,	1.8 ,	--- ,	--- ,	--- ,	5.9 ,	6.7 ,	--- ,	--- ,	8.4 ,	--- ,	11.5]
[--- ,	1.1 ,	1.8 ,	--- ,	--- ,	--- ,	5.9 ,	6.7 ,	--- ,	--- ,	8.4 ,	10.5,	11.5]
[--- ,	1.1 ,	1.8 ,	--- ,	--- ,	--- ,	5.9 ,	6.1 ,	6.7 ,	--- ,	8.4 ,	10.5,	11.5]
[--- ,	1.1 ,	1.8 ,	--- ,	--- ,	4.8 ,	5.9 ,	6.1 ,	6.7 ,	--- ,	8.4 ,	10.5,	11.5]
[--- ,	1.1 ,	1.8 ,	--- ,	3.7 ,	4.8 ,	5.9 ,	6.1 ,	6.7 ,	--- ,	8.4 ,	10.5,	11.5]
[--- ,	1.1 ,	1.8 ,	--- ,	3.7 ,	4.8 ,	5.9 ,	6.1 ,	6.7 ,	7.3 ,	8.4 ,	10.5,	11.5]
[0.4 ,	1.1 ,	1.8 ,	--- ,	3.7 ,	4.8 ,	5.9 ,	6.1 ,	6.7 ,	7.3 ,	8.4 ,	10.5,	11.5]
[0.4 ,	1.1 ,	1.2 ,	--- ,	3.7 ,	4.8 ,	5.9 ,	6.1 ,	6.7 ,	7.3 ,	8.4 ,	10.5,	11.5]
[0.4 ,	1.1 ,	1.2 ,	1.8 ,	3.7 ,	4.8 ,	5.9 ,	6.1 ,	6.7 ,	7.3 ,	8.4 ,	10.5,	11.5]

Final Sorted Array A

0	1	2	3	4	5	6	7	8	9	10	11	12
[0.4 ,	1.1 ,	1.2 ,	1.8 ,	3.7 ,	4.8 ,	5.9 ,	6.1 ,	6.7 ,	7.3 ,	8.4 ,	10.5,	11.5]

Figure 13.31 *In Situ* Rearrangement of Keys in *A*

Note, for example, what happens on the first few rearrangements, in Fig. 13.31. Assume that the proxmap and the future insertion locations have been computed, and that the algorithm has reached the stage where it is ready to move keys in A by the musical chairs rearrangement process. The first key to be considered is the not-yet-moved key, $A[0] == 6.7$. This is moved into location 7 (using the future insertion location $L[0] == 7$). However, when 6.7 is placed into location $A[7]$, it displaces the not-yet-moved key, 1.1. Thus the displaced key 1.1 is the next key to be moved (as if it had been bumped out of its seat in a musical chairs game). When 1.1 is inserted into its future location, $A[1]$, it bumps the key 5.9, which was previously located in $A[1]$. So key 5.9 is the next key to be moved, and so on.

inserting keys by the
musical chairs process

The details of this process, which are somewhat subtle, are given in Program 13.32. Before looking at this program, however, we have to redesign the items in array A, to hold new information in addition to the keys to be sorted, such as the status flags, the future insertion locations, and the values of the proxmap. We do this by defining a ProxmapSortingArray to replace the simple SortingArray used in the earlier comparison-based sorting methods. Each ProxmapSortingArray is an array of n *slots*, where each slot is a struct having a Status member, two Proxmap and InsertionLoc members containing integers, and a Key member, containing the key to be sorted. The following C declarations define these new data types for use in ProxmapSort:

```
/*symbolic constant and type definitions used in ProxmapSort */

#define n AnyArbitrarySize

typedef   enum {Empty, NotYetMoved, Moved} OccupantStatus;

typedef   struct {
              OccupantStatus  Status;
              int             Proxmap;
              int             InsertionLoc;
              KeyType         Key;
          } Slot;

typedef   Slot  ProxmapSortingArray[n];
```

In Program 13.32, we have economized on the use of time and storage a bit by (a) using the Proxmap member of each slot to store the *hit counts* before they are converted to a proxmap, instead of defining and using a separate hit count member in each slot, and (b) saving the values of MapKey(A[i].Key) in the InsertionLoc members of each slot, so they need not be recomputed (at possibly considerable expense) during the later computation of the insertion locations. This allows us to compute MapKey(A[i].Key) only once for each key during the execution of the program.

saving time and storage

Designing the MapKey Function

The function MapKey(K) should be designed to map keys, K, chosen from the full range of possible keys, onto the entire set of array indexes for array A. Let's look at two cases to see how MapKey(K) can be designed properly.

```
void ProxmapSort(ProxmapSortingArray A)
{
        /* assume: typedef  enum  {false, true} Boolean; has been declared */

        int             i, j, RunningTotal, TempInt;
        KeyType         KeyToInsert, TempKey;
        Boolean         NotInserted;

        /* Initialize Status and Proxmap */
        for (i = 0; i < n; ++i) {
                A[i].Proxmap = 0;             /* initialize all Proxmap entries to zero */
                A[i].Status = NotYetMoved;          /* initialize status of each slot */
        }

        /* Count hits when keys are mapped into MapKey locations */
        for (i = 0; i < n; ++i) {
                j = MapKey(A[i].Key);
                A[i].InsertionLoc = j;             /* save value of MapKey for later use */
                A[j].Proxmap++;                 /* store hit counts in Proxmap field */
        }

        /* Convert hit counts to a Proxmap */
        RunningTotal = 0;
        for (i = 0; i < n; ++i) {
                if (A[i].Proxmap > 0) {                  /* any nonzero hit count is */
                        TempInt = A[i].Proxmap;        /* converted to a proxmap entry */
                        A[i].Proxmap = RunningTotal;         /* by substituting the */
                        RunningTotal += TempInt;             /* running total */
                }
        }

        /* Compute insertion locations */
        for (i = 0; i < n; ++i) {
                A[i].InsertionLoc = A[A[i].InsertionLoc].Proxmap;
        }

        /* Now, A[i].InsertionLoc gives the insertion location for A[i].Key */
        /* and A[i].Status is NotYetMoved for all i in 0:n − 1 */

        /* Rearrange A[i] in situ in A into ascending sorted order */
        for (i = 0; i < n; ++i) {

                /* Find next key in ascending order of i that is NotYetMoved */
                if (A[i].Status == NotYetMoved) {
                        j = A[i].InsertionLoc;
                        KeyToInsert = A[i].Key;       /* pick up A[i]'s Key as KeyToInsert */
                        A[i].Status = Empty;      /* and plan to insert it in A[j], where j is */
                        NotInserted = true;                  /* its insertion location */
```

Program 13.32 ProxmapSort (continued)

Program 13.32 **ProxmapSort** (continued)

```
50 |                    while (NotInserted) {
   |                        if (A[j].Status == NotYetMoved)  {
   |
   |                            TempKey = A[j].Key;              /* swap KeyToInsert */
   |                            A[j].Key = KeyToInsert;               /* with A[j]'s key. */
55 |                            KeyToInsert = TempKey;  /* mark A[j] as moved, and */
   |                            A[j].Status = Moved;/* plan to insert the KeyToInsert */
   |                            j = A[j].InsertionLoc;        /* in its insertion location, j */
   |
   |                        } else if (A[j].Status == Moved) {     /* insertion sort the */
60 |                                                               /* KeyToInsert */
   |                            if (KeyToInsert < A[j].Key) {    /* in the subarray of A */
   |                                                           /* beginning at j. If */
   |                                TempKey = A[j].Key;   /* KeyToInsert < A[j].Key */
   |                                A[j].Key = KeyToInsert;    /* swap KeyToInsert */
65 |                                KeyToInsert = TempKey;       /* with A[j]'s key */
   |                            }
   |
   |                            j ++;                    /* and move to next Key at A[j+1] */
   |
70 |                        } else {                                /* A[j].Status == Empty */
   |                            A[j].Key = KeyToInsert;             /* insert KeyToInsert */
   |                            A[j].Status = Moved;                /* in the empty entry */
   |                            NotInserted = false;
   |                        }
75 |                    }
   |                }
   |            }
   |        }
```

First, suppose the keys, K, are floating point numbers in the range $0 \le K < 1$, and suppose that the index range of array $A[0{:}n-1]$ is $0 \le i < n$. Then, a good definition for **MapKey**(K) is

MapKey = floor(n * K);   /* where floor(x) == $\lfloor x \rfloor$ */

This mapping will send the key K == 0.0 onto 0, and will send the key K == 0.99999 onto $n-1$ (provided $n \le 100{,}000$). A key value of 0.50 will tend to map close to 50 percent of the way between 0 and $n-1$, and a key value of 0.75 will tend to map close to 75 percent of the way between 0 and $n-1$.

Now let's suppose that our keys are three-letter airport codes, such as ACK (for Nantucket, Massachusetts), MEX (for Mexico City, Mexico), or ZRH (for Zürich, Switzerland). We could consider the three-letter airport codes to be base-26 numbers, chosen from a range of keys having a maximum value of ZZZ_{26} == 17575 and a minimum value of AAA_{26} == 0. The value of the key, K, as a base-26 number is given by Program 13.33, where it is assumed that the type **AirportCodeKey** is defined by **char AirportCodeKey[4]**.

```
  |    int value(char L)
  |    {
  |        return (int)(L) − (int)('A');        /* returns value of the letter 'L', base 26 */
  |    }
5 |
  |    int Base26Value(AirportCodeKey K)
  |    {
  |        return value(K[0])*26*26 +  value(K[1])*26 +  value(K[2]);
  |    }
```

Program 13.33 Base-26 Value of an Airport Code Key

Using Program 13.33, we get the following values:

```
Base26Value('AAA')  =        0
Base26Value('ZZZ')  =    17575
Base26Value('ACK')  =       62
Base26Value('MEX')  =     8239
Base26Value('ZRH')  =    17349
```

We can map an airport code, K, into a real number, $r(K)$, in the range $0 \leq r(K) < 1$, by dividing K's base-26 value by one plus the base-26 value of 'ZZZ' according to the formula

$$r(K) = \text{Base26Value}(K) \, / \, (1 + \text{Base26Value}('ZZZ')).$$

In other words, we could convert the base-26 values of ACK, MEX, and ZRH into floating point numbers in the range $0 \leq r(K) < 1$ by dividing their base-26 values by 17576 (which equals 26^3). This yields $r(\text{ACK}) == 0.00353$, $r(\text{MEX}) == 0.46876$, and $r(\text{ZRH}) == 0.98708$.

Suppose, now, that the array, A[0:14], had $n == 15$ positions in it, and that we wanted to map ACK, MEX, and ZRH into locations in A, using a suitable **MapKey** function. We could then use the assignment statement

    MapKey = floor(n * r(K));   /* where floor(x) == $\lfloor x \rfloor$ */

to accomplish this. In this case, **MapKey**(ACK) == 0, **MapKey**(MEX) == 7, and **MapKey**(ZRH) == 14. This seems acceptable, since (a) we wanted ACK to map into a location near the beginning of A (because ACK is near the beginning of its key space in key order), (b) we wanted MEX to map somewhere near the middle of A (since MEX is near the middle of its key space in key order), and (c) we wanted ZRH to map to a location near the end of A (since ZRH is near the end of its key space in key order).

However, in the interest of efficiency, a better idea for computing **MapKey**(K), for an airport code key, K, is to compute a *scale factor*, s, consisting of the size, n, of the index range of array A, divided by 26^3, the number of possible keys in the key space. That is, $s == n/26^3$. After the scale factor, s, is precomputed, **MapKey**(K) can be computed simply by using the assignment statement

using a single scale factor

    MapKey = floor(s * Base26Value(K));   /* where s is a scale factor */

In the case of the array $A[0:14]$ with $n == 15$ positions and three-letter airport codes, K, taken as base-26 numbers, the scale factor is $s = 0.000853437$.

It is important that MapKey(K) be computed efficiently (in relation to the cost of comparing keys) in order to make ProxmapSort competitive in running time with the best comparison-based sorting methods.

Analysis of ProxmapSort**

In the worst case, ProxmapSort can take time $O(n^2)$. This occurs, for example, when all keys in A have an equal value, forcing MapKey to map them into the same location in A. In this case, the future subarray reserved for inserting all of these equal-valued keys becomes the entire array, and all keys are insertion-sorted into A, which takes time $O(n^2)$.

a nonrigorous argument

Even though a rigorous mathematical argument for why ProxmapSort runs on the average in time $O(n)$ is beyond the scope of this book, a rough, partial, and intuitive argument as to why this is so can be offered.

Suppose that the array A contains keys, K, drawn randomly and uniformly from the space of all possible keys, and suppose that MapKey(K) is defined to map keys onto the full range, $0{:}n - 1$, of index locations of array, A. If we are extremely lucky, all unsorted keys in the original unsorted array A will map onto separate locations in the final sorted array, A. In this case, the insertion locations for rearrangement of the unsorted keys in A will all be separate, and four linear passes through A (to compute hit counts, to compute the proxmap, to compute insertion locations, and finally, to relocate keys) will suffice to sort A.

However, we are rarely so lucky as to have hit counts that are all 1. Instead, some hit counts will be zero, and others will be greater than 1. In the case of hit counts greater than one, such as, $c > 1$, the proxmap will reserve a subarray of c locations in A where c keys will eventually be insertion-sorted, at a cost of $O(c^2)$.

In the case of an array A with n keys chosen randomly and uniformly, we can choose a value of c, such that it almost never occurs that some subset of c keys will collide at the same MapKey location to create a hit count of c. For example, if we have $n = 1000$ keys in A, then it is of very small probability that a hit count will ever be greater than $c = 50$. So suppose that we divide the $n = 1000$ locations into $n/c = 20$ separate reserved subarrays, and that we insertion-sort each of the $n/c = 20$ subarrays. This would cost $(n/c) \, O(c^2)$, since each such reserved subarray takes time $O(c^2)$ to sort, using insertion sorting. Supposing that the $O(c^2)$ function actually required is of the form: $O(c^2) = a \, c^2 + b \, c + f$, then $(n/c) \, O(c^2) = (n/c) \, (a \, c^2 + b \, c + f) = (n \, a \, c + n \, b + n \, f \, / \, c)$, which is $O(n)$.

In the average case, where the proxmap for the array A normally divides A up into reserved subarrays smaller than subarrays of size c, each such smaller reserved subarray, of size $d < c$, will be insertion-sorted in time $a \, d^2 + b \, d + f$, which will be less than $a \, c^2 + b \, c + f$. Moreover, the total time to sort an array A composed of smaller reserved subarrays will always be less than the time to sort an array A composed of larger reserved subarrays.

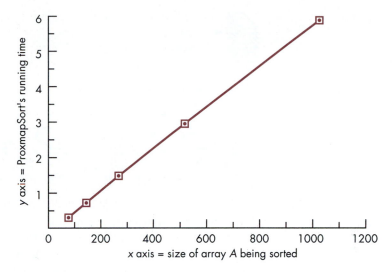

Figure 13.34 Graph of ProxmapSort's Running Times

Since, in the improbable case of n/c subarrays of size c, we can sort A in total time O(n), it follows that we can sort any collection of smaller subarrays also in time at most O(n). In conclusion, in the average case, **Proxmap** must run in time O(n)—because only could an unusual nonaverage case be worse than the case of sorting n/c subarrays of size c, in order to exceed the O(n) barrier established for sorting n/c subarrays of size c.

If you graph the actual measured sorting times for **ProxmapSort** (given later in Table 13.47 in Section 13.8) reproduced here

n =	64	128	256	512	1024
ProxmapSort	0.38	0.75	1.51	3.00	5.99

you will find that they actually lie very close to the straight line shown in Fig. 13.34. This suggests that the O(n) characterization of **ProxmapSort**'s sorting time can indeed be verified experimentally. For example, graphing the actual measured times given above, results in the graph shown in Fig. 13.34.

RadixSort

how the card sorter works

Radix sorting is a process that was used on electromechanical, punched-card sorting equipment of an earlier generation. To get a rough idea of how it works, let's consider an example. Suppose we have a set of 3-digit numerical keys, where each 3-digit key is punched on a separate card in a deck of cards. The deck of cards to be sorted is placed in a hopper on the card-sorter machine, and cards to be sorted are fed, one at a time, from the bottom of the deck. A crank on the sorting machine can be set to

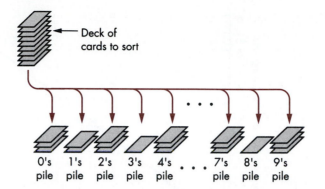

Figure 13.35 Card Sorter

sort either the first digit, the middle digit, or the last digit, of the 3-digit key. Suppose C is the card on the bottom of the deck that is currently being read by the sorting machine. If the digit currently selected in C is a 0, then C is fed mechanically to a bin where it drops down on top of the pile of cards containing 0's digits. This is called the *0's pile* in Fig. 13.35. Similarly, if C's currently selected digit, *d*, is 1 through 9, it is fed to the respective bin numbered *d*, where it drops on top of the respective *digit-d-pile*.

When the entire deck is processed, the piles of cards in the digit bins are stacked to reconstitute a new deck, with the 9's pile on the bottom, the 8's pile next to the bottom, and so on, until the 0's pile is placed on top of the deck. This deck is fed through the sorting machine another time, with a different digit selected for sorting. By a process that we will illustrate in a moment, the entire original unsorted deck can be sorted in three passes.

how RadixSort works

Now, let's study an example in which we have used columns of 3-digit numbers to represent the keys on the cards in the decks. Figure 13.36 shows the various stages

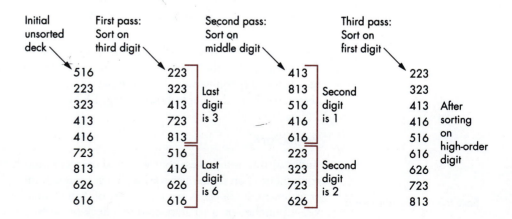

Figure 13.36 Stages of the RadixSorting Process

of the **RadixSort** process. An unsorted deck of keys is shown as the leftmost column of 3-digit numbers. On the first pass through the deck, the third (or least significant) digit is selected for sorting. Taking keys one at a time from the bottom of the deck and passing them through the sorting machine of Fig. 13.35, you can see that the keys will end up either in the 6's pile or the 3's pile, since the keys end either in 3 or in 6. After the entire deck has been processed in bottom-to-top order, the keys in the 3's pile are placed on top of the keys in the 6's pile, to give the new deck shown in column 2 of Fig. 13.36.

On the second pass, the middle digit is selected, and the keys are sorted so that the keys with a middle 1's digit are on top of those with a middle 2's digit in the deck that results (shown as the third column in Fig. 13.36). On the third and final pass, the first digit is selected for sorting, and the keys are sorted in the order of their first digits. The keys in the fourth column of Fig. 13.36 result from this last pass, after the separate digit piles are reassembled into the final sorted deck.

In the numbers in the fourth (and last) column of Fig. 13.36, you can see that competitions between the third digit (such as between the third digit of keys 413 and 416) have been resolved correctly, as have competitions between values of the second digit (such as between the second digit of keys 616 and 626).

Analysis of RadixSort**

RadixSort is an $O(n)$ sorting process because it makes exactly k linear passes through the deck of n keys when the keys have k digits.

13.6 Review Questions

1. Describe roughly how **ProxmapSort** works.
2. Describe roughly how **RadixSort** works.
3. Explain why **RadixSort** runs in time $O(n)$.

13.6 Exercises

1. From the rough outline of **RadixSort** explained in the last subsection, implement a version of **RadixSort** on three-letter airport code keys, using 26 separate "bins," each of which is a doubly linked list containing records with airport code keys and links to the next and previous records.
2. Compute the hit counts, the proxmap, and the insertion locations for an unsorted array of 13 keys, A, using the method illustrated in the example in the text, when A is the array:

$$A = [\, 3.5,\ 12.3,\ 4.2,\ 1.5,\ 5.7,\ 12.6,\ 4.7,\ 7.2,\ 12.1,\ 2.9,\ 0.7,\ 8.1,\ 9.3 \,]$$

13.7 Other Methods

Learning Objectives

1. To explore ShellSort, which is called a "diminishing increment sorting method," and BubbleSort, which is called a "transposition sorting method."
2. To learn why to avoid using BubbleSort.

The two methods considered in this section do not fit neatly into any of the other main categories shown in Fig. 13.1. Nonetheless, they are important and interesting. ShellSort's performance can be competitive with some of the $O(n \log n)$ methods, and BubbleSort's performance can be disastrously bad, even though it is simple to program.

ShellSort

A good way to introduce **ShellSort** is to consider an example. For instance, suppose we are attempting to sort an array, A, containing 14 integer keys, such as the one shown in Fig. 13.37.

We are going to use a sequence of increments: 5, 3, and 1. The current increment that we will use at a given moment will be given by the value of the variable, **delta**. Thus we begin by setting the value of the variable **delta** to five, **delta = 5**.

The current increment, **delta**, is used to partition the keys in A[0:n – 1] into several subsequences of keys. Then each subsequence is sorted using an insertion-sort process. Each subsequence consists of keys in A that are an equal distance, **delta**, apart from their left and right neighbors. Using **delta == 5**, the subsequences of keys in array, A, five spaces apart from each other are shown in Fig. 13.38.

i	0	1	2	3	4	5	6	7	8	9	10	11	12	13
A[i] =	13	3	4	12	14	10	5	1	8	2	7	9	11	6

Figure 13.37 An Initially Unsorted Array, A[0:13]

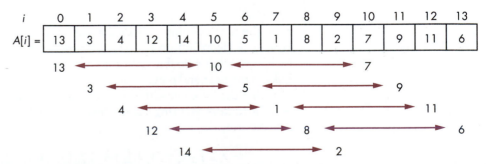

Figure 13.38 Five Unsorted Delta-5 Subsequences

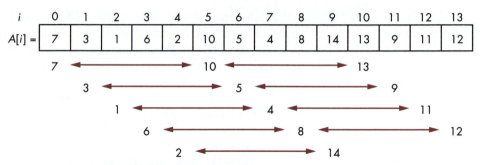

Figure 13.39 Five Sorted Delta-5 Subsequences

For example, the delta-5 subsequence of A beginning at A[0] consists of the subsequence of keys 13, 10, and 7, which are contained in the array locations A[0], A[5], and A[10], respectively. These array locations are five spaces apart.

After each of these five unsorted delta-5 subsequences is sorted separately, using an insertion-sorting process, the array A is converted to the configuration shown in Fig. 13.39. Note how each delta-5 subsequence in this figure is the sorted version of the corresponding subsequence in Fig. 13.38.

Next, the value of delta is changed from its previous value of 5 to a new smaller value of 3: **delta = 3**. Then, the unsorted delta-3 subsequences of A, as shown in Fig. 13.40 are considered. These unsorted delta-3 subsequences are individually sorted separately from one another, using an insertion-sorting process, yielding the configuration shown in Fig. 13.41.

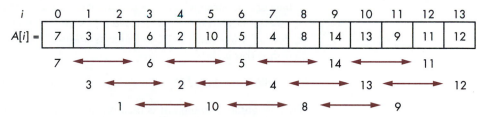

Figure 13.40 Three Unsorted Delta-3 Subsequences

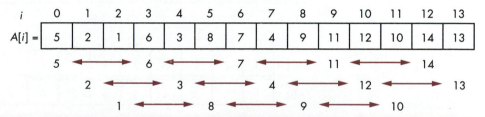

Figure 13.41 Three Sorted Delta-3 Subsequences

Finally, the value of delta is changed from 3 to 1, using **delta = 1**. There is only one subsequence of the array A consisting of keys spaced a distance of one apart from their left and right neighbors, and this consists of the entire array A itself. Thus, in the final stage of the process, the entire array is insertion-sorted. The final transformation is shown in Fig. 13.42.

How can ShellSort do better than $O(n^2)$?

You might wonder how a sorting process that repeatedly applies an insertion sorting technique could possibly be efficient, given that insertion sorting is known to take time $O(n^2)$ on the average. Part of the answer is that, initially, when delta has a fairly large value, insertion sorting takes place on subsequences containing few keys, and it tends to move keys large distances in the array A so that they land near to their eventual final sorted positions, whereas when delta's value is small, the insertion-sort process tends to move keys locally over short distances, which does not require very many key comparisons and key movements.

Figure 13.43 presents four views of the array A above when it is unsorted, delta-5 sorted, delta-3 sorted, and delta-1 sorted. If A[i] contains the key K, then K is shown as a small solid square at a height of K on the y-axis and at position i on the x-axis. Consequently, the completely sorted array, which is the same as the delta-1 sorted array shown in the rightmost diagram in Fig. 13.43, is simply a diagonal arrangement of solid squares (with key A[0] == 1 shown as the solid square at coordinates (1,1), key A[1] == 2, shown as the solid square at coordinates (2,2), and, in general, key A[i − 1] == i shown as the solid square at coordinates (i,i)). You can see how the values in A get closer and closer to their final positions (which lie on the diagonal of the square) each time a new smaller delta increment is used.

ShellSort is sometimes called a *diminishing increment sort*, since the values of the increment, **delta**, diminish in a sequence toward the final value, 1, starting from some initial value.

One way to compute the diminishing increments assigned to be the successive values of the variable **delta**, is to start with a value of **delta** close to one-third of the number of keys in the array A, **delta** ≈ $n/3$, and then to replace **delta** with one-third of its former value each time its value is diminished. An assignment statement which performs this is

delta = 1 + delta / 3;

This assignment statement is used on line 8 of Program 13.44 to compute a value for **delta** before the insertion sorting process is applied to the ith delta subsequence in A using the subroutine call **DeltaInsertionSort(A,i,delta)**. All of the separate delta subsequences in A are insertion-sorted using the for-statement on lines 10:12.

i	0	1	2	3	4	5	6	7	8	9	10	11	12	13
A[i] =	5	2	1	6	3	8	7	4	9	11	12	10	14	13
A[i] =	1	2	3	4	5	6	7	8	9	10	11	12	13	14

Figure 13.42 Unsorted and Sorted Delta-1 Array, A

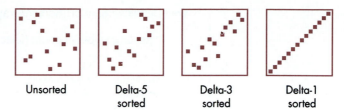

| Unsorted | Delta-5 sorted | Delta-3 sorted | Delta-1 sorted |

Figure 13.43 Snapshots of ShellSort

The subroutine that insertion-sorts the ith delta subsequences in A is given in Program 13.45. The strategy for the insertion sorting used in this program is identical to that of the insertion-sorting algorithm given in Program 13.21, except that the distance between keys being insertion-sorted is **delta** in Program 13.45 and 1 in Program 13.21.

Analysis of ShellSort**

Unfortunately, **ShellSort**'s performance has been hard to characterize analytically. However, experimental measurements suggest that, on the average, **ShellSort** runs in time $O(n^{1.25})$.

BubbleSort

the main idea

Given that the array $A[0:n-1]$ initially contains unsorted keys, suppose we make repeated passes through A, starting at $A[0]$ and moving toward $A[n-1]$, each time exchanging any adjacent pair of keys, $(A[i], A[i+1])$, that are not in sorted order. If we make enough passes, eventually the keys in A will be rearranged in ascending order. This is the idea behind **BubbleSort**.

```
    |    void ShellSort(SortingArray A)
    |    {
    |        int   i, delta;
    |
5   |        delta = n;
    |
    |        do {
    |            delta = 1 + delta / 3;
    |
10  |            for (i = 0; i < delta; ++i) {
    |                DeltaInsertionSort(A,i,delta);
    |            }
    |
    |        } while (delta > 1);
    |    }
```

Program 13.44 Main Procedure for **ShellSort**

```
 1  |    void DeltaInsertionSort(SortingArray A, int i, int delta)
    |    {
    |        /* assume: typedef enum {false, true} Boolean; has been declared */
    |
 5  |        int          j,k;
    |        KeyType      KeyToInsert;
    |        Boolean      NotDone;
    |
    |        j = i + delta;
10  |
    |        while (j < n) {
    |
    |            /* obtain a new KeyToInsert */
    |                KeyToInsert = A[j];
15  |
    |            /* move each Key > KeyToInsert rightward by delta spaces */
    |            /* to open up a hole in which to place the KeyToInsert */
    |                k = j;
    |                NotDone = true;
20  |                do {
    |                    if (A[k − delta] <= KeyToInsert) {
    |                        NotDone = false;
    |                    } else {
    |                        A[k] = A[k − delta];
25  |                        k −= delta;
    |                        if (k == i) NotDone = false;
    |                    }
    |                } while (NotDone);
    |
30  |            /* put KeyToInsert in hole A[k] opened by moving */
    |            /* keys > KeyToInsert rightward */
    |                A[k] = KeyToInsert;
    |
    |            /* consider next KeyToInsert at an increment of delta to the right */
35  |                j += delta;
    |
    |        }
    |    }
```

Program 13.45 Subroutine to **InsertionSort** ith Delta Subsequence in A

Program 13.46 gives the algorithm for **BubbleSort**. On line 6, the Boolean flag, **NotDone**, is set to *false*. On any given pass through the array A, if an out-of-order pair of keys, $(A[i], A[i + 1])$, is encountered, the Boolean flag, **NotDone**, is set to *true*, to indicate that at least one unordered pair was swapped and that another pass will be needed. If a complete pass is made without finding and exchanging any unordered pair of keys, then **NotDone** will remain *false*, and the do-while loop, on lines 5:15 of Program 13.46 will terminate. This is the proper moment for termination since no pair of keys was found to be out of sorted order on the last pass through the array A.

```
    |       void BubbleSort(SortingArray A)
    |       {
    |           int i; KeyType Temp; Boolean NotDone;
    |
  5 |           do {
    |               NotDone = false;                /* initially, assume NotDone is false */
    |               for (i = 0; i < n−1; ++i) {
    |                   if (A[i] > A[i+1]) {        /* the pair (A[i], A[i + 1]) is out of order */
    |                       /* exchange A[i] and A[i + 1] to put them in sorted order */
 10 |                       Temp = A[i]; A[i] = A[i + 1]; A[i + 1] =Temp;
    |                       /* if you swapped you need another pass */
    |                       NotDone = true;
    |                   }
    |               }
 15 |           } while (NotDone);                  /* NotDone == false iff no pair of keys was */
    |       }                                       /* swapped on the last pass */
```

Program 13.46 BubbleSort

Analysis of BubbleSort**

Unfortunately, **BubbleSort** is renowned to be one of the most inefficient sorting algorithms known unless it is applied to an array, A, that is only slightly out of order.

An O-notation analysis of **BubbleSort** is fairly simple. On each pass, **BubbleSort** is guaranteed to move at least one key into its final position in sorted order, and not to move that key on subsequent passes. Therefore, after at most n passes, all n keys will be in their final sorted order. On each pass, **BubbleSort** performs $(n - 1)$ comparisons of keys. Therefore the total number of comparisons performed is at most $n*(n - 1)$, which is $O(n^2)$.

BubbleSort runs in time $O(n^2)$

The actual performance of **BubbleSort** will be compared to that of the other $O(n^2)$ sorting algorithms, and indeed to other sorting algorithms that run in times $O(n \log n)$, $O(n^{1.25})$, and $O(n)$, in Section 13.8. There, data will show that in the average case, **BubbleSort** is by far the worst among the $O(n^2)$ sorting algorithms, and, in fact, is the worst sorting algorithm overall.

13.7 Review Questions

1. Describe how **ShellSort** works. Why is it called a "diminishing increment sorting method"?
2. Describe how **BubbleSort** works. Why is it called a "transposition sorting method"?
3. What is the O-notation for **BubbleSort**'s running time?

13.7 Exercises

1. Can you improve **BubbleSort** to run twice as fast by scanning from $0:i - 1$ on each pass, instead of from $0:n - 1$? Write an improved version of **BubbleSort** using this hint, and compare its performance to the original, given in Program 13.46.

2. Cocktail Shaker Sort is a variation of transposition sorting in which passes are alternately made in ascending order and then in descending order of the array indices of array A, transposing out-of-order pairs of keys on each pass. Write a program for Cocktail Shaker Sort, and compare its performance to that of the improved **BubbleSort** you implemented as your answer to Exercise 1 above.

≡ **13.8** Comparison and Perspective

Learning Objectives

1. To compare some experimental data that measure the performance of several of the sorting methods introduced in this chapter.
2. To learn from the comparisons when to use and when not to use various sorting methods.

Table 13.47 shows the results of running an experiment that measured sorting times for several of the sorting algorithms described in this chapter.

Five different sizes were used for the array, A, to be sorted: 64, 128, 256, 512, and 1024. On each trial, A was filled with floating point numbers chosen uniformly and randomly in the interval $0 \leq r < 1$. The running times given in Table 13.47 are measured in ticks (where a tick is a 60th of a second) and constitute averages taken over 100 different runs of each algorithm.

To get the numbers in Table 13.47, floating point compare operations and floating point multiply operations were compiled by a C compiler to run on a 68881 floating point chip. The relative times for three operations on keys used in sorting were also measured under these conditions. They are shown in Table 13.48.

As you can see from Table 13.47, even with the cost of a **MapKey** operation being about three and a third times greater than the cost of comparing two keys, **ProxmapSort** beats its nearest competitor, **QuickSort**, by a factor of 1.8 for an average array of 1024 keys. **ShellSort** and **HeapSort** are also good sorting techniques to use under these conditions.

and the winner is...

Table 13.47 Measured Sorting Times for Various Array Sizes

Array Size $n =$	64	128	256	512	1024
QuickSort	0.40	0.98	2.22	4.94	10.86
HeapSort	0.61	1.43	3.28	7.43	16.57
ProxmapSort	0.38	0.75	1.51	3.00	5.99
ShellSort	0.42	1.04	2.37	5.44	11.97
BubbleSort	2.76	11.36	46.42	189.35	766.22
InsertionSort	1.12	4.47	17.58	69.89	280.27
SelectionSort	1.40	5.56	22.18	88.66	354.48
MergeSort	0.99	2.28	5.13	11.45	25.11

Average move	0.26 milliticks
Average compare	0.56 milliticks
Average MapKey	1.85 milliticks

Table 13.48 Cost of Floating Point Operations Used in Sorting Floats (a millitick = a 60,000[th] of a second)

The $O(n^2)$ techniques are clearly the worst among the methods compared in Table 13.47, with **InsertionSort** beating **SelectionSort** by a factor of 1.26 and beating **BubbleSort** by a factor of 2.73 on arrays of size 1024.

Among the comparison-based methods, the best method, **QuickSort**, beats the worst method, **BubbleSort**, by a factor of over 70 on arrays of size 1024.

Although the data in Table 13.47 do not show it, nor do the analyses in this chapter cover it, one fact worth mentioning is that even though **HeapSort**'s average running time is about twice that of **QuickSort**, **HeapSort** has both an $O(n \log n)$ worst case running time and a tighter spread between its various running times than does **QuickSort**, whose worst case time is $O(n^2)$. This means that if you want to use a sorting technique that is guaranteed to run in time $O(n \log n)$, and whose overall average running time is not too shabby, then **HeapSort** is a good choice. For example, **HeapSort** would be a safe technique to use if you were trying to guarantee that your software could meet a real-time schedule deadline in, say, a real-time radar air traffic control system.

when it makes sense to use HeapSort

Although **ProxmapSort** is the fastest technique, under the circumstances in the experiments used to derive the measurements in Table 13.47, there are some circumstances in which it is not the best. One of these is if the keys in the array A to be sorted are bunched together in one portion of the key space (as in sorting all names in the phone book beginning with the letter M), or consist of several bunches that are each tightly clustered in the key space. Another circumstance is when the cost of computing the **MapKey** function is high in relation to the cost of comparing and moving keys. For example, suppose that C integer keys are used on a small personal computer on which floating point operations are simulated in software, rather than being performed by special floating point hardware. Under these circumstances, the floating point multiply operation used to multiply the scale factor, s, by the integer key, K, in **MapKey**(K), can take over 50 times longer than simple comparison of two integer keys (such as comparing $K_1 > K_2$). Table 13.49 gives one set of experimentally measured circumstances in which this is the case.

when ProxmapSort is not good to use

In the case of Table 13.49 the **MapKey** function costs over 185 times more than a comparison between two keys. Under these circumstances, the measured average sorting time for **QuickSort** and **ProxmapSort** turned out as shown in Table 13.50. Here,

Average move	0.26 milliticks
Average compare	0.17 milliticks
Average MapKey	31.47 milliticks

Table 13.49 Cost of Operations Used in Sorting Integers—Second Case

Table 13.50 Measured Sorting Times for Integer Keys Using Simulated Floating Point Operations

Array Size n =	64	128	256	512	1024
QuickSort	0.48	1.09	2.40	5.23	11.32
ProxmapSort	2.25	4.50	9.01	17.99	36.00

since **QuickSort** uses only relatively cheap key comparison and movement operations, it beats **ProxmapSort** by a factor of about 3.2 for arrays of size 1024.

On the other hand, for floating point keys (such as single-precision C **floats**), if both key comparisons and floating point multiplies are simulated in software, the advantage of **ProxmapSort** over **QuickSort** can become even more pronounced. For example, Table 13.51 gives the relative cost of operations for single-precision C floating point numbers, when both floating point compares and floating point multiplies are simulated in software. The **MapKey** function now costs only 3.5 times more than a comparison between two keys. Under these circumstances, the measured average sorting time for **QuickSort** and **ProxmapSort** turned out as shown in Table 13.52.

Under these conditions, the advantage of **ProxmapSort** over **QuickSort** is compelling. **QuickSort** takes over 2.88 times longer to finish than **ProxmapSort** on an average array, A, containing 1024 keys. Circumstances comparable to those shown in Table 13.51 might be typical of some sorting problems that use keys, such as long strings of characters requiring the use of software-based key comparisons and software-based **MapKey** functions, each of which will take much longer than the time required to move simple single-precision real keys or short integer keys.

One disadvantage of **ProxmapSort** is that, in addition to the space required to store keys, it requires space for two extra integer fields and for an extra two-bit status field in every struct of every entry in the array, A, to be sorted. If this extra space is not available, some of the efficient $O(n \log n)$ techniques might be preferable to use.

If space is at a premium, then even **QuickSort** may not be the best $O(n \log n)$ technique to use, since it implicitly eats up stack space when it calls itself recursively. Instead, **HeapSort** may be the best bet, since it runs in bounded workspace.

If the array A is only slightly out of order, then **BubbleSort** and **InsertionSort** will often quickly eliminate any minor disorders in which keys are only a few transpositions away from their final sorted order, and both algorithms will terminate quickly. However, one rule of thumb used by some good programmers is: "Never use **BubbleSort**." These programmers maintain that when they are tempted to use **BubbleSort** to restore order in a slightly disordered array, they have found it safer, in the long run, to use **InsertionSort** instead.

ProxmapSort wins when floating point operations are simulated

space disadvantage of ProxmapSort

if space is scarce, use HeapSort

Average move	0.22 milliticks
Average compare	10.80 milliticks
Average MapKey	37.32 milliticks

Table 13.51 Cost of Operations Used in Sorting Floats—Third Case

Table 13.52 Measured Sorting Times for Float Keys Using Simulated Floating Point Operations

Array Size n =	64	128	256	512	1024
QuickSort	5.73	13.63	31.38	70.84	155.98
ProxmapSort	3.39	6.76	13.51	27.07	54.12

Some Simple Wisdom

Finally, when you are faced with a new sorting problem, sometimes it pays to examine the situation carefully to see if some special, simple solution might apply.

For example, suppose you have an array A containing 100 keys, K, which are guaranteed to be distinct small integers in the range: $101 \leq K \leq 200$. Then it is a simple matter to map each key to its final sorted position in A[0:99], using a mapping that sends key K into location A[K − 101].

looking for special cases with simple solutions

Similarly, suppose you have keys representing cards in a deck of cards, where each key is a pair (S, V) consisting of a card's suit, S ∈ {♣, ♦, ♥, ♠}, and its face value, V ∈ {A, 2, 3, 4, 5, 6, 7, 8, 9, 10, J, Q, K}. Then, to sort a deck of 52 cards, each card with key (S, V) can be mapped onto its final sorted position in A[0:51] by devising a mapping which sends (S, V) into A[13*(int)(S) + (int)(V)], where the suit and face value have been represented by C enumeration types.

Under most circumstances, it may not be crucial which sorting algorithm you choose, assuming that you use reasonable wisdom to avoid the pitifully inefficient methods. For an overall conclusion, however, the two morals of the story are: (a) "If you absolutely need to select the best sorting algorithm, use measurement and tuning to discover it," and (b) "Under differing circumstances, different sorting algorithms will be the best. There is no single best sorting algorithm that beats all the others all of the time."

13.8 Review Questions

1. Which is the best among the $O(n^2)$ sorting techniques, according to the data in Table 13.47?
2. Which is the best among the $O(n \log n)$ sorting techniques, according to the data in Table 13.47?
3. Describe some special conditions under which it is not advantageous to use any of the sorting techniques mentioned in Table 13.47.

13.8 Exercises

1. Run some experiments in which you compare the running times of **BubbleSort** and **InsertionSort** when sorting arrays that are only "slightly" out of order. Which ones perform the best under which circumstances? How did you define what it means for an array of keys to be "slightly" out of order?

2. Which of the sorting methods of Table 13.47 would run fastest on an array, A, that is already sorted?
3. Are there hybrid techniques that will run faster than the single techniques shown in Table 13.47? For example, can you improve **QuickSort** by making a hybrid of **QuickSort** and **InsertionSort** in which **InsertionSort** is used to sort all subarrays of three or fewer keys, whereas ordinary **QuickSort** is used to sort subarrays containing four or more keys?

Pitfalls

- *Using* **BubbleSort**

  You might be tempted to use **BubbleSort** if the keys to be sorted are only slightly out of order. Don't do it. Instead, use **InsertionSort**, and if the keys are randomly arranged, then use one of the better $O(n)$ or $O(n \log n)$ sorting methods.

Tips and Techniques

- *Take advantage of special circumstances for a quick solution if they exist*

  Sometimes the keys used in a sorting problem are a simple permutation of the integer indexes of the sorting array, A, or they can be mapped into A's index range by a simple 1–1, onto function. Under these circumstances, it pays to use a mapping that sends each key onto its final position in A, instead of using one of the more elaborate and costly sorting methods studied in this chapter.

- *If you absolutely have to use the fastest possible technique…*

  And if the circumstances are favorable for applying the **ProxmapSort** method, then the guaranteed $O(n)$ behavior of **ProxmapSort**, plus its superior observed experimental running times, may suggest using it as the best possible solution. But remember, **ProxmapSort** will not perform well unless (a) the keys to be sorted in array A are reasonably close to a distribution chosen uniformly and randomly from the entire key space, (b) the **MapKey** function sends keys K onto the entire index range of array A and does so uniformly with respect to keys in the key space, and (c) the cost of the **MapKey** operation is not vastly more expensive than the cost of the key comparison operation that could be used to implement competing comparison-based sorting methods.

- *If you absolutely have to use the fastest possible technique…*

  Use measurement and tuning to measure and tune several candidate solutions before concluding that you know for certain that you have selected the best method.

- *If you absolutely have to use the fastest possible technique...*

    Be careful about what happens in the worst cases when you use some of the fastest techniques. For example, **QuickSort** and **ProxmapSort** each have worst case running times of $O(n^2)$, even though they are the fastest techniques to use under average circumstances. **HeapSort**, though a tad slower than **QuickSort**, has much better worst case times than **QuickSort**, and so it can be relied upon under widely ranging conditions to perform within a comparatively narrow range of overall sorting times.

References for Further Study

classical reference

Donald E. Knuth, *The Art of Computer Programming*, vol. 3: *Searching and Sorting*, Addison-Wesley, Reading, Mass., (1973).
The classical reference on sorting.

Chapter Summary

why the sorting problem is important

The problem of sorting an initially unsorted collection of keys into sorted order is a rich one that has fascinated serious computer scientists for many decades. Decades of intensive investigation have yielded crucial insights and illustrate the kind of progress computer science has made in the last half-century on an important central topic.

the *n* log *n* barrier

If a sorting method, M, sorts an array, A, of n keys, relying only on comparisons between pairs of keys and on moving keys to new positions in A, then method M's average running time can be no faster than proportional to $n \log n$. This crucial fact can be proven using *comparison trees*. However, the fact that comparison-based methods can sort in average time no faster than $n \log n$ does not mean that there do not exist other methods that can break the $n \log n$ barrier. In fact, there are known methods, such as **ProxmapSort** and **RadixSort**, based on address calculations, that can sort in average time $O(n)$. At least one of the address-calculation methods, **ProxmapSort**, is competitive with the fastest $O(n \log n)$ method, **QuickSort**, under certain circumstances.

different categories of sorting methods

One way to organize sorting methods for study and presentation is to classify them into categories such as (a) priority queue methods, (a) divide-and-conquer methods, (c) methods that insert keys and keep them sorted, (d) address-calculation methods, (e) diminishing increment methods, and (f) transposition sorting methods.

Two priority queue sorting methods are **SelectionSort** and **HeapSort**. Each method divides an array, A, into a subarray, *PQ*, representing a priority queue, and a subarray, *Q*, representing an ordinary output queue. The idea is to find the largest key among the yet-to-be-sorted keys in *PQ*, and to move it to the end of the output queue, *Q*. When keys are removed from *PQ* in decreasing order and are inserted at the end of *Q* in arrival order, they form a sorted arrangement of keys in *Q*.

SelectionSort

In **SelectionSort**, the subarray *PQ* represents a priority queue by using the unsorted array representation of *PQ*, in which, to identify the largest key in *PQ* to remove, we scan all keys in *PQ* to locate the position of the largest key. Because of this representation, **SelectionSort** runs in time $O(n^2)$.

HeapSort

HeapSort uses the sequential array representation of a heap to represent the priority queue, *PQ*. Because of this, the initial unsorted array A can be organized into a heap in time $O(n)$, and the largest key can be removed from a heap of k keys in time $O(\log k)$. Since the times required to remove keys from successively smaller and smaller heaps of sizes n, $(n-1)$, $(n-2)$, ... , 2, is no larger than a sum of numbers of the form: $a * \sum_{(1 < i \le n)} \lg i$, (for some constant of proportionality a), **HeapSort**'s dominant running time component is determined by the sum of the logarithms of the numbers from 2 to n, which can be shown to be of the form $O(n \log n)$. Moreover, **HeapSort**'s running times are clustered narrowly in a band around $O(n \log n)$, and are not dispersed as widely as, for instance, the running times for **QuickSort**, which can even deteriorate to times that are $O(n^2)$ in **QuickSort**'s worst case. **HeapSort** is therefore a good technique to use when an $O(n \log n)$ worst case running time is desirable.

divide-and-conquer methods

The divide-and-conquer sorting methods work by dividing the original unsorted array, A, into two smaller subarrays, L and R, sorting these two smaller subarrays using recursive calls, and then combining the sorted subarrays, L and R to yield the final sorted result, A.

MergeSort

MergeSort divides the array A into two half-arrays, $L = A[0:middle]$ and $R = A[middle + 1:n - 1]$, and combines the sorted versions of L and R by merging them together into a single sorted result, A. It runs in time $O(n \log n)$.

QuickSort

At the outset, **QuickSort** chooses a key in A, called the *pivot*, to use in separating A into two subarrays, L and R, where L contains keys $\le pivot$, and R contains keys $\ge pivot$. A partitioning process is used to accomplish this separation of A into subarrays L and R. Once L and R are sorted (by recursively applying **QuickSort** to them), no further actions are needed to produce a sorted final array, A, since L and R already occupy their final positions as subarrays of A the moment they are formed by the partitioning process.

QuickSort is the fastest known comparison-based sorting method, on the average, under favorable circumstances, and it is known to run in average time $O(n \log n)$, even though its worst case running time is $O(n^2)$.

InsertionSort and **TreeSort** are two sorting methods that work by inserting keys of the initial unsorted array, A, into an initially empty container, C, and by always maintaining the keys in C in sorted order. When all keys of A have been inserted into C, the keys can be read out of C in sorted order.

TreeSort

In **TreeSort**, the keys in A are inserted into an initially empty binary search tree, C. As new keys are inserted into C they are placed into the binary search tree in binary-search-tree order. When C is full, its keys can be read out in sorted order by performing an InOrder traversal of C. **TreeSort** is an $O(n \log n)$ method, in the average case.

InsertionSort

InsertionSort works by letting C be a subarray of the array A. Initially, C, consists of just one key. As each of the remaining $(n-1)$ keys, K, of A is inserted into C, K is placed into C so as to maintain all keys inside C in sorted order. This can be accomplished by moving all keys in C greater than K one space to the right, opening up a hole in C in which to insert K. Eventually, when all unsorted keys of A have been inserted into C, the subarray C occupies the entire array A, so that A is then completely sorted. **InsertionSort** runs in time $O(n^2)$ on the average, although it will terminate fairly quickly when applied to an array A that is only slightly out-of-order initially.

address-calculation
methods

Two sorting methods that run in average time $O(n)$, breaking the $n \log n$ barrier for comparison-based methods, are **ProxmapSort** and **RadixSort**. These methods work using techniques of address calculation.

ProxmapSort

In **ProxmapSort**, a proxmap is computed that calculates and reserves subarrays of the final sorted array A in which to move each key, K, of the original unsorted array, A. The word *proxmap* is short for "proximity map" because it is used to determine, for each key, K, a location in A, called the *insertion location* at the beginning of a reserved subarray of A, in which to insert key K, which is in *proximity* to the final position of K in the sorted array A.

When keys K are inserted into their reserved subarrays of A, starting at their insertion locations, they are insertion-sorted so that each reserved subarray always contains keys in ascending sorted order. **ProxmapSort** can be shown to run in time $O(n)$ in the average case, even though its worst case takes running time $O(n^2)$. Under certain circumstances, **ProxmapSort** runs considerably faster than **QuickSort**. However, **ProxmapSort** requires more space than **QuickSort** in the form of some extra members in each struct of A in order to hold the proxmap and the insertion locations for each key.

RadixSort

RadixSort is an older technique used with electromechanical punched-card sorting machines. If a key has d-digits, **RadixSort** makes d linear passes through the keys to be sorted. On the ith pass, it separates them into piles containing common values of the ith digit among the d-digit keys. These piles are reassembled into a "deck" with the high-digit piles on the bottom and the low-digit piles on the top, in preparation for the next pass. During each pass, keys are removed from the "bottom" of the deck and are placed on the "top" of the appropriate separate piles for the different digits. **RadixSort** runs in time $O(n)$ since it makes d linear passes, each requiring an amount of time proportional to the n keys to be sorted.

ShellSort

The last two sorting methods investigated in this chapter are **ShellSort** and **BubbleSort**. **ShellSort** is sometimes called a *diminishing increment sort*, since it uses a sequence of diminishing increments (such as **delta** == 14, 5, 2, 1) on successive passes through the array, A. Using the current value of the increment, **delta**, it considers delta different subsequences of the array, A, each of which contains keys separated by a distance of **delta** from its left and right neighbors in the subsequence. It uses insertion-sorting to sort each such subsequence of keys, spaced **delta** keys apart from one another. On each subsequent pass, a smaller value for **delta** is used. Eventually, the increment **delta** == 1, is used, in which case, **ShellSort** performs ordinary insertion-sorting, and rearranges A into its final sorted order. **ShellSort** has been hard to analyze, but empirical data suggest that it runs in time $O(n^{1.25})$. In actual experimental measurements, **ShellSort** is competitive with the better $O(n \log n)$ sorting techniques under favorable circumstances.

BubbleSort

BubbleSort is the final sorting method considered. It is sometimes called a *transposition sorting method*, since it works by making repeated passes through the array, A, *transposing* (i.e., swapping) any pair of adjacent keys, ($A[i]$, $A[i + 1]$), that are not in sorted order. Eventually, it makes a pass in which it finds no pair is out of order, at which point, it terminates. **BubbleSort** runs in time $O(n^2)$ in the average case. Unfortunately, it is renowned to be one of the worst sorting methods ever discovered.

Although it can be efficient when applied to an array that is only slightly out of order, many programmers recommend that it never be used.

looking for direct, simple sorting solutions
Under some circumstances, direct methods can be applied to rearrange an array into sorted order. For instance, if an array, $A[0:n - 1]$, contains n keys that are a permutation of the set of integers: $0:n - 1$, each key, K, can be sent directly to location $A[K]$. In other similar circumstances, a simple 1–1, onto mapping can be used to send keys onto final sorted array locations in A. You should always be ready to seize upon the opportunity to use such a direct method, if the circumstances warrant, since such direct methods are vastly simpler and more efficient than the general-purpose sorting methods.

conclusion

In the end, to choose a good sorting method, you might need to rely on measurement and tuning. No single sorting method performs best under all circumstances. Instead, differing circumstances favor the use of one method over the others, and different methods perform best under different conditions.

14

Advanced Recursion

Introduction and Motivation

Let's spend a moment recalling the aspects of recursion that have been discussed in previous chapters so we can get our bearings and see clearly where we are about to go to finish the journey. In Chapter 1 we saw that *recursion* was one of the *recurring concepts* of computer science that serves as an important unifying conceptual thread. Chapter 3 served as a gradual introduction to recursion, using a progression of examples to help you learn to "think recursively." Chapters 3 and 6, explored the connection between recursion and analysis of algorithms by showing how the recurrence relations for the running time of a recursive algorithm often closely reflect the structure of the algorithm itself.

finding our way

In Chapter 5, we discussed program transformations for eliminating tail recursion in order to transform a recursive program into an equivalent iterative one. We applied the tail-recursion elimination transformation to transform a recursive SelectionSort program into an iterative one. In Chapter 7, we saw how C implements recursion using run-time push-down stacks. Thus we learned that *recursion = stacks + iteration*.

581

using recursion for
describing and
recognizing things

In this chapter we will learn how recursion can be used for two additional important tasks: (1) *describing things* and (2) *recognizing things*. We will discover how to use recursion to describe the grammar of arithmetic expressions and how to use a recursive descent parser to recognize the structure of arithmetic expressions. Modifying the recursive descent parser to serve as an infix-to-postfix translator will enable us to provide a complete working arithmetic expression evaluation unit for use in completing our *pocket calculator project*.

Recall that in Chapter 4 we introduced a pocket calculator program composed of modules—one module handled the user interface, and the other evaluated an arithmetic expression and displayed its value. Then, in Chapter 7, we showed how to use a push-down stack to evaluate postfix arithmetic expressions. If we could discover how to translate an infix arithmetic expression given by the user of a pocket calculator into a postfix expression, we would have filled in a missing piece in our step-by-step attempt to build a complete pocket calculator.

recursion induction

In Chapter 5, not only did we discuss the execution time penalties associated with the use of recursion versus iteration, but we also discussed how to prove programs correct. When we attempt to prove the correctness of recursive programs, it sometimes pays to use an inductive proof technique called *recursion induction*. As the last task of this chapter, we will define recursion induction and show how to apply it to the task of proving recursive programs correct.

Plan for the Chapter

Section 14.2 shows how to use recursive definitions to define precisely the structure of arithmetic expressions, such as those that can be recognized and evaluated by an advanced pocket calculator. The device used to accomplish this is called a *context-free grammar* (or CFG, for short). As we will see, CFGs tend to be inherently recursive anytime they are defined to generate an unbounded set of expressions. CFGs *generate* arithmetic expressions by applying a set of substitution rules to a single starting symbol.

context-free grammars

Section 14.3 shows how to define a set of *mutually recursive procedures* to act as a recursive-descent parser for arithmetic expressions. A *directly recursive procedure*, P, is one in which P calls itself within itself. By contrast, a set of four mutually recursive procedures, $\{P_1, P_2, P_3, P_4\}$, is one in which, for instance, P_1 calls P_2, P_2 calls P_3, P_3 calls P_4, and P_4 calls P_1 again, in a circular fashion. While none of the four procedures, P_i, is directly recursive, nevertheless, each of the procedures can call itself indirectly via an indirect sequence of calls using the other procedures. The recursive-descent parser for arithmetic expressions given in Section 14.3 consists of four mutually recursive procedures.

recursive-descent parsers

A parser for a set of arithmetic expressions is a device that recognizes the structure of the subexpressions in an arithmetic expression according to the grammar that defines the structure. As we will see, the process of *parsing* (or *recognition*) is the inverse of the process of *generation* using a CFG.

translating infix into postfix

After we define the recursive-descent parser for arithmetic expressions, we will modify it to act as a translator that translates infix arithmetic expressions into postfix expressions. After translating an infix expression into the corresponding postfix expression, we can apply the postfix evaluator, defined in Chapter 7, to determine the value of the expression. Section 14.4 presents the modification of the recursive-descent parser that converts it into an infix-to-postfix translator. Once we are able to accept an infix arithmetic expression string, translate it to a postfix string, and evaluate the postfix string, we can complete the implementation of the pocket calculator module, left undefined as Program 4.12, called YourCalculationModule, in Chapter 4, which accepts an arithmetic expression string and returns its value for display in the calculator window.

Section 14.5 discusses a proof technique called *recursion induction*, useful for proving the correctness of recursive programs. Relying on a slightly different form of mathematical induction than the one usually learned first, recursion induction helps prove the correctness of a recursive program, P, when applied to a problem of a given size, n, assuming the correctness of the results of applying P to any smaller problem of size $k < n$. In this case, recursion has been applied to a *proof technique*, showing that recursion is useful for *proving things*.

Thus the chapter completes the coverage of recursion in this book by showing how to use recursion for *defining things*, *recognizing things*, and *proving things*.

14.2 Recursion as a Descriptive Method

Learning Objectives

1. To learn about context-free grammars.
2. To understand how to generate sentences using context-free grammars.
3. To understand how context-free grammars can employ recursion to describe an unbounded set of sentences using a finite description.

Let's begin by studying an example of a context-free grammar for arithmetic expressions. In what follows, we will use the single letters E, T, F, and P to stand for the words *Expression*, *Term*, *Factor*, and *Primary*. Figure 14.1 presents the *production rules* for the grammar. [*Note:* Here, the up-arrow operator (↑) signifies exponentiation, as it did in some of the early programming languages. The caret character (^) is sometimes used in ASCII character sets for this purpose.]

productions are substitution rules

The production rules, or *productions* for short, are a set of substitution rules that allow us to replace a symbol on the left of an arrow (→) with the symbols on the right of the arrow. For example, the first rule, E → E + T, says that any occurrence of

E → E + T	E → E − T	E → T
T → T * F	T → T / F	T → F
F → F ↑ P	F → P	
P → (E)	P → a	

Figure 14.1 Grammar for Arithmetic Expressions

Starting with E	Apply production
	E → T
To rewrite it as T	T → T / F
T / F	F → P
T / P	P → (E)
T / (E)	E → E – T
T / (E – T)	T → F
T / (E – F)	F → P
T / (E – P)	P → a
T / (E – a)	E → T
T / (T – a)	T → F
T / (F – a)	F → P
T / (P – a)	P → a
T / (a – a)	T → T ∗ F
T ∗ F / (a – a)	F → F ↑ P
T ∗ F ↑ P / (a – a)	P → a
T ∗ F ↑ a / (a – a)	F → P
T ∗ P ↑ a / (a – a)	P → a
T ∗ a ↑ a / (a – a)	T → F
F ∗ a ↑ a / (a – a)	F → P
P ∗ a ↑ a / (a – a)	P → a
a ∗ a ↑ a / (a – a)	

Figure 14.2 Derivation of a ∗ a ↑ a / (a – a)

an E can be replaced by E + T, and the rule, F → F ↑ P, says that any occurrence of an F can be replaced by F ↑ P.

These production rules are used to *generate* sentences in the language defined by the grammar. We begin with the *start symbol* of the grammar, which is the symbol E, and we apply production rules to rewrite E and its derivatives again and again until no more rules can be applied. The result is a string of symbols consisting of one of the *sentences* in the language defined by the grammar.

generating sentences

Let's look at Fig. 14.2, in which each line is rewritten as the next line by applying a production to the *rightmost* occurrence of a capital letter.

Now, note that the string a ∗ a ↑ a / (a – a) on the last line cannot be rewritten any further, since it does not contain any of the letters that are on the left sides of the productions. The symbols used in this last line are called *terminal symbols*, since they cannot be rewritten further. Any symbol in the grammar that is not on the left side of some production is a *terminal* symbol. By contrast, the letters {E, T, F, and P} on the left sides of the productions are called *nonterminal symbols*. To describe an entire

what a context-free grammar contains

grammar, G, completely, we need to give four items (S, V_N, V_T, P) where S is the *start symbol*, V_N is the set of *nonterminals*, V_T is the set of *terminals*, and P is the set of *productions*. In the case of the grammar of Fig. 14.1, $V_N = \{E, T, F, P\}$, $V_T = \{+, -, *, /, \uparrow, (,), a\}$ and $S = E$.

Productions always specify how to rewrite occurrences of nonterminal symbols as strings that use either terminals or nonterminals or both. The successively rewritten strings in the left column of Fig. 14.2 are called *sentential forms*. When a sentential form no longer contains any nonterminal symbols that can be rewritten and consists only of terminal symbols that cannot be rewritten, it is called a *sentence* of the language generated by the grammar. We can then say that the *language L(G)* generated by the grammar G is the set of all such sentences that can be generated from the start symbol of the grammar G, using productions in G. The sequence of sentential forms in the left column of Fig. 14.2 is called a *rightmost derivation* of the sentence a * a ↑ a / (a – a), starting from the start symbol, E, since the *rightmost* nonterminal in each line is always the one to be derived further.

Note that several of the productions are *directly recursive*, in that the symbol being defined on the left is used on the right. For example, $E \rightarrow E - T$, could be read as saying, "An *Expression* can derive to an *Expression* minus a *Term*." Still other sets of productions are *indirectly recursive* (or *mutually recursive*). For example, consider the set of productions, $\{ E \rightarrow T , T \rightarrow F , F \rightarrow P , P \rightarrow (E) \}$. By applying these four productions in sequence, we can derive an E to (E), or an F to (F), etc. Although none of the set of indirectly recursive productions is itself directly recursive, the effect of direct recursion can nevertheless be obtained by applying several of the productions in sequence.

Recursive context-free grammars can be used to provide a clean, simple way of giving a *finite* description for an *infinite* set of possible sentences. We conclude that recursion can be useful for defining things whose structure has parts that can contain instances of themselves. A programming language like C is just such an entity, since it contains many kinds of parts that can contain themselves, as in defining: subexpressions inside expressions, blocks inside blocks, and statements inside compound statements inside yet other statements, etc.

the language generated by a grammar

direct and indirect recursion

14.2 Review Questions

1. What is a context-free grammar?
2. Explain how productions of a CFG can be directly and indirectly recursive.
3. What is a rightmost derivation of a sentence with respect to a context-free grammar G?
4. How do you define the language, $L(G)$, generated by the context-free grammar G?

14.2 Exercises

1. Give a rightmost derivation of the sentence (a – a) ↑ a + a * a in the grammar G of Fig. 14.1.

2. Extend the grammar G of Fig. 14.1 to include the capability of generating arithmetic expressions with unary minus, as in the expressions: a ∗ − a↑a + a or − a + a ∗ a.

3. The typedefs of C structs using pointer members can be recursive. Give an example of a recursive C typedef of a struct, involving a pointer member, that can be used to define an unbounded set of pointer data structures. [*Hint:* Consider the definitions of binary trees or linked lists from earlier chapters.] Is such a recursive struct typedef an instance of a finite definition of an unbounded set of objects?

14.3 Using Recursion to Build a Parser

Learning Objectives

1. To learn how to build a recursive-descent parser for recognizing sentences in the language *L*(*G*) generated by a context-free grammar, *G*.
2. To see another example of the utility of mutual recursion.
3. To learn how to transform the productions of a context-free grammar into railroad diagrams, and how to transform the railroad diagrams into a recursive-descent parser.

The process of *parsing* a sentence is the process of discovering its grammatical structure with respect to a given grammar. Parsing a sentence is also the reverse of the process of generating it. Roughly speaking, in parsing, we start with a sentence and we try to go backward to collapse it to the start symbol of the grammar, by successively replacing subexpressions with their names. Each subexpression to be replaced

recursion is good for recognizing things, too

is identical to the right side β of some production N → β, and the name N used to replace it is the nonterminal on the left side of the production, N → β. By successively replacing subexpressions with their names, we perform stepwise reductions of the sentence being recognized, creating a sequence of intermediate collapsing sentential forms, until we get the start symbol, E, of the grammar, which cannot be collapsed any further. We then say that the sentence has been *recognized* as belonging to the language *L*(G).

The sequence of sentential forms produced by the parsing process is exactly the *reverse* of the sequence produced by the derivation process, if we observe two restrictions: (1) we always replace the *leftmost* subexpression β by its name N, using the production N → β, during parsing, and (2) we always substitute β for the *rightmost* occurrence of N during derivation.

parsing and generation are inverses

Another way to display the results of parsing a sentence is to draw a *parse tree*. In Fig. 14.3, the parse tree for the sentence a ∗ a ↑ a / (a − a) is shown above the dotted line, and another sentence, y ∗ x ↑ 2 / (z − 3), which is further derived from a ∗ a ↑ a / (a − a), is shown below the dotted line.

You can see how the tree above the dotted line is constructed from the derivation in Fig. 14.2 by noting that each of the productions used in the derivation, such as T → T ∗ F, can be applied to hang from the rightmost occurrence of the leaf, T, in the tree being constructed, each of the direct descendants T, ∗, and F, with lines traveling downward.

how to construct the parse tree

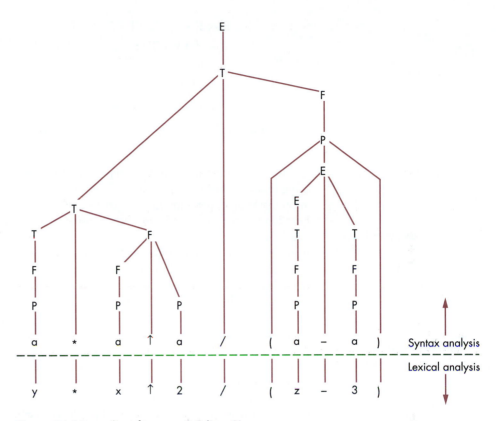

Figure 14.3 Parse Tree for y * x ↑ 2/(z − 3)

If we let the symbol "a" in the sentence, a * a ↑ a / (a − a), stand for "any letter or digit," and we replace different occurrences of "a" by different letters and digits, we can derive the further sentence, y * x ↑ 2 / (z − 3). This last sentence is shown below the dotted line in Fig. 14.3.

In many actual compilers, the process of translating an input program into a set of machine language instructions is divided into several phases. The first two phases of the translation process usually consist of *lexical analysis* followed by *syntax analysis*. The input program can be thought of as a sequence of raw characters, which may be viewed as a sequence of saved-up keystrokes typed by the programmer who wrote the program. During lexical analysis, this sequence of characters is divided into what are called *lexemes* (or sometimes *tokens*). Typically, lexemes consist of numbers, identifiers, operators, punctuation, reserved words, and possibly various kinds of literal constants (such as string or character literals).

Lexemes are the lowest units of organization in the program above the level of raw input characters. The lexemes in the input program are detected by a lexical analyzer, and they are fed one by one to the syntax analyzer. The job of the syntax analyzer is to discover the grammatical structure of this sequence of lexemes with respect to the grammar of the programming language.

lexical analysis

the syntax analyzer's job

$$E \rightarrow E + T \mid E - T \mid T$$
$$T \rightarrow T * F \mid T / F \mid F$$
$$F \rightarrow F \uparrow P \mid P$$
$$P \rightarrow (E) \mid a$$

where "a" stands for any letter or digit

Figure 14.4 Context-Free Grammar, Condensed Form

In our tiny example, we have represented the process of lexical analysis by imagining that *any* single letter or single digit is replaced by the letter "a" and that punctuation marks and operators stand for themselves. We also imagine that the lexical analyzer ignores sequences of blanks between separate lexemes in the input and does not pass blanks on to the syntax analyzer. (The lexical analysis routines that will be used in the recursive-descent parser in Program 14.6 are arranged so that they have these properties.) In Fig. 14.3, this process of lexical analysis is symbolized by the substitutions shown below the dotted line. (This is admittedly somewhat of an oversimplified caricature of the lexical analysis process, but it will serve as an organizational *placeholder* in the program design that can be replaced with a more elaborate version later.)

our lexical analyzer is only a placeholder

Now let's develop a *recursive-descent parser* for sentences in the language generated by the grammar of Fig. 14.1. We do this in three stages in which we transform the grammar of Fig. 14.1 first into a *condensed description*, then into a set of *railroad diagrams*, and finally into a C *program* for the parser.

developing a recursive-descent parser

Starting with the grammar of Fig. 14.1, we can group together all of the productions starting with E into a condensed production whose right side contains alternatives separated by vertical bars (|). For instance, the three productions $E \rightarrow E + T$, $E \rightarrow E - T$, and $E \rightarrow T$, can be rewritten as: $E \rightarrow E + T \mid E - T \mid T$. This latter condensed form is read as, "An E can derive *either* to an E + T *or* to an E − T *or* to a T." Applying a similar condensation process to the other groups of productions that begin with the same left sides, we get the condensed form of the grammar shown in Fig. 14.4.

condensing the grammar

Let's now look at what kind of sentential forms can be derived from the condensed rule, $E \rightarrow E + T \mid E - T \mid T$. We see that an initial E can be rewritten either as E + T or E − T, which we symbolize by E ± T. The leftmost E in E ± T can be further rewritten as E ± T giving E ± T ± T, and we can keep on doing this any number of times getting E ± T ± . . . ± T. Finally, we can rewrite the leftmost E as a T, getting T ± T ± . . . ± T. We could summarize the general effect of applying the condensed rule, $E \rightarrow E + T \mid E - T \mid T$, as saying that it permits an E to be rewritten as a sequence of one or more T's connected by pluses or minuses. This could be symbolized by a rule such as $E \rightarrow T \{ \pm T \}$, where $\{ \pm T \}$ stands for "a sequence of zero or more occurrences of ± T." In this form, we say that we have *eliminated* left recursion. The rule $E \rightarrow E + T$ is *left-recursive*, since a recursive use of E appears on the left side of E + T. By contrast, the rule $E \rightarrow T \{ \pm T \}$ is not recursive, since E does not appear on the right side of the rule. It is then easy to convert the rule $E \rightarrow T \{ \pm T \}$ into a railroad diagram in which, when we enter the diagram and travel around it in the direc-

eliminating left recursion

making railroad diagrams

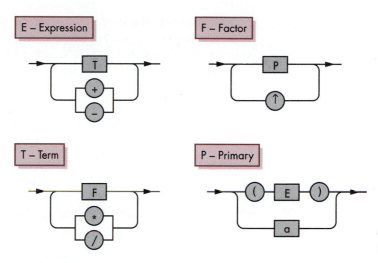

Figure 14.5 Railroad Diagrams

tion indicated by the arrows, we travel through boxes or circles that give us "a T possibly followed by one or more occurrences of ± T." The *railroad diagram* for an E, as shown in Fig. 14.5, recognizes any such sequence T { ± T}, provided we interpret the act of traveling through a box with a T inside as "recognizing an instance of a T."

Railroad diagrams such as these are sometimes used to describe the syntax of entire programming languages, such as Pascal and Modula 2. The railroad diagrams for T, F, and P are derived from the condensed grammar of Fig. 14.4 by a process similar to the one used for deriving the railroad diagram for E. For instance, the condensed rule for a term T, which is T → T * F | T / F | F, can be rewritten after eliminating left recursion, as T → F { */ F }, which directly generates the railroad diagram for T. Likewise, the condensed rule for an F, which is F → F ↑ P | P, can be rewritten as F → P { ↑ P }, which directly generates the railroad diagram for F.

now for the final phase

The stage is now set for the final phase of our conversion—generating a recursive-descent parser in C, using the railroad diagrams as a guide.

First, however, we need to introduce a package of software components that serve as building blocks for the parser. Our parser will belong to the class of parsers called *shift-reduce parsers with a lookahead of 1.* The three basic actions needed are *shifting,* *reducing,* and *looking ahead* into the input one lexeme in advance. Suppose we have a sentential form being collapsed stepwise into the start symbol of the grammar. Let's say

but first, we need some building blocks

it consists of a sequence of symbols: c_n, c_{n-1}, . . . , c_3, c_2, c_1. The action **Reduce**(3,L), when applied to this sequence, consists of replacing the last three symbols c_3, c_2, c_1 by an L, (and writing out the production, L → c_3 c_2 c_1, to record the fact that the reduction consisted of replacing the right side of the production, L → c_3 c_2 c_1, with its left side). In general, **Reduce**(k,L) means to replace the last k symbols by an L and to write out the production in which L derives to these last k symbols. The action, **Shift**(c), means to shift the next lexeme c from the beginning of the input onto the right end of the sentential form being parsed, and, afterward, to set the variable, **Next**, to contain the next lexeme in the input. The use of the variable, **Next**, enables us to look ahead one lexeme into the input. For example, suppose that, at an intermediate point in the parsing process, the initial part of the sentential form being parsed is T ∗ F ↑ , and that the remainder of the input to be shifted in is 2 / (z − 3). Here, **Next** == 2, since 2 is the next lexeme in the input:

String being parsed	*Remainder of input before shifting*
T ∗ F↑	2 / (z − 3)
	↑
	Next == 2

performing a shift

The last few lexemes of the string being parsed do not form the right side of any production and cannot be reduced. Whenever we cannot reduce these rightmost lexemes, we shift the next lexeme in the input onto the right part of the string being parsed (as in shifting the 2 in **Next** onto the right end of T ∗ F ↑). Performing this shift changes the picture above into the following:

String being parsed	*Remainder of input after shifting*
T ∗ F↑2	/ (z − 3)
	↑
	Next == /

then reducing once

Since the "2" is an instance of an "a" (meaning any letter or digit) and since the production, P → a, is the only one that could have generated it, we can make the call **Reduce**(1,P) to reduce the "2" to a P. After making this call, the picture is as follows:

String being parsed	*Remainder of input after calling* **Reduce**(1,P)
T ∗ F↑P	/ (z − 3)
	↑
	Next == /

reducing again

Now the rightmost three characters of the string being parsed are identical to the right side of the production F → F ↑ P, so we can make the call **Reduce**(3,F) to replace F ↑ P with F. This creates the following picture:

String being parsed	*Remainder of input after calling* **Reduce**(3,F)
T ∗ F	/ (z − 3)
	↑
	Next == /

and again

Again, since the last three lexemes of the string being parsed are T * F, which is the right hand side of the production $T \to T * F$, we can perform **Reduce**(3,T), getting:

String being parsed	Remainder of input after calling **Reduce**(3,T)
T	/ ($z - 3$)
	↑
	Next == /

and finally shifting

At this point, we could continue to reduce the T to an E, using $E \to T$, but doing so would turn out to be a mistake. Instead, we need to shift in the division sign ' / ' that is next in the input, getting:

String being parsed	Remainder of input after doing **Shift**(' / ')
T /	($z - 3$)
	↑
	Next == (

The process of parsing continues in this fashion performing either *shifts* or *reduces*. But then the interesting question arises, "How do you know when it is correct to shift or reduce when both moves are possible?" For example, we commented that it was possible either to reduce T to E or to shift in ' / ' from the input in the case immediately preceding the last one above. If it can always be decided whether to shift or reduce by looking ahead one lexeme in the input string, it is said that a shift-reduce parser is a *deterministic lookahead(1) parser*.

The recursive-descent parser we are about to construct is an example of such a deterministic lookahead(1) parser, because it can always decide whether to shift or reduce on the basis of looking at the value of the variable, Next, which contains the next lexeme in the input. Now it is time to show how the railroad diagrams in Fig. 14.5 can be used as a guide for writing the C functions to do recursive-descent parsing. These C functions are given as Program 14.6.

building the parser

Let's take a look at just two of these functions, ParseP (for parsing a Primary) and ParseT (to parse a Term). The remaining ones are similar and will be easy to understand once we have understood the first two.

how to write these functions

Starting with ParseP, we look at the railroad diagram for a Primary in Fig. 14.5. We observe that an instance of a Primary can be either of the form "(E)" or of the form "a" where an "a" is a single letter or digit. We can decide which of these two alternatives is going to come next in the remainder of the input string by looking at its first character. If this first character is '(', that is if the value of the variable Next == '(', then we know we can expect to parse an instance of the "(E)" alternative among the lexemes next in the input. Otherwise, we can expect to parse an instance of an "a."

Looking at the text of the function ParseP (on line 13 of Program 14.6), we see this is exactly the decision that is examined. On line 13, if Next == '(', then we proceed to parse "(E)" by first shifting in the left parenthesis, using Shift('('), then parsing

```
/* ---------------------------------------------------------------------- */

            /* Assume that the variable Next and the functions Reduce(k,L) */
            /* and Shift(c) are defined externally. */

  5  |       extern void ParseE(void);          /* extern needed for functions that are */
     |                                          /* called before they are declared */

/* ---------------------------------------------------------------------- */

 10  |
     |       void ParseP(void)                                    /* parse a Primary */
     |       {
     |           if (Next == '(' ) {
     |               Shift('(');
 15  |               ParseE( );
     |               Shift(')');
     |               Reduce(3,'P');                               /* P → ( E ) */
     |           } else {
     |               Shift('a');                /* 'a' stands for any letter or digit */
 20  |               Reduce(1,'P');                               /* P → a */
     |           }
     |       }
     |

/* ---------------------------------------------------------------------- */

     |       void ParseF(void)                                    /* parse a Factor */
     |       {
     |           ParseP( );
 30  |           Reduce(1,'F');                                   /* F → P */
     |           while (Next == '↑' ) {
     |               Shift(Next);
     |               ParseP( );
     |               Reduce(3,'F');                               /* F → F ↑ P */
 35  |           }
     |       }

/* ---------------------------------------------------------------------- */

 40  |       void ParseT(void)                                    /* parse a Term */
     |       {
     |           ParseF( );
     |           Reduce(1,'T');                                   /* T → F */
     |           while ( (Next == '*') || (Next == '/') ) {
 45  |               Shift(Next);
     |               ParseF( );
     |               Reduce(3,'T');                               /* T → T * / F */
     |           }
     |       }

/* ---------------------------------------------------------------------- */
```

Program 14.6 Recursive-Descent Parser (continued)

Program 14.6 Recursive-Descent Parser (continued)

```
       |    void ParseE(void)                                    /* parse an Expression */
       |    {
   55  |        ParseT( );
       |        Reduce(1,'E');                                                 /* E → T */
       |        while ( (Next == '+') || (Next == '–') ) {
       |            Shift(Next);
       |            ParseT( );
   60  |            Reduce(3,'E');                                         /* E → E ± T */
       |        }
       |    }


/* ------------------------------------------------------------------------------- */


       |    int main(void)
       |    {
       |        do {
       |            GetInputFromUser( );
   70  |            ParseE( );              /* call the parser to parse the input string */
       |        } while (UserWantsToContinue( ));
       |    }
```

an instance of an E that comes after the left parenthesis, using **ParseE( )**, followed by shifting in the right parenthesis, using **Shift(')')**, and finally, by reducing the three last lexemes "(E)" to a P, using the call **Reduce(3,'P')**.

Here, it is essential to "think recursively" by imagining that **ParseE( )** is a unit of action that reliably finds an instance of an E next in the input, shifts it in, and reduces it to a single letter E. Thinking recursively, in this case, means imagining that the subproblem of finding and reducing an E is successfully solved by **ParseE( )**, and proceeding to imagine how to combine the solution to this solved subproblem into the solution of the immediate problem at hand, which is to parse a Primary.

thinking recursively is essential

The other alternative of **ParseP** is to parse an "a" as a P. This is accomplished on lines 19 and 20 of Program 14.6 by shifting in a single letter or digit, using **Shift('a')**, and then reducing it to a P, using **Reduce(1,'P')**. Comparing the function **ParseP** with the railroad diagram for a Primary in Fig. 14.5, we see that **ParseP** faithfully implements the railroad diagram first by deciding whether to follow the "(E)" track or the "a" track on the basis of whether or not **Next == '('**, and then making appropriate calls to shift and reduce the expected items on each alternative track.

faithfully implementing the railroad diagram

The function **ParseT**, to parse a Term, on lines 40:49 of Program 14.6 works according to a second pattern. When we come into the railroad diagram for a Term in Fig. 14.5, we first encounter a Factor, F. Since this happens inevitably, the first thing to do in order to parse a T, is to parse the initial F. In order to do this, we again need to "think recursively," and imagine that calling the function **ParseF( )** will reliably shift in all the lexemes of an instance of an F in the input and will reduce them to the letter F. We make the call on **ParseF( )** on line 42 of Program 14.6 and on line 43, we call **Reduce(1,'T')** to replace the F with a T (and to output the production used to derive this change). We are now confident we have a T sitting at the end of the string being parsed.

how to parse a Term

According to the railroad diagram for a Term, after we have parsed an F, we can either exit, or we can encounter a multiplication or division sign that indicates we should follow the loop around the railroad diagram again. Consequently, by examining whether (**Next** == '*') or (**Next** == '/'), we can decide whether to exit or to go around the loop. The form that this loop takes is the while-loop on lines 44:48 of Program 14.6. Each time we encounter (**Next** == '*') or (**Next** == '/'), we need to shift in the multiplication or division sign, parse the instance of the factor F that is required to follow it, and reduce three lexemes of the form T */ F to a T. The latter is accomplished by making the call **Reduce(3,'T')** on line 47 of Program 14.6.

ParseF and ParseE are similar

Constructing the functions for **ParseF** and **ParseE** from their railroad diagrams involves the same sort of reasoning we have just used to construct the function **ParseT**. In each case, the railroad diagrams involve loops to travel if the next lexemes are identical to certain operators, and each such loop is implemented with a while-loop similar in form to the one just discussed for **ParseT**.

mutually recursive functions

We should note that the functions **ParseE**, **ParseT**, **ParseF**, and **ParseP** form a collection of *mutually recursive* functions. Note that **ParseP** calls **ParseE**, which calls **ParseT**, which calls **ParseF**, which calls **ParseP** again—all in a big cycle: **ParseP** ⊃ **ParseE** ⊃ **ParseT** ⊃ **ParseF** ⊃ **ParseP**. No matter which of these functions we declare first in C, at least one of them has to call another function that has not been declared yet. To break the cycle, we use the extern declaration on line 5 of Program 14.6.

Now it is time to run our recursive-descent parser on an actual input string. Figure 14.7 illustrates what happens.

```
=========== Syntax Analyzer Output ===========

give input string: y * x↑2 / (z-3)
        P   →       a       { where a = y }
        F   →       P
        T   →       F
        P   →       a       { where a = x }
        F   →       P
        P   →       a       { where a = 2 }
        F   →     F ↑ P
        T   →     T * F
        P   →       a       { where a = z }
        F   →       P
        T   →       F
        E   →       T
        P   →       a       { where a = 3 }
        F   →       P
        T   →       F
        E   →     E - T
        P   →     ( E )
        F   →       P
        T   →     T / F
        E   →       T

Do you want to give another string? (y/n)
```

Figure 14.7 Output of Recursive-Descent Parser

Now the reader should compare the productions output by the parser in Fig. 14.7 to parse the sentence y * x ↑ 2 / (z − 3) with the productions used in generating the sentence a * a ↑ a / (a − a) in Fig. 14.2. *Result:* the list of productions used in parsing is the same as the list of productions used in the derivation in *reverse* order. *Rightmost derivations* (in which the rightmost nonterminal is rewritten using some production) are *inverses* of *leftmost parses* (in which the leftmost subexpression, which is equal to the right side of some production, is replaced by the name used on the left side of that production). This result is proven in books that discuss the theory of context-free grammars and that develop the theory of parsing, translation, and compiling.

once again, parsing and derivation are inverses

We conclude that recursion can be a powerful tool for *recognizing things*. In fact, recursive-descent parsers are used in several fast contemporary compilers.

14.3 Review Questions

1. Explain what it means to parse a sentence in the language $L(G)$ generated by a context-free grammar G.
2. How does the parser of Program 14.6 use recursion? Define mutual recursion.
3. What is meant by saying that rightmost derivations and leftmost parses are inverses?

14.3 Exercises

1. Define a C module called **ParserUtilities.c**, which implements the following undefined items in Program 14.6: **Reduce(k,L)**, **Shift(c)**, the variable **Next**, the function **GetInputFromUser**, and the function **UserWantsToContinue**. Show where to place an include directive in Program 14.6 to invoke the services of the **ParserUtilities** module you have defined. Arrange for your parser utilities to find the next nonblank character in the input string to be the value of the variable, **Next**, so that you can put blanks in your input string (for spacing) that the parser will ignore.
2. Consider the following grammar, G_1, whose productions are

$$E \rightarrow 0 E 0 \quad E \rightarrow 1 E 1 \quad E \rightarrow 2.$$

Give a railroad diagram for E, then write a recursive-descent parsing routine, **ParseE**, to parse sentences generated by the grammar. (Use the variable **Next**, and the routines **Shift** and **Reduce**, used in the recursive-descent parser Program 14.6.)
3. The sentences generated by the grammar, G_1, of the previous exercise are of the form: 2, 020, 121, 00200, 01210, 10201, 11211, etc. They are called marked palindromes. Palindromes are words such as "ada" and "radar," that are the same when they are spelled backward. Marked palindromes are palindromes whose center is marked by a special character (such as 2 in the case of the grammar G_1). Consider now a grammar G_2 for a language of unmarked palindromes:

$$E \rightarrow a E a \quad E \rightarrow b E b \quad E \rightarrow a \quad E \rightarrow b.$$

Can you write a recursive-descent parser to parse these unmarked palindromes with respect to the grammar G_2?

4. Define a grammar, G_3, that generates the language 110, 111100, ..., $1^{2n}0^n$, whose sentences consist of an even number of ones followed by half that many zeros. In symbols, $L(G_3) = \{ 1^{2n}0^n \mid n \geq 1 \}$.

5. What is wrong with the following grammar?

$$S \rightarrow 0\,A\,0 \qquad S \rightarrow 1\,B\,1$$
$$B \rightarrow 1\,A\,1 \qquad A \rightarrow 0\,B\,0.$$

14.4 Translating from Infix to Postfix

Learning Objective

1. To learn how to augment the recursive-descent parser program so that it will translate any infix arithmetic string it is parsing into an equivalent postfix output string, suitable for evaluation by a postfix interpreter.

thinking recursively again

By "thinking recursively," for a moment, we can discover how to convert the recursive-descent parser of Program 14.6 into a *translator* that translates the arithmetic infix input string being parsed into an equivalent postfix output string.

To translate an infix expression, $x_1 \, \alpha \, x_2$, into a postfix expression, $\underline{x_1} \, \underline{x_2} \, \alpha$, where α is an arithmetic operator, where x_1 and x_2 are infix subexpressions, and where $\underline{x_1}$ and $\underline{x_2}$ are their respective postfix translations, we could pursue the following four-step strategy: (1) parse and translate the left subexpression, x_1, into a postfix string, p; (2) recognize and save the infix operator α that comes after x_1 in the input string; (3) parse and translate the right subexpression, x_2, into a postfix string, q, appended to the end of the previous string, p; and (4) append the saved operator α to the end of the string pq.

the strategy for translation

Suppose we start off with an empty output string, called, **PostfixString**, and suppose that we have augmented the four parsing routines: **ParseP**, **ParseF**, **ParseT**, and **ParseE**, so that they append the postfix translation of the infix subexpression they are parsing to the end of **PostfixString**. (*Note*: We have now begun to "think recursively" by imagining that the four routines **ParseP**, **ParseF**, **ParseT**, and **ParseE** already serve as postfix translators for the subexpressions they parse. That is, we have decided to make the assumption that all four subroutines solve subproblems of smaller size, before we start to write these subroutines themselves.)

For example, suppose we are trying to translate an infix expression of the form, $x_1 \uparrow x_2$, into its postfix translation, $\underline{x_1} \, \underline{x_2} \uparrow$. The function **ParseF** first calls **ParseP** to parse the subexpression x_1, which is the left operand of the binary operator, $\uparrow$, and it reduces x_1 to the letter F in its "string being parsed," (which, incidentally, behaves like a pushdown stack, since insertions and deletions are made only at its right end). Now, by the assumption we have made in thinking recursively, **ParseP** also appends the postfix translation, $\underline{x_1}$, of the infix input string x_1, to the end of the empty output string, **PostfixString**.

At this moment in the parsing process, the variable, **Next**, points to the binary operator, ↑, in the input string. **ParseF** can be augmented to save this binary operator in a local variable, called **Operator**, for later use. **ParseP** then proceeds to parse the right operand, x_2, of the binary operator, ↑, by calling **ParseP** again. Not only does this reduce x_2 to a P on the parser's stack, it also appends its postfix translation, $\underline{x_2}$, to the end of the output string, **PostfixString**.

At this moment, we are close to our goal, because the output string, **PostfixString**, contains $\underline{x_1}$ $\underline{x_2}$, and we have saved the binary operator, ↑, in the variable, **Operator**. To complete the translation, we can append the binary operator, ↑, which is the value of the variable, **Operator**, to the end of the output string, **PostfixString**, which will then have the value, $\underline{x_1}$ $\underline{x_2}$ ↑. By this means, **ParseF** will become a unit of action that parses an instance of a factor, F, in the input string and appends its postfix translation to the end of the output string, **PostfixString**.

By studying the other functions, **ParseP**, **ParseT**, and **ParseE**, in Program 14.8, you can see how the following theme is applied to complete the design of the infix-to-postfix translator. *Theme*: To translate an expression containing a binary infix operator into postfix, first parse the subexpression for the left operand and append its postfix translation to the end of the output string, save the binary operator, parse the subexpression for the right operand and append its postfix translation to the end of the output string, and finally, append the operator to the end of the output string. Simple, isn't it?—provided you "think recursively."

In the comments in Program 14.8, we use the notation that $\underline{X}$ stands for the postfix translation of the input string **X**.

Figure 14.9 shows the output of the infix-to-postfix translation process when Program 14.8 is applied to the input string $(x - y)\uparrow 2 + 5*z$. Each time a new character is appended to the end of the postfix output string, the entire postfix output string is shown in the right column of Fig. 14.9.

```
/* -------------------------------------------------------------------- */

     /* Assume that the variable Next and the functions Reduce(k,L) */
     /* and Shift(c) are defined externally. */
5
          extern char *PostfixString;  /* PostfixString holds the output of the translation */

     /* -------------------------------------------------------------------- */

10   |    void AppendToOutput(char x)        /* append x to end of PostfixString */
     |    {
     |         /* performs Concatenate(PostfixString,x, ' ');  */
     |    }

     /* -------------------------------------------------------------------- */

     |    extern void ParseE(void);           /* extern needed for functions that are */
                                              /* called before they are declared */
```

Program 14.8 Infix to Postfix Translator (continued)

Figure 14.8 Infix to Postfix Translator (continued)

```
      /* --------------------------------------------------------------------- */

   |      void ParseP(void)                              /* translate a Primary into postfix */
   |      {
   |          char Operand;
25 |
   |          if ( Next == '(' ) {
   |              Shift('(');
   |              ParseE( );                              /* ( E ) → E */
   |              Shift(')');
30 |              Reduce(3,'P');
   |          } else {
   |              Operand = Next;
   |              Shift('a');                             /* 'a' stands for any letter or digit */
   |              Reduce(1,'P');
35 |              AppendToOutput(Operand);                /* a → a */
   |          }
   |      }

      /* --------------------------------------------------------------------- */

   |      void ParseF(void)                              /* translate a Factor into postfix */
   |      {                                              /* F ↑ P → F P ↑ */
   |          char Operator;
   |
45 |          ParseP( );                                 /* F → F */
   |          Reduce(1,'F');
   |          while ( Next == '↑' ) {
   |              Operator = Next;
   |              Shift(Next);
50 |              ParseP( );                             /* P → P */
   |              Reduce(3,'F');
   |              AppendToOutput(Operator);              /* F P → F P ↑ */
   |          }
   |      }

      /* --------------------------------------------------------------------- */

   |      void ParseT(void)                              /* translate a Term into postfix */
   |      {                                              /* T */ F → T F */  */
60 |          char Operator;
   |
   |          ParseF( );                                 /* T → T */
   |          Reduce(1,'T');
   |          while ( (Next == '*') || (Next == '/') ) {
65 |              Operator = Next;
   |              Shift(Next);
   |              ParseF( );                             /* F → F */
   |              Reduce(3,'T');
   |              AppendToOutput(Operator);              /* T F → T F * /  */
70 |          }
   |      }
```

Figure 14.8 Infix to Postfix Translator (continued)

```
/* -------------------------------------------------------------------- */

   |     void ParseE(void)                          /* translate an Expression into postfix */
75 |     {                                                        /* E ± T → E T ± */
   |         char Operator;
   |
   |         ParseT( );
   |         Reduce(1,'E');                                              /* E → E */
80 |         while ( (Next == '+') || (Next == '–') ) {
   |             Operator = Next;
   |             Shift(Next);
   |             ParseT( );                                              /* T → T */
   |             Reduce(3,'E');
85 |             AppendToOutput(Operator);                    /* E T → E T ± */
   |         }
   |     }


/* -------------------------------------------------------------------- */

   |     int main(void)
   |     {
   |         do {
   |             PostfixString = " ";   /* initialize PostfixString to be the empty string */
95 |             GetInputFromUser( );
   |             ParseE( );                         /* call the parser to parse the input string */
   |             printf("output = %s\n", PostfixString);     /* output the PostfixString */
   |         } while (UserWantsToContinue( ) );
   |     }
```

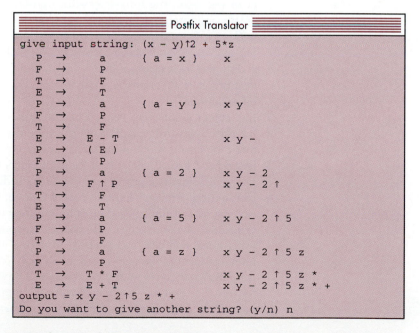

Figure 14.9 Infix to Postfix Translation Results

Once we are able to translate infix to postfix, we can accept an infix input string from the user, translate it to postfix, and then determine its value by applying the postfix interpreter given in Program 7.7 of Chapter 7. By combining these results, we can implement Program 4.12, called YourCalculationModule, which was a central component of the pocket calculator program given in Chapter 4.

14.4 Review Questions

1. In your own words, explain how the infix-to-postfix translator given in Program 14.8 works.
2. What is the main "theme" used in accomplishing this translation and how does it involve "recursive thinking"?
3. Are the functions in Program 14.8 mutually recursive?

14.4 Exercises

1. In Fig. 4.9, a calculator interface is shown that accepts a slightly more general class of arithmetic expressions than the parser in Program 14.8, since unary minus operators can be parsed and evaluated. Taking the results of Exercise 14.2.2, in which you extended the grammar of Fig. 14.1 to include unary minus operators, augment the railroad diagrams of Fig. 14.5, the recursive-descent parser of Fig. 14.6, the infix-to-postfix translator of Program 14.8, and finally, the postfix interpreter of Program 7.7, to handle unary minus operators. [*Hint:* When outputing a unary minus operator to the postfix output string, use a new character, such as '~', to represent unary minus, such that the unary minus character '~' is different from binary minus '–'. This will make it easier to augment the postfix interpreter of Program 7.7 to distinguish the interpretations of unary minus and binary minus.]
2. Implement a complete version of the C module, YourCalculationModule, whose interface is given in Program 4.12. Ensure that your unit can evaluate infix arithmetic expressions containing blanks and unary minus operators.
3. Extend the lexical analyzer of YourCalculationModule to recognize numbers consisting of strings of digits instead of just single digit characters.
4. (Substantial Project) Extend YourCalculationModule to recognize and evaluate expressions containing floating point numbers instead of just integers.
5. (Pocket Calculator Project) Implement a complete *advanced pocket calculator* by using a suitable windows package to define and implement a pocket calculator interface, such as the one shown in Fig. 4.9. [*Note:* It is possible that the computer laboratory associated with your course will have implemented this pocket calculator interface unit as a predefined and precompiled unit, in which case, all you will have to do is to call it from your main program and link it in.]

≡ **14.5** Recursion and Program Verification

Learning Objectives

1. To learn about the technique of recursion induction.
2. To learn how to apply recursion induction to prove the correctness of recursive programs.

ordinary mathematical induction

We have already used the ordinary form of *mathematical induction* to prove the correctness of iterative programs, such as **FindMax**, given as Program 5.21 in connection with proving the correctness of **SelectionSort**. Recall that in the ordinary form of mathematical induction, we try to prove that a proposition, P(n), depending on the integer n, is true for all non-negative values of n by means of the process shown in Fig. 14.10.

Step 1 is called the *base case* for the induction, and step 2 is called the *induction step*.

alternative principle of mathematical induction

Another form of the principle of mathematical induction, which is equivalent to that given in Fig. 14.10, is shown in Fig. 14.11. This second form often comes in handy when we want to prove that a recursive program works correctly. We treat P(n) as some proposition asserting the truth of some property about a subproblem of size n. After first proving P(0), we try to prove that P(n) is true of a given problem of size n, whenever P(k) is true for subproblems of all possible smaller sizes $k < n$. Assuming the truth of P(k), for $k < n$, amounts to assuming that the recursive calls solve smaller subproblems. If, having assumed this, we can establish that we can combine the solutions to the subproblems into a solution to the overall problem of size n, then we have proven that the recursive algorithm works for structures of all possible sizes (and sometimes all possible shapes, which is quite a nice conclusion to be able to draw).

Proving That Recursive Tree Reversal Works Correctly

Suppose we want to prove that a binary tree reversal algorithm (given as Program 14.13) actually works correctly for any binary tree T of any possible size and shape.

To prove P(n) is true for all $n \geq 0$:
1. First, prove P(0).
2. Then, assuming that P(n) is true for n, prove P(n + 1) is true.

Figure 14.10 Ordinary Principle of Mathematical Induction

To prove P(n) is true for all $n \geq 0$:
1. Prove P(0).
2. Assuming P(k) is true for all $0 \leq k < n$, prove P(n) is true.

Figure 14.11 Alternative Principle of Mathematical Induction

ordinary mathematical
induction does not
apply easily

Note that the ordinary mathematical induction technique does not apply easily to this task, since the trees being reversed come in all possible sizes and shapes,
and since there is no natural progression of binary trees with n nodes, $n + 1$ nodes,
$n + 2$ nodes, etc., on which to apply ordinary mathematical induction. For example, Fig. 14.12 illustrates some binary tree shapes and the shapes of their reversals.
In what follows, we'll agree to use the following data type definitions for binary
tree nodes:

```
typedef   char AirportCode[4];

typedef   struct TreeNodeTag {
              AirportCode           Airport;
              struct TreeNodeTag    *LeftLink;
              struct TreeNodeTag    *RightLink;
          } TreeNode;

typedef   TreeNode *TreeNodePointer;
```

However, we will think about these binary trees in a new way by agreeing to equate
mentally a pointer to a tree with the entire tree it points to.

Thus let T be a binary tree. If T is not the empty tree, we can agree to denote its
structure by an expression of the form, ([L] N [R]), where L is the left subtree, N is the

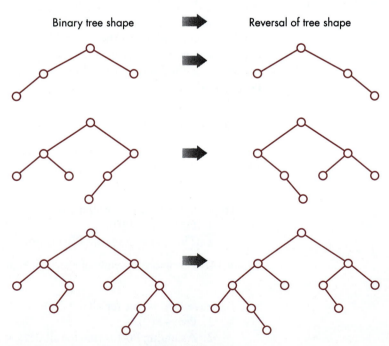

Figure 14.12 Binary Tree Shapes and Their Reversals

root node, and R is the right subtree. We can then define, $\rho(T)$, the reverse of a tree T, as follows:

The **Reverse**, $\rho(T)$, of a Binary Tree, T:

$$\rho(T) == T, \qquad\qquad \text{if } T == NULL$$
$$\rho(([L] \text{ N } [R])) == ([\rho(R)] \text{ N } [\rho(L)]), \qquad \text{if } T \mathrel{!=} NULL$$

Note that these two equations are statements in a logical language of relation and assertion. They are not statements of command in a programming language. Recall that in program verification, we always state the *preconditions* and *postconditions* in a language for making assertions, and then prove that an algorithm written in a language of command accomplishes the state changes described by the assertions. Thus, if Algorithm A is the tree reversal algorithm, ReverseTree(T), of Program 14.13, what we might strive to prove is that given the *precondition* {T is a binary tree}, then after S = ReverseTree(T) is executed, the *postcondition* {S is the reverse of T} is true.

precise formulation

Now that we have developed a bit of descriptive notation, we can formulate our problem precisely. We need to construct a mathematical proof of the following:

{ T is a binary tree }	precondition
S = ReverseTree(T);	algorithm
{ S == $\rho(T)$ }	postcondition

To prove: Given that the precondition is true beforehand, then after executing the algorithm, the postcondition must be true afterward.

recursion induction

We reason by using *recursion induction*. In recursion induction, we apply the second form of mathematical induction, given in Fig. 14.11, to a proposition, $P(n)$,

```
   |    TreeNodePointer ReverseTree(TreeNodePointer T)
   |    {
   |        TreeNodePointer Temp;
   |
 5 |        if (T == NULL) {
   |            return NULL;        /* the reversal of the empty tree is the empty tree */
   |        } else {
   |            Temp = T->LeftLink;                     /* save left subtree in Temp */
   |            T->LeftLink = ReverseTree(T->RightLink);
10 |            T->RightLink = ReverseTree(Temp);
   |            return T;
   |        }
   |
   |    }
```

Program 14.13 Reversing a Binary Tree T

where n is a measure of the possible sizes of substructures of data structures used in the algorithm. In this case, n is the number of nodes in a subtree of any shape in a binary tree.

Since the precondition asserts that T is a binary tree, T is either an empty tree, T == NULL, or a nonempty tree, T != NULL. So we can split the subsequent proof into two cases. First, the *base case*: Suppose T is the empty tree, so that T == NULL. Then according to the definition of reversal, ρ(T) == NULL. So we need to prove that S == ρ(T) == NULL, after executing the assignment, S = ReverseTree(T). Looking at Program 14.13, we see that if T == NULL on line 5, then, on line 6, NULL is returned as the value of the function call ReverseTree(T). So the base case is established.

Now consider the *recursion induction step*. Assume, by induction, that for any sub-tree Y containing k nodes, where $k < n$, ReverseTree(Y) == ρ(Y). Suppose now that T is a nonempty binary tree containing n nodes, where $n > 0$. Then T can be written in the form, ([L] N [R]), where L and R are (possibly empty) left and right subtrees. Now, when we compute the value, ReverseTree(([L] N [R])), Program 14.13 first saves the left subtree, L, in a variable Temp (on line 8). It then computes ReverseTree(R), which equals ρ(R) by recursion induction (since R has fewer nodes in it than T), and makes ρ(R) into the new left subtree of T (on line 9). Next, it changes the right sub-tree of T into ReverseTree(Temp) (on line 10). But since Temp contained L, and L has fewer nodes in it than T, we can conclude, by recursion induction, that ReverseTree(Temp) == ReverseTree(L) == ρ(L). Consequently, the right subtree of T has been changed to be ρ(L). Since the root node N of T was never changed, the original structure of T has been changed into ([ρ(R)] N [ρ(L)]). Finally, a pointer to this structure is returned by the function call ReverseTree(T) (on line 11), and becomes the value of S, using the assignment, S = ReverseTree(T). In short, if the value of T before executing this assignment was T == ([L] N [R]), then the value of S after executing the assignment has become ([ρ(R)] N [ρ(L)]). However, this last quantity is exactly equal to ρ(T), according to the definition of reversal. Putting the two cases together, and applying the second induction principle of Fig. 14.11, we conclude that ReverseTree(T) yields the value ρ(T), for trees of *any shape* having *any number* of nodes $n \geq 0$.

Oftentimes, readers who are introduced to proofs of program correctness, and who must struggle to make the effort to construct proofs are inclined to ask, "Was this effort worth it?" Well, maybe the answer to this question depends on the value placed on having a correct tree reversal algorithm. Suppose that a radar air traffic control system cannot work correctly unless its tree reversal software component is guaranteed to work correctly in all cases. Or suppose that a software product, such as an architectural drawing program, does not sell well to architects in the marketplace because it contains annoying bugs. People's lives or a company's commercial success might well depend on having correct software components. So to answer the question, "Was it worth the effort to verify this algorithm?" we need to be able to provide a payoff function that assigns values to achieving and not achieving the results. This foreshadows the discussion of the topic of the role of risk assessment in a software effort—a subject that we will explore further in Chapter 16.

proving the recursion induction step

was it worth it?

14.5 Review Questions

1. Describe two alternative principles of mathematical induction that are equivalent to one another.
2. What is recursion induction?
3. In your own words, describe how you apply recursion induction to prove that a proposition, P(n), is true of a recursive function F(t), where t is a structure of size n.

14.5 Exercises

1. Consider the following C function:

```
  |   int f(int n)                          /* let n be any positive integer */
  |   {
  |       if (n == 1) {
  |           return 1;
5 |       } else if ( (n%2) == 0 ) {        /* n is even iff (n % 2) == 0 */
  |           return f(n / 2);
  |       } else {                          /* otherwise, if n is odd */
  |           return f(3*n + 1);
  |       }
  |   }
```

For example, $f(13) == f(40) == f(20) == f(10) == f(5) == f(16) == f(8) == f(4) == f(2) == f(1) == 1$. If you play with enough examples, you will see that for any positive integer n, either $f(n) == 1$, or $f(n)$ causes an infinite regress of recursive calls which never converges. If a recursive function $f(n)$ is defined (i.e., converges to a defined result) for all $n \geq 1$, it is said to be an *entire function*. What difficulties do you encounter when trying to apply recursion induction to prove that $f(n) == 1$ is an entire function for all $n \geq 1$?

2. Let A[0:n – 1] be an array of n numbers. Another version of the **Partition** algorithm used as a subroutine of **QuickSort** can be used to find the kth smallest number in the array A, according to the following program strategy, in which **Find(A,k,m,n)** finds the kth smallest item in A[m:n]:

```
  |    void Find(ItemArray A, int k, int m, int n)
  |    {
  |
  |        /* to move the kth smallest item in A[m:n] */
5 |        /* into the kth position */
  |
  |        if (there is more than one item in A[m:n] ) {
  |
  |            (Partition A[m:n] into a LeftPartition A[m:j] and a)
10 |           (RightPartition A[i:n] such that i == j + 1)
  |
  |            if (the kth item is in the LeftPartition) {
  |                (Find the kth item of the LeftPartition A[m:j])
```

```
15 |                } else {
   |                        (Find the (k – ( j – m + 1))th item of the RightPartition A[i:n])
   |                }
   |        }
   |    }
```

Implement another version of the **Partition** function (given as Program 13.15) such that your new **Partition** function satisfies the conditions on lines 9:10 of the program strategy for **Find** above. Fill in the outline given by the above program strategy to obtain an actual C program for finding the kth smallest number in A. Then use recursion induction to prove the correctness of your program.

3. Use recursion induction to prove that the following program prints all $n!$ permutations of the first n objects in an array $A[0:n-1]$ of distinct objects.

```
   | /* --------------------------------------------------------- */
   |
   | void Perm(PermutationArray A, int m, int n)
   | {
 5 |     int i;
   |
   |     if ( m == 0 ) {
   |
   |         PrintPerm(A,n);                    /* prints the first n objects in A */
10 |
   |     } else {
   |
   |         for (i = 0; i < m; ++i ) {
   |             Exchange(A,i,m – 1);           /* swaps A[i] ↔ A[m – 1] */
15 |             Perm(A,m – 1,n);
   |             Exchange(A,m – 1,i);           /* swaps A[m – 1] ↔ A[i] */
   |         }
   |     }
   | }
20 |
   | /* --------------------------------------------------------- */
   |
   | void Permute(PermutationArray A, int n)
   | {
25 |     InitPermArray(A,n);         /* fills array A[0:n – 1] with n distinct objects */
   |     Perm(A,n,n); /* calls subroutine to print the n! permutations of A[0:n – 1] */
   | }
```

Pitfalls

- *Not exercising care when applying recursion induction*

    When trying to prove the correctness of a recursive program using recursion induction it is easy to be careless and to ignore certain subtle points.

In addition to making sure to prove all the base cases correct, it is important to ensure that the recursive calls to solve smaller subproblems eventually result in calls on the base cases, and that the supposedly smaller subproblems are in fact smaller than the original problem given.

Tips and Techniques

- *How to design a recursive-descent parser*

  Recursive-descent parsers are popular and can be designed to parse efficiently the sentences in the language, $L(G)$, generated by a context-free grammar, G.

  Generally speaking, if $L(G)$ contains infinitely many sentences, then the grammar, G, will be either directly recursive or indirectly recursive, or both. If some of the productions of G are left-recursive, it is important to eliminate left-recursion using the technique illustrated in Section 14.3. After this has been done, it may be possible to convert the productions of G into a set of railroad diagrams. When a railroad diagram contains a "fork in the railroad tracks" it is necessary to be able to look ahead either one lexeme or a few lexemes in the input to distinguish which fork to travel. If the railroad diagrams do not have this property, it is time to go back and alter the grammar, G, if possible, so that G generates the same language, $L(G)$, but can be converted to railroad diagrams in which k-lexeme lookaheads can be used to decide which tracks to follow at forks in the railroad diagrams.

  After a suitable set of railroad diagrams has been obtained, it is often possible to translate them into a collection of mutually recursive procedures that perform deterministic shift-reduce parsing, using a lookahead of k-lexemes in the input. The example in Section 14.3 illustrates some, but not all, techniques for accomplishing this.

References for Further Study

A. V. Aho and J. D. Ullman, *The Theory of Parsing, Translation and Compiling*, 2 vols., Prentice-Hall, Englewood Cliffs, NJ, (1972).

parsing theory

A good pair of books that presents more about different methods for parsing and translating context-free languages.

J. E. Hopcroft and J. D. Ullman, *Formal Languages and Their Relation to Automata*, Addison-Wesley, Reading, Mass., (1969).

context-free languages

A good book covering the theory of context-free grammars and context-free languages.

Chapter Summary

direct and indirect recursion

Recursion can be either direct or indirect. In *direct recursion*, the recursive entity being defined calls itself directly inside its own definition. By contrast, *indirect recursion* occurs when a collection of definitions is *mutually recursive*, meaning that the definitions can call each other in a cyclic manner in which a given entity can call itself indirectly using a chain of calls through the other definitions.

defining, recognizing, and
proving things with
recursion

In this chapter, we study examples of how recursion can be used for *defining things* and for *recognizing things*. We also study an additional technique, called *recursion induction*, useful for proving that recursive programs are correct, especially when the recursive programs are designed to work using arguments drawn from an unbounded collection of structures of differing sizes and shapes to which the ordinary familiar kind of mathematical induction does not apply easily.

the utility of recursive
definitions

Both direct and indirect recursion can occur among a collection of recursive functions declared in a program, in the data type declarations in a program, in the productions defining the grammar of a context-free language, and in other collections of definitions that define entities capable of containing instances of themselves as parts. Recursion thus becomes a powerful tool for providing finite descriptions of unbounded sets of objects that contain instances of themselves as parts.

context-free languages

Context-free languages are commonly used to define precisely the syntax of programming languages. A *context-free language*, $L(G)$, is a set of sentences generated from a *context-free grammar*, G. A context-free grammar, $G = (S, V_N, V_T, P)$, is a four-tuple consisting of a set, V_N, of nonterminal symbols, another set, V_T, of terminal symbols (distinct from the symbols in V_N), a special start symbol, S in V_N, and a set of productions, P, where each production in P is of the form, $X \rightarrow \alpha$, such that $X \in V_N$, and α is a string of symbols in $V_N \cup V_T$.

You use a context-free grammar, G, to derive sentences in $L(G)$ by repeatedly applying the production rules in P starting with the start symbol S. Each production, $X \rightarrow \alpha$, is a substitution rule that can be used to replace an instance of the symbol X on its left with the string α on its right. A string of symbols derived by application of the productions in this fashion is called a *sentential form*. When a sentential form no longer contains any nonterminal symbols that can be derived further through substitutions, using the productions in P, and thus contains only terminal symbols in V_T, it is called a *sentence* of the language $L(G)$, generated by the context-free grammar, G. In fact, $L(G)$ consists exactly of all the sentences that can be derived from the start symbol S, using productions in P.

recursive-descent parsers

A *recursive-descent parser* can often be constructed from a context-free grammar, G. A recursive-descent parser is a collection of mutually recursive procedures that typically can call one another in a cyclical fashion. Such a parser uses a push-down stack and typically performs two kinds of actions: *shifting* and *reducing*. Shifting means detaching a new symbol from the front of the remainder of the input string being parsed and pushing it on the top of a push-down stack. Reducing with respect to a production, $X \rightarrow \alpha$, means replacing the topmost symbols on the push-down stack matching the string on the right side, α, of the production, $X \rightarrow \alpha$, with the symbol, X, on the left side of the production. In effect, reducing consists of replacing a subexpression, α, with its name, X. By repeatedly replacing subexpressions with their names, the entire input string is progressively collapsed back into the start symbol, S, of the grammar G. Sometimes it may be necessary to look ahead k symbols into the remainder of the input string to make a decision about whether to *shift* or to *reduce* (when both actions are possible). If it is possible to construct a shift-reduce parser by looking ahead k symbols into the input string, the result is called a *deterministic, shift-reduce parser with lookahead k*.

A practical way to construct a recursive-descent parser is first to try to convert the context-free grammar, G, into a set of railroad diagrams (with a distinct railroad diagram corresponding to each nonterminal symbol in V_N). If it is possible to decide which tracks to follow at forks in the railroad diagrams, using suitable k-symbol lookaheads into the input string, it is usually possible to convert the railroad diagrams into a collection of mutually recursive functions forming a recursive-descent parser.

infix-to-postfix translators

Such a parser can be augmented to perform the task of *translating* the input string into a suitable output (or into an intermediate form of some sort) useful in processes of compiling and interpreting programming languages. An example was given in Section 14.4, in which infix arithmetic expressions were translated into corresponding postfix arithmetic expressions, suitable for evaluation using a push-down-stack-based, postfix interpreter developed earlier in Chapter 7.

recursion induction

Recursion induction is a technique that is often useful when attempting to prove the correctness of a recursive program. The idea is to "think recursively" in the construction of the proof as well as in the design of the program. To apply the technique of recursion induction, we first try to establish the correctness of the base cases of program P. Then, when applying P to an input of a given size, n, we assume the correctness of the results of recursive calls inside P, when applied to any subproblem of smaller size, $k < n$. On the assumption that all subproblems are correctly solved by these recursive calls, we try to prove that P correctly produces its own output.

15

Object-Oriented Programming

15.1 Introduction and Motivation

origins of object-oriented programming

Although the origins of *object-oriented programming* (OOP) stretch back three decades —to the introduction of the SIMULA and SMALLTALK programming languages—OOP's popularity as a practical programming technique has become widespread only in the last decade.

At its heart, object-oriented programming provides another set of concepts for modular programming that differ slightly from the modular programming concepts covered earlier in Chapter 4. A C module (or the similar concepts of an Ada *package* or a Pascal *unit*), is that of a section of text inside a bigger program which has its own internal data structures and functions and exports a carefully defined set of functions and data through its interface, while keeping its other internal mechanics hidden.

objects are dynamic

An *object* in an object-oriented programming system is similar to a C module, in that it has its own data and functions and can make them available through its interface. In contrast to a C module, however, an object's existence is dynamic. Rather than being a portion of a larger program text (as is the case with a C module), an

610

object is brought into being by an act of storage allocation during the running of a program. Moreover, its existence can be made to expire by freeing up its data storage while the program is running.

An object's data storage region can be a value of a variable or can be referred to by a pointer. Pointers that refer to other objects may be stored as values of variables and as struct members. This permits dynamically created objects to be linked into larger data structures and permits objects to refer to other objects dynamically via pointer references.

object references

C++ is an extension of C, defined by Bjarne Stroustrup of AT&T Bell Laboratories. In C++, the type of an object must first be defined using an object class definition. An individual instance of an object can then be created by allocating storage for it in the heap, using its class type definition as a declarator. This process is almost identical to the creation in the heap of a pointer to an instance of a C struct type, in that both structs and objects can have data members where their internal data values are stored. There are only two differences: (1) in addition to struct data members, objects can have locally defined function members associated with them, and (2) an object's class, T_1, can be derived from another object's class, T_2, in which case an object of type T_1 can access the data and local functions defined for objects that are of type T_2.

C++

It is then said that an object's class definition, T_2, specifies the *class* of objects that are the instances of T_2, created dynamically at run-time. Moreover, if object class, T_1, is derived from object class, T_2, then the object instances of T_1, created at run-time, are said to be a *subclass* of the class of objects that are instances of T_2. The objects in the subclass, T_1, are said to *inherit* the data and functions of the class T_2, and T_2 is said to be a *base class* for the derivation of T_1.

classes and inheritance

The act of deriving a subclass of objects is called *subclassing*. Subclassing is a powerful way to define new kinds of objects because all you need to do is to define a new class T_1 as a derived class of T_2, in which case T_1 inherits all of T_2's defined data and functions, following which, you can define some new individual features local to T_1 that differ from the features of T_2. This is called *customization*. In effect, defining new objects by customization is equivalent to defining new things using *differences*—you merely say, "I want this new kind of object, T_1, to be exactly like that other kind of object, T_2, except that I want my new kind of object to have the following new features,"—whereupon you provide the new data members and local functions that are individual to T_1 that make it *different* from T_2. But since T_1 is derived from T_2, it inherits, and can use, the data and functions defined for T_2.

derived classes and object customization

Occasionally, however, you want to define a function F that operates on T_1 to have the same name and parameter types as an identical function F that is common to a base class T_2, but you want the version of F that operates locally on T_1 to have a special local behavior and meaning. To do this, you arrange to define F when it applies to T_1 to supply a different locally defined meaning for function F. The virtual function F thus acts like a "blank slot" common to all derived classes of T_2 that gets filled in differently for each different class derived from T_2.

virtual functions

To sum up the essence of object-oriented programming: (1) it provides for packaging of both data and functions together into struct-like objects; (2) classes of objects can be defined having the three features: *subclass derivation*, *inheritance*, and *customization*; and (3) instances of objects can be created dynamically during the running of a program and can be referenced by pointers.

methods,
instance variables,
and message passing

There is some special vocabulary that has evolved and has become popular in connection with object-oriented programming, which we will introduce and use in this chapter along with the equivalent C++ terminology. Familiarity with this vocabulary will ease the reader's burden when attempting to decode books and articles on object-oriented programming elsewhere. In particular, the struct data members of an object are called *instance variables*, and the function members of an object are called *methods*. When you *call a method* (i.e., a function), $F(a_1, a_2, \ldots, a_n)$, in an object, O_2, you say that you have sent O_2 the *message*, $F(a_1, a_2, \ldots, a_n)$.

You might visualize a set of objects as a collection of factories that send each other messages. When one factory sends another factory a message, the receiving factory invokes a local manufacturing method named in the message to carry out an internal process, which may result in storing new values internally in the factory's *instance variables*, sending messages to other factories, or operating on the outside world to alter its structure in some defined fashion.

some benefits of object-
oriented programming

Object-oriented programming offers substantial benefits for organizing software that is built from reusable components. In the next chapter, we will review why software reuse has important economic benefits in reducing the cost of software development and maintenance. When reusable software components are provided in object libraries, it becomes easier to assemble them into big software systems than is the case with ordinary modular programming techniques, in part, because objects can be customized and modified to exhibit slightly different behavior only by expressing the new differences. In short, objects are easier to modify so that they become plug-compatible with other components than is the case for ordinary functions, data, and software modules.

Plan for the Chapter

Section 15.2 introduces object-oriented programming by means of a sequence of three progressive examples. The first stage example inscribes three kinds of shapes inside an enclosing rectangle: (1) ovals, (2) rectangles with rounded corners, and (3) ordinary rectangles themselves. Since only the "wire frames" of these shapes are drawn, these shapes are said to be "hollow shapes." The first stage illustrates how to derive customized subclasses of a single base class, **TShape**, to express the different drawing methods for ovals, rectangles, and rounded rectangles. Each of the subclasses *customizes* the virtual **Draw** method of the base class **TShape** to provide its own distinct drawing method.

studying three
progressive examples

In the second stage example, three subclasses of the original hollow shapes are defined to draw "filled shapes." In addition to having a wire frame in the shape of an oval, rectangle, or rounded rectangle, the interior of a filled shape is shaded. Filled shapes define their own local *customized* **Draw** methods to fill their interiors, but then make calls on the **Draw** methods of their immediate ancestors to draw the wire frames around their filled interiors.

In the third stage example, a list of shape objects is saved, and these saved shapes are redrawn in another location relative to the coordinate system of the overall drawing. The third stage illustrates how to store pointers to objects inside data structures such as linked lists, and how to apply the **Draw** method to all objects on a list. This is interesting because, even though the same draw message is sent to each object on the list, a different individual drawing method for each object in the list is invoked depending on its particular subclass. This illustrates one of the powers of object-oriented programming to perform what is called *dynamic binding*. Moreover, it is shown how the type system in C++ is more general and powerful than that of ordinary C, since object variables can store values from any derived subclass.

In Section 15.3, we investigate how to use object-oriented programming techniques to build software systems and how to use object editors to build graphical user interfaces with vastly reduced effort in comparison to that required when using ordinary programming techniques.

In Section 15.4, we discuss the advantages and disadvantages of object-oriented programming, and we comment on some of the drawbacks of using an object-oriented system lacking mature class browsers and run-time object debugging.

15.2 Exploring OOP Through Progressive Examples

Learning Objectives

1. To learn how to define an object class in C++.
2. To learn how to use class derivation, inheritance, and customization.
3. To learn how to use object pointers and how to send a message to each of a collection of objects dynamically.
4. To appreciate how to organize object-oriented modules and the programs that use them in C++.

drawing shapes

We are going to develop a small object-oriented drawing program that draws some shapes in a Cartesian coordinate system (having an *x*-axis and a *y*-axis in the normal fashion). There are three shapes: (1) rectangles, (2) ovals, and (3) rounded rectangles, as illustrated in Fig. 15.1.

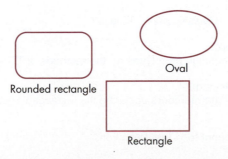

Figure 15.1 Three Kinds of Shapes

Rounded rectangle

Oval

Rectangle

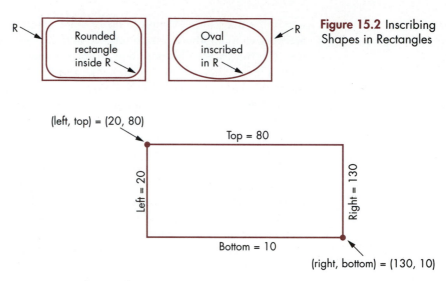

Figure 15.2 Inscribing Shapes in Rectangles

Figure 15.3 A Rectangle

```
typedef   struct {
              int   left, top, right, bottom;
          } Rect;
```

Figure 15.4 A Typedef for a Rectangle in C

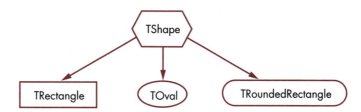

Figure 15.5 Subclasses of TShape

```
    |    class TClassX : public TClassY {
    |
    |       public:
    |           (function prototypes for the methods of TClassX)
  5 |
    |       protected:
    |           (data members declaring the instance variables of TClassX)
    |    };
```

Figure 15.6 Format for Class Definitions

We assume the existence of some basic graphics routines that can accept a rectangle, R, as a parameter and can draw R itself, or draw the oval or rounded rectangle inscribed inside R. These three routines are FrameRect(&R), FrameOval(&R), and FrameRoundRect(&R,a,b), where a and b are integers defining the curvature of the corners of the rounded rectangle. Figure 15.2 illustrates how FrameOval(&R) and FrameRoundRect(&R,20,20) inscribe ovals and rounded rectangles inside an enclosing rectangle, R.

A rectangle, R, can be defined by giving the coordinates of two points (x_1, y_1) and (x_2, y_2), where (x_1, y_1) is the point at the top left corner of R and (x_2, y_2) is the point at the bottom right corner of R. Figure 15.3 illustrates a rectangle whose top-left corner is at the point $(x_1, y_1) = (20, 80)$ and whose bottom-right corner is at the point $(x_2, y_2) = (130, 10)$.

The C data structure for a rectangle is simply a struct declared by the struct typedef shown in Fig. 15.4.

Now we are ready to use C++ to define a Shapes module, which defines a class of shape objects, called TShape, having three derived subclasses defining rectangles, ovals, and rounded rectangles. Figure 15.5 depicts these subclass relationships.

Figure 15.6 gives the format we shall use in this chapter to define a class of objects, TClassX, as a derived class of the base class of objects TClassY. Such a definition implies that an object X of type TClassX inherits all the methods and data members (or instance variables) of objects of type TClassY. In addition, X has its own data members and methods, as specified in the TClassX declaration.

The labels public: and protected: on lines 3 and 6 of Fig. 15.6 specify that the members listed after them have certain visibilities. Members declared in the public section are visible to (and can be used by) users external to the class. Members declared in the protected section are visible to (and can be used by) users in subclasses derived from the given base class TClassX. Members in a private section (used on line 12 of Program 15.19) are visible only within the class and cannot be used externally.

Let's now look at the Shapes module in Program 15.7. Note first that comments in C++ begin with two slashes (//) and extend to the end of the line. Focusing on the type declaration for TShape found on lines 6:19, line 6 declares the class of objects

```
     |    // ------------< begin Shapes.h header file >------------ //
     |
     |    // Shapes.h defines an abstract base class TShape and three derived
     |    // subclasses: TRectangle, TOval, and TRoundedRectangle.
   5 |
     |    class TShape {
     |
     |      public:
     |        // SetEnclosingRect sets the coordinates of the EnclosingRectangle.
  10 |            void SetEnclosingRect (int x1, int y1, int x2, int y2);
     |
     |        // Calling the Draw( ) method draws the shape. Each derived subclass
     |        // must give its own customized definition of the virtual Draw( ) method.
     |            virtual void Draw( );
```

Program 15.7 Shapes Module (continued)

Program 15.7 Shapes Module (continued)

```
15          protected:
                Rect EnclosingRectangle;          // The rectangle that encloses the shape

            };
20
            class TRectangle : public TShape {
                public: void Draw( );
            };

25          class TOval : public TShape {
                public: void Draw( );
            };

            class TRoundedRectangle : public TShape {
30              public: void Draw( );
            };

            // ------------< end-of-file Shapes.h >------------ //
            // ------------< begin file Shapes.c >------------ //
35
            #include "Shapes.h"

            void TShape : : SetEnclosingRect(int x1, int y1, int x2, int y2)
            {
40              EnclosingRectangle.top = 100 − y1;    // transform to a normal Cartesian
                EnclosingRectangle.left = 150 + x1;              // coordinate system with
                EnclosingRectangle.bottom = 100 − y2;      // origin at (x,y) = (100,150)
                EnclosingRectangle.right = 150 + x2;           // in the Drawing Window
            }
45
            void TShape : : Draw( )
            {
                printf("Impossible call on virtual Draw method of TShape.\n");
            }
50
            void TRectangle : : Draw( )
            {
                FrameRect(&EnclosingRectangle);
            }
55
            void TOval : : Draw( )
            {
                FrameOval(&EnclosingRectangle);
            }
60
            void TRoundedRectangle : : Draw( )
            {
                FrameRoundRect(&EnclosingRectangle, 20, 20);
            }
65
            // ------------< end-of-file Shapes.c >------------ //
```

TShape as a *base class* (which is not a derived subclass of any other class). It will be used as an *abstract class* from which further specific subclasses will be derived.

declaring an object's methods

In the public section following the introduction of the base class name the prototypes for the function members defining the object's *methods* are given. An *object method* is just another term for a function that applies to instances of the object.

On lines 10 and 14 of the declaration for TShape in Program 15.7, two method prototype declarations are given:

```
void SetEnclosingRect (int x1, int y1, int x2, int y2);
```

and

```
virtual void Draw( );
```

sending messages to call methods

These two prototypes specify that every object of type TShape has two methods that apply to it: SetEnclosingRect and Draw. Suppose Ob1 is an instance of an object of type TShape. To apply the Draw method to Ob1, you use the expression Ob1.Draw( ). In object-oriented programming terminology, this is called, "sending the Draw message to the object Ob1." A good way to think of it is to envisage two objects: a *sender object*, S, and a *receiver object*, R. When S sends the Draw message to R, by using the expression R.Draw( ), it is as if S tells R to "*draw yourself*." The format is, "Hey you . Do this," meaning that to the left of the dot, you designate the object instance that is to receive the message, and then to the right of the dot you give a message naming a method for the receiver to perform (which must name one of the receiver's own methods).

As another example, if you wanted to tell Ob1 to set its enclosing rectangle to be the rectangle bounded by the point (x1, y1) on the top-left and (x2, y2) on the bottom-right, you would write, Ob1.SetEnclosingRect (x1, y1, x2, y2). This would send a message to the object instance Ob1 to perform its own SetEnclosingRect method, using the parameters (x1, y1, x2, y2) sent in the message.

Just like the function prototypes defined in the interface header file of a C module, the function prototypes specified inside an object class definition require that their implementations be given later in the source file for the module. In Program 15.7, lines 34:66 provide the implementations of the SetEnclosingRect and Draw methods for objects of type TShape.

On line 17, the expression Rect EnclosingRectangle; declares that each instance of an object of type TShape has a data member called EnclosingRectangle, which contains a value of type Rect. The data member name EnclosingRectangle is said to be an *instance variable* in one of the variants of object-oriented programming terminology used elsewhere. Thus, an instance variable is the same as a struct data member.

instance variables use dot notation

Dot notation is used to select instance variables of an object. Suppose Ob1 is an *instance* of an object declared to be of object class TClass1, and suppose that the object class definition for TClass1 defines instance variables (i.e., struct data members), type1 member1; type2 member2; . . . ; type$_n$ member$_n$;. Then if Ob1 is a variable holding an instance of TClass1, you can access the values in the instance variables of Ob1, using the dot notation Ob1.member1, Ob1.member2, . . . , Ob1.member$_n$.

In the case of objects of type TShape, as declared on lines 6:19 of Program 15.7, if Shape1 has been created to be an instance of the object class TShape, then

Shape1.EnclosingRectangle, gives a data value of type Rect, which is a rectangle that encloses the shape defined by the object.

When the Rect EnclosingRectangle; data member is declared on line 17 in the *protected section* of its class definition beginning with the specifier protected: on line 16, it means that the EnclosingRectangle data member will become a visible data member of each of the derived subclasses of the base class TShape.

Defining Derived Classes

abstract classes

The class TShape is set up to function as an *abstract class*, meaning that it is a device to collect the derived subclasses defining rectangles, ovals, and rounded rectangles, even though nobody will ever create an actual instance of an object in the class TShape itself. The reason why this is a clever thing to do will become apparent in the subsequent stages of the shape-drawing example.

In particular, we will now derive three classes of the class TShape, which are the subclasses TRectangle, TOval, and TRoundedRectangle.

For example, the object type definition for TOval is given on lines 25:27 of Program 15.7 and is of the form

```
|     class TOval : public TShape {
|
|           public:
|                 void Draw( );
|     };
```

derived classes

The first line, class TOval : public TShape, defines the derived class of objects TOval to be a *subclass* of the base class, TShape. The class TOval has no instance variables of its own, since its class definition specifies no data member declarations, but it does have one method, given by the line, void Draw( ). This defines the Draw method for a TOval object to be a special local customized version of the identically named virtual Draw method for a TShape. Each class derived from the base class TShape must supply its own local definition of the virtual Draw( ) method. Thus, the virtual Draw( ) method behaves like an "empty slot" which must be filled in by a different local drawing method in each of the different classes derived from the base class TShape.

The object type definitions for TRectangle and TRoundedRectangle on lines 21:23 and 29:31 of Program 15.7 follow a similar format, and each is defined to have its own local Draw method, which supplies a local customized meaning for the virtual Draw method declared in the base class TShape.

In effect, what we have defined at this moment are three subclasses of TShape, each having its own local Draw method and each inheriting the EnclosingRectangle instance variable and the SetEnclosingRectangle method from the base class TShape.

defining method implementations

The Shapes.c implementation file of the Shapes module (see lines 34:66 of Program 15.7) now defines the operational meaning of each of the Draw methods for TRectangle, TOval, and TRoundedRectangle, as well as defining the SetEnclosingRectangle method for a general TShape. The key thing to notice is that inside any of the method implementations, you can use the name of an instance variable, V, and expect it to have as its value the contents of the data member V of the object instance to which the given method is being applied.

For example, let's look at the implementation of the TOval::Draw( ) method on lines 56:59 of Program 15.7.

```
|    void TOval : : Draw( )
|    {
|        FrameOval(&EnclosingRectangle);
|    }
```

distinguishing which
method is being defined

Note that you have to give the name of the method you are implementing as TOval::Draw, to distinguish it from TRectangle::Draw, TRoundedRectangle::Draw and TShape::Draw. If you just gave the header as void Draw( ), C++ would not know which Draw method you were attempting to define, since several of the classes and derived classes (four to be exact) have identically named Draw methods specifying individually different locally defined behaviors for the virtual Draw method.

The behavior you want for TOval::Draw, when applied to an object instance, Ob1, of type TOval, is to draw an oval inside Ob1's enclosing rectangle. The way you make TOval::Draw do this is to issue the call FrameOval(&EnclosingRectangle), given on line 58. Here, the parameter EnclosingRectangle is a data member (or an instance variable), inherited from TOval's base class TShape, having as its value the rectangle enclosing the oval you are asking FrameOval to draw for you. Its effect, when executed, is to draw a wire frame oval inscribed in the space designated by the coordinates of the enclosing rectangle.

Using the Shapes Module in the Main Program

Now we are ready to introduce the main program that uses the services of the **Shapes** module defined in Program 15.7. In effect, Program 15.7 has defined four classes of objects consisting of a base class, **TShape**, which has three derived subclasses, as depicted by Figure 15.5. Once we have created an instance, **Ob1**, of any of the three subclasses, we can set the coordinates of its enclosing rectangle by sending it a message of the form **Ob1.SetEnclosingRectangle(x1, y1, x2, y2)**, following which we can cause it to draw a wire-frame image of itself, by sending it a message of the form **Ob1.Draw( )**. We will see in a moment how this works. Now it is time to introduce the main program, given as Program 15.8.

```
   |    / /      First Stage Example of Shape Drawing
   |    / /      to draw three kinds of hollow shapes
   |
   |    #include <stdio.h>
 5 |    #include <string.h>
   |    # include "Shapes.h"
   |
   |    / / assume that typedef enum {false, true} Boolean; has been given
   |
```

Program 15.8 First Stage Example of Shape Drawing (continued)

Program 15.8 First Stage Example of Shape Drawing (continued)

```
10  |       Boolean UserDesignatesShape(TShape **theShape)
    |       {
    |           char *reply = "          ";
    |
    |           printf("Designate one of: Q)uit, O)val, R)ectangle,\n");
15  |           printf(" RR)oundedRectangle: ");
    |           gets(reply);                                    // get a reply string from the user
    |
    |           if ( (reply[0] == 'Q') || (reply[0] == 'q') ) {
    |               return false;
20  |           } else {
    |               switch (reply[0]) {
    |               case 'O': case 'o': *theShape = new TOval;
    |                                   return true;
    |               case 'R': case 'r':  if (strlen(reply) == 1) {
25  |                                         *theShape = new TRectangle;
    |                                     } else {                       // if (reply[2] is 'R' or 'r'
    |                                         *theShape = new TRoundedRectangle;
    |                                     }
    |                                     return true;
30  |               default: *theShape = NULL; return true;
    |               }
    |           }
    |       }
    |
35  |       void DrawCoordinateSystem( )                                    // details omitted
    |       {
    |           // Draws x-axis, y-axis, origin and boundaries of coordinate system
    |       }
    |
40  |       int main( )
    |       {
    |           TShape  *theShape;
    |           short    x1, y1, x2, y2;
    |
45  |           SetUpWindows( );      // displays Console Window and Drawing Window
    |           DrawCoordinateSystem( );       // draws x and y axes in Drawing Window
    |
    |           while (UserDesignatesShape(&theShape)) {
    |               if (theShape == NULL) {
50  |                   printf("unknown shape\n");
    |               } else {
    |                   printf("Give Coordinates of Enclosing Rectangle: \n");
    |                   printf("left top right bottom: ");
    |                   scanf("%hd%hd%hd%hd", &x1, &y1, &x2, &y2);
55  |                   theShape–>SetEnclosingRect(x1, y1, x2, y2);
    |                   theShape–>Draw( );
    |               }
    |           }
60  |       }
    |
```

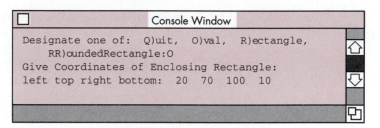

Figure 15.9 Console Window Dialog to Choose an Oval

Let's dive right in and explore how the main program section of Program 15.8 works. First of all, since the Shapes.h file has been invoked by the include directive on line 6, all of the methods and instance variables for the shape objects defined in Program 15.7 are available for service.

The main program section (given on lines 40:60) starts by executing lines 45:46, which display a console text window and a Drawing Window, in which a Cartesian coordinate system is drawn. Subsequent calls to printf will display text in the console window, where a normal C text dialog can take place with the user. Moreover, all drawing of shapes will take place in the coordinate system in the Drawing Window.

Execution of the main program now proceeds to the while-loop on lines 48:58. First, the Boolean function UserDesignatesShape(&theShape) is evaluated as the while-condition. This carries on a dialog with the user in the console window by asking the user to type some letter combinations to choose a shape or to quit the program. If the user types R, O, or RR, the respective shapes Rectangle, Oval, or RoundedRectangle are chosen. If the user types Q, the program quits.

Let's suppose that the user has chosen an Oval shape by typing an O in reply to the dialog in the Console Window, as shown in Fig. 15.9. Typing O causes lines 22:23 of the function UserDesignatesShape to be executed, which performs the assignment *theShape = new TOval;. Note that theShape is a variable of type TShape**. The operator new X allocates a new object of class X in the heap and returns a pointer to that object. In this case, the type of the new object created is TOval. Moreover, a pointer to the new object of type TOval is assigned to be the value of *theShape, which places a pointer to the new TOval object in the variable theShape defined on line 42 and used in the while-loop on lines 48:58.

creating a new object instance

This illustrates one of C++'s powerful features. A variable of type TShape* is capable of containing not only pointers to objects of type TShape* but also pointers to objects of any of the derived subclasses of TShape. In this case, the variable theShape, which is of type TShape*, is set to a pointer to a new instance of an object of subtype TOval, which is a subtype of the base type TShape.

When the user types other letter combinations in the console window, such as R, for Rectangle, or RR, for RoundedRectangle, new object instances of types TRectangle or TRoundedRectangle are created in the heap and pointers to them are assigned to be the value of the variable theShape by executing the assignments *theShape = new TRectangle; on line 25 and *theShape = new TRoundedRectangle; on line 27, respectively.

When the user selects a shape in the console window, in addition to assigning a pointer to a new object of one of the subtypes of shapes to be the value of the variable, theShape, the Boolean value returned by UserDesignatesShape(theShape) is set to *true*. This causes the body of the while-loop on lines 49:57 to be executed. The critical actions happen on lines 52:56. First, the user is asked to supply the coordinates of the enclosing rectangle for the shape (which are read from the console dialog and are assigned to be the values of x1, y1, x2, and y2). Next, on line 55, the following method call is made:

theShape–>SetEnclosingRect(x1, y1, x2, y2);

This sends the message SetEnclosingRect(x1, y1, x2, y2) to the object that is the value of the pointer variable theShape. Since this object is an object of type TOval, the SetEnclosingRect(x1, y1, x2, y2) method of TOval is called. In this case, since the SetEnclosingRect method of the class TOval is inherited from the base class TShape, the SetEnclosingRect method of the class TShape is executed, and this causes the (inherited) instance variable EnclosingRectangle of the TOval object to be set to the coordinates (x1, y1, x2, y2) passed in the message SetEnclosingRect(x1, y1, x2, y2).

setting the enclosing rectangle's coordinates

The net result is that the oval object now has the coordinates of its (inherited) enclosing rectangle set to the coordinates designated by the user in the console dialog immediately beforehand.

Now comes the final action—drawing the oval object itself. To do this, Program 15.8 sends the Draw message to the oval object that is the value of the variable theShape, using the statement theShape–>Draw( ); on line 56. In effect, the main program sends the message "Draw yourself" to the oval object.

When the object that is the value of the variable theShape receives this Draw message, the actual drawing action taken will be determined by the subtype of the object—TOval objects will be drawn as ovals, TRectangle objects will be drawn as rectangles, and TRoundedRectangle objects will be drawn as rounded rectangles. The specific action of the Draw method is thus determined dynamically at run-time, depending on the subtype of the object receiving the Draw message. This is called *dynamic binding.* You might imagine that each object that is a subtype of TShape has a different way to respond to the virtual Draw( ) message by invoking its own local customized drawing method that was supplied in its definition to "fill-in the blank" for the virtual Draw( ) method specified in the abstract TShape class definition.

drawing the oval shape

What happens in this case is that since the oval object indeed has its own local customized drawing method, it executes this local Draw method, resulting in the drawing of an oval inscribed inside the bounds given by the EnclosingRectangle instance variable.

Figure 15.10 shows the oval drawn as a result of executing theShape–>Draw( ) on line 56 of Program 15.8. After the oval is drawn, the while-loop on lines 48:58 of Program 15.8 repeats. Each time the user designates a rectangle, oval, or rounded rectangle, by typing R, O, or RR, in the console dialog, the program asks for coordinates of the enclosing rectangle and draws the designated shape inside it.

executing customized draw methods

When a rounded rectangle shape is designated by the user, executing theShape–>Draw( ); on line 56 sends the Draw message to a TRoundedRectangle object, referenced by the pointer value of theShape. This results in drawing a rounded

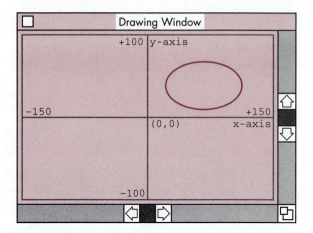

Figure 15.10 An Oval Drawn in the Drawing Window

rectangle, since rounded rectangle objects process the **Draw** message by using it to trigger the execution of the customized rounded rectangle drawing method internal to their object definitions. A similar case occurs for pure rectangle objects.

Eventually, the user types the letter **Q** in the console dialog window, and the program quits. Figure 15.11 shows the appearance of the **Drawing Window** after the user has designated an oval, a rounded rectangle, and a rectangle at coordinates: (20, 70, 130, 30), (−140, −10, −30, −70), and (−70, 20, 70, 10).

Our first stage example of object-oriented programming is now complete. We have seen how to define the C module, **Shapes**, having an abstract class, **TShape**, and three derived subclasses of **TShape**, defining ovals, rounded rectangles, and rectangles. We have seen how to define **Draw** methods for the subclasses that *customize* the virtual **Draw** method of the abstract class, and define different local drawing behaviors for each subtype of objects. We also saw how to create object instances of each subtype, set their enclosing rectangles in response to coordinates given in a user dialog, and get them to draw their specialized shapes in the **Drawing Window**.

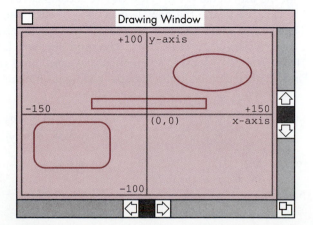

Figure 15.11 Three Shapes in the Drawing Window

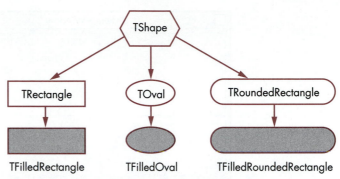

Figure 15.12 Class Inheritance Hierarchy for Shape Classes

Drawing Filled Shapes—The Second Stage OOP Example

We now proceed to the second stage example, which defines derived subclasses of the oval, rounded rectangle, and rectangle classes that draw *filled shapes* instead of *hollow* (or wire-frame) shapes. Each of the filled shapes defines its own local drawing method to fill its own special shape with a gray pattern, yet it still calls on the **Draw** method of its parent class to draw the wire frame around the filled object. Figure 15.12 illustrates the class inheritance hierarchy for the new derived shape classes. Let's concentrate on the hollow and filled oval classes to illustrate the new class type definitions. The cases for the other hollow and filled shapes are similar.

drawing filled shapes

To draw an oval filled with a light gray (**LtGray**) pattern, we can call the built-in graphics routine, **FillOval(&EnclosingRectangle,LtGray)**. Figure 15.13 shows how this routine fills in the interior of an oval inside an enclosing rectangle, **R**.

Suppose we decide that the filled oval of Fig. 15.13 lacks a crisply defined border, and that we want to draw a wire-frame oval border around it. We could accomplish this by calling the **Draw** method of the previously defined hollow oval type, **TOval**. So, we would like to define a derived class of the original class, **TOval**, called **TFilledOval**, which has its own **Draw** method that fills the oval inside its enclosing rectangle with light gray, and then calls the **Draw** method of its parent class, **TOval**, to draw the wire-frame border. How can we accomplish this?

drawing wire frames around filled ovals

First, we define the new derived class, **TFilledOval**, as shown in Program 15.14. The first line, **class TFilledOval : public TOval**, declares the new class **TFilledOval** to be a derived class of the class **TOval**. The third line, **void Draw( );** declares that the class **TFilledOval** has a local **Draw** method that customizes the identically named virtual **Draw** method defined in the **TShape** inheritance hierarchy.

Figure 15.13 The Result of Calling FillOval(&R, LtGray)

```
class TFilledOval : public TOval {
    public:
        void Draw( );
}
```

Program 15.14 Derived Class for TFilledOval

calling a parent's draw method

Program 15.15 gives the implementation of the **Draw** method for **TFilledOval**. Its first action is to fill in the oval inside its **EnclosingRectangle** with a light gray pattern. Then, to draw the wire-frame border around this light gray oval, it calls the **Draw** method of its parent class, **TOval**, using **TOval::Draw( )**.

Figure 15.16 illustrates the net result of executing the **Draw** method of **TFilledOval**. The gray pattern inside the oval is drawn by **FillOval(&EnclosingRectangle,LtGray)**, following which the border is drawn by calling **TOval::Draw( )**.

inheriting from grandparents and from all ancestors

Note that the instance variable **EnclosingRectangle** is available inside the body of the implementation of **TFilledOval::Draw**. This instance variable is defined in the grandparent class **TShape**, not in the immediate parent class **TOval** (see Fig. 15.12 and the class type definitions in Program 15.7). In other words, a given class inherits not only the methods and instance variables of its immediate parent class but also all methods and instance variables of each of its ancestors (no matter how many generations removed). This implies that **TShape**'s method, **SetEnclosingRectangle(x1, y1, x2, y2)**, is also available to object instances of type, **TFilledOval**, since it is a grandparent method that is passed down to all descendant classes of the **TShape** class.

To extend the **Shapes** module of Program 15.7 to incorporate filled shapes as well as hollow shapes, you can insert the object class type definitions of Program 15.17 at line 32 of Program 15.7, and insert the implementations of Program 15.18 at line 65 of Program 15.7.

programming with differences

Note that these extensions to the **Shapes** module illustrate what is meant by the phrase, "programming by specifying differences." All we did was to specify some new shapes that filled themselves with gray and called the drawing methods of their parents to draw their borders. All the other aspects of the ancestral class **TShape** are inherited

```
void TFilledOval : : Draw( )
{
    FillOval(&EnclosingRectangle, LtGray);
    TOval : : Draw( );                          // call Draw method of TOval
}
```

Program 15.15 Implementation of Draw Method for **TFilledOval**

Figure 15.16 The Result of Executing TFilledOval::Draw( );

```
     |
     |   class TFilledRectangle : public TRectangle  {
     |       public: void Draw( );
35   |   };
     |
     |   class TFilledOval : public TOval  {
     |       public: void Draw( );
     |   };
40   |
     |   class TFilledRoundedRectangle : public TRoundedRectangle  {
     |       public: void Draw( );
     |   };
     |
```

Program 15.17 Filled Shape Class Definitions

by the new filled shape classes. Specifically, the method for setting the coordinates of the enclosing rectangle and the instance variable for the enclosing rectangle itself were each inherited by the new filled shape classes. The **SetEnclosingRectangle** method therefore automatically applies to the new filled shapes without our having to define anything new.

The final step in building the second stage example is to extend the Boolean function **UserDesignatesShape(&theShape)** on lines 10:33 of Program 15.8, to handle an extended dialog with the user, so that the user can designate not only which kind of shape to draw but also whether the shape is to be drawn *hollow* or *filled*. A

```
     |
     |   void TFilledRectangle : : Draw( )
     |   {
     |       FillRect(&EnclosingRectangle, LtGray);
     |       TRectangle : : Draw( );                    / / call Draw method of TRectangle
70   |   }
     |
     |   void TFilledOval : : Draw( )
     |   {
     |       FillOval(&EnclosingRectangle, LtGray);
75   |       TOval : : Draw( );                         / / call Draw method of TOval
     |   }
     |
     |   void TFilledRoundedRectangle : : Draw( )
     |   {
80   |       FillRoundRect(&EnclosingRectangle, 20, 20, LtGray);
     |       TRoundedRectangle : : Draw( );             / / call Draw method of
     |   }                                              / / TRoundedRectangle
     |
```

Program 15.18 Filled Shape Draw Method Implementations

reasonable choice of letters for the user to give in the console window dialog might be **HR** for hollow rectangle, **FR** for filled rectangle, **HO** for hollow oval, **FO** for filled oval, **HRR** for hollow rounded rectangle, and **FRR** for filled rounded rectangle. We leave the extension of this subroutine as an exercise for the reader in Exercise 15.2.1.

Once the **UserDesignatesShape** function has been extended to obtain new shape codes from the user, and once it has been correctly extended to create instances of new shape objects (as in using ***theShape = new TFilledOval;** to create a filled oval object), then the rest of Program 15.8 runs correctly without change. In particular, the while-loop on lines 48:58 of Program 15.8 does not need to be extended to set the coordinates of the enclosing rectangle or to draw the new kinds of filled objects that have been added. This is a fairly impressive result when compared to the ordinary way of doing business in C, since in ordinary C, you might have to extend the while-loop to perform additional case analysis (perhaps based on a struct shapecode member) in order to know which drawing procedure to call to draw the new kinds of filled objects added in the extension.

Conclusion: Under appropriate circumstances, object-oriented programming can lead to ease of extension and modification of a program. Lowering the cost of software maintenance and modification and increasing the ease of using reusable software components is a key goal of contemporary software engineering. OOP techniques can assist in achieving these goals under the proper conditions.

an example of ease of extension

Building and Moving Lists of Shapes—The Third Stage OOP Example

To construct the third stage of the shape drawing program, we extend our second stage shape drawing program again. This time, we will build lists of shape objects by adding a new shape to a global list called **theShapeList** at the moment that the new shape is created. We can then *draw* every shape in the saved list of shapes by sending the **Draw** message to each shape on the list. We can also *move* all shapes on the list to a new location by sending an appropriate message of the form **Move(deltaX, deltaY)** to each shape on the shape list.

building and moving a list of shapes

Thus in our new third stage shape drawing program, we will be able to move the list of previously drawn shapes to a new location, and then draw the entire list of shapes in that new location. Our goal is to learn about how data structures can be built from different kinds of subobjects, and to learn how to apply general moving and drawing methods to entire lists of objects.

Once we have completed the third stage shape drawing extension, we will have learned enough of the basic ideas of object-oriented programming to begin to understand how to use OOP techniques to implement serious professional software, such as drawing programs for desktop computers. (On the other hand, we will not have gone all the way in exploring the rich set of programming features of C++, which include special techniques for input/output streams, adding new meanings to existing operators and functions using overloading, and using templates to define new functions.)

We start by defining a new **ShapeList** module, given as Program 15.19, to define the data and operations of a class of list objects that can be used to provide services for lists of shapes.

lists of shapes

```
|   // ------------< begin file ShapeList.h >------------ //
|
|   class TList                                    // define the ShapeList base class
|   {
5 |       public:
|           void InitShapeList( );                          // initialize the Shape List
|           void Append (TShape *theShape);
|           void Move(int deltaX, int deltaY);
|           void Draw( );
10 |          Boolean IsNonEmpty( );
|
|       private:
|           TShape        *Shape;
|           TList         *Link;
15 |  };
|
|   // ------------< end-of-file ShapeList.h >------------ //
|
|   // ------------< begin file ShapeList.c >------------ //
20 |
|   #include "Shapes.h"
|   #include "ShapeList.h"
|
|   void TList : : InitShapeList( );
25 |  {
|       Shape = NULL;          // Convention: A list node with a NULL Shape is an
|       Link = NULL;           // empty list awaiting a non-null Shape to be assigned
|   }
|
30 |  void TList : : Append (TShape *theShape)          // to add a new shape
|   {                                                 // to the end of a shape list
|       TList *LastNode, *NewNode;
|
|       if (Shape == NULL) {          // overwrite an "empty" shape with theShape
35 |          Shape = theShape;                        // to fill in the empty slot
|       } else {
|           NewNode = new  TList;                      // create a new list node
|           NewNode–>Shape = theShape;                 // store theShape in it
|           NewNode–>Link = NULL;           // and link it onto the end of the
40 |          LastNode = this;                              // shape list
|           while (LastNode–>Link != NULL) LastNode = LastNode–>Link;
|           LastNode–>Link = NewNode;
|       }
|   }
```

Program 15.19 The Shape List Module (continued)

Program 15.19 The Shape List Module (continued)

```
45  |    void TList : : Move(int deltaX, int deltaY)        // sends Move message
    |    {                                                  // to each Shape in the list
    |        TList    *TempNode;
    |        TShape *theShape;
    |
50  |        TempNode = this;
    |
    |        while (TempNode != NULL) {
    |            theShape = TempNode–>Shape;         // extract Shape from list node
    |            theShape–>Move(deltaX, deltaY);     // call theShape's Move method
55  |            TempNode = TempNode–>Link;          // advance to next node on list
    |        }
    |    }
    |
    |    void TList : : Draw( )
60  |    {
    |        TList  *TempNode;
    |
    |        TempNode = this;
    |
65  |        while (TempNode != NULL) {                      // send the Draw message
    |            TempNode–>Shape–>Draw( );                   // to each shape on the list
    |            TempNode = TempNode–>Link;                  // advance to next node on list
    |        }
    |    }
70  |
    |    Boolean TList : : IsNonEmpty( )                     // a NULL Shape in
    |    {                                                   // the first list node signifies
    |        return (Shape != NULL);                         // an empty list, by convention
    |    }
75  |
    |    // ------------<end-of-file ShapeList.c >------------ //
```

Lines 3:15 give the class definition for a class of **TList** objects. Each object instance of type **TList** has two instance variables, consisting of a **Shape** (which is a pointer to a shape object) and a **Link** (which is a link to another **TList** object). Thus **TList** objects function like list nodes in an ordinary linked list.

However, in addition to these two data members, each **TList** object has five methods defined on it: (1) **InitShapeList**, which initializes a shape list; (2) **Append(theShape)**, which appends a new shape to the end of a shape list; (3) **Move(deltaX, deltaY)**, which moves every shape in a list of shapes horizontally by an amount, **deltaX**, and vertically by an amount, **deltaY**; (4) **Draw( )**, which draws each shape in the list of shapes; and (5) **IsNonEmpty( )**, which is true only when the list of shapes contains one or more shapes.

defining five list methods

By convention, an empty **TList** consists of an object of type **TList** whose **Shape** instance variable (or, equivalently, whose **Shape** data member) has the value **NULL** (signifying the empty shape). The **InitShapeList** method, defined on lines 24:28, is applied to a newly created object of type **TList**, and sets both its **Shape** and its **Link** instance variables to be **NULL**, which is equivalent to initializing it to be the empty list, according to the convention just explained. The Boolean method **IsNonEmpty** on lines 71:74 checks whether the **Shape** instance variable of a **TList** object contains **NULL**, and concludes that the list object is nonempty if and only if the **Shape** instance variable contains a non-null shape value.

The method **Append(theShape)** given on lines 30:44 appends a shape object, referenced by the pointer value of the parameter **theShape** to the end of a shape list. It does this as follows. Let **L** be the **TList** object to which the **Append** method is applied. If **L**'s **Shape** instance variable contains **NULL**, then the current list object designates an empty list (by our convention) and **theShape** can be assigned to be the value of the **Shape** instance variable, converting **L** into a nonempty list containing one shape object. The assignment statement on line 35 performs this action. On the other hand, if **L** is a nonempty list, a new list node, **NewNode**, is created on line 37, its **Shape** and **Link** instance variables are set to contain **theShape** and **NULL** respectively (on lines 38:39), and a search is made on lines 40:41 to locate the last node, **LastNode**, of the current shape list. Once **LastNode** is identified, its **Link** instance variable is set to **NewNode**, making **NewNode** the new last node of the shape list. This serves to **Append** the new shape node to the end of the shape list.

There are some subtleties in lines 40:41, which are important to note. On line 40, we see the assignment statement, **LastNode = this;** which uses the C++ keyword, **this**, which we have not seen before. The keyword, **this**, is a variable whose value points to the object to which the current method is being applied. Thus the effect of executing the assignment **LastNode = this;** is to set the variable **LastNode** to point to the **TList** object to which the **Append** method has been applied—namely, to the first node of the shape list.

Once a pointer to a current list node object has been assigned to be the value of the variable **LastNode**, the while-statement on line 41 repeatedly advances down the list of nodes (linked together by pointers in their **Link** fields) until finding the first node having a **NULL Link** member. At this moment, the pointer in **LastNode** points to the last node of the original list.

When you give the name of any instance variable of the object inside the body of the method implementation, you are directly referring to the contents of the instance variable, as if it were a variable defined locally in the header of the method function, and as if it had been initialized after entering the method to the contents of the corresponding instance variable of the object.

appending the new last node of the list

After setting **LastNode** to be a pointer referencing the last list node on the current shape list, line 42 executes the assignment, **LastNode–>Link = NewNode;** which places a pointer to the **NewNode** in the **Link** field of the last node of the list.

Now let's tackle the explanations of the last two methods defined in the **ShapeList** module of Program 15.19. First, let's look at the **TList::Draw** method whose implementation is given on lines 59:69. Informally, the idea behind this method is to scan down the shape list and send the **Draw** message to every shape object on the list. It is as if we had enumerated each shape on the list and had given it the message, "Draw yourself."

drawing objects on the
shape list

The way the TList::Draw method works is to initialize a temporary node pointer variable **TempNode** to point to the first node of the shape list, using **TempNode = this;** on line 63. Then it advances down the list, node by node, following the pointers in the **Link** member, and at each list node it sends the **Draw** message to the shape referenced by the pointer in the **Shape** field, using the method call **TempNode–>Shape–>Draw( );** on line 66.

moving objects on the
shape list

The TList::Move(deltaX, deltaY) method works in a similar fashion. It scans down the shape list, node by node, and sends the message, "Move yourself horizontally by **deltaX** and vertically by **deltaY**," to each shape on the list. In a moment, we will define a **Move(deltaX, deltaY)** method to apply to individual shapes. The effect of applying **Move(deltaX, deltaY)** to an individual shape object is to modify the horizontal (or x-coordinates) of its enclosing rectangle by adding **deltaX**, and to add **deltaY** to the vertical (or y-coordinates) of its enclosing rectangle. The net effect is to move it horizontally by **deltaX** and vertically by **deltaY**. When the shape is drawn after having been moved, it will be drawn in its new location. When a list of shapes is drawn after the entire list has been moved, the effect is to draw the entire collection of previously defined objects in the new location.

Program 15.20 presents the modifications to the **Shapes** module giving the final version for the third stage shape drawing example. This program incorporates the changes of Programs 15.17 and 15.18 defining the behavior of the filled shapes (that was specified in the second stage shape drawing example). In addition, a **TShape::Move(deltaX, deltaY)** method has been added to the **TShape** object class definition (on line 8), and its implementation has been specified on lines 51:57. This **Move** method simply moves the coordinates of the enclosing rectangle for the shape a horizontal distance of **deltaX** and a vertical distance of **deltaY** in the Cartesian coordinate system.

We are now ready to present the final piece of the third stage shape drawing program—consisting of the main program itself. This is given as Program 15.21. The principal new feature of this program is that it accepts a code letter **M** in the console window dialog from the user to designate that the user wants to move and redraw the entire list of previously drawn shapes.

The procedure **MoveShapes** on lines 10:20 is called from line 37 when the first letter of the user's reply code is the letter **M**. **MoveShapes** asks the user to supply **deltaX** and **deltaY** displacements in the console window dialog. It then sends the **Move(deltaX, deltaY)** message to the shape list object, using the method call **theShapeList–>Move(deltaX, deltaY)** on line 17. As we have seen, applying the **Move** method to a list of shapes causes the **Move(deltaX, deltaY)** method to be sent to each individual shape object on the list, and this, in turn, causes each individual shape object to move itself a distance of **deltaX** horizontally and **deltaY** vertically.

drawing shapes after
moving them

After the entire shape list is moved on line 17, the list of shapes is then redrawn in its new location, by sending the **Draw** message to **theShapeList** on line 18. This causes each shape on the shape list to draw itself in its new location.

Before accepting descriptions of shapes to draw from the user, it is important to create and initialize the list of shapes. This is performed by the statements on lines 84:85 of Program 15.21. The statement **theShapeList = new TList;** on line 84 creates a new **TList** object and assigns it to be the value of the variable **theShapeList**. Line 85 calls the initialization method for this shape list object.

The Boolean function **UserDesignatesShape**, defined on lines 22:69, conducts a dialog with the user in the console window. It first prints instructions specifying the choices for the reply codes (on lines 28:30), following which it obtains a reply string from the user (by executing the function call **gets(reply)** on line 31).

It returns the function value *false* if the user gives the reply code **'Q'** to quit the program (see lines 34:35). In all other cases it returns the value *true*, which causes the main program to engage in additional dialog cycles in which the user can continue to specify additional shapes or can move the entire list of previously specified shapes. The Boolean value returned by the function call **UserDesignatesShape(&theShape)** becomes the value of the while-condition on line 87, in which a *false* return value exits the while-loop on lines 87:98 and a *true* return value causes the body of the while-loop to be executed.

In cases in which the function returns the value *true*, an additional result of calling the function is to set the contents of the pointer variable **theShape** (declared on line 78) to contain either the **NULL** pointer or a non-**NULL** pointer to a newly created shape object. The **NULL** pointer becomes the value of the variable **theShape** either when unknown shape code letters were given (see line 63) or when the user gave the **'M'** code to move the list of shapes (see lines 36:39).

In every case in which **theShape** was set to contain a non-**NULL** pointer, the body of the if-statement within the while-loop (on lines 90:95) will be executed to engage in additional dialog with the user to determine the coordinates of the enclosing rectangle for a newly designated shape, following which the shape will be drawn inside its enclosing rectangle. The method call:

```
theShape–>Draw( );
```

given on line 94, is the place where the (virtual) **Draw( )** message is sent to the object designating one of the six possible subtypes of shapes, causing the object's own customized local drawing method to be invoked in order to draw it in its own individually specified manner, even though an identical (virtual) draw message is passed in every case.

The case analysis in the switch statement on lines 41:65 breaks apart the letters of the shape code given by the user as the value of the reply string, and creates a pointer to a new shape object of the type the user has designated. This pointer to the new shape object is stored as the value of the shape variable **theShape** (see lines 43, 45, 50, 52, 56 and 58:59) for use in the method calls on lines 93:95.

The only other significant new feature of the third stage shape drawing program is shown on line 95 of Program 15.21. This specifies that immediately after drawing a shape specified for the first time by the user, the new shape is appended to the end of the shape list, using the method call:

```
theShapeList–>Append(theShape);
```

```
// ------------< begin Shapes.h header file >------------ //

class TShape {                          // the abstract class from which all actual
                                        // Shape classes are derivatives
    public:
        void SetEnclosingRect (int x1, int y1, int x2, int y2);
        virtual void Draw( );
        void Move(int deltaX, int deltaY);

    protected:
        Rect    EnclosingRectangle;     // the rectangle that encloses
};                                      // the shape

class TRectangle : public TShape {
    public: void Draw( );
};

class TOval : public TShape {
    public: void Draw( );
};

class TRoundedRectangle : public TShape {
    public: void Draw( );
};

class TFilledRectangle : public TRectangle {
    public: void Draw( );
};

class TFilledOval : public TOval {
    public: void Draw( );
};

class TFilledRoundedRectangle : public TRoundedRectangle {
    public: void Draw( );
};

// ------------<end-of-file Shapes.h >------------ //

// ------------<begin file Shapes.c >------------ //

#include "Shapes.h"

void TShape : : SetEnclosingRect(int x1, int y1 ,int x2, int y2)
{                                          // transform to a normal
        SetEnclosingRect.top = 100 – y1;   // Cartesian coordinate
        SetEnclosingRect.left = 150 + x1;  // system with origin at
        SetEnclosingRect.bottom = 100 – y2; // (x,y) = (150,100) in
        SetEnclosingRect.right = 150 + x2; // the Drawing Window
}
```

Program 15.20 Final Version of the **Shapes** Module (continued)

Program 15.20 Final Version of the **Shapes** Module (continued)

```
       void TShape : : Move(int deltaX, int deltaY)
       {
              EnclosingRectangle.top -= deltaY;      // deltaY is subtracted because
              EnclosingRectangle.left += deltaX;        // the coordinate system for
55            EnclosingRectangle.bottom -= deltaY;         // the built-in drawing
              EnclosingRectangle.right += deltaX;          // routines is upside-down
       }


       void TShape : : Draw( )
60     {
           printf("Impossible call on virtual Draw method of TShape.\n");
       }


       void TRectangle : : Draw( )
65     {
           FrameRect(&EnclosingRectangle);
       }


       void TOval : : Draw( )
70     {
           FrameOval(&EnclosingRectangle);
       }


       void TRoundedRectangle : : Draw( )
75     {
           FrameRoundRect(&EnclosingRectangle, 20, 20);
       }


       void TFilledRectangle : : Draw( )
80     {
           FillRect(&EnclosingRectangle, LtGray);
           TRectangle : : Draw( );               // call Draw method of TRectangle
       }


85     void TFilledOval : : Draw( )
       {
           FillOval(&EnclosingRectangle, LtGray);
           TOval : : Draw( );                    // call Draw method of TOval
       }
90
       void TFilledRoundedRectangle : : Draw( )
       {
           FillRoundRect(&EnclosingRectangle, 20, 20, LtGray);
           TRoundedRectangle : : Draw( );              // call Draw method of
95     }                                                // TRoundedRectangle


       // ------------< end-of-file Shapes.c >------------ //
```

```
  |    //  Final Stage 3 Shape Drawing Program
  |
  |    #include <stdio.h>
  |    #include <string.h>
5 |    #include "Shapes.h"
  |    #include "ShapeList.h"
  |
  |        TList      *theShapeList;      // global variable that contains the Shape list
  |
10|    void MoveShapes( )
  |    {
  |        short deltaX, deltaY;
  |
  |        if ( theShapeList–>IsNonEmpty( ) ) {              // move shapes only if
15|            printf("deltaX deltaY : ");                   // theShapeList
  |            scanf("%hd%hd", &deltaX, &deltaY);            // is nonempty
  |            theShapeList–>Move(deltaX, deltaY);
  |            theShapeList–>Draw( );
  |        }
20|    }
  |
  |    Boolean UserDesignatesShape(TShape **theShape)
  |    {
  |        char      *reply = "        "; // blank string to store user's reply to prompt
25|        int       ReplyLength;
  |
  |      while (1) {
  |          printf("Designate one of: Q = Quit, M = Move shapes, HO = Hollow Oval,\n");
  |          printf("FO = Filled Oval, HR = Hollow Rectangle, FR = Filled Rectangle,\n");
30|          printf("HRR = Hollow Rounded Rectangle,FRR = Filled Rounded Rectangle:");
  |          gets(reply);
  |          ReplyLength = strlen(reply);
  |
  |          if ( (reply[0] == 'Q') || (reply[0] == 'q') ) {
35|              return false;
  |          } else if ( (reply[0] == 'M') || (reply[0] == 'm') ) {     // if user gave 'M'
  |              MoveShapes( );                                // then move the list of shapes
  |              *theShape = NULL;
  |              return true;                                          // stay in the loop
40|          } else {
  |              switch (reply[1]) {
  |              case 'O': case 'o': if ( (reply[0] == 'H') || (reply[0] == 'h') ) {
  |                                      *theShape = new TOval;      // treat cases
  |                                  } else {              // for hollow and filled ovals
45|                                      *theShape = new TFilledOval;
  |                                  }
  |                                  return true;
```

Program 15.21 Final Stage-3 Shape Drawing Program (continued)

Program 15.21 Final Stage-3 Shape Drawing Program (continued)

```
                        case 'R': case 'r': if (ReplyLength < 3) {        // then had HR or FR
                                                if ( (reply[0] == 'H') || (reply[0] == 'h') ) {
50                                                  *theShape = new TRectangle;
                                                } else {
                                                    *theShape = new TFilledRectangle;
                                                }
                                            } else {          // had HRR or FRR if length(reply) ≥3
55                                              if ( (reply[0] == 'H') || (reply[0] == 'h') ) {
                                                    *theShape = new TRoundedRectangle;
                                                } else {
                                                    *theShape =
                                                        new TFilledRoundedRectangle;
60                                              }
                                            }
                                            return true;                      // stay in the loop
                        default:  *theShape = NULL;
                                  return true;                                // stay in the loop
65                  }                                                         // end switch
            }                                                                 // end if

        }                                                                     // end while
    }                                                                         // end UserDesignatesShape
70
    void DrawCoordinateSystem( )          // details omitted
    {
        // Draws x-axis, y-axis, origin and boundaries of coordinate system
    }
75
    int main( )
    {
        TShape  *theShape;
        short    x1, y1, x2, y2;
80
        SetUpWindows( );        // displays a Text Window and a Drawing Window
        DrawCoordinateSystem( );        // draws x and y axes in Drawing Window

        theShapeList = new TList;                     // create a new shape list node
85      theShapeList->InitShapeList( );   // initialize it to designate the empty list

        while (UserDesignatesShape(&theShape)) {
            if (theShape != NULL) {     // user neither moved shape list nor gave
                                        // unknown shape code letters
90              printf("Give Coordinates of Enclosing Rectangle: \n");
                printf("left top right bottom: ");
                scanf("%hd%hd%hd%hd", &x1, &y1, &x2, &y2);
                theShape->SetEnclosingRect(x1, y1, x2, y2);
                theShape->Draw( );
95              theShapeList->Append(theShape);

            }
        }
    }
```

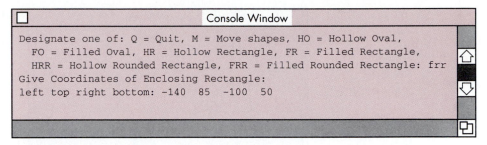

Figure 15.22 Initial Dialog with User

adding new shapes to the list

New shapes accumulate at the end of **theShapeList** each time the user designates a new shape. At any time, using the **M** code, the user can move and redraw the entire list of shapes accumulated so far in a new relative location.

Let's fire up the main program now, and give an example of how it operates. Figure 15.22 shows the initial part of a dialog with the user in the console window. In this dialog, the user has asked the third stage shape drawing program to draw a filled rounded rectangle (**frr**) within the enclosing rectangle (–140, 85, –100, 50). Figure 15.23 shows the drawing in the **Drawing Window** after the user has specified that a filled oval (**fo**) should be drawn at (–90, 40, –10, 10), and that a hollow rectangle (**hr**) should be drawn at (–80, 85, –10, 55). Note that all three shapes lie in the upper-left quadrant of the Cartesian coordinate system in the **Drawing Window**.

Now suppose that the user gives the **M** code and decides to move all the shapes into the lower-right quadrant of the **Drawing Window**. To do this, the user gives **deltaX = 150** and **deltaY = –100**, in response to the dialog query in the console window. The effect on the drawing in the **Drawing Window** is shown in Fig. 15.24 (where the solid color arrows and the expression **Move(+150, –100)** in the upper-right quadrant have been added by an artist, not by the program itself).

We have now completed the explanation of the third stage shape drawing program. In the process, we have covered quite a few object-oriented programming fea-

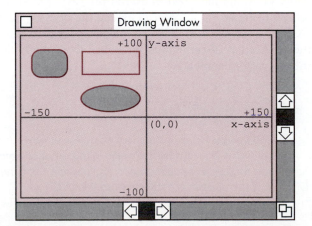

Figure 15.23 Three Shapes in the Upper-Left Quadrant

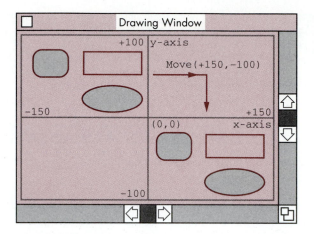

Figure 15.24 Moving Three Shapes to the Lower-Right Quadrant

tures of C++. One C++ feature we did not cover, but should mention now for completeness, was the method for disposing of the storage for an object, **Ob1** of type **TClassX**, after we are finished with it. This is done by applying the **delete** operator, **delete Ob1**. Here it is assumed that **Ob1** is a variable containing a pointer to the storage for an object **X** and that space for object **X** was allocated by applying the **new** operator to **TClassX** as in the assignment statement **Ob1 = new TClassX;**.

We are now ready to draw some conclusions.

Conclusions

Object-oriented programming can provide for smooth extension of a program when we need to add new classes of individually customized objects that share some general behaviors. For example, we were able to add new kinds of filled shape objects to the first stage shape drawing program by specifying new derived subclasses having new individual drawing methods, without having to alter any of the superstructure that called the drawing methods for the previously defined objects. In ordinary programming, we would have had to extend the case analysis that switches on the types of objects being drawn in order to extend the drawing behaviors for all objects. But in OOP, the extension of this case analysis is handled automatically for us by means of the application of customized individual **Draw** methods to individual objects when the program is being run.

15.2 Review Questions

1. How do you create an instance of an object of object type **T**?
2. Explain what is meant by the *methods* and *instance variables* of an object.
3. Explain *derived classes, inheritance,* and *customizing virtual methods* in OOP.
4. What is the meaning of the keyword **this** in C++?
5. Explain how C++ allocates space for object instances and how it uses pointers to

reference these objects. Explain how to use the **new** and **delete** operators in C++ and give an example of their use.

15.2 Exercises

1. Extend the Boolean function **UserDesignatesShape(theShape)** on lines 10:33 of Program 15.8 to analyze the reply given by the user in the console window dialog so that the following letter combinations designate hollow and filled shapes: **HR** for hollow rectangle, **FR** for filled rectangle, **HO** for hollow oval, **FO** for filled oval, **HRR** for hollow rounded rectangle, and **FRR** for filled rounded rectangle. Be sure to use the proper object types when creating a pointer to a new object, as in using ***theShape = new TFilledOval;** to create a pointer to a filled oval object.

2. Suppose you desire to extend the third stage shape drawing program so that filled shapes can be drawn with one of three fill-patterns: **LtGray**, **CrossHatch**, and **HorizontalLines**. Show how to add an instance variable, called **itsPattern**, to the filled object class definitions having a pattern as its value, and modify the program to let the user choose which fill-pattern to use when creating a filled object to draw.

15.3 Building Systems Using Object-Oriented Programming

Learning Objectives

1. To learn how object-oriented programming techniques are used to build software systems.
2. To learn how object-oriented programming can help make reusable software components easier to use.
3. To learn how object editors can be used to help build user interfaces in software systems.

imagining how to build a complete drawing program

Object-oriented programming techniques offer some advantages to software system builders. In this section, we will first use our imaginations to see how we could expand the third stage shape drawing example of Section 15.2 to become a full-blown object-oriented drawing application. Then we will comment on how the use of prefabricated software components taken from an object-oriented programming library could help complete the construction of the system by adding features such as a file subsystem and a printing subsystem. We will then explore how object-oriented editors can help build user interfaces to systems.

Imagining a Drawing Application

Perhaps you have been exposed to contemporary drawing software applications that are in widespread use on desktop computers. Basically, such programs consist of computer graphics software that permits users to compose drawings by creating and

Palette

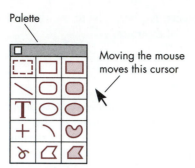

Moving the mouse
moves this cursor

Figure 15.25 A Drawing Tools Palette

arranging various kinds of graphic elements, such as lines, rectangles, ovals, polygons, curves, arrows, and regions of printed text.

Frequently, such drawing programs are used in conjunction with a pointing device, such as a *mouse*. Moving the mouse on a desktop causes an associated cursor to move around the computer screen. Buttons on top of the mouse can be depressed to signify shifts in the mode of an intended action, or to designate a choice among several alternatives in a menu or palette on the screen.

using pointing devices

The choices of elementary objects to draw are often presented in a menu or palette. Some drawing applications have palettes around the border of the screen, displaying choices of miniature models of various shapes that can be drawn. Other drawing applications have menus or floating palettes that can be made to appear and which present the choices of shapes to draw. Figure 15.25 illustrates one such palette of drawing tools. The miniature tool pictures show that it is possible to draw both hollow and filled ovals, rectangles, and rounded rectangles, as we did in the shape drawing program of Section 15.2. In addition, however, it is possible to draw curves, polygons, lines, and text. To select a particular kind of shape, S, to draw, the user moves the arrow cursor (shown to the right of the palette in Fig. 15.25) over the small picture of the shape, S, by moving the mouse on the desktop in the same direction that the user wants the arrow to move on the screen. When the tip of the arrow is over the picture of the shape, S, the user depresses a mouse button and the picture of shape, S, *highlights* (i.e., turns dark, or inverts, or changes color in some fashion), in order to give the user feedback that shape S has been successfully selected. This is the signal that the user, "has chosen the S drawing tool," and can now create an instance of shape S in the drawing window by *dragging* the mouse (or, in the case of the text tool (T), by clicking the mouse button when the cursor is positioned at the beginning of the text and then typing the characters of the text on the keyboard, which then appear on the screen in the designated position).

Figure 15.26 shows the result of selecting the hollow oval drawing tool, by clicking the mouse button when the arrow cursor is over the miniature hollow oval picture. The hollow oval has been highlighted by inverting it (i.e., changing white to color and color to white, just like a photographic negative).

Once the hollow oval drawing tool is selected and the cursor is moved to the drawing area, the cursor changes shape to become a crosshair (+). The crosshair cursor is then dragged with the mouse to create the shape. Dragging the mouse means

Figure 15.26 Palette with Hollow Oval Drawing Tool Selected

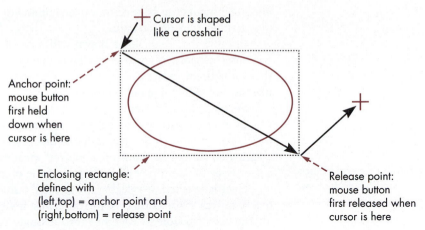

Figure 15.27 Symbolic Depiction of Dragging the Mouse

moving the mouse along the desktop with one of the mouse buttons held down. At the place where the mouse button is first depressed, the top-left corner of the enclosing rectangle for the oval is established. (This is sometimes called the *anchor point*.) As the mouse is moved with the button still held down, the position of the cursor gives the position of the bottom-right corner of the enclosing rectangle. When the mouse button is finally released, the position of the bottom-right corner is taken to be the current position of the cursor, and a hollow oval is drawn inside the enclosing rectangle defined by the *anchor point* (i.e., the point where the mouse button was first pressed down), and the *release point* (i.e., the point where the mouse button was finally released after having been held down continuously while the mouse was being dragged across the desktop). Figure 15.27 gives a symbolic description of the action of dragging the mouse to create an enclosing rectangle in which to draw the hollow oval.

The mouse and cursor can be used in slightly different ways to draw the shapes designated by the other drawing tools shown in Fig. 15.25. For example, to draw a polygon, the mouse button is *clicked* (i.e., pressed and released quickly) when the cursor is positioned over each corner of the polygon being drawn. For the straight line tool, the mouse is dragged to establish the beginning of the straight line at the anchor point and the end of the line at the release point. Straight lines can be modified by selecting options from menus that, for example, designate that they will have arrowheads at one or both ends, or that they will appear dashed instead of solid, and so on. For the text tool (T), the mouse is clicked when the cursor is positioned at the desired beginning point for the text, and the characters of the text are typed on the keyboard.

You can see that, in conjunction with a drawing tools palette, the actions of the mouse (i.e., pointing, clicking, and dragging) can become a substitute for typing character codes in the console window dialog in order to designate shapes to draw, as we did in the shape drawing example given in Section 15.2.

Now that we have imagined a slightly extended version of the shape drawing program developed in Section 15.2, let's further imagine how object-oriented program-

using other drawing tools

ming techniques can be used to implement additional features common to contemporary desktop drawing software.

Imagine that each shape drawn with one of the drawing tools exists inside the computer memory as an object instance having an enclosing rectangle. Imagine further that there exists a list, called theShapeList, which contains all the object instances of all the shapes in the drawing.

Suppose the user wants to *group* some of the shapes together into a single object (for example, grouping together some lines and rectangles forming a picture of the front of a house). To do this, the user first selects the objects to group together, by clicking on them. (To "click on an object" means to click the mouse button when the cursor is sitting on top of a visible part of the object's drawing on the screen.) When an object is selected, it is *highlighted* in some fashion—for instance, by showing small black squares at the corners of its (otherwise invisible) enclosing rectangle. To group all the selected objects together into a single new object, a "group" command is selected from an appropriate command menu, or a keyboard character sequence designating the "group" command is typed.

The underlying software then scans down theShapeList, removing the selected objects from theShapeList, and appending them to a new list, L. Then a new object, Ob1, is created as an instance of an object of type TGroupedObject. The enclosing rectangle of this grouped object is now determined by scanning list L and computing the smallest rectangle that encloses all of the enclosing rectangles of the objects on list L. The list of subobjects, L, is then inserted into a data field of object, Ob1, by making it the value of Ob1's subobject list instance variable, and the object, Ob1, itself is appended to the end of theShapeList. The meaning of the Draw method has to be defined for an object of type TGroupedObject by causing a Draw message to be sent to each of the subobjects on its subobject list L, just as we did in the third stage shape drawing example in Section 15.2. This implies that when the Draw method is sent to theShapeList (containing all visible shapes in the drawing on the screen), all grouped objects on theShapeList will be drawn, along with all ordinary ungrouped primitive shape objects. In effect, the introduction of grouped objects has turned theShapeList into a list structure, instead of its being just an ordinary linear, linked list.

Many of the commands in a drawing program apply transformations to a selected object (or group of selected objects). For example, you can *shrink*, *expand*, or *rotate* a selected object, and you can *move* a group of selected objects to a new location by dragging the mouse on the desktop. Also, you can *flip* objects to replace them with their horizontal or vertical mirror images. You can imagine how some of these transformations could be implemented by applying the relevant transformation mathematically to the enclosing rectangle of an object, after which it could be redrawn. In the case of grouped objects, the transformation would be given in the form of a message to be passed to each subobject on the list of subobjects in the grouped object. This message would apply the relevant transformation to each of the subobjects on the list, in the same manner as we sent the message Move(deltaX, deltaY) to each object on a TList object in the third stage shape drawing program of Section 15.2. Also, for instance, the displacement of a move command could be detected by measuring the difference, (deltaX, deltaY), between the anchor point and the release point of a mouse drag action specifying the direction and magnitude of the move on the screen.

grouping several objects
into a single object

aligning objects

Another type of command consists of *aligning* several selected objects by moving them so that their bottoms (or tops, or centers, etc.) are all on the same horizontal (or vertical) line. Perhaps you can imagine how to compute and move all the objects in a list of selected objects in this fashion.

front-to-back ordering of objects

Yet another command that changes the appearance of a drawing composed of objects on theShapeList is one that alters the front-to-back ordering of objects. When theShapeList is drawn, a Draw message is sent to every object on it in list order, starting at the front and proceeding toward the rear of the list. This implies that objects on theShapeList will be drawn in back-to-front order, with the objects at the front of the list drawn in the background layers of the drawing, and the object at the end of the list drawn last, in the frontmost layer of the drawing. If drawn objects overlap, this could be important, because an object drawn in the foreground may hide (i.e., block from view) a portion of an underlying object that it overlaps.

Thus many drawing systems permit users to select objects and then to apply commands that move the relative position of the object either toward the foreground or toward the background of the drawing. You can imagine how to implement such commands by simply changing the relative position of an object on theShapeList, and then by erasing and redrawing all objects whose enclosing rectangles intersect with the enclosing rectangle of the object that has just been moved forward or backward.

changing an object's features

Another category of drawing commands available in most contemporary drawing systems involves changing the features of a drawn object. For example, it is possible to change the fill-pattern of a filled object by selecting a new fill pattern from a palette (or a menu) of patterns. Or, it is possible to change the thickness of a line or a drawn border of an object, by selecting a new line thickness from a palette or menu offering choices of line widths. Obviously, in order for a filled object to be able to change its fill-pattern, the fill-pattern must be saved in an instance variable inside the object.

zooming and scrolling

Finally, most contemporary drawing applications permit users to change the view of the drawing by zooming in or out, to magnify a portion of the drawing in order to work more precisely on local details, or to perform operations on a large portion of the drawing lying outside the screen in one of the magnified views. When drawings are displayed inside windows, it is usually possible to scroll the window or otherwise to move the window so that it sits over another portion of the drawing.

Knowing what you know from studying the three stages of the shape drawing examples in Section 15.2, and from the brief descriptions given in this section, you should be able to imagine how object-oriented programming techniques could be used to perform many of the commands available in contemporary drawing applications when they are applied to lists of shape objects appearing in a drawing.

Implementing File and Printing Subsystems Using Object-Oriented Programming

filing and printing

When you build a software application intended for commercial use, such as the drawing program we have been discussing, it is important that it be full-featured with respect to capabilities such as being able to print drawings on various printers, and being able to save and read files on disks. Oftentimes, a team of programmers is assigned to implement such a software system, and sometimes, a particular programmer will be assigned the task of writing the *printing subsystem* or the *file subsystem*.

If you have never implemented a printing or filing subsystem for a mature software application before, it may take you six months or so to discover how to do it properly. There are many subtleties, and these must often be learned by experience, as there is seldom any publicly available literature of sufficient depth that tells you how to proceed. In fact, what often happens is that you implement a first version of the subsystem thinking it will be the final version, and along the way you discover that you have used a fundamentally flawed design. The best thing to do is to throw away your first version and start over. In effect, your first version becomes a prototype that provides you with the opportunity to learn how to do it right the second time.

programs are like waffles— the first one should be thrown away

Let's discuss for a moment why implementing a subsystem, such as the file subsystem, can be challenging. First of all, a typical operating system will furnish you with many building blocks from which to build your file subsystem. These building blocks will enable you to access a storage device (such as a floppy disk or a hard disk), read its file directory, determine the amount of unused space on the device, write a stream of bytes as a new file, name the file, close the file, and so forth. Your job is to fashion these building blocks into a file subsystem that integrates smoothly with the application you are building and that has some desirable properties. Among the desirable properties might be the following: (1) Allow more than one file to be open at one time, so that users can transfer portions of drawings from one file to another; (2) Warn the user if there is insufficient space on a storage device for writing a given file and allow the user to take alternate action (rather than crashing halfway through a file write operation when storage space becomes exhausted, causing the user to lose the file); (3) If failures are encountered, such as disk read errors, provide instructions for recoveries or work-arounds.

handling error conditions

Along with the software building blocks that an operating system provides, you will typically encounter a long list of operating system error conditions that can occur when you call the software building blocks to perform elementary file operations for you. For example, one contemporary operating system lists over 90 error conditions that can arise when dealing with files and storage devices. These errors are things such as media failures of various sorts (as in disk read or write errors), bad file directories or file names, duplicate file names or names that are too long, insufficient free storage on a storage device for writing a file, and so on.

When you write your file subsystem, you will have to take all such possible error conditions into consideration, and you will have to implement a sensible plan for helping the user to deal with them. For example, when you replace an old version of a file, F_1, on a disk by writing a new version, F_2, to replace it, it is good practice to write F_2 first, and only after F_2 has been successfully written, to delete the version F_1, which is being replaced. Of course, if there is not enough space to hold both F_1 and F_2 on the disk at the same time, you should inform the user, and let the user choose whether or not to delete F_1 before attempting to write F_2, or to abort the intended operation and give the user the option of choosing another disk that is less full.

Designing good policies to implement in these many exceptional circumstances is a painstaking task. It takes time, experience, and very detailed, careful consideration to come up with a mature, effective design. It is also challenging to "come up the learning curve" the first time, since you have to deal with hundreds of new concepts, complexities, and irritating details that are difficult to master.

This is a circumstance in which *object-oriented class libraries* can become a big win for the software system builder. One of the components that is frequently offered in an object-oriented class library is a complete *prefabricated file system*, which comes in the form of a big object with *blanks* for you to fill in. For example, assuming that a file is defined as a sequence of bytes of any length, all you may need to do is fill in two missing pieces—a **SendByteStream** piece, which converts the internal data to be saved in a file into a sequence of bytes to be output to the file, and a **ReceiveByteStream** piece, which converts a sequence of bytes being read from a file into internal data structures in primary computer memory suitable for manipulation by your software system.

using object-oriented class libraries

All the rest of the file system capabilities—including naming files, reading them, writing them, opening them, closing them, and responding to all error and warning conditions—are provided in prefabricated form by the file system object, once the two missing pieces are filled in.

The way that you fill in the missing pieces is (you guessed it) by defining local methods in a **TFile** object that customize virtual (or fill-in) methods defined in the **TFile** object. We saw an instance of this principle in the shape drawing example earlier, when a virtual **Draw** method was defined for an abstract object of type **TShape**. The virtual **TShape::Draw** method was merely a place-holder, or a blank slot, to be filled in, using customization, by every actual derived class of the **TShape** base class. Later we saw that each actual shape class, such as **TOval**, defined its own local **Draw** method by defining its own special customized **Draw** method. Yet each actual derived shape class inherited many useful general methods from the **TShape** class, such as the **SetEnclosingRectangle** and **Move** methods.

Likewise, when you supply customized methods for the virtual **SendByteStream** and **ReceiveByteStream** methods of a **TFile** object, you allow the superstructure of the prefabricated file system to call on your application in the two critical cases where specific actions are needed to translate internal data structures into and out of byte stream format used in files. All the rest of the file operations and file system behavior is inherited in prefabricated form, mostly by means of inherited methods of a **TFile** object.

If you like the prefabricated design of the file system object (as well you might since it is built to handle all those contingencies that are so hard to enumerate and handle in a properly integrated, smooth fashion), you have saved yourself six months or more of system programming agony. If you do not like the way the file system object is designed, you can often customize its behavior by defining derived classes, inheriting features you do like, and then redesigning and customizing features you want to change.

building a printing subsystem

Building a printing subsystem can offer challenges similar in difficulty to those encountered when building a file subsystem. Complexities abound when there are many different kinds of printer device types to handle (such as dot-matrix printers, ink-jet printers, laser printers, and printer spoolers in the file system). Not only are there many error and exception conditions to handle (such as "printer is out of paper," etc.), but also there may be device specific characteristics that have to be addressed when sending a page image to various different kinds of devices.

Again, object-oriented class libraries often supply complete prefabricated printing subsystem objects with slots for you to fill in. In a printing subsystem, the key slot to fill in is the **Draw** method for drawing the contents of a page image. If all you have to do is to implement a few drawing methods for page images, your cost in building the printing subsystem can be reduced dramatically when compared to the cost of building the entire printing subsystem from the ground up by yourself.

You can see that object-oriented programming techniques can offer significant cost-reduction advantages and software reliability advantages when compared to approaches that do not use reusable software components.

Developing User Interfaces Using Object-Oriented Programming

Another powerful advantage of using object-oriented programming techniques has emerged recently in the area of building user interfaces to software systems. The *user interface* of a system is the part of the system that the user interacts with in order to direct the activities of the system and to receive output results. A *graphical user interface* (GUI) is one that uses computer graphics, such as windows, menus, icons, palettes, and perhaps a desktop metaphor, to help the user interact with the system, using an output screen and various input devices.

In order to make the ideas more crisp, let's look at a specific example of a system a user might need to build to study the behavior of an economic model. Suppose that Jeannie G. Economist is an employee of an economic research firm who has been assigned the task of studying the impact of consumer debt levels on the recovery of the national economy from a recent recession. She has available a sophisticated economic model in the form of a system of equations that predict the magnitudes of some performance output variables using values of input variables measuring various status and rate indicators characteristic of the economy. She would like to build a system to allow her to vary rates of consumer debt, while holding all other inputs equal, in order to see what effect the model predicts that changes in consumer debt rates will have on economic growth.

In particular, Jeannie is skeptical about a claim by the Federal Reserve Board (the Fed) that consumer debt levels have been steadily declining as consumers pay off auto loans, home mortgages, credit card debt, and other kinds of consumer debt. Jeannie has collected new evidence that consumers have, in fact, been shifting their debt burdens to other kinds of borrowing, such as home equity loans and auto leases, both of which are not measured by the Fed in its tally of consumer debt. An auto lease, for example, is not, strictly speaking, a form of debt, since it consists of a series of rental payments to rent the use of a car. However, Jeannie believes that auto lease payments act as substitutes for auto loan payments, and she notes that 25 percent of cars delivered this year will be leased instead of bought on loan, in part because leases require little or no money down and have low monthly payments. Moreover, Jeannie recently learned that the Consumer Banking Association released a statement in which it claimed that home equity loans grew by 14 percent last year to a total of $130 billion, of which a third was used to consolidate existing debt and 11 percent was used to finance car purchases.

So while the Federal Reserve Board Chairman was testifying to Congress that consumer debt payments had fallen to 16.7 percent of every after-tax dollar from a prior percentage of 18.2 percent eighteen months ago, heralding good news for the economic recovery, Jeannie believes that an accurate measure of consumer debt payments could be obtained by including auto lease payments and home equity loan payments, in which case it would measure 25.8 percent of every after-tax dollar, instead of just 16.7 percent. So Jeannie wants to run her firm's economic model to let her ask what the effect on the recovery will be if the consumer debt level is set to 25.8 percent instead of the Fed Chairman's claimed 16.7 percent. Will the recovery be aborted or delayed under these circumstances—all other things being equal?

Jeannie cranks up her desktop computer and invokes an object-oriented system for running economic models and building user interfaces to them. She first needs to design a control panel for her planned inquiry. Figure 15.28 shows the control panel object that Jeannie designed. The way Jeannie designs this panel is to use the object drawing features of her system. First, she creates a blank color background object (using the tool for drawing filled rectangles). Then she inserts three *buttons*, labeled Start, Stop, and Reset, which she intends to hook up to the economic model to set it in motion, stop it, and start it over, if she needs to. To do this, a button drawing tool is selected from an object drawing palette, three button objects are drawn on the control panel background, and a text editing feature is used to type in the button names. (The three buttons appear on the left side of the panel in Fig. 15.28.)

Next, Jeannie inserts a *slider control*, by choosing the "draw slider tool," from her system's tool palette, after which she stretches it and moves it to fit neatly into the right side of the panel. Finally, she labels the slider as a control for the consumer debt rate, and adjusts its scale to indicate percentages between 0 percent and 100 percent. The slider indicator in Fig. 15.28 shows the debt rate set initially at 50 percent (which is artificially high, and has not been set yet to a proper value).

designing a control panel

inserting a slider control

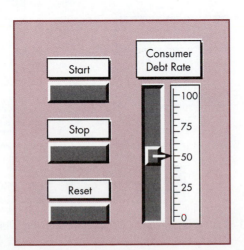

Figure 15.28 Control Panel for Economic Study

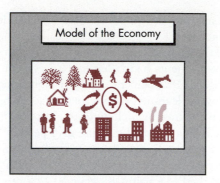
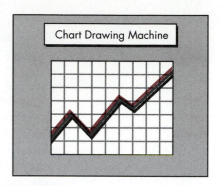

Figure 15.29 Economic Model and Chart Drawing Objects

Jeannie next retrieves her firm's economic model object and a chart drawing object with which to record the performance outputs of the model. Figure 15.29 shows these two retrieved objects as they appear on Jeannie's computer screen. Now comes the important step. Jeannie must connect these objects, so that the control panel controls the operation of the economic model, and so that the chart drawing machine graphs the economic performance of the model over time.

connecting the components

To make the connections, Jeannie invokes an object connection command that asks for the objects on the *input-side* and the *output-side* of the connection to be made. Jeannie specifies the control panel object as the *input* to the connection and the economic model as the *output* from the connection. For each of the three buttons and the slider on the control panel, Jeannie makes a selection from a menu of input messages that the economic model can receive. These input messages on the menu are just a list of the methods that the economic model object has defined for itself. Figure 15.30 shows a portion of this menu.

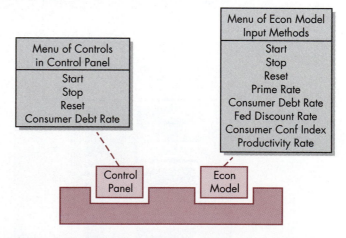

Figure 15.30 Making Connections Using the Receiving Object's Methods

For example, Jeannie directs that the output value selected on the slider's scale measuring consumer debt should be sent as a value change message to the economic model, invoking its **ConsumerDebtRate** method, each time the slider's scale is changed on the control panel to indicate a new consumer debt rate value. She does this by selecting the "Consumer Debt Rate" choice on both the output menu for the control panel, and the input menu for the economic model. By making other menu choices, Jeannie hooks up the start, stop, and reset buttons on the control panel so that they send start, stop, and reset messages to the economic model (thereby invoking the model's start, stop, and reset methods).

You can imagine how Jeannie makes similar connections from the outputs of the model to the inputs of the chart drawing machine, in order to get the chart drawing machine to produce a graph of the outputs of the model's economic performance indicators.

running the model

Now it is time for Jeannie to run the system she has built. First, she sets the slider on the consumer debt rate control to indicate 25.8 percent—the rate she believes is an accurate assessment of the percentage of each after-tax dollar that consumers are spending to service either debt or substitute debt in the form of leases. Then she presses the "Start" button on the control panel, and—*ka-chunk, ka-chunk*—the model is set into motion. Figure 15.31 shows the model with the start button pressed in, as it appears on Jeannie's screen.

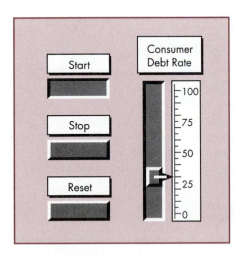
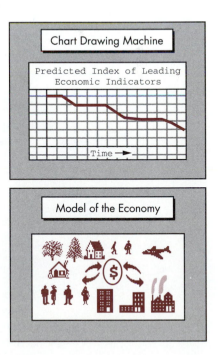

Figure 15.31 Economic Model in Motion

getting results without
letting the computer get in
the way

After displaying the graph showing the performance of the predicted Index of Leading Economic Indicators, Jeannie believes she might have discovered something significant. She believes that artificially optimistic yet misleading measures of consumer debt levels have led the Fed to make overly optimistic predictions about the speed of the economic recovery. After defining a concept, called the *effective consumer debt measure*, she predicts that its effect on the recovery will be to forestall the operation of factors that have historically led to recovery, such as consumers taking on new debt to finance purchases of autos, housing, and durable goods. She believes it is possible that the recovery will stall, or will at the very least not be a traditional recovery led by increased levels of consumer spending.

If you compare Jeannie's method for building a user interface with the traditional methods used by systems programmers, you will find that Jeannie's method has reduced the cost and complexity of building a user interface by an enormously significant amount.

The key idea is to couple the capabilities of an object-oriented graphics drawing program (to design the appearance of user interface objects) with an object interconnection and execution system. The drawing system functions as a graphics object editor, capable of specifying the order and arrangement of interface objects. But objects retrieved from the object library are not merely graphics objects, having only appearances, but no other capabilities. Instead, they are endowed with significant behaviors, which can be called upon by invoking their built-in methods. By interconnecting graphics interface objects, designed and edited by the user to library objects having interesting and powerful computational behaviors, a system can be assembled, at low expense to the designer, having both a powerful user interface and significant behaviors controlled by it.

15.3 Review Questions

1. Explain how an object-oriented graphics drawing system can group a list of selected shape objects into a single grouped object.
2. What is a user interface to a system?
3. How can object-oriented programming techniques be used to advantage to create file and printing subsystems for a software application?
4. How can object-oriented programming techniques be applied to build a user interface allowing a user to control the behavior of an economic model?

15.3 Exercises

1. Describe how to compute the smallest rectangle that encloses all enclosing rectangles of the objects on a list, L, of objects, each of which has its own enclosing rectangle.
2. Describe how you would implement an *ungroup* command that applies to a grouped object and resolves it into a collection of separate drawn objects residing on **theShapeList** of a drawing application.

3. Given a list of shapes, L, compute how to *align* them either horizontally or vertically, so that their bottoms, centers, or tops lie on the same horizontal line or their centers, right sides, or left sides lie on the same vertical line. (Here, define the *left*, *bottom*, *right*, *top*, and *center* of an object with respect to its enclosing rectangle.) After computing an alignment command by scanning a shape list, L, define an **Align** method to send an **Align** message to all objects on L, and then define how to apply the **Align** method to an individual shape, S.

≡ 15.4 Advantages and Disadvantages of Object-Oriented Programming

Learning Objectives

1. To understand the hidden costs incurred when using object-oriented programming techniques.
2. To understand the importance of object browsers.
3. To learn how to assess the circumstances under which the use of object-oriented programming techniques yields payoffs.

The discussion of object-oriented programming examples in the previous sections covered the following *advantages* of using object-oriented programming: (1) Providing a clear modular software structure at a level of organization finer than that of the C module, in which objects themselves each have clearly defined interfaces and information hiding behaviors; (2) Providing a framework in which reusable software components can be expressed and can be conveniently used, such as the objects in a class library that can be customized to provide the file and printing subsystems of a system; (3) Providing for ease of maintenance and modification of a program by permitting a style of programming in which new objects and new behaviors can be introduced merely by expressing the differences they exhibit when compared to existing objects; (4) Providing convenient avenues for natural growth of a system via the introduction of new derived classes of customized objects that nonetheless share inherited common behaviors with other similar classes of objects; and (5) Providing for fast, easy definition of graphical user interfaces to a system.

first, the advantages

As is often the case in computer science, we face tradeoffs, one of the most notable being the tradeoff between generality and efficiency. In the case of object-oriented programming techniques, the advantages of increased generality must be purchased in the coinage of reduced efficiency. Since objects are often allocated in heaps using dynamic storage allocation techniques, and since they are often referenced by pointers, their use incurs a notable memory allocation policy cost (because heaps require search times to identify and allocate suitable blocks of storage in the heap).

generality versus efficiency

In addition, the dynamic binding of method calls can incur run-time penalties. For example, a message **M** sent to an object **Ob1**, may trigger the application of a locally defined method in object **Ob1** that implements a customized meaning for a virtual method **M** specified in an abstract base class **B**. To know what method to invoke when message **M** is sent to an object that is the value of a variable of type **B**,

run-time penalties

the run-time system may need to perform a run-time case analysis. This incurs a run-time type switching penalty.

Finally, if full object debugging features are turned on, the display update time penalties and associated additional debugging time and memory costs can make a complex object-oriented program run slowly when it is being debugged. (Of course, the debugging options can be turned off and the final production version of the system can be compiled without debugging features, which can increase its efficiency considerably.)

While the memory and time penalties associated with object-oriented programming often severely taxed the meager resources of the earlier generation of personal and desktop computers (and tended to degrade the performance of object-oriented programs unacceptably), the more powerful recent generation of desktop computers seems to have enough additional memory and processor speed to compensate for the earlier OOP performance drawbacks. It is possible that in the future the increased software benefits associated with OOP techniques together with a reduction in their unacceptable performance penalties will imply an increase in the popularity and acceptance of object-oriented programming.

The Importance of Using Good Class Browsers

There is an important recommendation to consider when using object-oriented programming techniques on large software systems: You should try if at all possible to use an object-oriented programming system that provides a good *class browser*.

Suppose you are attempting to extend an object-oriented program consisting of 40,000 lines of code and having 200 separate object classes defined in it. (These numbers might be typical of a mature contemporary software application for a desktop computer). Typically, such a program has an extensive class inheritance hierarchy spanning many levels of derived classes. A given subclass typically inherits methods and instance variables from many ancestors defined in textually separate locations throughout the program text.

consider a complex object-oriented system

For example, in a mature drawing program, numerous objects will have **Draw** methods defined on them—since drawing methods are invoked anytime you want to display the visual appearance of an object on the screen, or anytime you want to draw an object in a page image before printing the page on a printing device. This implies, for instance, that windows, menus, control buttons, scroll bars, and all manner of user-drawn objects will each be expressed as objects having individual local **Draw** methods defined on them.

using ordinary C cross-reference methods is unhelpful

If you use an ordinary C cross-reference listing program to list all identifiers used in your program together with the list of line numbers of the lines in which these identifiers appear, you will find that the cross-reference index has an entry for the identifier, **Draw**, followed by a huge list of line numbers, giving every line on which a **Draw** method was defined or called. This tends to be of very little help when you want to locate the **Draw** method of a particular object class, **Ob1**, in which you are interested at a given moment, since only a very small percentage of the **Draw** references will refer to the **Ob1::Draw** method, while most will reference the **Draw** methods of the

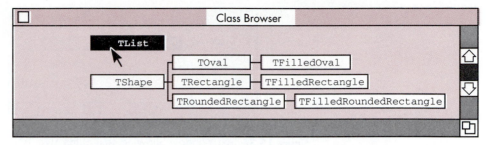

Figure 15.32 Class Inheritance Hierarchy for Stage-3 Shape Drawing Program

many other kinds of objects also having **Draw** methods. The inadequacy of the ordinary cross-reference index can become highly irritating when the programmer, engaged in the quest of trying to discover how an object behaves, is forced to search for scraps of inherited methods, scattered all over the program listing, using the cross-reference index's nearly totally useless clues.

A good solution to this problem—if not an essential tool for the professional object-oriented programmer—is a *class browser*, which is a dynamic search device that locates references to class definitions and methods and which portrays the class hierarchy graphically, allowing visual identification of the ancestors of a given object class, and subsequent fast access to the texts of their implementations. Figure 15.32 shows the class hierarchy for the third stage shape drawing program of Section 15.2, as portrayed by one of the better commercially available C++ systems.

accessing a class definition

To access the text of the class definition for **TList** in Fig. 15.32, you can click the mouse twice when the cursor is over the rectangle containing the identifier, **TList**. When you do this, a text window opens up and shows the definition's text in which the identifier **TList** has been highlighted. Even more impressively, if you hold the mouse button down when the cursor is over **TList**, a menu pops up giving a list of all methods defined on **TList** objects in alphabetical order. If you then drag down the menu and select a method name, then, when you release the mouse button, the text of the method is accessed and displayed in another text window.

Figure 15.33 shows the result of choosing the **IsNonEmpty** method name from the menu of method names of a **TList** object. As a result of making this choice, a new text

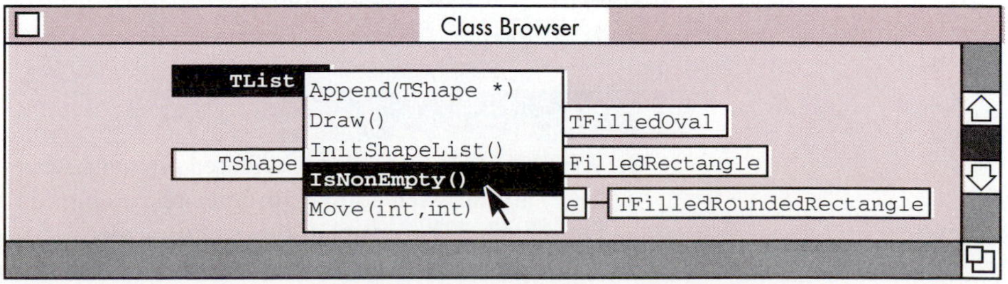

Figure 15.33 Accessing the Method Names Menu for the TList Object

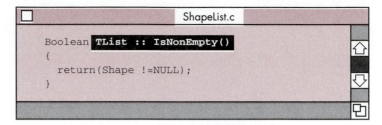

```
┌─────────────────────────────────────────────┐
│ □                 ShapeList.c              │ │
├─────────────────────────────────────────────┤
│  Boolean ███████████████████████            │▲│
│          █TList :: IsNonEmpty()█            ├─┤
│  {                                          │ │
│     return(Shape !=NULL);                   ├─┤
│  }                                          │▼│
│                                             ├─┤
│                                             │▣│
└─────────────────────────────────────────────┘
```

Figure 15.34 Text Window Showing Text of the TList::IsNonEmpty Method

window opens up and automatically scrolls to the text of the **TList::IsNonEmpty** method with the method name highlighted, as shown in Fig. 15.34.

fast, accurate search is important

Professional object-oriented programmers quickly learn to appreciate the value of a good class browser capability such as this. Its use enables them to locate quickly the text of object class definitions and method definitions, and to leap around nimbly and efficiently in the many text files defining a typical, large object-oriented system.

Also of considerable value are run-time debugging facilities for objects. Using a run-time debugger, a window opens up that displays the instance variables and method names for object instances existing at run time. It is possible to follow the pointer references to other object instances dynamically and to display the contents of those object instances. As discussed earlier in Section 5.5, formatted debugging aids are worth their weight in gold when trying to track down obscure errors. The appearance of run-time object debuggers in several of the contemporary, commercially available, object-oriented programming systems provides the professional programmer with excellent, state-of-the-art tools for debugging ambitious, complex, new software systems.

formatted debugging aids for objects are critical, too

15.4 Review Questions

1. List some advantages of using object-oriented programming techniques.
2. Discuss the storage and time penalties associated with the use of object-oriented programming techniques.
3. What is the value of using class browsers when trying to understand how a large object-oriented program works?

15.4 Exercises

1. When compiling an object-oriented program, what information would you have to keep, and in what format in order to be able (1) to draw the class hierarchy of Fig. 15.32; (2) to display the menu of method names of Fig. 15.33; and (3) to access and display the text of the method shown in Fig. 15.34, or the text of the object class definition for a **TList** (not shown in any figure in this section)?

 Pitfalls

- *Attempting to build a large OOP system without class browsers and debuggers*

  It is a nearly fatal mistake to assume that you can successfully build a large object-oriented programming system without the benefit of convenient, efficient class browsers and dynamic object debuggers. Remember the lessons learned from the early days of software engineering that the use of formatted debugging aids can cut system debugging times in half. Follow the words of the wise who have found class browsers to be essential to their attempts to comprehend how complex object-oriented programs work.

Tips and Techniques

- *Use OOP techniques to build prototypes of user interfaces*

  User interfaces tend to be risk-prone portions of a software system because it is hard to anticipate whether users will find them convenient and suitable. To reduce the risk that a user interface design will turn out to be inadequate, you can build a prototype rapidly and then test it on actual users to try to identify its shortcomings, if any, and to collect suggestions for improvements. If you have graphics object editors and user-directed object assembly systems available for your use, you will likely find that it is easy and cheap to build a rapid prototype of your user interface.

- *Use OOP software component libraries to build key subsystems*

  Object-oriented class libraries often contain objects that can be customized to generate major subsystems of a system, such as the printing or filing subsystems. You customize them by specifying local behaviors for virtual methods that give you blanks to fill in by supplying missing details from your program. (Filling in these empty slots specifies the necessary connections to your program.) Using this approach, the cost of building key subsystems can be greatly reduced, and the reliability and user-convenience of the result can be greatly increased, compared to conventional systems programming techniques.

- *Use OOP techniques to structure your software system for ease of modification*

  Software maintenance and modification activities occupy a major fraction of the lifecycle of a large software system, and typically constitute from 70 percent to 90 percent of the system's lifetime cost. By using OOP techniques to structure your software system, you often provide for ease of future modification and upgrade, since you can introduce new derived classes that inherit the behaviors you want to retain while expressing new modifications of behaviors using new method definitions.

References for Further Study

a C++ primer

Stanley B. Lippman, C++ *Primer, 2nd Edition*, Addison-Wesley, Reading, Mass. (1991).

A good introduction to object-oriented programming covering all the features of the latest version of ANSI C++.

C++

Think C/Symantec C++ User's Guide, Symantec Corporation, Cupertino, Calif., (1993).

An explanation of how to use a good class browser and debugger, as well as how to use many other features of a mature C++ programming system.

Chapter Summary

object classes

As its name implies, object-oriented programming focuses on a style of programming involving various classes of objects. These classes can be arranged in inheritance hierarchies in which *subclasses* are derived from *base classes*.

methods, instance variables, and inheritance

An object can be thought of as a C struct, having ordinary struct data members, that is extended to have local function members, called *methods*, attached to it, and that *inherits* (i.e., has access to) the data members and methods of the objects in its ancestral base classes. The data members of an object are sometimes referred to as *instance variables* in some variants of object-oriented programming terminology.

customization of virtual methods

Suppose the class of objects of type X is defined to be a derived class of the base class of objects of type Y. Then, not only does an X inherit all the instance variables and methods of objects of type Y, but also, an X can have a local method, M, defined for it, which has the same name as a virtual method, named M, defined for Y. In this case, X's local method, M, gives a customized local meaning for method M when applied to objects of subtype X.

OOP in a nutshell

In a nutshell, then, we could say that *object-oriented programming* consists of manipulating classes of objects, each of which can have its own *instance variables* and *methods*, and in which separate classes can be related to one another by *class derivation*, *inheritance*, and local *customization* of shared *virtual methods*.

object pointers

Ordinarily, storage for specific instances of a particular type of object is allocated in a heap storage zone, using a suitable dynamic memory allocation policy, and *pointers* are used to reference object instances in the heap.

drawing a list of shapes

Suppose L is a variable containing a pointer to a list of shape objects, and S is a shape object. Furthermore, suppose we want to draw the entire list of shape objects, L, on a computer screen. To do this, we could send a **Draw** message to the list, L, using the notation, L–>Draw( ). This would call the **Draw** method of the list object L. Suppose further that the implementation of the **Draw** method for L involves sending a **Draw** message to every shape object, S, on the list. Thus the method S.Draw( ) would be called for each shape S on the list L. Each individual shape object could react differently to its receipt of the **Draw** message by drawing the particular individual type of shape it represents on the screen. As objects are drawn in first-to-last order on the list L, they are drawn in back-to-front order on the screen.

Thus in object-oriented programming the metaphor of *message passing* between objects is used to designate the action in which one object calls another object's method. Moreover, many different kinds of objects can each have their own versions of an identically named virtual method (such as the virtual **Draw** method), and each can perform its own different individual action in response to the call of this identically named method.

If Y is a base class from which class X is derived, then a variable of type Y can hold values of type X, implying that C++'s rules for variables and their permissible value types are more general than those for ordinary C. This added generality can be quite useful when applying shared virtual method names to collections of objects having different derived subtypes. Also, it would be possible to define a general linked list object capable of containing pointers to list items of a general class **TClass**, meaning that any object created in the system could become a value that could be stored in such a general linked list.

Object-oriented programming can be used to express the structure of a system of objects in a clean modular fashion, particularly at the level of individual objects, each of which is defined to have a clean interface. Class libraries can furnish useful reusable software components, such as objects that allow you to generate complete file and printing subsystems. To use these library objects, you define individual methods that customize the virtual (or blank fill-in) methods in the library objects in order to establish the necessary connections with the rest of your system. Successful use of such library objects allows you to take advantage of a great deal of prefabricated labor without having to master the details of building such subsystems for yourself.

When a software system is built using object-oriented programming techniques, it often exhibits an enhanced capacity to tolerate change and modification. New modifications can be introduced by establishing new derived classes of objects and by defining customized local methods to exhibit the desired behavior changes. Not only is object-oriented programming efficient because it permits you to program by expressing only the changes you desire, it also tends to reduce the costs of system maintenance and modification because it structures the system in a way that accommodates changes more easily than that achievable through traditional programming techniques (which require many distributed, nonlocal program text changes to express the same changes that can be expressed locally using object-oriented programming).

Some contemporary software systems come equipped with object-oriented systems for defining and building graphical user interfaces. Object editors can be used to assemble and adjust user interface objects, such as control panels, palettes, menus, windows, and the like. Such objects are not only graphical, they can also perform control actions in response to user inputs, and they can communicate their control actions by calling on the methods of other objects to which they can be connected. Such systems allow rapid, easy construction of graphical user interfaces, which can be especially helpful in the activity of rapid prototyping.

It is important to select an object-oriented programming system offering good class browsers and run-time object debuggers, if you are planning to build a large object-oriented software system. A good class browser allows you to inspect a visual model of the class hierarchy and to access rapidly both the program text of each

---

the message passing metaphor

the useful generality of C++'s type system

class libraries with reusable software components

ease of modification

fast construction of graphical user interfaces

the importance of good class browsers and debuggers

object class definition and each method implementation for that object class. Without the services of a good class browser, it is exceedingly difficult to understand the behavior of a system of objects and their methods, since the fragments of text defining the method behaviors tend to be scattered across a large listing, rather than being concentrated in one place. (While the declarations for a single object class are usually concentrated in one portion of the text, the parts of the text defining the behavior of a virtual method with a given name, M, which applies to many kinds of objects, tends to be scattered across the texts of all objects for which the inheritance hierarchies for method M are defined. A good browser can provide rapid access to the different customized local method definitions for virtual method M.)

Although the use of object-oriented programming techniques incurs some storage and time penalties in a running program, these penalties seem less debilitating as computers increase in power and come with bigger memories. As more programmers learn about the advantages of object-oriented programming, it is possible that its popularity and utility will increase in coming years.

16

Advanced Software Engineering Concepts

the challenge of large-scale programming

Programming-in-the-large—i.e., building big software systems—is a fascinating topic for study, in part because, in the past, it has been such a formidable challenge. Large software systems may be among the most complex artifacts ever built by humankind.

early failures

In the early days of software engineering, it was not unusual for big software projects to exceed their budgets and deadlines, and even to be canceled for lack of ability to meet their system requirements. For example, in the 1960s, IBM's TSS (Time Sharing System) for the IBM 360 model 67 mainframe computer was canceled after the expenditure of over 500 person-years of effort.

fascinating phenomena

As experience accumulated, many fascinating software engineering phenomena began to be observed. For example, you might think that if your project is running late, you could add more programmers to get it back on schedule. But *Brooks' Law* states, "Adding manpower to a late software project makes it later." Software engineers have discovered quantitative limits on how much you can compress the schedule for a project by adding new personnel. Project managers should know about these

659

limits, since they define when it is impossible to shorten a project's completion time.

Although the early days of software engineering were tarnished by failure and frustration, the field advanced rapidly as it learned from experience. Among the improvements we can note when comparing present-day practice to the situation that prevailed in those early days are the following: (1) A more mature understanding of the software development process and how to manage it properly, (2) More accurate techniques for estimating the time and effort required to build a software system, and (3) Dozens of proven practical techniques for ensuring that software can be built to meet its requirements on schedule and within budget.

recent advances in the field

Today, the evolution of advanced software engineering is still vigorous. For example, promising new risk-based software management methods have emerged only within the last decade.

In a single chapter such as this, we can give only a brief glimpse of some of the findings and approaches of contemporary software engineering. Nonetheless, it will be possible for you to develop an appreciation for many of the issues by reading just these few pages. Perhaps this will whet your appetite for further study of software engineering.

Plan for the Chapter

Section 16.2 presents the phases of the *software lifecycle*. The software lifecycle is a span of time that stretches from the initial conception of a software system, through its development and active use, to the time when the system is retired from active use. Typical phases of a software lifecycle include: requirements analysis, specification, design, coding and debugging, testing, release for actual use, and software maintenance and upgrade during the period of operational use.

the software lifecycle

We study factors affecting *software productivity* in Section 16.3. The most important factor affecting productivity is programmer and team capability. We'll talk about *the software learning* curve in connection with the impact of programmer experience.

software productivity

Section 16.4 discusses two *software process models:* the traditional *Waterfall Model* and a new risk-based *Spiral Model*. The Waterfall Model has been in use for many years, but recently some of its disadvantages have become apparent. The Spiral Model is an interesting new process model that uses risk-management techniques to control activities during software development.

software process models

≡ **16.2** The Software Lifecycle

Learning Objectives

1. To learn about the phases of the software lifecycle.
2. To understand the high cost of maintenance in the lifecycle of typical long-lived systems.
3. To understand why software system design is an important lifecycle activity.

the toolshed theorem

Suppose you had 1000 construction workers and you divided them into 100 groups of ten each. Suppose you gave each group of ten some boards and nails and said, "Go build me a toolshed." You'd probably get 100 very reasonable toolsheds. But suppose you then supplied construction materials to the entire group of 1000 workers and said, "Now build me a hotel." You'd probably get a pretty lousy hotel. The point of this example is that the construction of a complex artifact with many complex interacting parts by many people requires levels of design, specification, coordination, and management that simple artifacts do not require.

By a large, long-lived software system, we mean one that is over 100,000 lines of code long and whose useful service lifetime is 25 years or more. Because such large, long-lived software systems are incredibly complex, they demand, during their development, careful adherence to disciplines that have proven successful for managing the complexity of the construction process and coordinating the efforts of many individuals who must cooperate effectively to achieve successful results.

adherence to management disciplines

Figure 16.1 shows the phases of the software lifecycle. The subsections that follow will describe each of these lifecycle phases in sequence.

Requirements Analysis

definition of requirements analysis

In *requirements analysis* we try to formulate a high-quality statement of the true capabilities and properties of the system that are needed by its users and operators. The result of this process is usually a "requirements document," having many numbered sections and subsections, which enumerates all the requirements the system will have to meet.

For example, suppose we are trying to analyze the requirements for an on-line banking information system for a large bank with 120 branches in 70 cities. Suppose this system is to be designed to perform the following functions: (1) handle all customer checking and savings accounts; (2) handle dial-in inquiries by customers who want to know their current account balances and give computer-generated voice out-

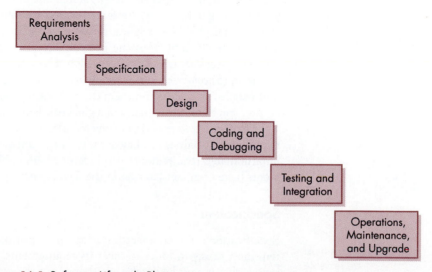

Figure 16.1 Software Lifecycle Phases

put to answer customers over the phone; and (3) handle all transactions for all tellers at all branch banks when such transactions are punched into special on-line video-display terminals at each teller's window.

general requirements

The system might have many general requirements. For example, we would like it to be reliable, correct, efficient, user-friendly, expandable, and as cheap as possible, given the other constraints.

Suppose we are dealing with a numbered item in the requirements document, "Item 12: User-Friendliness." Under Item 12, we might find "Item 12c: Tellers' On-Line Terminals," and under this item, we might find, "Item 12c4: Responsiveness— When a teller has completed entry of a transaction at a teller terminal, the system shall respond rapidly and without delay to acknowledge the acceptance of the transaction or to indicate an error condition in the transaction entry. Any information requested in the transaction shall be computed rapidly and shall be rapidly delivered to the teller." You can see how Item 12c4, has defined the meaning of the "responsiveness" requirement for tellers' terminals, under the general heading of user-friendliness requirements.

characteristics of a good requirements analysis

In general, in a good requirements analysis, we are trying to conceive of everything that is relevant and nothing more. We attempt to generate a set of requirements statements with at least the following properties: (1) *completeness*, (2) *consistency*, (3) *unambiguity*, (4) *correctness*, and (5) *comprehensibility*.

For example, (2) *consistency* means there should be no contradictions in the requirements. As an example of two inconsistent requirements, suppose that under the heading of "Item 6: Efficiency," there was an "Item 6d3: Mainframe Efficiency," reading, "The central processing unit shall be completely engaged in processing transactions and shall never sit idle and waste computer cycles." A consequence of this

an example of inconsistent requirements

would be that queues of incoming transactions would have to be pending awaiting processing. But this would mean that transactions would spend time waiting to get processed, so the responsiveness requirement under Item 12c4 might not be met. If you are going to have very short transaction waiting times, or even zero waiting times, your central processor is going to have to run in an undersaturated condition. This may not be efficient from the perspective of optimal mainframe utilization, but it might be necessary to guarantee quick transaction turn-around times.

Item (5) *comprehensibility* simply means that the requirements should be written so that people can understand them easily. Writing comprehensible requirements is harder than you think, particularly in a gibberish-laden field such as systems programming.

Good requirements do not overconstrain the set of valid implementations. Good requirements analysis is a key activity in the software lifecycle, because ill-structured, unfathomable requirements preclude our being able to determine that the requirements have been met later on in the development process.

Specification

specifications must be testable

Specification is the enumeration of specific, quantitative behavioral constraints a system must satisfy in order to meet its requirements. A key property of a specification item is that it must be *testable* whether or not the system satisfies it.

Such specific measurable properties are necessary to provide operational tests later in the lifecycle in order to determine whether or not designs and implementations satisfy the system requirements.

For example, requirements Item 12c4 demanded that the system respond rapidly after a teller enters a transaction at a teller terminal. But what does it mean to have the system respond rapidly, and how can we test whether this requirement has been achieved? A specification corresponding to requirements Item 12c4 might read, "The system shall respond within $1/_2$ second for 95 percent of the tellers' transactions entered, and shall respond within 2 seconds for 99.8 percent of the tellers' transactions entered. In all remaining cases, the system shall respond within five seconds."

You can see how this specification is testable. A system could monitor the response times the system takes to answer the teller transaction requests and could print a report giving the distribution of response times and some statistical summaries making it easy to answer whether or not the response-time specification had been met.

Good specifications are (1) *complete*, (2) *unambiguous*, (3) *minimal*, (4) *comprehensible*, and (5) sufficiently specific and well-quantified to be *testable* whether or not they are satisfied.

Specification is a key activity in the software lifecycle because in the absence of specific measurable properties a system must exhibit to meet its requirements, determining whether a system satisfies the requirements may not be testable.

relating specifications and requirements

Generally speaking, it is often useful to give a specification in the form of a document having numbered items such that the specification items are indexed to corresponding numbered requirements items in the requirements document. Here, it is intended that if the test corresponding to the specification item is met, then the corresponding requirements item(s) will be deemed to have been satisfied.

Design

A *design* is a representation of an artifact or a system. For example, architects use blueprints to communicate a design for a house that is being constructed. Construction workers can interpret these blueprints and can build the house that they represent. Similarly, a software design is a representation of a full software system suitable for programmers to use to implement it. *Designing* is the art of constructing and evaluating designs to meet constraints and satisfy purposes.

what are designs?

design representations and PDLs

A popular form of software system design is to sketch the system's modules and module components using a *program design language* (PDL). The *program strategies* found throughout this book are examples of programs written in a PDL. The PDL, in this case, consists of normal C control structures with high-level comments substituted for portions of actual executable C code.

You can see that, if a software design were expressed entirely as a collection of program strategies in a suitable PDL, programmers could implement the actual system, just as we used program strategies to guide our implementation of actual running C programs by refining the outlines given by those strategies.

design goals

In the software lifecycle, we try to produce designs (1) to satisfy the specifications and requirements, (2) to help prescribe further implementation activities, and (3) to exhibit certain useful properties, namely (a) *completeness*, (b) *consistency*, (c) *comprehensibility*, (d) *technical feasibility*, (e) *unambiguity*, and (f) *susceptibility to analysis and evaluation*.

Given a complete design, we can often devise a *work breakdown structure* (WBS), and we can formulate tasks and schedules for subsequent implementation, testing, integration, and validation activities.

analyzing designs

We also attempt to produce designs that are susceptible to forms of analysis such as cost estimation, performance estimation, and determination of physical system characteristics (as in the activity of *computer sizing estimation*, in which we attempt to predict how big and fast computers and peripherals will need to be to run the system in a way that enables it to meet its specifications).

Good design is a key activity in the software lifecycle because (1) it provides a key input helpful for organizing subsequent stages and activities, (2) it permits certain kinds of errors to be caught at early stages where correction is relatively inexpensive in comparison to the cost of repair downstream, (3) it enables task schedules, communication disciplines, and preliminary resource and performance estimation to take place, and (4) it supports early validation and improvement of requirements specifications.

catching errors early has high payoff

Item (2) is worth further emphasis. Namely, if we can catch an error in the design stage during design review, it is often much less costly to fix the error by redesigning a portion of the system than it is to let implementation proceed and fix the error later after the error has been discovered in the testing stage. The reason this is so has to do with *sunk cost*. If we catch and fix the error early in the lifecycle, we have much less sunk cost invested than if we catch it later during testing after the cost of implementation has already been incurred. Cost multiples of tens or hundreds are not uncommon when comparing the cost of early detection and repair versus late detection and repair in the software lifecycle.

design walkthroughs

Consequently, after finishing a design, a useful practice is to conduct a *design walkthrough*. In a design walkthrough, the designers try to explain the design to a critical (but friendly) team of design reviewers (who should be distinct from the actual designers, themselves). The idea is to go over the design with a fine-toothed comb to attempt to catch errors and problems early in the lifecycle before investing in costly implementations that will be thrown away.

Coding and Debugging

During the *coding and debugging phase* of the software lifecycle (sometimes called the *implementation phase*), we construct and debug a working executable representation of the system design.

implementation goals

During implementation, we try not only to produce a concrete design realization in a suitable programming language that satisfies the specifications and meets the requirements, we also attempt to produce an artifact that enhances the ease of subsequent maintenance and modification. That is, we attempt to construct the artifact in such a manner that its pieces can be readily understood and which has the capacity to sustain future variation in response to changing requirements. Clear consistent *documentation* explaining how the parts work is essential at this stage and should always be considered an integral part of the implementation process.

dealing with indispensable programmers

It is during this phase that we often run into the phenomenon of the "indispensable whiz programmer." Perhaps you have met such a person at one time or another in your programming experience. The whiz is incredibly knowledgeable about how the underlying operating system works, knows all manner of miraculous programming tricks, and can lay down miles of undocumented code at a rate that could win a gold medal at the Olympics, if programming were ever admitted as an Olympic sport. But the way in which the code works is kept as a mystery in the whiz's head and is never offered in the form of program comments or in conversation to associates.

Sometimes the whiz's code will be almost correct, but just short of perfect, and because the whiz must perpetually devote scarce time to the solution of other critical problems, which nobody else has been able to solve, it will fall to some poor associate to try to debug the whiz's splendid creation. It is at that moment that the true cost of having a whiz on a project will begin to be revealed.

the impact of brilliant, undocumented code on maintainers

Again, later in the software lifecycle, when the whiz has turned to some other project, it will be the responsibility of maintenance programmers to attempt to understand and modify the code the whiz originally wrote. And because this code is brilliant, obscure, and undocumented, they won't understand it. Even if the code is efficient and correct, the maintenance programmers will tend to rip it out and replace it with something comprehensible, even if the replacement is less efficient than the original, in order to achieve the goal of having, in hand, a program that they are confident they understand and can modify to do something new and useful.

These observations have lead many a seasoned (and humane) software manager to recommend maxims such as the following: (1) If you have a whiz programmer on your project, make sure the whiz documents all code written, and then test that documentation with the same rigor that you test the code by having a second group of programmers try to understand the program and explain how it works satisfactorily to a third group of programmers; and (2) If you have an indispensable programmer on your project, fire him or her immediately.

Testing and Integration

During module testing and integration, we attempt to ensure that modules have correct behavior, that they satisfy performance specifications, and that they cooperate correctly together to achieve overall system performance.

Testing and integration is a key phase of the software lifecycle because it ensures that software quality requirements are met prior to system release.

unit testing and integration testing

Often, testing is broken down into *unit testing* and *integration testing*. In unit testing, we test the operation of a module apart from its interconnection to and cooperation with other separate units. In the integration testing phase, we test a connected system of previously tested units to see if they can cooperate successfully together. A common error in software effort estimation is to underestimate the amount of time and effort that need to be spent on integration testing.

Because considerable attention was given to testing in Chapter 5, we will not emphasize it further in this chapter.

Operations, Maintenance, and Upgrade

After a system has passed its *acceptance test*, it is usually released into operational use. At this moment, its *useful service lifetime* begins. As its service lifetime progresses, it is nearly inevitable that the conditions of its use will change unpredictably, and that new needs will arise to modify or extend the system to behave in some new, important manner. Also, bugs will be detected, and either the bugs will have to be repaired, or workarounds will have to be discovered to enable users to avoid unacceptable results.

a system's useful
service lifetime

Thus, during the maintenance and upgrade phase of the lifecycle, we attempt to alter the system either to remedy defective properties revealed during system usage experience, or to meet new behavioral requirements.

repair and upgrade

The activities involved during maintenance may repeat any and all of the previous lifecycle activities. For example, attempting to modify the system to meet a new requirement may entail reenactment of requirements analysis activities, which in turn can lead to respecification, redesign, and reimplementation of parts of the system and to new test and integration activities. On the other hand, fixing an implementation bug may entail only reimplementation, retesting, and integration, not redesign.

Typically, when a lifecycle decision is remade, it causes all successor lifecycle activities to be reenacted incrementally, whereas none of the predecessor activities need to be considered.

An important point about the maintenance and upgrade phase of the lifecycle is that it typically comprises 70 to 90 percent of the total lifecycle cost of a large, long-lived software system. In other words, maintenance is enormously expensive. This implies that spending extra time and effort in the prerelease phases of the software lifecycle, in order to decrease downstream maintenance costs, can produce significant cost-avoidance results.

maintenance often costs 70
to 90 percent of the total
lifecycle cost

For example, by one estimate, only 17 percent of the time spent in the maintenance phase is attributable to debugging, but over 50 percent of the time is spent by programmers trying to understand the system they need to repair or extend. If software understanding constitutes 50 percent or more of the maintenance activities, then a key prerelease, cost-avoidance activity is producing clear documentation (or other types of system understanding aids such as videotapes of key designers and implementers explaining what was going through their minds when they built the system).

cost-avoidance through
good documentation

The maintenance phase of the lifecycle tends to take on a distinct operational flavor of its own that is distinct from that of the other prerelease phases. For example, there is often emphasis on (1) collection, analysis, and prioritization of software trouble reports from users, (2) troubleshooting the highest priority problems on the prioritized list, (3) managing the installation of new system releases from the originating software development organization, (4) communicating user's manual changes, and new usage procedures to users, (5) updating system documentation to keep it current, (6) managing configuration control issues (which relate to how the software system maps onto the specific mix of computers and peripherals on which a given version of the system is being run—as in generating a new version of the system to run on a new hardware configuration when new printers, new disk drives, more memory, or new central processing units are added), and (7) training new maintenance personnel—a constant activity since the duration on the job of most maintenance personnel is short in comparison to the service lifetime of the system.

16.2 Review Questions

1. Describe each of the phases of the software lifecycle.
2. What are the properties of a good software system design?
3. What is a design walkthrough and what role does it play in the software lifecycle?
4. What is the most expensive phase of the software lifecycle, and what measures can be taken to avoid its costs?

16.2 Exercises

1. Enumerate some sensible requirements for a bank data processing system that performs the following functions at over 100 geographically dispersed branch banks of a single banking corporation: (1) handles transactions at teller windows; (2) handles automatic cash dispenser machines; (3) prints and mails monthly statements to checking and savings account customers; (4) processes instant cash transaction requests from bankcard computers and debits customers' checking accounts or denies payment in the case of insufficient funds; (5) prints monthly management reports; (6) offers on-line access to bank personnel to establish or close customer accounts, change bankcard passwords, and provide current account balances; and (7) accepts dial-in inquiries over touch-tone phones by customers, and after a password check, uses voice-generation equipment to give customer account balances over the phone.
2. Take two items from the requirements you generated in your answer to Exercise 1 and generate specific, quantitative, testable specification items from them.

16.3 Software Productivity

Learning Objectives

1. To learn how software productivity is defined.
2. To learn how to estimate the software effort (in person-months) and the total development time (in months) of a proposed software project.
3. To learn how productivity audits can be used to develop a strategy for improving a software organization's productivity.
4. To become familiar with the surprising lessons of software engineering.

Productivity is a measure of the output achieved from spending a given unit's worth of input effort. With regard to a software system, you might measure it by dividing the number of delivered source instructions (DSIs) in an operational software system by the number of person-months (PMs) it took to build the system prior to its release into service. For example, if System A took 85.3 person-months to build and consisted of 30,000 lines of documented delivered source code, then the productivity of System A's project team was 352 lines of code per person-month.

All other things being equal, if your software project team can adopt techniques that increase its productivity, then it will complete its system building task with less effort (and therefore at less cost) than would otherwise be the case. For this reason, software engineers have had a healthy curiosity about factors affecting software productivity stretching back to the earliest days of the field.

early findings

Among the early findings were several astonishing facts concerning (1) the effect of experience, (2) the high variance in productivity among individual programmers, and (3) the difference in productivity between programmers working on different kinds of projects. In the next three subsections, we will comment on these three early categories of findings.

The Software Learning Curve

When a team of programmers implements a given type of software, such as a FORTRAN compiler, over and over again under slightly changing circumstances, such as implementing the compiler on each of three new brands of computers, not only does the team's performance get better with practice, but also it tends to get better at estimating how much time it will take to complete the job.

improvements in actual and estimated performance

Figure 16.2 shows the actual effort and estimated effort taken by the same team of programmers to implement three FORTRAN compilers on three successive occasions. The first time the team implemented a FORTRAN compiler, they estimated it would take 24 person-months, but in fact it took 48 months. The third time around, however, they estimated it would take 12 person-months and it took them 14. Thus the

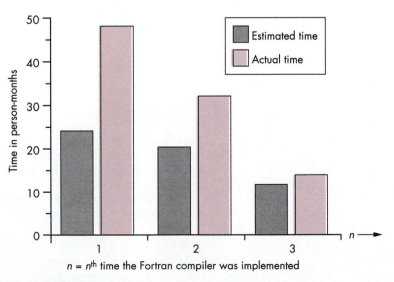

Figure 16.2 The Software Learning Curve

last time around, they were 3.4 times more productive, and their estimates were only 17 percent off instead of 100 percent off.

You can imagine that the first time the team tried implementing a FORTRAN compiler, they may have been unsure of what they were doing, and they may have had to use a trial-and-error process to experiment with several approaches before finding ones that worked when building various subsystems. However, their trial-and-error approach was most likely replaced with a "tried-and-true" approach when building the last of the three compilers. They had learned from experience what would likely work, and the cost of exploration to determine new models and methods was reduced dramatically the third time around.

trial-and-error gives way to tried-and-true

In applying the lessons of the software learning curve to actual project effort estimation, it is important to be cautious and ask, "Does the team's experience really scale-up under the new circumstances of the proposed new project?" A few decades ago, there was a company who had a very good reputation for building FORTRAN compilers. They used table-driven software generators that accepted input parameters and generated components of the final system. It was almost as if they had produced powdered FORTRAN compilers for which an appropriate ad might have read, "Just add water and stir."

but does it scale-up?

This company won a contract to produce a PL/I compiler for various models of IBM mainframe computers. (PL/I was a new, multipurpose programming language IBM had introduced shortly before.) Alas, the model of compiler building that the company depended on, which worked so well for FORTRAN compilers, did not stretch to fit the new requirements of PL/I compilers. The company failed to deliver an acceptable PL/I compiler and went out of business as a result of their financial losses on the contract. The moral of the story is that you should perform a careful risk analysis to determine if your team's experienced approaches and methods actually scale-up to fit the new circumstances of a given new project. Will their team experience be a rich source of helpful new insights, or will it ossify them into an old-fashioned way of doing business that won't stretch to meet the demands of the new situation?

High Variance in Individual Productivity

In 1966, time-sharing systems had just appeared on the scene, and controversy arose as to whether their use made programmers more productive than the use of traditional batch systems. Intense but speculative arguments arose on both sides of the issue, so Sackman, Ericson, and Grant performed an experiment in which they attempted to measure the difference in productivity between a time-shared system and a batch system.

One of the most unusual aspects of their findings was that the performance of individual programmers varied enormously. Among the things they measured were the time it took a programmer to write a program solving a particular problem, the debugging time, the size of the program, the speed of the program, and the number of errors found during debugging. They found that these measures correlated very strongly for given programmers. For example, if a programmer wrote a program in a very short time, it tended to be easy to debug, to run fast, and to consume very little memory. But if a programmer took a long time to write the program, it tended to be big, to have many errors, to run slowly, and to consume a generous amount of memory.

A key result was that the best programmers were up to twenty times better than the worst programmers on these various measures of productivity. This finding has been confirmed in subsequent studies by other investigators.

Other studies of human productivity in various contexts have revealed a surprising result, sometimes called the *principle of top talent*. This principle states that about 50 percent of the productivity comes from 20 percent of the participants, and, moreover, the bottom 50 percent of the participants contribute only 20 percent of the productivity.

the principle of top talent

For example, 50 percent of the touchdowns in football are scored by 20 percent of the players, 50 percent of the arrests are made by 20 percent of the police, and 50 percent of the aerial combat kills were made by 20 percent of the RAF World War II pilots. Sometimes the productivity is skewed even further to what is called an 80–20 rule. For example, 80 percent of charitable giving comes from 20 percent of the donors. Generally speaking, these results are characterized by a family of skewed distributions called Zipf distributions. Other examples of Zipf distributions are the distribution of personal incomes, the distribution of city sizes, the frequency of use of natural language words versus their length, and database accesses. In the last case, for example, 80 percent of the accesses in a database are to the most active 20 percent of the records.

skewed productivity distributions

In the next section, when we study factors affecting productivity in Barry Boehm's Cocomo model, it should not surprise us to find that the factor that most affects productivity, among those Boehm identified, was what he called *personnel and team capability*. That is, the experience and capability of the individual programmer, as well as that of the programming team, is the factor that provides the biggest multiplier effect on the Cocomo model's baseline productivity estimate, among all productivity-affecting factors that Boehm's model identified.

Productivity Differences as a Measure of Comparative Difficulty Among Projects

Another of the early discoveries about productivity related to apparent differences in the difficulty of the type of programming being attempted. For example, an early study characterized programmers writing operating systems as having a typical average productivity of about 500 lines of documented, debugged code per person-year. Those writing compilers produced about 1500 lines per year, and those writing straightforward scientific applications programs produced about 15,000 lines per year. Clearly, there are important differences in the difficulty of the type of programming being attempted.

Boehm's Cocomo Model

Until the appearance of Boehm's Cocomo model and some similar contemporary models, making productivity estimates and software effort estimates was a mysterious art. However, use of the Cocomo model has helped to make solving such estimation

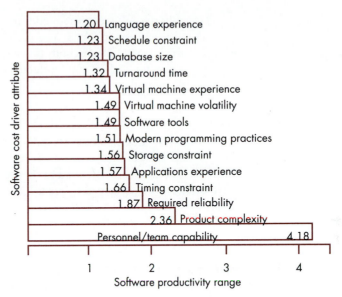

Figure 16.3 Cocomo Software Productivity Ranges (reprinted by permission of Prentice-Hall, Inc., Englewood Cliffs, NJ, from p. 642 of *Software Engineering Economics* by Barry W. Boehm, copyright © 1981.)

problems more of a science than an art, as Boehm makes clear in his book, *Software Economics* (see the references at the end of this chapter).

Figure 16.3 shows various factors affecting software productivity in the Cocomo model. Recall, from Chapter 5, that the Cocomo model works by starting with a *baseline estimate* of the number of person-months (PMs) that it will take to complete the most familiar class of software project of a given estimated size measured in Kilo-Delivered Source Instructions (KDSI), according to the relationship, PM = $2.4*(KDSI)^{1.05}$. The baseline estimate is then adjusted using *multipliers*. Each multiplier is derived from a rating scale that rates one of the attributes shown in Fig. 16.3.

PMs = baseline estimate times productivity multipliers

The *software productivity ranges* for the various attributes shown in Fig. 16.3 are ratios between the highest and lowest measures on the Cocomo rating scales for each of the attributes. For example, take the *software tools attribute*. Suppose you have two software projects (Project A and Project B) having every productivity attribute at the nominal (or baseline) level except for the software tools attribute. Suppose Project A has a very high level of software tool support, and suppose it gets the highest rating on the Cocomo software tools rating sheet—a rating of 0.83. Now suppose Project B has a very low level of software tool support, and suppose it gets the lowest possible rating of 1.24 on the Cocomo software tools rating sheet. The ratio 1.49 = 1.24/0.83 is computed by dividing the Cocomo rating for the lowest level of tool support by the Cocomo rating for the highest level of tool support. The number 1.49 is called a *software productivity range*, and is shown in Fig. 16.3 opposite the software tools attribute.

In effect, what the software tools productivity range says is that there can be up to a 1.49 multiple in the number of person-months required by a low-support-tools project when compared to the number of person-months required by a high-tool-support project—all other things being equal.

applying the full
Cocomo model

To apply the full Cocomo model to a proposed software project, you first estimate the software size, in KDSI. You then rate all of the software cost-driver attributes in Fig. 16.3, using Cocomo rating scales, to obtain a series of multipliers: m_1, m_2, ..., m_{14}—one for each of the fourteen Cocomo attributes in Fig. 16.3. Finally, you compute the formula

$$\text{PM} = m_1 * m_2 * \ldots * m_{14} * 2.4 * (\text{KDSI})^{1.05}. \qquad (16.1)$$

Cocomo Estimate for Software Effort in Person-Months

The Cocomo model was derived to fit a database of 63 sets of actual software project attributes, and was observed to predict the software effort (in PMs) to within 20 percent in over 70 percent of the cases.

Estimating the Development Time

the nominal
development time

Once you have estimated the number of person-months (PMs) required for your software project, using Eq. 16.1, you can apply an additional formula to estimate the total development time. The Cocomo baseline formula for the nominal development time in months, T_d, is given by

$$T_d = 2.5 * \sqrt[3]{\text{PM}}. \qquad (16.2)$$

Cocomo Nominal Development Time

For instance, returning to the example of System A above, which consisted of 30,000 lines of delivered source instructions and which was estimated to take 85.3 PMs to build, we can compute System A's nominal development time as 11 months, using Eq. 16.2 as follows:

$$11 \text{ months} = T_d = 2.5 * \sqrt[3]{85.3}.$$

It has been discovered by Boehm and others that it is nearly impossible to compress the development schedule below 75 percent of the nominal estimate given by Eq. 16.2. That is, when you plot the actual development times taken by many projects versus the total number of person-months they required for development, the data points almost invariably fall above a curve given by $y = 75\% * T_d$.

Brooks' Law

One of the early maxims of software engineering, called *Brooks' Law*, stated by Fred Brooks in his book, *The Mythical Man-Month*, is shown in Fig. 16.4. Brooks had

Adding manpower to a late project makes it later.

Figure 16.4 Brooks' Law

observed that when software project managers saw that their projects were running behind schedule and were in danger of missing their deadlines, a natural tendency was for the managers to believe that by adding more programmers, their late projects could be brought back on schedule. The idea was that since "many hands make light work," the labor could somehow be divided more finely into smaller pieces, which could then be accomplished faster using more personnel. Brooks observed that when this strategy was tried in actual practice, something funny occurred, and the project was made even later than it would have been had the new personnel not been added.

By adding new personnel late in the schedule, the already overworked original personnel often had to drop what they were doing to train the new personnel and get them up-to-speed so they could contribute. Also, the work breakdown structure of the project often had to be reorganized to give the new personnel something to do, and the new task breakdowns did not often fit terribly well with the one already under development. The delays encountered as a result of such reorganization and such assimilation of new personnel often made the late project even later than it would have been in the absence of the last-minute attempt at salvation.

using COCOMO equations to determine when Brooks' Law applies

The COCOMO development time estimate, given in Eq. 16.2, makes Brooks' Law into more of a science than would have been the case if Brooks' Law had remained in the form of a verbal maxim. For example, it is not always the case that adding manpower to a late project makes it later. To take a trivial and extreme example, suppose you have a project estimated to require 100 person-years (or 1200 PMs), whose nominal development time is estimated to be T_d = 26.6 months.

are you near the danger zone?

Suppose you have a deadline of 5 years, but you can only afford to put 10 programmers on the project. Then, since it will take these 10 programmers 10 years to contribute the required 100 person-years, you will finish 5 years late. In this case, you can double the number of programmers to 20, and you will be able to finish in five years and meet the five-year deadline on schedule (all other things being equal). In choosing to do this, you have come nowhere near the minimal schedule compression limit of 75% of T_d = 20 months, so you are not near the danger zone where Brooks' Law comes into play.

you must pay a cost, if you want to compress your schedule

By the way, if you do want to compress your schedule to meet a deadline, and you are not tampering with adventuring into the "zone of impossibility" by attempting to compress it below 75% of T_d, you will still have to pay a price for accomplishing an achievable level of schedule compression. For example, compared to the nominal schedule time, T_d, COCOMO predicts that you will have to use 23 percent added effort (in PMs) to compress your nominal T_d to the 75%*T_d limit. Be careful, however. Experience shows that if you attempt to accommodate more than 1.64 times the nominal project's personnel staffing level, you run the danger of straining your project's ability to coordinate its various parts to an extreme degree.

Improving Software Productivity

You can use Boehm's COCOMO model to improve the software productivity, and hence the competitive advantage, of your software development organization.

You can begin by noting that some of the cost-driver attributes shown in Fig. 16.3 are manipulable (or controllable) while other attributes must be taken as given because of the requirements of particular software projects. It may be possible to make judicious investments that improve the software productivity ratings of various attri-butes in your software organization.

software productivity audits

To begin with, you could conduct a *software productivity audit* of your software organization by rating its software productivity attributes using the rating sheets in the COCOMO model.

Then you could identify several manipulable cost-drivers found as a result of your audit to have low productivity ratings. For example, suppose three such low-rated attributes were (1) turnaround time, (2) software tools, and (3) modern programming practices. You could improve the ratings in these three areas by (1) installing more computer equipment to improve turnaround time, (2) purchasing advanced software tools, and (3) instituting a training program for your programmers in modern programming practices.

performing a cost-benefit
analysis to determine
the ROI

You could then estimate both the cost of making these three investments and the improvements on the software productivity attribute rating scales that would result. This would enable you to provide a cost-benefit analysis for your management, showing the return on investment (ROI) from investing in making improvements in these three areas assuming the productivity increases were in effect for some period of time afterward. If your management were persuaded that these improvements had payoff, and if they had investment capital to spare, they might well go along with you by agreeing to fund your proposed improvements.

Reusable Software Components

In Chapter 5, we already showed how to apply the COCOMO baseline estimate (PM = $2.4*(KDSI)^{1.05}$) to the task of helping to decide whether it was advantageous to build a proposed software system from scratch, or to attempt to employ reusable software components drawn from a suitable software library or a commercial off-the-shelf package. Note that the size of the software is the biggest cost-driver in Eq. 16.1, because the software effort in PMs is an *exponential* function of the size, but is not an exponential function of the other software productivity attribute ratings. Consequently, if you can reduce the size of the software that needs to be written by employing reusable software components or by using software generators, you may be able to reduce the estimated effort for your project quite substantially.

Object-oriented programming techniques, such as those introduced in the last chapter, may furnish promising avenues for employing reusable software components that have affordable costs for the integration and customization needed to adapt them to serve as components in your system.

16.3 Review Questions

1. Define the term *software productivity*.
2. What is the software learning curve?

3. Describe how to use a software productivity audit to improve the productivity of a software development organization.

4. When do software engineering effort and schedule equations favor employing reusable software components?

16.3 Exercises

1. Your software development organization has performed a software sizing estimate that has concluded that it would take 100,000 lines of code to develop a proposed new *Super-Spreadsheet* program. You need to estimate the software effort (in person-months) needed to develop the spreadsheet, and you need to estimate its nominal development time, T_d. You fill out the COCOMO software attribute rating sheets and conclude that all productivity attributes are nominal, except for *personnel/team capability*, which has a multiplier of $m_{14} = 0.83$ (because you have an exceptionally capable and experienced team of programmers) and *software tools*, which has a multiplier of $m_7 = 0.93$ because you intend to use an advanced object-oriented programming environment. Use Eqs. 16.1 and 16.2 to estimate the software development effort required to develop your spreadsheet system in person-months and to estimate the development time in months.

2. Your boss has obtained an industrial intelligence report that has revealed that a competitor is working on a spreadsheet program that will compete with yours. If your organization does not market its product first, it stands to lose 15 percent market share. Your boss wants you to compress the development schedule to meet a release deadline of one year from now. Would it be possible to meet this deadline? If so, what would be the additional software effort (in PMs) to meet a deadline 11.54 months from now?

16.4 Software Process Models

Learning Objectives

1. To learn about several software process models.
2. To learn about the Waterfall Model and its drawbacks.
3. To learn about risk-based process models, such as the Spiral Model.
4. To learn about risk management techniques such as risk assessment, risk-item prioritization, and risk-item resolution strategies.

A *software process model* is a scheme for organizing the activities that take place during the software lifecycle. Such a model attempts to define the various different stages of the software development process, and the criteria by which a software development team should transition from one stage to the next. Such a model answers questions like: "What should we be doing now?," "How much longer should we continue doing it?," and "What should we do next?"

what is a software process model?

One of the earliest models might be termed the *Code-and-Fix Model*. This was used in the earliest days of software engineering and consisted essentially of the

```
|    do {
|        (write some code)
|        (identify and fix problems in the code)
|    } while (substantial problems remain in the code);
```

Program Strategy 16.5 The Code-and-Fix Model

process illustrated by Program Strategy 16.5. This model consisted of laying down some code first, and then of thinking about the system requirements, design, testing, documentation, and maintenance later. One of the problems with this model was that even when the code produced by its process could eventually have been considered to be well-designed, it often happened that the resulting system was poorly matched to the real needs of the system's users. The result was that the system was either rejected by its intended clients or had to be redeveloped at great expense to be more responsive to the actual users' requirements. After a number of costly failures using the Code-and-Fix Model, the need for a requirements analysis process preceding design and coding became compelling.

discovering the need for requirements analysis

Another problem with the Code-and-Fix Model was that premature selection of various data structures and algorithms led to a rigid system structure that was expensive to revise if the need arose to switch to different data structures and algorithms. This underscored the need for using a design process that postponed certain decisions at the detailed-implementation level until enough information could be developed to make these decisions successfully.

the need for design

Again poor preparation for testing, debugging, and revision made it unnecessarily expensive to debug and fix code in the later stages of its development, and pointed toward the advantage of having explicit stages in the software development process to prepare for and to conduct testing, debugging, and code improvement.

The *Waterfall Model* resulted from an attempt to learn lessons from these early difficulties with the Code-and-Test Model. It incorporated separate and explicit phases for requirements analysis, design, coding, and testing. It soon became the dominant model used in most software acquisition contracts by large organizations. In fact those software acquisition contracts often contained provisions requiring that each of the software development phases should result in a *deliverable document* expressing the results of that phase in concrete written form.

The Waterfall Model

Figure 16.6 gives a diagram of a preliminary *Waterfall Model*, which is obtained from Fig. 16.1 by adding feed-forward arrows from one box to the next. If you imagine each box as filling with water and spilling its overflow into the next lower box along a path indicated by the arrows, you will be able to visualize the image that led to use of the word "waterfall" as a descriptive adjective for the model.

preventing coding before the design was completed

You can see how the Waterfall Model might offer advantages in avoiding the ills of the Code-and-Fix Model in that it certainly avoids many of the problems resulting from coding up the first approach that comes to mind and hoping that it can be patched or progressively debugged into a satisfactory complete system. In fact, many

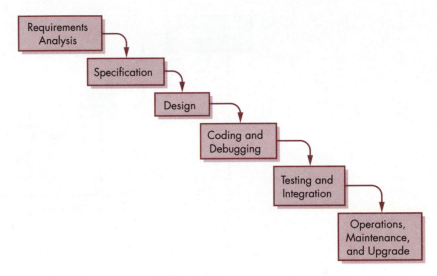

Figure 16.6 The Preliminary Waterfall Model

of the contracts written to enforce the Waterfall Model not only demanded that specific requirements documents and design documents be delivered in order to receive partial payments for work performed, they also explicitly forbade writing any code until after delivery and acceptance of the design document, in order to prevent developers from *writing code before completing the design* (in apparent recognition that the early tendency to do so was so strong).

When a software development organization takes on a contract to build a software system using the Waterfall Model, it usually agrees to provisions to deliver documents at the completion of each phase on certain dates. These are called the *deliverables* of the contract. For example, a contract might specify that the completed requirements document be delivered on March 1, that the design document be delivered on September 1, and that the completed, tested system must pass an *acceptance test* to be specified by the client, in order for the system to be considered as formally delivered to the client, by March 1 of the following year.

the deliverables

Such contracting disciplines, especially when written into legal directives and enforced by major government software acquisition agencies, tend to make software development under the Waterfall Model into a *document-driven* process. Under the influence of this process, a great deal of the software development organization's time and effort tends to go into the preparation of the *documents* to be produced by various deadlines in order to satisfy the provisions of the contract. The result can be that when a document has been signed off and has been accepted, its authoring team considers the corresponding software process to be finished, and moves on to other tasks or disbands so its participants can be assigned to new work elsewhere.

*the waterfall model is
document-driven*

The trouble with this top-down, feed-forward process is that we live in an imperfect world where requirements are never likely to be complete or accurate, designs are never likely to be correct, and implementations are never likely to satisfy the require-

living in an imperfect world

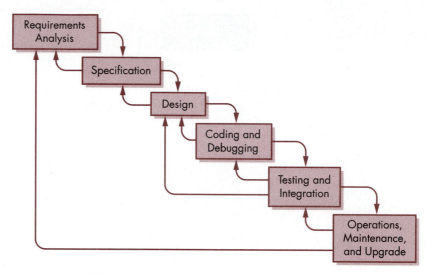

Figure 16.7 Waterfall Model with Feedback Loops

ments and reflect the design intentions perfectly. So we must deal with imperfection in each of the software lifecycle stages or products, and we must resort to special measures in order to improve quality progressively.

Thus, at a deeper level, feedback loops must connect stages of the lifecycle in the Waterfall Model, to allow us incrementally to improve the understanding and quality achieved at each stage. Figure 16.7 illustrates this more mature understanding of the Waterfall Model, which shows explicit feedback loops.

The feedback arrows in Fig. 16.7 go from each box to its predecessor, suggesting that experience gathered at each stage could reveal errors in the product of the preceding stage that need to be corrected, leading to the modification of the preceding stage's document. The most common example is that, during testing, you discover bugs, which need to be fixed by revising the system code document produced as a result of the coding stage. Again, an attempt to code a portion of the system design may reveal that the design strategy was infeasible or implied unacceptable performance penalties. This new information would demand that the design document be modified incrementally to try an alternative approach.

feedback and incremental improvement

It can also happen that the feedback arrows jump backward across many stages. For example, you may discover only after the release of the completed system into actual service that its users do not like it. Then you may have to conclude that your original requirements statements did not capture the true user needs accurately. This is perhaps the worst and most expensive kind of delayed feedback that can be experienced in the Waterfall Model, but it is by no means uncommon. There have been many systems whose users cannot articulate their true needs verbally in the form of a set of requirements statements. They are being completely candid and open when they say, "I don't know how to describe what I want, but I'll know it when you show one to me."

feedback across many stages is often costly

Thus we may only really begin to understand the true requirements of a system when we are exposed to the behavior of an implementation. Cyclical exposure to the behavior of the artifacts we build may be necessary to achieve understanding of the true requirements, especially for a system we are attempting to build for the first time.

user interfaces are often risk-laden

The risk of misunderstanding has been historically high for user interfaces. Document-driven software-development practices have forced many projects to write elaborate requirements and specification documents for poorly understood user interfaces. Following this, large quantities of user interface code get written, and eventually the user interface is released for use to actual end-users, who then reject it as unresponsive to their needs.

Two Case Histories

The author witnessed two actual software developments in the 1960s and 1970s that illustrated differing approaches to these problems in user interface design in the area of air traffic control systems. The first of the systems was called the National Airspace System, Stage A (or NAS, Stage A). It has been used by all of the enroute radar air traffic control systems in the United States since the 1960s.

NAS, Stage A

The system design specified that each radar target under the control of a given radar controller in a given sector would have a data block attached to it on the radar screen. Under the old system that was being replaced by NAS, Stage A, the controllers used to write flight data on little chips of plastic, called *shrimp boats*, which were then placed over the radar targets on a flat, horizontal radar screen and which were pushed along by hand to remain over the moving targets.

An early release of NAS, Stage A was tried out on real radar controllers in Jacksonville, Florida at the Enroute Air Traffic Control Center in the small hours of the morning. The controllers absolutely hated it, so much so that over four hundred controllers signed a petition to have the system permanently removed. They complained that when warning and error conditions arose, they had to take their eyes and minds off the radar screen, type commands at a keyboard, and suffer either delays or insults from the system, which used an unfamiliar and (to them) inconvenient command syntax and often argued back if they typed command syntax errors—chewing up precious time and distracting them from the mentally demanding tasks of controlling real airplanes. A common complaint they voiced was, "My pencil doesn't argue back with me, but this darn computer does." In short, the user interface failed to satisfy the true needs of the end users.

the failure of an early system release

Controller productivity was later measured to have been reduced by NAS, Stage A, which was, of course, installed nationally over the Jacksonville controllers' objections. The NAS system has now been scheduled for replacement for, among other reasons, that the accumulation of software errors has become so serious that the current system is practically unmaintainable and that it suffers from ongoing operational errors and computer outages.

controller productivity fell

Another system developed during that period was the ARTS III terminal air traffic control system. It allowed approach and departure radar controllers to control the arriving and departing traffic within a forty-to-fifty nautical mile radius of a given

ARTS III

major airport (or for several airports clustered in the same geographical area). An early version of ARTS III (pronounced "*arts three*") was tried out in the control room of Atlanta, Georgia's Hartsfield Airport. The controllers became actively involved in suggesting improvements to the system implementers who were conveniently located in the next room.

In the old system, when one controller would accept a "radar hand-off" from another controller, they used to have to shout across the room, "Hey, Joe, I'm handing you United Airlines flight 354 at 8,000 feet." And the receiving controller would have to acknowledge receiving the hand-off, by saying something like, "Okay, I got him." This verbal communication traffic shouted across the room was happening at the same time as the controllers were trying to talk to pilots in the airplanes they were controlling through the controllers' individual microphones and headsets. Needless to say the distractions of attending to more than one communication channel were annoying, if not dangerous.

So the Atlanta controllers suggested to the ARTS III prime contractor that they plot different alphabetical symbols on the screen, with a different letter being used for each different controller, instead of plotting the usual slash that had been traditional for designating a radar target. Then the computer could arrange to perform the hand-offs by blinking the symbol for one controller and changing it to the symbol for another controller as the hand-off airplane crossed the hand-off boundary between controller jurisdictions.

For example, suppose Atlanta's north-arrival sector controller had all airplanes under his or her control designated by the letter, V. When a target designated by a V neared the hand-off boundary where it needed to be handed-off to the Atlanta south-arrival controller, the V would blink briefly, and then change to the H symbol for the south-arrival controller.

The author once visited the Atlanta radar control room and heard a controller describe one of the important contributions he had made. He said that in an early stage of development, when the computer blinked the hand-off target symbols, it was flashing them on and off at a very fast rate, "on/off/on/off . . . ," suggesting alarm and panic. The controller recommended to the prime contractors that they should blink the targets at a much more relaxed rate, "on—pause—off—pause—on," and so forth. He explained to the programmers that life was enough of a panic in the control room that another source of anxiety was not welcome. Substituting a soft, relaxing blink rate would be much better, in the controller's opinion, since there was no chance that they would fail to notice the blinking target, no matter its blink rate, but a slow blink rate would make the atmosphere of the whole radar scope seem more orderly and under control, contributing to the system's overall goal of keeping traffic flow safe, orderly, and efficient.

The programmers installed and tried the change suggested by the controller and the controllers loved it. ARTS III evolved into one of the most admired and useful systems in radar air traffic control.

The moral of this story is that in a high-risk area, such as the design of a user interface, an effective strategy for reducing risk of design concept failure is to build a prototype system and try it out with actual end users, being prepared to accept and try suggestions from the end users, and being prepared to let the circumstances of actual

automating radar hand-offs

relying on end users' expertise to improve the prototype

risk-resolution by trial use of prototypes by end users

trial use reveal aspects of the user interface problem that were ill-understood during the original requirements analysis process.

Of course, building and trying prototypes of subsystem components is forbidden by the strict rules of the feed-forward version of the Waterfall Model, which strictly forbids any code-and-fix activities until after complete requirements, specification, and design documents have been completed and delivered.

the evolutionary development model

In effect, the ARTS III software developers were following a different software process model, sometimes called the *Evolutionary Development Model* (or the Incremental Build Model). Its stages consist of expanding an initial partial working solution in increments, using directions for expansion determined by experience with the working system.

Thus, while use of the Waterfall Model tended to cure earlier ills with budget and schedule unpredictability and control, it sometimes ran afoul of not detecting the danger that its early stages were seriously off track in some respects. Often, the requirements and design documents in the waterfall process would provide elaborate detail for well-understood parts of the project, while giving little elaboration of poorly understood, high-risk parts. The result was to give a software project the illusion of progress (since all the required documents were being produced on schedule and within budget), while, in fact, the project was headed for disaster.

good software project managers were good risk managers

These difficulties with the Waterfall Model stimulated leading software engineering researchers, such as Barry Boehm, to begin to rethink the software process problem anew. Boehm decided to try to identify the characteristics of good software managers who had successfully completed many software projects. He came to the conclusion that the best managers were *good risk managers*. They had a well-tuned sense of the risks that their projects faced, and they aggressively sought to identify, prioritize, and resolve risks threatening their projects' successful conclusions.

Thus was born the *Spiral Model* of the software process. The Spiral Model is a *risk-driven* process model, as opposed to being *document-driven* like the Waterfall Model, or *code-driven* like the Code-and-Fix Model.

The Spiral Model

The Spiral Model consists of a number of iterations, or passes, of a multipass process, shown as spirals in the diagram of Fig. 16.8. The Spiral Model can be specialized to behave like other predecessor models. It works by using multiple passes, shown as the successively wider spirals (or *cycles*, as Boehm calls them) in Fig. 16.8. It also provides guidance as to which of the previous models to use under various circumstances within a larger project.

Each cycle of the spiral involves a sequence of steps that addresses the same set of concerns. To start a given cycle, you identify the following:

1. The *objectives* of the portion of the system being elaborated (e.g., performance, functionality, user acceptance, modifiability, etc.).
2. The *alternatives* for implementing this portion of the system (e.g., buy commercial off-the-shelf (or COTS) components, reuse components from a software library, implement design-1, implement design-2, etc.).

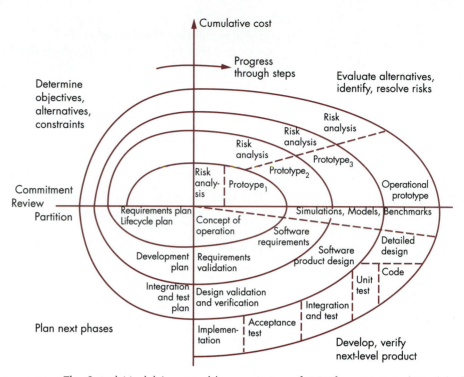

Figure 16.8 The Spiral Model (reprinted by permission of IEEE from "A Spiral Model of Software Development and Enhancement," by Barry W. Boehm, *IEEE Computer*, (May 1988), pp. 61–72, © 1988 IEEE.)

3. The *constraints* imposed when the alternatives are pursued (e.g., schedule, cost, interface requirements, etc.).

risk analysis

The next step is to conduct a *risk analysis* by evaluating the alternatives, from step (2), with respect to the objectives, from step (1), and the constraints, from step (3). The idea is to identify uncertainties that are significant sources of risk to the project.

The risk analysis yields a list of risk items. These risk items are then prioritized in the order of greatest-to-least risk. Then, cost-effective strategies are formulated for resolving the risk items. Thus the next three steps are as follows:

4. Risk item identification.
5. Risk item prioritization.
6. Devising cost-effective risk item resolution strategies.

risk-item prioritization and resolution

After the identification and evaluation of the risks, in steps (4–6), the next step is determined by the relative nature of the risks. For example, if a user interface risk or a system performance risk is dominant, and risks such as program development risks or internal interface-control risks are analyzed to be of lesser priority, then the next spiral cycle may follow the Evolutionary Development Model.

For instance, if uncertainties about the user interface dominate, the evolutionary development strategy would call for building a prototype user interface and evaluating it in trial use with real users to attempt to resolve the risk that the user interface is ill-understood and runs a great risk of being unacceptable to end users. In essence, prototyping plays the role of buying information to reduce risk and is a risk-resolution strategy.

You can see how this was the strategy actually followed in the development of the ARTS III system and that helped lead to its success. Conversely, failure to follow this strategy in an area of high risk, and rigid adherence to the Waterfall Model may well have contributed substantially to the unsatisfactory nature of the NAS, Stage A radar controller user interface.

Again, if system performance is identified as a high-risk item, then simulations or benchmarking of trial implementations of risky portions of the system may be strategically wise as a risk-resolution strategy. For example, in the Space Shuttle project, the flight control software had to send control inputs to the ailerons and other control surfaces at least 25 times per second, otherwise the Space Shuttle would be uncontrollable and could not be flown to a landing. A prototype flight control module was implemented and was benchmarked on a computer identical to the one that would fly in the Shuttle. The trials resulted in the conclusion that the software could only send updates at a rate of 24 times a second or slower. So the Space Shuttle engineers reimplemented the trigonometry routines to use table lookups and fixed point arithmetic, instead of trig calculation subroutines and floating point numbers. The performance was then improved to output control signals faster than 25 times per second, and this risk item was resolved.

If, for example, the user interface prototype turned out to be a big hit with the trial end users, and if it were flexible enough to serve as a low-risk kernel for future system evolution, the follow-on risk-driven steps might consist of the evolution of a sequence of evolutionary prototypes (shown as **prototype$_2$**, **prototype$_3$**, etc. immediately above the x-axis in Fig. 16.8). In this case, the option of writing user interface specifications would be addressed but would not be exercised. Consequently, risk analysis can result in a project's implementing only a subset of all of the Spiral Model's potential steps. By implementing subsets of potential steps in various orders, the Spiral Model specializes itself to behave like the other software process models under appropriate risk conditions.

As another example, suppose that previous prototyping efforts have already resolved all of the user interface risks, or that simulation, benchmarking, and reimplementation have resolved all of the previous performance risks. Suppose that a new cycle of the Spiral Model is about to begin, during which the remaining highest priority risks are in the areas of internal component-interface risks (i.e., the risk that the system modules will not be properly plug-compatible and will not be able to cooperate smoothly together), or cost or schedule risks that the budget or deadline for the project may be overrun.

In this case, the next cycle of the spiral might follow the basic waterfall process, with its relatively predictable costs and schedules (given the low-risk circumstances that requirements volatility and performance inadequacies have been eliminated by previous risk-resolution activities). In this latter cycle, the options to model, simulate, prototype, and benchmark have been considered, but have not been adopted, leading to a different set of steps being selected. You can see then, how the Spiral Model specializes itself on different cycles to act like the other models—but only when risk analysis indicates that such a course of action is the proper one to adopt under the circumstances.

how cycles end

Each cycle of the Spiral Model terminates with a review culminating in a plan and a commitment for the next cycle. The end-of-cycle review covers all developments and approaches undertaken in the cycle. Then plans for the next cycle are formulated and resources required to carry them out are determined. Finally, an attempt is made to bring all major parties on board to commit to the approach to be used on the next cycle.

Use of the Spiral Model can help improve a software development organization's productivity by allowing it to escape the risk of costly reworking of those parts of a system that were built before their failure risks were properly addressed by appropriate risk-resolution strategies. It can also take advantage of cost avoidance by not engaging in the motions of low-risk lifecycle activities that have little or no payoff. For example, in the waterfall process, requirements and design documents are often developed to elaborate but uniform levels of detail. But if experienced experts design a subsystem that is familiar to them and the same experts implement it using familiar equipment, it is just plain wasteful to elaborate the design to its fullest possible detail, even though that is what the deliverable in the Waterfall Model, and perhaps the software development contract, calls for. Under these conditions, the Spiral Model would opt not to pursue full elaboration of low-risk detail.

failure of the waterfall process to resolve risks

The flip side of the coin is that in the Waterfall Model, an ill-understood, high-risk part of the system might receive insufficient attention at the requirements and design stages, while elaborate effort might be spent providing detail for well-understood parts of the system, in order to produce requirements and design documents to deliver on schedule. This pattern is one that is typical of failed software projects for which the waterfall process provided an illusion of progress that concealed a looming disaster. The Spiral Model is much more apt to avoid getting trapped in illusions that can be induced by an easy reliance on the document-driven approach, since it focuses on risk identification, prioritization, and resolution.

16.4 Review Questions

1. What is a software process model?
2. Explain the characteristics of the Code-and-Fix Model, the Waterfall Model, the Evolutionary Development Model, and the Spiral Model.
3. Explain what is meant by risk analysis, risk-item prioritization, and risk-item resolution.
4. In what sense can prototyping activities or simulation activities used in the Evolutionary Development Model be considered as risk-resolution strategies?

16.4 Exercises

1. Give an example of a software project with a high risk element that the use of the Waterfall Model does not address well but to which the use of the Spiral Model is well-adapted.

2. Did the development of the ARTS III system follow the Waterfall Model? How do you know? If so, why? If not, then what software process model did it appear to follow?

Pitfalls

- *Unforeseen risks in software development projects*

  Many software development projects have come to grief because they failed to identify and resolve significant risks early in the project lifecycle.

  A particularly notorious form of risk is to prepare requirements and design documents that provide elaborate detail on well-understood parts of the system, but provide scant detail on ill-understood parts, creating the illusion of satisfactory progress under a document-driven software model, while actually heading for disaster. Use of risk-item identification, prioritization, and resolution techniques can help avoid these pitfalls, even if practiced alongside a compulsory document-driven discipline imposed by a software development contract.

- *Compressing the delivery schedule into the zone of impossibility*

  While it is often possible to accelerate a software development schedule (at the cost of a predictable increase in effort), it is sometimes nearly impossible. Use the COCOMO model's software effort and schedule equations to estimate your project's development time, and make sure you do not try to compress your schedule below 75 percent of the nominal development estimate. Otherwise, you may venture into the zone of impossibility, where Brooks' Law applies.

Tips and Techniques

- *Make sure to spin-up on software management concepts before attempting to manage*

  If history is any guide, there is a significant chance that you will be promoted to a job requiring software management and team leadership abilities after an average of only 1.8 years practicing as an entry-level programmer in a large software organization. If you are tempted to accept such a promotion, but you have not had an opportunity to educate yourself in software management techniques, then taking a crash course in software management is highly recommended. If none is available in your area, then reading Boehm's two books, *Software Engineering Economics* and *Software Risk Management*, is an excellent alternative. Don't leave home without them on the day you accept promotion to a software management position.

- *Learn to use risk management techniques in all of your software efforts*

  Whether you are building software as an individual, as a member of a small team, or as part of a huge software organization, software risk-management techniques are highly recommended for optimally raising your probability of success. It has been observed that good software managers who have impressive track records making intelligent management decisions tend to be excellent risk managers.

In particular, consider using the Spiral Model to guide your software development process, since it is risk-management-driven, and since its various passes can be specialized to behave like the other software process models under appropriate risk conditions. It thus encompasses the advantages of the other models but employs them only when the risk-resolution circumstances have been assessed to be favorable.

References for Further Study

COCOMO Model

Barry W. Boehm, *Software Engineering Economics*, Prentice-Hall, Englewood Cliffs, NJ, (1981).

Provides full details of the COCOMO Model for software effort and schedule estimation.

Spiral Model

————, *Software Risk Management*, IEEE Computer Society Press, Washington, DC, (1989).

An excellent tutorial on risk-based software management, which includes a reprint of Boehm's article on the Spiral Model.

compressing schedules

Frederick P. Brooks, *The Mythical Man-Month*, Addison-Wesley, Reading, Mass., (1975).

An entertaining and insightful look at software engineering issues.

Chapter Summary

building big software is
challenging

Building large, long-lived software systems—which may be among the most complex artifacts ever created in the history of civilization—has turned out to be a formidable challenge, and many surprising lessons have been learned from early failures.

The *software lifecycle* is the span of time that starts with the initial conception of a software system and ends with its retirement from use, following its useful service lifetime.

software lifecycle phases

The software lifecycle can be divided into various stages involving activities such as *requirements analysis, specification, design, coding and debugging, testing and integration,* and *operations and maintenance.* The maintenance phase of the lifecycle tends to consume from 70 to 90 percent of the total lifecycle cost, and actually includes *system upgrade*—an activity in which the system is modified to meet the changing circumstances of its use, typically over a period of twenty-five or more years.

the software learning curve

The *software learning curve* refers to an observed phenomenon in which, if a given team of programmers reimplements the same or a substantially similar system over and over again, then both the resources consumed and their estimates of the resources they will need tend to fall dramatically on successive iterations as they replace their initial expensive *trial-and-error* behavior with lean, efficient *tried-and-true* methods.

Software productivity can be measured by dividing the number of lines of delivered source instructions (DSIs) by the number of person-months (PMs) of effort needed to develop a given software system. There tends to be enormous variance in the productivity of individual programmers with observed ratios between the productivities of the best and worst programmers approaching 20:1. Also, the difficulty of a software project greatly affects the productivity of those working on it. Meeting difficult constraints in real-time performance or storage, or achieving high levels of required system reliability tend to correlate with lower levels of software productivity.

software productivity

The *Constructive Cost Model* (or COCOMO model) provides equations and procedures for calculating a software project's estimated development effort (in person-months, PMs) and its estimated development time (in months). You start with an initial (or baseline) effort estimate, which is a function of the expected software size (in DSIs). Then you multiply it by multipliers derived from software productivity rating scales for a number of factors whose individual effect sizes have been calculated from a factor analysis of a large database of actual project attribute measures. The nominal development time (in months) is then estimated to be a multiple of the cube root of the effort (measured in PMs).

the COCOMO model

If you want to compress the development schedule, it is possible to add more project personnel to do so, but it is nearly impossible to compress the schedule below 75 percent of the nominal schedule estimate given by the COCOMO equation. It costs 23 percent more effort to reduce the schedule from the nominal time to 75 percent of the nominal time, all other things being equal.

schedule compression

Since the size of the software is the biggest cost-driver in the COCOMO software effort equations, you can reduce your software effort substantially if you can take advantage of *reusable software components* or table-driven software generation techniques, provided that they can be made to satisfy the requirements of your project.

reusable components

You can improve the productivity of your software organization by conducting a *software productivity audit* in which you rate your organization's productivity using the COCOMO cost-driver attribute rating scales, and then make judicious investments to improve those attributes that are controllable.

software productivity audits

Software process models prescribe various activities and stages of effort during the software development process and the software service lifetime. A software process model tells your software organization what it should be doing at a given stage, how long it should be doing it, and what to do next.

software process models

Among the software process models are the Code-and-Fix Model, the Waterfall Model, the Evolutionary Development Model, and the Spiral Model.

The *Code-and-Fix Model* is a *code-driven* process in which you repeatedly write some code and fix it, until a satisfactory system is produced.

The *Waterfall Model* tends to be a *document-driven* process in which, often under contract, a software development organization must produce a requirements document, a specification document, a design document, a system code document, and various users manuals and system maintenance manuals. It incorporates validation activities such as design walkthroughs, unit testing, integration testing, and acceptance testing.

the waterfall model

the evolutionary
development model

In the *Evolutionary Development Model*, you build a sequence of prototypes, each of which is modified by assessing its defects using a risk-identification strategy and which is improved using a suitable risk-resolution strategy. The last completely evolved prototype in the sequence of prototypes becomes the final system that is released for use.

the spiral model

The *Spiral Model* uses a *risk-management-driven* process, built upon the notion of using multiple passes (or cycles of a spiral), each of which incorporates risk analysis, risk-item identification, risk-item prioritization, and risk-item resolution. Each cycle of the spiral identifies and addresses a high-priority risk item, until, after several cycles, the risk items have been resolved, and a finished system emerges. The Spiral Model can specialize any given cycle of the spiral to behave like one of the other software process models by ignoring some optional steps and adopting others.

Appendix

Math Reference
and Tutorial

Arithmetic Progressions

Arithmetic and geometric progressions occur quite frequently in the analysis of algorithms, and you should know how to find their sums. Let's start by considering three examples of arithmetic progressions, A_1, A_2, and A_3:

A_1:	3	5	7	9	11	13	15
A_2:	100	85	70	55	40	25	10
A_3:	2.1	3.2	4.3	5.4	6.5	7.6	8.7

An arithmetic progression is an ordered sequence of terms in which the difference between any two neighboring terms is always the same amount. This difference, d, is called a *constant difference*, because the amount of the difference remains *constant* (that is, it never *varies* or changes).

For example, in arithmetic progression A_1, the constant difference is 2. In A_2 it is

689

–15, and in A_3 it is 1.1. To calculate the constant difference, d, you can take any two neighboring terms in the arithmetic progression, say t_i and t_{i+1}, and subtract the first from the second, getting $d = t_{i+1} - t_i$. (Try verifying that this formula for d gives the constant differences: 2, –15, and 1.1 for A_1, A_2, and A_3, as claimed.)

Let's suppose that there are n terms in some arithmetic progression A, that A's first term is a, and that A's last term is l. How can we calculate the value of the sum, S, of all of the terms in A, knowing only n, a, and l? Try memorizing Memory Jog A.1 to help you remember the answer.

Memory Jog A.1 Sum of an Arithmetic Progression

> The sum of an arithmetic progression is given by the product of
> the number of terms
> times
> the average of the first and last terms.

In symbols,

$$S = n\left(\frac{a+l}{2}\right).$$

The *average* of the first and last terms is obtained by adding the first and last terms, $a + l$, and then dividing this sum by two.

Let's take an example. Suppose we want to find the sum, S, of the terms in A_1. Write down two copies of S, one *forward* and one *backward*. Then add the two copies together:

S	=	3	+	5	+	7	+	9	+	11	+	13	+	15
S	=	15	+	13	+	11	+	9	+	7	+	5	+	3
2S	=	18	+	18	+	18	+	18	+	18	+	18	+	18

Since the right side of the sum 2 S consists of 7 copies of 18, the last line is the same as 2 S = 7 * 18. Solving for S gives, S = 7 * (18/2) = 7 * 9 = 63. Here, the number of terms is 7, and the average of the first and last terms is (3 + 15)/2 = 9. So we see that the sum, S = 63, is the product of the number of terms (7) times the average of the first and last terms (9).

In the general case, suppose A is an arithmetic progression having n terms, and having a as its first term, l as its last term, and d as the constant difference between terms. First write down one copy of the sum S for A in the forward direction, and underneath, write down another copy of S in the backward direction. Then add the two copies together:

S	=	a	+	$(a + d)$	+	$(a + 2d)$	+	...	+	$(l - 2d)$	+	$(l - d)$	+	l
S	=	l	+	$(l - d)$	+	$(l - 2d)$	+	...	+	$(a + 2d)$	+	$(a + d)$	+	a
2S	=	$(a + l)$	+	$(a + l)$	+	$(a + l)$	+	...	+	$(a + l)$	+	$(a + l)$	+	$(a + l)$

But since there are n terms, the right side of the sum for 2 S is $n*(a + l)$. Now, solving for S in the equation $2S = n*(a + l)$ gives the final result:

$$S = n\left(\frac{a+l}{2}\right).$$
(A.1)

Sum of an Arithmetic Progression

Why does each column in the sum for 2 S add up to $(a + l)$? The reason can be seen as follows. The first column adds up to $(a + l)$ because the first row starts with the first term, a, in the forward direction, and the second row starts with l, in the backward direction. Now each time you move from a given column to the next column to its right, the top row's term *increases* by d in the forward direction, while the bottom row *decreases* by d in the backward direction. These increases and decreases of $+d$ and $-d$ exactly cancel one another when the column is added up. Consequently, all columns have the same sum $(a + l)$. There are exactly n columns, so the sum of two copies of S is $n*(a + l)$.

You might want to remember how this derivation is carried out, since it uses a trick that is easy to remember (even easier to remember than Memory Jog A.1). If you get stuck and cannot remember the formula for the sum, you will find it is easy to re-derive the formula yourself whenever you need it, provided you can remember the trick. [*Remember:* The trick is to *add up two copies of the sum of the terms with one copy written backward.*]

Now suppose you do not know the last term of the arithmetic progression, A, but you do know the first term (a), the number of terms (n), and the constant difference (d). How do you find the sum? One way might be to try first to derive a formula for the last term, l, and then to plug the result into the formula we just derived. Let's try this.

The terms, t_i, of A, starting at a, are: $t_1 = a$, $t_2 = a + d$, $t_3 = a + 2d$, and so on. The key thing to notice about the "and so on" part is that the ith term t_i is the first term a plus $(i - 1)$ copies of the difference d. That is, $t_i = a + (i - 1)d$. If there are n terms, then the last term, $l = t_n$, so, setting $i = n$ in $t_i = a + (i - 1)d$ gives us the formula for the last term,

$$l = a + (n - 1)d.$$
(A.2)

Last Term of an Arithmetic Progression

If we now use this formula to substitute for l in $S = n((a + l)/2)$, we get

$$S = n((a + l)/2) \quad \Rightarrow \quad S = n((a + a + (n - 1)d)/2).$$

This last equation simplifies to the familiar formula for the sum S that is given in most scientific handbooks and in many high school algebra books:

$$S = \frac{n}{2}\left\{2a + (n-1)d\right\}.$$
(A.3)

Sum of an Arithmetic Progression

Applying the Formulas for Arithmetic Progressions

Let's now apply the formulas we have derived to find the sums of some arithmetic progressions.

First, what are the sums of arithmetic progressions A_2 and A_3 on p. 689? In this case, A_2 and A_3 both have seven terms, and their first and last terms are known, so it is easy to apply Eq. A.1. The sum S_2 for A_2 is just $S_2 = 7*((100 + 10)/2)$ or $S_2 = 7*55 = 385$. The sum S_3 for A_3 is $S_3 = 7*((2.1 + 8.7)/2) = 7*((10.8)/2) = 7*5.4 = 37.8$.

One situation that comes up repeatedly in the analysis of algorithms is the problem of finding the sum of all the numbers from 1 to n:

$$S = 1 + 2 + 3 + \ldots + n.$$

Using Eq. A.1, this sum is easy to calculate:

$$S = n\left(\frac{n+1}{2}\right). \tag{A.4}$$

Sum of the Integers from 1 to n

Eq. A.4 is used often enough that it is worthwhile memorizing it.

Now suppose you know that there are 110 terms in a particular arithmetic progression A, which begins with $6^2/_3$ as its first term and has a constant difference of $^1/_3$ between successive terms. What is the sum S of the terms in A? Here is a case where it pays to use Eq. A.3, since you do not have the last term of A immediately in hand. Substituting appropriately in Eq. A.3 gives

$$S = \frac{110}{2}\left\{2*6\frac{2}{3} + (110-1)*\frac{1}{3}\right\}.$$

This simplifies to

$$S = 55\left\{13\frac{1}{3} + 36\frac{1}{3}\right\},$$

and yields the final result $S = 2731^2/_3$.

Let's now consider a variety of arithmetic progressions that occur in algorithm analysis, in which we know the first few terms exactly, but for which the last term is known only in terms of a formula for n. For example, suppose we are asked to find the sum of a number of iterations of an inner for-loop in a program, which is under the control of an outer for-loop of the form for (j = 3; j < n; ++j). When j == 3, the inner for-loop takes 4 steps, when j == 4, it takes 6 steps, when j == 5, it takes 8 steps, and when j == n − 1 it takes $2(n-2)$ steps. How many steps in all does the inner for-loop take as a function of n? The problem is equivalent to finding the sum of an arithmetic progression in which

$$S = 4 + 6 + 8 + \ldots + 2(n-2).$$

If we knew how many terms there were, we could easily apply Eq. A.1. But the outer for-loop can be analyzed to determine the number of terms. This outer for-loop starts at j == 3 and finishes at j == n − 1. It increments j in steps of 1. There are exactly $(n-3)$ numbers in the range 3:n − 1. It is easy to figure this out if you know the formula for the number of integers in an integer range in C:

$$\text{There are exactly } (n - m + 1) \text{ integers in the range } m{:}n \qquad \text{(A.5)}$$

$$\text{Number of Integers in the Range m:n} = \{ \, i \mid m \le i \le n \, \}$$

Eq. A.5 is also a good formula to memorize, since it is used so often in the analysis of algorithms. A handy memory jog for remembering it is "the number of integers in the range *bottom:top* is one more than the difference (*top–bottom*)." If you are uncertain you have recalled this fact correctly, you can check yourself by trying it out on a familiar range of numbers, such as the range 1:100. (For instance, try saying to yourself, "there are 100 numbers in the range 1:100, because one plus top minus bottom equals $1 + 100 - 1$, which is 100.")

Given that there are $(n-3)$ terms in an arithmetic progression whose first term is 4 and whose last term is $2(n-2)$, we can apply Eq. A.1 to find the sum

$$S = (n-3)\left(\frac{4 + 2(n-2)}{2} \right).$$

This simplifies to the rather tidy sum, $S = n(n-3)$.

Another way to cross-check yourself on deriving a result such as this is to attempt to derive the result a second way. For instance, you could look at the sum

$$S = 4 + 6 + 8 + \ldots + 2(n-2)$$

and reason to yourself as follows: "suppose I were to factor a 2 out of each term of this sum S. This would give

$$S = 2 * [2 + 3 + 4 + \ldots + (n-2)].$$

But if I add a new first term, 1, to the quantity $[2 + 3 + 4 + \ldots + (n-2)]$ getting $[1 + 2 + 3 + 6 + \ldots + (n-2)]$, then I've got the sum of the first $(n-2)$ numbers, which is just $(n-2)(n-1)/2$ {from applying Eq. A.4}. Hence, the sum S must be given by S =

$2\left(\left[(n-2)(n-1)/2\right]-1\right)$. If I simplify this, I get

$$S = 2\left\{\frac{(n-2)(n-1)}{2} - 1\right\}$$
$$= (n-2)(n-1) - 2$$
$$= n^2 - 3n + 2 - 2$$
$$= n^2 - 3n$$
$$= n(n-3).$$

But this gives the same results as the other method I tried. So using this method of cross-checking, I have raised my confidence that my result is correct."

You're almost there. After you finish answering the review questions and doing the exercises that immediately follow, you'll be an expert on the subject of arithmetic progressions. And you'll be ready to tackle all of them that come up in the context of analysis of algorithms.

A.1 Review Questions

1. What is an arithmetic progression?
2. Give the formula for the sum of the first n integers, $1 + 2 + 3 + \ldots + n$.
3. What is the formula for the sum of n terms of an arithmetic progression with first term a and last term l?
4. What is a trick for deriving the sum in question 3, if you have forgotten the formula?
5. How many integers are there in the integer range bottom:top?

A.1 Exercises

1. There are 99 bottles of beer on the wall. Because of previous unruly behavior in the beer hall, they are only partly full. The first bottle has 1 cubic centimeter (cc) of beer in it, the last bottle has 99 cc's of beer in it, and each of the other bottles in sequence has one more cc of beer in it than its immediate predecessor does. How many cc's of beer are there in all 99 bottles of beer on the wall?
2. Suppose you have an arithmetic progression, A, for which you know the last term, l, the constant difference, d, and the number of terms, n, but you do not know the first term, a. Derive a formula for the sum S of the terms in A in terms of n, l, and d. [*Hint:* Solve Eq. A.2 for a and use the result in Eq. A.1. Then simplify.]
3. Suppose you have an arithmetic progression, A, for which you know the first term, a, the last term, l, and the constant difference, d, but you do not know

the number of terms, n. Derive a formula for the sum S of the terms in A in terms of a, l, and d. [*Hint:* Solve Eq. A.2 for n and use the result in Eq. A.1. Then simplify.]

4. An inner **while-loop** in an algorithm is executed $9 + 12 + 15 + \ldots + 3(n - 1)$ times. Give a closed formula in terms of n, for the total number of times this **while-loop** is executed. [*Hint:* Use the formula you derived for the previous exercise.]

5. What is the sum of the even numbers from 2 to $2n$? Give a formula in terms of n.

6. What is the sum of the odd numbers $7 + 9 + 11 + \ldots + (2n + 1)$? Give a formula in terms of n.

7. An arithmetic progression A consists of 101 terms. The last term is $(2n + 150)$ and the constant difference is 3. What is the sum of A's terms? Give a formula in terms of n.

A.2 Geometric Progressions

In a *geometric progression*, each new term is a multiple of the previous one. If you divide a given term by the immediately preceding term, you get a ratio, r, called the *common ratio* between terms. The ratio r is identical for all pairs of adjacent terms, which is why it is called the "common" ratio. G_1, G_2, and G_3 below are three examples of geometric progressions:

G_1:	1	2	4	8	16	32	64
G_2:	1	$1/2$	$1/4$	$1/8$	$1/16$	$1/32$	$1/64$
G_3:	5	15	45	135	405	1215	3645

In geometric progression G_1, the common ratio, r, is 2. In G_2, $r = 1/2$, and in G_3, $r = 3$. You can see that if the common ratio is greater than one, the successive terms of the geometric progression get bigger and bigger. Here, $r > 1$ is a multiplier that increases each new term by making it a multiple of its predecessor. However, if $r < 1$, then each new term is a fraction of its predecessor, and the successive terms get smaller and smaller. This gives us a convenient boundary to use to separate geometric progressions into two cases: (1) increasing geometric progressions—those for which $r > 1$, and (2) decreasing geometric progressions—those for which $r < 1$.

If the first term of a geometric progression is a, if the common ratio is r, and if there are n terms, then the sum, S, is

$$S = a + ar + ar^2 + \ldots + ar^{n-1}.$$

To derive the closed formula for this sum, we can apply a useful trick. If you can remember this trick, you will always be able to rederive the formula for the sum. The idea is to take two copies of the above equation for S, multiply the second by r, and then subtract the first from the second. Here's how this works:

$$S = a + a\,r + a\,r^2 + \ldots + a\,r^{n-1}$$

$$r\,S = a\,r + a\,r^2 + \ldots + a\,r^{n-1} + a\,r^n.$$

Now, subtract the first from the second:

$$
\begin{aligned}
r\,S &= \qquad a\,r + a\,r^2 + \ldots + a\,r^{n-1} + a\,r^n \\
-S &= -a - a\,r - a\,r^2 - \ldots - a\,r^{n-1} \\
\hline
r\,S - S &= a\,r^n - a
\end{aligned}
$$

You can see that all the pairs of terms $(a\,r - a\,r)$, $(a\,r^2 - a\,r^2)$, ..., $(a\,r^{n-1} - a\,r^{n-1})$ cancel each other out, leaving only the last term of the top equation, $a\,r^n$, minus the first term, a, of the bottom equation. We can now solve for S, as follows:

$$r\,S - S = ar^n - a \qquad \text{\{now, factor out S on left and } a \text{ on right\}}$$

$$S(r-1) = a(r^n - 1) \qquad \text{\{then, divide through by } (r-1), \text{ giving\}}$$

$$S = a\left(\frac{r^n - 1}{r - 1}\right). \qquad\qquad\qquad\qquad (A.6)$$

The Sum of a Geometric Progression

Applying this formula to G_1 above, with $a = 1$, $r = 2$, and $n = 7$, gives

$$S_1 = 1\left(\frac{2^7 - 1}{2 - 1}\right)$$

$$= \left(\frac{128 - 1}{1}\right)$$

$$= 127.$$

When the common ratio r is less than one ($r < 1$), and we have a decreasing geometric series, it is convenient to use a second form of Eq. A.6, in which we multiply the top and bottom of the fraction $(r^n - 1) / (r - 1)$ by -1 to reverse the signs, getting

$$S = a\left(\frac{1 - r^n}{1 - r}\right). \qquad\qquad\qquad\qquad (A.7)$$

The Sum of a Decreasing Geometric Progression

When this formula is applied to geometric progression G_2 above, with $a = 1$, $r = 1/2$, and $n = 7$, it gives

$$S_2 = 1 \left(\frac{1 - (1/2)^7}{1 - 1/2} \right)$$

$$= \left(\frac{1 - (1/128)}{1/2} \right)$$

$$= 2 - \frac{1}{64}$$

$$= 1\frac{63}{64}.$$

Let's pause for a moment and think about adding up powers of $1/2$. Have you ever thought about a process in which you start, say, one foot (or one meter) from a wall, and take a first step of 1/2 foot (or a half a meter), then a next step of 1/4 foot (meter), and a next step of 1/8 foot (meter), . . . , and so on—so that at each step, you advance half the remaining distance to the wall? You never reach the wall, right? But you keep getting closer and closer.

A geometric progression similar to G_2 above, which starts with first term $a = 1/2$, and keeps adding new terms of the form $(1/2^i)$ until reaching a last term of the form $(1/2^n)$ is a model for this process. Its sum, S, takes the following form:

$$S = 1/2 + 1/4 + 1/8 + \ldots + 1/2^i + \ldots + 1/2^n.$$

On the basis of our imaginary thought experiment, we would predict that (1) the sum S never reaches 1 (since 1 represents the distance from the starting point to the wall), and (2) the sum S must be, $1 - (1/2^n)$, since the distance remaining to go to the wall is the same as the size of the last step taken toward the wall. We could apply Eq. A.7 to verify these conclusions.

Now, in a slight digression, let's look at another special case of the formula for a geometric progression that appears sufficiently often that it is worth giving it special emphasis. Suppose we are trying to calculate the following sum:

$$S = 1 + r + r^2 + r^3 + \ldots + r^n.$$

There are actually $(n + 1)$ terms in this sum, instead of n (check carefully to see why). In closed form, the sum S is $(r^{n+1} - 1) / (r - 1)$ for the increasing geometric progression, or, $(1 - r^{n+1}) / (1 - r)$ for the decreasing geometric progression. We note these sums as Eq. A.8 for special emphasis, as follows:

$$\text{if} \quad S = 1 + r + r^2 + r^3 + \ldots + r^n, \quad \text{then}$$

$$S = \frac{r^{n+1} - 1}{r - 1}, \quad \text{or}$$

$$S = \frac{1 - r^{n+1}}{1 - r}. \tag{A.8}$$

Special Cases of the Sum of a Geometric Progression

The reason that Eq. A.8 arises so often is that if we take the general sum for a geometric progression $S = a + ar + ar^2 + \ldots + ar^n$, and we factor out the first term a, we get $S = a(1 + r + \ldots + r^n)$. After factoring out the first term, if you then know the power, n, of the common ratio, r, used in the last term, you can directly write the closed formula for the sum S. It is just the first term times a fraction whose numerator is the common ratio raised to the $(n + 1)$st power minus one, divided by a denominator equal to the common ratio minus 1. That is,

$$\text{if} \quad S = a + ar + ar^2 + ar^3 + \ldots + ar^n, \quad \text{then}$$

$$S = a\left(\frac{r^{n+1} - 1}{r - 1}\right). \tag{A.9}$$

Sum of Alternative Form of Geometric Progression

Note that the power of r used in this last formula is one greater than the power of r in Eq. A.6. You have to be just a tad cautious in applying these formulas to check that you are starting at the correct place and that you are using the correct power of r in the final result. The power of r is always exactly equal to the number of terms. But if you factor out a, then starting with $r^0 = 1$, and ending with r^n, involves $(n + 1)$ terms.

Applications of Geometric Progressions

Suppose we have a balanced tree with one node at its root (at the top), and with each node having b children directly under it. (Here, b is called the branching factor of the tree.) We agree that the top level containing the root is called level 0. Figure A.2 shows a balanced tree with an unspecified branching factor, b.

For example, if $b = 3$, we would have one node (the root) at level 0, three children on level 1, and nine children on level 2 (since each of the three children on level 1 has 3 children of its own), and so on. Now, let's ask two questions: (1) How many nodes are on level l? (2) How many nodes are there in total in all levels of a balanced tree with nodes in each position at each of its l levels?

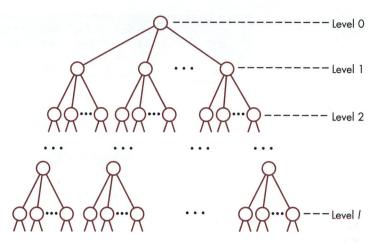

Figure A.2 Balanced Trees with Branching Factor b

You can see that there is $b^0 = 1$ node at level 0. Then level 1 has b^1 nodes, since the root has b children. There are b^i nodes at level i. In general, the number of nodes goes up by a multiple of b as we go from a given level down to the next lower level, since each node in the upper level has b children. So we have a geometric progression with a common ratio b that describes the number of nodes on each level. At level l, we must have b^l nodes. In an entire tree of l levels, the total number of nodes must be equal to the sum, $S = 1 + b + b^2 + \ldots + b^l$. Applying Eq. A.9 enables us immediately to conclude that $S = (b^{l+1} - 1)/(b - 1)$.

Binary trees, where each node has exactly two children (i.e., where $b = 2$), constitute an important special case. Here, a balanced binary tree with n levels has a number of nodes given by $S = 2^{n+1} - 1$.

As a second example, suppose we have a code segment in a program involving the for-statement shown in Program A.3.

Suppose we want to obtain a formula, in closed form, for the sum accumulated in the variable S at the conclusion of executing this program fragment. How might we proceed?

Table A.4 gives the values of S for the first three iterations and the last iteration of the for-statement in Program A.3. Using the last line in this table, it is easy to apply Eq. A.9 to conclude that $S = a\,(r^{n+1} - 1)/(r - 1)$.

```
|    S = a;                                              /* initialization */
|
|    for ( i = 1; i <= n; ++i ) {
|        S = a + r*S;                                    /* body of for-statement */
|    }
```

Program A.3 A For-Statement

On each trip through the for-statement, multiply the last value of S by r, and then add a	
Value of i	**Value of S at end of for-statement**
1	$S = a + a\,r^1$
2	$S = a + a\,r^1 + a\,r^2$
3	$S = a + a\,r^1 + a\,r^2 + a\,r^3$
. . .	. . .
n	$S = a + a\,r^1 + a\,r^2 + \ldots + a\,r^n$

Table A.4 Values of S in a For-Statement

A.2 Review Questions

1. What is a geometric progression?
2. If you forgot the formula for the sum of a geometric progression, what trick can you use to rederive the result for yourself?
3. If you add the terms $1/2 + 1/4 + 1/8 + \ldots + 1/2^i + \ldots + 1/2^n$, does the sum increase without bound as n increases, or is the sum bounded above by some sort of upper limit?
4. What is the branching factor in a tree?

A.2 Exercises

1. Show that the sum of the powers of two starting with 2^0 and ending with 2^n is just one less than the next power of two past the last term. That is, show $2^0 + 2^1 + 2^2 + \ldots + 2^n = 2^{n+1} - 1$.
2. Apply your solution to Exercise 1 to compute the total number of nodes in a completely balanced binary tree with nodes in all possible positions in each row, where the tree has l levels. [*Caution:* The root is at level 0, not level 1.]
3. Find a closed formula for the sum $1/8 + 1/16 + 1/32 + \ldots + 1/2^n$.
4. Find a closed formula for the sum $1/2^j + 1/2^{j+1} + \ldots + 1/2^k$.
5. Determine a closed formula for the sum $1/2^1 + 2/2^2 + \ldots + k/2^k$. [*Hint:* Expand each individual term, $i/2^i$, into a row of i copies of $1/2^i$. Then sum the columns using the result of Exercise 4. Finally, add the sums of the columns, again using the result of Exercise 4.]
6. Each year for 10 years, you make a contribution (on January 1) of $100 to a savings account which pays 9 percent annual interest. On December 31, the interest each year is added to the value of the account. What is the value of the account after 10 years.
7. Find a formula in closed form for the value of S after the following for-statement is executed:

```
S = a;
for ( j = k – 1; j < n; ++j ) {
    S = a + r*S;
}
```

[*Hint:* Don't forget about Eq. A.5 in the previous section.]

A.3 Floors and Ceilings

Suppose x is a real number, such as 2.31 or –5.68. The *floor* of x, denoted by $\lfloor x \rfloor$, is the largest integer less than or equal to x. At first, you might think that to find the floor of x, all you have to do is throw away the fractional part of x. That is, to find the floor of 2.31, you just throw away the fractional part .31, leaving 2, since it is true that $\lfloor 2.31 \rfloor = 2$. While this rule works for positive real numbers, it gives the wrong answer for negative real numbers such as –5.68. Thus it is not true that $\lfloor -5.68 \rfloor = -5$. What is instead true is that $\lfloor -5.68 \rfloor = -6$. So taking floors of numbers is not the same as "rounding them toward zero," as you might at first expect. Because this is just slightly subtle, it is worth trying to develop and use a suitable *mental model*.

Think of a building with many storeys, with some extending upward above the ground, and with some underground storeys going downward into the earth. Suppose you think of the street level as level 0, and you number the divisions between the storeys with +1, +2, etc., going upward above ground, and –1, –2, etc., as you go downward into the earth. See Fig. A.5 for a diagram of this situation. You can also think of the left vertical wall of the building as the y-axis of a two-dimensional graph in which the integer points on the y-axis correspond to the division points between the storeys of the building.

On such a graph, a point 2.31 units up on the y-axis would fall 0.31 units above the second floor of the building. (By definition, let's say that the second floor is the floor labeled with +2 on the y-axis). The floor of 2.31 would then be the integer label on the y-axis of the floor of the building immediately beneath the point 2.31. For a point such as 2.00, which lies directly on the floor 2, the floor of 2.00 is identical to 2.

Now let's apply this reasoning to the point –5.68. The point labeled –5.68 lies 0.32 units above the floor of the building labeled –6 in Fig. A.5. In this method of picturing things, $\lfloor -5.68 \rfloor$ is the floor of the building directly below the location of

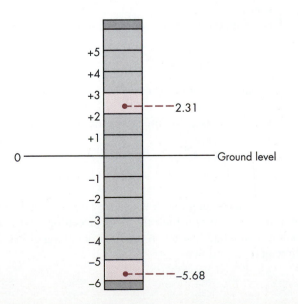

Figure A.5 A Building with Above-Ground and Underground Storeys

the point -5.68. So we have $\lfloor -5.68 \rfloor = -6$. Again, in the case of a negative integer value, such as -6.00, the floor of -6.00 is identical to -6.

Ceilings are similar to floors, only we go *upward* from a point, x, to find the label of the ceiling of a room in which x is located in order to determine the ceiling of x. The ceiling of x is denoted by $\lceil x \rceil$. From this, you can see that the ceiling of the real number x is the smallest integer greater than or equal to x.

In Fig. A.5, it is obvious that $\lceil 2.31 \rceil = 3$. If you use this way of picturing things, it is also clear that $\lceil -5.68 \rceil = -5$. However, if you forget to picture the relationship, and you forget the meaning of the definition, it is easy to make a mistake and conclude that $\lceil -5.68 \rceil = -6$, since it seems natural to "round away from zero" thereby increasing the absolute value of a number to get its ceiling. This rule works for positive real numbers, but it gives the wrong result for negative real numbers.

We are now ready for the formal definitions of the floor and ceiling.

Let x be a real number.
The *floor* of x, denoted $\lfloor x \rfloor$, is the largest integer y, such that $y \leq x$.
The *ceiling* of x, denoted $\lceil x \rceil$, is the smallest integer y, such that $y \geq x$.

Definition of the Floor and Ceiling of x

Manipulating Floors and Ceilings

To manipulate floors and ceilings in expressions, it is worthwhile developing a few rules. These can help in dealing with expressions involving floors and ceilings, and can make their mechanical transformation accurate.

In what follows, suppose that x and y are real numbers, and suppose that a and b are integers.

First of all, the floor and ceiling of an integer is always the same integer:

$$\lfloor a \rfloor = \lceil a \rceil = a.$$

That's because the largest (or smallest) integer equal to a given integer is the integer itself.

You can always move integers inside and outside of floor and ceiling brackets:

$$\lfloor x \pm a \rfloor = \lfloor x \rfloor \pm a \text{ and}$$
$$\lceil x \pm a \rceil = \lceil x \rceil \pm a.$$

This is just like saying that if you moved a point x a distance of a storeys up or down a building and then you took the floor or ceiling, you would have obtained the same result as if you had first taken the floor or ceiling of x and then had moved a distance of a storeys up or down.

There are some inequalities that are also significant and useful. Can you see why each of the following are true?

$$\lfloor x + y \rfloor \geq \lfloor x \rfloor + \lfloor y \rfloor \text{ and}$$
$$\lceil x + y \rceil \leq \lceil x \rceil + \lceil y \rceil.$$

Let's take $x = 3.6$ and $y = 4.6$ and substitute in the inequality $\lfloor x + y \rfloor \geq \lfloor x \rfloor + \lfloor y \rfloor$. This gives $\lfloor 3.6 + 4.6 \rfloor \geq \lfloor 3.6 \rfloor + \lfloor 4.6 \rfloor$, which becomes $\lfloor 8.2 \rfloor \geq \lfloor 3.6 \rfloor + \lfloor 4.6 \rfloor$. Then taking floors gives, $8 \geq 3 + 4$, and finally adding on the right gives, $8 \geq 7$. A condition under which this inequality can become a strict inequality ($>$) is when both x and y are positive and have fractional parts that add to more than one. In such a case, adding x and y and then taking the floor yields an integer one greater than the process in which x and y's fractional parts are first dropped, and then their sum is taken.

The example considered in the previous paragraph used positive x and y. Other cases need to be considered in which one or both of x and y is negative. For example, if $x = -4.1$ and $y = -3.1$, substitution in $\lfloor x + y \rfloor \geq \lfloor x \rfloor + \lfloor y \rfloor$, followed by simplification yields, $-8 \geq -9$. With more work, it is possible to verify the other cases, and the similar relationship involving the ceilings as well.

A useful symmetry principle is that the negative of operations on floors above ground zero is the same as the operations on the ceilings of the negatives below ground zero. Thus we can write

$$-\lfloor x \rfloor = \lceil -x \rceil \text{ and}$$
$$-\lceil x \rceil = \lfloor -x \rfloor.$$

Another form of this symmetry principle is

$$\lfloor x \rfloor = -\lceil -x \rceil \text{ and}$$
$$\lceil x \rceil = -\lfloor -x \rfloor.$$

Finally, it is useful to note that if $x \leq y$, then $\lfloor x \rfloor \leq \lfloor y \rfloor$ and $\lceil x \rceil \leq \lceil y \rceil$. Let's collect these laws for convenient reference into Table A.6.

Table A.6 Manipulation Laws for Floors and Ceilings

Floor and Ceiling Laws for reals x and y and integers a and b
$\lfloor a \rfloor = \lceil a \rceil = a$ $\lfloor x \pm a \rfloor = \lfloor x \rfloor \pm a$, and $\lceil x \pm a \rceil = \lceil x \rceil \pm a$ $\lfloor x \pm y \rfloor \geq \lfloor x \rfloor \pm \lfloor y \rfloor$, and $\lceil x \pm y \rceil \leq \lceil x \rceil \pm \lceil y \rceil$ $-\lfloor x \rfloor = \lceil -x \rceil$, and $-\lceil x \rceil = \lfloor -x \rfloor$ if $x \leq y$, then $\lfloor x \rfloor \leq \lfloor y \rfloor$ and $\lceil x \rceil \leq \lceil y \rceil$.

A.3 Review Questions

1. Define the floor and ceiling of a real number x.
2. How is the floor of x related to the ceiling of $-x$?
3. When is a number equal to both its floor and ceiling?
4. When is it not true that taking the floor of x is the same as discarding x's fractional part?

A.3 Exercises

1. Calculate: $\lfloor 3.99 \rfloor$, $\lceil -2.99 \rceil$, $-\lfloor -2.1 \rfloor$, and $\lceil 0.001 \rceil$.
2. Alf Witt has come up with a conjecture: "Whenever $\lfloor x \rfloor \le \lfloor y \rfloor$, we always have $x \le y$." Is this true? If so, prove it. If not, give a counterexample.
3. Is the following assertion true: $\lceil \lfloor x \pm y \rfloor \rceil = \lfloor x \pm y \rfloor$? If it is true, prove it. Otherwise, give a counterexample.

≡ A.4   Logarithms and Exponentials

In this section, we develop some laws for manipulating exponentials and logarithms. In the first subsection, we take up the subject of exponentials. In the second subsection, we develop logarithm manipulation laws.

Exponentials

When we multiply several copies of a quantity, x, together, we can use a shorthand to denote the number of times x is multiplied by itself. For example, taking five copies of x and multiplying them together, $x*x*x*x*x$, is denoted, x^5. The exponent (or power) of x in x^5 is 5. From this simple observation, we can proceed to derive some laws by which exponents (or powers) can be manipulated.

Let x and y be real numbers, and let a and b be integers (for the moment). Multiplying a copies of x together gives x^a, and multiplying b copies of x together gives x^b. If we now multiply x^a by x^b, as in the expression $x^a x^b$, how many copies of x would be multiplied together in all? The answer, of course, is $a + b$ copies, so we have the first law:

$$x^a x^b = x^{a+b}. \tag{A.10}$$

Assuming, for the moment that $a > b$, if we divide a copies of x by b copies of x, we would cancel out b copies of x in x^a, leaving us with $(a - b)$ copies of x. This leads to the companion law that when we divide terms, we subtract exponents:

$$\frac{x^a}{x^b} = x^{a-b}. \tag{A.11}$$

In Eq. A.11, if we take $a = b$ and then substitute a for every occurrence of b, we get $1 = x^a/x^a = x^{a-a} = x^0$. This is valid only if $x \neq 0$ (since division by 0 gives undefined results). Consequently, we have the law:

$$x^0 = 1, \text{ provided } x \neq 0. \tag{A.12}$$

Now letting a be zero in Eq. A.11 and applying Eq. A.12, $x^0/x^b = 1/x^b = x^{-b}$. So we have

$$x^{-b} = \frac{1}{x^b}. \tag{A.13}$$

We can continue in this fashion to develop laws for manipulating exponentials. For instance, we might want to develop laws for fractional exponents, such as $x^{1/2}$. Using Eq. A.10 with $a = b = 1/2$, gives, $x^{1/2} x^{1/2} = x^{1/2 + 1/2} = x^1 = x$. This implies that $x^{1/2}$ is a quantity which, when multiplied by itself, gives x. In other words, $x^{1/2}$ must be equal to $\sqrt{x}$ (the square root of x). Similar reasoning gives us the law for the nth root of x,

$$x^{1/n} = \sqrt[n]{x}. \tag{A.14}$$

Once we have fractional exponents (which are more general than integer exponents) we are led naturally to the generalization that considers exponents that can be rational numbers or real numbers. It turns out that the laws expressed by Eqs. A.10 through A.14 work for real exponents, a and b, without change.

Table A.7 summarizes some laws for manipulating exponents. Some new laws have been added that were not derived above (but which could be derived easily using derivations similar to the ones we have been illustrating).

Logarithms

Logarithms are exponents, in the following sense. The base-b logarithm of x, denoted $\log_b x$, is the power to which the base b must be raised to equal x. In symbols, if

Exponent Laws for reals x, y, a, and b
$x^a x^b = x^{a+b}$
$x^a/x^b = x^{a-b}$
$x^0 = 1$, provided $x \neq 0$
$x^{-b} = 1/x^b$
$x^{1/n} = \sqrt[n]{x}$
$1^a = 1$, and $x^1 = x$, for any a and x
$(x\,y)^a = x^a\, y^a$
$(x^a)^b = x^{ab}$
$(x/y)^a = x^a/y^a$

Table A.7 Manipulation Laws for Exponents

$y = \log_b x$, then $b^y = x$. This is the same as asserting

$$b^{\log_b x} = x.$$

The base of a logarithm, b, is a quantity that must always be greater than 1. Some popular bases in scientific work are 10 and e, where e is a special quantity with the value $e = 2.718281828$. The base-10 logarithm of x is written $\log_{10} x$, but the base e logarithm of x has a special notation, $\ln x$. Here "ln" is shorthand for "log natural" and stands for the "natural logarithm." (Natural logarithms arise in calculus, because when you calculate the area under the curve $y = 1/x$ starting at 1 and ending at x, you get $\ln x$. This has been called the "natural" way to define the logarithm.)

In computer science, we frequently use base-2 logarithms, as in $\log_2 x$. In fact, this is used so often that we define a special notation, $\lg x$, to stand for the base-2 logarithm of x.

The most important law for logarithms is that the logarithm of a product, $x\,y$, is the *sum* of the logarithms of x and y. (*Caution:* People often get this confused, and use invalid variations, which we will not spell out, since doing so might add to the confusion.)

$$\log_b(x\,y) = \log_b x + \log_b y \qquad (A.15)$$

Log of Product is Sum of Logs

The reason this is true is that raising the base b to the power $\log_b x + \log_b y$, and applying Eq. A.10 yields

$$b^{\log_b x + \log_b y} = b^{\log_b x}\, b^{\log_b y} = x\,y.$$

But $\log_b(x\,y)$ is just the power to which the base b must be raised to be equal to $x\,y$. So we also have, $x\,y = b^{\log_b xy}$. In other words, the sum of the logarithms of x and y add up to a power, p, which is the same as the power $p = \log_b(x\,y)$, and for which the base b raised to this power p equals the product $x\,y$, namely, $b^p = x\,y$. Hence, the logarithm of the product, $x\,y$, must be identical to the sum of the individual logarithms of x and y.

From Eq. A.15, we can obtain some other laws that are useful for manipulating expressions involving logarithms. For example, the logarithm of n copies of x multiplied together is the sum of n copies of the logarithm of x. Writing n copies of x multiplied together as x^n, and writing n copies of $\log_b x$ added together as $n \log_b x$, we have

$$\log_b(x^n) = n \log_b x. \qquad (A.16)$$

Equation A.16 also works not only when n is an integer but also when n is any real number. Let's derive a few consequences. For example, if $n = -1$ in Eq. A.16, then since $x^{-1} = 1/x$ (from Table A.7), we get

$$\log_b(1/x) = -\log_b x. \tag{A.17}$$

Similarly, we can derive the law for the logarithm of a fraction, by writing the fraction x/y in the form $x(1/y)$, and applying Eqs. A.15 and A.17 in succession. This yields

$$\log_b(x/y) = \log_b x - \log_b y. \tag{A.18}$$

In Eq. A.18, if we let $x = y$, replace y by x, and replace x/x with 1, we get

$$\log_b(1) = 0. \tag{A.19}$$

Also, since $b^1 = b$ (from Table A.7), the definition of the logarithm implies that

$$\log_b b = 1. \tag{A.20}$$

An important set of relationships for both the logarithmic and the exponential functions concerns being able to deduce equality and inequality in a certain fashion. In Eq. A.21, which illustrates preservation of equality and inequality by logs and exponentials, let the symbol, $\Leftrightarrow$, stand for "if and only if":

$$
\begin{aligned}
x = y &\Leftrightarrow \log_b x = \log_b y \\
x > y &\Leftrightarrow \log_b x > \log_b y \\
x < y &\Leftrightarrow \log_b x < \log_b y \\
x = y &\Leftrightarrow b^x = b^y \\
x > y &\Leftrightarrow b^x > b^y \\
x < y &\Leftrightarrow b^x < b^y
\end{aligned}
\tag{A.21}
$$

In other words, if two quantities are equal, then their logs and exponentials are also equal, and if two quantities are unequal, their logs and exponentials are unequal in the same order. Moreover, if the logs or exponentials of two quantities are equal (or unequal), then the quantities themselves are equal (or unequal in the same order). This principle is needed frequently in deducing facts and consequences involving logs and exponentials.

Let's now turn to the subject of changing the bases of logarithms. For example, suppose we have a natural logarithm, $\ln x$, and we want to change it into a base-2 logarithm, $\lg x$. How can we accomplish this conversion? We can deduce the base conversion formula for logarithms as follows. We start with the definition of the logarithm:

$$b^{\log_b x} = x.$$

We then take base-c logarithms of both sides of this equation, getting

$$\log_c(b^{\log_b x}) = \log_c x.$$

By applying Eq. A.16, we can move the exponent of b inside the parenthesis on the left side to a new position outside as a multiplier, getting

$$\log_b x * \log_c b = \log_c x.$$

Finally, we can divide both sides by $\log_c b$, getting

$$\log_b x = \frac{\log_c x}{\log_c b}. \tag{A.22}$$

Changing Bases of Logarithms

By setting $x = c$ in Eq. A.22, and noting that $\log_c c = 1$ from Eq. A.20, we can derive an additional useful formula:

$$\log_b c = \frac{1}{\log_c b}. \tag{A.23}$$

Let's now apply Eq. A.22 to change bases from a natural log to a base-2 log. Putting $b = 2$ and $c = e$ in Eq. A.22, gives

$$\log_2 x = \frac{\log_e x}{\log_e 2}.$$

Replacing $\log_e x$ with $\ln x$, $\log_e 2$ with $\ln 2$, and $\log_2 x$ with $\lg x$, gives

$$\lg x = \frac{\ln x}{\ln 2}. \tag{A.24}$$

Converting Natural Logs to Base-2 Logs

If you have a calculator that computes natural logarithms, you can always compute the value of a base-2 logarithm of x by dividing $\ln x$ by $\ln 2$. For example, the value of $\lg 8$ (which should be equal to 3, since $2^3 = 8$), is obtained by dividing $\ln 8 = 2.079441542$ by $\ln 2 = 0.69314718$. (In fact, $2.08/0.6931 = 3.0010$.)

Let's now summarize the rules we have discussed in tabular form. Table A.8 gives the results.

One more useful fact worth keeping in mind is that logarithms are defined only for positive arguments—i.e., $\log_b x$ is defined only if $x > 0$. The logarithm of 0 is minus infinity ($\log_b 0 = -\infty$).

Logarithm Laws
for reals x, y, n, and for $b > 1$, $c > 1$

$log_b(x\,y) = log_b x + log_b y$

$log_b(x/y) = log_b x - log_b y$

$log_b(1/x) = -log_b x$

$log_b(x^n) = n\,log_b x$

$log_b(1) = 0$

$log_b b = 1$

$x \,\Re\, y \Leftrightarrow log_b x \,\Re\, log_b y$, for $\Re \in \{=, \leq, <, >, \geq\}$

$$log_b x = \frac{log_c x}{log_c b}$$

$$log_b c = \frac{1}{log_c b}$$

Table A.8 Manipulation Laws for Logarithms

Application to Inequalities

Sometimes, when dealing with analysis of algorithms, we need to prove inequalities, such as the following:

$$\lg(n + 1) < \lg n + 1, \text{ whenever } n > 1.$$

How might we go about establishing such a fact? We could start with the conclusion and see if we can reason backward toward the initial conditions. To start with, let's apply Eq. A.21 by using the assertion that if $a < b$, then $2^a < 2^b$, where $a = \lg(n+1)$ and $b = \lg n + 1$. This gives

$$2^{\lg(n + 1)} < 2^{\lg n + 1}, \text{ whenever } n > 1.$$

But, by the definition of the logarithm, $2^{\lg(n + 1)} = (n + 1)$, and, by applying Eq. A.10, we observe that $2^{\lg n + 1} = 2^{\lg n}\, 2^1 = 2n$. Therefore the inequality above is true if and only if the following inequality is true:

$$(n + 1) < 2n, \text{ whenever } n > 1.$$

Subtracting n from both sides of the latter inequality yields

$$1 < n, \text{ whenever } n > 1.$$

Now, it turns out that each of the steps used in this chain of backward reasoning is reversible (since the reasoning steps in the other direction each have valid justifications, too). So we can reverse the steps to derive the conclusion we are seeking, starting from the initial condition $(n > 1)$. Thus, in compressed form: $(n > 1) \Leftrightarrow (1 < n)$ $\Leftrightarrow (n + 1) < 2n \Leftrightarrow \lg(n + 1) < \lg(2n) \Leftrightarrow \lg(n+1) < \lg 2 + \lg n \Leftrightarrow \lg(n+1) < \lg n + 1$.

A.4 Review Questions

1. Define the base-2 logarithm of a real number x.
2. How do you change the base of a logarithm?
3. What is the formula for $\log_b xy$ in terms of $\log_b y$ and $\log_b x$?

A.4 Exercises

1. Prove that for any $b > 2$, whenever $n > k$, we must have $\log_b(n + k) < \log_b n + 1$.
2. Show that $\lg 4x^2 = 2(\lg x + 1)$.
3. Show that $\ln(8x/y)/\ln 2 = 3 + \lg x - \lg y$.

A.5 Modular Arithmetic

We are all familiar with the notion of dividing one integer by another and getting a *quotient* and a *remainder*. To keep things simple, let's think of using positive integers a and b. Let's divide a by b, getting a quotient q and a remainder r. Then the quantities a, b, q, and r are related by

$$a = b\,q + r, \qquad \text{where } (0 \leq r < b). \tag{A.25}$$

Relation Between Quotients and Remainders

For example, if $a = 36$ and $b = 7$, then dividing 36 by 7 gives a quotient $q = 5$ and leaves a remainder of $r = 1$. Since seven fives are thirty-five, and adding one to thirty-five gives thirty-six, we have verified that Eq. (A.25) holds in this case ($36 = 7*5 + 1$).

When the remainder $r = 0$, we say that b divides evenly into a, and we write $b \mid a$ (which is pronounced "b divides a").

Suppose we take a divisor, such as 7, and we agree to perform a new kind of arithmetic in which we will agree to confine ourselves always to use "remainders after division by 7." To start with, we use only the numbers from 0 to 6 (which is the range in which the remainders after division by 7 are forced to lie on account of Eq. A.25). When we add or multiply two numbers in the range 0:6, and we get a new number outside the range 0:6, we *reduce* it to be a number back in the range 0:6, by replacing it with its remainder after division by 7. This is called *reducing a number modulo* 7. Here, 7 is called the *modulus*.

For example, suppose we multiply 4 by 5, getting 20. Since 20 is not in the range 0:6, we divide 20 by 7, getting a quotient of 2 and a remainder of 6. We then throw away the quotient, and keep the remainder as the result. Hence, we say 4 *times* 5 *equals* 6 *modulo* 7, and we write

$$4 * 5 \equiv 6 \ (\textit{modulo } 7).$$

Addition								Multiplication							
+	0	1	2	3	4	5	6	*	0	1	2	3	4	5	6
0	0	1	2	3	4	5	6	0	0	0	0	0	0	0	0
1	1	2	3	4	5	6	0	1	0	1	2	3	4	5	6
2	2	3	4	5	6	0	1	2	0	2	4	6	1	3	5
3	3	4	5	6	0	1	2	3	0	3	6	2	5	1	4
4	4	5	6	0	1	2	3	4	0	4	1	5	2	6	3
5	5	6	0	1	2	3	4	5	0	5	3	1	6	4	2
6	6	0	1	2	3	4	5	6	0	6	5	4	3	2	1

As another example, suppose we add 5 and 6 getting 11. Since 11 is not in the range 0:6, we divide by 7, getting the remainder 4. This means we can write

$$5 + 6 \equiv 4 \ (modulo\ 7).$$

If we make up an addition table and a multiplication table for these operations, we get what is shown in Table A.9.

Once we know how to define modular addition and modular multiplication we can find a way to define subtraction and division, using the concept of *inverses*. For instance, if we know that $a + b = c$, then we can define $c - b = a$. Thus, if $3 + 5 = 1$ (*modulo* 7) from Table A.9, then $1 - 5 = 3$ (*modulo* 7). This actually makes sense from the perspective of our "wrap around" arithmetic principle, if we try, in some sensible way, to extend the concept of "keeping the remainder after division by 7" to cases covering negative numbers. For example, $1 - 5 = -4$, using ordinary arithmetic. But what is the remainder of -4 after division by 7, wrapped around to be an appropriate number in the range 0:6? Applying Eq. A.25 in a strict sense, gives $-4 = 7*(-1) + 3$, where the quotient $q = -1$, and the remainder $r = 3$. (Recall that the remainder r is forced to lie in the range $0 \leq r < q$, which in this case means r must lie in the range 0:6.) We will not say much more about modular subtraction and division here, since we will not need it (except for a useful cancellation law, which we will talk about in a moment.)

One reason we need to know about modular arithmetic in the study of data structures is that it comes up when we try to create tables having a limited range of table indexes, for which we want to make sure that indexes into the table are kept in the appropriate range. For this purpose, we often use wrap-around arithmetic in which if we add (or subtract) a constant to a table index and get a new index that falls off one end of the table, we wrap it around so it falls back inside the table starting at the opposite end. For example, we might have a hash table, represented by an array T[0:M − 1] with entries T[i], where the table index i falls in the range $0 \leq i < M$. When we add a displacement c to i, getting $i + c$, to move from entry T[i] to another entry T[i + c], it may happen that $i + c \geq M$. In this case, we wrap around by computing a new index, $j = (i + c) - M$, and we access the wrap-around entry T[j]. Here you can see that j is just the remainder of $(i + c)$ after division by M, so we are using modular arithmetic to keep table indexes inside the proper index range $0:M - 1$.

It will turn out that when we reason about how to construct these table indexing schemes properly, we will need to know certain facts about modular arithmetic. For this reason (among others), we need to proceed to develop just a few more laws of modular arithmetic which will prove necessary and useful in our developments (particularly in Chapter 11).

Let's now take a small jump and define the binary operator *mod*, which is used in expressions such as $(a \bmod b)$, where a and b can be either integers or real numbers.

> The *mod* Operator:
>
> Let a and b be any two real numbers.
> We define $a \bmod 0 = a$, and if $b \neq 0$, we define
> $$a \bmod b = a - b \lfloor a/b \rfloor.$$

For example, if $a = 23$ and $b = 5$, we have $a/b = 23/5 = 4.6$. So $\lfloor a/b \rfloor = \lfloor 4.6 \rfloor = 4$. This implies that $a \bmod b = 23 \bmod 5 = 23 - 5\lfloor 23/5 \rfloor = 23 - 5*4 = 23 - 20 = 3$.

Thus, the *mod* operator gives the same result as "keeping the remainder after dividing a by the divisor b." (In C, if a and b are integers, $a \bmod b$ is written **a % b**.)

If we have a positive real number a with a fractional part, such as $a = 1.618$, then the expression $(a \bmod 1)$ gives the fractional part of a, since our definition of the *mod* operator causes us to subtract the floor of a from a itself, leaving the fractional part. Thus, if $a = 1.618$, then $(a \bmod 1) = a - 1\lfloor a/1 \rfloor = a - \lfloor a \rfloor = 1.618 - \lfloor 1.618 \rfloor = 1.618 - 1 = 0.618$.

Returning to our hypothetical discussion of a table T with entries T[$0:M - 1$], we see that all we need to consider are integers of the form $(i \bmod M)$ in order to maintain index values in the range $0:M - 1$.

Now, let's take a final step in this section, by defining what it means for two integers to be "congruent modulo m," and then by giving two laws that apply to the defined congruences.

We say that $a \equiv b$ (*modulo m*) if and only if $(a \bmod m) = (b \bmod m)$. We pronounce "$a \equiv b$ (*modulo m*)" as "a is congruent to b modulo m." This is also called a *congruence relation* between the integers a and b.

There are several important manipulation laws that apply to congruence relations, of which we will mention only two:

$$
\begin{aligned}
&\text{If } a \equiv b \ (modulo\ m) \quad \text{and} \quad r \equiv s \ (modulo\ m) \\
&\quad \text{then} \quad (a \pm r) \equiv (b \pm s) \ (modulo\ m) \\
&\quad \text{and} \quad (a\, r) \equiv (b\, s) \ (modulo\ m)
\end{aligned}
\tag{A.26}
$$

Addition, Subtraction, and Multiplication Law for Congruences

Before giving the next law, we have to pause for a moment and define what is meant by having two integers, m and n, that are *relatively prime* to one another. We say m and n are relatively prime if they have no common divisors other than 1. When you reduce a fraction of two integers to "least common terms" by removing common factors from the numerator and denominator, you obtain a numerator and denominator that are relatively prime. For example, 7 and 5 are relatively prime, since they have no common divisors. But 21 and 15 are not relatively prime, since they have a common divisor, 3. If you had the fraction 21/15, and you were asked to reduce it to least common terms, you would divide out the factor 3 from the numerator and denominator, getting 7/5. This reduced fraction in least common terms, has a relatively prime numerator and denominator.

In order to get a "division law" for congruences, we need to focus on the special case when the quantity, c, that we are dividing out, is relatively prime to the modulus m. Otherwise division may be invalid.

Provided c and m are *relatively prime*, (A.27)
if $a c \equiv b c$ (*modulo m*) then $a \equiv b$ (*modulo m*)

Cancellation Law for Congruences

As a memory jog, you can think of Eqs. A.26 and A.27 as telling you that addition, subtraction, and multiplication work modulo m, but that you can divide out a factor, c, modulo m, only if c and m have no common divisors themselves.

Chapter 11 shows how the modular arithmetic laws developed in this section are used as the basis for hash table searching having very good performance properties.

A.5 Review Questions

1. Define $a \bmod b$ for any two real numbers a and b.
2. What does the notation $a \equiv b$ (*modulo m*) mean?
3. What is the modulus in the expression $a \equiv b$ (*modulo m*)?
4. When can you cancel c in $ac \equiv bc$ (*modulo m*) to get $a \equiv b$ (*modulo m*)?

A.5 Exercises

1. Find the values of $(21 \bmod 6)$, $(-3 \bmod 7)$, and $(2.18 \bmod 2)$.
2. Let $n = 11$ be a table size for a table, T[0:10]. For the integers i in 0:10, compute $(i*5 \bmod 11)$ and show that all the integers in the table index range 0:10 are generated once and only once.

A.6 Sums

Mathematicians have been using a special notation for sums for over two centuries. The notation we will discuss and use was first introduced by the mathematician LaGrange in the 1770s. Up until this point, we have (for the most part) used three dots between plus signs (+ . . . +), to mean something informally equivalent to "and so on" as in, S = 3 + 5 + 7 + . . . + (2*n + 1).

We now seek a systematic way to "roll up" a sum into a single expression involving the tricks of combining a *general term*, and an *index* that is allowed to range over a set of values. The general term will usually (though not always) contain instances of the index.

Let's start by studying the summation notation for the example of the sum of the odd numbers, S, given at the end of the first paragraph of this section.

$$S = \sum_{i=1}^{n} (2*i+1) = 3+5+7+ \ldots +(2*n+1).$$

Summation notation involves the use of the Greek letter Σ. Below the Σ in the formula for S above, we have, $i = 1$, and above the Σ, we have n. This means that i is an *index variable* that starts at $i = 1$ and increases in steps of 1 until it reaches n. (Another name for an *index variable* is a *dummy variable*). Each time the index variable i takes on a distinct new value, v, this value is substituted for i in the general term $(2*i + 1)$, and each such substituted copy of the general term becomes one of the summands that are added up to form the sum, S.

Thus, when $i = 1$, we substitute $i = 1$ in the general term, $(2*i + 1)$, getting $(2*1 + 1) = 3$. So 3 becomes one of the summands of the sum S. Next, we increase i to become $i = 2$, and we substitute $i = 2$ in the general term, getting $(2*2 + 1) = 5$. So 5 becomes the next summand to be added together in the sum. We continue in this fashion, until we reach the upper limit of summation, $i = n$. When we substitute $i = n$ in the general term, we obtain the last summand, $(2*n + 1)$, to be added together in the sum, S.

One reason the index variable i is called a *dummy variable* is that if we systematically substitute some new distinct dummy variable, say j, for i, in the formula for S, we get a new formula that involves j instead of i, but which computes exactly the same sum, S. Thus we could write

$$S = \sum_{j=1}^{n} (2*j+1) = 3+5+7+ \ldots +(2*n+1).$$

Since it does not matter whether we have used i or j, and since neither i nor j really appears in the sum, once it is written out in full, i and j take on roles merely as "place holders" or "dummies" that stand for a range of values, but do not really stand for themselves. (This meaning of the word "dummy" is similar to the use of the word "dummy" in phrases like "a dummy corporation," which is a corporation set up to act in place of some other corporation—as a place holder, so to speak—to represent the other corporation's interests.) The dummy variable is thus a *place holder* that represents all the integers in the range specified below and above the Σ, and which does not represent itself.

Another more modern way to express summation notation is to use a relation on the index variable below the $\sum$ sign. Thus we could write

$$S = \sum (2*i+1) = 3+5+7+\ldots+(2*n+1)$$

Here, we use a relation of the form, $(1 \leq i \leq n)$, to constrain the values of the index variable used to generate all the instances of the general term that are to be taken as summands. In this book, we sometimes use this "relational" way of writing sums, especially when we need to write summation notation in-line in the text, and we write the relation in a subscript position immediately following the $\sum$ sign, but before the general term. Thus we write, $S = \sum_{(1 \leq i \leq n)} (2*i + 1)$.

Changing Index Variables

The relational way of writing sums is also useful when we need to change the index variable. You can replace an index variable i with an expression involving another index variable, provided the substitution accomplishes a *permutation of the range*. Here, a permutation of the range is simply a rearrangement of the integers in the range in which the integers in the range are given in some possibly different order. One useful type of permutation of the range can be obtained by replacing i with $(\pm j \pm c)$, where c is a constant.

For example, suppose we want to replace i with $(j + 1)$ in $S = \sum_{(1 \leq i \leq n)} (2*i + 1)$. To do this, we systematically substitute $(j + 1)$ for each occurrence of i both in the range $(1 \leq i \leq n)$ and in the expression for the general term $(2*i + 1)$. Without first simplifying, this would give $S = \sum_{1 \leq (j+1) \leq n} (2*(j+1) + 1)$. After some preliminary simplification, in which we simplify $(1 \leq j + 1 \leq n)$ to $0 \leq j \leq (n-1)$, and $(2*(j + 1) + 1)$ to $(2*j + 3)$, we get $S = \sum_{(0 \leq j \leq n-1)} (2*j + 3)$. If you try expanding the latter version of S, using j, into the full sum, by substituting values of j in the range, $0 \leq j \leq (n - 1)$, for the general term, $(2*j + 3)$, you find that you get an expansion into summands identical to that obtained by expanding the original version using the index variable i.

A way of stating a rule for change of index variables in a sum is as follows. Suppose we have a sum, $S = \sum_{R(i)} F(i)$, where $R(i)$ is a relation involving the index variable i, and $F(i)$ is a general term involving i. Then you can substitute $(\pm j \pm c)$ for each occurrence of i in, $\sum_{R(i)} F(i)$, provided j is either the same as i, or is a distinct new variable not previously used in $R(i)$ and $F(i)$. Here, if c is not a numerical constant but is instead a variable, it, too, must be distinct from the other variables used in $R(i)$ and $F(i)$.

Application

Let's work through an example of the use of a change of index variable transformation to show how it can be used to advantage. We choose a sum used in Chapter 9, when studying a special type of binary tree called a *heap*. The sum to be manipulated is

$$S = \sum_{i=0}^{n-1} (n-i) * 2^i.$$

Let's rewrite this, using relational notation, as

$$S = \sum_{0 \le i \le n-1} (n-i) * 2^i.$$

Then, let's substitute $(n-i)$ for i. (This will have the effect of exchanging the roles of $(n-i)$ and i.) First of all, when we replace i by $(n-i)$ in $(0 \le i \le (n-1))$, we get $(0 \le (n-i) \le n-1)$. By subtracting n, this changes to $(0 - n \le -i \le -1)$. Multiplying through by –1, and reversing the inequalities gives, $(1 \le i \le n)$.

Now we know how to rewrite the range. But what about the general term? If we substitute $(n-i)$ for i in $(n-i)*2^i$, we get, $(n - (n-i))2^{(n-i)}$, which is the same as $i*2^{(n-i)}$.

Consequently, the sum S can be rewritten as

$$S = \sum_{1 \le i \le n} i * 2^{(n-i)}.$$

In the latter sum, we can apply Eq. A.11 to note that $2^{(n-i)} = 2^n / 2^i$. Then, we can factor out 2^n, from each term in the sum, leaving us with

$$S = 2^n * \sum_{i=1}^{n} \frac{i}{2^i}.$$

It can be shown that

$$\sum_{i=1}^{n} \frac{i}{2^i} < 2$$

(see Exercise A.2.5 above, or stay tuned for a moment and we'll establish it directly in the subsection after the next one.) From this, it follows that, $S < 2^{(n+1)}$. In Chapter 9, proving this fact is crucial to establishing that n values in a binary tree can be arranged into a heap in an amount of time proportional to n. This in turn enables us to establish some astonishing performance properties of heaps.

Finding Closed Formulas for Sums

The problem of finding a closed form solution for a sum has so many variations that it would be impossible to cover them all, even if we wrote several books on the subject. So we will introduce just one technique in this subsection and leave it at that.

Suppose we have a sum of the form $S = \sum_{(1 \leq i \leq n)} F(i)$, where the general term, $F(i)$, is a polynomial of degree d in the index variable i. For example, suppose that $F(i) = (2i^2 - i + 1)$. Then $F(i)$ is a polynomial of degree 2, since the power of i in the highest order term is 2.

In the method for finding a closed form solution that we shall investigate, we assume that the solution will be a polynomial in n of degree $(d + 1)$. We will proceed to solve just one specific example, with the hope that the reader will be able to generalize the technique to other cases.

Let's find a closed formula for the sum $S = \sum_{(0 \leq i \leq n)} (2*i + 1)$. Since the general term, $2*i + 1$, is a polynomial in i of degree 1, we assume the solution is a polynomial in n (the upper index of summation) of degree 2, which takes the general form, $An^2 + Bn + C$, for suitable constants, A, B, and C. (Note that S is just a sum of odd numbers, starting at 1.) To start with, we write

$$S = \sum_{0 \leq i \leq n} (2*i + 1) = 1 + 3 + 5 + 7 + \ldots + (2*n + 1) = An^2 + Bn + C.$$

The idea is to set up and solve some simultaneous equations that determine the values of A, B, and C. To do this, we use values of the sum S for $n = 1$, $n = 2$, and $n = 3$. When $n = 1$, $S = 1 + 3 = 4$. Taking $n = 1$, and $S = 4$ in $S = An^2 + Bn + C$, gives us our first equation, $A*1^2 + B*1 + C = 4$. Similarly, for $n = 2$, $S = 9$, and for $n = 3$, $S = 16$. This enables us to write the three simultaneous equations,

$$A*1^2 + B*1 + C = 4$$
$$A*2^2 + B*2 + C = 9$$
$$A*3^2 + B*3 + C = 16.$$

Rewriting these equations in conventional form gives

$$1\,A + 1\,B + C = 4$$
$$4\,A + 2\,B + C = 9$$
$$9\,A + 3\,B + C = 16.$$

To solve these equations for A, B, and C, we can first subtract the first from the second, and then the second from the third, which gives us two new equations in which C has been eliminated,

$$3\,A + B = 5$$
$$5\,A + B = 7.$$

To eliminate B from these last two equations, we can subtract the first from the second giving

$$2\,A = 2.$$

From this, A = 1. We can now substitute A = 1 in 3 A + B = 5, and solve for B, to determine that B = 2. Finally, we can substitute A = 1 and B = 2 in A + B + C = 4 to determine that C = 1.

Now we can substitute A = 1, B = 2, and C = 1 in S = An^2 + Bn + C, getting

$$S = 1\,n^2 + 2\,n + 1.$$

This last result can be factored into the simpler form, S = $(n + 1)^2$. The end result is

$$S = \sum_{0 \le i \le n} (2*i + 1) = 1 + 3 + 5 + 7 + \ldots + (2*n + 1) = (n + 1)^2.$$

Let's check our results. We can try to use mathematical induction to prove that this formula for S is valid. First, for the base case, let $n = 0$. So S = $\sum_{(0 \le i \le 0)}(2i + 1)$ = $(2*0 + 1) = 1 = (0 + 1)^2 = 1^2 = 1$.

Now for the induction step, assume that the formula works for n, and let's see if we can establish that it works for $(n + 1)$. We need to show that

$$S = \sum_{0 \le i \le n+1} (2*i + 1) = ((n + 1) + 1)^2.$$

Working with the left side first, we can separate S into the last term plus the sum of all the terms except for the last term.

$$S = \sum_{0 \le i \le n+1} (2*i + 1) = \sum_{0 \le i \le n} (2*i + 1) + (2*(n + 1) + 1).$$

By the inductive hypothesis, the sum of the terms up to and including $i = n$ is given by $(n + 1)^2$. So we can write

$$S = \sum_{0 \le i \le n+1} (2*i + 1) = (n + 1)^2 + 2*(n + 1) + 1.$$

But this is the same as the expansion of $((n + 1) + 1)^2$, which can be obtained by applying the transformation, $(x + 1)^2 \Rightarrow x^2 + 2x + 1$, using $x = (n + 1)$.

Sums of Sums

Sometimes, we need to compute a sum of a sum of general terms. For instance, this could take the form S = $\sum_{(1 \le i \le n)}\sum_{(1 \le j \le m)} F(i,j)$.

As an example of this, let's explore the problem of finding a simpler form for the sum,

$$S = \sum_{i = 0}^{k} \frac{i}{2^i}.$$

If we write out an expanded version of S, we get

$$S = \frac{0}{2^0} + \frac{1}{2^1} + \frac{2}{2^2} + \ldots + \frac{k}{2^k}.$$

Taking each term, $R_i = i/2^i$, and expanding it into i copies of $1/2^i$, gives

$$R_i = \frac{i}{2^i} = \sum_{j=1}^{i} \frac{1}{2^i} = i \text{ copies of } \frac{1}{2^i} \text{ added together.}$$

The original sum, S, can then be written as a double sum,

$$S = \sum_{i=0}^{k} \frac{i}{2^i} = \sum_{i=0}^{k} R_i = \sum_{i=0}^{k} \left(\sum_{j=1}^{i} \frac{1}{2^i} \right).$$

Now let's write out this double sum as a triangular sequence of rows. Each row, R_i, will contain i copies of $1/2^i$. We will ignore the row, R_0, for $i = 0$, since its value is 0, and we will start at the row, R_1, for $i = 1$.

$$
\begin{array}{llllll}
S = 1/2 & + \\
1/4 & + & 1/4 & + \\
1/8 & + & 1/8 & + & 1/8 & + \\
+ & & \ldots \\
1/2^k & + & 1/2^k & + & 1/2^k & + \ldots + & 1/2^k.
\end{array}
$$

Here, for example, the row, R_3, for $i = 3$, expands $i/2^i$ which is $3/2^3 = 3/8$ into three copies of $1/8$. The row R_5, for $5/2^5$ would expand into five copies of $1/32$, and so on.

Now, let's change direction and take sums along the *columns*. Each column is a geometric progression. For example, the sum of the first column, C_1, is

$$C_1 = \frac{1}{2^1} + \frac{1}{2^2} + \ldots + \frac{1}{2^k}.$$

By applying Eq. A.7 for the sum of a geometric progression and simplifying a bit, you will be able to determine that the sum for $C_1 = 1 - 1/2^k$.

If, now, we let C_2 be the sum of the second column of the triangular expansion of S, we get, $C_2 = 1/2 - 1/2^k$. This follows either from Eq. A.7, or from the direct observation that C_2 must be $1/2$ less than C_1, since C_2 is identical to C_1, except that it does not have C_1's first term of $1/2$. Continuing in this fashion, it can be shown that the sum of the ith column is $C_i = 1/2^{(i-1)} - 1/2^k$.

Since there are exactly as many rows as columns, and since there are k rows, the sum S of the columns, is given by, $S = \sum_{(1 \le i \le k)} C_i = \sum_{(1 \le i \le k)} (1/2^{(i-1)} - 1/2^k)$.

Let's now simplify this latter sum,

$$S = \sum_{1 \le i \le k} \left(\frac{1}{2^{(i-1)}} - \frac{1}{2^k} \right)$$

$$= \sum_{1 \le i \le k} \frac{1}{2^{(i-1)}} - \sum_{1 \le i \le k} \frac{1}{2^k}.$$

On the last line containing two sums, the first is the sum of another geometric progression equal to $2 - 1/2(k-1)$, and the second is a sum of k copies of $1/2k$. This gives us

$$S = 2 - 1/2(k-1) - k/2k.$$

Some simplification gives us a result in final form,

$$S = 2 - \frac{(k+2)}{2^k}.$$

It is easy to see from this that $S < 2$ for any $k \ge 0$. Our results are summarized as Eq. A.28.

$$\sum_{i=0}^{k} \frac{i}{2^i} = 2 - \frac{(k+2)}{2^k}. \tag{A.28}$$

The Sum of $i/2^i$

Useful Formulas for Some Special Sums

In this section, we give a few formulas for some useful sums that we use in the earlier part of the book. Deriving some of these is within the reach of the techniques illustrated above in this section. Deriving the others is beyond the scope of this book, and so we just list them without derivation.

For example, two useful formulas are those for the sum of the squares and the sum of cubes of the first n integers, given by Eqs. A.29 and A.30, respectively.

$$\sum_{i=1}^{n} i^2 = \frac{n(n+1)(2n+1)}{6}. \tag{A.29}$$

The Sum of the Squares

Equations A.29 and A.30 tend to arise in analysis of algorithms that contain loops within loops. For example, if an inner loop takes the form, for (j=1; j<=i; ++j) S(j), and this is contained within an outer loop of the form for (i=1; i<=n; ++i) {the inner loop}, giving a nested loop structure

```
|    for ( i = 1; i <= n; ++i ) {
|        for ( j = 1; j <= i; ++j ) {
|            (some statements, S(j), that cost a*j to execute)
|        }
|    }
```

then we might try to analyze the cost of executing these nested loops. The cost of the inner loop is given by the sum, $S = \sum_{(1 \le j \le i)} a*j$, which is a simple arithmetic progression with sum, $S = a*i*(i+1) / 2$, (from Eq. A.4). Because this inner loop is nested inside an outer loop, it becomes the general term of a sum, T, for the outer loop having index variable i. Thus $T = \sum_{(1 \le i \le n)} (\sum_{(1 \le j \le i)} a*j)$.

Let's now manipulate the expression for the double sum, T.

$$T = \sum_{1 \le i \le n} \left(\sum_{1 \le j \le i} a*j \right)$$

$$= \sum_{1 \le i \le n} \left(a * \frac{i(i+1)}{2} \right)$$

$$= \left(\frac{a}{2} \right) * \sum_{1 \le i \le n} (i^2 + i)$$

$$= \left(\frac{a}{2} \right) * \left(\sum_{1 \le i \le n} i^2 + \sum_{1 \le i \le n} i \right)$$

$$= \left(\frac{a}{2} \right) * \left(\frac{n(n+1)(2n+1)}{6} + \frac{n(n+1)}{2} \right)$$

$$= \frac{an(n+1)(n+2)}{6}.$$

If the statements, S(j), in the innermost loop were to be replaced by another form of inner loop, such as for (k = 1; k <= j; ++k) S(k), and having an execution cost of the form $(j^2 + j)/2$, then the total cost of executing all three nested loops would involve a sum of cubes. In this case, Eq. A.30 would be useful.

$$\sum_{i=1}^{n} i^3 = \frac{n^2 (n+1)^2}{4}. \tag{A.30}$$

The Sum of the Cubes

The formula giving the sum of the floors of the base-2 logarithms of the numbers from 1 to n is also useful. This formula arises in the analysis of the running time of binary searching, and when we try to add up the levels of nodes in a binary tree. For example, what happens if we try to add up the numbers inside the nodes of the binary tree in Fig. A.10?

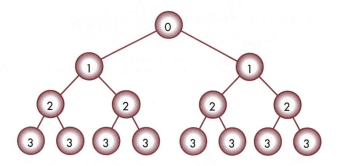

Figure A.10 Level Numbers in a Binary Tree

The sum we need is S = 0 + 1 + 1 + 2 + 2 + 2 + 2 + 3 + . . . + 3, which adds together one zero, two ones, four twos, eight threes, and so on. If you examine quantities in Table A.11, you will be able to see that the floors of the base-2 logarithms of the integers, $\lfloor \lg i \rfloor$, give us the terms we need in the sum S.

Thus, we can write S = $\sum_{(1 \le i \le n)} \lfloor \lg i \rfloor = \lfloor \lg 1 \rfloor + \lfloor \lg 2 \rfloor + \lfloor \lg 3 \rfloor + \ldots + \lfloor \lg n \rfloor =$ $\lfloor 0.0 \rfloor + \lfloor 1.0 \rfloor + \lfloor 1.585 \rfloor + \ldots + \lfloor \lg n \rfloor = 0 + 1 + 1 +$ four 2's + eight 3's + . . . + $\lfloor \lg n \rfloor$. This reveals that the sum S also takes the form, $\sum j\, 2^j$,

$$
\begin{aligned}
S &= 0*1 + 1*2 + 2*4 + 3*8 \\
&= 0*2^0 + 1*2^1 + 2*2^2 + 3*2^3.
\end{aligned}
$$

Elsewhere in the book, we use the symbol L_n to stand for the sum

$$\sum_{i=1}^{n} \lfloor \lg i \rfloor.$$

Deriving the formula for L_n in closed form is beyond the scope of this book. Nonetheless, it is important to have a formula for it. We give this as Eq. A.31.

Table A.11 The Relation Between i and $\lfloor \lg i \rfloor$

The Floors of the Base-2 Logarithms of the Integers		
i	$\lg i$	$\lfloor \lg i \rfloor$
1	0.000	0
2	1.000	1
3	1.585	1
4	2.000	2
5	2.322	2
6	2.585	2
7	2.807	2
8	3.000	3
9	3.170	3

$$L_n = \sum_{i=1}^{n} \left\lfloor \lg i \right\rfloor = (n+1)q - 2^{(q+1)} + 2, \quad \text{where } q = \left\lfloor \lg(n+1) \right\rfloor. \quad \text{(A.31)}$$

The Sum of the Floors of the Base-2 Logarithms

Another formula in this subsection concerns Harmonic numbers. The Harmonic number, H_n, is defined by $H_n = 1 + \frac{1}{2} + \frac{1}{3} + \ldots + \frac{1}{n}$. Using summation notation, we see that $H_n = \sum_{(1 \le i \le n)} \frac{1}{i}$. Eq. A.32 shows that the value of H_n is nearly equal to the natural logarithm of n plus a constant $\gamma = 0.57721566$, plus smaller terms, $O(1/n)$, which are "on the order of" $1/n$, and can be ignored for large n. The constant, γ, is called *Euler's constant*.

$$H_n = \sum_{i=1}^{n} \frac{1}{i} = \ln n + \gamma + O\left(\frac{1}{n}\right), \quad \text{where } \gamma = 0.57721566. \quad \text{(A.32)}$$

The nth Harmonic Number, H_n

The Harmonic number H_n arises in analysis of the performance of binary tree searching algorithms (among other places). Equation A.32 is used in Chapter 9 for this purpose.

The final formula in this subsection gives the closed form for a sum $\sum i \, d^i$. This is useful in solving recurrence relations.

$$\sum_{1 \le i \le n} i \, d^i = \left(\frac{d}{(d-1)^2}\right)[(nd-n-1)d^n + 1] \quad \text{(A.33)}$$

The Sum of $i{*}d^i$

Equation A.28 is a special case of Eq. A.33 for $d = \frac{1}{2}$ and $n = k$.

A.6 Review Questions

1. In the notation $\sum_{(1 \le i \le n)} F(i)$, what is the general term and what is the index variable?
2. Why is an index variable sometimes called a dummy variable?
3. What is the nth Harmonic number?
4. When can you systematically replace the index variable in a sum?

A.6 Exercises

1. Verify that Eq. A.28 can be derived from Eq. A.33.
2. Show that $1 + 3 + 5 + \ldots + (2n - 1) = n^2$.
3. Give a closed formula for the sum of the even numbers, $2 + 4 + 6 + \ldots + 2n$.

4. Find a closed formula for $S = \sum_{(1 \leq i \leq n)} \sum_{(1 \leq j \leq i)} j$. [*Hint:* Assume $S = An^3 + Bn^2 + Cn + D$, then set up and solve simultaneous equations.]
5. Is it true that $\sum_{(m \leq i \leq n)} 1/2^i = 2(1/2^m) - 1/2^n$?
6. Change i to $(j-1)$ in $\sum_{(-1 \leq i \leq n-1)} 2^{i+1}$, and simplify.

▤ **A.7** Recurrence Relations

Recurrence relations arise naturally in the analysis of algorithms—particularly recursive algorithms. Chapter 6 explores this topic in greater detail. Recurrence relations can be used to define a quantity, $T(n)$, usually by giving two rules. The first rule, usually called the *base case*, gives the value of $T(n)$ for some small constant value $n = c$. For example, for $n = 1$, we might have $T(1) = 5$. A second rule usually gives a *general case*, which defines the value of $T(n)$ in terms of previous values of T. Let's look at an example to help make this clear.

$$
\begin{aligned}
T(1) &= 1 \\
T(n) &= 1 + (1/2)\, T(n-1).
\end{aligned}
\tag{A.34}
$$

Recurrence Relations

Let's expand a few values of $T(n)$, for $n = 1$, $n = 2$, $n = 3$, and so on. You'll see a pattern will begin to emerge rather quickly.

First of all, $T(1) = 1$, from the base case. Now let's calculate $T(2)$. Using the formula for the general case, we have $T(2) = 1 + (1/2)\, T(2-1) = 1 + (1/2)\, T(1) = 1 + 1/2$. Now for $T(3)$, we see $T(3) = 1 + (1/2)\, T(2) = 1 + (1/2)*(1 + 1/2)$. So $T(3) = 1 + 1/2 + 1/4$. If we keep going, in this fashion, we discover that

$$
T(n) = 1 + 1/2 + 1/4 + \ldots + 1/2(n-1).
$$

If you studied geometric progressions carefully, this expansion of $T(n)$ might look familiar to you. We can apply the formula for a sum of a geometric progression to conclude that $T(n) = \sum_{(0 \leq i \leq n-1)} 1/2^i = 2 - 1/2(n-1)$.

Let's check this out, starting with the base case. If $n = 1$ in $T(n) = 2 - 1/2(n-1)$, then $T(1) = 2 - 1/2(1-1) = 2 - 1/2^0 = 2 - 1/1 = 1$. So our base case agrees with the first rule in Eqs. A.34. Now let's see if by plugging in the formula for $T(n-1)$ on the right side of $T(n) = 1 + (1/2)\, T(n-1)$, we can generate the formula for $T(n)$. Substituting $T(n-1) = 2 - 1/2(n-2)$, in $T(n)$ gives

$$
\begin{aligned}
T(n) &= 1 + (1/2)\, T(n-1) \\
&= 1 + (1/2) * (2 - 1/2(n-2)) \\
&= 1 + (2/2 - 1/2(n-1)) \\
&= 2 - 1/2(n-1).
\end{aligned}
$$

But the right hand side of the last line is exactly the closed formula for $T(n)$. So our solution works.

Sometimes, we are fortunate, and after expanding a few terms of $T(n)$, we can recognize the sum as an instance of a familiar formula. Other times, we are not so fortunate, and we need to resort to more general solution methods.

In Chapter 6, two methods for solving recurrence relations are given. One method involves looking at tables of solutions. Tables 6.18 and 6.21 give general parameterized solutions for two families of commonly occurring recurrence relations.

Another solution method covered in Chapter 6 is the method of unrolling and summing. This involves unrolling the general equation for $T(n)$ into a sum of terms, and then applying known formulas for sums. In effect, this is the method we used to solve Eqs. A.34.

Another method for solving recurrence relations (among many possible methods) is one using *summing factors*. This works somewhat like the familiar method for solving simultaneous equations. Let's take Eqs. A.34 and illustrate how to find their solution using the method of *summing factors*.

The idea is to build up what is called a *telescoping sum*—which has terms in the middle that fold up and collapse when they are added together. Here's how it works. We start with the general equation, $T(n) = 1 + (1/2) T(n - 1)$, and we subtract $(1/2) T(n - 1)$ from both sides. This gives

$$T(n) - (1/2) T(n - 1) = 1.$$

Now we write down a column of equations. The first equation in the column is the equation for $T(1)$. The second is the equation above with $n = 2$. The third is the above equation with $n = 3$, and so on.

$$
\begin{aligned}
T(1) & & = 1 \\
T(2) & - (1/2) T(1) & = 1 \\
T(3) & - (1/2) T(2) & = 1 \\
T(4) & - (1/2) T(3) & = 1 \\
\cdots & & \\
T(n) & - (1/2) T(n - 1) & = 1.
\end{aligned}
$$

Next we multiply the second through n^{th} of these equations by a multiplier (called a *summing factor*), which will cause the second term of the left side of the previous equation to cancel out when the column of equations is added up. This gives

$$
\begin{aligned}
T(1) & & = 1 & \\
2*T(2) & - (2/2) T(1) & = 2 & \quad \{\text{multiply through by 2}\} \\
4*T(3) & - (4/2) T(2) & = 4 & \quad \{\text{multiply through by 4}\} \\
8*T(4) & - (8/2) T(3) & = 8 & \quad \{\text{multiply through by 8}\} \\
\cdots & & & \\
2^{i-1}*T(i) & - (2^{i-1}/2) T(i - 1) & = 2^{i-1} & \quad \{\text{multiply by } 2^{i-1}\} \\
\cdots & & & \\
2^{n-1}*T(n) & - (2^{n-1}/2) T(n - 1) & = 2^{n-1} & \quad \{\text{multiply by } 2^{n-1}\}
\end{aligned}
$$

Now we add up all the equations, and note that the left sides form a telescoping sum, in which all terms but the last cancel one another.

$$
\begin{aligned}
\cancel{T(1)} &= 1 \\
2 * \cancel{T(2)} - 1 * \cancel{T(1)} &= 2 \\
4 * \cancel{T(3)} - 2 * \cancel{T(2)} &= 4 \\
8 * \cancel{T(4)} - 4 * \cancel{T(3)} &= 8 \\
\cdots & \\
2^{i-1} * \cancel{T(i)} - 2^{i-2} * \cancel{T(i-1)} &= 2^{i-1} \\
\cdots & \\
\underline{2^{n-1} * T(n) - 2^{n-2} * \cancel{T(n-1)}} &\underline{= 2^{n-1}} \\
2^{n-1} * T(n) = 1 + 2 + 4 + 8 + \ldots + 2^{n-1} & \quad \{\text{add up all equations}\}
\end{aligned}
$$

You can see that the sum on the right side of the bottom line is another familiar geometric series with sum, $1 + 2 + 4 + \ldots + 2^{n-1} = (2^n - 1) / (2 - 1)$. So we can rewrite the sum of all the equations in closed form as

$$2^{n-1} * T(n) = 2^n - 1.$$

Now, dividing both sides by 2^{n-1} gives

$$T(n) = \frac{2^n}{2^{n-1}} - \frac{1}{2^{n-1}}.$$

And this can be simplified to yield the final form,

$$T(n) = 2 - \frac{1}{2^{n-1}}.$$

The latter result is the same one we derived earlier by unrolling and summing.

The reader might find it challenging to try to solve the following general recurrence relations:

$$
\begin{aligned}
T(1) &= a \\
T(n) &= b + c\,T(n-1).
\end{aligned}
\tag{A.35}
$$

General Recurrence Relations

Using the method of summing factors, it is possible to derive the results in Table A.12 for these recurrence relations.

The results in Table A.12 are slightly less general than those in Table 6.18 in Chapter 6, and can be obtained from Table 6.18 by setting some parameters equal to zero while exchanging certain others.

Solutions to Some Recurrence Relations $T(n) = b + c\,T(n-1)$, where $T(1) = a$	
Condition	General Solution
$c = 1$	$T(n) = b\,n + (a - b)$
$c \neq 1$	$T(n) = \left(\dfrac{a-b}{c} + \dfrac{b}{c-1}\right) c^{\blacksquare} - \left(\dfrac{b}{c-1}\right)$

Table A.12 Some Solutions to Recurrence Relations

A.7 Review Questions

1. In the recurrence relations: $T(0) = a$ and $T(k) = 2 + \frac{1}{2} T(k/2)$, what is the base case and what is the general case?
2. What is a summing factor?
3. What is a telescoping sum?
4. What method can you use to verify that a proposed solution to some recurrence relations actually satisfies the recurrence relations correctly?

A.7 Exercises

1. In Table A.12, for $c = 1$, verify that $T(n) = b\,n + (a - b)$ satisfies Recurrence Relations A.35.
2. Show by expansion that $T(n)$ is a sum of a geometric progression if $T(0) = a$ and $T(n) = a + r\,T(n-1)$, and give a closed formula for $T(n)$.
3. Show by expansion that $T(n)$ is a sum of an arithmetic progression if $T(1) = a$ and $T(n) = n\,d + (a - d) + T(n-1)$, and give a closed formula for $T(n)$.
4. Solve the recurrence relations $T(1) = 3$ and $T(n) = 1 + 2T(n-1)$. [*Hint:* Use Table A.12.]
5. Derive the formulas in Table A.12 by using the method of summing factors to solve Recurrence Relations A.35.

A.8 Manipulating Logical Expressions

We can manipulate logical expressions by repeatedly applying exchange laws that show how to replace a given logical subexpression with an equivalent one.

In what follows, let a, b, and c stand for propositional variables, and let the operators $\wedge$, $\vee$ and $\sim$ stand for C's logical operators **&&** (and), **||** (or), and **!** (not). A propositional variable can stand for any logical subexpression of a C program. For example, the relational expression $(x \geq y)$ in C has a value which is either 1 (*true*) or 0 (*false*), and hence is a logical subexpression. If we let the variable a stand for $(x \geq y)$ and we let the variable b stand for $(y < z)$, then the logical expression, $a \wedge \sim b$, stands for $(x \geq y)$ **&&** $(! (y < z))$.

$a \wedge$ true $\equiv a$	$a \vee$ true $\equiv$ true
true $\wedge a \equiv a$	true $\vee a \equiv$ true
$a \wedge$ false $\equiv$ false	$a \vee$ false $\equiv a$
false $\wedge a \equiv$ false	false $\vee a \equiv a$
	$\sim$ true $\equiv$ false
	$\sim$ false $\equiv$ true

Table A.13 Laws for Eliminating true and false

The laws given in Table A.13 can be used to eliminate occurrences of the logical constants *true* (1) and *false* (0) when they occur in propositional expressions.

The laws given in Table A.14, can be used to manipulate logical expressions in order to simplify them or to show that they are equivalent to other logical expressions.

To see how these laws can be used to help simplify C programs, let's consider the following two problems.

Problem 1

A computer scientist looks at a C program and discovers the following if-statement, which uses the variables x and y:

Table A.14 Manipulation Laws for Propositional Logic

Exchange Laws for Propositional Variables a, b, and c	The Name of the Law
$a \wedge b \equiv b \wedge a$	Commutative law
$a \vee b \equiv b \vee a$	Commutative law
$a \wedge (b \wedge c) \equiv (a \wedge b) \wedge c$	Associative law
$a \vee (b \vee c) \equiv (a \vee b) \vee c$	Associative law
$a \wedge a \equiv a$	Idempotent law
$a \vee a \equiv a$	Idempotent law
$a \wedge (b \vee c) \equiv (a \wedge b) \vee (a \wedge c)$	Distributive law
$a \vee (b \wedge c) \equiv (a \vee b) \wedge (a \vee c)$	Distributive law
$\sim\sim a \equiv a$	Double negation
$\sim(a \wedge b) \equiv (\sim a) \vee (\sim b)$	DeMorgan's law
$\sim(a \vee b) \equiv (\sim a) \wedge (\sim b)$	DeMorgan's law
$a \wedge (a \vee b) \equiv a$	Subsumption law
$a \vee (a \wedge b) \equiv a$	Subsumption law
$\sim a \vee (a \wedge b) \equiv (\sim a) \vee b$	Cancellation law
$\sim a \wedge (a \vee b) \equiv (\sim a) \wedge b$	Cancellation law
$(a \wedge \sim b) \vee (a \wedge b) \equiv a$	Ground resolution
$(a \vee \sim b) \wedge (a \vee b) \equiv a$	Ground resolution
$(a \vee \sim a) \equiv$ true	Excluded middle
$(a \wedge \sim a) \equiv$ false	Contradiction law

```
if ( (x > y) && (y <= x ) ) y = 2*x;
```

She decides she can replace this statement with the simpler equivalent statement:

```
if (y < x)  y = 2*x;
```

Question: Was she justified in making this improvement?

The two statements will certainly be equivalent if the logical conditions following the keyword if are equivalent—i.e., provided that the condition $((x > y)$ && $(y \le x))$ is logically equivalent to the condition $(y < x)$. But is this the case?

We can make a logical argument, as follows. First, we expand the condition $((x > y)$ && $(y \le x))$ into the equivalent condition $(y < x)$ && $((y < x)$ || $(y == x))$, noting that we have replaced $(x > y)$ with the equivalent condition $(y < x)$. Now, if we substitute the propositional variable A for the condition $(y < x)$ and we substitute the propositional variable B for the condition $(y == x)$, we could ask whether the logical expression $(A$ && $(A$ || $B))$ is logically equivalent to the expression A. This is equivalent to asking whether $(A$ && $(A$ || $B)) \equiv A$ is always true in propositional logic. It follows immediately from the first of the two *subsumption laws* in Table A.14 that this equivalence is valid. So the improvement is justified.

Problem 2

While helping with a code review in a software project, a software manager discovered the following patch of code, written by one of the entry-level programmers. The manager has the intuition that this code gets into an endless loop.

```
 |    void ChangeClock(void)
 |    {
 |        /* Note: assume typedef enum {false, true} Boolean; has been declared */
 |
5 |        Boolean MouseDown;
 |
 |        MouseDown = false;
 |
 |        while ( ( ! MouseInWindow) ||
10 |              (MouseInWindow && ( ! MouseDown)) ) {
 |
 |            UpdateClock( );
 |            MouseInWindow = CheckMousePosition(CurrentWindow);
 |
15 |        }
 |
 |    }
```

First, the manager attempts to use logical simplification to help establish the conclusion by reasoning as follows. Since the Boolean variable **MouseDown** is set to *false* on line 7, and is not changed inside the while-loop on lines 9:15, the Boolean constant *false* can be substituted for it inside the while-loop. This implies that the while-condition

    (! MouseInWindow) | | (MouseInWindow && (! MouseDown))

simplifies to

    (! MouseInWindow) | | (MouseInWindow && (! false)).

By applying rules from Table A.13, this latter line simplifies first to

    (! MouseInWindow) | | (MouseInWindow && true).

and then to

    (! MouseInWindow) | | (MouseInWindow).

But the last line always has the value *true*, using the excluded middle law of Table A.14. Consequently, the while-loop on lines 9:15 has the form

```
while (true) {
     (statements inside while-loop)
}
```

When the manager shared this conclusion with the entry-level programmer, the programmer replied with the following argument. In the original while-condition:

    (! MouseInWindow) | | (MouseInWindow && (! MouseDown))

let the propositional variable **A** stand for **MouseInWindow** and let **B** stand for the logical subexpression (! **MouseDown**). With this substitution, the condition above becomes

    (! A) | | (A && B).

Now apply the first cancellation law from Table A.14, to conclude that the latter line is equivalent to

    (! A) | | B.

But if **B** always takes the value *true*, the last line is equivalent to

    (! A) | | true,

which is the same as (! A), by the laws of Table A.13. So the programmer asserts that the while-loop is really equivalent to:

```
while ( ! MouseInWindow) {
     (statements inside while-loop)
}
```

This latter while-loop does not get into an endless loop but rather terminates as soon as the mouse is moved into the window. The programmer complains that while, admittedly, the manager has helped simplify the original program (for which the programmer confesses gratitude), the original program nonetheless correctly updates the clock only when the mouse is outside the current window, or is moved outside the current window, which is what the programmer had intended.

Mystery: Who has correctly applied the laws of logic, and whose conclusion is the correct one? We leave this for the reader to solve in Exercise A.8.1.

Applications

The laws of logic given in Tables A.13 and A.14 are helpful in performing the manipulations needed to establish proofs of program correctness, as explained in Section 5.3 of Chapter 5.

They are also useful in designing algorithms starting from preconditions, postconditions, and loop invariants.

A.8 Review Questions

1. What expressions and subexpressions in a C program can be represented by propositional variables?
2. How can the laws in Tables A.13 and A.14 be used to help simplify logical expressions in a C program?

A.8 Exercises

1. Who has the correct solution to Problem 2, the manager or the programmer? Whose reasoning was incorrect, and why?
2. Simplify: $(x <= y)$ && $(! (y > x))$.
3. Simplify: $(((x{\to}top<=9)$ && $(x{\to}bottom !=2)) | | ((x{\to}top<=9)$ && $(x{\to}bottom == 2)))$.
4. In C, the logical operators && (and) and | | (or) do not always obey the commutative laws (given as the first two laws in Table A.14). In C, the expressions a && b and c | | d are evaluated according to "short circuit" rules in which the operands are evaluated in left-to-right order such that the evaluation terminates as soon as any operand is evaluated that determines the value of the expression. It is as if a && b were evaluated by evaluating the expression (a ? b : false), and c | | d were evaluated by evaluating the expression (c ? true : d). Under what conditions will the commutative laws a && b == b && a and c | | d == d | | c fail to hold when manipulating C programs? [*Hint*: Consider $(x == 0.0) | | (y/x > 15)$.]

Index

A

Abstract classes, 618
Abstract data types, 10, 19, 20, 23, 97
    for lists, 298
    for priority queues, 98
    for queues, 260
    for stacks, 260
    for strings, 313
    for tables, 453–454
    use by clients, 133
Abstract priority queue sorting, 534
Abstract sequences, 259
    linked representation, 261
    sequential representation, 261
    as structuring method, 259
Abstraction, 2, 8, 10, 18, 20, 93
    procedural, 132

Acceptance testing, 175–176, 203, 666
Access preservation, for nodes, 59
Activation records, 258, 276
Ada packages, 94, 610
Address calculation sorting, 551–565
Address range discrimination, 322
Addressable storage media, 24–25
Adjacency matrices, 412–414
    weighted, 423
Adjacency sets in graphs, 410–411
Adjacent vertices, 408–410
ADTs, 10, 19, 20, 23, 97, *see also*
    Abstract data types
  as data plus operations, 259
  for lists, 298
  for priority queues, 98
  for queues, 260

  for stacks, 260
  for strings, 313
  for tables, 453–454
Advanced recursion, 581
Advanced software engineering, 659
Affordability, 2, 12
Aho, Alfred V., 250, 607
Airport codes, 42
Algorithm analysis, 205, 225–247
    complexity classes, 252
    methods, 252
    precise analysis, 251
    transforming for ease of analysis, 250
    using abstraction in, 250
Algorithm performance, 206, 251
    yardstick for measuring, 206
Algorithms, of wrong complexity, 249

Aliases, 24, 30, 31
Aligning objects, 643
Allocating new nodes, 40–41, 116
Allocation failure, 30, 332
    in heaps, 327, 336
Allocation, static versus dynamic, 319
Almost balanced trees, 377
Analysis of algorithms, *see* Algorithm
    analysis
Analysis of binary searching, 241–245
Analyzing algorithms, *see* Algorithm
    analysis
Analyzing designs, 664
Ancestors in trees, 340
Annotated call trees, 69–70
Anonymous variables, 32
ANSI Standard C, 15
Appel, K., 442–443, 447
Arithmetic expression grammar, 583
Arithmetic progressions, 689–695
    last term, 691
    sum of, 690–691
Array searching, 16–17
Arrow notation, 37–38
    in pointer diagrams, 27
ARTS III, *see* Automated Radar
    Terminal System
Assertions, 138, 155
Atomic items, 305
Atomic value zone, 322
Automata, push-down, 256–257
Automated Radar Terminal System
    (ARTS III)
    case study, 679–680
Automatic storage reclamation, 321
Auxiliary functions, 73, 91
Avail, 115, 325
    available space list, 115
    pointer in heaps, 325
Available space lists, 115, 321
    creating, 115
AVL trees, 339, 376–388, 403
    balance factors, 383–384
    definition, 377–378
    as dynamic memory allocation index,
        388
    Fibonacci AVL trees, 385–387
    height, 377
    performance of, 384–387, 403

representation of List ADT, 387
representation of Table ADT,
    489–492
rotations, 378–382, 403
versus binary search trees, 401
worst case search, 387

B

B-trees, 391, 513–514
    branching factor, 391–392
    used for large files, 513–514
Baase, Sara, 251
Background on graphs, 439
Background on stacks, 256–259
Backtracking, 254
Balanced parentheses, 263–267
Base cases,
    of recursion, 66
    never called, 84
Base classes, 611, 615, 617–619
Benchmarks, 207
Bentley, Jon, 91
Berge, C., 447
Best solutions, 13
Best-fit policy, 326, 335
Binary search trees, 339, 365, 402
    AVL trees, 376–388
    external nodes, 368–369
    external path length, 368–369,
        529–530
    insertion in, 366
    internal path length, 367
    performance, 366–374, 403
    to achieve performance, 400–401
    when to use AVL trees, 401
Binary search tree property, 365
Binary search tree search
    average case, 366, 371–373
    best case, 366, 369–370
    comparison of methods, 373–374
    tables of results, 374
    worst case, 366, 370–371
Binary searching, 180–184, 217
    analysis of, 241–245
    comparisons used in, 243
    recurrence relations for, 244
    recursive versus iterative, 180–184
    running time, 217–218

Binary tree traversals
    InOrder, 360–361, 402
    LevelOrder, 363–364, 402
    PostOrder, 360–361, 402
    PreOrder, 360–361, 402
    using linked representations,
        361–364
    using queues, 363–364
    using stacks, 363–364
Binary trees, 338, 342–344, 359, 402
    binary search trees, 365
    complete, 343, 402
    contiguous sequential representation,
        344
    definition of, 342
    expression trees, 359
    extended, 342, 368–369
    external path length, 368–369,
        529–530
    full binary tree, 341, 402
    height, 377, 402–403
    Huffman coding trees, 394–399
    level order, 344
    linked, 56
    non-recursive traversals, 363–364
    sequential representation, 344–346
    traversals, 338–339, 359–364, 402
Binding times, 622
Birthday Paradox, 462
Block allocation, in heaps, 323
Boehm, Barry W., 186–189, 202, 670,
    681, 686
Bonar, J., 202
Bottom-up programming, 143, 186, 204
Bottom-up testing, 173–174
    order defined, 174
Boundary cases, 174
    caution for, 58
Boundary conditions,
    precautions, 294
Branches, of trees, 56
Branching factors, 699
    in B-trees, 391–392
    in trees, 699
Breadth-first order, 418
Breadth-first searching, 418, 448
Brooks, Frederick P., 659, 672–673, 686
Brooks' law, 659, 672–673
    and COCOMO equations, 673

BubbleSort, 527, 569–571, 579
  prohibition on use, 576
Buffers, 289
  implemented by queues, 290–291
Building recursive descent parsers,
  586–595

C

C modules, 94–95, 610
  compilation dependencies, 122
  header files for, 94
  how to use, 96
  implementation file, 94
  independent compilation of, 122
  interface, 94–95
  structure of, 95
  template for, 95
C program format, 15–17
C program style, 17
C programming language, 15
  ANSI Standard C, 15
C Strings, 335, 297, 314
C++ programming language, 16, 19,
  611, 657
  Symantec C++™, 656
Calculator, 107–108
  interface, 107
  interface file, 109
  program shell, 108
Call frames, 276–280
Call traces, 70–71, 91
Call trees, 69, 91
  annotated, 69–70
Catching errors early, 664
CD-ROM, 24
Cdr-direction linearization, 312
Ceilings, 701–704
  definition of, 702
Celsius temperatures, 213
Chaining, 452, 494
Challenging mathematics(**), 15
Changing object features, 643
Chayne, Daisee, 305
Children in trees, 340
Choosing hash functions, 486–489
Choosing wrong data representations
  for graphs, 446
Circular definitions, 63
Circular linked lists, 303, 325

Circular queues, 281–282, 294
  modular arithmetic in, 281–282, 294
Class browsers, 652–654, 657–658
Class debuggers, 657
Class libraries, 657
Classes of objects, 611, 618
Clicking a mouse, 640–641
Clients and servers, 133, 254
Cliques in graphs, 444
Clusters in linear probing, 467, 495
Coalescing in heaps, 327
Cocktail shaker sort, 572
COCOMO model, 186, 670–675, 685,
  687
  software productivity ranges, 671
  software tools rating sheet, 671
  development time equation, 672
  effort estimate, 672
  rating scales, 671
  see also Constructive cost model
Code and fix model, 675–676, 687
Coding, 20
Coding and debugging, 664, 686
Collections of data, external, 497
Collision resolution policy, 452,
  456–457, 462, 494
  separate chaining, 460
Collisions, 452, 456, 494
  definition, 462
Combinations, 74
Comments in C programs, 17
  color of, 17
  goal comments, 17
Compact disk, 24
Compacting in heaps, 328, 336
Comparing list representations,
  301–302
Comparison trees, 527–529
Comparison-based methods for sorting,
  531
Competitive advantage, 188–189
Compilation dependencies,
  among modules, 122, 124
Complete binary trees, 343, 402
  sequential representation, 344–346
Complete graphs, 444
Complexity classes, 210, 214, 251
  different running times for, 215
  exponential, 90

intuition for, 251
Computer science, 3–6, 205
  enduring principles in, 6–8
  precise laws of, 205
Computer sizing estimates, 664
Computing the proxmap, 554
Concatenation, 76–77
Concurrent tasks, 290
Congruences, 712–713
  definition of, 712
  laws for, 712–713
Connected components, 406, 408–410,
  447
Constant running time, 214, 219
Constants, 191
  naming of, 191
Constructive Cost Model, *see* COCOMO
  model
Consumer debt rate, 649
Context-free grammars, 5, 257,
  582–585, 608
  condensed form, 588–589
  formal definition, 584–585
  non-terminal symbols, 584–585
  productions, 583–585
  start symbol, 584–585
  terminal symbols, 584–585
Context-free language, 585, 608
Control panel design, 647–650
Converting bases of logarithms, 708
Correctness, 12
Correctness proofs, 20, 138, 203
Cost drivers, 187
Cost-benefit analysis, 674
Covering retrievals, 519
Creating an available space list, 115
Creating object instances, 621
Critical path, 429, 437, 448
  definition of, 429
Critical path algorithms, 431–438
Critical path problems, 428, 448
Cubic running time, 214, 219
Curve fitting, 209
Customization, 611
Cycles in graphs, 408–410

D

DAG, *see* Directed acyclic graph
Dahl, O. J., 202

Danger zone for schedule compression, 673, 685
Dangling pointers, 24, 30, 31, 57
Data abstraction, 18, 23, 93
   and generalized lists, 127
   levels of, 23
Data collections, large external, 497, 522
Data representations, 134
   of graphs, 407, 412–414, 447
   hiding, 111, 126
   layers of, 133
   linked, 18, 22–23
   for linked lists, 299–304, 334
   of lists, 297–304
   postponing choice of, 142, 144, 333
   of priority queues, 101–106, 346–359
   sequential binary trees, 344–346
   sequential lists, 298–299, 334
   of strings, 314–319, 335
   substitutability, 126
   of Table ADTs, 489–492
Data structures, 9, 253
   intermediate level, 9
   linear, 253
   queues, 253
   stacks, 253
Data types, for linked lists, 42
Databases, 517–523
   definition of, 519–520
Database systems, definition of, 519–520
Date, C. J., 521
Deallocation, failing to deallocate, 57
Defining derived classes, 618
Definitions
   of binary trees, 342
   of ceilings, 702
   of collisions, 462
   of congruences, 712
   of context-free grammars, 584–585
   of critical paths, 429
   of derived classes, 618
   of floors, 702
   of garbage, 31
   of graphs, 409
   of heaps, 320–321, 346
   of load factor, 465
   of *mod* operator, 712
   of O-notation, 221
   of pointers, 27

of priority queues, 98
Deleting last list node, 46
   program for, 49
   strategy for, 47
Delivered source instructions, 667
DeMorgan's laws, 162
Depth-first order, 417
Depth-first searching, 417, 448
Dereferencing, 27–32
   the null pointer, 57
   pointers, 32
Deriving object classes, 611, 618
Descendants in trees, 340
Describing things recursively, 582–583, 608
Designs, 4, 20, 663, 686
   analysis of, 664
   definition of, 663
   walkthroughs, 664
Deterministic shift-reduce parsers, 591, 608
Development time for software, 672
Diagramming notation, for pointers, 35
Digraph, 408–409
Dijsktra, Edsger, W., 202, 426
Dijkstra's shortest path algorithm, 426, 448
Diminishing increment sort, *see* **ShellSort**
Direct-access file organization, 521
Directed acyclic graph (DAG), 420
Directed graph, 408–409
Directly recursive procedures, 582, 607
Directories on a disk, 25–26
Discovery, 6
Discrimination nets, 403
   represented by tries, 392–393, 403
Disk, 501–504, 522
   average random access time, 503
   cylinders, 502–503
   directories, 25–26
   exchangeable disk packs, 502
   files, 25–26
   floppy disks, 501
   latency time, 498, 502, 522
   movable-head disks, 502
   random access costs, 504
   removable-disk packs, 502
   sectors, 501, 503

   seek time, 498, 502, 522
   seek time formula, 503
   transmission time, 498, 502, 522
   Winchester disks, 501–504, 522
Disposing of unused storage, 30–31
   for a node, 117
   function for recycling used storage, 30–31
Dissolution of universe, 86
Divide and conquer, 80, 525, 540–547
Documentation, 12, 20, 190–199, 204
   cost avoidance, 666
   for multiple audiences, 197
   and program comments, 198
   and program strategies, 201
   for test plans, 178
   undocumented code, 665
   use of program strategies in, 201
Dodd, M., 515–516, 522
Double dereferencing, 330
   of handles, 330
Double hashing, 452, 458, 466, 470, 474–476, 494–495
   clusters in, 467–468
   efficiency of, 479
   separate probe sequences, 475
Dragging a mouse, 640–641
Drawing
   applications in OOP, 639–646
   filled shapes, 624–627
   shapes, 613–639, 656
   shape lists, 627–638
   tools palette, 640
Drawing window, 623
Dynamic allocation, 319, 335
Dynamic binding, 613, 622
Dynamic memory allocation, 28, 31, 297, 319–332
   allocation failure, 336
   techniques, 297, 333–334
   hidden expense, 400
   using AVL tree index, 388
Dynamic storage, 32
   lifetime of, 41
Dynamic trees, 337

E

Earliest finishing time, 433
Earliest start time, 433

Early error detection, 664
Ease of extension, 627, 638, 657
    in OOP, 627, 638
Ease of modification, 132, 657
    of programs, 134
    of software systems, 135
Economic model, 646–650
    connecting components, 648–649
    running the model, 649–650
    user interface, 646–650
Economist, Jeannie G., 646–650
Edges in graphs, 408–409
Efficiency, 2, 11–12, 20, 297
    versus generality, 127, 311, 651
    measurement and tuning, 200
Elimination methods
    eliminating recursion, 166–172
    eliminating left recursion, 588
    eliminating tail recursion, 168–169,
        203
Empty entries in tables, 453
Empty key in hashing, 469
Empty tree, 341, 403
    precautions concerning, 399
Encapsulation, 126, 133
End of list marker, 58
    using NULL for, 58
Enduring principles, 6
Engineering, 3, 20
Ensuring complete table search,
        in hashing, 476–478, 495
Erlich, K., 202
Estimating development time, 672
Estimating software project costs, 187
Evaluating expressions, 254
    evaluating postfix expressions,
        267–270
    using stacks for, 294
Even, Shimon, 447
Event-driven programs, 109
Evolutionary development model, 681,
        687–688
Execution time profiles, 180
Exhaustive probe sequences, 476–478,
        495
Experiments, 5
Explicit deallocation, 321
Exponential complexity class, 90, 214
Exponential running time, 90

Exponentials, 704–705
    manipulation laws, 705
Exporting and importing declarations,
        133
Expression evaluation, 254, 294,
        267–270
Expression trees, 359
Extended binary trees, 342, 368–369
extern declaration, 96
External collections of data, 497
External nodes, 368–369
External path length, 368–369,
        529–530
External storage devices, 499–504

F

Factorial of n, 71, 529
    iterative, 72
    recursive, 72
    Stirling's approximation for, 530
    uses for, 74
Fahrenheit temperatures, 213
Faulty initialization, 332
Federal Reserve Board, 647
Feller, William, 295
Fibonacci AVL trees, 385–387
Fields of nodes, 35
FIFO (first-in, first-out), 258
File inversion techniques, 517–518, 523
File organization, direct access, 521
Files
    full inversion, 518, 523
    on a disk, 25–26
First-come first-served order, 291
First-fit policy, 325, 335
Fitting curves, 209
Floors and ceilings, 701–704
    definition of, 702
    manipulation laws, 702–703
Floppy disks, 501
Flow graphs, 406
Flow networks, 441–442
    max-flow, min-cut algorithm, 442
Forgetting to recycle used memory, 57
Formal definition of O-notation, 221
Formal logic, 161–166
Formatted debugging aids, 174–175,
        200, 654
Formulation and discovery, 6

Four color problem, 442
    Appel and Haken's proof, 442–443
Fragmentation in heaps, 327
free function, 30–31
    for recycling used storage, 30–31
Free trees, 409, 447
Freeing a node, 30–31, 117
Frequency counts, 394
Full binary tree, 341, 402
Fully inverted files, 518, 523

G

Gaining competitive advantage, 188
Game trees, 338
Garbage collection, 31, 311, 321–323,
        335–336
    gathering phase, 322–323
    incremental, 330–331, 336
    initialization phase, 322–323
    by marking and gathering, 321–323
    marking phase, 322–323
Garbage, 31
    defined, 31
    inaccessible storage, 24, 31
Generality versus efficiency, 127, 311,
        651
Generalized lists, 296–297, 305,
        334–335
    for algebraic expressions, 309–310
    applications of, 308–312
    and data abstraction, 127
    nodes, 306
    printing, 306–307
    shared sublists, 306
    supporting flexible data structures,
        309
Generalized traversal function,
        361–362
Generating sentences, 583–585
Geometric progressions, 695–700
    sums of, 696–698
    use of, 234, 239
Global variables, 147
Goal comments, 17
Golden ratio, 386–387
Grammar for arithmetic expressions,
        583
Graph representations, 407, 412–414,
        447

Graph searching, 415, 448
  breadth-first, 418, 448
  depth-first, 417, 448
  generalized, 418
  using queues, 418
  using stacks, 415–417
Graphical user interfaces, 657
Graphs, 405
  adjacency matrices, 412–414
  adjacency sets, 410–411
  adjacent vertices, 408–410
  background, 439
  basic anatomy, 447
  cliques, 444
  colorability, 442
  complete, 444
  connected components, 408–410,
    447
  connected vertices, 410
  critical path algorithms, 431–438
  critical path problems, 428, 448
  cycles in, 408–410
  digraph, 408–409
  directed acyclic graph (DAG), 420
  directed graph, 408–409
  edges in, 408–409
  edge origin, 409
  edge terminus, 409
  flows in, 406
  formal definition, 409
  free trees, 409, 447
  Hamiltonian circuits, 444
  linked adjacency lists, 413
  maximal connected component, 410
  paths, 408–410
  path length, 408–409
  planar, 442
  problems and known solutions,
    446–447
  searching in, 407, 448
  set representation, 413
  shortest paths, 423–428, 448
  shortest path algorithms, 407
  simple cycles, 408–410
  strongly connected, 410
  task networks, 407, 428, 448
  terminology, 408–411
  topological order, 407, 419, 448
  undirected, 408–409

  utility of, 405–406
  vertex covers, 444
  vertices, 408–409
  weakly connected, 410
  weighted, 423, 448
  wrong representations for, 446
Greedy algorithms, 440–441
Grouping objects, 642
Growth and combining laws, 23

H

Haken, W., 442–443, 447
Hamiltonian circuits, 444
Handles, 297, 328–330, 336
  double dereferencing of, 330
Handling error conditions, 644
Hard disks, *see* Winchester disks
Hardware changes, 7
Harmonic numbers, 546, 723
Hash address, 456
Hash functions, 452, 456, 496
  choosing, 486–489
  division method, 487–488
  folding, 488
  middle squaring, 488
  poor choice of, 492
  truncation, 488
Hashing, 451
  basic idea, 494
  buckets, 452, 494
  chaining, 452, 494
  checking performance of, 493
  choosing hash functions, 486–489
  clusters, 467, 495
  collisions, 452, 456, 462, 494
  collision resolution policies, 452,
    456–457, 462, 494
  comparing performance, 482–483,
    495
  double hashing, 452, 458, 466, 470,
    474–476, 494–495
  double hashing clusters, 468
  empty key, 469
  ensuring complete table search,
    476–478, 495
  exhaustive probe sequences,
    476–478, 495
  full table, 466
  hash address, 456

  hash functions, 452, 456, 496
  linear probing, 457, 470, 494–495
  load factor, 465, 495
  open addressing, 452, 458, 469–486,
    494–495
  perfect hash functions, 488–489
  performance comparisons, 482–483
  performance formulas, 478–482
  performance of double hashing, 479
  performance of linear probing, 479
  performance of separate chaining,
    479
  primary clustering, 466, 470–474,
    495
  probe sequence, 457
  quadratic probing, 484
  running time, 218
  tables of performance results,
    482–483
  triangle number hashing, 484–486
  with buckets, 460, 514–516
  with wrong probe decrements, 492
Header files in C modules, 94, 96
Header nodes, 304
Heapifying in linear time, 356–357
Heaps, 320–321, 323–332, 335, 338,
    346
  allocation failure in, 327
  best-fit policy, 325, 335
  block allocation in, 323
  coalescing, 327, 336
  compacting, 328, 336
  cost of heapifying, 356–357
  definition of, 320–321, 346
  for dynamic memory allocation,
    320–321, 335
  in dynamic memory allocation,
    323–332
  equilibrium in, 327
  first-fit policy, 325, 335
  fragmentation, 327, 336
  mathematical facts about, 355–358
  for priority queues, 402
  reheapifying, 350
  representation for priority queues, 338
  roving pointers, 327
  second meaning of, 346
  system heaps, 330
  to represent priority queues, 401

use of handles in, 328–330
use of two-way linked lists in, 325
user application heaps, 330
worst case deletion times, 356
worst case insertion times, 356
HeapSort, 352, 525–526, 537–539, 577–578
when to use, 573
Height of binary tree, 377, 402–403
Hiding data representations, 111, 134
Hiding representation-dependent notation, 113
Hierarchies, 2, 653
class inheritance hierarchies, 653
High-priority run queue, 286
Highlighting, 640–641
HitCounts in **ProxmapSort**, 553–554
Hoare, C. A. R., 202
Hopcroft, John E., 250, 607
Horowitz, E., 493
Huffman codes, 339, 394–399
coding trees, 394–399, 404
weighted path length, 398
Hypermedia systems, for documentation, 197–198

I

I/O buffers in operating systems, 290–291
I/O wait queue, 286
Imaginary line printer listings, 16, 21
Implementing file subsystems, 643–646
Implementing printing subsystems, 643–646
Implementing railroad diagrams, 593–594
Implementing recursion, 581
Implicit pointer variable notation, 36
Inaccessible storage, 24, 30
see also Garbage
include directive, 96
Incomplete assertions, 161
Inconsistent requirements, 662
Incremental garbage collection, 330–331, 336
Independent compilation of modules, 122
Index of Leading Economic Indicators, 650

Index Sequential Access Method (ISAM), 499, 509–513
cylinder surface index, 509–510
deletions, 513
file maintenance, 513
handling overflows, 512–513
master index, 510
overflow areas, 509–511
overflow tracks, 511
primary area, 509
prime cylinders, 510
prime tracks, 511
top-level index, 509
track index, 509–511
Indispensable programmers, 665
Induction proofs, 157–158
Infinite regresses, 63, 83, 90
Infix expressions, 267
Infix to postfix translator, program for, 597–599
results, 599
Infix, translating to postfix, 596–600, 609
Information hiding, 2, 10, 18, 20, 93, 132
in program design, 131
Information retrieval, 517–519, 523
covering retrievals, 519
multiattribute retrievals, 519
quantified queries, 519
query language, 519, 523
query types, 519
range queries, 519
similarity retrievals, 519
Inheritance, 19, 625, 656
from all ancestors, 625
from grandparents, 625
Inserting new last list node, 48
program for, 50
Insertions, 366, 389–390
in binary search trees, 366
in 2-3 trees, 389–390
InsertionSort, 527, 548–551, 578
Instance variables, 612, 615, 656
Integer ranges, 16
number of integers in, 693
Integration testing, 175, 203
Interfaces, 2, 20, 93–94
exporting and importing declarations, 133

for queues, 261–262
for stacks, 261–262
Intermediate expression swell, 309
Intermediate-level data structures, 9
Internal and external path length relationship, 369
Internal nodes in trees, 340
Internal path length, 367
Interpolation search, 491–492
Interpretation of postfix, 267–270
Intuition, 13, 24
behind O-notation, 13
for pointers, 24
Inverted files, 517–518
IPL IV programming language, 308
ISAM, *see* Index Sequential Access Method

K

Kernighan, Brian W., 60
Keys
comparisons in binary searching, 243
search keys, 338
with subscripts, 455
Kilo-delivered source instructions, 187
Knuth, Donald E., 60, 401, 493, 514–515, 522, 577

L

Language generated by a grammar, 585
Large data collections, 497, 522
using appropriate techniques, 521
Large external files, 507–509
sorting, 507–509
wrong techniques for, 521
Large scale programming, 659
Latency time, 498, 502, 522
Latest finishing time, 435–436
Latest start time, 435
Layers, 2, 9, 10
of data representations, 9, 133
of programs, 173
Leaves in trees, 56, 340
Leftmost parses, 586, 597
Level order, 344, 363–364, 402
in binary trees, 344
Levels in trees, 340
Levels of data abstraction, 23
Lexemes, 587

Lexical analysis, 587
Lifecycle, 12
Lifetime of dynamic storage, 41
LIFO (last-in, first-out), 258
   see also Stacks
Line numbers, 16–17, 21
Line starts, 317–318, 355
Linear data structures, 253
Linear linked lists, 24, 38
Linear probing, 457, 470, 494–495
   clusters, 467, 495
   efficiency, 479
Linear running time, 214, 219
Linked binary tree, 56
Linked data representations, 18, 22
Linked file directories, 25–26
Linked list node operations, 112
Linked list representations, 299–304,
   334
Linked lists, 24, 38, 42, 55, 118–121,
   304
   array-of-node-structs representation,
     118–119
   data types for, 42
   linear, 24
   parallel array representation,
     120–121
   symmetric, 55
   two-way, 55
   with header nodes, 304
Linked representations, 273–274,
   284–286
   of queues, 284–286
   of stacks, 273–274
Linking, 24–27
   in directories, 25–26
   of storage, 24
Links, 24, 35
Lippman, Stanley B., 656
LISP programming language,
   308–312
List ADT, 298
   AVL tree representation, 387
List representations, 297–304
   linked, 299–304
   sequential, 298–299
List reversal, 75–78
   iterative version, 75
   recursive version, 75–78

List searching, 43
   program for, 45
   strategy for, 43–44
List structures, *see* generalized lists
Lists, 296
   circular linked lists, 303
   comparing representations, 301–302
   concatenation, 76–77
   deleting last node of, 46
   generalized, 296–297
   linear linked, 38
   linked lists with header nodes, 304
   linked representations, 334
   printing, 48, 51
   reversal, 75
   searching for items in, 43
   sequential representations, 334
   of shapes, 628–638
   two-way linked lists, 303
   of windows, 25–26
Load factor, 465, 495
   definition of, 465
Local variables, 41
Logarithmic complexity class, 214
Logarithms and exponentials, 704–710
Logarithms, 705–710
   base conversion, 708
   ignoring bases of, 223
   inequalities, 709–710
   of products, 706
Logic, 161–166, 727–731
   eliminating *true* and *false*, 728
   formal, 161–166
   manipulation laws for, 163–164, 728
   predicate, 161–166
   propositional, 161
   quantifiers, 161–166
   symbols for, 163
Logical text files, 316–319
Loop invariants, 138, 157
Low-priority run queue, 286
Lueker, George S., 240, 251, 480
Lum, V. Y., 515–516, 522

M

Machine organization principles, 7
Maintenance, 12, 20, 665–666, 686
   costs, 666
   undocumented code problem, 665

malloc, memory allocation function, 28
Management disciplines, 661
Manipulation laws for logic, 163–164,
   727–731
MapKey function, 552, 558–562
Market share, 189
Marking bits, 322–323
Marking end of list, 58
Master pointers, *see* Handles
Math reference and tutorial, 689–731
Mathematical induction, 601–602
   alternative principle, 601–602
   ordinary principle, 601
Mathematics, 3, 13, 20, 205
   for practical programmers, 13
Maximal flow problem, 406
McCarthy, John, 334
Measurement and tuning, 64, 139,
   179–186, 203
   philosophy of, 179, 203
Merge sorting
   in external files, 508–509
MergeSort, 207, 526, 540, 578
   analysis of, 236–239
   running time, 239–240
Merging two lists, 237
Messages, 612, 617, 656–657
   sent to call methods, 612, 617,
     656–657
Methods, 612, 617, 656
   virtual, 618
Milestone charts, 428, 430
Minimal spanning trees, 439–440
Mod operator, 712
   definition of, 712
Modular arithmetic, 710–713
   congruence laws, 712–713
   definition of *mod* operator, 712
   use of, 477–478
Modular program designs, 131, 294
   ADTs for clean design, 294
Modularity, 18, 93
Module, 10, 93–95, 133, 610
   in C, 94–95
   private part, 94
Modulo, *see* Congruence
Modus tollendo ponens,
   law of logic, 164–165
Molodowitch, Mariko, 480

Mouse, 640
  clicking, 640–641
  dragging, 640–641
  dragging anchor point, 641
  dragging release point, 641
Multiattribute retrievals, 519
Mutually recursive procedures, 582,
    594, 607

N

n log n barrier for sorting, 524–525,
    531, 577
Naming constants, 191
National Airspace System (NAS) Stage
    A, case study, 679
Natural control structures, 195
  in programming languages, 195
Nested structures, 254
New nodes, 28, 40–41
  allocation of, 40–41
  storage allocation function, malloc,
    28
Nievergelt, J., 401
Node operations, 112
  on linked lists, 112
Nodes, 35, 42, 390
  fields of, 35, 42
  link fields of, 35
  overflows in 2-3 trees, 390
  structs, 42
  types, 42
Non-deterministic computers, 443
Non-recursive traversals, 363–364
  using queues, 363–364
  using stacks, 363
Notation
  arrows in pointer diagrams, 27
  for C programs, 15–17
  for dereferencing, 32
  for integer ranges, 16
  hiding representation-dependent
      notation, 113
  for pointer following, 32
  for pointer types, 32, 42
  for pointer variables, 36
  for pointers, 27, 32
  for unknown pointer values, 36
  for unknown values, 36
  O-notation, 13

pointer diagramming notation, 35
  representation-independent,
      111–112, 134
  two-star (**), 15
NP-complete problems, 443–445, 449
NULL, 35–36, 38, 43, 58
  to mark end of list, 58
Null pointer
  value of, 35–36, 38, 43
  dereferencing, 57

O

O(1) running time, 218
  for hashing, 218
  see also, Constant running time
O(n log n) complexity class, 214
O-notation, 13, 19, 206, 211, 220–225
    251–252
  definition of, 221
  dominant terms, 211, 233
  ignoring constants in, 211
  ignoring lesser terms, 222–223
  intuition behind, 213–219
  manipulation of, 222–225, 252
  proof of, 221–222
  shortcuts for, 222–225
  what it doesn't tell you, 247, 250,
      252
  when it is invalid, 247–248, 250,
      252
Object class definitions, 615
  private section, 615
  protected section, 615, 618
  public section, 615
Objects, 610–612, 656
  aligning, 643
  changing features, 643
  classes, 611
  class browsers, 652–655, 657–658
  class definitions, 611, 653–654
  class inheritance hierarchies, 653
  class libraries, 657
  debuggers, 657
  front-to-back ordering, 643
  grouping, 642
  making connections, 648–649
  methods, 612, 617, 656
  pointers, 611, 656
  references, 611, 656

Object-oriented programming, 16, 19,
    610
  abstract classes, 618
  advantages and disadvantages,
      651–654
  base classes, 611, 656
  class derivation, 611–612, 618, 656
  class inheritance hierarchies, 653
  creating drawing applications in,
      639–646
  creating object instances, 621
  customization, 611
  debuggers, 655
  developing user interfaces, 646–650,
      657
  drawing shapes, 613–639
  dynamic binding, 613
  ease of extension, 627, 638, 657
  ease of modification, 655, 657
  formatted debugging aids, 654
  implementing file subsystems,
      643–646
  implementing printing subsystems,
      643–646
  inheritance, 611–612, 625, 656
  instance variables, 612
  messages, 612, 617, 656–657
  methods, 612, 615, 656–657
  moving shape lists, 627–638
  objects, 611–612, 656
  prototyping user interfaces, 655
  run-time penalties, 651–652
  software component libraries, 655,
      657
  this, 630
  used to build systems, 639–646
OOP, *see* Object-oriented program-
    ming
Open addressing, 452, 458, 494–495
  in hashing, 469–486, 494–495
Operating systems, 286–287, 289–291
  time-shared, 286
Operations on linked-list nodes, 112
Operator precedence, 360
Optimizing programs, 139, 166, 203
Order for bottom-up testing, 174
Ordered pair zone, 322
Organizing a software project, 135
Origin of edges, 409

Overflows, 332
  in sequential list representations, 299
  in 2-3 tree nodes, 390
Overriding, 19

P

Packages, 133
  in Ada, 94
  of services, 127
Parents in trees, 340
Parnas, David L., 135
Parse trees, 586–587
Parsers
  deterministic lookahead(1), 591, 608
  implementing railroad diagrams,
      593–594
  lookahead in, 589
  reducing in, 589–594, 608
  shift-reduce, 589, 591
  shifting in, 589–594, 608
Parsing, 5, 254, 586
Partition algorithm
  finding k^{th} smallest number, 605–606
  in QuickSort, 541–543
Pascal strings, 297, 314–316, 335
Pascal units, 610
Paths in graphs, 408–410
  path length, 408–409
PDA, see Push-down automata
PDL, see Program design language
Perfect hash function, 488–489
Performance of hashing, 478–482
Permutations, 74, 529, 606
PERT charts, 428–429, 438
Physical text files, 316–319
Pivot in QuickSort, 541
Planar graphs, 442
Pocket calculator, 107
  project, 582
Pointer diagrams, 35, 58
  diagramming notation, 35
  during design, 58
Pointers, 22, 25, 27, 28
  dangling, 24, 31
  definition of, 27
  dereferencing, 29, 32
  diagramming notation, 35
  following, 32
  to integers, 28–29

to objects, 611, 656
intuition for, 24
notation for, 27, 32
null pointer, 38
to pointers, see Handles
types, 32, 42
unknown values for, 36–37
variable notation, 36
Pointing device, see Mouse
Polyphase merge sorting, 508–509
Popping stacks, 256, 295
Postconditions, 138, 155, 203, 603
Postfix expressions, 267
Postfix expression evaluation, 267–270
  using stacks, 267–270
Postfix, 339, 596–600, 609
  interpreter for, 339
  translating infix into, 596–600, 609
PostOrder traversal, 339
Postponed obligations, 363–364
Postponing choice of representations,
      142, 144, 333
  for tables, 493
Precise laws in computer science, 205
Preconditions, 138, 155, 203, 603
Predicate logic, 161–166
Preserving access to nodes, 59
Pretty printer, 17
Prim's algorithm, 440
Primary clustering, 466, 495
  examples, 470–474
Principle of top talent, 670
Principles of software engineering, 11
Print buffers, 289, 290
Printer spoolers, 290
Printing a list, 48, 51
Priority Queue ADT, 98, 101–106,
      346–359
  heap representation of, 346–355
Priority queue sorting, 99, 525,
      532–539, 577
  abstract, 534
Priority queues, 97, 338
  ADT for, 98
  comparing representations, 357–358
  defined, 98
  heap representation, 338, 346–355,
      401–402
  implementations, 101–107

interface, 98
represented as heaps, 401–402
sorted linked-list representation,
    101–104
unsorted array representation,
    104–106
used for sorting, 99, 525, 532–539,
    577
Probe sequence, 457, 475
Procedural abstraction, 132
Processing nested structures, 294
  using stacks, 294
Productions, 583–585
  in grammars, 583–585
  recursion in, 585
Productivity
  COCOMO productivity ranges, 671
  improvement method, 673–674
Profiler, 180
  for execution time measurement, 180
Profiles, 180
  execution time profiles, 180
Program
  comments in, 198
  complexity, 134
  correctness proofs, 138, 155, 203
  documentation, 204
  efficiency by measurement and tun-
      ing, 201
  format, 17
  global variables, 147
  layers, 173
  modularity, 147
  optimization, 139, 166, 203
  shell for calculator, 108
  shell for tic-tac-toe, 110
  specifications, 138
  strategies, 39, 202
  strategies, role in documentation,
      201
  strategies, used as PDL, 663
  structure, ease of modification, 132
  structuring, 190
  style, 17
  testing, 161, 172–179
  transformation, 139, 166–167, 203
  verification, 20, 155, 161, 203
Program design, 131
  information hiding in, 131

modularity in, 131
languages, 663
Program design language (PDL), 663
Program strategies, 39, 202
  defined, 39
  divide and conquer, 80
  role in documentation, 201
  used as PDL, 663
Program transformations, 139, 166–169, 203
  eliminating tail recursion, 168–169
Program verification, 20, 155, 203
  flaw in method of, 161
  use of recursion in, 601–605
Programming
  bottom-up, 143, 186
  large scale, 137, 202
  natural control structures, 195
  notation, 15–17
  object-oriented, *see* Object-oriented programming
  proverbs for, 190
  small scale, 137, 202
  by software reuse, 186, 188–189
  by stepwise refinement, 11, 19–20, 39, 138–155, 202
  structured, 190, 204
  style disciplines, 196, 201
  top-down, 11, 19, 39, 138–155, 202
  with reusable components, 186, 188–189
Programming-in-the-large, 11, 137, 202, 659
Programming-in-the-small, 11, 137, 202
Project Evaluation and Review Technique, *see* PERT charts
Project finishing time, 432–435
Project management software, 438
Project starting time, 432
Proofs of correctness, 20, 155, 203, 603
  postconditions, 138, 155, 203, 603
  preconditions, 138, 155, 203, 603
Propositional logic, 161
Prototyping, 12, 20, 655, 680–681
  user interfaces in OOP, 655
Proverbs for programming, 190
Proving things recursively, 582–583, 608
Proximity map, *see* Proxmap

Proxmap, 552–563
ProxmapSort, 527, 552–563, 577, 579
  computing the proxmap, 554
  HitCounts, 553–555
  MapKey function, 552, 558–562
  MapKey scale factor, 561–562
  performance of, 563, 572–575
  program for, 559–560
  proximity map, 552–563
  when to use, 573–574
Push-down automata, 256–257
Push-down stacks, 581
  see also Stacks
Pushing stacks, 256, 295

Q

Quadratic functions, 210
Quadratic running time, 214
Quantified queries, 519
Quantifiers, 161–166
Queries in information retrieval, 518, 523
Query languages, 519, 523
Query types, 519
Queue ADT, 260, 280–288
  circular track representation, 281–282, 294
  definition of, 260
  implementations of, 280–288
  linked representation, 284–286
  representations of, 280–288
  sequential representation, 281–283
Queues, 253, 259, 295–296
  ADT for, 260
  of clients, 291
  comparing sequential and linked, 286–287
  FIFO, 258
  interface for, 261–262
  in modeling, 254
  in operating systems, 254, 286–291
  for regulating O/S tasks, 294
  in simulation, 254, 291–293
  for synchronization, 294
  used in time-shared operating systems, 286–287, 289–291
  uses for, 295
Queuing theory, 293
QuickSort, 217, 220, 525, 540–547, 577–578

best case running time, 217
worst case running time, 217

R

RadixSort, 527, 563–565, 577, 579
Railroad diagrams, 588–589
Rainfall in New Haven, 193–195
Range queries, 519, 523
Ranges, integer, 16, 693
Rapid response to trivial requests, 286–287
Readers' and writers' problem, 290
Real-time applications, 330–331
Recognizing a sentence, 586
Recognizing things recursively, 582–583, 608
Rectangles, 614
Recurrence relations, 14, 89, 206, 225, 231, 233–246, 724–727
  base cases, 231
  for binary search tree search, 372–373
  for binary searching, 244
  for Fibonacci AVL trees, 386
  solution by unrolling and summing, 231–236
  solution tables, 236, 241, 727
  solving with summing factors, 725–726
  telescoping sums, 725
  for von Mises probability, 463
Recursion, 18
  advanced, 581
  base case, 66
  combining half-solutions, 67–68
  describing things, 582–583, 608
  direct recursion, 585, 607
  direct versus indirect, 585
  eliminating tail recursion, 168–169, 203
  elimination, 166–172
  for generating expressions, 583–585
  going-down recursion, 67
  going-up recursion, 67
  in grammar productions, 585
  indirect recursion, 585, 607
  mutual recursion, 585, 594, 607
  in C, implemented using stacks, 581
  and program verification, 601–605

proving things, 582–583, 608
recognizing things, 582–583, 608
recursion induction, 160, 582–583,
    603–604, 608–609
recursive descent parser, 586–595
stacks + iteration = recursion, 581
tail-recursion elimination, 168–169,
    203
used for generating languages, 582
used for parsing, 582, 594
used for recognition, 582
Recursion induction, 160, 582–583,
    603–604, 608–609
    base case, 604
    careless use of, 606–607
    induction step, 604
Recursive calls, 65
    traces of, 69
Recursive descent parser, 586–595,
    608
    how to design, 607
    output of, 594
Recursive procedure calls, using stacks
    to implement, 275–280
Recycling storage, 30–31, 57
Reference counts, 330–331, 336
Referents, 27
Regression testing, 175–176, 203
Regulating tasks in operating systems,
    294
    using queues, 294
Reheapifying a heap, 350
Reliability, 2, 12
Repair and upgrade, 666
Representation, 2, 9, 18, 20
    layers, 9
    linked data, 18
Representation-dependent notation,
    113
    hiding, 113
Representation-independent notation,
    111–112, 134
Representations
    of graphs, 407, 412–414, 447
    linked, 22–23
    linked lists, 334
    for List ADT, 298–304
    of lists, 297–304
    postponing choice of, 333

for Priority Queue ADT, 101–106,
    346–359
of priority queues, 101–106, 346–359
for Queue ADT, 280–287
of queues, 280–287
sequential, 23
sequential lists, 334
for Stack ADT, 271–274
for String ADT, 314–318
of strings, 314–319, 335
substitutability of, 126
for Table ADT, 489–492
Requirements analysis, 12, 20, 661, 686
    characteristics of, 662
Requirements
    for software, 190
    inconsistent, 662
Resource consumption, 2
    curves, 251
    patterns, 210
Return on investment (ROI), 674
Reusable software components, 139,
    186, 204, 657, 674, 687
    profitability, 674
    programming with, 188–189
Reversing data structures
    binary trees, 603
    lists, 75
    strings, 75, 78–79
Rightmost derivations, 585, 595
Risk analysis, 19
Risk item identification, 682
Risk item prioritization, 682
Risk item resolution, 19, 682
Risk management, 681
Risk-based process models, 19–20
    see also Spiral model
Ritchie, Dennis M., 60
Roberts, Eric S., 91
Root of tree, 56, 340
Rotations in AVL trees, 378–382, 403
Roving pointers, 327
Run queues,
    in time-shared operating systems, 286
Run-time stacks, 275
Running time
    exponential, 90
    linear, 214, 219
    table for MergeSort, 240

tables for SelectionSort, 208–209
tables for sorting methods, 572–575

S

Safety, 2, 12
Sahni, S., 493
Schedule compression, 673, 685, 687
    Brooks' Law, 672–673
    cost of, 673
    danger zone, 673, 685
Science of the Artificial, 3
Science, 3, 20
Scientific method, 5
Scope of control, 17
Search keys, 338
Search trees, 338
    2-3 trees, 388–391, 403
    AVL trees, 376–388
    B-trees, 391–392
    binary search trees, 365–375
    tries, 392–393, 403
Searching
    in 2-3 trees, 389
    in arrays, 16–17
    in binary trees, 365
    in graphs, 406–407, 415, 448
    in large files, 514–516
    in lists, 43
    in tables, 450
    in tries, 393
Seek time, 498, 502, 522
SelectionSort, 149–152, 207, 525–526,
    535–537, 577, 581
    analysis of, 227–232
    analysis of recursive, 230–232
    curve fitting, 209
    $O(n^2)$ running time, 214
    recursive, 231
    running time, 208–209, 230
Sending messages to call methods,
    617
Sentential forms, 585, 608
Separate chaining, 460, 479
    efficiency of, 479
Separate probe sequences, 475
Sequences, 296
Sequential binary tree representation,
    344–346
    leaf test, 345

locating children, 345
locating parents, 345
Sequential representations, 23
of complete binary trees, 344–346
of lists, 298–299, 334
of priority queues, 104–107
of queues, 281–283
of stacks, 271–273
Sequential search, 225
analysis of, 226–227
program for, 226
Servers and clients, 133, 254, 291–293
Service time distribution, 291
Service time interval, 291
Shape drawing, 622–623, 656
Shared sublists, 306
ShellSort, 527, 566–569, 579
Shift-reduce parsers, 589, 608
Shortest path, 405, 407, 423–428, 448
algorithm, 407
Dijkstra's algorithm, 426, 448
problem, 405
Sieve of Eratosthenes, 207
SiftUp procedure for HeapSort,
537–539
Similarity retrievals, 519, 523
Simple cycles, 408–409
Simula, 610
Simulation and modeling, 291–293
to assist design, 294
to predict performance, 255
using queues, 291–293
Slack time, 429, 437–438
sharing, 438
Slider control, 647–650
Smalltalk, 610
Software components, 186, 204
see also Reusable software compo-
nents
Software development projects, see
Software projects
Software development schedule com-
pression, see Schedule compression
Software development time equation,
672
Software economics, 186–189
Software engineering, 11, 659–688
advanced concepts, 659–688
early failures, 659

principles of, 11
recent advances, 660
Software effort estimate equation, 672
Software learning curve, 660, 668–669,
686
Software lifecycle, 12, 660, 686
Software lifecycle phases, 661, 686
coding and debugging, 664–665, 686
design, 663–664, 686
maintenance, 666–667, 686
operation and upgrade, 666, 686
requirements analysis, 661–662, 686
specification, 662–663, 686
testing and integration, 665, 686
Software process models, 660, 675–684,
687
code and fix model, 675–676, 681,
687
definition of, 675
evolutionary development model,
681, 687
prototyping in, 680–681
spiral model, 660, 681–684, 687–688
waterfall model, 660, 676–679, 681,
687
Software productivity, 660, 667–675,
687
audits, 674, 687
Cocomo estimating equation, 672
Cocomo rating scales, 671
comparative difficulty of projects, 670
cost-benefit analysis, 674
definition of, 667
high variance among individuals,
669–670
improvement of, 673–674
principle of top talent, 670
ranges, 671
return on investment (ROI), 674
skewed distributions, 670
software learning curve, 668–669
software tools attribute, 671
Software projects, 135–136, 685
costs, 187
estimating effort and schedule, 187,
672
organization, 135–136
unforeseen risks, 685
work breakdown structures, 135

Software requirements, 190
Software reuse, 186
Software size as cost driver, 187
Software system effort equation, 187,
672
Software system lifecycle, 12
Software system organization, 132
clean organization of, 135
Software system structure, 8
Software tools attribute, 671
Soloway, Elliot, 192–195, 202
Sorting
by address calculation, 551–565
analysis of BubbleSort, 571
analysis of HeapSort, 539
analysis of InsertionSort, 549–550
analysis of MergeSort, 236–241
analysis of ProxmapSort, 562–563
analysis of QuickSort, 543–547
analysis of RadixSort, 565
analysis of SelectionSort, 536–537
analysis of ShellSort, 569
analysis of TreeSort, 550
BubbleSort, 527, 569–571, 579
choosing best method, 575–577, 580
comparison of methods, 572–575
comparison trees, 527–529
comparison-based methods, 531
direct simple solutions, 580
divide and conquer, 525, 540–547
HeapSort, 525–526, 537–539,
577–578
insertion methods, 547–551
InsertionSort, 527, 548–551, 578
large external files, 507–509
MergeSort, 526, 540, 578
minimum average comparisons,
530–531
$n \log n$ barrier, 524–525, 531, 577
preliminary assumptions about,
532–533
ProxmapSort, 527, 552–563, 577, 579
QuickSort, 525, 540–547, 577–578
RadixSort, 527, 563–565, 577, 579
richness of sorting problem, 534
SelectionSort, 525–526, 535–537,
577
ShellSort, 527, 566–569, 579
special circumstances, 576

in Table ADT, 506
table of running times, 572
themes for, 525–527
TreeSort, 527, 550, 578
with priority queues, 99, 525,
    532–539, 577
worst case times, 525
Specifications, 662–663, 686
of programs, 138
testability of, 662–663
Spiral model, 660, 681–684, 687–688
cycles, 681
encompassing other models, 683–684
risk item identification in, 682
risk item prioritization in, 682
risk item resolution in, 682
risk-management driven, 681–685,
    688
Spooled file, 290
Spooler for printer, 290
Stack ADT, 260
implementations of, 271–275
linked representation, 273–274
sequential representation, 271–273
used to check for balanced parenthe-
    ses, 263–267
used to evaluate postfix expressions,
    267–270
Stacks, 253, 259, 295–296
of activation records, 258
ADT for, 260
background on, 256–259
frames, 276–280
holding postponed obligations, 258
for implementing recursive function
    calls, 275–280
interface for, 261–262
LIFO (last-in, first-out), 258
linked representation, 273–274
popping, 256, 295
for processing nested structures, 254
pushing, 256, 295
sequential representation, 271–273
uses for, 295
Standard C, 15
ANSI Standard C, 15
Standish, Thomas A., 334
Start symbol, 584
Static allocation, 319–320, 335

Static trees, 337
Stepwise refinement, 11, 19–20, 39,
    138–155, 202
Stirling's approximation, 530
Storage allocation in heaps, 325–326
Storage allocation policies, 30, 58, 325,
    327
allocation failure in, 30, 58, 327
best-fit policy, 325
coalescing, 327
first-fit policy, 325
fragmentation, 327
roving pointers in, 327
Storage allocation
malloc function for, 28, 30
static versus dynamic, 319–320
Storage devices, external, 499–504
Storage media, addressable, 24–25
Storage reclamation, see Garbage col-
    lection
Storage recycling, 30
Storage, 24, 30–31
allocation failure, 30
garbage, 24
inaccessible, 24, 30
reclamation, 30
recycling, 31
see also Storage allocation policies
String representations, 314–319, 335
in word processors, 316–319
Strings, 296, 312–319, 335
ADT for, 313
C strings, 297, 314, 335
concatenating strings, 315
Pascal strings, 297 314–316, 335
reversal, 78–79
Stroustrup, Bjarne, 611
Struct, members, 35
Structured programming, 11, 20, 139,
    190, 204
Structuring methods, 259
Stubs, 176–177
used in testing, 176–177
Style disciplines, in programming, 196
Subclassing, 19
Sublists, 306
in generalized lists, 306
Substitutability of data representations,
    126

Sums, 65–66, 713–723
of arithmetic progressions, 690–691
changing index variables, 715–716
closed formulas for, 716–718
of cubes, 721
dummy variable, 714
of floors of logarithms, 722–723
of geometric progressions, 696–698
Harmonic numbers, 723
index variable, 714
iterative program for sum of squares,
    65
of $i*d^i$, 723
of natural logarithms, 530
of squares, 720
recursive program for sum of squares,
    66
sums of sums, 718–720
use of in algorithm analysis, 225
useful formulas for, 720–723
Sunk costs, 664
Supercomputers, 498
Switching data representations, 126
Symantec C++™, 656
Symantec Corporation, 656
Symmetric linked lists, 55, 303
Synchronization problems, 290
Synchronizing concurrent tasks, 290,
    294
Syntax analysis, 587

T

Table ADT, 453–454, 489–494
AVL-tree representations, 489–492,
    505–506
comparative performance, 491
comparison of representations,
    489–492
comparison of searching methods,
    489–492
deletion in, 490
hash table representation, 489–492
poor performance, 505–507
poor techniques for, 505–507
sorted array representation, 489–492
sorting in, 506–509
Tables, 450–453
abstract storage device, 453
ADT for, see Table ADT

deleting entries, 450
empty entries, 453
enumerating entries, 450
representations, 451
retrieving entries, 450
searching, 450
updating entries, 450
Tagged type system, 310
Tail recursion elimination, 168–169, 203
Tapes, 499–501, 522
block addresses, 500
calibrated, 500
nine-track, 500
Task networks, 407, 428, 430–431, 448
graph representations, 430–431
topological order in, 432
Temperature scales, 213
conversion, 213
Terminal symbols, 584
Terminus of edges, 409
Test drivers, 174–175
Test files, 335
representations of, 316–319, 335
Test plans, 178, 203
documents, 178
Test suites, 176
Testing and integration, 665, 686
Testing and verification, 201
Testing, 20, 138–139, 161, 172–179, 203
acceptance testing, 175–176, 203
bottom-up, 173, 204
boundary cases, 174
of documentation, 200
integration testing, 175, 203
regression testing, 175–176, 203
specifications, 662–663
stubs, 176–177
test drivers, 175
test plans, 178, 203
test plan documents, 178
test suites, 176
top-down, 176–177
unit testing, 174, 203
and verification, 178–179, 201
Text representations, 317–319
advanced, 317–319
Think C™, 656

Thinking recursively, 63, 80, 91, 593
Throughput, 292
Tic-tac-toe, 110
program shell, 110
user interface, 110
Time-shared operating systems, 286
Toolshed theorem, 660–661
Top-down programming, 11, 19–20, 39, 138–155, 202
Top-down testing, 177
Topological order, 407, 419, 448
program strategy for, 422
use of, 432
Towers of Hanoi, 86
Traces, 91
of recursive calls, 70–71
Tradeoffs, 2, 11, 20, 297, 311
efficiency versus generality, 127, 311, 651
generality versus simplicity, 406
Transformations, 167, 203, 250
of algorithms for ease of analysis, 250
of programs, 167, 203
Translating infix to postfix, 596–600, 609
Transmission time, 498, 502, 522
Transposition sorting, see BubbleSort
Traveling salesperson problem, 218, 444
Tree traversals, 363–364, 399
caution for empty trees, 399
using queues, 363–364
using stacks, 363–364
Trees, 337
anatomy, 401
ancestors, 340
AVL trees, 339, 376–388
B-trees, 391
basic terminology, 339–341
binary trees, 338
branches, 56, 339
branching factor, 699
children, 340
comparison trees for sorting, 527–529
descendants, 340
dynamic, 337
edges in, 339
empty tree, 341, 403
external path length, 368–369, 529–530

family relationships, 340
free trees, 409, 447
game trees, 338
generalized traversal, 361–362
geometric relationships, 340–341
Huffman coding trees, 339, 394–399
internal nodes, 340
leaves, 56, 340
levels, 340, 402
minimal spanning trees, 439–440
parents, 340
path length in, 340
roots of, 56, 340
search trees, 338
static trees, 337
traversals of, 360–364, 402
tries, 339, 392–394, 403
2-3 trees, see Two-three trees
TreeSort, 527, 550, 578
Triangle number hashing, 484–486
Tries, 339, 392–394, 403
discrimination net, 392–393, 403
pronunciation of, 392
searching in, 393
TSP, see Traveling salesperson problem
Tuning, 179–186, 203
and measurement, 139
Two-star notation (**), 15
indicating challenging mathematics, 15
Two-three trees, 339, 388–392, 403
insertions in, 389–390
node overflows, 390
searching in, 389
Two-way linked lists, 55, 303, 325
in heaps, 325
Two-way ring, 55
Typeless languages, 308, 311

U

Ullman, Jeffrey D., 250, 607
Undirected graph, 408–409
Unforeseen risks, in software development, 685
Unit testing, 174, 203
Units, 133
in Pascal, 610
Universe, dissolution of, 86
Unknown pointers, 36–37